IN THE PRESS. VOLS. I. & II., DEMY 8vo.

THE
HISTORY OF THE POPES,

FROM THE CLOSE OF THE MIDDLE AGES.

DRAWN FROM THE SECRET ARCHIVES OF THE VATICAN AND OTHER ORIGINAL SOURCES.

BY Dr. LOUIS PASTOR,

PROFESSOR OF HISTORY IN THE UNIVERSITY OF INNSBRUCK.

TRANSLATED FROM THE GERMAN

BY FREDERICK ANTROBUS,

OF THE LONDON ORATORY.

———————

JOHN HODGES:
HENRIETTA STREET, COVENT GARDEN, LONDON.
1890.

BRIEF OF HIS HOLINESS POPE LEO XIII.
TO DR. L. PASTOR.

"Dilecto filio Ludovico Pastor Doctori historiæ tradendæ Ænipontem.

"Leo P.P. XIII.

"Dilecte fili, salutem et Apostolicam benedictionem. Ex historia Pontificum Romanorum, quam habes institutam, adlatum Nobis primum volumen est una cum litteris tuis. Quod rerum monumenta veterum, utique ex Tabulario Vaticano deprompta, usui tibi scribis fuisse, gratum est: nec fieri profecto potest, ut tanta supellex non magnum afferat ad investigandam antiquitatem lumen. Tu vero opus habes in manibus sane laboriosum idemque magna casuum varietate notabile sum ab exitu medii ævi exorsus, pergere ad hanc nostram ætatem contendas. Sed ab ista lucubrationum tuarum priore parte, cui quidem suffragium idoneorum virorum videmus non defuisse, conjecturam facere de reliquarum bonitate licet. Reddere crum alacritate, quæ restant, hortaremur, nisi Nobis esset cognitum tua te voluntate alacrem hortatione plane non indigere. Nec sane facultatem ingenii tui usquam poteras utilius sanctiusque collocare, quam in illustrandis diligenter ac sincere rebus gestis Pontificum maximorum, quorum laudibus tam sæpe invidere vel temporum iniuria consuevit vel hominum obtrectatio malevola. Cælestium munerum auspicem ac benevolentiæ Nostræ paternæ testem tibi Apostolicam benedictionem peramanter in Domino impertimus. Datum Romæ apud S. Petrum die XX. Januarii Anno 1887, Pontificatus Nostri nono.

"LEO P.P. XIII."

"To my beloved son Ludwig Pastor, Professor of History at Innspruck.

"Leo P.P. XIII.

"My beloved son.

"Health and Apostolic benediction!

"The first volume of your history of the Roman Pontiffs has reached us with your letter.

"We are pleased with what you report of your work upon ancient documents, and particulary upon those of the Vatican Archives. Such a store of material cannot fail to throw much light upon the study of old times. You are, indeed, undertaking a truly laborious work, and one which has to deal with a wonderful variety of occurrences, for you start from the beginning of the Middle Ages with the intention of bringing your work down to our own day. But as far as we may judge from this first portion of your labour, carrying with it the approval of capable critics, we augur favourably for the remaining part.

"We might have thought to encourage you in hastening to produce this remainder, but we are fully aware that your earnest zeal requires no kind of such encouragement.

"It is most true that your intellectual powers cannot be more usefully or piously applied than in this work of displaying with industrious candour the acts of those great Pontiffs, whose fame has so often been impaired either by the unjust severity of the time, or the malicious slander of individuals.

"In assurance of heavenly help, and in testimony of our fatherly good-will, we bestow the Apostolic Benediction with all love in the Lord.

"Given from Rome at St. Peter's, January 20, 1887, the ninth year of our Pontificate.

"LEO P.P. XIII."

DEMY 8vo.   PRICE 12s.

...ward VI. and the Book of Common Prayer.

...origin illustrated by hitherto unpublished documents.

...simile pages of the MS.

...By FRANCIS AIDAN GASQUET, O.S.B.,

...hor of "Henry VIII. and the English Monasteries",

and EDMUND BISHOP.

CONTENTS.

To the Reader.

APPENDIX.

JOHN HODGES, 25, HENRIETTA STREET, COVENT GARDEN, W.C.

Henry VIII, and the English Monasteries. An attempt to illustrate the History of their Suppression, with an Appendix and Maps showing the situation of the religious houses at the time of their dissolution. By Francis Aidan Gasquet, O.S.B. 2 Vols. 12s. each. *Fourth Edition, now ready.*

JOHN HODGES, 25, Henrietta Street, Covent Garden, W.C.

The Catholic Standard Library.

❧❧❧

Under this title is now issuing a series of Standard Works, consisting of Foreign Translations, Original Works, and Reprints, printed in the best style of the typographic art, bound in cloth, in demy 8vo, of from 450 to 500 pages, and issued at short intervals, price 12s. each Volume, *post free to any part of the world;* to subscribers, 25s. for three Vols., or post free 26s. 6d. Either of the works may be taken separately at 10s. per Vol., or twelve Vols. may be selected for £ 5, 5s., carriage paid.

The Great Commentary on the Gospels of Cornelius à
Lapide. Translated and Edited by the Rev. T. MOSSMAN, B.A., Oxon., assisted by various Scholars.

> SS. MATTHEW AND MARK'S GOSPELS. 3 Vols. *Fourth Edition.*
> S. JOHN'S GOSPEL AND THREE EPISTLES. 2 Vols. *Second Edition.*
> S. LUKE'S GOSPEL. 1 Vol. *Second Edition.*

"It would indeed be gilding the finest gold to bestow praise on the great Commentary of à Lapide. It is a work of unequalled—we should say unapproached—value. We specially entreat the clergy not to neglect obtaining so vast a treasure of saintly wisdom, even if, in so doing, they are obliged to sacrifice many volumes far inferior to it in real helpfulness." — *John Bull.*

"Mr. Mossman has done his part as an able and sympathetic scholar might be expected to do it, and the volume, both in translation and execution, is worthy of its author."— *Saturday Review.*

"It is the most erudite, the richest, and altogether the completest Commentary on the Holy Scriptures that has ever been written, and our best thanks are due to Mr. Mossman for having given us, in clear, terse, and vigorous English, the invaluable work of the Prince of Scripture Commentators." — *Dublin Review.*

"Really the Editor has succeeded in presenting the public with a charming book. We have been accustomed to regard à Lapide for consultation rather than to be read. But in the compressed form, clear and easy style, and excellent type in which it now appears, it is a book we can sit down to and enjoy." — *The Month.*

"We set a high store upon this commentary. There is about it a clearness of thought, a many-sided method of looking at truth, an insight into the deeper meaning, and a fearless devotion which lend a peculiar charm to all that he writes. The great value which his commentaries have for Bible students is in the fact that nowhere else can they find so great a store of patristic and scholastic exegesis." — *Literary World.*

"It is one of those few 'books which are books,' an unfailing magazine of instruction and devotion of the profoundest views of Holy Scripture and Theology in general, and one of the most valuable and important recently issued from the press." — *Church Review.*

"The translation is good, the sense is rendered truthfully and in good English; the sentences are terse and vigorous." — *Tablet.*

"Mr. MOSSMAN has done his work well, and we wish his enterprise the success it deserves." — *Guardian.*

"We have no hesitation in saying that this is the best and most able Commentary in the English language." — *Revisionist.*

Henry VIII. and the English Monasteries. An Attempt to illustrate the History of their Suppression, with an Appendix and Maps showing the situation of the religious houses at the time of their dissolution. By Francis Aidan Gasquet, O.S.B. 2 Vols. *Fourth Edition.*

"We may say in brief, if what we have already said is not sufficient to show it, that a very important chapter of English history is here treated with a fulness, minuteness, and lucidity which will not be found in previous accounts, and we sincerely congratulate Mr. Gasquet on having made such an important contribution to English historical literature." — *Athenæum.*

"The old scandals, universally discredited at the time, and believed in by a later generation only through prejudice and ignorance, are now dispelled for ever." — *Academy.* Signed, James Gairdner.

"A most valuable contribution to ecclesiastical history." — *Saturday Review.*

"A learned, careful, and successful vindication of the personal character of the monks. . . . In Mr. Gasquet's skilful hands the dissolution of the monasteries assumes the proportions of a Greek tragedy." — *Guardian.*

Historical Portraits of the Tudor Dynasty and the Reformation Period. By S. Hubert Burke. 4 Vols. *Second Edition.* "Time unveils all Truth."

"I have read the work with great interest, and I subscribe without hesitation to the eulogy passed on it by the *Daily Chronicle*, as making, as far as I know, a distinct and valuable addition to our knowledge of a remarkable period." — *From a Letter by* Mr. Gladstone.

"The greatest charm of these fascinating volumes is in the brightness of the style, for it reads more like a romance than a history." — *Land and Water.*

"We do not hesitate to avow that, in his estimate of character and events, Mr. Burke is seldom wrong. . . . We heartily wish it a large sale and an extensive circulation."— *The Academy.* Signed, Nicholas Pocock.

"They are full-length portraits, often so life-like, that when placed beside each other, we feel no difficulty in realizing the relations which Mr. Burke aims at establishing between them." — *Annual Register.*

"The author writes history as it should be written. The men and women that pass before us in these portraits are no hard lifeless outlines, but beings of flesh and blood, in whom, and in whose fate, we feel a keen and absorbing interest." — *Tablet.*

"This work will excite much interest, obtain many readers, and much extend the acquaintance with the period the author illustrates." — *Westminster Review.*

"We attach great importance to Mr. Burke's work, as it is, we believe, the first attempt on any considerable scale to collect and arrange in a living picture the men and women who made the England of to-day. . . . This effort, seriously and conscientiously undertaken, and aided by a graphic and attractive style, must do immense good." — *Dublin Review.*

"No honest student of a most memorable period can afford to neglect the aid of Mr. Burke's long and laborious researches, while the general public will find in his pages all the interest of a romance, and all the charm of novelty, about events more than three centuries old. He is also what is rare—an historian of absolute impartiality."— *Life.*

The History and Fate of Sacrilege. By Sir Henry Spelman. Kt. Edited, in part from two MSS., Revised and Corrected. With a Continuation, large Additions, and an Introductory Essay. By Two Priests of the Church of England. New Edition, with corrections, and some Additional Notes by Rev. S. J. Eales, D.C.L.

"All who are interested in Church endowments and property should get this work which will be found to be a mine of information on the point with which it deals." — *Newbery House Magazine.*

The Hierurgia; or, The Holy Sacrifice of the Mass. With Notes and Dissertations elucidating its Doctrines and Ceremonies. By Dr. DANIEL ROCK. 2 Vols. A New and thoroughly Revised Edition, with many new Illustrations. Edited, with a Preface, by W. H. JAMES WEALE. *In the Press.*

The Dark Ages: A Series of Essays illustrating the State of Religion and Literature in the Ninth, Tenth, Eleventh, and Twelfth Centuries. By the late DR. MAITLAND, Keeper of the MSS. at Lambeth. Fifth Edition, with an Introduction by FREDERICK STOKES, M.A.

"The essays as a whole are delightful; although they are full of learning, no one can find them dull or heavy; they abound in well-told stories, amusing quotations, and clever sarcasm. Whatever the previous knowledge of a reader may be, he will be stirred up by these essays to learn more of a subject they treat so pleasantly." — *Saturday Review.*

"No task could be more worthy of a scholar and divine so eminently distinguished as the author of this volume, than a vindication of institutions which had been misrepresented for centuries, and a defence of men who had been maligned by those to whom they had been generous benefactors. We have read this work both with pleasure and profit." — *Athenæum.*

"There is scant opportunity for prayer and repose in the restless, commonplace age in which we live. The whole atmosphere of the times is fatal to that spirit of faith which is the motive power of all real progress. The reading of Maitland's pages will greatly in convincing us of the accuracy of this conclusion." — *American Catholic Quarterly Review.*

Piconio (Bernardine à). Exposition on St. Paul's Epistles. Translated and Edited by A. H. PRICHARD, B.A., Merton College, Oxford. 3 Vols. *Vols. I. and II. ready. Vol. III. in the Press.*

"The learning, the piety, the spiritual-mindedness and loving charity of the author, which deservedly earned for him a high reputation in France, are everywhere conspicuous, and there is a freshness in the mode in which he presents much that is suggestive, helpful, and beautiful." — *National Church.*

"We desire to recommend this book to all. Of course to the priesthood any commendation of it is unnecessary; but among the laity there are many souls one of whose greatest drawbacks in the spiritual life is unfamiliarity with the Word of God. Let them read the Scriptures daily, if only for a few minutes, let them bear along with them such guides as Piconio, and the Spirit of God will illumine their minds and inflame their hearts with a freshness and vigour of Divine life altogether peculiar."— *New York Catholic World.*

A Commentary on the Holy Gospels. In 4 Vols. By JOHN MALDONATUS, S.J. Translated and Edited from the original Latin by GEORGE J. DAVIE, M.A., Exeter College, Oxford, one of the Translators of the Library of the Fathers. *Vols. I. and II. (St. Matthew's Gospel).*

"Maldonatus is as yet but little known to English readers, yet he was a man of far more ability than à Lapide, and is far more original in his remarks and explanations." — *Month.*

"To those who may not with facility be able to read the Latin, this English version will be a great boon. The Commentary is certainly one with which a Biblical student should make himself acquainted." — *Guardian.*

The History of the Popes, from the Close of the Middle Ages. Drawn from the Secret Archives of the Vatican and other Original Sources. By Dr. L. PASTOR, Professor of History in the University of Innsbruck. Translated from the German by FREDERICK ANTROBUS, of the London Oratory. Vols. I. and II. *In the Press.*

The Church of our Fathers, as seen in St. Osmund's rite for the Cathedral of Salisbury. By the late Rev. Dr. ROCK. A New and Revised Edition. By the Benedictines of Downside. 4 Vols. *Preparing.*

THE DARK AGES;

A SERIES OF ESSAYS,

INTENDED TO ILLUSTRATE THE

STATE OF RELIGION AND LITERATURE

IN THE

NINTH, TENTH, ELEVENTH, AND TWELFTH
CENTURIES.

BY

S. R. MAITLAND, D.D., F.R.S., & F.S.A.,

SOMETIME LIBRARIAN TO THE LATE ARCHBISHOP OF CANTERBURY
AND KEEPER OF THE MSS. AT LAMBETH.

Fifth Edition.

WITH AN INTRODUCTION BY FREDERICK STOKES M. A.

JOHN HODGES,
HENRIETTA STREET, COVENT GARDEN, LONDON.
1890.

PRINTED BY
H. C. A. THIEME
AT NIMEGUEN (HOLLAND)
AND
BILLITER SQUARE BUILDINGS
LONDON E. C.

INTRODUCTION.

It is by no means easy for even impartial men to arrive at clear and accurate knowledge of the social and mental conditions of peoples and classes living under different conditions from themselves. Even a selected body of men like a Royal Commission often ends by presenting widely different conclusions, drawn from precisely the same evidence as to the same facts. The actual condition, for instance, of the Irish peasantry is a subject of hot dispute among men of education and intelligence living under the same laws at the same time. When the class under consideration differs from its critics, as in the case of a foreign country, the difficulty is greatly increased. How many Englishmen are qualified to pronounce upon the social and economic conditions of Russia, or China, or, one might even add, of Ireland?

In truth, the judgments which men form are to a large extent subjective, and are determined not merely by evidence which may be the same for all, but by training, inclination, prejudice, sometimes even by heredity. In religious matters an impartial critic is the exception. The great majority of men inherit their faith, as they do their physique, from their parents. Hence it may be assumed as fairly certain that a Protestant writer dealing with the Dark Ages—a period when Christendom was Roman Catholic—will have a tendency to deal out something less than justice. Even if he be fair-minded—and many ultra-Protestant writers are not —there is the danger of what may be called involuntary bias. For most men unconsciously set up their own standards of happiness and enlightenment as the test by which others are to be judged. Rich men, as a class, take it for granted that their less favoured fellow creatures are necessarily miserable. Poor men too commonly accept the deplorable fallacy that to be rich is to be happy. The man of the world regards monastic life as a species of voluntary penal servitude. The monk, too often, assumes that there is no real happiness or virtue outside the cloister. Each decides not solely according to the objective truth of the matter, but more or less conformably to his own mental sympathies and tastes.

Perhaps no period of Christianity has been more misjudged than the Dark Ages—an epoch which, in the present work, is taken as comprising the ninth, tenth, eleventh, and twelfth centuries. The general tradition when Maitland wrote—a tradition which has been greatly modified by later historians like Hallam and Gasquet—was that these ages were almost wholly barbaric; ages of ignorance, superstition, oppression, and general misery. Perhaps writers of the twenty-first century will take a similar view of the nineteenth, and regar   as a time when the world was desolated by fa   , war, pestilence; when the condition of the poor   s as harsh as it has ever been; when men were subject to conscription, invasion, misgovernment. The writers of the first half of this century looked down with scorn upon the centuries before the Reformation, yet historians like Walpole pronounce an almost equally severe verdict upon the times when George the Third was king. The Anglican Churchmen of the last century were emphatic in their denunciations of the abuses of pre-Reformation times. The general verdict of Churchmen of our own times as to the state of the Church of England in the eighteenth century is the reverse of flattering. It would be easy, indeed, by treating the Anglican Church in the eighteenth century as many Protestant writers—notably Robertson—have treated the Church of the Middle Ages, to prove that it was as dark as any century of the Christian era.

And, in judging of any past age, it is necessary to remember that evil is more conspicuous than good; that one great criminal attracts more attention than thousands of men living quiet and virtuous lives. One year of war furnishes forth more matter for the historian than a decade of peace. Moreover, it is necessary to remember the Dark Ages were a time when Roman Catholicism was dominant, while the writers who formed the existing tradition were mostly Protestant. It is hardly too much to say that modern literature, as a whole, is Protestant. For whatever reason, a species of intellectual sterility seems to have fallen upon Roman Catholics within the last two hundred years. For a century past Roman Catholicism has produced perhaps three literary men of the first rank—Lamennais, Dollinger, and Rosmini,—and of these, two quitted the Church, and the third, now dead, has been condemned by the present Pope. [1] To anyone, however, acquainted with ecclesiastical history, the wonder will be not that Catholicism has party lost the creative power it possessed in mediæval times, but that it continues to exist at all. For a century past a series of hurricanes have swept upon the Western Church, which have reduced her policy to a desperate struggle for very existence. Perhaps no Church since the days of the Roman Empire has endured—and survived—so tremendous a persecution as that to which the Gallican Church was subjected at the close of the eighteenth century. In Italy a strong anti-Catholic movement, engendered by the secret societies, has culminated in the destruction of the Temporal Power, and is now again developing into a legislative policy, which will still further weaken and oppress the Italian clergy. In Germany the Catholics are just emerging from the obligations of the Falk laws. Everywhere education has passed out of the hands of the

---

[1] The condemnation is, however, limited to some posthumous works of Rosmini. The great bulk of his writings were examined and approved by Pius IX. Rosmini is one of the most brilliant and gifted philosophers that the Church of Rome has produced since the Reformation.

Church. The old universities are either Protestant or secularized, the primary schools are passing into the hands of the State. So complete is the de-Catholization of Europe, that at the Vatican Council—Rome's last appeal to the nations—representatives of the Catholic States were for the first time omitted from the Papal invitations. As Cardinal Antonelli said in his despatch to the Nuncio at Paris—"If the Holy See has not thought fit to invite Catholic princes to the Council, as it did on other occasions, everyone will easily understand that this is chiefly to be attributed to the changed circumstances of the times."

But it is not the Latin Church alone which is threatened. Christianity itself is menaced. We are face to face with a new phenomenon in the intellectual history of Europe—a religion without a God. Infidelity has developed into materialism, and materialism propounds to the world a philosophy which shall explain and solve the mysteries of the past and the future, which shall guide the thoughts and wills of men, but in which a Creator has no place. Man, according to the new Gospel, is a combination of chemical and physical atoms produced by evolution and dissolved by death. The moral effects of such a creed, when once established—and it is spreading daily—cannot but be disastrous. For without God there is no morality and no civilization, no joy in the past, no peace in the present, no hope for the future. Let us eat and drink, for to-morrow we die and death is the end of all things.

And this modern materialism comes upon us not as other religious movements have done with blare of trumpet and beat of drum; rather it steals upon men's minds like some poisonous malaria begotten of polluted river or unwholesome marsh, asphyxiating the conscience and corroding the intellect so that men find that faith is dead before they were conscious that it was in danger. Moreover, the germ of it is in every man's heart, from the theologian watching with perplexed spirit the perennial waves of human folly and misery, to the peasant sullenly gazing at his empty platter and fireless grate, and its spread is helped and furthered by the social and economic miseries of the times. More and more the great landlords and labour-lords are eating up the people as men eat bread, and grinding the faces of the poor. More and more the wealth of Europe, scanty in proportion to the needs and numbers of her population, is being garnered into the cellars of the banker and the safes of the usurer. More and more money is used not to satisfy the legitimate needs of humanity, but as coins in a vast system of public gambling, as bait for the unwary, as the minister of a luxury, upon which Caligula might have looked with envious eye. Is has been said and said truly that the rich are growing richer and the poor poorer and this coupled with the spread of democratic instructions is tending to a perilous state of things when wealth is in hands of the few and political power in the hands of the many.

The Dark Ages had their miseries, too. Since man first fell from his high estate of original innocence, happiness has not been the lot of any considerable community for any considerable time. The corruption, seemingly incurable, of human nature and the malice of the unseen enemies of our race have always and everywhere proved too strong to be overcome by any creed or constitution. But, on the other hand, these ages had many advantages which we do not enjoy. They were ages in which Christian faith was what a recent writer has called a "vivid dynamic reality." Whatever may be thought of the Crusades—and more than one great authority has held that they resulted in great political advantage to Europe—they were one of the most splendid displays of faith and manhood that the world has ever witnessed, except, perhaps, the earlier developments of Mahommedanism. Christ must have been believed in those days when half the manhood of Europe was willing to undergo indescribable hardship and peril to rescue only "the grave made with the rich," and there was more political unity and more theological liberty. Europe was a Christian confederacy under the primacy of Rome. There was indeed war, bloodshed, rivalry among the nations but there was unity of faith and universal recognition of the principles of morality. The Episcopate was a living authority, with power and capacity to rule and judge the peoples. The assembling of Provincial and General Councils was an ordinary feature of ecclesiastical government. The great theological schools were full of activity and intellectual life. It was during the very ages which moderns call dark that Christianity was formulated and systematized into its present shape. St. Thomas of Aquin, whose Summa has dominated the Latin Church for six centuries, did but reap where the earlier scholastics had sown. Moreover, the influence of the scholastics is not confined to the Roman Communion. In so far as Protestantism has a positive side, it owes it to the scholastics. The reformers pruned away much of mediæval Catholicism, but they added nothing of their own except the doctrine of justification by faith—one of the most dangerous delusions that Christianity has seen. The fundamental dogmas of the Trinity and the Incarnation of Heaven and Hell, of the immortality of the soul and the resurrection of the body, are held by the Reformed Churches in the same sense, almost in the same terms, as by the Roman Church, and although the later Jesuit writers have somewhat modernized and developed the scholastic methods, the approved theology in the Catholic Schools at the present day is substantially the same as in the so called Dark Ages. Rome is still moored to the Summa, which the present Pope has once again publicly approved and recommended to his clergy, and the Summa was but the codification and systematization of the work of the theological writers of the Dark Ages.

Nor were the early writers during these times so ignorant as is commonly supposed. They knew little of natural science, though an accurate theory about the glacial period is of much less practical importance than correct views of another period to come of a higher temperature. No man who is really grounded in the truths of Christianity can be truly said to be ignorant, and the practical teaching which the early writers of the Dark Ages obtained from the pulpit and the confessional was of far more real intellectual and moral value than the farrago of scraps of grammar and elementary arithmetic imparted to an unwilling generation in Board Schools and such like. "This," said Christ, "is life eternal to know Thee, the only true God, and Jesus Christ, whom Thou hast sent" (John xvii. 3), and this knowledge the men of the Dark Ages had in a degree which we, who live in times when the Church is traversing the vast desert which separates the devout faith of the past from the baptised science of the future, can hardly realize. For the poison of unbelief has affected even the Churches. Many of those who regard themselves as orthodox do not really believe, do not get beyond a nominal acceptance of Christian dogmas. The spectacle which Europe has witnessed for a whole generation of a professedly Catholic people like the Italians, living in open defiance of a succession of Papal anathemas, would have been as impossible in the Middle Ages as perhaps an interdict would be now. Much of the so-called morality of the present day is on a par with that of the estimable burglar who never stole what he did not want. Among the Reformed Churches, with the exception of the Catholic party in the Church of England, the spirit of asceticism is almost dead. Fasting, specifically named by Christ as a means of sanctification, has fallen into general disuse. It would perhaps savour too much of justification by works.

Lastly, the Dark Ages were distinguished for the

vigour and success with which the mission work of
the Church was carried on. During the ninth century,
Christianity, says Dean Milman (Lat. Chris. Vol. III. c.
viii.), "was gathering in nations of converts." The
Bulgarians were won to the Gospel by Cyril and
one of the first steps taken by the new Church was
to submit a list of no less than 106 questions to Pope
Nicholas I. Some of the Papal decisions indicate that
at Rome at least the standard of morals was by no
means a barbarous one. No violence was to be used
to those who adhered to Paganism. Torture, with the
object of obtaining evidence, was strictly forbidden,
as was also polygamy. The same century witnessed
the conversion of Moravia and Bohemia, and the
despatch of missionaries to Scandinavia, where the work
of conversion begun by Anschar (who was created
Archbishop of Hamburg) was carried on for a century
and a half, until, in the reign of Canute, who wore
the English and Danish crowns, the task was completed
by a band of English missionaries sent by the king.
During the tenth, eleventh, and twelfth centuries, the
Normans, Magyars, and a multitude of formidable tribes
were won to Christianity, and the havoc wrought in
Christendom by the ravages of these pitiless invaders
before their conversion were repaired. Nor was this
period intellectually barren. "The Church," says Milman,
"did not entirely rely on fixing the infamy of heretical
doctrine upon the more daring reasoners. She reasoned
herself by her sons with equal vigour, if with more
submissiveness, sounded with her antagonists the depths
of metaphysical inquiry, examined the inexhaustible
processes of human thought and language, till gradually
the gigantic bulwark of scholastic theology rose around
the Catholic doctrine." (Lat. Ch. Bk. VIII. c. v.) And
Milman was a writer who cannot be suspected of any
undue leaning towards Romanism.

It is much to be regretted that there are comparatively so few authentic records of the period from 800

to 1200. There were no newspapers, no printed books, no Royal Commissions, or Parliamentary debates (if these last can be really regarded as sources of information). Men worked, and fought, and argued, and preached, and died, leaving no other record than a tombstone. Hence a large part of the criticism of the Dark Ages is too often mere generalization and declamation, representing rather the prejudice of the writer than the verdict of the scholar. And the special merit of Maitland's book is that it is free from this tendency. He was essentially a scientific writer. His object was not to make out a case for or against the Dark Ages but to ascertain from such data as were accessible in his time what the real *status quo* was. He was to modify a well known saying, a Churchman if you please but above all a critic, resolute to find the truth and contemptuously indifferent to mere popular superstitions.

Perhaps the safest way to arrive at a just judgment of the Dark Ages will be to study some of the actual changes wrought in the condition of Europe during this epoch. Voltaire's traveller, wrecked, as he supposed, upon a desert island, was cheered by the sight of a gallows—to him a convincing proof that he was in a civilized country. In a less cynical spirit the student of history may see what actual modification of the condition of men was effected during the historic period under consideration. The age during which Westminster Abbey was built cannot have been architecturally blank. The men who built up the scholastic philosophy cannot have been wholly indifferent to learning and culture. The men who died in myriads on the plains of Syria to rescue the Holy Sepulchre can hardly have been devoid of love of Him who was laid there.

At the beginning of the ninth century the foundations of modern Europe had been laid. Three centuries earlier the Western Empire had perished before

the incursions of the barbarians, and during the interval
between the fall of the older Western Empire and its
restoration under Charlemagne, the history of Europe
had been an almost unbroken record of war, destruction, and ravage. The marvel is not that Christianity
should have been wanting in enlightenment, but that
the Christian Church survived those terrible centuries
when Europe was thrown into the crucible. In the
ninth century, however, the storm of anarchy and
ravage had begun to abate. The genius of Charlemagne
had united under a single sceptre the whole Western
part of Continental Europe, including what is now
France, Germany, Northern Italy, and the Western
part of Austria. England, heretofore split up into
several small kingdoms, founded by the Angles and
Saxons, and for the most part engaged in constant
warfare, was united by Egbert in a single kingdom.
Here, as on the Continent, the ages preceding the date
which Maitland takes as the beginning of the Dark
Ages—A.D. 800—had been times of invasion, slaughter
and conquest. There can be no doubt that the condition of England at the end of the eighth century
was far inferior in wealth and civilization to the state
in which it had been left at the withdrawal of the
Roman eagles. Almost every vestige of civilization
had perished under the attacks of the Teutonic invaders.
The work of founding a polity and a civilization had
to be recommenced, and this is one of the salient
facts to be borne in mind in judging of the Dark
Ages. The men of those ages had to recreate the
political and social world. They had to rebuild almost
from the foundation. Not quite; for Christianity, the
basis of European civilization had not only survived
the storms of the age of invasion, but had to a large
extent converted the barbarians themselves. In Spain,
indeed, the Moors were master from Gibraltar to the
Pyrenees, but, throughout the rest of Western Europe,
Christianity was dominant. To take our own country.

When the Dark Ages began, the Heptarchy was still standing; when it closed, the conquest of Ireland had begun. During the interval England had been welded into a single kingdom, and the main outlines of that Constitution, which has survived in its chief features down to our own days, had been formed. The Universities of Oxford and Cambridge had been founded. A code of laws was drawn up by Alfred the Great, and subsequently revised by Edward the Confessor—the last English king who obtained the honour of canonization. The Irish schools had a high reputation for learning and piety. These are only a few examples of the rapid and solid progress of Christendom during the Dark Ages. Others will be found recorded in Maitland's work, although the author's object may be said to be critical rather than constructive. Maitland was in truth one of those in whom the critical faculty existed in its highest perfection, and his ecclesiastical position enabled him to deal impartially with both sides of his subject.

One of the points upon which there is a strong contrast between our own times and the Dark Ages is the greater degree of individualism in the latter. We live in an age of machinery. Government is carried on by Parliaments, ballots, caucases—all machinery. We travel by machinery and fight by machinery. In the Dark Ages it was not so. It was a time when men were governed by men. The work that would nowadays be the platform of a party was accomplished then by princes, such as St. Louis of France, whom Hallam describes as "perhaps the most eminent pattern of unswerving probity and Christian strictness of conscience that ever held the sceptre in any country." ("Middle Ages," Vol. I., p. 40, 5th ed.) Whether the majority of men were better off under personal rule and simple civilization is a debatable question. It is doubtful whether any more terrible example of wide-spread suffering took place anywhere in the Dark Ages than the Irish famine of 1848. It is doubtful whether any population during the Dark Ages lived in more bitter and hopeless misery than do the sweated workers of London. Civilization has done much for the few, but it is questionable whether it has really benefited the many. Shelter, food, and clothing are the three great bodily wants of men, and the poorer classes in olden times were at least as well supplied with these in the Dark Ages as they are now. They had no votes, nor third class carriages, nor cheap newspapers, but they lived for the most part in the open country, not penned together like swine in huge cities. They had at least fresh air, and pure water, and healthful environment, which is more than can be said of the bulk of our city populations nowadays. Nor was their ignorance so deep as is commonly supposed. In those days faith was a vidid reality, and the confessional and the services of the Church in themselves constituted an education in that which is the most important of all knowledge— the knowledge how to live.

On the whole, one is tempted to believe that the Dark Ages were not so very dark, nor our own times so very full of light as some of the authors criticized by Maitland would have us believe. Men lived simpler and rougher lives, but it does not follow that they led less happy ones. It is doubtful whether the influences of the nineteenth century do not tend to degrade men rather than to elevate them. "The individual withers and the State is more and more." There is scant opportunity for prayer repose in the restless, commonplace age in which we live. The whole atmosphere of the times is fatal to that spirit of faith which is the motive power of all real progress.

PREFACE

FIRST EDITION.

NEARLY eight years have elapsed since the first of
the following essays was printed; and they have all
been more than five years before the public. I wish
the reader to be aware of this, not only because it
may account for some references ·to matters which
occurred during the period of their publication, but
because it will show that some things which may wear
that appearance, are not in reality allusions to more
recent occurrences.

My purpose in these essays, I stated very fully at
the outset; and the collateral objects which I had in
view, I mentioned as occasion offered. I need not,
therefore, here tell the reader over again what I meant
in writing them; but I do not like that this reprint
should issue without a few words of distinct statement
as to what I did *not* mean. It is *possible* that I may
have been misunderstood; though I think that no one
who fairly and candidly reads these essays can imagine
that I designed to hold up to imitation what has, since
I wrote them, been much talked of as "the mediæval
system." As to some superstitions and heresies, and a

B

thousand puerilities, which seem likely to creep into the
Church under that name, I do not feel it necessary to say
anything. I have never, I hope, written a line which
the most ingenious perversion could construe into a
recommendation or even a toleration of them. But there
is one great feature of the mediæval system of which I
feel, and of which I have spoken, very differently,
and in terms which may have been, though I can hardly
think that they really have been, misunderstood.

It is quite impossible to touch the subject of
MONASTICISM without rubbing off some of the dirt
which has been heaped upon it. It is impossible to get
even a superficial knowledge of the mediæval history
of Europe, without seeing how greatly the world of
that period was indebted to the Monastic Orders; and
feeling that, whether they were good or bad in other
matters, Monasteries were beyond all price in those
days of misrule and turbulence, as places where (it
may be imperfectly, yet better than elsewhere) God
was worshipped—as a quiet and religious refuge for
helpless infancy and old age, a shelter of respectful
sympathy for the orphan maiden and the desolate
widow—as central points whence agriculture was to
spread over bleak hills, and barren downs, and marshy
plains, and deal bread to millions perishing with hunger
and its pestilential train—as repositories of the learning
which then was, and well-springs for the learning
which was to be—as nurseries of art and science,
giving the stimulus, the means, and the reward to
invention, and aggregating around them every head
that could devise, and every hand that could execute—as
the nucleus of the city which in afterdays of pride
should crown its palaces and bulwarks with the towering
cross of its cathedral.

This I think no man can deny. I believe it is true,

and I love to think of it. I hope that I see the good hand of God in it, and the visible trace of His mercy that is over all His works. But if it is only a dream, however grateful, I shall be glad to be awakened from it; not indeed by the yelling of illiterate agitators, but by a quiet and sober proof that I have misunderstood the matter. In the meantime, let me thankfully believe that thousands of the persons at whom Robertson, and Jortin, and other such very miserable secondhand writers, have sneered, were men of enlarged minds, purified affections, and holy lives—that they were justly reverenced by men—and, above all, favourably accepted by God, and distinguished by the highest honour which He vouchsafes to those whom He has called into existence, that of being the channels of His love and mercy to their fellowcreatures.

But admitting all this, does it form any reason why we should endeavour to revive the monastic system in the present day, and in this country? This is a thing which has been very seriously proposed, and for which much that is specious may be said, without any violation of truth or fairness. But is it a proposition which should be listened to? Is it, in fact, one that *can* be carried into effect? Many others have, I suppose, as well as myself, received a circular letter, bearing no name, but supposed to emanate from persons entitled to respect, [1] and headed " Revival of monastic

---

[1] [It certainly was on this supposition that I wrote the observations in the text. The truth is that a mistake arose from an erroneous judgment respecting the handwriting of a document. I do not mean to insinuate, for I really do not believe, that any deception was intended. Neither do I pretend to say from what quarter the letters did emanate. Having, however, been led by the mistake to say what I did, and seeing no reason for retracting it, I let the observations remain, not without an impression that some things which have happened since they were published, may have tended to manifest their truth.—*Note to Third Ed.*]

and conventual institutions on a plan adapted to the exigencies of the reformed Catholic Church in England."

After a brief statement of what are considered as the objects, the means, and the constitution, the writer proceeds to say, " It is hoped and earnestly requested that the friends of primitive piety, order, and simplicity, into whose hands this paper may fall, will contribute their thoughts and endeavours towards expanding these hints, and devising some method of bringing them to a practical issue." No channel for the contribution of thoughts is, however, pointed out: but, for the reason which I have already stated, I wish to say something on the subject; and I will take the opportunity of offering some which have occurred to me; and I venture to hope, that, being fully convinced that the suggestion cannot be brought to any good " practical issue," I may be allowed to say so plainly, and without offence. I have no wish to dogmatize on the subject, but on the other hand, I know not how to speak of it with doubt or hesitation, and therefore wish to say, as decidedly as may be lawful, that the " monastic and conventual system " never can be adapted to meet the present exigencies of the Church of England; and that any attempt to revive that system in this time and country, can only prove a sad and mischievous failure.

When I say this, I do not mean to dispute that it would be easy to make a plan and raise money for the building, and even for the endowment, of a monastery and to settle all the details on paper; or to deny that a sufficient number of very good men might be found to inhabit it, on such terms as those who might have the settling of the matter would venture to propose. A few such institutions might, we may believe, be founded, and carried on for a longer or a shorter period. There is such variety in the minds and feelings of men, that such a scheme (indeed *any* scheme that had so much of both antiquity and novelty to recommend it) would immediately find supporters enough to keep it up for some little time, and a fresh supply of others to keep it up for some little time longer.

But even this must be done by "adaptation," as will be seen by the heading of the letter which I have quoted; or according to the language used in the body of that document, the proposal is for the " Revival of the Monastic and Conventual System *in a form* suited to the genius, character, and exigencies of the Church of England." But really this is (to use plain terms, which I hope will not offend, for I know of no others to express my meaning) mere playing at monkery ; if not quite like children playing at soldiers, yet something not much beyond the customary show and service of our rural militia. Anything like *real* monasticism, anything for which the use of such terms as " THE MONASTIC AND CONVENTUAL SYSTEM " is not a most unwarrantable and delusive usurpation, anything really calculated to produce its advantages, such as they were, or even such of them as are wanted or could be desired, in these days—an attempt to revive anything that can fairly be called the Monastic and Conventual System, on a scale of any magnitude and permanence, must, I think, fail, for want of one great thing—that thing on which, by the Divine appointment, it flourished, while it did flourish, as truly as man lives by the air he breathes—namely, that concurrence of men's minds which forming what is called the Spirit of the Age wants, desires, imagines, carries forward its own schemes, irresistibly bears down opposition, creates, protects, uses, and then, in its pro-

gress neglects, disowns, and tramples down its old
institutions, and knows no use in their ruins but to
furnish quarries or foundations for new ones.

It seems to me that we can no more revive the
Monastic System than the Feudal System. We cannot
recall the days of ancient republicanism, or mediæval
chivalry. The French republic was tragic enough; but
who does not feel,—who, except the lowest and weak-
est of the wretches whom it was meant to impose
on, did not feel at the time,—that all its archaism was
purely farcical? Why could not the French have what
Greece and Rome had had, if they liked? Simply for
the same reason that it could not be dealt with as a
matter of solemn propriety, if the Duke of Wellington
should go down to the house in complete armour, or
if Julius Cæsar should tread the stage in a field-mar-
shal's uniform. And why cannot we have tournaments
as our forefathers had? Why was the attempt to hold
one, a few years ago, so laughed at that the experiment has not been repeated? Why is that ridiculous
now, which was honorable and almost sacred four
hundred years ago? Why may not our nobles amuse
themselves as their ancestors did, without being laughed
at? I am not expressing any wish for the revival of such
a pastime; but merely asking *why* the attempt to revive
it is considered as actually absurd, and whether it is
because the thing itself is so very much less dignified and
worthy of great men, and so very much more ridiculous
in itself than a horse-race, a fox-hunt, or a steeple-chase.

I shall be told that the state of society is so different.
I know it. It is just what I am saying. Why it should
differ, and differ in that particular way, are questions
not so easily answered. Nor is it my present business
to attempt any answer to them. It is more to the purpose to offer one or two reasons for believing, that

the altered state of society renders the revival of monasticism altogether impracticable.

Do what he may, no man can strip himself of the circumstances, and concomitants, which it has pleased God to place around him. He may say, "I will be a monk;" and he may call himself, and get others to call him by the name; but if he says, "I will be a monk of the *fourth* century," or "a monk of the *twelfth* century," we can only assure him that he is mistaken, that the thing is impossible, and that if he is a monk at all nowadays, it must be of the *nineteenth* century. I am not speaking of either one of those centuries as better or worse than the others, but only mean that whatever character he may assume, he must take it in his own circumstances. They may be friendly or hostile; and, as it relates to the case now under consideration, they may be in the Church or in the world; in Christians or infidels; in others, whoever and whatever they may be, or in himself, such as he is naturally, or such as he has been made by education and habit: and nothing can be more clear than that any man, whether young or old, whether lay or clerical, a nobleman or tradesman, a soldier or sailor, a peasant or mechanic, a man rich or poor, single or married, who is now living in England, is, both as to externals, and as to the modification of himself, in very different circumstances from those in which he could have been placed, had he lived in the same character and station in the fourth or in the twelfth century. And for the English monk of the nineteenth century, there seem to be some peculiar obstacles. They may exist, and in some degree, more or less, they certainly do exist, in some other parts of Christendom, but they are particularly obvious and powerful in this country.

In the first place, consider how completely, and by what means, the monastic system has been put down in England. There is no need to enter into the matter of motives or proofs. The fact, which is all that we want, is, that popular indignation and hatred of the bitterest kind was excited, and has been studiously kept up, and that for centuries the general notion in this country has been that a monastery naturally, almost necessarily, is a place dedicated to idleness, gluttony, lewdness, hypocrisy, political intrigue, fraud, treachery, and blood; so that, as a matter of course, a nun is to be supposed something as bad as can be, and a monk no better. Now, certainly, no candid man will deny, that before the period of the Reformation, the monastic system in the Western Church hat got into a very bad state. Too many monasteries were really societies of dissolute men; and a vast many more had so far departed from their bounden discipline that there was nothing to restrain the vicious. That is, the monks lived in them under scarcely, if any, more control from vice than fellows of colleges do now. That under these circumstances, in a dissolute age, a great number of monks became profane and debauched, and a great many more secular and careless of religion, is not to be doubted; but that there ever was truth in the coarse and filthy abuse heaped upon the monastic order as a body by some who were forward in the business of the Reformation, is what I suppose never was believed by anyone who had a moderate knowledge of facts. The truth perhaps is, and it is such as should satisfy all but the infidel and profane, that if we take any period whatever in the history of Christianity, and compare the morals of the monks and clergy with those of the laity, we shall find that, however bad the former might be, the latter were worse. In fact, it appears to be the testimony of history, that the monks and clergy, whether bad or good in themselves, were in all times and places better than other people.

Be this as it may, however, the point with which we are concerned is, that this odium, just or unjust, does exist, and would form an obstacle to the revival of monastic institutions in this country. There are, perhaps, some lively young men who would reply, "We should like it all the better. We should enjoy being persecuted, especially as nobody would venture to harm us in life, or limb, or property, to burn us up as the Danes did, or sell us up as Henry VIII. did, or hang us up as Elizabeth did; and we should go about with shaved crowns and rope-girdles, and people would look at us, and come to hear us intone from our lecterns." Of this, one can only say, that in such hands the matter would soon be laughed out of countenance. But others, who deserve more respectful consideration, may tell us that we are not to truckle to the spirit of the age, but to do that which is right. That is plain enough, and I trust that no one will imagine that I am recommending a servile obsequiousness to popular notions and feelings. Of course we are not to shrink from duties, to compromise principles, to adopt or renounce doctrines or practices in mere compliment to the irreligious—but there is no need to repeat the string of truisms which are not only obvious to common sense, and instinctively felt by common honesty, but which must be familiar to most readers, as being perpetually in the mouths of those who are conscious that they are proposing or practising what the great body of the Church may deem eccentric or absurd.

But these truisms are inapplicable to the matter in hand, which involves no fulfilment or breach of any law human or divine. And in such a case it is a matter of wisdom and duty, and, practically speaking, of absolute necessity, to take into account the state of thought and feeling in which the great body of the Church has been brought up and exists. If any man is fully satisfied that there is a divine command, or a human law, by which he is bound to build a monastery and carry on monasticism, let him pursue his convictions, without troubling himself about the consequences. Or if he thinks that, though there may have been no command on the subject, yet, having developed itself, monasticism must be an essential and permanent part of the divine dispensation, I should not wish to discuss what appears to me so entirely unreasonable, and so incapable of being even approached in argument without the settlement of many previous questions. But those who believe with me that different states of society may render specific institutions, forming no part of the Church, though more or less connected with it, useful at one time, noxious at another, and incapable of existence at a third, I would beg to consider one or two features of the present time, as compared with the middle ages.

In the first place, as it regards *vows* of any kind, I do not know whether, among the advocates for the revival of Monasticism, there are any who would maintain them; but in the letter to which I have alluded they are fairly abandoned. In the adapted form there are to be "no vows; but a solemn declaration and engagement of obedience to the Superior, and of compliance with the rules of the Institution during residence." But this seems to be in fact giving up the whole thing. Surely no one who has at all considered the system of Monasticism, can doubt that the vow of perpetual selfdedication was the very root of the matter. The reserved power of change, even if encumbered with difficulties, would alter the whole thing. The monastic vow necessarily operates in two ways. First, in making all but the most thoughtless careful how they enter upon such a mode of life; and secondly, by making those who have taken it contented with a condition which they know to be unalterable, and in which, whatever other schemes of life may occur to their imagination as brighter than their own, they remain peacefully and cheerfully, because that very circumstance of perpetual obligation has given it somewhat the character of a divine dispensation. It is very well for political agitators, and makers of fancy tales, to tell us of raging monks and pining nuns, gnawing the chains of their spiritual bondage, because they were either in love commonly so called, or in love with the vanities of the world,—as if such persons, with very few exceptions, would not fairly run away, vow or no vow—but it is no part of human nature to be rendered permanently unhappy by unalterable dispensations. Generally men and women are satisfied with the sex, and the stature, assigned to them, and do not think of making themselves miserable about the circumstances of native country, parentage, or anything else which, they know, *cannot* be altered.

But the matter may be illustrated by a case in which a vow of perpetual obligation remains among us in the present day. No one can doubt that it would make a difference scarcely to be imagined if the marriage vow, instead of being perpetual and irrevocable, were only a "solemn declaration" that the parties would conduct themselves properly so long as they should see fit to continue man and wife. I do not mean merely that many unhappy marriages would be dissolved, and many unequallyyoked persons set at liberty, for it would certainly operate something far beyond this, and of quite a different nature. Thousands who are now living happily together, and who, if they ever thought of such a thing as separation, would consider it one of the greatest evils that could happen to them, would become unsettled, would be led to speculate, and tempted to experiment; the *possibility* would be present to their own minds, or perpetually suggested by others; a cross word or an angry look would be followed by divorce, and a state of things would follow, plainly showing that if the name of marriage was retained, its nature was changed, and its chief benefits were lost. I am not saying that the monastic vow was a good thing, or that those who took it did right; but, that without it the system could not have existed; and also, that without it neither the system, nor anything really like it, can be now established.

But there are, moreover, two particulars in the character assumed by the vow in question, which are strongly against its revival in the present age. In the early days of monasticism, a person selfdevoted by a vow to a life of celibacy was *on that account* looked up to with respect. But the *vow,* which was then in itself a ground of reverence, would in the present day expose any men or women who should be known to have taken it, to the suspicion, or the remonstrance, or the ridicule, not merely of the frivolous and thoughtless, but of nine out of ten of those whom they were brought up to love and honour, and to whom they were bound by every tie of affection and respect. And it must surely make some difference in the working of a system, whether those who adopt it become objects of esteem and veneration, or of contempt and suspicion. There may be those who would answer as before, that persecution from anybody would be delightful; but, beside other reasons for taking courage, we may comfort ourselves with the hope that they are not sufficiently numerous to fill more than one or two monasteries at the utmost, and that only for a very little while.

For let us just look at another point—the monastic vow was one of obedience; and in the proposed adaptation there are to be "no vows; but a solemn declaration and engagement of *obedience to the Superior,* and of compliance with the rules of the Institution during residence." But what are we to understand by "obedience to the Superior" in this revived monastic system? Is it, for instance, to be such as the Rule of St. Benedict required? The reader may see what that was in a following page [1]. Nothing of that sort, I

---

[1] See p. 190. No. 60. — The original of it is "Præceptis Abbatis in omnibus obedire, etiam si ipse aliter (quod absit) agat memores illud Dominicum præceptum, Quæ dicunt, facite : quæ autem faciunt, facere nolite."—*Cap.* iv. There is, indeed, in this Rule such a plain statement of the doctrine of passive obedience and non-resistance as would appear perfectly ridiculous in the present day. What would those who talk most about obedience say to such passages as these: " Primus humilitatis gradus, est obedientia *sine mora.* Hæc convenit his, qui nihil sibi a Christo carius aliquid existimant propter servitium sanctum quod professi sunt, seu propter metum gehennæ, vel gloriam vitæ æternæ ; *mox ut aliquid imperatum a majore fuerit, ac si divinitus imperetur, moram pati nesciunt in faciendo."* . . . "Sed hæc ipsa obedientia tunc acceptabilis erit Deo, et dulcis hominibus, si, quod jubetur, non trepide, non tarde, non tepide, aut cum murmure, vel cum responso nolentis efficiatur : quia *obedientia quæ majoribus præbetur, Deo exhibetur."—Cap.* v. And this was to extend, not merely to things specifically mentioned in statutes or Acts of Parliament, nor yet merely to things reasonable in themselves, but to such things as were grievous, and even impossible. The LXVIII. chapter is headed " Si fratri impossibilia injungantur ;" and it is as follows : "Si cui fratri aliqua forte gravia aut impossibilia injunguntur ; suscipiat quidem jubentis imperium, cum omni mansuetudine et obedientia. Quod si omnino virium suarum mensuram viderit pondus oneris excedere ; impossibilitatis suæ causas ei, qui sibi præest, patienter et opportune suggerat, non superbiendo aut resistendo vel contradicendo.

suppose, can be intended in this enlightened country;
and I am led by the disputes which I have heard for
many years past respecting canonical obedience to
our Bishops, to doubt whether the talk of obedience
has any real meaning. I am afraid that in the present
day nothing will give such a Superior *power,* except
law or money; and that only the latter will procure
for him anything which can properly be called *obedience.* In the former of these cases, where power is
given by law, the obedience will be rendered to the
law, and in no sense whatever to the Superior. If he
has an Act of Parliament hanging in his cell, consti-
tuting and appointing him Ruler over certain persons
named in the schedule A annexed, according to certain regulations set out in schedule B annexed, those
certain persons must obey (whether *him,* or the *law,*
is perhaps of no great consequence) so far as the law
goes; but beyond that the Superior has no power. On
the other hand, something further may perhaps be
procured for him in the way of obedience, by money.
I do not mean what lawyers call "monies numbered,"

Quod si post suggestionem suam in sua sententia Prioris imperium
perduraverit, sciat junior ita sibi expedire, et ex caritate confidens de
adjutorio Dei, OBEDIAT." Nor was this obedience to be confined to
the Abbot: "Obedientiæ bonum non solum Abbati exhibendum est ab
omnibus: sed etiam sibi invicem ita obediant fratres, scientes se per
hanc obedientiæ viam ituros ad Deum. ... Si quis autem Frater pro
quavis minima causa ab Abbate, vel a quocumque Priore suo corripiatur
quolibet modo; vel si leviter senserit animum Prioris cujuscumque contra
se iratum, vel commotum, quamvis modice; *mox sine mora tamdiu
prostratus in terra ante pedes ejus jaceat* satisfaciens, usque dum bene-
dictione sanetur illa commotio." — *Cap.* lxxi. I do not know whether
it is proposed to revive anything like this; but without it, how could
the monasteries of the dark ages have been what they were? In fact,
what did they become as this spirit of submission, now lost in that of
jealous independence, was gradually subsiding?

paid down in pence by the Superior to the monks for capping him, or doing what he bids; but money's worth, provided by the expense of money. There may be endowments such as will (according to the familiar phrase) make it worth men's while—worth the while of men nursed up in sensitive independence—to put up, at least for a time, with the degradation and annoyance of submission; or it may give a lift in society, smooth the way to holy orders, or more probably to a sectarian ministry; or it may hold out various other advantages which it is easy to imagine. But whatever they may be, the obedience thus purchased will be of little value, and the mode by which it is obtained will considerably qualify the nature of the society. It must, I suppose, consist chiefly of those to whom such advantages are an object; perhaps entirely, for men of higher motives may not like that sort of constant association, and close fellowship, with the sordid and scheming.

There is, I repeat, a want of power; a want which it is in the present day impossible to meet by any legitimate and reasonable means. How is it attempted in the plan to which I have so repeatedly alluded? The author of it seems to have been conscious that the Superior would be in rather a helpless predicament, and to have thought that as he could not be magnified, he should be multiplied. I am afraid I shall hardly be believed, when I say that under the head of "VISITATION," we are told that the proposed monasteries are to be visited, "monthly by the Parochial Minister, quarterly by the Rural Dean, half-yearly by the Archdeacon, yearly by the Bishop." I fear there would be "many masters." Will the reader be so good as to imagine monasteries in the parish, rural deanery, archdeaconry, and diocese, in which he lives and some three or four others which he may happen to know—to consider the probabilities—and charitably keep them to himself?

But let us look at the matter on a broader scale. It must be obvious to everyone who has reflected on the subject, that the progress of modern society—particularly English society—has been most decidedly against the possibility of reviving any institution in which men should live together in common.

The way of living in this country has long been receding more and more from anything like cœnobitic life; and has been characterized by an increasing tendency to independence, individualization, and (to use the words in a mild sense) the dissociation and disconnection of men. It will be remembered that I am not speaking of parties political or religious, or of joint-stock companies, but of the habits of domestic life. How will these prepare men for the *Refectory?* There is now no such thing as "the Meeting of Gallants at the Ordinarye," although such common tables "were long the universal resort of gentlemen;"[3] and indeed of all classes of society in England, as they still are in other countries of Europe. But the most striking illustration is furnished by the principal clubs which have been instituted in London within about twenty years. Most of them have some distinguishing charac-

---

[3] I borrow these words from Nares, who places the word Ordinary in his Glossary with some apology on account of its not having *quite* fallen into actual disuse. Perhaps every year since his book was published had given it a greater right to be included among the "words, phrases, and names" which, as his title page states, "have been thought to require illustration." It means, he tells us, "A public dinner, where each person pays his share. The word, in this sense, is certainly not obsolete; but it is here inserted for the sake of observing, that ordinaries were long the universal resort of gentlemen, particularly in the reign of James I."

ter; the Athenæum, for instance, as a literary club, the Carlton a political one, and in some others the name is a sufficient indication, as the United Service, the Junior United Service, the Travellers', the United University, the Oxford and Cambridge, the Reform. We may in all these cases imagine some degree of sympathy and congruity among the members of each club. At least, we may safely say, what is still more to our purpose, than an immense majority of members have at some time or other been used to eat what are significantly called "commons," in the hall of a College, or an Inn of Court, or at a Naval or Military mess-table. And yet I am informed that in only one of the institutions which I have mentioned is there anything in the nature of a *table d'hôte*; and that in that one it is only a recent experiment, of which it still remains to be seen whether it will succeed, or whether, like similar attempts in other clubs, it must be abandoned. So totally different is the usual course of things, that half a dozen gentlemen, it may be, are sitting together until the moment at which each has put down his name to dine on a particular joint; when it is ready, they go into another room, separate to six different tables, and the ambulatory joint seeks them out in their independent establishments, while each is not supposed to know of even the existence of the other five. Perhaps it would not be too much to say that, in the clubs which I have named, nearly a hundred thousand dinners (to say nothing of other meals) are annually served; and to add, that though eaten (as it regards each club) in the same room, and in company, yet nine out of ten are single, not to say solitary meals. [4]

---

[4] I do not know how far it might be right to consider the details of any one of the Institutions which I have named, as forming a ground

C

I am not finding fault with this. I shall probable be
told that it is much the best way; that it does not arise
from any want of good feeling, but that it is found to be,
on the whole, much more pleasant,—"you are more
independent." I really do not mean to contradict this, or
to argue about the comparative merits of the present,
and any former, system. I am only stating a fact, and
that only as an illustration; but I say that such a fact,
or its cause, whatever that may be, is something much
in the way of any attempt to revive cœnobitic life.
And if the habits in which the present generation
have been educated, have drifted them so far away
from the refectory, is it worth while to waste a word
about the dormitory? I will, therefore, here only ask
the reader to reflect on these two very important points,
and to draw out, for his own consideration, the details
respecting them ; unless indeed he should feel that he
cannot do that until he knows from what class of
society, or whether from all classes indiscriminately,
the monks are to be taken ; and on this point I am
not at present able to give him any satisfactory information, being extremely puzzled about it myself.

I hope I have convinced the reader that whether
the revival of Monasticism be practicable or impracticable, good or bad, I am no advocate for it; and
having said perhaps more than enough to vindicate
myself from the suspicion of any such design in the

for precise calculation respecting the others. But nothing of that sort
is here required; and though (as I suspect) the following statement
may exhibit proportions in a trifling degree more favourable to my
argument, than would be furnished from some of the clubs which I
have named, yet I think it will show the reader that I have not on
the whole exaggerated. In the month of June, 1843, the number of
dinners served at the Athenæum was 1,457, of which all but 36 were
single. Of the latter, 30 were served to two persons, five to three,
and one to four.

following Essays, will he indulge me in the further egotism of saying a very few words about the Essays themselves? They were originally published in the "British Magazine," between the months of March, 1835, and February, 1838. They were written at the request of my most dear, and honoured, and deeply-lamented friend, the Rev. Hugh James Rose, who was then, as he had been from its beginning, the editor of that work. After receiving the first, he wrote to me that he should "fully rely on a perennial, or, rather, *permensal* supply." I mention this, because, under the impression which it created, I was anxious that, throughout the whole series, whenever a paper appeared, another should be sent in time for the next number. In fact, the first thirteen were printed with no intermission; and though of course I do not mean that I had each month to begin the collection of materials *de novo*, yet the arrangement of raw materials is a work which takes some time and trouble, generally more than one expects, and which if it is hurried is likely to be ill-done. Some of the papers were written under disadvantages from want of health and leisure, and all without the help which many books, not within my reach at Gloucester, would have afforded. But chiefly they were written under that great disadvantage of anxiety to furnish a certain quantity, and only a certain quantity, by a given time, and therefore feeling obliged to select, and abridge, and condense, and cut up, and piece together, and omit, and copy over again hastily, and, in short, do all the things which were likely to present unfavourably, materials which I was sure were interesting in themselves. Such circumstances impress an indelible character on a work, which no subsequent labour can remove; but the reader may view it with more indulgence if he considers it as belonging to essays written under the disadvantages which I have described, and published in the pages of a monthly periodical work. I need scarcely add that, though printed much more accurately than I could have expected, such a mode of publishing such materials, of a great part of which I had no opportunity of correcting the press, ensured many typographical errors. Some, I fear, must have escaped, but I hope that the greater part are corrected.

ADVERTISEMENT

TO THE

THIRD EDITION.

THESE Essays have been again reprinted with very slight alteration. The little additions made in the two more recent editions, in the form of Notes, may be had separately by those who have the First edition.

THE DARK AGES.

Nº. I.

"I know nothing of those ages which knew nothing."

I REALLY forget to which of two eminent wits this saying belongs; but I have often thought that I should have liked to ask him how he came to know so curious and important a fact respecting ages of which he knew nothing. Was it merely by hearsay?

Everybody allows, however, that they were *dark* ages. Certainly; but what do we mean by darkness? Is not the term, as it is generally used, comparative? Suppose I were to say that I am writing "in a little *dark* room," would you understand me to mean that I could not see the paper before me? Or if I should say that I was writing "on a *dark* day," would you think I meant that the sun had not risen by noon? Well, then, let me beg you to remember this, when you and I use the term, *dark* ages. I am sorry to waste time about words; but it is so important that people should fully understand one another, and the sooner the better, that I must just notice another point. Do we always clearly know what we should understand—or, indeed, what we mean to express—when we hear or talk of the *dark* ages? Do we mean ages which were dark in themselves, and with respect to those who lived in

them? Or, do we mean that they are dark to us, and
that it is very difficult for us to form a clear idea of
them? I suppose that we sometimes mean one and
sometimes the other, and very frequently both—and,
in fact, both are true; but it is better not to confound
the two ideas, which are in themselves perfectly distinct.

Many causes—of some of which I hope to speak
hereafter—have concurred to render those ages very
dark to us; but, for the present, I feel it sufficient to
remind the reader, that darkness is quite a different
thing from shutting the eyes; and that we have no
right to complain that we can see but little until we
have used due diligence to see what we can.

As to the other point—that is, as to the degree of
darkness in which those ages were really involved, and
as to the mode and degree in which it affected those
who lived in them, I must express my belief, that it
has been a good deal exaggerated. There is no doubt
that those who lived in what are generally called the
"middle" or the "dark" ages, knew nothing of many
things which are familiar to us, and which we deem
essential to our comfort, and almost to our existence;
but still I doubt whether, even in this point of view,
they were so entirely dark as some would have us
suppose. I dare say you have observed, that, in a certain
state of twilight, as soon as you have lighted only a
taper in your chamber, it seems quite dark out of
doors. Yet, perhaps, you have only just come into the
house out of that which, if not broad day-light, was
nevertheless such good serviceable twilight as that,
while you were in it, you never once thought of darkness, or of losing your way, or not being able to see
what you were about; yet, I say, as soon as ever you
lighted, were it only a rushlight, in your chamber, all
the look-out was darkness. Were you ever so misled

as to open the window, and tell the people in the road
that they would certainly lose their way, and break
their shins—nay, even to condole with, or triumph over,
those inevitable consequences of their wandering about
in pitch-darkness? I very much doubt it; if you had
attempted it, I feel quite confident that, if from being
at a loss for an exordium, or for any other reason,
you had been obliged to wait with your head out at
window until your eyes had recovered from the glare
of your own little candle, you would have seen that
there was *some* light abroad—you would have begun
to distinguish houses, and highways, and sober people
going about their business in a way which showed
that they could see enough for common purposes—and
you would have held your tongue and drawn in your
head, rather pleased that you had not exposed yourself.

Certain it is that we are lighted up, and every man
who struts about in our gas light can see that it is
dark out of doors; and, to bring him to anything like
a right understanding of the case—not to prove to
him that it is as light out of doors as in, for I beg
the reader not to suspect me of any such folly—to
bring him, I say, to a right understanding of the case,
he must put his head out, and keep it out for some
time. "What then," says the reader, "are we to do?
Can he mean that one is to wade through all the
stuff that was written in the middle ages?" Certainly
not; for, in the first place, a good deal of it (and, I
suspect, much of what would be most interesting) is
not known to be in existence. I say *known,* because
who can take upon himself to say what is extant?
A good deal has been printed; and, as to MSS., we
know that there are a good many unpublished in the
British Museum, the Bodleian, and other libraries of
our kingdom; and I suppose that everybody who has

the privilege of using those collections, or the King of France's, and a thousand others, can find out specifically what manuscripts they contain. Some, I suppose, know what is in the Vatican, and in other of the less open libraries; but who knows what may be lurking up and down Christendom? Who knows what was hastily swept together when the libraries of suppressed monasteries, in some of the less frequented parts of Europe, were accumulated in large collections, without, perhaps, a full investigation of some of their less obvious and intelligible contents? Perhaps I underrate the pains that may have been bestowed on them; but the idea has been strongly impressed on my mind since I was, some time ago, in the midst of a collection drawn from such sources, in which the manuscripts alone amounted to sixty thousand. I cannot help thinking that a more thorough investigation of such collections may one day bring to light much that is not supposed to exist. But I am running on too fast; and all that was necessary was to assure the reader that, so far from requiring him to read all the works which were written in those ages, I by no means require him to read one-half of such of them as have been printed since; but by putting your head into the darkness, good reader, I do mean that you must, in some degree, make yourself acquainted with the original writers of the period. I have heard of a traveller at an inn, who wished to look out and see if it was day; and who returned to bed with a very wrong judgment on the matter, owing to his being in the dark himself, whereby he was led to open the glass door of a cupboard, instead of a window; and I must say, that, in trusting to the representations of some popular writers, you will be doing much the same thing.

This is a strong assertion; and it is one which I would not make if I were not fully prepared to defend it by sufficient examples, which I hope to give in subsequent papers. And, now I think of it, the reader may, perhaps, desire some account of my plan: and I shall be very glad to take the opportunity of assuring him that I have no plan whatsoever—that I do most absolutely and entirely disclaim everything of the sort—and that I would rather put this very pen into the fire, than undertake to draw out a plan and keep to it in such a matter as this must needs be. I wish this to be understood at the outset, that the reader may not charge me with digressing—a thing to which I am exceedingly prone, whenever restriction makes it practicable. For, to say the truth, I have seldom taken much trouble to find any one thing, that I was not rewarded by finding at least two or three which I was not looking for; and I cannot help digressing myself, and wishing to carry the reader along with me, when anything turns up which interests me, and which I think may amuse or instruct others.

But while I thus disclaim all *plan*, let me say, that I do not write without *purpose;* and this purpose I wish to be fully understood. It is to furnish some materials towards forming a right judgment of the real state of learning, knowledge, and literature during the dark ages. The *period* which I have more particularly in view is that extending from A.D. 800 to A.D. 1200; and to this period I wish the reader to apply any general statement or remark which I may offer respecting the dark or middle ages. At the same time, I do not consider myself as restricted to that precise period, or precluded from adducing proofs or illustrations which may be somewhat more ancient or modern. The subject I have endeavoured to state in terms as comprehensive as possible, by saying, "learning, knowledge, and literature;" for I did not know how else to include the variety of miscellaneous matter into which it is my purpose to inquire, or which, having incidentally met with it in such inquiries, has appeared to me worthy of notice. It will not, however, be understood that I am pretending to write a literary history of that period. All that I propose in these papers is, to bring forward some facts illustrative of the points already mentioned. For this reason a great part of the inquiry will, of course, turn on *books;* and I consider nothing relating to them as foreign to my purpose, which includes any notices that may throw light upon their number, value, and materials—the means employed by proprietors, librarians, and scribes for their multiplication, correction, embellishment, and preservation—any hints tending to show what books were most in request—any notices of the love of books, or of the sale, loan, or gift of them—of the means employed to qualify or cause people to read them—anything in the shape of catalogues of libraries, or collections of books, during that period.

This looks so fine now I have put it on paper, that I must again beg the reader to understand that I am as far as possible from pretending to give a full account of these matters; but I think that by bringing together and offering to notice some hints which lie scattered in various writers of those times, I may—I do not say enable him to form, but—assist him in forming an estimate of the learning, knowledge, and literature of the dark ages; and on this point I will only add, that though he may probably find (and if so, I hope pardon) some errors and mistakes, yet he may rely on my never intentionally copying a reference—that is, whenever I give a reference he will understand (unless the contrary is stated) that I copy immediately from the book to

which I refer. Those who have had any practice in
verifying quotations will know what I mean, and I believe that they will have found reason to join me in
wishing that all authors, great and small, would do
the same.

It must be obvious to everyone who has any acquaintance whatever with the subject, that the learning respecting which I inquire was chiefly sacred or ecclesiastical
—this, I say, is obvious as a matter of fact; but I wish
it to be distinctly understood, that it is particularly with
a view to such learning that I now offer these desultory
notices to the public. My object is to inquire what
knowledge, and what means of knowledge, the Christian Church actually had during the dark ages, and
what was, in fact, the real state of the Church on these
points during that period. All which does not *directly*
tend to this is purely incidental, and is admitted with
a view to another object in which I feel deeply interested—the promotion of the study of ecclesiastical history.

There is no difficulty in knowing where to begin,
for before we can think of building, we must clear
away the rubbish—or, to recur to the figure which I
have already used, before we can possibly look out
of the window, we must open the shutters ; for, if we
only go to "windows that exclude the light," we might
aswell keep our eyes shut. I feel it necessary to do
this, because statements extremely false have been handed
about from one popular writer to another, and it is
quite impossible to form any correct opinion on the
subject without knowing that they are false. At the
same time I cannot persuade myself to begin the business
without begging the reader not to consider me as the
advocate of ignorance, superstition, and error—not to
suppose that I wish to hold up the dark ages as golden

ages—not to think that I undervalue the real improvements which have been made in learning and science. I do not want to maintain any such silly paradox; but I do want to contradict falsehood, and to bate down exaggeration into at least something like truth. Indeed, I cannot help wishing that the reader who has formed his idea of the dark ages only from some modern popular writers—I do not mean those who have written professedly on the subject—could be at once fairly thrown back into the midst of them. I cannot help thinking that he would feel very much as I did the first time that I found myself in a foreign country. A thousand novelties attracted my attention; many were strange, and some displeasing; and there was more or less that seemed foreign in everything. For this I was prepared; but I was not prepared for another feeling which very soon, and quite unexpectedly, sprung up in my mind— "How much is different, and go where I may, for ever changing! True; but how much is the same everywhere!" It was almost a surprise to me to find that the sun and moon went on much the same way as at home —that there were roads, and rivers, and fields, and woods, and towns, and cities, and streets, and houses filled with people who might, perhaps, talk some other language, and dress in some other fashion from mine, but who had evidently much the same notions as to the necessaries of life, and the substantials of society; and, without losing all my pride, or patriotism, or prejudice, I got a new idea of the unity of nature. I felt that He had "made of one blood all nations of men for to dwell on all the face of the earth"—it brought with it a kind of home-feeling—a sense that, wherever I wandered, I was but moving in the hollow of His hand among my own brethren.

Well, and these old folks of the dark ages were our

grandfathers and grandmothers ; and, in a good many points, vastly like ourselves, though we may not at first see the resemblance in the few smoky family pictures which have come down to us ; but had they "not eyes?" had they "not hands, organs, dimensions, senses, affections, passions—fed with the same food, hurt with the same weapons, subject to the same diseases, healed by the same means, warmed and cooled by the same winter and summer" as we are? "Yes ; but they knew nothing." Well, then, it is strange to think how they could do and say so much as they did without any knowledge. But you do not mean quite *nothing*—you will allow that they knew the *Pater-noster* and *Credo*, and that is *something*—nay, a good deal, in itself, and the pledge of a great deal more.

Nº. II.

" 'Amongst so many Bishops,' says Fleury, 'there was not one critic,
who knew how to discern true from false Records '— Critic! quoth
he. It is well if there was one amongst them who could write
his own name." — JORTIN.

I HAVE said, that the state of things during the dark
ages has been misrepresented by some popular writers;
and also that, in making that charge, I did not mean
to reflect on those who had professedly written on
those times. Indeed, as far as I know, the opinions of
men in general on the subject are less frequently formed from these writers, than from those who, having
obtained popularity on some other grounds, treat incidentally of the subject, or here and there give a passing sneer to the dark ages. Few books have been
more popular, or more generally read by thousands
who never thought of asking for authorities, than Robertson's "History of Charles the Fifth;" and, perhaps,
I cannot do better than take some proofs and illustrations of what I have said from that work. Some remarks on his statements may not only tend to obviate
those prejudices which have been raised by him, and
by other writers, but may also furnish a sort of introduction absolutely required by those who have not
given any attention to the subject.

In his "View of the Progress of Society," prefixed
to his History, Robertson says:—

" Literature, science, taste, were words scarce in use during the ages
we are contemplating; or if they occur at any time, eminence in them
is ascribed to persons and productions so contemptible that it appears
their true import was little understood. Persons of the highest rank,

and in the most eminent stations could not read or write. Many of the clergy did not understand the Breviary which they were obliged daily to recite; some of them could scarce read it."—(Vol. i. p. 18.)

On this statement Robertson adds a note, containing "proofs and illustrations;" but, before I come to it, let me observe by the way, that he is professedly speaking of the period "from the *seventh* to the *eleventh* century;" and, that unless we understand him to mean "from the seventh" to quite the *end* of the "eleventh century," it is not wonderful that the clergy did not understand the "Breviary," or true that they were obliged to recite it; for it did not exist. The fact is, indeed, unimportant: because the question is, not whether there was, at that period, a book called the "Breviary," but whether, supposing there were such a book, the clergy could have read it, or anything else. I notice the matter, however, as one of the proofs which Robertson gives that he was not very familiar with a subject on which he ventured to speak in very broad and general terms, but evidently without scrupulous exactness. The note, however, begins in the following manner:—

"Innumerable proofs of this might be produced. Many charters granted by persons of the highest rank are preserved, from which it appears that they could not subscribe their name. It was usual for persons who could not write, to make the sign of the cross in confirmation of a charter. Several of these remain, where kings and persons of great eminence affix *signum crucis manu propria pro ignoratione literarum.* Du Cange, voc. Crux, vol. iii. p. 1191. From this is derived the phrase of signing instead of subscribing a paper. In the ninth century, Herbaud Comes Palatii, though supreme judge of the empire by virtue of his office, could not subscribe his name. Nouveau Traité de Diplomatique par deux Bénédictins, 4to. tom. ii. p. 422."—Note X. p. 232.

It is extremely difficult to meet broad general assertions which it is, in the nature of things, impossible to

D

disprove; but we may reasonably call for evidence of
their truth, and, if it is not produced, we may be allowed to doubt and to dispute them. If "*many* charters" are preserved in which "kings and persons of
great eminence" avow their ignorance, surely many
might be, and, I think, would have been, produced.
The ignorance of the dark ages has long been a matter
of triumphant retrospect; and such regal curiosities of
literature or illiterature, would have been highly interesting to an enlightened public. Perhaps, indeed, "many"
instances have been adduced; but I do not remember
to have seen, or specifically heard of, more than four.
One of them is, I believe, less commonly known; but
the other three have been repeatedly paraded in decla-
mations on this subject.

First—WITHRED, King of Kent, who reigned from
A.D. 671 to A.D. 725, and one of whose charters is
subscribed "Ego Withredus Rex Cantiæ omnia supra
scripta confirmavi, atque a me dictata propria manu
signum Sanctæ Crucis pro ignorantia litterarum ex-
pressi."

Secondly—TASSILO, Duke of Bavaria, in the eighth
century, subscribed a charter containing a grant to
Atto, abbot of Saltzburg, "quod manu propria, ut potui,
characteres chirographi inchoando depinxi corom judi-
cibus atque optimatibus meis. Signum manus meæ pro-
priæ Tassilonis," etc.

Thirdly—HERIBAUD, Comte du Palais under Lewis
II., subscribed a charter in A.D. 873, "Signum Heribaldi
Comitis Sacri Palatii, qui ibi fui et propter ignorantiam
litterarum, signum sanctæ crucis feci."[1]

---

1 These three instances were given by Mabillon (De Re Diplom.
p. 163, 544), and were thence transferred to vol. ii. (not iii.) of the
Benedictine edition of Du Cange. I write here with reference to the
statement of Robertson; for the reader will observe, that two out of

Fourthly—The authors of the *"Nouveau Traité de Diplomatique,"* after arguing against those who considered such ignorance as incredible, say, "L'usage d'avouer pareille ignorance est attesté par tant de traits historiques, que toutes les chicanes de l'esprit humain ne pourront en obscurcir l'éclat. Il suffira d'en rappeler quelques-uns dans les notes." In a note on this passage they exhibit poor Withred "Roi de Cantorberi," and the "Comte du Palais," already mentioned, and add the case of GUI GUERRA, Count of Tuscany, who was reduced to the same necessity, "quia scribere nesciebat." "Il seroit superflu," say they, "d'accumuler un plus grand nombre de faits, pour vérifier un usage, dont la certitude est démontrée."[2]

To me it appears that three or four instances, occurring between the eighth and twelfth centuries, are so far from demonstrating the certainty of a custom, that they do not prove that anything which can properly be called a custom existed; unless, indeed, these writers meant (as perhaps their language elsewhere might almost incline us to believe) that these instances prove the *usage* of kings and great men, when they could not write, to state that fact on the face of the instrument. There is, however, no need to pursue this point; for, of course, I do not mean to deny that there was, in those days, a much greater ignorance of writing than in ours, and that men of rank were much more frequently unable to write then than they are now. But when Robertson talks of "*innumerable* proofs," and tells us that "*many*" charters are preserved, from which "it *appears*" that such persons could not sign

---

the three cases are earlier than the period which I have specified—that is, A.D. 800—1200.

[2] Tom. ii. p. 426.

their names, I feel it right to question his statement.
Had he seen the original charters? I very much doubt
it. If he had seen them, would it have enabled him to
decide the point? I am sure that it would not; and I
feel this certainty, not only because I do not give him
credit for so much research *in re diplomatica* as that
he should bring forward "innumerable proofs" when
Mabillon, and Toustain, and Tassin, gave only four
between them, but from the very nature of the case.
The fact that a man's name was subscribed to a document by another, was, in those days, no proof that he
could not have done it himself; and though, in the
present day, we should hardly give anyone credit for
being able to write if we found that he had only made
his mark, yet we must not entirely judge of other ages
by our own.

Mabillon has given and discussed four reasons why
charters were frequently signed by proxy:—(1.) The
inability of the parties to write; which was, of course,
a very common reason, and may well be supposed,
upon the great scale, to have been the most frequent.
Under this head he gives the well-known story of
Theodoric, and the three cases first mentioned above.
(2.) Physical inability, arising from blindness, disease, or
old age; as in the case of Eugenius, at the council of
Constantinople, in the year 536, who subscribed by the
hand of Paul, a deacon of his monastery, ὡς μὴ δυ-
νάμενος διὰ τὸ γῆρας;[3] of St. Omer, whose will was
subscribed—"Hæc abocellis feci, et alius manum meam
tenens scripsit et subscripsit;" and of some others whom
he mentions. (3.) An affectation of dignity, through
which many high official persons chose that their names
should be written by the notary. (4.) What is most to

---

[3] Conc. Tom. V. p. 136.

our purpose, a custom growing out of this, and extending so far as that by the eleventh century it had become almost universal. In imitation of their superiors, almost all persons—all at least who could pretend to any kind of distinction or title—preferred having their names written by the notary (who could say of them what it might have seemed ostentatious to say of themselves), and then adding, or sometimes omitting to add, their mark—that is, the sign of the cross made with their own hands. It will be obvious, therefore, that it does not "appear" in all cases, even from the original document, whether the parties *could* write their names. Indeed, if it dit not suppose an almost incredible degree of ignorance, one would be tempted to think that Heribaud's affixing the sign of the cross, "pro ignoratione litterarum," had led Robertson to infer, that all persons who made the sign of the cross on such occasions did it for the same reasons; for he says, it was usual "*for persons who could not write* to make the sign of the cross in confirmation of a charter." No doubt; but it was also usual for those who *could* write. The sign of the cross was, in fact, "*the* confirmation and the signature"[4] and

---

[4] Take, by way of specimen, the subscription to the will of Hagano, Canon of St. Martin's at Tours in A.D. 819 : — " Hagano diaconus cessionem a me factam sub signum Sanctæ Crucis confirmavi."—*(Martene, Thesaurus Novus Anecdotorum*, vol. i. p. 23.) (And here let me say, by the way, that as I hope to make frequent reference to this work, as well as to the " Veterum Scriptorum et Monumentorum Amplissima Collectio," edited by *Martene and Durand*, I shall be glad to be allowed, for brevity's sake, to refer to the former as " *Mart.*," and the latter as " *M. & D.*") A charter, too, of Robert, Abbot of St. Martin's in the same city, and of the year 897, is subscribed " Robertus Comes et inclytæ congregationis S. Martini Abbas, per hoc signum Sanctæ Crucis subterfirmare studuit." (*Mart.* i. 57.) Or, to take a subscription belonging to our own country, which may, at the same time, be a specimen of notarial eloquence :—" Anno Incarnationis Dominicæ nongentesimo sexagesimo sexto scripta est hujus privilegii syngrapha, his

the subscriber, in thus making the sign of his holy
religion, was considered as taking an oath. He was, in
fact, said *manu jurare;*[5] and, for greater solemnity, the
cross was sometimes made with the consecrated wine.[6]
The subscriber's adding his name was no essential part
of the confirmation, but simply a declaration and noti-
fication that the person, whose name was there written,
was he who had thus bound himself by his *signature*.
If he was unable, or if he did not choose, to do the
writing for himself, it was done for him by the notary.

I beg the reader not to suppose that I wish to do
more than to moderate the extravagance of Robertson's
statement, and to show that he made it without sufficient grounds. Does he not, in fact, show this himself
when he proceeds to say—

---

testibus consentientibus, quorum inferius nomina ordinatim charaxantur;"
and then follow the subscriptions—"Ego, EDGAR, divina largiente
gratia, Anglorum Basileus, hoc privilegii donum nostro largiens Redemptori
locoque ejus sanctissimo, primus omnium regum, monachorum inibi
collegium constituens, *manu propria signum hagiæ crucis imprimens
confirmavi*—Ego, DUNSTAN, Dorobernensis ecclesiæ archiepiscopus, lar-
gifluam benevoli Regis donationem venerans, *crucis signaculo corroboravi*—
Ego, EADMUND, clytos legitimus præfati filius, *crucis signaculum*, infan-
tuli florens ætate, *propria indidi manu*—Ego EDWARD, eodem rege
clyto procreatus, præfatam patris munificentiam *crucis signo consolidavi*—
Ego ÆLFTHRYTH, legitima præfati regis conjux, mea legatione monachos
eodem loco rege annuente constituens, *crucem impressi*—Ego EADGIFA
prædicti regis ava hoc opus egregium *crucis thaumate consolidavi;*"
and Athelwold, Bishop of Winchester, says, " *crucis signaculo benedixi*."
(Conc. tom. ix. 673.)

⁵ "Comes Tolosanus hanc eandem donationem ibi deveniens rogatu
nostro corroboravit, firmavit, *manuque propria juravit*, id est, subscrip-
tione crucis. "—(*Du Cange in v.* Crux.)

⁶ " Interdum quo solemnius ac firmius esset pactum, quod scribebatur,
cruces ipsæ exarabantur calamo in pretioso Christi sanguine intincto."
(*Du Cange, ibid.*) See also Odo Aribertus (cited by Baluze in his notes
on Agobard, p. 129), who says, " Pace itaque cum sanguine eucharis-
tico separatim per Regem et Comitem firmata et obsignata," etc.

" So late as the fourteenth century, Du Guesclin, Constable of France, the greatest man in the state, and one of the greatest men of his age, could neither read nor write. St. Palaye Mémoires sur l'ancienne Chevalerie, t. ii. p. 82."

Well, then surely two instances in the eighth century, one in the ninth, and one in the twelfth, of men of rank who could not *write*—it does not appear, and really does not follow, that they could not *read*—form too slender a ground for such broad assertions as Robertson has ventured to make respecting the state of letters.

Having, however, disposed of the laity, he proceeds:—

" Nor was this ignorance confined to laymen; the *greater part* of the clergy was not many degrees superior to them in science. *Many* dignified ecclesiastics could not subscribe the canons of those councils in which they sat as members. Nouv. Traité de Diplom., tom. ii. p. 424."

If the reader turns to the authority cited, he will find some general statements respecting the ignorance of the *laity* as to writing (with no specific instances, however, except those already named), but no mention of ecclesiastics. It is true, that, in the succeeding pages, the bishops and other ecclesiastical persons are mentioned, and several are named in a note at page 426; but Robertson should have observed, what is there so plainly stated, " *Tous ces exemples sont antérieurs au VII*ᵉ *Siècle.*" I do not say that later instances might not be produced; but I do not remember to have seen any. He proceeds:—

" One of the questions appointed by the canons to be put to persons who were candidates for orders was this, ' Whether they could read the Gospels and Epistles, and explain the sense of them, at least literally?' Regino Prumiensis ap. Bruck. Hist. Philos. v. iii. p. 631."

I am sorry to say that I have not the Abbot of Prum's book; and I must, therefore, answer as well as I can without it; and perhaps some reader who has it, or who is so happy as to have access to a public library, will be kind enough to give me an extract, or some information as to the specific canon to which Robertson (or rather Brucker) refers. In the meantime I must observe—

First, that supposing all which Robertson meant to convey to the reader were true, still such a canon would show that, bad as things were, there was some attempt to mend them. Granting that up to about the year 900, when Regino wrote, all bishops, priests, and deacons had been entirely ignorant and illiterate—granting that these very canons were written by those who could not write, for the use of those who could not read, still they would be a standing proof that the heads of the church did, at that time, require even from candidates for orders, what Robertson would lead us to consider as rather an unusual accomplishment in a bishop.

Secondly, though I have not Regino's book, I have Brucker's, from whence Robertson professes to borrow the quotation; but, on turning to it, I find a very important difference. The reader will observe that the question, even as Robertson gives it, is, in fact, whether the candidate could read *Latin* publicly, and explain the meaning; but, beside this, the inquiry was really essentially different. It was not whether the candidate had *learned to read,* nor even whether he could *read Latin;* but whether he could read Latin *well.* The words, as quoted by Brucker, are— "Si Evangelium et Epistolam *bene* legere possit, atque saltim ad literam sensus ejus manifestare. Item, si sermonem S. Athanasii de fide SS. Trinitatis memoriter teneat, et sensum ejus intelligat, et verbis communibus enuntiare sciat." Surely there was no proof of brutal ignorance in inquiring whether a candidate for holy orders could read Latin well in public—could repeat, understand, and explain the Athanasian Creed, and preach the doctrine contained in it, in the vernacular tongue. The question did not imply the slightest doubt whether the man could read; but only directed an inquiry whether he could do that which many a man of the present day, who has chuckled over the ignorance of the dark ages, could not do.

Thirdly, if my object were merely to answer Robertson, I should think that I had said enough on this point; but having a farther and more important design, let me, without at present entering very fully into the subject, give a few extracts from "the canons," and one or two writers of the dark ages, or at least of the period to which Robertson refers.

Isidore, Archbishop of Seville, who lived until the year 636, in his work on Ecclesiastical Offices, has a chapter of rules for the clergy, in which he says, that they should be "continually occupied in teaching, in reading, in psalms, and hymns, and spiritual songs;"[7] which seems to imply, at least, that in his time it was no uncommon thing for the clergy to be able to read.

At the eighth council of Toledo, held in A.D. 653, regret was expressed that persons had been admitted into holy orders who were altogether incompetent to the discharge of clerical duties; and it was expressly provided, that no one should be admitted to any degree of ecclesiastical dignity unless he knew the whole Psalter, the hymns of the church, and the office for baptism; and that those who had been admitted without such necessary knowledge should forthwith set to work to acquire it, or be made to do so by their superiors. "For," says the canon, "it is absurd that they who are ignorant of the law of God, and not at least moderately

---

[7] Bib. Pat. x. 203.

learned, should be promoted to any degree of orders, or ecclesiastical office, in which it is their business to teach simple and lay persons, to whom they ought to be mirrors of life and discipline. Let no one, then, who is unlearned, approach to meddle with the holy mysteries of God[8].... none who is blinded by the darkness of ignorance; but let him only come who is adorned with innocence of life and splendour of learning. Otherwise the vengeance of God, and of His church, will hereafter fall on both the ordainers and the ordained."[9]

Whether the council of Nantes, to which the following canon belongs, was held in the year 658, or more than two centuries after, has been disputed; but, either way, it falls within Robertson's period, and is in itself worth notice:—"When a bishop purposes to hold an ordination, all those who are candidates for holy orders are to be cited to the city on the Wednesday preceding, together with the archpresbyters, who are to present them. And then the bishop is to appoint priests and other prudent men, skilled in the divine law, and conversant with the ecclesiastical sanctions, who shall diligently inquire as to the life, family, country, age, and education of the candidates; and as to the place where they were educated, whether they have made good progress in learning (*si sint bene literati*), and are instructed in the law of the Lord. Above all things, whether they firmly hold the catholic faith, and are able to set it forth in plain language. Those, however, to whom this is entrusted must take care that they do not depart from the faith, either from favour or for interest, so as to present to the bishop any unworthy or unfit person

---

[8] There is apparently some hiatus in the MSS.

[9] Conc. vi. 406.

to receive holy orders; for should they do this, he who has unworthily approached the altar shall be removed from it; and they who have attempted to sell the gift of the Holy Ghost, being already condemned in the sight of God, shall be deprived of their ecclesiastical dignity. They shall, therefore, be diligently examined during three following days, and then those who are approved shall be presented to the bishop on the Saturday." [1]

To come to our own country, it was decreed by the sixth canon of the council held at Cliffe, or Cloveshou, near Rochester, in the year 747, "that the bishops shall ordain no man, either of clerks or monks, to the holy degree of priesthood without public inquiry as to his previous life, and his present purity of morals, and knowledge of the faith. For how can he preach to others the whole faith, minister the word of knowledge, and appoint to sinners the measure of penance, unless he first, with studious care, according to the measure of his capacity, takes pains to learn, so that, according to the apostle, he may be able to 'exhort according to sound doctrine?'" The seventh canon directs, "that bishops, abbots, and abbesses . . . shall study and provide, with diligent care, that the custom of continual reading may be practised in their societies, and may become more common, to the benefit of souls and the praise of the eternal King. For it is a lamentable thing to say that, in these times, very few are to be found who are carried away by a thoroughly hearty love of holy learning (*qui ex intimo corde sacræ scientiæ rapiantur amore*), and they are scarcely willing to take much pains to learn anything; but rather from their youth they are occupied with divers vanities, and lusts

---

[1] Conc. ix. 471.

of vain glory; and, with wandering minds, they seek after the unstable things of this world rather than the unchangeable things of holy scripture. Let them, therefore, be compelled; and let the children in the schools be brought up to the love of sacred learning, that, by these means, welleducated persons may be found for every kind of service in the Church of God. Nor let their earthly rulers be so tenacious of their services as that the House of God should fall into contempt, being destitute of all spiritual ornament." [2]

This brings us to the time of Charlemagne, of whose exertions in the cause of literature I hope to say more hereafter; but, in the mean time, I must just notice his Capitulary of Aix-la-Chapelle, addressed to the ecclesiastical authorities in A. D. 789. He says, "We beseech your piety, that the ministers of God's altar may adorn their ministry by good morals—whether, as canons, by the observance of their order, or, as monks, by the performance of their vow—we entreat that they may maintain a good and laudable life and conversation, as our Lord in the gospel commands, 'Let your light so shine before men, that they may see your good works, and glorify your Father which is in heaven;' so that, by their good conversation, many may be drawn to God. And let them collect and keep under their care *(adgregent sibique socient),* not only children of servile condition, but those belonging to persons of better rank; and let there be schools of reading boys. In all monasteries and dioceses, let them learn the Psalms, the musical notes, the chants, the calendar, [3] and grammar. But let

---

[2] Conc. vi. 1575.

[3] " Chants and calendar" is not a very satisfactory translation of " cantus et compotus." To call the latter (as I have seen it called) "the compost" would not be very intelligible to the English reader. Still calendar does not express the thing, which was rather that learn-

them have catholic books well corrected; because frequently, when they desire to pray for anything very
properly, they ask amiss, by reason of incorrect books.
And do not suffer your boys to spoil the books, by
either their reading and writing; and if you want a
gospel or a missal to be written, let it be done by men
of mature age, with all diligence."[4] Again, in the *Capitula data Presbyteris,* in the year 804, he says, " I would
admonish you, my brethren and sons, to give attention
to these few capitula which follow:—first, that a priest
of God should be learned in holy scripture, and rightly
believe, and teach to others, the faith of the Trinity,
and be able properly to fulfil his office. Secondly, that
he should have the whole Psalter by heart. Thirdly,
that he should know by heart the Creed and the office
for Baptism. Fourthly, that he should be learned in the
Canons, and well know his Penitential. Fifthly, that he
should know the Chants and the Calendar."[5] More might
be quoted from this source, but perhaps it is not necessary for my present purpose,—which is, to show that
it was pretty commonly taken for granted that a clerk
could read.

But, in case any reader should have thought that I
lay undue stress on the word *bene,* and should suppose
(as it is charitable to hope that Robertson did when he
left it out), that it was a mere expletive, I will here give

---

ing, that *compotus,* or *computus,* which would enable a *computista,* or
artis computatoriæ magister, to make a calendar, or *computorium ;* and
some of which (enough to show its nature) the reader may find in
the beginning of his Prayer Book. I may, however, perhaps, be allowed at present to pass over some words without explanation, of which
I hope to speak more fully hereafter. What is implied in knowing the
cantus, compotus, grammatica, and penitential, will then more fully
appear.

[4] Capit. Reg. Fr. edit. Baluz., tom. i. 237.   [5] Ibid. p. 417.

an extract from a writer of this period, from which it will appear that the inquiry as to reading *well* was one actually and particularly made. Rabanus Maurus, who was afterwards Archbishop of Mentz, and who wrote his book *De Institutione Clericorum* in the year 819, says, "The canons and the decrees of Pope Zosimus have decided, that a clerk proceeding to holy orders shall continue five years among the readers, or exorcists; and, after that, shall be an acolyte, or subdeacon, four years. That he shall not be admitted to deacon's orders before he is twenty-five years of age; and that if, during five years, he ministers irreproachably, he may be promoted to priest's orders; but on no account before he is thirty years of age, even though he should be peculiarly qualified, for our Lord himself did not begin to preach until he had attained that age."[6] Now, as Rabanus had just before remarked, "*Lectores*" are so-called "*a legendo;*" and if a man was to fill that office for five years before he became even a subdeacon, we may reasonably suppose that, when he came to be examined for, what the Romish church calls, "greater Orders," it might be taken for granted that he had learned to read; but as to reading *well* (I hope no offence to modern times), it certainly was then quite another question, and one to which some attention was paid. "He," says Rabanus, "who would rightly and properly perform the duty of a Reader, must be imbued with learning, and conversant with books, and instructed in the meaning of words, and the knowledge of words themselves; so that he may understand the divisions of sentences, where a clause ends, where the sense is carried on, and where the sentence closes. Being thus prepared, he will obtain such a power of reading as

---

[6] Lib. i. c. xiii. ap. Bib. Pat. tom. x. 572.

that, by various modes of delivery—now simply narrating, now lamenting, now angry, now rebuking, exhorting, pitying, inquiring, and the like, according to circumstances—he will affect the understanding and feelings of all his hearers. For there are many things in the scriptures, which, if they are not properly pronounced, give a wrong sense; as that of the apostle—'Who shall lay anything to the charge of God's elect? God who justifieth.'—Now if, instead of pronouncing this properly, it were to be delivered confirmatively, it would create great error. It is, therefore, to be so pronounced as that the first clause may be a *percontation,* and the second an *interrogation.* Between a percontation and interrogation, the ancients made this distinction—that the former admitted a variety of answers, while the latter must be replied to by 'yes' or 'no.' It must, therefore, be so read that, after the percontation— 'Who shall lay anything to the charge of God's elect?' —that which follows be pronounced in an interrogatory manner—'God that justifieth?'—that there may be a tacit answer, 'no.' And again we have the percontation—'Who is he that condemneth?' and again we interrogate—'Christ that died? or rather that is risen again? who is at the right hand of God? who also maketh intercession for us?' At each of which there is a tacit answer in the negative. But in that passage where he says, 'What shall we then say? that the Gentiles, which followed not after righteousness, have attained to righteousness,' unless after the percontation— 'What shall we say then?'—the answer were added— 'that the Gentiles which followed not after righteousness have attained to righteousness,' the connexion with what follows would be destroyed. And there are many other parts which, in like manner, require to be distinguished by the manner of pronouncing them. Beside this, a reader ought to understand the force of the accents, that he may know what syllables he is to lengthen ; for there are many words which can only be prevented from conveying a wrong meaning by being pronounced with the proper accent. But these things he must learn from the grammarians. Moreover the voice of a reader should be pure and clear, and adapted to every style of speaking, full of manly strength, and free from all that is rude or countrified. Not low, nor yet too high ; not broken, not weak, and by no means feminine; not with inflated or gasping articulation, or words mouthed about in his jaws, or echoing through his empty mouth ; not harsh from his grinding his teeth ; not projected from a wide-open mouth,—but distinctly, equally, mildly pronounced ; so that each letter shall have its proper sound, and each word its proper quantity, and that the matter be not spoiled by any affectation." [7]

It is true that Rabanus Maurus has taken the substance of this from Isidore of Seville,[8] who wrote more than two hundred years before, though he has improved it; but if it was good, why should it not be repeated? So thought Ivo, Bishop of Chartres, who gave it again in his discourses *De Rebus Ecclesiasticis*,[9] nearly three hundred years after Rabanus wrote—and I cannot help suspecting that if Robertson had gone to the Archbishop of Seville in the seventh century, the Archbishop of Mayence in the ninth, or the Bishop of Chartres in the eleventh, for holy orders, he would have found the examination rather more than he expected. If I have failed to convince the reader of this,

---

[7] Lib. ii. c. lii. Bib. Pat. x. 616.

[8] De Eccles. Office., lib. ii. c. xi., Bib. Pat. x. 209.

[9] Serm. ii. ap. Bib. Pat. x. 774.

by the extracts already given, I shall hope to do so
hereafter; but I think that what has been said must
be sufficient to show that it was not a very uncommon
thing, even in the dark ages, for the clergy to be able
to read and write.

E

Nº. III.

" —— nil dulcius est, bene quam munīta tenere
  Edita doctrina sapientum templa serena;
  Despicere unde queas alios, passimque videre
  Errare, atque viam palanteis quærere vitæ."—LUCRETIUS.

" Rivers of waters run down mine eyes, because they keep not thy law."—Ps. cxix.

WHEN I began the preceding paper, I had no idea of replying to Robertson's character of the clergy during the dark ages at such length; and meant only to notice, very briefly, such parts of his statement as are absolutely untrue. I intended, until I should have thus gone through his remarks, to say little or nothing on matters which may be more conveniently, intelligibly, and convincingly, discussed after untruths have been exposed, and the prejudices created and fostered by them removed; and also, after a variety of facts have been adduced, which may be referred to for proof or illustration. Perhaps enough has been already said to show that the clergy of the period to which Robertson refers were not so universally, or even so entirely, ignorant as might be supposed from his language; yet, having said so much, and considering that it all tends to the elucidation of our subject in more than one way, I feel desirous (without professing here to enter fully into the matter) to add one or two more extracts, which are not, I think, in themselves uninteresting.

From the Constitutions of Reculfus, who became Bishop of Soissons in A.D. 879, and who is supposed to have issued these instructions to his clergy ten years afterwards, it appears as if he took it for granted that they could, not only read, but write. The fourth, fifth, and. sixth sections are as follows:—"Know, therefore, that this is addressed to you, 'Be ye clean, ye that bear the vessels of the Lord;'[1] which you must not suppose to refer only to the cleansing of the chalice and paten, wherein the body and blood of Christ is consecrated, but also to personal cleanliness and mental purity. For, as St. Gregory says, in treating of the parable of the ten virgins, "Our vessels are our hearts, wherein we bear about with us all our thoughts.'[2] We have, therefore, a frail vessel, that is, our body, which we ought always to keep clean, with the most scrupulous care; so that, while we offer 'pure offerings,' we also ourselves may be acceptable sacrifices before his holy altar. Also we admonish that each one of you should endeavour to have by heart, truly and correctly, the Psalms, the Discourse on the Catholic Faith which begins 'Quicumque vult,' etc., and the Canon of the Mass, and the Chants, and the Calendar. The office for Baptism (both for male and female children, and also singular and plural), as well as the offices for consecrating fonts, water to be sprinkled in houses, the commendation of the soul, and the prayers at the burial of the dead, you are to have distinctly and correctly written out; and, by frequent study, you are to qualify yourselves to perform them correctly and unblameably for both men and women. As to the aforesaid office for the baptism of infants, we would that you should write it out in a fourfold manner; that is to say, the singular masculine and the singular feminine; the plural masculine and the plural feminine; as we, if Christ

---

[1] "Mundamini qui fertis vasa Domini." Isaiah lii. 11. I give the words of our translation; and wish to mention that I do so wherever there is not any material variation.

[2] Hom. in Evan. XII., t. ii. p. 357.

permit, will furnish you with a copy. Also we admonish that each one of you should be careful to have a Missal, Lectionary, a Book of the Gospels, a Martyrology, an Antiphonary, Psalter, and a Book of Forty Homilies of St. Gregory, corrected and pointed by our copies which we use in the holy mother church. And, also, fail not to have as many sacred and ecclesiastical books as you can get; for from them you shall receive food and condiment for your souls, our Lord himself having declared, 'Man doth not live by bread alone; but by every word that proceedeth out of the mouth of God.' If, however, any one of you is not able to obtain all the books of the Old Testament, at least let him diligently take pains to transcribe for himself correctly the first book of the whole sacred history, that is, Genesis; by reading which he may come to understand the creation of the world."[3]

This, as I have observed, seems to imply that the priests in the diocese of Soissons, in the ninth century, could both read and write; and, indeed, from the sixteenth section, it appears that the secular clergy in that diocese kept schools; and so not only read and wrote themselves, but were the causes of reading and writing in others. But this is anticipating; for what reader of Robertson is prepared to believe that the schoolmaster was abroad in the ninth century? I will, therefore, only here add one more extract on this subject, and that shall be from the history of our own country. The Canons of Ælfric, whether we owe them to the archbishop or the grammarian, or whether they were one and the same person, were written between the years 950 and 1000. They were addressed to Wulfin, Bishop of Sherborn; and written in such a form as that he might communicate

---

[3] Conc. ix. p. 418.

them to his clergy as a kind of episcopal charge. The twenty-first canon orders—"Every priest, also, before he is ordained, must have the arms belonging to his spiritual work; that is, the holy books—namely, the Psalter, the Book of Epistles, and the Book of Gospels, the Missal, the Book of Hymns, the Manual, the Calendar,[4] the Passional, the Pœnitential, and the Lectionary. These books a priest requires, and cannot do without, if he would properly fulfil his office, and desires to teach the law to the people belonging to him. And let him carefully see. that they are well written."

The passage of Regino, quoted by Robertson—of which, in this long reply, I am afraid the reader has almost lost sight—tempts me to add the twenty-third canon—"The mass-priest shall, on Sundays and on mass-days, explain the Gospel in English to the people; and, by the Lord's Prayer and the Creed, he shall, as often as he can, stir them up to faith and the maintenance of Christianity. Let the teacher be warned to avoid that which the prophet has said—'*Canes muti*

---

[4] The Latin translation in Wilkins's Councils has *numerale;* that in Labbe's preserves the original Anglo-Saxon *gerim;* and I translate it *calendar*, because I have no doubt that it means the *compotus*, which I have before (somewhat improperly) so translated. It occurs in a "Calendarium seu Menologium Poeticum," given by Hickes, *Thes. Ling. Vett. Sept.*, tom. i. p. 203, from a MS. in the Cottonian Library, at the 18th line "Ianuaɲiuɼ ʒeɲim," where it is translated "Januarium Calendarii;" and in a note on it, at p. 209, he says, "Sic enim ʒeɲim, ut ɼiɪɪm apud veteres *calendarium, fastos, ephemerida* denotat." Considering the purpose for which I write, it may be worth while to state that Collier, in his *Ecclesiastical History*, vol. i. p. 207, gives this canon, thus:—"By the one-and-twentieth, 'Every priest, before his ordination, was obliged to be furnished with church books, that is, with a Psalter; a Book of Epistles and Gospels; a Missale; a Book of Church Hymns: a Penitentiale, and a Lectionarie, or Ræding Boc,'" etc., thus leaving out the Gerim, Manual, and Passional; a convenient way of quoting.

non possunt latrare'—'Dumb dogs, they cannot bark.'
We ought to bark and preach to the laity, lest per-
chance we should cause them to perish for lack of
knowledge. Christ saith in his Gospel of ignorant teachers, 'if the blind lead the blind, both fall into the
ditch.' Blind is the teacher if he is illiterate, and deceives the laity by his ignorance. Beware of this, as
your office requires." [5]

To proceed, however, with Robertson:—

"Alfred the Great complained that, from the Humber to the Thames,
there was not a priest who understood the liturgy in his mother tongue,
or who could translate the easiest piece of Latin; and that, from the
Thames to the sea, the ecclesiastics were still more ignorant. Asserus
de rebus gestis Alfredi, ap. Camdeni. Anglica, &c., p. 25. The ignorance of the clergy is quaintly described by an author of the dark
ages. ' Potius dediti gulæ quam Glossæ; potius colligunt libras quam
legunt libros; libentius intuentur Martham quam Marcum; malunt legere
in Salmone quam in Solomone.' Alanas de art. Prædicat. ap. Lebeuf.
Dissert. tom. ii. p. 21".— p. 233.

I will not here run into what must necessarily be
a long discourse about Alfred, and which would anticipate what I may more properly say when some facts
shall have come under notice which may enable us to
form a better judgment of the state of things in England during the reign of that monarch, as well as before
and after it. Here I only observe that, supposing Robertson's statement to be quite correct, [6] it only shows
that the Anglo-Saxons were at that period behind their
neighbours on the continent of Europe; which nobody
would think of disputing. Let us, therefore, with Robertson, leap over about *three centuries*, and into Flanders,

---

[5] Wilkins's Conc., i. 250.

[6] Which, by the way, it is not. Alfred said "very few," which is
quite a different thing, if I may trust the Latin translation of Wise
(p. 87) — " paucissimi ;" and Mr. Sharon Turner's English translation
"very few," in his History of the Anglo-Saxons, vol. ii. p. 277.

to see how quaintly "the ignorance of the clergy" was described by Alanus. Are we to take this as the character of "the clergy" generally in all places during the dark ages? or only of "the clergy" in the time and neighbourhood of Alanus? And is it by jumping over time and space in this manner, to pick out parts of sentences, that we can hope to understand the matter aright?

Though, after taking and giving some trouble, I am not at present able to say whether this passage has been correctly and fairly quoted either by or from Lebeuf, yet I feel authorized by what I have seen of Alanus to suspect that he did not speak in these terms of "the clergy" in general. Of this, however, one cannot judge without seeing what is to agree with "dediti;" and, indeed, the whole connexion of the sentence. Yet it matters little: the words may be there; and whether they are or not, and whether they meant all that Robertson pretends, is of no consequence. It is of more importance to observe the taste and the spirit which are manifested in the citation of such ribaldry. I notice it the rather, because I have remarked that so many moderns seem disposed to speak and write with self-satisfied glee of their dark ancestors; and to be much amused with the quaint humour which describes and exaggerates their ignorance, barbarism, and vice. I believe the feeling is natural to man—it was avowed with infernal candour by the heathen whose hackneyed lines I have placed at the head of this paper—but it is one which we might expect to find disavowed with abhorrence by every man pretending to be a Christian. That men were wandering in error, and seeking in vain "the way of life," with such guides as Alanus has "quaintly described," can be no subject of mirth to a Christian mind. Superstition may put on a ridiculous form, and ignorance may commit ludicrous blunders—we *may* laugh, for, by the law of our nature, we *must* laugh at some of these things—but to find amusement in the brutal and degraded state of the ministers of religion at any time, and, indeed, I may say of any religion, must, I think, be peculiar to bad men.

It is, however, very important, and very much to our present purpose, to add a few words on this subject; because I apprehend that, for the want of a little consideration, many persons have been led into a mistaken view of the case. There were in the dark ages (as well as at other times) two sets of persons, from whose writings it is easy to cull passages describing "the clergy" as less learned and religious than they were bound to be; and each set tempted to detail, and perhaps to exaggerate, the vices of ecclesiastics.

First, there were those who hated the religion which the clergy maintained, and who envied the property, privileges, and influence which they enjoyed; and which (whatever the personal character of some of them might be) they generally employed to check the licentiousness of others. Among these there have perhaps always been facetious persons who have considered religion and its ministers as fit subjects for their drollery; and who have delighted to represent the clergy as a vile race of knaves and fools, characterized only by pride, sensuality, avarice, and ambition, except where all these, and all that was better, was kept under by idiot superstition. Yet, as far as I know, there was but little of this ribaldry during the period of which Robertson writes. He talks of the *seventh to the eleventh* century; but for the single instance which he gives (and I cannot but doubt whether it properly belongs to this class) he goes to, at least, the middle of the twelfth century. Without entering into the dispute about the precise period, or the identity of Alanus, this is the earliest date that can be assigned to him; and, in fact, it is to the thirteenth, and yet more to the fourteenth and fifteenth, century that we must go for quaint descriptions of the corrupted church. I should like very much to bring forward some of these, with the remarks of some modern writers on them; but I am afraid that, notwithstanding all I have said, such a proceeding really would be a digression; and, therefore, it may suffice, for the present, to say that what we know of the incapacity or vices of the clergy or the monks during the period in question, we derive principally from their own confession; or, at least, from their own statements.

The second set of writers to whom I have alluded, are those who either under pretence, or with the real object, of producing reformation, have been vigilant to spy out, and forward to publish, the vices of churchmen. If there were but few of the former class of writers during the period more immediately under our consideration, there were some (I hope to be able to show ground for believing that there were many) virtuous, pious, and comparatively enlightened persons [7] who belonged to this class; and who, when their lot was cast among ecclesiastics who disgraced their profession by ignorance and vice, did seriously desire (and were joined or imitated by others who pretended to desire) a reformation of such evils. But I need not say that the zeal of reformers, whether real or pretended, has often

---

[7] I use this qualification in deference to the popular view of the subject; for I cannot tell why, in things pertaining to the kingdom of God, and on which man can be enlightened only by the word and Spirit of God, they might not be as truly, and even as fully enlightened as any of mankind before or after their time.

exaggerated the evils which it desired to redress; sometimes by describing them as greater, and oftener by representing them as more general, than they really were.

From both these sets of writers very strong statements may be extracted; and the testimony which they apparently give will seem, to the young student of ecclesiastical history, to be confirmed by the proceedings of Councils, and the tenor of their canons, as well as by a good deal of what he will find in the works of secular historians, even supposing that he does go to original sources. He must, however, remember that sin, in some shape or other, is the great staple of history, and the sole object of law; and he must expect, from both the historian and the legislator, to hear more of one turbulent prelate, or one set of factious or licentious monks, than of a hundred societies, or a thousand scattered clergy, living in the quiet decency suited to their profession. Yet even of such societies, passing through the year, and the century, in orderly obscurity, annals are not wanting—"but they are generally written in very shocking Latin"—very true.

However, to illustrate what I have said, let me recur to the canons of Ælfric, of which I have already spoken. One might find words in his address to Wulfin, from which it would seem as if he meant to testify, that the wickedness of the clergy was such, as that they had completely destroyed the church. "You ought," he says, "frequently to talk to your clergy, and to rebuke their negligence; for, by their perverseness, the laws, religion, and learning of the church are almost destroyed. Therefore deliver your soul; and tell them what are the duties of priests and ministers of Christ, lest you likewise perish, being counted as a dumb dog. We have written this epistle which follows in English, as if spoken by you, and you had addressed it to the clergy of your diocese, beginning thus:—'I myself tell you priests, that I will not put up with your negligence in your ministry; but, in truth, I will tell you what is the law concerning your order,'" etc. Fuller illustration I hope to give hereafter; [8] in the meantime I wish to get through Robertson's statement. He goes on to say—

" To the obvious causes of such universal ignorance arising from the state of government and manners, from the seventh to the eleventh century, we may add the scarcity of books, and the difficulty of rendering them more common during that period. The Romans wrote their books either on parchment or on paper made of the Egyptian

---

[8] To pursue this point here would lead us into what is, perhaps, a much wider field than some readers may suppose—the subject of *church reform* in the middle ages. To me it has appeared extremely interesting, and I hope to give some extracts, which may lead us to believe that, bad as things were, there were always some who were trying to mend them. Conceive a bishop of the tenth century writing to two archbishops in such terms as these:—" Relicto penitus eo qui nos proposuit mundo, relicto omni præter nomen officio, ipsi ita specialius deservimus ceteris mundo, ut dum ceteri Deo quæ Dei, mundo quæ mundi sunt contendunt reddere, nos e contra mundo quæ Dei, id est omnigenum amorem et cultum; Deoque quæ debuerant mundo reddi, reddamus, id est omnigenum despectum et contemtum, et ut ipsi alligemur arctius, ne quando scilicet, dum ab eo non recognoscimur, despiciamur, relicto ritu cultu, habitu quoque nostro, ipsius mundi consuetudine atque studiis, amictibus etiam in tantum utimur, ut solo, ut ita eloquar, barbirasio et corona, et quod non a nobis ut ab eis ducuntur uxores, qualescumque etiam, quas Domino ore tantummodo, et hoc rarissime, reddere videmur, laudes, in nullo alio sæcularibus videamur dissimiles; ita ut de nobis, proh nefas! dictum prophetiæ possit credi quod continent tempora præsentis ævi : ' Et erit sicut populus, sic sacerdos,'" etc. And he presently afterwards relates an anecdote which I must translate, though for the other matter I wished the reader to have the bishop's own words. A certain priest who saw his bishop playing at dice, shook his head in a scornful manner. The prelate perceiving it, was very angry (justly enough, says the bishop who relates it, if his anger had been directed against the right person), and

papyrus; the latter, being the cheapest, was of course the most commonly used. But after the Saracens conquered Egypt, in the seventh century, the communication between that country and the people settled in Italy, or in other parts of Europe, was almost entirely broken off, and the papyrus was no longer in use among them. They were obliged, on that account, to write all their books upon parchment, and as the price of that was high, books became extremely rare, and of great value. We may judge of the scarcity of the materials for writing them from one circumstance. There still remain several manuscripts of the eighth, ninth, and following centuries, wrote on parchment, from which some former writing had been erased, in order to substitute a new composition in its place. In this manner, it is probable, that several works of the ancients perished. A book of Livy, or of Tacitus, might be erased to make room for the legendary tale of a saint, or the superstitious prayers of a missal. Murat. Anti. Ital. v. iii., p. 833. P. de Montfaucon affirms, that the greater part of the manuscripts on parchment which he had seen, those of an ancient date excepted, are written on parchment from which some former treatise had been erased. Mém. de l'Acad. des inscript. tom. ix., p. 325. As the want of materials

---

told the priest, that if he did not show him that what he was doing was forbidden by the canon law, he would immediately send him to gaol. The priest, with an aspect of horror, fell at his feet, and said, "Pardon me, my lord, I am so overwhelmed with fear that I could not repeat even the first verse of the first psalm" (the very alphabet of a priest in those days), "nor any one decree from the canons; but I beseech you, most pious prelate, that you would recal to my mind what in my terror I have quite lost." On this the bishop, and the rest of the company, began to laugh and jest; but, the priest being still urgent, the Bishop yielded to his entreaties, and repeated a couple of verses: — "Blessed is the man that walketh not in the counsel of the ungodly, nor standeth in the way of sinners, nor sitteth in the seat of the scornful; but his delight is in the law of the Lord; and in his law doth he meditate day and night." — "Very right, most holy father," cried the priest, "and then the rest of your time you may play at dice."

As to the zealous bishop, who relates this story, are we to take his words respecting the state of the church as a plain statement of facts, and set them down as cold-blooded history? or do the very act and circumstances of his writing them constrain us to receive them with some qualification?

for writing is one reason why so many of the works of the ancients have perished, it accounts likewise for the small number of manuscripts, of any kind, previous to the eleventh century, when they began to multiply, from a cause which shall be mentioned. Hist. Liter. de France, tom. vi., p. 6."

Much of the foregoing, which relates to the materials, value, and scarcity of books during the period in question, would lead us into multifarious discussion; yet it is so interwoven with the specific statements with which it is my object at present to deal, that I know not how to convince the reader that I am acting fairly, or even to make the matter intelligible, except by thus quoting the whole passage. I do not know whether there ever was a time when readers looked out the passages referred to, or granted the writer's request that they would, "see," "compare," etc., such-and-such things, which for brevity's sake he would not transcribe: but if readers ever did this, I am morally certain that they have long since ceased to do it; and, therefore, where I feel it necessary that the reader should know what has been said, I dare not content myself with merely referring even to so common a book as Robertson's.

As to the specific statements, allow me to say— but perhaps the reader would be offended at my saying all that I might be inclined to say on the subject—it brings us on rather tender ground, and he may think that I am as bad as the monks ; and, besides, one is really ashamed to say, in the nineteenth century, what they might have been allowed to say a thousand years ago. Let me rather suppose some monk, of the period to which Robertson refers, to rise in defence of his order. He may say what he pleases ; and if he should talk nonsense, the enlightened reader will smile and forgive him. Let him be as absurd and wretched

a creature as modern taste can conceive—such as,
from his own description, we may suppose the historian
Ditmar to have been[9], or the Prior of Grandmont, whose

> " Frequens genuflexio nasum oblicavit,
>   Genibus et manibus callum concreavit."

Let us suppose such a person brought to light, and
blinking in our sunshine, and at length made to understand the nature of the charge preferred against him
and his brethren. He might, perhaps, answer—"Truly,
Dr. Robertson, you are rather hard upon us. To be
sure, some part of what you say cannot be denied—
a book of Tacitus or Livy *may* have been erased to
make room for a legend, or a missal—it is, as you
say, a peradventure ; but it *may* have been so ; and,
if it was, people could do better without books of
Tacitus and Livy than without prayer-books. Nay, you
who go on to tell us that in those days 'even monasteries of considerable note had only one missal,'—you
who profess yourself to be a Christian minister (which
many of us were not), ought to applaud us for spoiling
the Egyptians, and serving ourselves of the heathen.
We *may* have destroyed a book of Tacitus or Livy,
to preserve a legend, or make a missal ; or it *may*
have been the other way. We *may* have saved the
youth of Christendom from some heathen obscenity,
and preserved a valuable treatise of Jerome, Ambrose,
or Augustine—or, if these names only provoke a sneer,
we *may* have thus preserved some of those Annals to
which you modern historians are indebted (not imme-

---

[9] " Agnosce, lector, proceritatem, et videbis in me parvum homun-
cionem, maxilla deformem leva, et latere eodem, quia hinc olim erupit
semper turgescens fistula. Nasus in pueritia fractus ridiculum me facit,
idque totum nil questus essem, si interius aliquid splendiscerem."— *Lib.*
IV. *ap. Leibn. Scr. Bruns. Tom.* I. *p.* 364.

diately, I fear, in most cases) for whatever is true in
your works; and which, in grateful return, some of
you love to describe as dull, stupid, barbarous, musty,
old records, with which you have condescended to defile
yourselves for the public good. But then, as to our
substituting the *legendary tales* of the saints—under
favour, doctor, I cannot help thinking, from the way
in which you write, that you have not quite a correct
idea of the time when what are commonly known to
Protestants as the legends of the Roman Church were
principally written. We, who lived between the seventh
and eleventh centuries, had comparatively little to do
with the matter. We plead guilty to great ignorance,
bad Latin, and blunders; to much nonsense, some lies,
and a good deal that was, in fact, legendary—but as
to what your readers would understand by legendary
tales of saints, you must look to a later period,—you
must go forward to the times when (as that so good
inquisitor and bishop, Bernard Guido, says) 'Frater
Jacobus de Voragine Lombardus, postmodum Archiepiscopus Januensis, suam conflavit compilationem *more
suo* in *vitis* sanctorum *novis*, sicut et de aliis sanctis
fecit, prout ibiden patet.'[1] You must talk to writers of
the thirteenth century; you may go on, and talk to the
Council of Trent, and the Congregation of the Index,
and ask them why they never expurgated the Golden
Legend, why they never even weeded out its barbarous
blunders, to say nothing of its lies. Yes, to the horrible
disgrace of our church, you may ask why they never
stretched out the hand of correction, or restriction—
never even directed the slightest breath of censure—
towards it, and the thousand and one lying books that
began to be made, and circulated, and devoured, as soon

---

[1] Libellus de Magist. Ord. Prædic. *M. & D.* VI., 405.

as what you are pleased to call the revival of letters had set men to read the monstrous figments, the foul and scandalous obscenities of the pagan poets. Then you may go on with Ribadaneira, and a host of moderns,— but do not accuse *us,*—look for yourself, and see what we *did* write; and I am persuaded that, though you may sometimes see a legendary tale of a saint, and sometimes a superstitious prayer of a missal, you will find comparatively little for which it would have been so very sinful to scrape a parchment, which might, or might not, contain a book of Tacitus or Livy.

"Moreover, in case we should not come to anything like an agreement as to relative value, led me add, that as we are not the people principally concerned in concocting the legends, so we are not the people who were most addicted to scraping parchments. I do not mean to deny that what you say is true as to the letter, and that 'there still remain *several* manuscripts of the eighth, ninth, and *following* centuries,' which have been so treated. There are, I confess, *several* such specimens; but you know, though you slur over (not to say misrepresent) his words, by saying 'of ancient date,' that Montfaucon expressly limits his statement to manuscripts written *since* the *twelfth* century;[2] and therefore I put

---

[2] Not having it in my power to verify the citation of Montfaucon, I applied to a learned friend who has access to a public library He replied, "This reference is wrong—there is nothing, in the volume referred to, by Montfaucon, nor any mention of him in the page given above. I therefore looked to the index, where, under Montfaucon's name, I got a reference to a paper of his, vol. vi. p. 592, entitled, 'Dissertation sur la plante appelée Papyrus, sur le papier d'Egypte, sur le papier de coton, et sur celuy dont on se sert aujourd'huy.' In p. 606 is the following passage, which, I presume, gave rise to Robertson's statement. After having mentioned the fact, that 'depuis le xiie Siècle,' ancient writings were erased to make way for books of the church—and thus that Polybius, Dio, Diodorus, etc. were converted into Triodions,

it to your own conscience, whether it is not probable
that we were more sinned against than sinning in this
matter—whether those who wanted writing materials
were likely to prefer parchment which was older than
our time, to that which we had used—and whether our
works were not more exposed to erasure than those of
earlier writers? I have said that you know this—for I
cannot affect to suppose that you did not see the words
which you have omitted or altered—but I doubt whether
you do know, that a great part of the scraping of manuscripts was not owing to our writing legends or missals,
but was perpetrated in order to carry on the ungodly
quarrels, or worldly business, of secular men; so that
as late as the fourteenth and fifteenth centuries notaries
were restricted from practising, until they had taken
an oath to use none but new parchment."

I do not mean to make myself responsible for all that
a monk under such circumstances might say; but yet
I cannot suppress my opinion, that if any of that fraternity had so addressed Robertson, his most prudent and
popular course would have been to turn short round
on the opposite tact, and to reply—"Ah! you sensual,
ignorant, lazy monks; you could not read or write—
potius dediti gulæ quam glossæ," etc.

Pentecostaries, Homilies, etc. he says, 'Après une exacte recherche, je
puis assurer que des livres écrits sur du parchemin *depuis le xii Siècle*,
j'en ay plus trouvé dont on avoit raclé l'ancienne écriture, que d'autres."

Nº. IV.

Bibliothekar. Haben sie des *Muratorius* seine Werke nicht gelesen ?
P. Priszilian In meinem Leben nicht; ich kenne sie gar nicht.

DIE HEILIGEN.

I HAVE already observed that there is often great difficulty in meeting broad general assertions, even when one is sure that they are untrue; and I may add that it is as difficult—perhaps it is impossible—to prevent, or remove, the erroneous impressions likely to arise from statements which though really false are *verbally* true. My meaning will be illustrated by considering the statement with which Robertson follows those already discussed.

" Many circumstances prove the scarcity of books during these ages. Private persons seldom possessed any books whatever. Even monasteries of considerable note had only one missal. Murat. Antiq. v. ix. p. 789."

Certainly there needs no proof that books were scarce during the middle ages. No doubt the scarcity, as compared with the plenty, and even surfeit, of the present day, was great indeed. Yet, great as it was, I cannot help suspecting that it has been exaggerated; and I think we shall find ground to doubt the truth of the assertion that "private persons seldom possessed any books whatever"—or if, by assigning a lax, and comparative, meaning to "seldom," the statement should be turned into a notorious truth not worth uttering, we shall see reason for believing that the impression which it was calculated to convey, and probably has conveyed to most readers, is erroneous.

To come, however, to the specific statement, backed by the authority of Muratori—for my present business

is chiefly with it—"even monasteries of considerable
note had only one missal." In the first place, will
anybody tell me what they wanted with more? "Monasteries of considerable note" had but one church, or
chapel, and not more inmates than that one building
would contain; and might not mass be said every hour
of every day all the year round, out of *one* missal, as
well as if there had been fifty? "Yes," it may be said
"but one is accustomed to look on monasteries as having
been, in some small and comparative degree, places
where there was *some* learning, and some appearance
at least of religion; and one is surprised to hear of
their being so ill provided with books." I know it—I
know that no man who has any tolerable acquaintance
with history, sacred or secular, can help having some
idea—perhaps a very vague and discouraged idea—that,
in those ages, the monastery was the refuge of want
and weakness, the nursery of art, the depository of
learning, and the sanctuary of religion. This, I say, every
man who is moderately acquainted with history must
know; even though he should not be aware of the less
obvious, but not less certain influence of monastic institutions on agriculture, commerce, and those comforts
and pleasures of social life from which their inmates
were themselves excluded. Something like this, I repeat,
every tolerably educated man does feel; but a strange
sort of vague contradiction is thrown over it by such
foolish statements as that which I have quoted from
Robertson. Half the readers of his History of Charles V.
do not know what a Missal is, or why the monks wanted
any, or what they did with that single one which they
are admitted to have had; but yet, from the way in
which it is stated, they take it for granted that it was
a horrible delinquency in "monasteries of considerable
note," to have only one missal—and if *they* were so

wretchedly off, in what state were the thousands of monasteries which were of inconsiderable note, or of no note at all?

But, to say the truth, all this, though not I hope untrue or entirely useless, is not to our present purpose; as the reader will find if he refers to Muratori, or favours me with his attention to a brief statement of the grounds on which Robertson ventured to make his assertion.

The Abbot Bonus appears to have been born about the year 990; and though the place of his birth is not certainly known, it seems probable that he was a native of Pisa. At all events we are informed that he became a monk at Nonantula, and that he, and his uncle Peter, came from thence in the year 1018, to Pisa, where they laid the foundation of the monastery of St. Michael, which certainly was afterwards "of considerable note." Bonus presided over it for thirty years; after which period some dispute or dissension (it does not clearly appear of what nature, but it seems not to have been any quarrel with his monks) caused him to quit his monastery, and set off for Corsica, where some property had been bequeathed to him, and where he proposed to live as a private person. Stopping, however, on his voyage at the island of Gorgona, where there was a monastery, he found the monks greatly distressed by the recent loss of their Abbot. They unanimously called on Bonus to take his place. He resisted for some time; but overcome by their importunity, he consented; requesting only leave to return to Pisa, in order to bid farewell to his old associates, and to exhort them with respect to the choice of a successor. Having obtained permission, and executed his purpose, he returned to Gorgona, and undertook the office of abbot there, which he

held until his death in the year 1070. On quitting the
monastery at Pisa, however, he wrote a statement of
what he had done in the matter of founding and maintaining it; and it is to this "Breve Recordationis,"
printed by Muratori, in the fourth volume (not the
ninth, for there are but six), of his *Antiquitates Italicæ
medii ævi* that Robertson refers. [1]

I by no means suppose that the Abbot did, or could
foresee what inferences would be drawn from a fact
which he relates; but really, if he had, he could hardly
have told his story in terms more adapted to preclude
the possibility of such perversion. The monastery "of
considerable note" (that is, as the Abbot says, in the
pride of his heart many years afterwards, " que *nunc*
est cœnobium ") was *then* no monastery at all, but a
chapel near Pisa *(capella, que tunc temporis detinebatur
a presbyteris),* which was in a most deplorable and
destitute condition, when "Senior Stephanus," I presume
the principal authority in Pisa, procured this poor monk
to come and perform divine service. Not only does
Bonus call it simply a chapel, but he tells us that
when he came there he found *neither monk nor abbot,*
nor any decent dwelling place, and in fact nothing
but a hut. *(Neque monachun, neque abbatem ibidem
inveni; et non casam neque mansionem sed tantummodo unum tugurium, ubi cepi habitare cum avunculo
meo.)* He then proceeds to detail the destitute state
of the place as to service-books, vestments, bells, and

---

1 It was, I believe, first printed by Mabillon; then by Grandius (an
abbot of St. Michael's, who, after seven centuries, erected a statue in
honour of his predecessor, Bonus); by Muratori, to whom Robertson
refers; and, fourthly, by Mitarelli and Costadoni, in their " Annales
Camaldulenses." This latter work contains, I believe, the fullest account
of the abbot, and to it I am indebted for the facts and extracts which
I here give. [The " Breve Recordationis " at full length will be found
at the end of this paper.]

all the requisites for the performance of divine service; and, having given a lamentable picture, he breaks out, with honest pride—may I not hope with real and pious gratitude? — "Now hear, and understand, how that place is improved by the help of Almighty God, and by mine, and by that of my monks, and that of the good Christians of our city." After five years he set to work on the church, and went to Rome, where he bought columns for it; and then made a belfry, which he furnished with two bells. Fifteen years afterwards, this belfry gave place to one much handsomer, containing seven bells, the largest of which weighed twelve hundred pounds. The vestments, by the time when the Abbot wrote, had not only increased in number, but some of them were so costly that, as he tells us, the bishop of the diocese might have said mass in them on Easter Sunday, "cum honore"—the single tin cup had been exchanged for four chalices, one of gold and three of silver—the single hut had expanded into a monastery, with all suitable offices and appendages, and a considerable estate in land; and, what is more to our purpose, instead of the "single missal," the monks of the monastery of St. Michael rejoiced in a library consisting of thirty-four volumes. But this requires more specific notice, for it is the ground of Robertson's statement.

In describing the destitute state of the chapel as he originally found it, the Abbot tells us, "in ipsa ecclesia non inveni aliud nisi unum missale;" and afterwards he repeats, "quando veni in ipsum locum non legebatur in ipsa ecclesia, per totum fere annum, nisi epistole et evangelia quia non habebatur nisi unum missale."

Now, the first thing to observe is, that there is no pretence for calling the place a "Monastery" at all at the time when it had only one missal.

Secondly, that in speaking thus of "one missal," Robertson obviously misunderstands the drift of the Abbot's complaint, which was not that the chapel had *only one* missal, but that it had no other service-book *but* a missal; and that, therefore, only that service could be performed which was contained in the Missals. *Unus*, in writers of that period, whether Italian, French, or German, no more implies definite singularity than the corresponding word in either of those languages now does. We alone, I believe, have discarded it, or turned it into "a," and are apt to smile when our foreign friends very naturally say, "Here is one book," etc.

Thirdly, be it observed, that as soon as this place did become a monastery it began to have books. And this seems to me the more creditable, because, during a great part of the time, the monks were in want of the comforts, and even perhaps of the necessaries, of life; and what they got was principally obtained by begging. The great and ruling passion of the poor Abbot seems to have been to form a monastery, and provide it with everything needful; and, as to himself, he tells us, that for the first two years he had only a single shirt per annum, and used to lie in bed while it was washed; and that during the wholo thirty years he was never possessed of two suits of clothes, or a horse.

As to the books, however, I must give the list in his own words, grammar, and spelling :—

Sermonum liber unus quem ego scripsi solus cum Priore meo, sicut habetur domui Sancte Marie, valde optimus.

Liber Historiarum unus, ubi continetur quidquid in sancta ecclesia pertinet ad legendum per totum annum

Textum Evangeliorum unum, valde optime scriptum, cum tabule de argento valde bone.

Passionarium unum novum, ubi sunt omnes passiones ecclesiastice.

Tractatum super Genesis, Sancti Augustini liber unus.

Dialogorum, liber unus.

Moralium Job, liber unus.

Summum bonum, liber unus.
Diadema, liber unus.
Paradisi, liber unus.
Glossarum, liber unus.
Canones, liber unus.
Sancti Benedicti Regula, liber unus.
Pastorale, liber unus.
Antiphonarii VIII.
Quinque Diurnales.

Tres Nocturnales.
Liber Bibliothece[2] novum quod est comparatum libras decem.
Missales quinque; unum missale valde optimum, quod semper in arca manebit, valentem solidos C.
Super Ezechiel, liber unus.
Libri Psalmorum valde optimi V.

I am aware that this catalogue may provoke a smile from those who are conversant with modern collections; but I am not ashamed to say that I honour the man who, under such circumstances, had the spirit, and found the means, to rebuild or enlarge his church, to provide all things necessary for the honourable performance of divine service, to annex a monastery, and make a beginning for a school of learning. Let me also (partly to illustrate what I have said in the preceding number, and partly to prepare the way for what I hope more fully to show) request the reader to observe the nature of the books in this little list— are they legendary tales of saints? mere lies and rubbish? But more of this, I hope, hereafter.

Having said so much of the Abbot Bonus, I am anxious to proceed to the account which Robertson gives of the Abbot Lupus; but I wish first to add a few words respecting the canons and the Abbot Regino. In the second number I stated that I had not got the

---

[2] I hope to give some catalogues relating to the period with which we are engaged, which will offer a fitter opportunity for saying something of these and other books; but I am apprehensive that some readers may not know that *Bibliotheca* was, in those days, the latin, or at least the name, for a Bible. Will the protestant reader give the abbot and his monks any credit for buying it, in so early a period of their monastery, at so great a price? and, honestly (but quite between ourselves), would he have expected to find *that* book in the list?

original work of the Abbot, but since that number
was printed, the kindness of a learned friend has furnished me with the book, and I am desirous to give
the passage as it really stands. Besides, I am induced
to recur to the subject because, after I had written
the preceding part of this paper, I happened to take
up a "History of Switzerland, designed for young persons," published by Harvey and Darton in 1825, which
tells the rising generation that, " so small were the
qualifications thought requisite for the priesthood before
the Reformation, that candidates were admitted to holy
orders if they could only read and tolerably understand what they read," p. 237. This, I presume, is taken
from Robertson's statement, that " one of the questions
appointed to be put to candidates for orders, was this,
'Whether they could read the Gospels and Epistles,
and explain the sense of them, at least, literally.'" It
may be said (and is very likely to be said by anybody
who may take the trouble to read such a paper as
this) that though this history of Switzerland costs six
shillings, it is only a child's book, that they never heard
of it, and that it is not worth notice. To this I answer,
first, that children's books are not read by children
only, and it was not in the hands of a child that I
found this book; and also that, in my opinion, even
children should not be set to read lies; secondly, I
confess that I never saw the book until this very day,
but I do hold it to be very well worth notice as an
instance of the way in which the errors of popular
writers are copied and disseminated, and dribbled down
in minor publications.

To come, however, to the point, the inquiry does
not at all respect candidates for orders, but is one
which a bishop is directed to make in all the cures
in his diocese. I may have to recur to it, but for

the present it is enough to say that it is entitled,
" Inquisitio de his quæ Episcopus vel ejus ministri in
suo districtu vel territorio inquirere debeant per vicos,
pagos, atque parrœchias suæ dioceseos." It suggests
ninety-five points of inquiry, of which the first fifteen
relate to the church, its state of repair, and the requisites for the performance of divine service. No. 16—73,
concern the life and conservation of the priest. No. 74—80,
respect points on which the priest was to be personally questioned; that is, as to his parentage,
place of birth, by what bishop he was ordained, etc.
No. 81—95, relate to his ministry (Posthæc de minis-
terio sibi commisso inquirendum est) and it is that part
of the 83rd and 85th which I mark by italics that is
quoted by Brucker, [3] but I must extract the two which
precede:—"Si expositionem symboli atque orationis dominicæ juxta traditionem orthodoxorum patrum penes
se scriptam habeat, et eam pleniter intellegat, et inde
prædicando populum sibi commissum sedulo instruat.
82. Si orationes Missarum, præfationem quoque canonis,
et eundem canonem bene intellegat, et memoriter ac
distincte proferre valeat. 83. *Si epistolam et evangelium
bene legere possit atque saltem ad litteram ejus sensum
manifestare.* 84. Si psalmorum verba et distinctiones
regulariter ex corde cum canticis consuetudinariis pro-
nuntiare sciat. 85. *Si sermonem Athanasii Episcopi de
fide Sanctæ Trinitatis* cujus initium est 'Quicunque vult
salvus esse' *memoriter teneat, et sensum illius intellegat, et verbis communibus enuntiare sciat.*" The remaining ten questions inquire minutely as to his capability to perform different parts of the service, and the

---

[3] Of this, indeed, Robertson ought to have been aware, for Brucker
introduces it as a formula inquisitionis ... "secundum quam inquirere
debebat Episcopus per vicos, etc. ... In ea enim *inter alia* circa *pres-
byteros* jubetur inquiri, 'Si,'" etc.

94th inquires, " Si habeat quadraginta homilias Gregorii et eos studiose legat atque intellegat." To say nothing of the erroneous application of this document to the examination of candidates for orders, is it not most extraordinary that it should have been brought forward to prove that the clergy could not read?

Let us, however, proceed to another case. Robertson goes on to say:—

> "Lupus, Abbot of Ferrieres, in a letter to the Pope, A.D. 855, be-seeches him to lend him a copy of Cicero de Oratore, and Quintilian's Institutions. 'For,' says he, 'although we have parts of those books, there is no complete copy of them in all France.' Murat. Antiq. v. iii. p. 835."

The plain matter of fact is, that two monks, named Adulphus and Acaricus, having resolved on a pilgrim-age, the Abbot took the opportunity of sending to Rome what was in fact a letter of introduction as it respected them, a tender of his own humble service to the Pope, and a request that his Holiness would lend him some books, in order that he might have them copied for the library of his monastery. From the part of the letter which relates to this latter point, [4] it ap-

---

[4] " Cæterum quia parentes thesaurizare debent filiis, ut doctor gentium manifestat, nosque vobis obsequentissimi filii esse cupimus, commentarios beati Hieronymi in Hieremiam, post sextum librum usque in finem prædicti prophetæ per eosdem fratres nobis mitti deposcimus in codice reverendæ veritatis, vestræ sanctitati, si id obtinuerimus, postquam celeriter exscriptus fuerit sine dubio remittendos Nam in nostris regionibus nus-quam ullus post sextum commentarium potuit inveniri; et optamus in vobis recuperare quicquid parvitati nostræ deesse sentimus. Petimus etiam Tullium de Oratore et XII libros Institutionum Oratoriarum Quintiliani, qui uno, nec ingenti, volumine continentur: quorum utriusque auctorum partes habemus, verum plenitudinem per vos desideramus obtinere. Pari intentione Donati Commentum in Terentium flagitamus. Quæ auctorum opera si vestra liberalitas nobis largita fuerit, Deo annuente, cum memo-rato Sancti Hieronymi codice, fideliter omnino restituenda curabimus."— *Ep.* 103, *edit. Baluz.*, p. 155.

pears, in the first place, that Lupus says nothing about
"all France;" though here, I confess, that Robertson
seems to have been misled by Muratori, who, after
quoting a part of the letter, says, "Hæc Lupus, in cujus
verbis non solum animadvertere possumus codicum ra-
ritatem, quum supra memoratos *universa Gallia* suppe-
ditare Lupo non posset, iique *in tam remota regione*
quærendi essent, sed, etc." Lupus, however, only says,
of certain works of Cicero and Quintilian, "*we* have
parts, but desire through you to obtain the whole;"
and by "we," he obviously meant his own monastery.
Why Robertson did not mention that the request included Donatus on Terence, I do not know; but what
he says of "all France"—though obviously a very exaggerated translation of *nostris regionibus*, considering
the state of things in those days—applies *not* to the
books which Robertson mentions, but to the Commentaries of Jerome on Jeremiah, from the sixth book to
the end.

Now as to the Abbot's not having a complete copy
of these books of Cicero and Quintilian, and his pre-
ferring, als he had so good an opportunity, to borrow
a volume of no great bulk which he knew to contain
all that he wanted *from Rome*, to sending about in his
own country, even if that had been equally easy, or
even practicable ; and indeed, generally, as to the sort
of half-contraband trade which was carried on about
the classics by the more learned ecclesiastics of those
days—as to this point, which is not uninteresting when
viewed in connexion with our subject, I hope to speak
more fully elsewhere; here it is only worth while to
notice that, according to the Abbot Lupus, the commentaries of Jerome on Jeremiah, from the sixth book
to the end, were not to be found "in regionibus nostris ;"
and whether we interpret this to mean what a modern

reader would understand by "all France," or restrict it to more reasonable limits, it was still a very broad assertion. Might not the Abbot be mistaken as to the fact? With all due respect for the Abbot of Ferrieres, and on some grounds he deserved not a little, are we bound to believe that he knew of *all* the books "in regionibus nostris," whatever we may suppose that phrase to mean? Robertson elsewhere says:—

"Many proofs occur in history of the little intercourse between nations during the middle ages;" [and it is rather a singular coincidence, that he states in proof of this,] "Even so late as the beginning of the twelfth century, the monks of *Ferrieres*, in the diocese of Sens, did not know that there was such a city as Tournay in Flanders; and the monks of St. Martin, of Tournay, were equally unacquainted with the situation of Ferrieres. A transaction in which they were both concerned made it necessary for them to have some intercourse. The mutual interest of both monasteries prompted each to find out the situation of the other. After a long search, which is particularly described, the discovery was made by accident. Herimannus Abbas de Restauratione St. Martini Tornacensis ap. Dach. Spicel. vol. xii., p. 400."[5]

I am induced to make this extract, not only because it states what is, under proper and reasonable limitations, an acknowledged truth, and one which it is very necessary to bear in mind, but because it incidentally furnishes another instance of what I hope it is true, as well as charitable, to call the extreme carelessness with which Robertson quoted. No doubt monks situated at places as far distant, and as little connected, as Ferrieres and Tournay were not likely to know much about each other; but the view which Robertson gives of the matter is quite erroneous. It would occupy too much space to show this in detail; but I must just observe, that so far from its appearing that the monks of Ferrieres did not know that there was such a city as Tournay—which

---

[5] See note [FF.] No. XIX., p. 325.

is indeed a supposition altogether absurd, especially as
the conversation between the two monks which brought
about an understanding and intercourse between the
monasteries took place at Courtray, and he of Ferrieres
must have passed comparatively near to Tournay to
get there, as anybody may see by the map—it is perfectly
clear, from Heriman's account, that they *did* know of
the existence of Tournay and where to find it ; and
that the place which they did *not* know, and could *not*
find, was a certain monastery of St. Martin, said to
be at Tournay. They had in their possession old documents
relating to it, but of the place itself as existing they
could learn nothing—and why ? simply because, though
there had been such a place, it had ceased to exist for
some centuries, insomuch that some, perhaps most people,
disputed whether it had ever existed at all. The monks
of Ferrieres had no " interest " (but rather the contrary)
in finding out the place, but they had some curiosity
on the subject ; and when one of them being at Courtray
accidentally met with a monk, who told him that he
belonged to the monastery of St. Martin, at Tournay,
he was surprised, and asked him where in the world
it was, for they had never been able to find it. It did
not probably appear strange to the monk of Tournay
(and it will not seem strange to any reflecting person)
that the monks of Ferrieres should not have heard how
Master Odo and his clerks had revived this monastery
of St. Martin—that is, had settled down on the old
foundation (like Bonus and his uncle at Pisa), and dragged
on about twenty years of miserable poverty and obscurity,
in restoring, or rather refounding, what in after ages
became most eminently a " monastery of considerable
note." He answered (truly, we may believe, as far as
he knew) that it was quite a recent foundation ; and
he seems not to have known, or not to have cared,

about its claim to antiquity, or to have made any farther inquiries when the monk of Ferrieres told him that they had documents relating to its former existence. When, however, he returned to his monastery at Tournay, and related to his brethren what he had heard, they lost no time in sending to Courtray for farther information ; but the monk of Ferrieres was gone, and it is true that they did not know how to follow him. How Heriman hunted for the Abbot of Ferrieres, and found him at the Council of Rheims, and how he followed him, by his direction, to Ferrieres, and found that by that time he had changed his mind as to parting with the documents, or giving information on the subject, from fear, as it seemed, of giving offence to one or more of his neighbours, by setting on foot a claim to property which was supposed to belong to St. Martin's, at Tournay, but which had got into other hands ; these, and many curious and interesting particulars, the reader may find in Heriman's own account of the matter to which Robertson refers, but they would be out of place here.

I quote the statement, as I have already said, not to question so notorious a fact as that intercourse between distant places was comparatively small at that period, and attended with difficulties unknown in these days, but to show the carelessness with which Robertson quoted,—and moreover the inconsistency with which he argued, for if the monks of Ferrieres in the twelfth century did not know that there was such a city as Tournay, could we suppose that an Abbot of Ferrieres, more than two centuries and a half before, was competent to say that any given book was not to be found "in all France?"

My own feelings with regard to this letter of Lupus are much like those expressed by Fleury respecting another of his epistles. After having said, that "Dans une autre lettre il prie un ami de lui apporter les guerres de Catilina et le Jugurtha de Salluste, et les Verrines de Cicéron," he adds, "C'est la curiosité de ces savans abbez, et le travail de leurs moines, qui nous ont conservé les livres de la bonne antiquité ecclésiastique et prophane."[6] Indeed, when Robertson had Muratori before him, and adopted that part of his remarks on Lupus which I have already extracted, I wish he had also attended to what Muratori proceeded to say. After remarking on the scarcity of books, in the terms which I have quoted, and on the assurance of the abbot in asking that such treasures should be exposed to the perils of such a journey, Muratori says, *"Potius tamen hinc discendum nobis,* quamplurimas iis ipsis monachis habendas esse gratias, quum ferme eorum tantummodo cura, quidquid librorum veterum superest, nos habeamus; et majores quidem nostros excusatione dignos, si plura in literis excolendis non præstitere; nos vero indignos, qui in tanta librorum copia adhuc desides et indocti esse pergimus."[7]

---

[6] Tom. x. p. 609.

[7] I hope I may be forgiven if there is any vanity mixed with the feelings which induce me to retain the note which my dear and partial friend the Editor annexed to this paper when it was first printed in the "British Magazine" for June, 1835 :—["The following passages from the letters of Gerbert, afterwards created pope in A.D. 998, by the name of Silvester II., may afford some confirmation and illustration to the very interesting and valuable paper in the text He was abbot of Bobbio during part of the time when they were written. In his 130th letter, to Rainald, a monk, written long before his elevation, he says, 'I entreat you to render me one service, which you can do without danger or injury to yourself, and which will bind me most closely to you. *You know with what zeal I seek for copies of books from all quarters; and you know how many writers there are everywhere, both in the cities and the country parts of Italy.* I entreat you then, that, *without any other persons knowing it,* and at your own cost, transcripts

be made for me of M. Manilius de Astrologia, Victorinus de Rhetorica, Demosthenes Ophthalmicus.' (This is explained by another letter.) 'I promise you most faithfully that this kind service shall be kept in sacred secrecy, and that whatever you lay out I will pay you to the full, according to your accounts, and whenever you require it.' In letter 123 he writes to Thietmar of Mayence, for a part of one of the works of Boetius, which was wanting in his copy. In letter 9, to the Abbot Giselbert, he writes respecting deficiencies at the end of his MS. of the oration of Cicero, ' Pro Rege Dejotaro,' and at the beginning of a treatise of Demosthenes the Philosopher, called '*Ophthalmicus*.' In letter 8, to the Archbishop of Rheims, he requests that prelate to borrow for him, from Azo, an Abbot, a copy of Cæsar. In return, he promises to communicate whatever literary treasures he had, especially eight volumes of Boetius on astrology, some very beautiful geometrical figures, and other things not less to be admired. In letter 7, he requests a friend (Airard) to attend to other business of the same kind—the correction, as it would seem, of a MS. of Pliny (*Plinius emendetur*), and the transcribing MSS. (not named) which were kept at two different places. Again, in letter 44, to Egbert, the Abbot of Tours, he mentions his own diligent study of philosophy, and of the arts of eloquence, and states, that with a view to them, he had been very busy in collecting a library; that he had been paying, for a long time, transcribers at Rome, and other parts of Italy, in Germany and Belgium, and buying copies of authors at great expense, by the aid of friends in his own country. He then goes on to beg the abbot to assist him in the same pursuit in *his* country; adding, that he gives a list, at the end of his letter, of the works which he wishes transcribed (unfortunately lost, or not printed), and will supply parchment, and other necessary costs, at the abbot's demand. In many other letters he mentions his own works on rhetoric, arithmetic, and his completion of a sphere. But if in the tenth century we find the work of transcribing so common, that there were writers everywhere, in the cities and country places in Italy, and, as it would seem from other letters, no difficulty in finding them elsewhere, if the collection of a library was so great a matter, that many were ready to assist, surely matters were far different from our common notions.—ED."]

THE "BREVE RECORDATIONIS" OF THE ABBOT BONUS.

Referred to p. 69.

This document would have been too long for insertion in a magazine; but I hope it is not out of place here; and I cannot resist the temptation to give it entire, not only because it seems to be the fairest way of dealing in the matter, but also because it is really a curious document, both as to facts and style. No translation would do it justice. The good abbot does indeed

> " From settled rules with brave disorder part,
> And snatch a grace beyond the reach of art."

The dignified, though unpretending, simplicity with which he breaks his way through the little restraints of grammar, and gratefully uses the first case or tense that comes to hand, will probably be new to most readers, and will, I trust, convince those who are suspicious, that I am not upholding the pure latinity of the Dark Ages.

" In nomine Domini nostri Jesu Christi Dei eterni. Breve recordationis facio ego Bonus Abbas, qualiter ab initio inchoavi conversari in Ecclesia Sancti Michaelis, *que nunc est cenobium.* Fecit me venire Senior Stephanus de Nonantulis, cum avunculo meo Petro, et investivit me de *ista capella,* que tunc temporis detinebatur a presbyteris, et *neque monachum, neque Abbatem ibidem inveni;* et non casam, neque mansionem, sed tantummodo unum tugurium, ubi cepi habitare cum avunculo meo. Et operabatur tunc temporis in turre ipsius ecclesiæ, et quod habebam, et habere potui dedi in restaurationem ipsius turris ad magistros et ad manuales, et ad quod necesse erat. Et cessavit ipse Stefanus laborare in

ecclesia post unum mensem quam ego cepi habitare in ipso loco, et
non levavit in altitudinem ipsam turrem nisi tantummodo unum passum
super ipsam ecclesiam. Et post hec finitus est annus quod ipsa ecclesia
fuit offerta ad honorem Dei et Sancti Michaelis, et ad officium Sancti
Benedicti, et ad ipsius regulam monachis ibidem in perpetuum conver-
sandis. Et hoc vobis notum sit, quia *in ipsa ecclesia non inveni aliud
nisi unum missale,* et unum calicem de stagno, et unum camisum cum
amicto, et unam stolam de lino, et unam planetulam, que nunc superest.[8] ... quia non inveni in ipso loco neque squillam, neque campanam,
sed tantummodo unam tabulam et cum ipsa tabula ... ipsa ecclesia
quatuor ... nunc audite et intelligite qualiter melioratus est locus ipse
cum auxilio Omnipotentis Dei, et meo, et de meis monachis, et de
bonis christianis nostre civitatis. Post quinque annos cepi laborare in
ipsam turrim quam nunc videtis de helemosina bonorum hominum que
nobis dabatur, et edificavi in ipsa turre ecclesiam que nunc videtur ab
omnibus et perrexi ad Romam per columnas ipsius ecclesiæ, et comparavi,
et feci eas venire in navim per mare, de nostro pretio; et post hoc
edificavi super ipsam ecclesiam campanilem. Cum autem consummatum
fuisset ipsum campanilem cum turris et ecclesia, ambulavi per civitatem
nostram cum Burello quondam bone memorie, et cum Landulfo parente
ipsius et cum tribus aliis religiosis hominibus, et acquisivimus ipsa die
centrum solidos, quos dedi pro pretio ad magistros, et posui in ipsum
campanile duas campanas. Et post quindecim annos videbatur mihi et
fratribus meis ipsum campanilem parvum et rusticior, et everti eum a
fundamentis, et feci fabricare illum quomodo videtis valde pulchrior,
et posui in ipsum campanas septem, quos omnes de helemosinis fecit
Domnus Dominicus meus Prior,[9] quem ego enutrivi, et nunc est Abbas

---

[8] I give the document as I find it, presuming that such marks here
and elsewhere indicate an hiatus in the MS.

[9] The authors of the Annales Camaldulenses combat what they suppose to be the mistake of thinking that the Prior cast the bells himself; but I confess I so understand the Abbot, and am rather jealous
of any attempt to rob the Prior of the credit due to him for this work
of art. Who else was so likely to be able to do it? Of an Archdeacon of Verona, nearly two hundred years before, we are told:

> "Quicquid auro, vel argento, et metallis ceteris,
> Quicquid lignis ex diversis, et marmore candido,
> Nullus unquam sic peritus in tantis operibus;"

and plenty of such instances will occur to those who have paid any
attention to the subject; but I notice it because I do not like to pass-

Monasterii Sancti Zenonis: et omnes facte sunt de helemosinis, que
nobis facte sunt, et de missis, quas ego et monachi mei decantaverunt. . . .
Et habent in se ipse campane libras metallorum tantas. Una campana
major est ponderis M.CC. . . . alia quingentarum, tertia trecentarum,
quarta ducentarum, quinta centum, sexta et septima quinquagintarum.
Quando veni in ipsum locum, non inveni, sicut superius memoravimus,
nisi unum camisum cum planetula et stola sua linea. Nunc autem
hàbemus in istum locum sanctum camisi XIII cum amictis suis. Et tres
camisi sunt tam perfecti et optimi ut Episcopus Opizus [1] domui Sancte
Marie possit cum honore cantare missas in die Pasche. Et tres planetas,
duo de pallio, una valentes solidos centum, alia valentes solidos XXX,
tertia de castanea, et tres stolas optimas cum manipulis suis, due de
purpure, et alia de pallio et tres corporales de pallio valde optimo.
Unum corporale de ipsis tribus est de brusco deaurato valente solidos XX
quem fecit Leo Papa quarto Romanus, et habet in se depicta imago
Salvatoris nostri de brusco, et ex una parte imago Sancti Petri Apostoli,
et ex alia parte Sancti Johannis Evangeliste, et unum pluviale de pur-
pura, et alium de pallio valde bonum. *Quando veni in ipsum locum non
legebatur in ipsa ecclesia per totum fere annum nisi epistole et evangelia
quia non habebatur nisi unum missale.* Nunc autem scitote quod melioratus est de libris ipsum locum.

[Here follows the list of books already given at p. 71.]

" Quot sunt insuper totum numeris XXXIV. Quando veni in ipsa
ecclesia non inveni nisi unum calicem de stagno. Modo, autem, cum
auxilio Domini, habentur ibi calices IIII. Unum de auro, valde bonus,
et habet uncias XI. Alius de argento major, et habet libras III et
mediam. Alii duo habentes in se libram unam de argento per unam-
quemque. Quando veni in ipsum locum non inveni nisi unum parvam
domum, et postquam cepi commorari cum meis monachis, feci levare
mansiones ibidem novas, et post decem annos disrumpebantur ipse
mansiones quas feci, quoniam erant de ligno de mala generatione, hoc
est fuere de cerro. Et dejeci ipse mansiones a fundamentis. Et hedi-

---

an opportunity of telling the march-of-intellect gentlemen, how much
they are indebted to the monks for even what they are pleased to call
" useful knowledge " in contradistinction to that knowledge which, to
be sure, is of no more *use* to them than Alnwick or Chatsworth is to
me. Of the same Archdeacon I read, " Horologium nocturnum nullus
ante viderat " — but I hope to say more of him another time.

[1] He was Bishop of Pisa in A D. 1044 See Ughelli, Italia Sacra,
tom. iii. p. 407.

ficavi alias mansiones de lignis castanietis quas venire feci per mare de Luni. Et non post multum tempus comparavi da Erigo filio Eritii terram, ubi nunc ipsum monasterium consistit, et dedi in ipsa terra libras XLII, et post hec hedificavi ipsam domum a petra et calcina, ubi sunt omnes officines, sicut abbatia habere debet; et est tam perfecta domus, ut in tota Marcha melior non est, cum columnas, quas de Insula Ilba et de Luni adduci feci. Et hoc sciatis, quia quando veni in ipsum locum non dedit amplius terre Stefanus in offersionem in ipsa ecclesia, nisi stariorum sex in loco Sejo de valde mala, et stariorum XXIIII ad Tramarice et similiter mala. Nunc audite qualiter, adjuvante Domino, amplificatus est locus ipse de bona terra. Habet Monasterium Sancti Michaelis modo DC stariorum de terra. Dedimus nos pretium in ipsa terra, quod nobis Dominus dedit magnam partem, videlicet libras C valde modice minus, et de alie terre cantavimus et promissimus ad ipsos parentes, que in ipsum locum dari fecerunt in manibus nostris, multe misse decantari. Cui mille, cui quingente, cui trescente, cui centum, et adjutorium el consilium habuimus in aliquantulum de nostris senioribus. Et dedit Albertus de Acuto in ipsum locum curtem unam in Corsica, propter amorem et servitium quod fecit Johannes nepoti meo ad predicto Alberto; et promisi dare predicto Johanni servitium X libr. ut me adjuvaret, et non tulit mihi propter meum amorem nisi solid. XX et fecit mihi dare hanc curtem, et detinet ipsam curtem, inter montes et colles et planities et agros sistariorum innumerabiles. Hoc est malum quod ego feci cum monachis meis per annos XXX in ipsum locum; et non vobis abscondam verecundiam meam, quoniam quando inchoavi habitare in eodem loco, tam pauper erat locus, in duobus annis non habui nisi unam stamineam per annum, et tempore estatis in meridie, quando dormire pergebam, ipsam stamineam ad lavandum dabam: et quando surgebam, predicta lota staminea induebar. Et nunquam habui equum, sicut ceteri abbates habent, et etiam viles monachi. Sed si necesse erat in silva ambulare, aut in aliquo loco, pedibus meis ambu-labam; et non duplicia vestimenta desideravi, sed quando novum induebar, neque per Pascha neque per Natalem, alium mutavi usque dum scin-deretur, quia consideravi paupertatem loci, ut cum debito non maneret. Et multa alia feci, que commemorare longum est ... argenteum et alium ereum, quando elongavi ecclesiam Sancti Michaelis expendi in ipsa ecclesia solidos mille sine pane, et sine vino, et sine carne, et sine pisces. Omnia ista expensaria in breve habentur scripta." p. 123.

N⁰. V.

"Sed quis pejerat hoc? Non Muratorius hercle
Maffejusve, et Averanius, non qui Calepinum
Restituit nuper."—L. SECTANUS.

" Scientia fere omnis exolevit : et ubique locorum non mediocris ignorantia successit. Quod cum aio, non est mihi animus significandi,
Italiam in Lapponiam tum fuisse conversam, literasque adeo sublatas,
ut neque legere neque scribere quisquam nosset. Aut delirantis, aut
infantissimi plane hominis hæc opinio foret."—MURATORIUS.

PROCEEDING with his proofs and illustrations of the
extreme darkness of the middle ages, Robertson tells
us —

" The price of books became so high, that persons of a moderate
fortune could not afford to purchase them. The Countess of Anjou
paid for a copy of the Homilies of Haimon, Bishop of Halberstadt,
two hundred sheep, five quarters of wheat, and the same quantity of
rye and millet. Histoire Littéraire de France, par des Religieux Bénédictins, tom. vii. p. 3."

Of course we are to understand that this was somewhere about the market price of a volume of homilies ;
and a price arising out of the scarcity of the article,
and the consequent difficulty of procuring it ; and, if
this was the case, it is quite clear that in those days
most people must either have made homilies for themselves, or gone without them. The story is, however,
so very good that one would be tempted, at first sight,
to suspect it of not being true. Let us see what the
price stated by Robertson actually was, for it is fortu-
nately given in terms more intelligible—at least in such
a way as that we are more likely to come at a true
notion of value—than if it had been stated in terms of
money. The scribe, it is said, received two hundred
sheep, and fifteen quarters (that is, thirty sacks) of grain.

It may reasonably be presumed that the sheep were
alive, and likely to increase; that they had wool, which
was worth something; or, at any rate, two hundred
skins, which would, of themselves, be a little fortune to
a man who lived upon parchment. But waiving all this,
and considering the sheep as mere mutton, the scribe
would be furnished with almost half a sheep, and more
than half a bushel of grain, per week for four years.
Was there nobody who would transcribe a few homilies
on more reasonable terms? Surely, from that time forth,
every man in Anjou, and everywhere else, who heard
of the transaction, set about learning the art of penmanship, which must have been, beyond all comparison,
the most lucrative which had ever been practised, and
which might fairly vie with alchemy itself.

Let us, however, look at the authorities. Robertson
refers to "the Histoire Littéraire de France," where the
story is thus told:—"Un trait que l'histoire nous a conservé touchant le prix excessif des livres en ce temps
là, nous doit faire juger de leur rareté. Encore s'agit-il
d'un auteur ecclésiastique, le recueil des homilies d'Haimon d'Halberstadt. Grécie, Comtesse d'Anjou, l'acheta
deux cents brebis, un muid de froment, un autre de
seigle, un troisième de millet, et un certain nombre de
peaux de martres. Il falloit être riche pour former de
nombreuses bibliothèques au même prix." Perhaps nobody will dispute the inference which these historians
draw from the story; but some will be surprised that
Robertson omitted the "certain nombre de peaux de
martres." This certain (that is, of course, uncertain)
number may be supposed to stand for any quantity of
rich and costly furs, and increases the price and the
wonder greatly. [1]

---

[1] It is a happy thing that some failings and vices carry with them
to a certain extent, and so far as regards the general mischief which

But let us retrograde another step, and look at the authority to which the authors of the "Histoire Littéraire" refer. Mabillon, having occasion, in his "Benedictine Annals," to mention the Countess Grecia as a subscribing witness to a charter of about the year 1056, by which Geoffry Martel, Count of Anjou, granted certain privileges to the monks of St. Nicholas at Angers, adds, that she was the second wife of that Count, and married to him after his divorce from his first Countess, Agnes of Burgundy. He farther says, that the divorce is mentioned in a letter from a monk to the Abbot Oderic, who had asked him about a certain homilary of Haymo; and remarks, that though not very important in itself, the monk's letter is worth transcribing, because it shows both the high price of books and the estimation in which these homilies were held at that period. He then gives the letter, which is as follows:—

"To his Lord the Abbot O. brother R. offers his prayers in Christ. Most dear father, I would have you to know that the Countess bought the book of which you have heard, for a great price, of Martin, who is now a bishop. On one occasion she gave him a hundred sheep on account of that book; at another time, on account of that same book, a *modius* of wheat, another of rye, and a third of millet. Again, on the same account, a hundred sheep; at another time, some marten

---

they are calculated to produce, their own antidote or mitigation. Certainly the same carelessness which gives rise to a great part of the mistakes and misquotations of popular writers prevents them from making the best of a good story when they have got one. Mr. James Petit Andrews, F.A.S., in his "History of Great Britain connected with the Chronology of Europe"—"an undertaking which had probably been blighted in the bud if he had foreseen the toil that would attend it"— tells us that it was "a large parcel of rich furs," p. 87; but unaccountably (unless he suspected a blunder which he did not kwow how to correct) says nothing of the wheat, rye, and millet. He professes to quote from Henault—that is, I suppose, from the English translation of Henault, in which, if I remember right, the French *muid* stands untranslated.

skins. And when she separated herself from the Count he received from her four pounds to buy sheep. But afterwards, when she asked him for the change, he began to complain about the book. She immediately gave up to him what he owed her."[2]

On this letter I would observe—

1. If there is really any reference to the divorce, it seems obvious that it must have been Agnes (who separated herself), and not Grecia (her successor), who purchased the book. I cannot help doubting, however, whether there is any such reference; though I have

---

[2] Mabillon's words are—"De hoc divortio fit mentio in quadam epistola cujusdam monachi ad Odericum Abbatem qui monachum illum de homilario Haimonis percontatus fuerat. Hæc epistola, tametsi in speciem non magni momenti, hic referenda videtur, ex qua nimirum intelligitur, quanti tunc temporis constarent libri, quantique hoc homilarium haberetur. Sic autem habet illa Epistola.

"Domno suo Abbati O., frater R. orationes in Christo. Pater carissime, scire vos volumus, quod codicem, de quo audivisti, pretio magno a Martino, qui est modo præsul, Comitissa emit. Una vice libri causa centum oves illi dedit: altera vice causa ipsius libri unum modium frumenti, et alterum sigalis, et tertium de milio. Iterum hac eadem causa centum oves: altera vice quasdam pelles martirinas. Cumque separavit se a Comite, quatuor libratas, ovium emendi causa, ab illa accepit. Postquam autem requisivit denarios, ille conqueri cœpit de libro. Illa statim dimisit illi quod sibi debebat."

Mabillon proceeds to say—"Martinus ille præsul, capellanus fuerat Gaufridi Comitis et Agnetis, postmodum Episcopus Trecorensis, ut superius vidimus ex quadam charta eorundem quam scripsit Martinus tunc Capellanus, postea Treguerensis Episcopus." *Lib. LXI, No. 6, p.* 528.

Mabillon gives no authority, that I see, for the letter, and may therefore be presumed to quote from the original. It will be observed that the letter itself mentions neither *homilary* nor *Haymo*. Mabillon says both; I should like to know why he says that the codex contained the homilies of *Haymon*; for I cannot help thinking that the CODEX might be that service-book which was then more properly and strictly, and commonly too (if not exclusively) called a Homilary; and, if it was a book got up for the church service, in any such way as some which will be described presently, the price is not so remarkable.

so far deferred to Mabillon as to translate *separavit se*, by "*she* separated," and *accepit*, by "*he* received." We learn, from the subscription to another charter, that Martin had been the Count's chaplain; and, from this letter, that he had ceased to be so; and I cannot but think that the "*separavit se*" may mean when he quitted the Count's service.

2. It is more to our present purpose to observe, that his book of homilies was a peculiar volume, which was the subject of particular inquiry. The Abbot was asking about it, and the monk, who knew its history, describes it as the volume which the Countess bought at "a great price." So that what she gave was *then* considered extraordinary.

3. The price was paid at different times, and in so strange a manner, that it looks rather as if the chaplain was some skilful artist who was honoured on account of his talents, and took advantage of them to work on the liberality of his patroness.

4. As to the quantity of grain—I suffer *modius* to stand, because, if I were to translate it, I should be inclined to say "one bushel" instead of "five quarters," which would, of course, divide Robertson's quantity by *forty*. I do not mean to say that the English bushel is the exact representative of the *modius* here spoken of, for what that was precisely I really do not know; and whoever looks into the subject of weights and measures will perceive that it is not very easy to determine; but I am inclined to think that I should be giving very good measure.

Now let me appeal to every rational and reflecting person, whether it is from such cases that we can judge of the price of books in general, or of the comparative ease or difficulty of procuring them? Are we to form our ideas from the sums paid or given by royal and

noble patrons and patronesses to artists, whose skill
in writing, illuminating, and embellishing manuscripts,
enabled them to ask what they pleased, and get whatever they asked? [3]

Suppose, however, that there was no fine writing in
the case, it is still very possible that, on other grounds,
the book might have been worth twice, or twenty
times, as much as the Countess gave for it, without
proving that books in general were so outrageously
scarce and dear. From such cases, indeed, we cannot,
as I have already said, prove anything. Will it not be
quite as fair for some writer a few centuries hence to
bring forward the enormous and absurd prices which
have been paid by some modern collectors for single
volumes, as an evidence of the price of books in our
age? May he not tell his gaping readers (at a time,
too, when the march of intellect has got past the age
of cumbersome and expensive penny magazines, and
is revelling in farthing cyclopædias) that in the year
1812, one of our nobility gave £ 2,260, and another,
£ 1,060 10 s. for a single volume? and that the next
year, a Johnson's Dictionary was sold by public auc-
tion, to a plebeian purchaser, for £ 200? A few such
facts would quite set up some future Robertson, whose
readers would never dream that we could get better

---

[3] Look at the state of things in countries which are now similarly
circumstanced. "The art of printing," says Morier, "is unknown in
Persia, and beautiful writing, therefore, is considered a high accomplishment. It is carefully taught in the schools, and those who excel
in it are almost classed with literary men. They are employed to copy
books, and some have attained to such eminence in this art, that a few
lines written by one of these celebrated penmen are often sold for a
considerable sum." (*History of Persia*, vol. ii., p. 582) He adds in a
note, "I have known *seven pounds* given for *four lines* written by
Dervish Musjeed, a celebrated penman, who has been dead some time,
and whose beautiful specimens of writing are now scarce."

reading, and plenty of it, much cheaper at that very time. The simple fact is, that there has always been such a thing as bibliomania since there have been books in the world; and no member of the Roxburgh Club has yet equalled the Elector of Bavaria, who gave a town for a single manuscript—unless, indeed, it be argued that it was a more pure, disinterested, and brilliant display of the ruling passion, a more devoted and heroic sacrifice of property and respect, to give £ 2,000 for an unique specimen of obscene trash, than to part with a German town for a copy of the New Testament.

Intrinsic value of this description, however, does not enter into the question, though another species of it does, and it is necessary to say a few words about it, which I hope to do presently. In the meantime let me ask, does not Robertson proceed to state in his very next sentence what might, by itself, show his readers that the transaction which he had just recorded was not peculiarly characteristic of the age in which it occurred. He goes on to say:—

" Even so late as the year 1471, when Louis XI. borrowed the works of Rasis, the Arabian Physician, from the Faculty of Medicine in Paris, he not only deposited as a pledge a considerable quantity of plate, but was obliged to procure a nobleman to join with him as surety in a deed, binding himself under a great forfeiture to restore it. Gabr. Naudè Addit. à l'histoire de Louys XI. par Comines. edit. de Fresnoy, tom. iv. p. 281. Many curious circumstances with respect to the extravagant price of books in the middle ages, are collected by that industrious compiler, to whom I refer such of my readers as deem this small branch of literary history an object of curiosity."

Might I not add, that "even so late as" two centuries after the occurrence mentioned by Robertson, when Selden wished to borrow a MS. from the Bodleian Library, he was required to give a bond for A THOUSAND POUNDS?

but does it follow that in that dark age he could not have got as much good reading on easier terms?

I have said, however, that there was frequently an intrinsic value in books independent of that which might arise from their subject; and I mean that which was inseparable from the nature of the costly materials of which they were composed, as well as from the art and labour bestowed in making them. This value was often, I apprehend, much greater than many of Robertson's readers would imagine; and if they think of a book as nothing but a thing to read, and (looking back to the dark ages) as only a cramped illegible scrawl on dirty parchment, they will form a very erroneous opinion on the whole matter. Books, and especially those used in the church service (of which, by the way, general readers are most likely to hear, and to which class, I suspect, as I have said, that this Homilary belonged), were frequently written with great care and pains, illuminated and gilded with almost incredible industry, bound in, or covered with plates of gold, silver, or carved ivory, adorned with gems, and even enriched with relics. Missals of a later date than the period with which we are at present concerned were, some years ago, the objects of eager competition among collectors, and some of them must always be admired for the exquisite beauty of their embellishments. I am not going to compare the graphic performances of the ninth and tenth centuries with those of the thirteenth and fourteenth; in this point of view it may suffice to say, that they were the finest specimens of art which those who purchased them had ever seen, and in all matters of taste and fancy this is saying a good deal. As to the value of books, however, which arose from the costly materials of which they were made, or the labour, industry, and taste, with which they were embellished, I hope I shall find a more proper

place to speak. For our present purpose this general
reference to the subject is quite sufficient.

But there was another species of value attaching
to some books in those ages which does not present
itself to our minds so obviously or forcibly. The
multiplication of books, by printing, has not only
rendered them much cheaper by reducing the labour
required for the production of a large number of
copies, but it has provided that each one of that large
number should be a fac-simile of all the rest. He who
sees one copy of an edition sees all: that edition is
dispersed among those who can best judge of its value;
it receives from their suffrages a certain character; and
from that time forth, if we see the title-page, we know
what are the contents or the errors of every other page
in the book. Among those who are likely to want it,
it is sufficient to mention the time and place of its
publication, and if we admire the correctness and read-
ableness of our own edition of a Father or a Classic,
we recommend our friends to get it, well knowing that
as there is one there are many; or that, at least, our
own copy is not likely to be *unique*, or we should
infallibly have heard of it from our bookseller. Now,
in those days *every* copy was unique—every one, if
I may so speak, stood upon its own individual character; and the correctness of a particular manuscript
was no pledge for even those which were copied immediately from it. In fact, the correctness of every
single copy could only be ascertained by minute and
laborious collation, and by the same sort of tedious
and wearisome process which is now required from
the editor who, with infinitely more ease and better
helps, revises the text of an ancient writer. We may,
therefore, naturally suppose that if a manuscript was
known to be the work of a good and careful scribe—if

it came out of the Scriptorium of some well-respected monastery—if it had passed through learned hands, and had been found, by the scrutiny which it was then necessary to give to each individual copy, to be an accurate work which might be safely trusted as a copy for future transcripts—if all this was known and attested, it would form another and a very good reason why a book should fetch an extraordinary price.

But to return to Robertson—

" When any person made a present of a book to a church or a monastery, in which were the only libraries during these ages, it was deemed a donative of such value, that he offered it on the altar *pro remedio animæ suæ*, in order to obtain the forgiveness of his sins. Murat. vol. iii. p. 836. Hist. Littér. de France, t. vi. p. 6. Nouv. Traité. du Diplomat, par deux Bénédictins, 4to. tom. i. p. 481."

Now really if a book was to cost two hundred sheep and fifteen quarters of grain (to say nothing of the furs and money), I do not see anything very absurd in its being treated as a donative of value; at least, I wish that people would make gifts of the same value to churches nowadays, and I believe they would find that they were not considered quite contemptible. I think I have seen in a parish church a board (whether gilt or not, I do not remember) informing the world that Esquire somebody had given "forty shillings a year for ever to the poor of the parish—viz., to the vicar, five shillings," for preaching an annual sermon to commemorate his bounty, and so forth.

But let me say a few words, first, as to the authorities, and then as to the fact.

First, then, as to the authorities, which it will be most convenient to notice in an inverted order. In the part of the Nouv. Traité du Diplom. referred to, I cannot find anything to the purpose, and I can only suppose that there is some mistake in the reference. To the Histoire Littéraire de France, I have not at present access; [4] but the passage of Muratori referred to is as follows:—"Rari ergo quum olim forent, multoque ære redimerentur codices MSti, hinc intelligimus, cur tanti fieret eorum donatio, ut si quando vel ipsi Romani Pontifices ejusmodi munera sacris templis offerebant, ad eorum gloriam de iis mentio in historia haberetur. Stephanus V. Papa, ut est in ejus Vita, tom. iii. pag. 272, Rer. Italicar. circiter annum Christi DCCCLXXXVI. præter alios libros ibi commemoratos 'pro animæ suæ remedio contulit ecclesiæ Sancti Pauli cantharam exauratam unam (fortasse, cantharum) Lib. Comment. I. Prophetarum, Lib. I. Gestarum Rerum Lib. II.'"

---

[4] Since this was published I have referred to the passage, which is as follows :—

" D'autres ne croïoient pas faire aux églises et aux monastères de plus excellents dons, que de leur offrir des livres. [How could they get such an idea in the dark ages?] Et pour mieux marquer le cas qu'ils en faisoient, ils les déposoient ordinairement sur l'Autel, comme une chose sacrée. L'usage de les offrir de la sorte devint assés commun en ce siècle.[a] On ne trouve des vestiges à la tête d'un recueil manuscrit des Conciles généraux et des Décretales des Papes, où se lit une inscription qui porte, que ce livre fut offert à l'Autel de Nôtre-Dame du Puy par Adalard qui en étoit Evêque en 919.[b] S. Maieul, Abbé de Cluny, aïant fait copier le Commentaire de S. Ambroise sur S. Luc, et celui de Raban Maur sur Jérémie, les offrit de même à son Monastère, en les mettant sur l'Autel de S. Pierre.[c] Letald nous apprend la même chose de Pierre, sçavant Moine de Mici son contemporain, qui y donna divers recueils d'histoire après les avoir déposés sur l'Autel de S. Etienne le jour du Jeudi saint."

I give the passage, to show what it is; it is not perhaps worth while to add any remark. It will be observed that the second of these authorities (which is in fact to the *Itinerar. Burgund.*) I had myself noticed, and quoted in the next paragraph with rather a different view.

---

[a] Gall. chr. nov. t. 2. p. 693.   [b] Mab. opusc. t 2. p. 22.
[c] Act. B. t. 1. p. 598. n. 3

Here it will be obvious that the drift of Muratori's remark, which has been misapprehended by Robertson, is, not that the books given to churches were offered on the altar, or that they were offered *pro remedio animæ,* though the instance which he quotes happens to contain the words *"pro remedio animæ suæ,"* to which he undoubtedly attached no importance, as well knowing, and expecting everybody to understand, that this was, in all such cases, implied, if not expressed; but that, when given even by popes, it was thought worth while to record the donation in history, that is, in their lives. Even this remark, however, surprises me as coming from a writer who must have known that the gifts of some of the popes to various churches and monasteries were scrupulously registered, and have been unmercifully detailed by their biographers; and, indeed, some of the books which occur in such lists might well be considered "donatives" of great value, even by those who could not read. For instance, when Leo III., in the beginning of the ninth century, gave a copy of the Gospels so ornamented with gold and precious stones that it weighed seventeen pounds, four ounces; [5] or, when Benedict III. gave one to the church of St. Calistus, adorned with gold and silver of nearly the same weight. [6] Surely when such books, or even books of

---

[5] "Hic fecit B. Petro apostolo fautori suo, Evangelia aurea cum gemmis prasinis atque hyacinthinis et albis miræ magnitudinis in circuitu ornata, pensantia libras decem et septem et uncias quatuor." See a list of his donations to various churches, occupying nearly twelve of the large close printed, double-columned pages of Labbe's Councils, tom. vii. c. 1090.

[6] "Ad laudem et gloriam ipsius Ecclesiæ fecit Evangelium argento auroque perfusum unum pensans libras quindecim ... et in ecclesia beatæ Balbinæ Martyris obtulit evangelium ex argento purissimo ... et

less value, were given, it was as natural to record the donation as that of a silver chalice, or a silk vestment. We may also believe that when books—especially such books—were formally presented to churches, they were offered on the altar, though I have met with very few instances of it;[7] and, indeed, with scarcely any charter or deed of gift conveying such things as books at all. The reason is plain, for churches and monasteries not merely (as Robertson observes very truly, if not taken strictly) had the only libraries, but they were the great and almost the only manufactories of books. Still books might be, and sometimes were, presented; and, on such occasions, were likely to be offered on the altar, though neither because they were books, nor because they were peculiarly rare or costly, but for another reason which is worthy of notice.

The false view which Robertson gives, and which I wish to expose and remove, arises from appropriating to a particular case what was in principle, and as far as could be in practice, general and universal. Ro-

---

in titulo beati Cyriaci Martyris obtulit evangelium unum ex argento purrissimo ad laudem et gloriam ipsius ecclesiæ."—*Ibid.*, tom. viii. p. 230.

[7] Mabillon thought it worth while to mention that he found in the library at Cluny a copy of St Ambrose on Luke, at the end of which was written, " Liber oblatus ad Altare S. Petri Cluniensis Cœnobii ex voto Domni atque Reverentissimi Maioli Abbatis." And he remarks upon it, " Sic libros offerebant veteres ad altare, et ad sepulcra sanc-torum, quemadmodum de Mammone S. Augendi præposito superius vidimus." In this he refers to a book which he had mentioned as being in the Boherian Library at Dijon, and of which he had said, " Hic codex voto bonæ memoriæ Mammonis, ad sepulchrum Sancti Augendi oblatus est regnante Carolo Calvo, uti et Epistolæ Paschales, quæ ibidem habentur pluresque alii codices, quos in varias Bibliothecas dispersos deprehendimus."— *Itinerar. Burgund.*, p. 9, 22. That of which such a man as Mabillon thus spoke, could scarcely have been at any period general and notorious custom in the church.

bertson would have spoken more correctly, though
not to his purpose, if, instead of saying, "When any
person made a present of *a book,*" he had said, "When
any person made a present of *anything* to a church,"
he offered it on the altar, etc. That he offered it *pro
remedio animæ suæ,* or for the spiritual benefit of
some other person, was always understood, though
not always expressed; [8] and that he should offer it
on the altar was perfectly natural when we consider
to whom the donation was made. We, indeed, commonly say that a man gave property "to the monastery
of St. Bertin," or "the monks of St. Martin," or "the
canons of Lille," and a donor then might say so in
his deed of gift for brevity's sake; for, as we have
heard often enough, and I pretend not to deny, parchment was expensive in those days. Many charters run in
that form—as Hildebert, Bishop of Avignon, in 1006,
"donamus monachis qui in Cœnobio S. Andreæ et S.
Martini.... modo famulantur Deo," [9] etc.; but, in fact,
the donation was not made to the church or the monastery—the canons or monks had no property in it,
and nothing to do with it, except as servants and
stewards to provide for its safe keeping. The gift was
to God and the patron saint; and, therefore, it was
laid on the altar erected in honour of both. Nothing
could be more natural or reasonable as it respects Him

---

[8] This is not, however, to be understood as having exclusive reference to purgatory. Pommeraye has very well observed :— "Le motif
plus ordinaire qu'apportoient dans leurs chartres les bien-faiteurs, étoit
afin que l'aumosne qu'ils faisoient servist au soulagement de leurs ames
et de celles de leurs parens et amis : c'étoit aussi quelquefois pour
estre associez aux prières et aux bonnes œuvres des monastères, dont
les seigneurs et les personnes de piété recherchoient très soigneusement
la participation."—*Hist. de l'Abbaye de S. Catharine du mont de Rouen,*
p. 84

[9] Dach. Spic., iii. 384.

who, though He dwelleth not in temples made with
hands, was once pleased to dwell between the cherubim,
and who, of all that He has framed for man, or given
him skill to fashion, reserves only the altar for Himself, and sets it over against His mercy-seat as the
symbol of that glory which He will not give to another.

Beside this, the superstition of the age supposed
the glorified saint to know what was going on in
the world, and to feel a deep interest and possess a
considerable power in the church militant on earth.
I believe that they who thought so were altogether
mistaken, and I lament and abhor, and am amazed
at the superstitions, blasphemies, and idolatries which
have grown out of that opinion; but as to the notion
itself, I do not know that it was wicked, and I almost
envy those whose credulous simplicity so realized the
communion of saints, and anticipated the period when
"the whole family in heaven and earth" shall be gathered
together in one. Be this as it may, however, they did
in fact conceive of the saint as a being still conversant
among mortals—hearing their prayers, assisting them
in their need, acknowledging their gifts by intercession
and protection, and not unfrequently making his presence known, and even visible, among them—and his
altar was naturally the place where all business relating to his property in this world, or his patronage in
another, was transacted.

The form of such deeds of gift naturally varied at
different times and in different places; and even according
to the taste of individual scribes and notaries. I have
already said that the gift was sometimes described as
made to the monks,—sometimes, but I think comparatively
seldom, to the monastery,—more frequently to God,
and the patron saint, and the abbot,—as frequently the
abbot was omitted, and still more frequently, perhaps,

the saint only was mentioned, and he was sometimes
actually addressed as a party to the conveyance. [1]

It was very natural that what was thus given to
the saint should be offered on his altar, for how else

[1] It may illustrate what I have here said, and perhaps amuse some
readers, if I throw together a few specimens of the different forms taken
at random from the various charters, the dates of which are indicated
by the numbers in parenthesis :—" Dono ad monasterium sancti Bonifacii "
(759).—*Schannat.*, *Trad. Fuld.*, p. 8. "Trado ad sanctum Bonifatium
et ad monasterium quod dicitur Fulda" (759).—*Ibid.* "Tradidit Deo et
sanctissimo martiri ejus Bonifacio, necnon et venerando Abbati Eggeberto
ceterisque fratribus sanctæ Fuldensis Ecclesiæ" (1058).—*Ibid.*, p. 255.
In these cases the trusteeship was fully understood; but sometimes it
was expressed, as by Poncius, Count of Gervaudan and Forez, in a
charter to the church of Brioude (1010). After saying—" Reddo Creatori omnium Domino Regi Regum, et Domino dominantium, necnon
et cedo gloriosissimo Martyri Juliano," etc., he describes the property,
and adds—" Omnipotenti Deo reddo, Sanctoque Juliano, ut, a die
præsenti et deinceps, omnes res suprascriptas sub tuitione ac potestate
sanctissimi martyris Juliani, et Canonicorum ibidem Christo militantium,
sint omni tempore," etc.—*Dach. Spicil.*, iii. 385.—And an early form
from the same Chartulary (945) runs, " totum et ad integrum reddo
Creatori omnium Domino, et sub dominatione et potestate libenti animo
committo beati Juliani, Canonicorumque suorum."—*Ibid.*, 373. More
frequently, however, as I have said, it was to God and the patron
saint, as in the donation of Amalric, to the schools of St. Martin's, at
Tours (cir. 843)—" Offero Creatori Deo, necnon Sancto Martino Domino
meo gloriosissimo quem toto affectu diligo," etc.—*Mart.* i. 33 ; or, as
Gulfrad, the deacon to the same church (cir. 930)—" Offero, dono,
trado atque confirmo Omnipotenti Deo necnon Sancto Martino Confessori
suo egregio," etc.—*Ibid.*, 68. Or, the saint only, as—" In Dei nomine.
Ego Theothart trado in elemosinam meam ad sanctum Bonifatium Man-
cipia IIII. id est uxorem Altrati cum tribus filiis et cum omni substantia
sua " (824).—*Schannat.*, p. 150. Of this, innumerable instances might
be given; but sometimes the matter was put in a still more business-like
form by addressing the saint as a party to the conveyance, as—" Domno
sancto et apostolico Patri Bonifatio Episcopo ego Adalberdus ; constat
me nulli cogentis imperio, sed proprio voluntatis arbitrio vobis vendidisse
et ita vendidi vineam unam," etc. (754).—*Schannat.*, p. 1. The emperor,
in the year 962, began a diploma thus—" Ego Otto Dei gratia Imperator
Augustus, una cum Ottone glorioso rege filio nostro, spondemus atque

was the donor to present it? It was, I say, *general*, not
meaning that every trivial donation was there offered,
but that, when property of any considerable value was
given, this was the common course of proceeding. If
that property consisted of moveable chattels, such as
money, plate, etc., it was actually placed on the altar;
or, if this could not be conveniently or decently done,
they came as near to it as they could. For instance,
the rule of St. Benedict directed that when a novice
had passed through the prescribed trials, and was to be
received, he should present a written petition, containing the promise which he had already made; and
that, at the time of his actual reception, he should lay
it on the altar—"De qua promissione sua faciat petitionem
ad nomen sanctorum, quorum reliquiæ ibi sunt, et abbatis
præsentis. Quam petitionem manu sua scribat: aut certe

promittimus per hoc pactum confirmationis nostræ tibi beato Petro principi
Apostolorum et clavigero regni cœlorum, et per te vicario tuo Domno
Joanni summo Pontifici," etc.—*Conc.* ix. 643. Again, in 1014—"Ego
Henricus Dei gratia Imperator Augustus spondeo atque promitto per hoc
pactum confirmationis nostræ, tibi beato Petro," etc.—*Ibid.*, 813. Leo
IX., about 1050, began a diploma bij which he granted a tenth of the
oblations made at the altar of St. Peter, to the saint himself (or, as
we should say, set apart that proportion for the repairs of the church)
with the following words—"Beate Petre Apostole, ego Leo Episcopus
servus tuus et omnium servorum Dei, de tuis donis aliquam tibi offero
particulam," etc.—*Ibid.*, 985. In fact, numberless examples of various
forms of speech might be given; and, without them—at least, without
some familiarity with the modes of expression which were perpetually
used—it is impossible to form an idea of the real spirit and character
of the times. With this view, I venture to add to this long note one
or two phrases from the charters of the Abbey of St. Peter, at Con-
dom—"Ego Amalbinus .... facio chartam de una pecia de vinea ....
ad opus sancti Petri."—*Dach. Sp.*, ii. 591. "In alio loco possidet
sanctus Petrus aliam vineam"—"in villa quæ dicitur Inzlota habet beatus
Petrus casalem unum."—*Ibid.*, p. 596. "Quædam nobilissima fœmina ..
suprascriptam ecclesiam violenter beato arripuit Petro."—*Ibid.*, 585.
"Molendinum quod construxit familia beati Petri"—*Ibid.*, 596.

si non scit literas, alter ab eo rogatus scribat : et ille
novitius signum faciat, et manu sua eam *super altare*
ponat." (c. 58.) It was, in fact, offering himself ; and, as
he did it, he began the 116th verse of the 119th
Psalm—"Uphold me (suscipe) according unto thy word,
that I may live ; and let me not be ashamed of my
hope." To this the congregation thrice responded by
repeating the verse and adding the *Gloria Patri.* If a
child was to be received, his hand was wrapped in the
hanging of the altar, "and thus," says the rule of St.
Benedict, "let them offer him." The words are—"Si
quis forte de nobilibus offert filium suum Deo in monasterio, si ipse puer minore ætate est, parentes ejus faciant
petitionem quam supra diximus. Et cum oblatione, ipsam
petitionem et manum pueri involvant *in palla altaris*,
et sic eum offerant."[2] (c. 59). Thus the idea of offering
at the altar was kept up ; and, indeed, though I know
of no rule for it, nor that it was a usual practice, yet
I apprehend that sometimes the matter was carried still
farther. The Abbot Heriman (of whom I have already
had occasion to speak in connexion with the Abbot
Lupus[3]) tells us that, in the year 1055, his mother took
him and his brothers to the monastery of which he was
afterwards abbot—"She went to St. Martin's, and
delivered over her sons to God, placing the little one in
his cradle upon the altar, amidst the tears of many
bystanders." At the same time, she placed on the altar
two hundred marks of silver, and gave to the monastery
two mills and the rest of her property.

Thus the offering on the altar was performed, in
most cases, as literally as could be ; and even when
the property was immoveable, as houses or lands—or

---

[2] See an "Antiqua Formula Oblationis Puerorum in Monasteriis,"
IX. M. &. D., p. 158.

[3] See p. 78, 79.

impalpable, as rights of toll or tithe, or market—it
was sometimes spoken of as if really laid on the
altar. Thus, in a charter of about A.D. 1120, Hugh de
Belmont says, "Ego ipse Hugo *dexteræ manus meæ
juramento* firmavi [I quote these words as confirming
my statement at p. 35, that he who made the sign of
the cross was considered *manu jurare*], et insuper ne
successorum aliqua redeat in futurum calumnia, Deo
et Sancto Petro, et Fratribus Besuensis ecclesiæ quicquid est, vel erat, quod meum jus juste aut injuste
possederat de hoc mercato, *totum super altare posui,* et
ipsum mercatum dono donavi."[4] Gertrude also, with her
daughter and son-in-law, "obtulerunt Deo et sancto
Petro Besuensis ecclesiæ, *super altare* in Vetus vineis
villa," a moiety of a house, six acres of land, and two
serfs named Tetbert and Oltrude.[5] In such cases, I
need not say, the property was not really placed on
the altar; but it is probable, and, indeed, almost certain, that either the deed of gift or some other symbol
was actually so placed. Du Cange alone supplies an
immense number and variety of examples; from which
I will extract a few scraps by way of farther illustrating
this matter.[6] Very commonly, especially in cases of
land, a turf or a twig, or a bough of a tree, was laid
on the altar (obtulit super altare B. Petri per cespitem—
propriis manibus prædictam oblationem ramo et cespite
posuerunt super altare beatissimæ Mariæ). Sometimes
by a knife (ipsi tres eumdem cultellum super altare
Dominicum S. Nicolai portaverunt); and very frequently,
either that it might be preserved from being stolen
or from getting into common use by being, in fact,

---

[4] Chron. Besuen. ap. Dach. Spicil., tom. ii. p. 452.

[5] *Ibid.*, p. 441.

[6] Those examples which are in parenthesis may be found under
the word *Investitura.*

rendered useless, or, perhaps also, that the act might
be remembered, the knife was bent before the witnesses
(posuit super altare per cultellum in hujus rei memoriam
plicatum—posito super altare præscripti Confessoris
cultello incurvato), and, in some cases, it seems to
have been broken, as Fulk, Count of Anjou, in A.D.
1096, in a charter giving a forest, says, "Super altare
Sancti Nicolai ipsam chartam pono, et cum cultello
Roberti Monachi quem ante ipsum altare frango, cum
eadem charta donum supradictæ forestæ concedens
pono." [7] Very commonly a book, either merely because
books were at hand, or perhaps also because the books
belonging to the altar might be supposed to give a
greater degree of solemnity to the act (has omnes
elemosynas.... cum libro super altare posuerunt—cum
libro missali eam super altare ibidem obtulerunt—de
hoc dono revestivit Quirmarhocus et duo filii ejus,
Gradelonem Monachum S. Nicholai in ecclesia S. Petri
Namnetensis, et osculati sunt eum de hac donatione
per fidem, librum quoque quo revestierunt monachum
posuerunt pro signo super altare S. Petri). It was not,
however, necessary that it should be one of the service
books; for I find in a charter giving to the church
of Beze, already repeatedly mentioned, "quinque homines, tres mares, et duas fœminas," that the donor
"propria manu donum roboravit super altare per librum
qui vocatur Regula S. Benedicti, coram multis testibus." [8] In short, it might be by anything—by a glove,
or a girdle, or a candlestick, or a purse, or a spoon,
or whatever came to hand,—per wantonem, per was-
onem, super altare posui—candelabro pro more illius
temporis (12 sæc.) super altare posito—super altare

---

[7] Brevic. S. Nic. Andeg., p. 30.
[8] II. Dach. Spicil. p. 442.

ipsius ecclesiæ per eleemosynariam [a beautiful name
for a purse] meam, lapidem berillum intus habentem,
propria manu imposui—donum decimæ quam habebat
apud Atheiam posuit super altare per cochlear de
turibulo—accipiens in manibus particulam marmorei
lapidis, quæ ibi forte reperta est, venit cum ea ante
altare et tenentes omnes simul.... obtulerunt eam super
altare.

Surely these instances are sufficient to show the
absurdity of making it a wonder that books should
be sometimes offered on the altar of churches to which
they were presented, as if other things were not so
offered, and as if it arose from their great rarity, and
the mere circumstance that they were books; while
the simple fact is, that the church and the cloister
were, in all ages, the places where books were kept,
and made, and copied, and from whence they were
issued to the rest of the world; as, indeed, Robertson
had just admitted in terms which would scarcely allow
his readers to believe it possible that anybody, out
of a church or monastery, should have any book to
present.

Nº. VI.

"Assem para, et accipe *auream* fabulam: fabulas immo, nam me
priorum nova admonuit."—PLINIUS.

ONCE upon a time there was a certain king who took
it into his head to have a throne, or a chair, or a saddle,
of some peculiar pattern, which, as far as I know, has
never been described; [1] but whatever it might be, he
could find no artificer who would undertake to execute
his conceptions.

Now it so happened that shortly before this time
a young artist had come to the place where the king
held his court. He had been brought up, and for some
years employed, by an eminent goldsmith, who was

---

[1] " Sella aurea "—but the learned are not farther agreed than that
it was something to sit on. Fleury and Ceillier say, "un *siége* magnifi-
que;" and Butler, "a magnificent chair of state." Pommeraye, with
more caution, calls it, "un ouvrage," and adds in the margin, "Sella
aurea, qui se peut entendre, d'une selle de cheval selon l'opinion com-
mune, ou d'un trône royal selon l'explication de M. de Montigni en
ses annotations," etc. I am inclined to vote for the saddle, because I
think that agrees best with a subsequent part of the story, which seems
to imply something more portable, and producible, and concealable
than a throne or a magnificent chair of state. I do not know how
much of the saddle was made of gold, for, indeed, I am not very well
acquainted with the history and use of such things ; but, without wishing
tediously to detain the reader on a subject which I never get upon
without extreme reluctance, I must add that Du Cange quotes a passage
which mentions, " equos cum sellis aureis " (*in v.* Sella). That is,
indeed, from a period considerably later than the king mentioned in
my story; but I find it mentioned elsewhere that when a rogue, named
Winegard, robbed a bishop, who was almost a contemporary of the
king, of the " ministerium ecclesiasticum aureum," which he carried
with him on his missionary excursions, " de calice et patena fecit sibi
fieri *sellam 'auream ;*" which I presume was a saddle.

master of the mint in what might then be called another country. I do not find any reason assigned for
this migration of the young workman, who perhaps
only went (like the mechanics of a great part of Europe
even now) on a *wanderschaft* to acquire more perfect
knowledge of his art. He seems, however, to have left
home with a good character, as one who was loved
and respected by those among whom he lived, not only
for extraordinary skill as a workman, but for the simplicity of his manners, and his strict and regular piety.
Whether he owed it to his professional skill, or to his
character, or to some introduction which is not recorded, I do not know. But in a few days after his arrival
at the place where the court was, he was taken under
the patronage of the king's treasurer, under whose
protection he set to work at his business, and soon
made friends of all around him. The treasurer was naturally consulted by his royal master on the golden
project which filled his mind, and he, as naturally,
thought of the young stranger. He conferred with him,
and reported to the king that he had found an artist
who would undertake the business.

The king was delighted, and gave an order to the
treasurer for an ample quantity of gold, which he faithfully delivered to the goldsmith, who immediately set
to work. He wrought with great diligence, and with
such ingenuity and honesty that, from the materials
which he received for one saddle he made two. This,
though apparently impossible, he was able to do, because he not only used the materials very skilfully,
but abstained from the common practice of cheating
under pretence of waste occasioned by cutting, filing,
and melting. When he had completed them, he took
one of the saddles to the king, who was filled with
admiration. He praised the elegance of the work, and

ordered a suitable reward to be given to the artist; who thereupon brought forth the other saddle, and told his majesty that he had thought it better to make up what was over in that manner than to waste it. The king was astonished, and, at first, incredulous; but, finding that he had really made both saddles from the materials delivered to him for one, he not only praised his skill, but assured him that he should from thenceforth consider him worthy of confidence in greater matters. In fact, this was the first step of his advancement at court; and, from that time forward, he not only rose to the highest eminence in his art, but increased in favour with the king and his nobles. In a word, he seems to have been in much the same circumstances as those of George Heriot at the court of our James, and to have enjoyed the same personal favour, or perhaps I should say, royal friendship.

It appears to have been soon after this, and it was probably on occasion of his being appointed to some confidential situation, or employed in some business of state, that he was required to take an oath on the relics of the saints in the presence of his sovereign. "I do not know how it happened," says his friend and biographer, "that I was present at the time; but it may be naturally supposed that I was likely to be there in the way of my duty, for I was brought up in my childhood at that king's court;" and he proceeds to relate that the goldsmith respectfully, but firmly, refused to comply with the requisition. [2] His majesty was

---

[2] "Divinum intuitum verens," says his biographer. I really do not understand it; or know how far a modern writer may be correct in saying that his relutance arose from the fear of taking what he considered as an *unnecessary* oath. Indeed, I can hardly suppose that to have been the case; and still less that his reluctance proceeded (as has been suggested) from a superstitious dread of meddling with relics.

urgent; and the poor goldsmith, seeing no alternative but to disobey either God or the king (and each was considered a sin in those days), burst into tears. The king had the good sense to give way—to speak to him in a kind and soothing manner—and to dismiss him with a cheerful countenance, and an assurance that he should feel more confidence in him than if he had sworn all sorts of oaths—"pollicens se plus eum ex hoc jam crediturum quam si multimoda tunc dedisset juramenta."

Shortly after this, he seems to have entered on a more strictly religious life, which he commenced by a general confession of his sins, and a course of great austerity. "Having arrived," says his biographer, "at the age of full maturity, he desired to manifest himself as a vessel sanctified for the service of God;" and he adds, that "he began stoutly to resist the striving of the flesh by the fervour of the Spirit," that is, according to the apostle, in labours, in watchings, in fastings, in chastity, in much patience, and in charity unfeigned; for in opposition to the present desires of the flesh, he set before him the fires of future punishment, and the consideration of the fire of hell kept out the heat of concupiscence. He prayed without ceasing for heavenly gifts, and offered his supplications to God by day and by night, frequently repeating from the book of Job—"I would seek unto God, and unto God would I commit my cause, which doeth great things and unsearchable; marvellous things

---

To this, I presume, his business must have accustomed him; but I notice the matter because I have been led, by other circumstances, to suppose that there have been persons in every age who doubted of the lawfulness of oaths in general; and it seems not improbable that he may have been one of them.

without number.... to set up on high those that be
low; that those which mourn may be exalted to safety."[3]
He restricted himself from fulness of bread that he
might gain the bread of heaven. His face, indeed, was
pale with fasting, his body dry and withered; but his
mind glowed with ever-increasing love of his heavenly
country. The consideration of more heavy evils made
him bear light afflictions with patience; for, habitually
looking forward to the end of his present life, he fer-
ed the future sentence of God, and His tremendous
judgment, knowing that it is written, "Happy is the
man that feareth alway," (Prov. xxviii. 14), and that of
the apostle, "Work out your own salvation with fear
and trembling." (Philip. ii. 12.) Also that saying of Job,
"For I have alway feared God like as the waves swell-
ing over me." (c. xxxi. 23[4].) By night he would lie at
the feet of his Lord, smiting his breast with his hands,
and watering his cheeks with tears; and with eyes
uplifted and suppressed sighs did he look to Him whom
he feared to have offended—and many a time did he
repeat, "Against thee only have I sinned"—"have mercy
upon me according to thy lovingkindness" (Ps. li. 4, 1);
and that of Job, "O remember that my life is wind"
(viii. 7), and "let me alone, for my days are vanity"
(17); and, being as it were out of himself, he pictured
to his own mind that which eye hath not seen, nor
ear heard, nor hath entered into the heart of man, but
which God hath prepared for those who love Him.

Whatever may be my motive for running into this
story, it certainly is not to set up the goldsmith as a
perfect model of doctrine and practice. If the reader

---

[3] Job. v. 8.—Ego deprecabor Dominum, et ad Deum ponam eloquium
meum : Qui facit magna et inscrutabilia, et mirabilia absque numero.
Qui ponit humiles in sublime, et mœrentes erigit sospitate.

[4] "Semper enim quasi tumentes super me fluctus timui Dominum."

should think him foolish, or pharisaical, or heterodox,
it is no fault of mine—at least if I succeed in what
is really my wish, and faithfully repeat an old story.
I do not want to conceal that the goldsmith's religion
—for I cannot help thinking that he had some—was
mixed with superstition. He had relics hanging up in
his chamber, and he saw and smelt, or said (and I
really believe thought) that he saw and smelt, a fra-
grant balsam distilling from them; and he took this to
be an answer to the earnest and fervent prayer which
he had poured forth beneath them, that God would
vouchsafe to give him some sign that his repentance
was accepted. "Remembering his prayer," says his
biographer, "and utterly astonished at the goodness
of the divine bounty, with deep groaning from his
inmost soul, he blessed Christ the faithful rewarder,
who hath never forsaken those who have trusted in
Him. This, therefore, was the beginning of his goodness, or rather of Almighty God's, from whom all
derive power for all things"—hoc ergo fuit initium
virtutum ejus, imo omnipotentis Dei, per quem omnes
omnia possunt.

The reader is not, however, to suppose that the
artist, and the man of business and active benevolence,
was lost in the ascetic. The goldsmith, it is true, came
to have a very monkish appearance, and was commonly to be seen in very mean clothes, with a rope
for his girdle. His biographer confesses that when he
first came to court, he did, indeed, somewhat ruffle it
in the bravery of silk, and gold, and gems; but even
then, adds this bosom friend, who was in all his secrets,
and who was, as I have said, brought up at the court—
who was, in fact, a little scion of nobility, and induced
by his admiration of the goldsmith to embrace a religious life, and who, with his brother, became, as he

tells us, one heart and one soul with him—even then, says his biographer, his finery concealed a hair shirt. Still, however, though his finery was laid aside, and his dress and manners approached to the monastic, he was not less diligent in business than fervent in spirit. He wrought incessantly with his own hands at his trade, with a book open before him, having, it seems, constructed for this purpose a sort of revolving desk, by means of which he could bring before him a number of books in succession; [5] and moreover, though a working man, and a reading man, and a man high in office and in court favour, he appears to have been always ready for, and constantly engaged in, works of active benevolence.

It is not my present business to enter into all the details of the goldsmith's life; or to tell how the favour

---

[5] "Fabricabat in usum Regis utensilia quamplurima ex auro et gemmis: sedebat fabricans indefesso, et contra eum * * * * vernaculus ejus . . . . qui magistri sequens vestigia, et ipse postmodum venerabilem vitam duxit. Sedens ergo * * * * ad opus prædictum, codicem sibimet præ oculis præparabat apertum, ut quoquo genere laborans divinum perciperet mandatum." His biographer farther says, "Habebat itaque in cubiculo suo multa sanctorum dependentia pignora, necnon et sacros libros in gyro per axem plurimos, quos post psalmodiam et orationem revolvens, et quasi apis prudentissima diversos ex diversis flores legens, in alvearium sui pectoris optima quæque recondebat." I cannot help supposing that this revolving was more than what is usually meant by turning over the leaves of a book, and refers to some contrivance by which he could bring a variety of books within his reach; though it does not appear to have been so understood by any moderns whose notice of him I have seen. Perhaps I may have some readers to whom it is right to state that, in writers of the middle age, such an expression as "sacros libros," even if it had been "scripturam sacram," would not necessarily imply the Bible. I do not doubt that what we properly call Holy Scripture was meant to be included in this case, and elsewhere in this history; but without being aware that such phrases were used to designate "religious books" in general, the student of church history would be liable to fall into error.

I

and confidence of his first royal master was continued by his son and successor. I pass over the accounts which his biographer gives of the favours which his sovereign heaped upon him, and which he so freely bestowed in acts of charity, that, if a stranger inquired for him (and what stranger came to that city who did not?) the natural answer was, "Go into such a quarter, and where you see a crowd of poor people you will find him." It might be imagined that such lavish bounty was sufficient to exhaust even all the means which could be obtained from an extensive business and from royal munificence; though the king seldom refused him any request, not so much, I am afraid, from any real zeal for religion as from an hereditary attachment to the goldsmith, and because he knew that in giving him anything he was conferring a benefit, not on one, but on many. But, in fact, the goldsmith had other and, I suppose, much greater expenses. One of these arose from what his time and circumstances rendered a very obvious Christian duty. His mode of performing it might now be considered singular and unwise; and perhaps, as it was not adopted by some of those who have, in modern times, felt most strongly (or, at least, talked and written most fiercely) about the abolition of slavery, it may be liable to serious objections, which I do not perceive. To me, a very poor judge in such matters, and perhaps somewhat prejudiced, it seems that his plan, whatever faults it might have, was the most simple, certain, and expeditious—he put his hand in his pocket, and paid the price of redemption. It was not the grandest way of doing the thing; but he lived in a dark age, when, even if the thing itself could have been successfully carried on, the collateral benefits of philanthropy and political agitation were little understood. Right or wrong, however, his biogra-

pher tells us that when he heard of a sale of slaves,
he set off immediately, and bought as many as twenty
or thirty, or even fifty or an hundred at a time. When
he had got them, the next business was to carry them
before the king, and set them at full liberty with all
the forms of law. When they had thus become their
own masters, he suggested to them three courses, and
helped them to take which they pleased, if they chose
to take either. In the first place, if they chose to
return home, he was ready to give them all the
assistance in his power, — secondly, any who wished
to remain with him, he willingly allowed to do so;
and it was rather on the footing of brethren than of
servants,—thirdly, if he could persuade them to become
monks, he treated them with great respect, honoured
them as a class superior to that to which he belonged,
supplied them with clothes, and all other necessaries,
sent them to different monasteries, and took a great
deal of care of them.

All this was, no doubt, very expensive; but it was
not all. He asked the king to give him a certain town
that he might there build a ladder by which they might
both get to heaven. His majesty granted it at once ; and
he built a monastery capable of receiving a hundred and
fifty monks. He spent upon it " all that he had, all that he
could get from the king, all that he could honestly come
by in any way, and all that the great were willing to
give." His biographer says, "You might see waggons
heavily laden with vessels of brass and wood for all
purposes, bedding, table linen, a great number of religious books, and, indeed, everything necessary for the
monastery ; in so much that some evil-minded persons
were moved to envy ;" [6] and, having himself inspected

---

[6] Ipse vero tanta se devotione, tantoque amore eodem loco diffudit,
ut quidquid, habere potuisset, ut quidquid Regi auferre, quidquid digne

the place, he speaks in high terms of the order and
discipline maintained in it. He adds, "There is now
a great company there, adorned with all the flowers
of various graces. There are also many artificers skilled
in divers arts, who, being perfected in the fear of Christ,
are always prepared to yield ready obedience. No man
there claims anything as his own; but (as we read in
the Acts of the Apostles) all things are, in all respects,
common. And the place is so fertile and so beautiful
that anybody going there, amidst its wide orchards
and pleasant gardens, might well exclaim, 'How goodly
are thy tents, O Jacob, and thy tabernacles, O Israel!
like shady woods, as cedar trees beside the waters, as
gardens by the river side.' It is of such that Solomon
has said, 'The habitations of the righteous shall be
blessed;'" [7] and he goes on to describe how it was
surrounded by an enclosure (not, indeed, a stone wall,
but a bank, with hedge and ditch—sphærico muro, non
quidem lapideo; sed fossatum sepe munitum), about a mile
and a quarter in circumference; and how the excellent
river on which it was situated, with all the beauties
of wood, water, and precipice, combined (perhaps one
should say contrasted) with the enclosure of the monastery, entirely filled with fruitbearing trees, might
almost make the spectator fancy that he saw paradise
before him.

"Yes, the monks took care to make themselves
comfortable." No doubt they did; and I dare say, if

---

comparare, quidquid etiam gratuito ei a potentibus largitum esset, cuncta,
prædicto loco destinaret. Videres plaustra vehere onera copiosa vascula
utique usibus necessaria, ærea simul et lignea : vestimenta etiam lectuaria
ac linteamina mensalia, necnon et *volumina sacrarum scripturarum
quamplurima*, sed et omnia quæ erant Monasterii usibus necessaria, in
tantum ut pravi quique ingenti ex hoc succenderentur invidia.

[7] Prov. iii. 33.

the truth were known, the reader does the same; and I
believe that, if he observes the course of things, he
will find that no man can rationally seek his own
comfort without promoting the comfort of others. At
any rate, I restrain myself with difficulty from expressing a very familiar train of thought, now excited by
this peep at the enclosed monastery. Very often it has
been awakened; and I know of nothing in the history
of the dark ages more admirable and adorable than
the visible Providence of God over-ruling not only the
better sense and feelings, but even the weakness and
whims, the folly, the fanaticism, the sin, of the monks,
and actually making their infirmities and vices the
means of spreading not only religion, but civilization;
and setting forth in a dark and desolate age, in lands
ravaged by fire and sword, among men wild and turbulent and cruel—setting forth, in characters of peace
and sunshine, the great truth that godliness hath the
promise of this life as well as of that to come. I hope,
some time or other, to show this, with no other difficulty than what arises from selecting out of the abundant materials which are furnished by monastic history.

To return, therefore, to the goldsmith; and it will
be a very natural mode of transition if I say a few
words of his foreman—at least I suppose him to have
held that rank from his being placed first in the list
of the goldsmith's workmen, which his biographer
gives, and the statement that he used to sit opposite
his master at work, as may be seen in a foregoing
note. He was a foreigner of good family, who had
been brought away from his own country in his
childhood, and sold as a slave. Happily for him, he
was purchased by the goldsmith, who sent him to
this new monastery which he had founded, to be
educated, and then took him back, and they worked

and read together. [8] So matters went on, until the
goldsmith gave up business; and then what could the
foreman do but go back to the scene of his youth,
and turn monk? At least he did so; and, by direction
of his old master, he became a priest also. Whether
it was out of respect to their founder, or whether the
same qualities which had endeared him to his master
won the affection and respect of the abbot and monks,
or whether it was commanded by the mild virtues and
rigid austerities which had become habitual to him, I
cannot tell; but, in fact, he received so much attention
and honour that he did not know what to do with
himself in the monastery, [9] and seems to have remained
there only out of respect for his benefactor; for, as
soon as ever he heard of his death, he fairly ran away.
Two texts of Scripture seem to have harassed his
mind, and made him fear lest in his popularity with
men he should lose the favour of God [1] — "They
that please men; they are ashamed because God hath
despised them" (Ps. liii. 5); and the words of the
Apostle— "If I yet pleased men, I should not be the
servant of Christ." (Gal. i. 10.) He wandered alone

---

[8] "Quem vir sanctus" — that is, the abbot (says the biographer
of the foreman) "sicut in mandatis acceperat, cum omni diligentia sub
pietatis studio enutrivit, sacris literis erudivit, evangelicis atque apostolicis
documentis roboravit;" and then sent him back to his master, to work
at his business. He kept him constantly about his person; and the
young captive "alter Eliséus, Eliæ felix virtutum ejus heres et successor,
Deo donante futurus famulabatur obsequiis. Fabricabant ambo simul
indefesse apertos præ ocellis semper codices habentes, geminum inde
fructum capientes, ut videlicet manus usibus hominum, mentes vero
usibus manciparentur divinis."

[9] Whether they made him abbot I do not know. Who is to decide
when Mabillon and the Bollandists disagree?

[1] "Qui hominibus placent confusi sunt quoniam Deus sprevit eos." —
Vulg.

through desert places until he found a remote, and
almost inaccessible, spot among the rocks, which he
could only approach on his hands and knees, but
which offered the necessary supply of wild fruits and
water. "There he lived," says his biographer, "always
singing in his heart that of David— 'Oh that I had
wings like a dove; for then would I fly away, and
be at rest. Lo! then would I wander afar off, and
remain in the wilderness'[2]— 'As the hart panteth
after the water brooks, so panteth my soul after thee,
O God. My soul thirsteth for God, for the living God:
when shall I come and appear before God?' For he
was such a man as Jeremiah describes when he says,
'It is good for a man that he bear the yoke in his
youth. He sitteth alone and keepeth silence, because
he hath borne it upon him;'[3] and elsewhere, 'I sat
alone because of thy hand, for thou hast filled me with
indignation.'"[4] Knowing, however, the dangers of idleness, and the apostolic injunction, that he who would
not work should not eat, he employed himself in cultivating the earth; and soon found farther occupation in
preaching to the multitudes who came to visit him,
and to seek his prayers and instruction. I believe that
only one of his sermons is in print. That it is quite
original I do not vouch; neither will I take upon me
to say that it contains all and omits nothing that it
should contain, for that is more than I can say of any
sermon that I ever saw or heard; but I am not writing
controversially, and merely wish, on this occasion, to
tell the reader, as a matter of fact, what he did say;
and according to the specimen given by his biographer,

---

[2] Ps. lv. 6.
[3] Lam. iii. 27, 28.
[4] Jer. xv. 17.

it was as follows:—"Brethren, hear what I say with attention; and sedulously meditate on it in your hearts. God the Father, and his Son our Lord Jesus Christ, who gave his precious blood for us, you must love with all your soul, and with all your mind. Keep your hearts clean from wicked and impure thoughts; maintain brotherly love among yourselves, and love not the things that are in the world. Do not think about what you *have*, but what you *are*. Do you desire to hear what you are? The prophet tells you, saying—'All flesh is grass; all the goodliness thereof as the flower of the field.'[5] Consider how short the present life is; always fearing, have the day of judgment before your eyes. While there is opportunity, redeem your sins by alms and good works." Such, says his biographer, were his discourses; and if the reader cannot agree with him in adding, "sermo ejus mellifluus sufficienti sale erat conditus," he may yet join me in hoping that he spoke truly in saying, that "no corrupt or idle discourse at any time proceeded out of his mouth; never was anything on his lips but Christ, and peace, and mercy."

As he grew old, his thoughts turned again to the monastery which he had twice left, and he besought the abbot to build a little cell near it in honour of its founder, and to let him live there. The abbot accordingly built one, rather more than half a mile from the monastery; and there the old man lived, constantly employed in reading or praying, or some work of Christian duty or benevolence, or some handicraft until he was ninety-four years old. I do not know that he ever pretended to work miracles. One of his biographers gives them to him by whole-sale; but another

---

[5] Is. xl. 6.

account is not only very sparing on that point, but relates an anecdote which has quite an opposite aspect. When a certain woman, who was grievously wounded, went to the gate of the monastery, asking to see him, "he would by no means see her, but sent her back this message:—'Woman, why do you ask my help? I am a mortal, and your associate in infirmity; but, if you believe in Christ, whom I serve, go away and pray to God according to your faith, and you will be healed.' Immediately she went away believing; and having without delay called on Jesus, returned home healed."

To proceed, however, with our story. Up to the point at which we digressed from the goldsmith's affairs, one history might have served for master and man; but then a great difference began. When the servant became a monk, the master became a bishop. But I ought to have mentioned several things before this, only I write under a constant dread of being tedious. One hears so much of "wading through"—not thick folios and cubical quartos—but even magazine articles on subjects more popular than mine, that I am always tempted to omit those details which in my own opinion give interest to history, and enable one to understand, and remember, and use it. But for this I should have told of the opposition which the goldsmith and his noble convert and biographer, though both laymen, made to the simony which was too prevalent in their part of the world—how they also opposed heresy, and drove it out of the kingdom without personal injury to the heretics—and how the goldsmith converted a mansion in the capital, which his royal master had given him, into a convent for three hundred nuns, who lived there under the superintendence of an abbess, who was appropriately (but, as

far as I see, accidentally) named *Aurea*. She was not,
I believe, the daughter of the goldsmith, nor do I
find or suppose that he had any children; but he is
said to have had a god-daughter; and were it not
for the reasons just mentioned, I should run into a
story about her. As it is, even, I cannot help briefly
mentioning one or two particulars of her history; for
the truth of which, however, as to matter of fact, I
by no means vouch. I quote it for the illustration of
our subject; should it be a contemporary and literally
true story, it is worth our attention—or indeed whether
it is truth or fiction; and if it belongs to a later period
(of which, I suppose, there can be no doubt), it is
still more deserving of notice. It is, I mean, more to
our purpose to read the romance, if it be one, of a
writer of any period within the limits to which the
production in question must belong than to learn the
real adventures of a young woman.

I pass over the account of her noble birth, and
her betrothal in her infancy to one of equal rank,
and how at a marriageable age she persuaded him
to accompany her to Rome; and how, while he was
rambling about to see the rarities of the city, she
took the opportunity of throwing herself at the pope's
feet, and declaring her determination to become a
nun—it is sufficient to say that she did so, and that
after returning thanks to God, his holiness addressed
her:—"'Of what nation art thou, and from what
country dost thou come, maiden? And say also, what
is thy name, and the creed of thy people; for I suppose thee to have been born of noble race, and
instructed in sacred learning from thine infancy.'
Whereupon she, with most serene mind and countenance, and with downcast look, began:—'If you
inquire, O father and lord, concerning my nation, I

am a * * * * my name is * * * * I was born in
the district of * * * *, whence I came hither. I was
educated by Christian parents; and, contrary to my
own will (and I believe to the will of God), I was
betrothed to a young man, whom I give up, and turn
from, being bound by the love of Christ, through
whose guidance and favour I remain free from all
pollution in body and mind. I devote myself to Him
who created all things; and that faith of which you
inquire, I keep unbroken to Him—which faith, if
you really wish to hear it, most excellent father, I
will rehearse; for though I am a barbarian by nation,
we, notwithstanding, profess that true and holy faith
which was brought to us in the end of time from
this holy apostolical see and catholic mother church.
For truly, when your holiness inquires after our creed,
it seems like Christ's asking water from the Samaritan
woman, in that while He vouchsafed to honour her
with such a discourse, He covertly insinuated that no
nation could exclude anyone from the faith. As, therefore, we blush not for our creed, so we are not confounded by reason of our nation; for David commands
that all peoples should clap their hands, and rejoice
before God with the voice of praise, &c. But since we
are admonished by the apostolical injunction to give
a reason concerning the hope and charity that is in
us to all who ask us, I will no longer delay to set
forth before your holiness, in few words, the glory of
our faith. We believe, then, and confess a chief and
unlimited (summum et incircumscriptum) Spirit, without
beginning of time or ending, to be the one omnipotent
God; as Moses has said, 'Hear, O Israel, the Lord
thy God is one." There is, I say, one Father, unbe-
gotten; one Son, his only begotten; one Holy Spirit,
proceeding from both, co-eternal with the Father and

the Son; but that always the Father is God; the Son, God; and the Holy Ghost, God; by whom, through whom, and in whom, are all things, and without whom nothing was made. This tripartite conjunction, and conjunct division, both excludes unity in the persons, and produces unity notwithstanding the distinction of persons. But while we believe in three persons, we do not believe in three Gods; but we confess one Godhead in three persons. We believe in a Holy Trinity of subsistent persons; but in an unity as to the nature, majesty, and substance of God. We, therefore, divide all that exists into two parts; and, except only the Trinity, all that has power, action, or motion in heaven, earth, or sea, we believe and confess to be a creature, and God the only Creator. Moreover, we believe that the Son of God was, in the last times, conceived of the Holy Ghost, and born of the Virgin Mary, and took upon him the flesh and soul of human nature. In which flesh we believe and confess that he was crucified and buried, and arose from the dead; and that in that same flesh, though of another glory, after his resurrection, he ascended into heaven, from whence we expect him to come as the Judge of the quick and the dead. We also confess an entire and perfect resurrection of our flesh in which we now live and move in this present life; and that in it we shall either receive the reward of good things for good actions, or sustain punishment for evil actions. Repentance of sins we confess with the fullest faith, and receive as a second grace, according to what the apostle says to the Corinthians—'I was minded to come unto you before, that ye might have a second benefit' [6] (*secundam gratiam*). This is the treasure of our faith, which we

---

[6] 2 Cor. i. 15.

keep sealed with the seal of the creed of the church which we received in baptism. Thus before God we believe with our hearts; thus before all men we confess with our mouths; that the knowledge of it may give faith to men, and that his image may bear testimony to God."

Such, we are told, was this virgin's confession; and I have endeavoured to translate it as literally as possible, without addition or diminution. Should any reader observe that she did not say (or, if he pleases, that the more modern, lying, forging, legend-maker, does not make her say) anything about transubstantiation, or purgatory, or prayers for the dead, or worshipping the Virgin Mary, or the saints, or relics, or indeed any of the subjects with which it might have been supposed that a candidate for the veil would have entertained the pope in a "barbarous age" like hers, when "religion lay expiring under a motley and enormous heap of superstitious inventions," I cannot help it. Neither am I concerned to explain to system-makers how it was that the great western Antichrist, instead of opening his "mouth, speaking great things" to blaspheme God and his saints, should have given utterance to the prayer which followed her confession— or, rather, the benediction of her veil, and the other habits which she was to assume:—"'Look down, O Lord, on this thine handmaid, that the purpose of holy virginity which, by thy inspiration, she hath formed, she may, under thy governance, keep. May there be in her, O Lord, by the gift of thy Spirit, a prudent modesty, a serious gentleness, a chaste freedom. May she be fervent in charity, and love nothing beside Thee (*extra te*). May she study so to live as that she may deserve praise without being ambitious of it. In thy fear, may she love Thee above all things, and in love

may she fear Thee in all things. Be thou, O Lord,
her rejoicing; thou her comfort in sorrow; thou her
counsel in doubt. Be thou her defence against injury;
in poverty, abundance; in fasting, food; in sickness,
medicine. What she has professed, may she keep; so
that she may overcome the old enemy, and purify
herself from the defilement of sin ; that she may be
adorned with fruit an hundredfold, with virgin beauty,
and the lamps of virtues, and may be counted worthy
to join the company of the elect virgins.' And when
they had all answered 'Amen,' the holy pontiff, kissing
the forehead of the holy virgin * * * *, dismissed her
in peace."

As to all these collateral matters, however, I content myself, for the present, with noticing them more
briefly than I could wish. This paper is already longer
than I expected it to have been, and than it ought to
be, considering that it is written in what I hope
the reader considers the worst possible style—without
any name of person or place, or any date, or a
single reference to any authority whatever. If he has
fairly got thus far, there is perhaps little use—I wish
there may be any courtesy—in telling him that he
might have skipped it; that it is entirely parenthetical,
and intended only as an introduction to another paper,
in which I hope to explain why I have written it, and
to excuse myself for writing it in such a manner.

No. VII.

"Vir bonus est quis?"—Hor.

THE goldsmith, [1] as I have already said, became a bishop. It is not very surprising, and some perhaps will say, "Yes, that was, of course, what he was aiming at." For my own part I should very much doubt it; at least, if he desired a bishopric, I do not see any reason to suppose that he did so from sordid or unworthy motives. The lowest calculation (for the point is disputed) makes him more than fifty years of age when he was consecrated—of money he seems to have possessed unlimited command—the love of power, if he had it (though I really know of nothing to show that he had), might have been better gratified at court than in his diocese, which can scarcely be supposed to have contained such luxuries as the times afforded,

---

[1] Here again I trust that I shall be pardoned if I retain the note which Mr Rose appended to this paper, at its first publication. "It may be doubted whether anything will induce many persons in *this* age to read for themselves. If anything could, surely the simple statement in this paper ought to have that effect. Here we find not only an individual *traduced*, but, through him, the religious character of a whole age *misrepresented*, and this misrepresentation now *generally believed*. We find men leaving out what a writer says, and then reproaching him and his age *for not saying it*. We find Mosheim, Maclaine, Robertson, Jortin, White, *mangling*, misusing, and (some of them) traducing a writer whose works not one of them, except Mosheim (if even he), *had ever seen*. These things are very serious. We may just as well, or better, not read at all, if we read only second-hand writers, or do not take care that those whom we do trust read for themselves, and report honestly. We, in short, trust a painter who paints that *black* which is *white*, and then think we have a clear idea of the object.—ED."

and as he might have enjoyed where he was. There is, moreover, another circumstance to which I cannot help attaching considerable importance, both as it regards this point, and as a mark of his character in general. On the proposal being made, and whatever reluctance he might feel being overcome, he insisted on a delay of two years, and during that period he exercised the office of an ordinary priest. From a consideration of all these circumstances, I am not inclined to believe that he had any flagrant desire to become a bishop, or was influenced by any sordid or ambitious motive.

But, after all, how much there is in a name. No doubt it is correct to say that he became a bishop; but the real idea would be much better conveyed by saying that he turned missionary; and, forsaking all that the world had to offer, went to preach the gospel among pagan barbarians. In fact, having received episcopal consecration at the same time as his noble young convert, he set off for his diocese, and began to visit it diligently. At first, we are told, the people, sunk in idolatry, received him with hostility; but, being gradually softened by his preaching, a great part of them renounced idolatry, and embraced Christianity.

But from this point what need is there to pursue the details of his history? The rest is known, perhaps, at the antipodes; at least, from the Ohio to the Ganges, every reader of popular books has been told *how* he preached. It is really curious to observe by what apparently trifling incidents people become notorious. Comparatively few persons take the trouble to read about Clotaire and Dagobert, and their goldsmith, and his noble convert Dado (or St. Owen), and his foreman Tillo or St. Theau the Saxon, and his god-daughter St. Hunegundis, and the Abbess St. Aurea. But what reader of Robertson's Charles the Fifth, or Mosheim's History, or Jortin's Remarks, or White's Bampton Lectures, or other popular books (to say nothing of living writers), has not heard of St. Eligius or Eloy, Bishop of Noyon? And all because Mosheim—the only one of the writers mentioned who can be suspected of knowing anything about him—was pleased to record that he had preached a bad sermon, and to give a specimen of it. This scrap, as Dr. Lingard has truly said, "holds a distinguished place in every invective which has been published against the clergy of former ages; and the definition of a good Christian has been echoed a thousand times by the credulity of writers and their readers." [2] Indeed, the story has been so widely circulated, and, I apprehend, so influential, that on coming to Robertson's statement in the note next to that on which I have been hitherto commenting,

---

[2] I copy these words from a note signed "Editor", and printed on a cancel in the edition of Mosheim, Lond. 1826, vol. ii. p. 159. When the leaf was changed I do not know, as it is only lately that I met with the copy in which I saw it. I wish I could give the space which the whole note would require ; but the following certificate in favour of Dr. Lingard I cannot persuade myself to omit, not for his sake, but for the reader's :—"We are bound to state, because we have ascertained the point, that he [Dr. Lingard] has quoted the original *fairly* and *correctly*, according to the best edition of the Spicilegium.— (Paris, 1723, 3 vols. folio.) We are induced to mention this circumstance because some protestant divines have been so eager to exculpate Dr. Mosheim, that they have accused Dr. Lingard of following a spurious edition, in which various interpolations *might have been* made by the Romanists to support the credit of the early church. We are aware that papists *seem* to have a fellow-feeling with their religious ancestors [something, I suppose, connected with what an old document calls "the communion of saints"], and are frequently hurried by their zeal into misrepresentation, sometimes into gross deviations from truth; but it is certainly illiberal to suspect them without cause [which he says there is], or to condemn them without inquiry."

K

I cannot help wishing and endeavouring to put the matter in a truer light. Though, strictly speaking, it does not immediately relate to that period of which I professedly write, yet this "hack story" should be exposed, because many persons have read it without knowing or attending to its date, and also because many—perhaps most—of those who do know its date, have a general idea that matters, far from improving, grew worse and worse for some centuries. It seemed, however, desirable first to give some account of this most unfortunate bishop, and accordingly I did so in the preceding number, in which I ventured to give his story anonymously, because I was afraid that in some, at least, I should excite unconquerable prejudice, if I mentioned a name which has acquired such evil notoriety. [3]

But let us now inquire about his preaching. Robertson had said in his text:—

"Even the *Christian religion*, though its precepts are delivered, and its institutions are fixed in Scripture with a precision which should have exempted them from being misinterpreted or corrupted, degenerated during those ages of darkness into an *illiberal superstition*. The barbarous nations when converted to Christianity changed the object, not the spirit of their religious worship. They endeavoured to conciliate the favour of the true God by means not unlike to those which they had employed in order to appease their false deities. Instead of aspiring to sanctity and virtue, which alone can render men acceptable to the great author of order and of excellence, they imagined that they satisfied *every obligation* of duty by a scrupulous observance of external ceremonies. Religion, according to their conception of it, comprehended *nothing else;* and the rites, by which they persuaded themselves that they could gain the favour of Heaven, were of such a nature as might

---

[3] The facts which I have stated respecting St. Eloy are to be found in his Life, written by St. Owen, Archbishop of Rouen, in D'Achery's Spicilegium, tom. ii. p. 76. Those which relate to St. Tillo, or Theau, the foreman, and St. Hunegundis, the goddaughter, are in the second volume of Mabillon's A. S., 954, 977.

have been expected from the rude ideas of the ages which devised and introduced them. They were either so unmeaning as to be altogether unworthy of the Being to whose honour they were consecrated, or so absurd as to be a disgrace to reason and humanity."—(p. 19.)

A sad picture of religion truly, when it comprehended *nothing else* beside what was either *unmeaning*, or so *absurd* as to disgrace reason and humanity; but it is a note on the word "ceremonies," in the foregoing passage, with which we are at present concerned; he begins it by saying—

"*All* the religious *maxims* and *practices* of the dark ages are a proof of this. I shall produce one remarkable testimony in confirmation of it, from an author canonized by the church of Rome, S. Eloy or Egidius, [4] Bishop of Noyon, in the seventh century."—(p. 236.)

---

[4] So it stands in the original edition; whether it has been corrected in those which have followed I do not know; nor can I tell whether Robertson (who was not, I imagine, very familiar with either St. Eloy or St. Giles) thought that he was correcting a mistake by turning *Eligius* into *Egidius ;* but I cannot help suspecting Maclaine of some such conceit when he turned the *S. Piato* of Mosheim into *St. Plato*, as it stands in all editions which I know, Cent. VII. part ii. c. 3, in a note which by itself might settle the character of the "learned and judicious translator," as Robertson calls him. It affords matter highly illustrative not only of his learning and judgment, but of his taste. [The note referred to is retained in the new edition of Dr. Murdock, edited by Mr. Soames, since these papers were published, but with some diminution of its low and filthy blackguardism ; but even as it now stands, is such a phrase as "carcass-hunter of saints" proper ? Surely the most bitter puritanism might be satisfied to direct its wrath against those who give undue, or give any, reverence to the relics of God's saints; but is it right to speak thus of the bodies in which the Apostles of Christ shall be raised ? But how singular it is that those who write in this way generally stamp their performances with some plain mark of ignorance. None of the parties to the translation seem to have heard of Father D'Achery. Maclaine takes it as it stands in Mosheim, and speaks of "Dacherius' Spicilegium." Dr. Murdock, I suppose, translated at a venture; but reinforced himself a little from the original, where he found LVCAE DACHERII, which (without assigning a full equivalent to the Christian name) he put down as "Lu. Dachier."

But as he, and everybody else I believe, was indebted to Mosheim, it may be as well at once to give the original as it stands in his work, placing beside it the passage as it stands in Robertson's work:—

Mosheim.

"Bonus Christianus est, qui ad ecclesiam frequentius venit, et oblationem, quæ in altari Deo offeratur, exhibet, qui de fructibus suis non gustat, nisi prius Deo aliquid offerat, qui quoties sanctæ solemnitates adveniunt, ante dies plures castitatem etiam cum propria uxore custodit, ut secura conscientia ad Domini altare accedere possit, qui postremo symbolum vel orationem Dominicam memoriter tenet. - - - Redimite animas vestras de pœna dum habetis in potestate remedia - - oblationes et decimas ecclesiis offerte, luminaria sanctis locis juxta quod habetis exhibete - ad ecclesiam quoque frequentius convenite, sanctorum patrocinia humiliter expetite - - - Quod si observaveritis, securi in die judicii ante tribunal æterni judicis venientes dicetis : Da, Domine, quia dedimus."—p. 269.

Robertson.

"He is a good Christian who comes frequently to church; who presents the oblation which is offered to God upon the altar; who doth not taste of the fruits of his own industry until he has consecrated a part of them to God; who, when the holy festivals shall approach, lives chastely even with his own wife during several days, that with a safe conscience he may draw near to the altar of God; and who, in the last place, can repeat the creed and the Lord's prayer. Redeem, then, your souls from destruction while you have the means in your power; offer *presents* and tythes to *churchmen;* come more frequently to church; humbly implore the patronage of the saints; for if you observe these things, you may come with security in the day to the tribunal of the eternal Judge, and say, 'Give to us, O Lord, for we have given *unto Thee.*'"—Vol. i p. 236.

This, then, according to Robertson, is a "remarkable testimony in confirmation" of his assertion that "*all* the maxims and practices of the dark ages" are a proof

---

Of course there is no credit in knowing Father D'Achery's works, and no discredit in not knowing them; but can those who really do not know his name, have qualified themselves (whatever their erudition of other kinds may be) with *such* knowledge as is needed to write, to translate, or even to edit the Church History of the middle ages?]

that men "instead of aspiring to sanctity and virtue,....
imagined that they had satisfied *every obligation* of duty
by a scrupulous observance of external ceremonies."
Let us, then, look at it as it stands. Some of it appears
to me quite unobjectionable, and indeed, as far as I
can judge, there are only, or (to say the least) chiefly,
three points at which protestants would take offence.

1. "Redeem, then, your souls from destruction while
the means are in your power; offer presents and tithes
to churchmen." Pretty advice, truly—it shows the cloven
foot at once; and the sordid, grasping churchman stands
out as plain as Robertson, or Jortin, or any modern
radical, could wish. I say nothing, however, of Robertson's translating "oblationes et decimas ecclesiis offerte,"
by "offer *presents* and tithes to *churchmen*," for that
(however indicative of the *animus*) is quite unimportant
compared with his connecting the two things in such
a way as if Eligius had made the gift of presents and
tithes to churchmen the means of redeeming men's
souls. Mosheim acts more fairly, for he places two
hyphens after the word "remedia," from which his
copyists should have learned that something was omitted.
In fact, the sentence stands. "Redimite animas vestras
de pœna dum habetis in potestate remedia; eleemosynam
juxta vires facite," &c., and the reference is evidently
to Dan. iv. 24 (our version 27), "peccata tua eleemosynis
redime."

2. "Humbly implore the patronage of the saints," is
certainly an injunction which may properly offend
protestants; but I need not, I presume, say that it is
not peculiar to St. Eligius or the dark ages—that the
error which it countenances had assumed foul shapes
of sin centuries before he was born, and still flourishes
in these enlightened days. I am not undertaking to
defend all that Eligius said, but only to show the

absurdity of bringing it forward as peculiarly characteristic of *his* preaching, or of *his* age. That it was not so, will as clearly appear from the next point.

3. "Give to us, O Lord, for we have given unto Thee." The words "unto Thee," are neither expressed nor implied in the original, but inserted by Robertson without any warrant whatever. The idea, however, and even the mode of expressing it, was not characteristic of the age of St. Eligius. Strange as it may seem in these days of high education and profuse literature, it cannot be denied that during the dark ages preachers did sometimes make bold to borrow a homily, or part of one, from their predecessors; and, in fact, this sermon of St. Eligius (or part of it, including that with which we are at present concerned) had belonged to Cæsarius, Bishop of Arles, who died about a hundred years before Eligius became a bishop. [5] He begins a Homily on Almsgiving by saying that a gracious and merciful God has provided a variety of ways by which men may be enabled to procure the pardon of their sins— "quibus possumus sine grandi labore ac difficultate peccata nostra redimere," and he afterwards says, "Let him to whom God has given more than necessaries hasten to redeem his sins with his superfluity; and let him who has it not in his power to redeem captives, or to feed or clothe the poor, harbour no hatred in his

---

[5] Cæsarius was born in A.D. 469, and became Bishop of Arles in A.D. 502, and died A.D. 542. Eligius became Bishop of Noyon, according to the earliest date which I have seen assigned, in A.D. 635 (*Chron. Elnon. ap. III. Mart.* 1392); or, according to the latest, which Cave states to be the most common, in the year 646. He thinks, however, that Le Cointe has proved that the right date is 640; and adds, that according to the same authority, Eloy lived until A.D. 659; according to the most commonly received opinion till 665; and according to others till 663.

heart against any man; but let him love, and never cease to pray for them; certain of the promise, or the mercy of his Lord, with a free conscience he will be able to say, 'Give, Lord, for I have given; forgive, for I have forgiven.'" [6]

This was the language of Cæsarius; and I adduce it merely to show the absurdity of bringing forward the words as characteristic of St. Eloy and his age, and in this view it may be worth while to add that the language of some earlier, and more respected, fathers did not, as far as I can see, very materially differ from it.

The charge, however, against Eligius is not only, and perhaps not principally, that his doctrine is popishly heretical, but that it is grossly defective; he is much to blame, we are told, for what he says, but much more to blame for what he does not say. Robertson tells us, "The *learned* and *judicious* translator of Dr. Mosheim's Ecclesiastical History, from one of whose additional notes I have borrowed this passage, subjoins a *very proper* reflection—'We see here a *large and ample* description of a good Christian, in which there is not the least mention of the love of God, resignation to his will, obedience to his laws, or of justice, benevolence, and charity towards men.'" Jortin says, "As to true religion, here is the *sum and substance* of it as it is drawn up for us by Eligius, one of the principal saints of that age;" and, in his table of contents, this scrap is referred to as "Eligius's *system of religion.*" White, in the notes to his Bampton Lectures (if they should be called his), tells us that, "no representation can convey stronger ideas of the melancholy state of religion in the seventh century than the description

---

[6] Bib. Pat. ii. 285.

of the character of a good Christian by St. Eligius, or Eloi, Bishop of Noyon." [7]

As to defectiveness, then, let it be observed in the first place, that this scrap is but a very small part—as nearly as I can calculate not a hundredth part—of a very long sermon; or rather, as one might suppose, from its prolixity and tautology, even if the language of St. Eloy's biographer did not suggest it, of several sermons mixed up into one great homily. If it were printed like Bishop Horsley's Sermons, it would, I believe occupy just about the fifty-six octavo pages which contain the first three of them. Candour would suggest a possibility that the other ninety-nine parts might contain something that would go towards supplying the deficiencies of the scrap.

But this is not all; or even what is most important. Mosheim printed the passage in such a way as to show that there were *some* omissions, though he did not indicate *all*. In Jortin's *translation* only one mark of omission is retained; and that is, between the words "prayer" and "Redeem." In the *version* given by Robertson, *all* such indications are removed, and the scrap stands as one continuous passage. White goes a step farther, and prints the *Latin text* without any break or hint of omission. Let us, therefore, see what is omitted in the part which is professedly quoted; and as that part is not far advanced in the sermon, it will be best to begin at the beginning. The part actually extracted by Mosheim I mark by *italics*:—

"I beseech you, most dear brethern, and admonish you with great humility, that you would listen attentively to those things which I desire to suggest to you for your salvation. For Almighty God knows that I offer them with fervent love towards you, and were I to do otherwise

---

[7] Bampton Lectures, notes, p. 5.

I should undoubtedly be held to have failed in my duty. Receive, then, what I say, not for my sake, who am of little account, but for your own salvation, willingly ; at least, in such a way that what you receive by the ear you may fulfil in practice, so that I may be counted worthy to rejoice with you in the kingdom of heaven, not only by my obedience, but through your profiting by it. If there is any one of you who is displeased that I persist in preaching to you so frequently, I beg him not to be offended with me, but rather to consider the danger to which I am exposed, and to listen to the fearful threatening which the Lord had addressed to priests by his prophet, — 'If thou dost not speak to warn the wicked from his way, that wicked man shall die in his iniquity ; but his blood will I require at thine hand. Nevertheless, if thou warn the wicked of his way to turn from it ; if he do not turn from his way, he shall die in his iniquity ; but thou hast delivered thy soul.'—Ezek. xxxiii. 8. And that, 'Cry aloud, spare not, and show my people their sins,'—Is. lviii. 1.

"Consider therefore, brethren, that it is my duty incessantly to stir up your minds to fear the judgment of God, and to desire the heavenly reward, that, together with you, I may be counted worthy to enjoy perpetual peace in the company of angels. I ask you, therefore, always to hold in dread the day of judgment ; and every day to keep before your eyes the day of your death.

"Consider how far you would be fit to be presented before angels, or what you would receive in return for your deserts, and whether you will be able in that day to show that the promise of your baptism has been kept unbroken. Remember that you then made a covenant with God, and that you promised in the very sacrament of baptism to renounce the Devil and all his works. Whosoever was able then made this promise in his own person and for himself. If any was unable, his sponsor, that is, he who received him at his baptism, made these promises to God for him, and in his name.

"Consider, therefore, what a covenant you have made with God, and examine yourselves whether after that promise you have been following that wicked Devil whom you renounced. For you did renounce the Devil, and all his pomps and his works ; that is, idols, divinations, auguries, thefts, frauds, fornications, drunkenness, and lies, for these are his works and pomps. On the contrary, you promised to believe in God the Father Almighty, and in Jesus Christ, his only Son, our Lord, conceived of the Holy Ghost, born of the Virgin Mary ; that he suffered under Pontius Pilate, rose from the dead on the third day, and ascended into heaven ; and then you promised that you would believe also in the Holy Ghost, the holy catholic church, the remission of sins, the resur-

rection of the body, and the life everlasting. Without all doubt this
your covenant and confession which you then made will never be lost
sight of by God; and, therefore, most dearly beloved, I warn you that
this your confession or promise should always be kept in your own
memory, that so your bearing the Christian name, instead of rising in
judgment against you, may be for your salvation. For you are made
Christians to this end, that you may always do the works of Christ;
that is, that you may love chastity, avoid lewdness and drunkenness,
maintain humility, and detest pride, because our Lord Christ both showed
humility by example and taught it by words, saying—'Learn of me,
for I am meek and lowly in heart; and ye shall find rest to your
souls.' (Matt. xi. 30.) You must also renounce envy, have charity among
yourselves, and always think of the future world, and of eternal blessedness, and labour rather for the soul than for the body. For the flesh
will be only a short time in this world; whereas the soul, if it does
well, will reign for ever in heaven; but, if it does wickedly, it will
burn without mercy in hell. He, indeed, who thinks only of this life
is like the beasts and brute animals.

"It is not enough, most dearly beloved, for you to have received the
name of Christians, if you do not do Christian works. To be called a
Christian profits him who always retains in his mind, and fulfils in his
actions, the commands of Christ; that is, who does not commit theft,
does not bear false witness, who neither tells lies nor swears falsely,
who does not commit adultery, who does not hate anybody, but loves
all men as himself, who does not render evil to his enemies, but rather
prays for them, who does not stir up strife, but restores peace between
hose who are at variance. For these precepts Christ himself has deigned
to give by his own mouth, in the gospel, saying—'Thou shalt do no
murder, Thou shalt not commit adultery, Thou shalt not steal, Thou
shalt not bear false witness, Thou shalt not swear falsely nor commit
fraud, Honour thy father and thy mother: and, Thou shalt love thy
neighbour as thyself.' (Matt. xix. 18, 19.) And also, 'All things whatsoever ye would that men should do to you; do ye even so to them:
for this is the law and the prophets.' (Matt. vii. 12.)

"And he has given yet greater, but very strong and fruitful (valde
fortia atque fructifera) commands, saying—'Love your enemies, do
good to them that hate you,' and 'pray for them which despitefully
use you and persecute you.' (Matt. v. 44.) Behold, this is a strong
commandment, and to men it seems a hard one; but it has a great
reward; hear what it is—'That ye may be,' he saith, 'the children
of your Father which is in heaven.' Oh, how great grace! Of ourselves
we are not even worthy servants; and by loving our enemies we become

sons of God. Therefore, my brethren, both love your friends in God, and your enemies for God; for 'he that loveth his neighbour,' as saith the apostle, 'hath fulfilled the law.' (Rom. xiii. 8.) For he who will be a true Christian must needs keep these commandments; because, if he does not keep them, he deceives himself. He, therefore, is a good Christian who puts faith in no charms or diabolical inventions, but places all his hope in Christ alone; who receives strangers with joy, even as if it were Christ himself, because he will say — 'I was a stranger, and ye took me in,' and, 'inasmuch as ye have done it unto one of the least of these my brethren, ye have done it unto me.' *He*, I say, *is a good Christian* who washes the feet of strangers, and loves them as most dear relations; who, according to his means, gives alms to the poor; *who comes frequently to church: who presents the oblation which is offered to God upon the altar; who doth not taste of his fruits before he hath offered somewhat to God;* who has not a false balance or deceitful measures; who hath not given his money to usury; who both lives chastely himself, and teaches his sons and his neighbours to live chastely and in the fear of God; *and, as often as the holy festivals occur, lives continently even with his own wife for some days previously, that he may, with safe conscience, draw near to the altar of God; finally, who can repeat the Creed or the Lord's Prayer*, and teaches the same to his sons and servants. He who is such an one, is, without doubt, a true Christian, and Christ also dwelleth in him, who hath said, 'I and the Father will come and make our abode with him.' (John xiv. 23.) And, in like manner, he saith, by the prophet, 'I will dwell in them, and walk in them, and I will be their God, and they shall be my people.' (2 Cor. vi. 16.)

"Behold, brethren, ye have heard what sort of persons are good Christians; and therefore labour as much as you can, with God's assistance, that the Christian name may not be falsely applied to you; but, in order that you may be true Christians, always meditate in your hearts on the commands of Christ, and fulfil them in your practice; *redeem your souls from punishment while you have the means in your power;* give alms according to your means, maintain peace and charity, restore harmony among those who are at strife, avoid lying, abhor perjury, bear no false witness, commit no theft, *offer oblations and gifts to churches, provide lights for sacred places according to your means*, retain in your memory the Creed and the Lord's Prayer, and teach them to your sons. Moreover, teach and chastise those children for whom you are sponsors, that they may always live with the fear of God. Know that you are sponsors for them with God. *Come frequently also to church; humbly seek the patronage of the saints;* keep the

Lord's day in reverence of the resurrection of Christ, without any servile work; celebrate the festivals of the saints with devout feeling; love your neighbours as yourselves; what you would desire to be done to you by others, that do to others; what you would not have done to you, do to no one; before all things have charity, for charity covereth a multitude of sins; be hospitable, humble, casting all your care upon God, for he careth for you; visit the sick, seek out the captives, receive strangers, feed the hungry, clothe the naked; set at nought soothsayers and magicians, let your weights and measures be fair, your balance just, your bushel and your pint fair; nor must you claim back more than you gave, nor exact from any one usury for money lent. *Which, if you observe, coming with security before the tribunal of the eternal Judge, in the day of Judgment, you may say ' Give, Lord, for we have given;* show mercy, for we have shown mercy; we have fulfilled what thou hast commanded, do thou give what thou hast promised.' "

I feel that by this extract I do very imperfect justice to the sermon of St. Eloy; of which, indeed, I might say that it seems to have been written as if he had anticipated all and each of Mosheim's and Maclaine's charges, and intended to furnish a pointed answer to almost every one. I feel it to be most important to our forming a right view of the dark ages, that such false statements respecting the means of instruction and of grace should be exposed; but with so wide a field before us, I am unwilling, at present, to give more space than this to one case, especially as I am anxious to get beyond that part of the subject which consists in merely contradicting misstatement; but I cannot do so until I have offered some remarks on the work of a popular historian whom I have not as yet noticed.

(*Addition to the Second Edition.*)

The passage in Mosheim which gave rise to this paper is still retained without qualification or explanation in the "New and literal translation from the

original Latin, with copious additional notes, original
and selected, by James Murdock, D.D., edited, with
additions, by Henry Soames, M.A., rector of Stapleford
Tawney, with Thoydon Mount, Essex," and published
by Messrs. Longman and others in the year 1841. I am
tempted, therefore, to give some further extracts which
I made when the paper was written, but which would
have occupied too much room in the magazine. But
for this I should then have produced proofs and illustrations of my statement, that the sermon seemed as
if it had been written to anticipate and refute the
charges of Mosheim.

In this new translation the passage to which the
note on St. Eligius is appended, stands as follows:—

"During this century, true religion lay buried under
a senseless mass of superstitions; and was unable to
raise her head. The earlier Christians had worshipped
only God, and his Son; but those called Christians in
this age, worshipped the wood of a cross, the images
of holy men, and bones of dubious origin. The early
Christians placed heaven and hell before the view of
men; these latter depicted a certain fire prepared to
burn off the imperfections of the soul. The former
taught, that Christ had made expiation for the sins of
men, by his death and his blood; the latter seemed to
inculcate, that the gates of heaven would be closed
against none who should enrich the clergy or the
church with their donations."—Vol. ii. p. 93.

Now at this distance of time I do not pretend to
speak positively respecting the contents of this long
rambling discourse, which it is not worth while to
search over again minutely, in order to say whether
it contains one word about the wood of the cross, or
the images of the saints, or the dubious bones. I really
believe there is nothing of the kind; but the extracts

which I have by me were, I think, made to meet the statement that instead of having heaven and hell set before them, the people were told about a certain fire that was "to burn off the imperfections of the soul." The reader will therefore understand that I give them as illustrative of the preacher's doctrine (if he can be said to have had any) of purgatory; though at the same time they may show us what he taught on some other subjects; and lead the reader very reasonably to disbelieve the other charges made against him, all of which could hardly be answered without extracting the greater part of the Homily.

"Those whom you see to be good, do you imitate; those whom you see to be bad, chasten and rebuke; that you may have a double reward. And let him who has hitherto lived free from the aforesaid evils rejoice, and give God thanks, and take care for the future, and persevere with alacrity in good works; but let him who has hitherto lived in sin, quickly correct himself, and repent with his whole heart before he departs this life; for if he dies without repentance he will not enter into rest, but will be cast into hell fire (in gehennam ignis), whence he will never get out through all eternity" (unde nunquam exiet in sæculorum).—p. 98 a.

After addressing magistrates, he says—"Considering these things, brethren, both you who govern and you who are subject, ground yourselves in the fear of God. Retain what has been said, do what is commanded, have Christ always in your mind, and his mark on your forehead. Know that you have many adversaries who are eager to impede your course; therefore in all places and at all times arm yourselves with the sign of the cross, fortify yourselves with the standard of the cross; for this alone they fear, this alone they dread, and this is given you as a shield whereby you may quench all the fiery darts of the wicked one. For the mark of Christ is a great thing and the cross of Christ, but it profits those only who keep the precepts of Christ. That it may profit you, therefore, strive to fulfil his precepts with all your might; and whether you sit or walk, or eat, or go to bed, or get up, always let the mark of Christ guard your forehead, that by the recollection of God it may both protect you while waking and keep you while asleep; and as often as you wake in the night and sleep flies from your eyes, immediately let the sign of the cross occur to your lips and let your minds be occupied in prayers, and revolve the commandments of God in your hearts, lest the enemy should suddenly creep into your stupid breasts, or the eager adversary twist himself into your soul through your foolish carelessness. And when he suggests to your sense any evil thought, set before yourself the future judgment of God, the punishment of hell, the pains of Gehenna, the darkness of Tartarus, which the wicked endure. If you do this, the evil thought will immediately vanish, and the power of Christ will not desert you; for that which the prophet has said is true, 'He that trusteth in the Lord, mercy shall compass him about.'" (Ps. xxxii. 10). —p. 98 *b*.

"Redeem yourselves while you live, for after death no one can redeem you" (quia post mortem nemo vos redimere potest).—p. 99 *b*.

"In all these works of goodness which the Lord has commanded you to perform, he seeks nothing from you but the salvation of your souls, and that you may fear him always and keep his commandments [then after referring to and in great measure repeating the blessing and the curse given by Moses, he proceeds :] These things, therefore, brethren, always keep in mind, these words repeat to your sons and your neighbours, remember them when you sit in your houses, and when you walk, neither forget them in your prosperity, but always fear God, and serve him alone, lest his fury be kindled against you. Know that he keepeth covenant and mercy towards those who love him and keep his commandments, and heals all their sicknesses. Consider that, as the apostle John forewarns, 'it is the last hour,' and therefore do not now love the world, for it soon passeth away, and all the lust thereof with it. But, do you do the will of God, that you may remain for ever, and may have confidence when he shall appear, and not be confounded at his coming. Let no man deceive you. He that doeth righteousness is righteous, and he that committeth sin is of the devil; and certainly every sin, whether theft, or adultery, or lying, is not committed without diabolical agency. Consider, I beseech you, what a destructive thing it is to do the works of the devil, and to become partaker with him, not in rest, but in the punishment of gehenna. Therefore, whenever you sin, do not wait in mortiferous security until your wounds putrefy, nor add others to them, but immediately by the confession of repentance hasten to obtain a remedy."—p. 100 *a*.

"Now, according to his unspeakable mercy, the Lord not only admonishes, but entreats that we would be converted to him. Let us therefore listen to him when he asks, lest if we do not, he should not listen to us when he judges. Let us listen also to the Scripture, which crieth out, 'My son, have pity on thine own soul, pleasing

God.'[8] What wilt thou answer to this, O human frailty? God entreats thee to pity thyself, and thou wilt not; how shall he hear thee supplicating in the day of necessity, when thou wilt not hear him entreating for thyself? If you now neglect these things, brethren, what will you do in the day of judgment, or to what refuge will you fly? If, I say, you now neglect such exhortations of God, you will not then escape the torments of hell, nor can gold or silver deliver you, nor those riches which you now secrete in corners, and through the pride of which you become negligent of your salvation. For hence, God saith by the prophet, 'I will visit you with evil, and I will cause the arrogancy of the wicked to cease, and will lay low the haughtiness of the terrible.' (Is. xiii. 11.) And again he admonishes, saying, ' Bring it again to mind, O ye transgressors; cease to do evil, learn to do well; relieve the oppressed, defend the poor, and the widow, and the orphan; deal not by oppression with the stranger.' [9] These things, therefore, brethren, keep in mind. Hasten to observe them with all your might. Fight as those who are separated from the devil. Be joined to God, who has redeemed you. Let the Gentiles be astonished at your conversation, and if they slander you, and even if they mock you for performing the duties of Christianity, let not that trouble you, for they shall give an account to God. Place, therefore, all your hope in the mercy of Christ, and not only abstain from every impure act, but also guard your minds from evil thoughts; for the Lord God is a righteous judge, and judgeth of evil thoughts."—p. 101 *b*.

"Moreover, that which is threatened by the voice of truth in the gospel: 'they,' it saith, 'that do iniquity shall be cast into a furnace of fire, where there shall be weeping and gnashing of teeth." Consider, then, how fierce, how much to be dreaded that fire is; and let him who could not now bear to put even one of his fingers in the fire, fear to be tormented there with his whole body for ever" (in sæcula). —p. 102 *b*.

"But know that the soul when it is separated from the body, is either immediately placed in paradise for its good deserts, or certainly precipitated directly into hell for its sins."—p. 103 *b*.

---

[8] "Miserere animæ tuæ placeus Deo." Eccles. xxx. 23. Our English version is, "Love thine own soul, and comfort thy heart; remove sorrow far from thee." v. 23. I give the Douay in the text.

[9] The passage stands, "Redite prævaricatores ad cor; quiescite agere perverse, discite benefacere; succurrite oppresso, defendite pauperem et viduam, et pupillum; et advenam nolite calumniari." It will be seen that it is made up from Is. xlvi. 8, and i. 16, 17, and Ezek. xxii. 7.

Love therefore with all your hearts that eternal life which through all ages you shall never bring to an end. Hasten thither, where you shall ever live, and never fear death. For if you love this wretched, fleeting life which you maintain with such labour — in which by running about and bustling, by the sweat of your brow, and working yourselves out of breath, you can scarcely provide the necessaries of life — how much more should you love eternal life in which you shall have no labour at all, where there is always the highest security, secure happiness, happy freedom, free blessedness ; where shall be fulfilled that which our Lord saith in the gospel, 'Men shall be like unto the angels;' like, indeed, not in substance, but in blessedness ? And that, 'then shall the just shine forth as the sun in the kingdom of their Father.' What, think you, will then be the splendour of souls, when the light of bodies shall have the brightness of the sun ? There shall then be no sorrow, no labour, no grief, no death ; but perpetual health shall endure. There no evil shall arise, no misery of the flesh, no sickness, no need of any kind ; there shall be no hunger, no thirst, no cold, no heat, no faintness of fasting, nor any temptation of the enemy ; nor then any will to sin, any possibility of defection ; but there shall be fulness of joy, and exultation in all things ; and men, associated with angels, shall be ever young in freedom from all fleshly infirmity. There, therefore, shall be solid joy, there secure rest, there pleasure infinite ; where if it be once attained, there shall be no chance of losing it throughout eternity, in that blessedness in which what is once gained shall be kept for ever. Nothing is there more magnificent than that place, nothing more glorious, nothing more bright, more beautiful, more true, more noble, nothing more pure in excellence, nothing more abundant in fulness. There always peace and the highest rejoicing. There is true and certain happiness. There shall no longer be feared that most fierce enemy who continually desires to destroy souls, nor shall the fiery darts of the devil, or any temptations of the adversary, be any longer dreaded. The cruelty of barbarians shall no more strike terror, nor shall any adversity be thenceforth apprehended. There shall be no fear of the sword, of fire, or the savage countenance of the tormentor. No one in that glorious place shall want clothing; for there is there no cold nor heat, nor any change of climate. No one there hungers, none is sad, none is a stranger; but all who shall be counted worthy to attain to that place shall live secure as in their own country. The flesh shall no longer war against the spirit, nor shall any danger be feared, but unspeakable rewards with the angels shall be given by Christ; and 'what the eye hath not seen,' saith the apostle, 'nor the ear heard, neither hath it entered into the heart of man to conceive, what God

L

hath prepared for those who love him.' Behold what blessedness he
will lose who refuses now while he hath opportunity to amend himself.
Let us therefore, brethren, for whom so great blessedness is prepared
in heaven, disdain (the Lord being our helper) to be any longer the
servants of sin. While, then, there is time, let us hasten to obtain the
favour of God, let us despise earthly things, that we may gain those
which are heavenly; let us think of ourselves as pilgrims in this world,
that we may the more cheerfully hasten towards heaven; for all the
things which are here seen quickly pass away, and will be gone like
a shadow."—p. 103 *b*.

After quoting Matt. xxv. of our Lord's advent, he
proceeds:—

"Then when all are looking, he will show the wounds and the
holes of the nails in that body undoubtedly the same in which he
was wounded for our transgressions; and addressing the sinners he
will then say—'I formed thee, O man, with my hands from the dust
of the earth, and placed thee amidst the delights of a paradise, which
thou didst not deserve; but thou, despising me and my commands,
didst prefer to follow a deceiver; wherefore, being condemned to just
punishment, thou wast appointed to the torments of hell. Afterwards,
pitying thee, I became incarnate, I dwelt on earth among sinners, I
bare scorn and stripes for thee. That I might save thee, I underwent
blows and spitting. That I might gain for thee the sweets of paradise,
I drank vinegar and gall. For thee I was crowned with thorns, fastened to the cross, wounded with the spear. For thee I died, was laid
in the grave, and descended into hell. That I might bring thee back
to paradise, I went to the gates of hell; that thou mightest reign in
heaven, I penetrated the infernal deep. Acknowledge, then, oh human
impiety, how much I have suffered for thee. Behold the wounds which
I received for thee, behold the holes of those nails fastened by which
I hanged on the cross. I bare thy griefs, that I might heal thee; I
underwent punishment, that I might give thee glory; I submitted to death,
that thou mightest live for ever; I lay in the sepulchre, that thou mightest
reign in heaven. All these things I bare for you; what more than these
things should I have done for you that I have not done? Tell me now,
or show me, what you have suffered for me, or what good you have done
for yourselves. I when I was invisible did, of my own will, become
incarnate on your account; though I was impassible, for you I condescended to suffer; when I was rich, for your sakes I became poor.
But you, always despising both my humility and my commandments,
have followed the seducer rather than me; and now behold my justice

cannot adjudge to you anything else than what your works deserve to receive. Take, then, what you have chosen; you have despised light, possess darkness; you have loved death, go into perdition; you have followed the devil, go with him into eternal fire.' What, think you, will then be the grief, what the lamentation, what the sadness, what the distress, when this sentence shall be given against the wicked? For then shall be to the wicked a grievous separation from the sweet company of the saints; and, being delivered over to the power of demons, they will go in their own bodies with the devil into eternal punishment, and will remain for ever in lamentation and groaning. For being far exiled from the blessed country of Paradise, they will be tormented in hell, never again to see light, never to obtain a time of refreshing, never to end their punishment, never to arrive at rest; but through thousands of thousands of years to be tormented in hell, nor ever, through all eternity, to be delivered. Where he that torments is never tired, and he that is tormented never dies. For there the fire so consumes that it still reserves; torments are so inflicted as that they may be for ever renewed. According to the quality of his crimes, however, each one will there suffer the punishments of hell; and those who are guilty of the like sins will be associated together in punishment. Nothing will be heard there but weeping, and wailing, and gnashing of teeth. There will be no consolation, nothing but flames and the terrors of punishments, and the wretched ones will burn without end in eternal fire through all ages. But the just shall go into life eternal, and without doubt in that very same flesh which they here had, and shall be associated with holy angels in the kingdom of God, appointed to perpetual joys, never again to die, no more to see corruption, but always filled with the joy and sweetness of Christ, they shall shine as the sun in the brightness and glory which God has prepared for those who love him. And the more obedient to God any one hath been in this life, so much the larger reward shall he receive; and the more he hath loved God here, the more nearly shall he then see him.

"Behold, most dearly beloved, I have foretold you plainly, so that you may understand what things shall happen to every one. No one can now plead ignorance, for life and death are set before you; the punishments of the wicked and the glory of the just are told you,— now it remains for your choice to take which you please; for each will surely then possess that which he hath desired and endeavoured after here."—p. 104 *b*.

These are not all the passages which might be quoted to the same effect; but surely they are more than

enough, and such in quality as to warrant my saying
that they seem as if they had been written purposely
to anticipate, and refute, the charge that the preachers,
of whom St. Eloy is given as a specimen, instead of
placing "heaven and hell before the view of men,"
only "depicted a certain fire prepared to burn off the
imperfections of the soul."

No. VIII.

"A modern author, who writes the history of ancient times, can have no personal knowledge of the events of which he writes; and consequently he can have no title to the credit and confidence of the public, merely on his own authority. If he does not write romance instead of history, he must have received his information from tradition — from authentic monuments, original records, or the memoirs of more ancient writers — and therefore it is but just to acquaint his readers from whence he *actually* received it."—HENRY.

IN the preceding paper, I expressed my design to go on from Robertson to another popular writer; and I now beg to call the reader's attention to the historian from whom I have borrowed my motto. In that part of his History of England which treats of the tenth century, Henry compassionately says:—

"That we may not entertain too contemptible an opinion of our forefathers, who flourished in the benighted ages which we are now examining, it is necessary to pay due attention to their unhappy circumstances. To say nothing of that contempt for letters which they derived from their ancestors, and of the almost incessant wars in which they were engaged, it was difficult, or rather impossible, for any but the clergy, and a very few of the most wealthy among the laity, to obtain the least smattering of learning; because all the means of acquiring it were far beyond their reach. It is impossible to learn to read and write even our own native tongue, which is now hardly esteemed a part of learning, without books, masters, and materials for writing; but in those ages, all these were so extremely scarce and dear, that none but great princes and wealthy prelates could procure them. We have already heard of a large estate given by a king of Northumberland for a single volume; and the history of the middle ages abounds with examples of that kind. How, then, was it possible for persons of a moderate fortune to procure so much as one book, much less such a number of books as to make their learning to read an accomplishment that would reward their trouble? It was then as difficult to borrow books as to buy them. It is a sufficient proof of this that the king of France was obliged to deposit a considerable quantity of plate, and

to get one of his nobility to join with him in a bond, under a high
penalty, to return it, before he could procure the loan of one volume,
which may now be purchased for a few shillings. Materials for writing
were also very scarce and dear, which made few persons think of
learning that art. This was one reason of the scarcity of books; and
that great estates were often transferred from one owner to another by
a mere verbal agreement, and the delivery of earth and stone, before
witnesses, without any written deed. Parchment, in particular, on which
all their books were written, was so difficult to be procured, that many
of the MSS. of the middle ages, which are still preserved, appear to
have been written on parchment from which some former writing had
been erased."—Book ii. ch. iv. vol. iv. p. 80.

After what I have said in former papers, it is, I
trust, quite unnecessary to make a single remark on
all this; which I transcribe and set before the reader,
instead of asking him, as I should otherwise have done,
to turn back to the statements of Robertson, which I
have from time to time quoted, and to see how far,
when read off without any explanation, they are calculated to give a true view of things. Henry has,
however, one "hack story," of which I must take particular notice; for, notwithstanding the false impression
conveyed by such absurd matter as that which I have
just quoted, there is really more mischief done by the
little pointed anecdotes with which some popular writers
pretend to prove or to illustrate their sweeping statements. These stories are remembered by their readers,
and the semblance of particular and detailed truth in
one instance, gives sanction and weight to a whole
string of false and foolish assertions about the general
state of things. Perhaps it might be enough to refer
the reader back to the instance of the Abbot Bonus; [1]
but instead of that we will have an entirely new story,
from Henry.

---

[1] See No. IV. p. 63.

Having told us that—

"All the nations of Europe were involved in such profound darkness during the whole course of the tenth century, that the writers of literary history are at a loss for words to paint the ignorance, stupidity, and barbarism of that age"—(Book ii. c. 4. vol. iv. p. 67).

and having, in proof of this, referred to "Cave Histor. Literar. p. 571, Brucker Hist. Philosoph. t. 3. p. 632," he adds on the next page—

"The clergy in this age were almost as illiterate as the laity. Some who filled the highest stations in the church could not so much as read; while others, who pretended to be better scholars, and attempted to perform the public offices, committed the most egregious blunders; of which the reader will find one example, *out of many*, quoted below."

At the foot of the page, we find the following note:—

"Meinwerc, Bishop of Paderborn, in this century, in reading the public prayers, used to say,—'Benedic Domine regibus et reginis mulis et mulabis [*sic*] tuis:—' instead of 'famulis et famulabis; [*sic*]' which made it a very ludicrous petition.—*Leibniz Coll. Script. Brunswic.*, t. i. p. 555."

Very ludicrous indeed—What an odd person Bishop Meinwerc must have been, and what a very strange habit to fall into—but, without attempting to account for it, farther than by saying, "it was his way," may we not draw three inferences from it—first, that if Meinwerc habitually made this blunder, he made a thousand others like it; secondly, that what *he* did, all the other bishops did; thirdly, that if the bishops were so ignorant, the priests and deacons, to say nothing of the laity, were infinitely worse? Are not these fair deductions?

And yet, to say the truth, when I consider that my inquiry is not whether there were any ignorant, stupid, incompetent persons in the dark ages; but whether there were not some of a different character, I feel inclined to claim, or at least to cross-examine, this witness. I cannot but think that the story, even as it stands, may be fairly made to say something in my favour. If the bishop did make this blunder, it seems that he had, at least, one hearer who knew that it was a blunder, and who thought it worth while to note it down as such; which, moreover, that hearer would hardly have done if conscious that he was the only person capable of seeing its absurdity. Besides, if this is only "one example out of many," there must have been persons in various places equally competent to detect such errors; and who, like the critic of Paderborn, thought them worth recording. So that, in proportion as the recorded blunders of this kind are numerous, we may be led to suspect a thicker and more extensive sprinkle of better-instructed persons. I know not how else to account for the fact that such things were seen and recorded as errors; unless, indeed, we assume the existence of some one individual "George Seacoal," whose reading and writing in this dark age came "by nature;" and suppose him to have circuited about with "the lanthorn" which he had in charge, in order to "comprehend all vagrom men" who broke the bounds of grammar, and who has certainly acted up to the very letter of his instructions, by letting his reading and writing "appear where there is no need of such vanity;" for what in the world did it matter to Bishop Meinwerc's flock whether he said *mulis* or *famulis*, if neither he nor they knew the difference?

We cannot, however, well understand this story without paying some attention to the circumstances of the bishop; and it is quite within the limits—indeed in the very heart—of our subject, to inquire into the proceedings of any prelate who was born in the tenth century, though not (as Henry makes him) a bishop until the eleventh. I might fairly inflict on the reader a long pedigree, and trace up the Bishop of Paderborn to the great Duke Witikind; but it may suffice for our present purpose to say, that he was born in the reign of the Emperor Otho II., and was his second cousin once removed; Theoderic, the father of the Empress Matilda, the wife of Henry the Fowler, being their common ancestor. His father, Imed, intending that Thiederic, the elder of his two sons, should succeed him in his honours and possessions, devoted Meinwerc, at an early age, to the clerical function, and offered him, in his childhood, in the Church of St. Stephen, at Halberstadt. There he received the first rudiments of his education; but was afterwards removed to Hildesheim, where, among many other schoolfellows, who afterwards took a leading part in the world, he had his third cousin, Henry, Duke of Bavaria, afterwards Emperor, better known under the tittle of St. Henry. [2]

Otho II. died in A.D. 983, and was succeeded by his son, Otho III.; who called his kinsman, Meinwerc, to court, and made him his chaplain. In this situation he

---

[2] I should have thought that there was such a difference between the ages of Meinwerc and the emperor, as could not have allowed of their being school-fellows. But the author of the life to which Henry refers, so distinctly states not only that it was so, but that it was in the time of Otho the *Second*, that I do not know how to dispute it, though I cannot reconcile it even with the dates which he gives himself in various parts of his work. He says that Meinwerc went to Hildesheim, "ubi Henricus filius Ducis Bajoariæ Henrici, cum aliis plurimis honori et decori ecclesiæ Christi suo tempore profuturis, secum theoriæ studiis continuam operam dedit. . . . Acceptus autem de scholis, vixit in prædicta Halverstadensi Ecclesia sub Præposito canonicæ legis, omnibus carus et amabilis, aspectu et colloquio affabilis, actu et eloquio irreprehensibilis. Eo tempore monarchiam Romani Imperii Otto ejusdem nominis *secundus* strenue gubernabat."—p. 519. It is not worth while to discuss the chronology of the matter. If it be a mistake to suppose that the emperor and the bishop were school-fellows, it is beyond all doubt that they were cousins and play-fellows.

is said to have been esteemed and respected by all, and particularly beloved by his royal master and cousin, who enriched him with most liberal presents, in proof of his affection—"quod videlicet suam vitam diligeret ut propriam." On the death of that Emperor, in A.D. 1002, among many candidates for the empire, the successful one was Henry of Bavaria, who was related to Meinwerc in precisely the same degree as his predecessor in the empire had been, and who was perhaps bound to him by what is often the closer and stronger tie of school-fellowship. The chaplain became the inseparable companion of his royal master—"de Karo fit Karissimus; factusque est ei in negotiis publicis et privatis comes irremotissimus."

After some time—that is to say, in the year 1009 —the see of Paderborn became vacant by the death of Rhetarius, who had been bishop for twenty years. Messengers from the church announced the fact to the emperor, who was then at Goslar, and prayed him to appoint a successor. This, however, was not so easy a matter; for, about nine years before, the city of Paderborn had been burned; and the noble monastery, containing the cathedral, had been all but entirely destroyed. Rhetarius had, indeed, done what he could with the pope, and the Emperor Otho III.; and had obtained from them (what was, no doubt, very important as far as it went) a full confirmation to the church of all the rights and property which it had possessed before the conflagration; but it does not appear that he got anything from them towards repairing losses. When, however, Henry, his successor, came to the throne of the empire, he made it his study and his business to advance the interests of the church; and when Rhetarius applied to him, he gave him a forest. When he came at another time to beg for his church,

the emperor not having (as the historian says with
great simplicity) at the moment anything which he
could conveniently give him (rege autem in promptu
quod daret non habente), his chaplain, Meinwerc, gave
his royal master a farm, which belonged to himself,
which the emperor immediately transferred to the
bishop.

Still, notwithstanding the exertions of Rhetarius, the
see remained in a state of wretched poverty as long
as he lived; and it was difficult to know how to fill
up the vacancy occasioned by his death. The emperor
having, however, convened such bishops and princes
as attended him at Goslar, consulted with them as to
the appointment of a bishop who should be most suited
to the circumstances of time and place. After long
deliberation, and canvassing the merits of a good many
persons, all agreed that Meinwerc was the fittest man.
In coming to this decision, they were avowedly influenced by his rank and wealth; but it is only justice
to him to say, that I find nothing against his moral
character, nor even anything which should authorize
me to say that he had not a true zeal for God, though
it might not be, in all respects, according to knowledge. The council, however, were unanimous; and the
emperor (faventibus et congratulantibus omnibus) sent
for the chaplain; and, when he came, smiling with his
usual kindness, he held out a glove, and said—"Take
this." Meinwerc, who can hardly be supposed to have
been quite ignorant of what was going on, and who
understood the nature of the symbol, inquired what
he was to take. " The see of Paderborn," replied the
emperor. The chaplain, with all the freedom of a kinsman
and old school-fellow, asked his royal master how he
could suppose that he wished for such a bishopric,
when he had property enough of his own to endow

a better. The emperor, with equal frankness, replied that that was just the very thing that he was thinking of—that his reason for selecting him was that he might take pity on that desolate church, and help it in its need. "Well, then," said Meinwerc, heartily, "I will take it on those terms;" and then and there—namely, at Goslar, on the next Sunday, being the second Sunday in Lent, and the thirteenth of March, 1009—he was consecrated Bishop of Paderborn, by Willigisus, Archbishop of Mentz, and the other bishops who were there.

"Being therefore," says his biographer, "raised to the episcopal office, he constantly watched over the flock committed to him; and, fearing lest he should incur the reproach of the slothful servant, who hid his lord's money in a napkin, he did nothing remissly. As to external duties, in the general government of the clergy and people, he laboured diligently with heart and body in his episcopal superintendence; and, as to internal labours, he without ceasing made intercession to God for them all, by watchings, fastings, and the sacrifice of prayers." He immediately made over his hereditary property to the see; and on the third day after his arrival he pulled down the mean beginnings of a cathedral, which his predecessor had built up, and erected one at great expense, and with singular magnificence — sumptu ingenti et magnificentia singulari. His personal attention to the work, and his kindness to the workmen, made the building go on rapidly; and he did not fail to call upon the emperor, who frequently came to Paderborn, and took great interest in its proceedings, for his full share of the expense; and Henry and his empress, Chunigunda, contributed largely and willingly.

A circumstance which occurred during one of the

emperor's visits tends so much to illustrate the character
of the bishop, and of the times, that I am induced to
transcribe it. It quite belongs to our subject; and,
indeed, to our immediate purpose, so far as it shows
that Meinwerc was rather a severe disciplinarian, and that
if he performed the services of the church disreputably
himself, he did not allow others to do it, or even to
run the risque of it, with impunity. There was in those
days an eccentric saint—or the church of Rome has
made him one since—named Heimrad. He was a native
of Swabia, and, as far as I know, a good sort of
fanatic. After wandering about, and doing a great many
strange things, he settled down in a little cell, or hut,
at Hasungen. Previously to this, however, in the course
of his rambles, he came to Paderborn, and suddenly
made his appearance before the bishop; who, being
startled at the sight of his sickly countenance and his
long figure, rendered ghastly and unsightly by fasting
and rags, inquired whence "that devil" had risen.
Heimrad having meekly replied that he was not a devil,
the bishop inquired if he was a priest; and learning
that he had that day celebrated mass, he immediately
ordered that the books which he had used should be
produced. Finding that they were written in a slovenly
manner, and were of no value (incomptos et neglectos
et nullius ponderis aut pretii), he caused them to be
immediately put in the fire; and, by command of the
Empress, who sympathized with the "just zeal" of the
bishop, he farther ordered that the unlucky priest should
be flogged.

After this, Count Dodico, of Warburg (a person of
some consequence in the early history of the see of
Paderborn), invited the bishop to keep the feast of
St. Andrew, at his castle; and on the very eve of the
festival, whom should the bishop see seated opposite

to him, at supper, but this identical Heimrad. He was
not a little moved, and inquired what could induce a
man of his host's respectability to keep such company;
and then, breaking out into severe abuse of the poor
solitary, he called him a crazy apostate. Heimrad
took it all very quietly, and said not a word; but
Count Dodico began to apologize to the bishop, for
whom he had a sincere respect, and endeavoured to
soothe him by assurances that he had no idea that the
recluse was in any way offensive to him. All his
endeavours were, however, in vain, and the bishop was
not to be appeased. On the contrary, he declared that
as people chose to consider Heimrad as a saint, he
would put him to the test; and, in the presence of all
the company, he ordered that he should sing the *Hal-
lelujah* at mass the next day, on pain of being flogged.
The Count at first attempted to beg him off; but finding that he only added fuel to the flame, he took the
recluse apart, as soon as lauds were over, and endeavoured to console him. He besought him to bear this
trial as one of those which are appointed for the puri-
fication of the saints—to make the attempt, beginning
in the name of the Trinity, and trusting in God for
the event. Heimrad did not at all like the prospect, and
earnestly requested leave to creep away quietly to his
cell at Hasungen; but at length, overcome by the
Count's entreaties, he acquiesced. When the time came,
another attempt was made to beg him off; but the
bishop continuing inexorable, he began, and in fact
chanted the whole with such propriety, and in so agreeable a manner, that the company were astonished, and
declared that they had never heard sweeter modulation
from any man. The bishop, as soon as mass was over,
taking Heimrad aside, fell at his feet, and having
humbly asked, and quickly obtained, pardon for his

conduct towards him, became, from that time forth, his constant and faithful friend.

But, though I give these anecdotes as characteristic of the bishop and the times, and therefore illustrative of our subject, it will be more immediately to our present purpose to give one or two which show the terms on which the bishop stood with the emperor, and some passages which occurred between them. Those terms cannot, perhaps, be more briefly or more clearly explained, than by saying that these two school-fellows still behaved to each other rather more in the manner of schoolboys than was quite becoming in a bishop and an emperor, as will appear; but first, let me premise that from the time when he became Bishop of Paderborn, Meinwerc seems to have devoted him-self—that is, his property, his time, his thoughts, words, and deeds,—to the aggrandizement of his see. He was, his biographer tells us, skilful in getting all that was to be had, as well as faithful in taking care of what he had got—"in acquirendis utilis, in conservandis fidelis." [3]

As to the latter point, many stories are recorded which show that he laboured most energetically in conducting the affairs of his diocese, which he seems to have governed with an extraordinary degree both of severity and kindness, so as to have been, in a peculiar degree, a terror to evil-doers, and a praise to those who did well. He superintended, in person,

---

[3] It might perhaps be said of him, as it was of an abbot of much the same period—"cum esset vir strenuus, et suam rempublicam semper augmentare toto anhelaret desiderio."—*Mab.* A. S. *tom.* vi. p. 405. Such hints as these contain a good deal, and are a key to a good deal more, and must be borne in mind when we read such notes as I have adverted to in the note, p. 131, about carcass-hunting bishops who wanted "to amass riches." What did they want the riches for?

the buildings which the circumstances already mentioned
required, until he had got them so far advanced that
he could be spared to look after the country estates
of the diocese; and then perpetually visiting them,
from time to time, he took care that all things were
managed decently and in order, and raised the serfs
to a degree of comfort which they had not before
enjoyed. Once, riding through one of the farms belonging
to the bishopric, he told some of his companions to
ride their own, or to turn some loose, horses into some
corn, which was being thrashed under cover; saying,
that if the serfs were faithful, they would resist them,
but if they were unfaithful to the steward, they would
rejoice in a mischief which would bring loss upon him.
The serfs, however, under pretence of paying their
obeisance to the bishop, all ran away; and the horses
began to devour and trample on the corn. The bishop
immediately taxed the labourers with their want of
faith, had them severely flogged, and then gave them
an uncommonly good dinner (ciborum copiis abundan-
tissime reficiens), and a paternal admonition on fidelity
to their master; all which together had so excellent
an effect, that when he next visited the place he found
himself shut out by their faithful vigilance, and was
obliged to make his way into the premises by stealth.
Having done so, he heard the woman of the house
complaining that the labourers on that farm had nothing
but a very spare allowance of meal; whereupon he
ordered that two of the gammons of bacon which the
steward was bound to furnish every year should be
detained for them.

I should like to gossip on with an account of his
visits to other farms, and to tell how he once got
into the kitchen of his monastery by himself, and
investigated the contents of the pots which were boiling

at the fire, in order to see that his monks had proper food; and how, at another time, he went there in a lay habit, to have a little chat on the same subject with the cook, who, in reply to his inquiries, informed him that the living there was very good as concerning the soul, but very poor in respect of the body; and how—for he seems always to have been on the alert—he went through his diocese in the disguise of a pedlar, in order that he might see for himself how things were going on. I should like, I say, to transcribe some of these anecdotes, for they are really—not like some which we find produced as such—characteristic of the times; but I am afraid of being tedious; and whatever might be his care in preserving, it is more to our purpose to show that he was diligent in acquiring. In that matter, he did not spare his imperial school-fellow. Indeed, there seems to have been an understanding—or, in the language of the schools, they seem to have "made it fair"—between them, that the bishop should get all he could by force or fraud, and that in return the emperor should love him heartily, growl at him occasionally, and now and then make a fool of him. As to the latter point, however, the emperor seems generally to have had the worst of it in the long run, as will appear from one or two instances.

Once, when Henry was going to hear mass at the cathedral, he ordered the altar to be decked with the costly apparatus of royalty, and bade his people keep a sharp look-out, lest the bishop should get hold of anything, as he was very apt to do. Meinwerc said mass himself, and after the *Agnus Dei*, he entered the pulpit, and began to discuss the difference between the imperial and sacerdotal dignity, and the superiority of the latter, affirming that matters of divine right

M

were above human authority, and showing by the
canons that whatsoever was consecrated to the uses
of divine service was under the sacerdotal jurisdiction.
He therefore put under a bann all the ecclesiastical
ornaments and priestly vestments which had just been
used, and threatened with excommunication any person
who should remove them.

On another occasion, the emperor sent him, after
vespers, his own golden cup, of exquisite workmanship, full of drink,[4] charging the messenger not to
see his face again without the cup. The bishop received
the present with many thanks, and got the messenger
into a long chat, during which he seems to have
forgotten the business which brought him there, and
the emperor's charge—at least, somehow or other, he
went away without the cup—and the bishop, taking
care to have the doors fastened after him, sent immediately for his goldsmiths, Brunhard, and his son,
Erpho, and in the course of the night, which immediately preceded Christmas-day, the cup was converted
into a chalice. One of the emperor's chaplains, who
officiated as sub-deacon at mass the next day, recog-
nized the cup, and took it to the emperor, who charged
the bishop with theft, and told him that God abhorred
robbery for burnt-offering. Meinwerc replied that he
had only robbed the vanity and avarice of Henry, by
consecrating their subject to the service of God; and
dared him to take it away. "I will not," said the
emperor, "take away that which has been devoted to
the service of God; but I will myself humbly offer
to him that which is my own property; and do you

---

[4] The laxity with which writers of this age use the word "sicera"
sanctions the ambiguous expression which I use. If not very elegant,
it is better than talking of beer between such parties.

honour the Lord, who vouchsafed as on this night to
be born for the salvation of all men, by the performance of your own duties."

At another time, the emperor had a mantle of marvellous beauty, and exquisite workmanship. Meinwerc
had often begged it for his church in vain ; and
therefore, on one occasion, when the emperor was
intent on some particular business, he fairly snatched
it from his person, and made off with it. The emperor
charged him with robbery, and threatened to pay
him off for it some time or other. Meinwerc replied
that it was much more proper that such a mantle should
hang in the temple of God, than on his mortel body,
and that he did not care for his threats. They were,
however, carried into execution in the following manner :—" The emperor knowing that the bishop, being
occupied in a great variety of secular business, was
now and then guilty of a barbarism, both in speaking
and in reading Latin, with the help of his chaplain
effaced the syllable *fa* from the words *famulis* and
famulabus, which form part of a collect in the service
for the defunct, in the missal ; and then called on the
bishop to say a mass for the souls of his father and
mother. Meinwerc, therefore, being unexpectedly called
on to perform the service, and hastening to do it, read
on as he found written, *mulis* and *mulabus*, but, perceiving the mistake, he repeated the words correctly.
After mass, the emperor said, in a sarcastic manner,
to the bishop, 'I asked you to say mass for my father
and mother, not for my male and female mules.' But
he replied, 'By the mother of our Lord, you have been
at your old tricks, and have made a fool of me again ;
and now, in no common way, but in the service of
our God. This he who is my Judge has declared that
he will avenge ; for that which is done to him he will

not pass by unpunished.' Thereupon, he immediately convened the canons in the chapter-house of the cathedral, ordered the emperor's chaplain, who had been a party to the trick, to be most severely flogged; and then, having dressed him in new clothes, sent him back to the emperor to tell him what had happened." [5]

And here, good reader, you have, I believe, the whole and sole foundation for the notable story of Bishop Meinwerc and his mules. If you have been at church so often as you should have been in these five years past, perhaps you have heard King George prayed for by men who were neither stupid nor careless; but who were officiating from a book which had not been corrected. I am sure I have heard it within these six months;—but there is no need to apologize for the bishop.

"Oh! but he '*used* to say' this." Well, that is one of those things which, as they admit of only one reply,

---

[5] "Sciens autem Imperator, episcopum sæcularibus negotiis multipliciter occupatum, tam latinitatis locutione quam in lectione barbarismi vitia non semel incurrere, de missali in quadam collecta pro defunctis *fa* de *famulis*, et *famulabus*, cum capellano suo delevit, et episcopum pro requie animarum patris sui et matris missam celebrare rogavit. Episcopus igitur ex improviso missam celebrare accelerans, ut scriptum reperit *mulis* et *mulabus* dixit; sed errorem recognoscens, repetitis verbis, quod male dixerat, correxit. Post missam insultans Imperator Pontifici, 'Ego,' inquit, 'patri meo et matri, non mulis et mulabus meis, missam celebrari rogavi.' At ille, 'Per matrem,' ait, 'Domini, tu more solito iterum illusisti mihi, et non quoquo modo, verum in Dei nostri servitio. Cujus ero vindex, en promittit meus judex. Namque sibi factum non pertransibit inultum.' Illico canonicis in capitolium principalis ecclesiæ convocatis, capellanum Imperatoris, hujus rei conscium, durissime verberibus castigari jussit, castigatumque novis vestibus indutum ad Imperatorem, nuntiaturum quæ facta fuerant, remisit." I suspect that the reply of Meinwerc, from the word "Cujus," &c., is a quotation from some hymn; though it is printed like prose, and certainly can hardly be called verse.

very commonly receive none at all from civil people.
"But it is only 'one example out of *many*.'" Perhaps so;
but I really do not recollect any story like it, except
the notorious *mumpsimus*, and one which looks almost
like another version of what we have just had, and which
I know only from its being quoted by Lomeier,[6] in
connection with another dark-age anecdote which is
too good to be passed by, and which shows, in dismal
colours, the horrible ignorance of the clergy. "A certain
bishop, named Otto, is said to have recommended a
clerk to another bishop for an ecclesiastical office in
these terms—' *Otto Dei gratia, rogat vestram clementiam,
ut velitis istum clericum conducere ad vestrum dia-
conum.*' The words being abbreviated, the clerk, who
was directed to read it to the bishop, read thus:—
' *Otto Dei gram rogat vestram clam ut velit istum
clincum clancum convertere in vivum diabolum.*'" The
other story is of a clerk, who turned Sueno, king of
Norway, into a mule by the same mistake as Meinwerc's.
As to the truth or falsehood of these statements, I have
never inquired; and I have not, at present, the means
of consulting the author to whom Lomeier refers.

But is it not lamentable that learned men should

---

[6] De Bibliothecis, cap. viii., de Bibliothecis sub ipsa barbarie, p. 147
[It is a pity not to have as many such good stories as we can, and
therefore I add one which I have met with since I wrote the foregoing
paragraph. Bruno, in his account of the Emperor Henry IV., who
reigned from A. D. 1056 to A. D. 1106, tells us, that among his other
wicked deeds, he appointed to the see of Bamberg (tam rebus exterius
divitem, quam sapientibus personis intus venerabilem) an ignoramus, who
read out in divine service (coram sapientibus clericis) that the earth,
instead of being void, *vacua*, was a cow, *vacca*. "Ipse," adds the indignant historian, "nimirum, licet bipes, *vacca* bruta et omni probitate
vacua."—(*Saxon. Belli Hist. ap. Freh. Ger. Rer. Scr.* Tom. I. p. 179;
old Ed. p. 105.) Surely there must have been *some* critical ears in those
days.]

credit and circulate such stories? I do not mean Henry; [7]
for, notwithstanding what he says, and what I have
quoted at the head of this paper, I do not believe that
he really took the story from the book to which he
refers. I think I know where he picked it up; and I
believe it is more charitable—at least it is imputing
what is, of the two, least disgraceful—to suppose that
he took the story (notwithstanding his profession quoted
as the motto to this paper) from a respectable writer,
than to suppose that he made up the falsehood himself
from such an original as he refers to, and I have just
transcribed. He had (as I have stated near the beginning
of this paper, p. 143) almost immediately before quoted
Brucker's History of Philosophy, Vol. III. p. 632, and
on the 634th page of that same volume, and in the
section entitled "Facies literarum et philosophiæ sæculo
X.," stand this very story of Meinwerc in these terms—
"Meinwercum episcopum Paderbornensem ne recte
legere quidem potuisse, et in psalterio legisse: *Benedic
Domine regibus et reginis mulis et mulabus tuis*, pro
famulis et famulabus tuis." Brucker's reference is, "In
eius vita in LEIBNIZ. Coll. Script. Brunsuic. T. I. p. 555."
And, really, if it were in any way possible, I should
believe that Brucker had had some other edition, or
some other authority, for the story. He tells us that
it was in the *psalter*, and affects to give us the words.
Henry seems to have been sensible of the absurdity
of this; and, not knowing what particular part to
substitute, he says, it was "in the public prayers." I

---

[7] And still less Mr. Andrews, already introduced to the reader as a
retailer of such things. He prefaces this perverted story by saying, "The
prelates set examples of the most gross want of common literature.
Mein-*hard*, Bishop of Paderborn, used to read," &c. Yet he gives no
reference but to the original. Does anybody believe that he had seen it?

speak thus, because I cannot doubt that he took it from Brucker, though not perhaps immediately; and my belief is strengthened by a trifling circumstance, which is perhaps worth mentioning, because it is desirable to trace error when we can. Who has not heard of Leibnitz? Thousands have known the philosopher by name or character, who never took the trouble to learn that he was librarian of the Royal and Electoral Library of Brunswick-Luneburg, and who never had the pleasure of reading his three folios containing the "Scriptores Rerum Brunsvicensium illustrationi inservientes;"—his name is familiar; but how often have they seen it spelt (by any writer of English, to say the least) without a *t*? He calls himself, on the title-page of this work, "Leibnitius;" and I do not remember ever to have seen his name without the *t*, except in this very volume of Brucker, and in Henry's reference.

I must, however, notice that Brucker adds to his account of the matter, "unde vix credi potest quod idem vitæ Meinwerci scriptor refert, '*studiorum multiplicia sub eo floruisse excercitia, et bonæ indolis juvenes et pueros strenue fuisse institutos.*'" Incredible as this might appear to Brucker, it is certainly true that the same authority which tells us that Meinwerc was guilty of occasional barbarisms in speaking and reading Latin (which implies that he was not unfrequently called on to do both), also assures us that he was a promoter of education. Indeed, the foolish trick which has given rise to all this discussion, was not such as to have been worth playing, or as was likely to have been even thought of, among perfectly illiterate barbarians. What wit or fun could there be in leading a man into a blunder, which nobody could know to be a blunder? The same authority tells us, that the schools

of Paderborn, then founded, became more famous in
the time of Imadus, who was the nephew and successor
of Meinwerc, and brought up by him; "sub quo in
Patherbornensi ecclesia publica floruerunt studia: quando
ibi *musici* fuerunt et *dialectici,* enituerunt *rhetorici,*
clarique *grammatici;* quando magistri artium exerce-
bant *trivium,* quibus omne studium erat circa *quadri-*
vium; ubi *mathematici* claruerunt et *astronomici,*
habebantur *physici,* et *geometrici:* viguit *Horatius,*
magnus et *Virgilius, Crispus* ac *Salustius* et *Urbanus*
Statius: Ludusque fuit omnibus insudare versibus, et
dictaminibus jocundisque cantibus. Quorum in *scriptura*
et *pictura* jugis instantia claret multipliciter hodierna
experientia dum studium nobilium clericorum usu per-
penditur utilium librorum." Make what allowance you
like for exaggeration, but let the words have *some*
meaning; and if you do this you will never be able
to make them square with the letter, still less with the
spirit, of these absurd stories.

No. IX.

"*LI.* Attate! modo hercle in mentem venit.
Nimis vellem habere perticam. *LE.* Quoi rei? *LI.* Quî verberarem
Asinos."—PLAUTUS.

THERE is one of Robertson's proofs and illustrations,
which I intended to notice, but I really forgot it when
I passed on to Henry's history of England—a blunder
the more stupid, because it is another note immediately
following the note respecting St. Eloy; and I actually
quoted the text to which it belongs, and in which
Robertson tells us, that "the external ceremonies, which
then formed the whole of religion, were either so
unmeaning as to be altogether unworthy of the Being
to whose honour they were consecrated, or so absurd
as to be a disgrace to reason and humanity." The note
is as follows:—

"It is no inconsiderable misfortune to the church of Rome, whose
doctrine of infallibility renders all such institutions and ceremonies as
have been once universally received immutable and everlasting, that she
must continue to observe in enlightened times those rites which were
introduced during the ages of darkness and credulity. What delighted
and edified the latter, must disgust and shock the former. Many of
these rites appear manifestly to have been introduced by a superstition
of the lowest and most illiberal species. Many of them were borrowed,
with little variation, from the religious ceremonies established among the
ancient heathens. Some were so ridiculous, that, if every age did not
furnish instances of the fascinating influence of superstition, as well as
of the whimsical forms which it assumes, it must appear incredible that
they should ever be received or tolerated. In several churches of
France, they celebrated a festival in commemoration of the Virgin
Mary's flight into Egypt. It was called the feast of the Ass. A young
girl richly dressed, with a child in her arms, was set upon an ass
superbly caparisoned. The ass was led to the altar in solemn procession.
High mass was said with great pomp. The ass was taught to kneel at

proper places; a hymn no less childish than impious was sung in his praise: And, when the ceremony was ended, the priest, instead of the usual words with which he dismissed the people, brayed three times like an ass; and the people, instead of their usual response, We bless the Lord, brayed three times in the same manner. Du Cange, voc. Festum v. iii. p. 424. This ridiculous ceremony was not, like the festival of fools, and some other pageants of those ages, a mere farcical entertainment exhibited in a church, and mingled, as was then the custom, with an imitation of some religious rites; it was an act of devotion, performed by the ministers of religion, and by the authority of the church. However, as this practice did not prevail universally in the Catholic Church, its absurdity contributed at last to abolish it."— p. 237.

I copy this note, not so much as a specimen of broad, barefaced falsehood, or gross mistake, such as I have before presented to the reader's notice,—though, as it regards the misrepresentation of facts, it is worth looking at,—as for some other reasons, which will, I hope, appear satisfactory.

First, however, as to the fact,—which it is always well to examine in such cases,—that is, in all "wonderful-if-true" stories, told by persons of whose knowledge or veracity we have any doubt. The reader is welcome to put this rule in practice with regard to myself, and my communication, for he may naturally be somewhat incredulous when I tell him that the Feast of the Ass was not "a festival in commemoration of the Virgin Mary's flight into Egypt,"—that the Virgin Mary had nothing to do with the matter, and, so far as appears, was not even mentioned in it,—and that the Ass from whom the festival derived its name was not that on which she fled into Egypt (if, indeed, any such ass ever existed), but the ass of Balaam. Of this whoever pleases may satisfy himself by turning to Du Cange, as cited by Robertson.

Secondly, as to the fact.—Though Robertson cites

Du Cange, it is not for the Feast of the Ass, but for
the story about the "young girl richly dressed," &c.;
which (though Robertson has confounded the two things)
had nothing whatever to do with the Feast of the
Ass, and is not mentioned, or even alluded to, by Du
Cange. I do not mean to be hypercritical, or quibbling.
There is an account of this folly at the volume and
page of the book which we may familiarly call "Du
Cange,"—that is, the Benedictine edition of Du Cange's
Glossary, which expanded his three folios into ten,—
but it is important to observe, that the account of this
custom formed no part of the original work ; and that,
therefore, the custom itself may be presumed to have
been unknown to Du Cange; and how far anything
of that kind, which was at all general, or of long
standing, was likely to have escaped him, those who
are even slightly acquainted with his Glossary will be
able to judge.

Thirdly, as to the fact.—Du Cange does give, from
the Ordinal of the Cathedral of Rouen, the office (or
more properly, the rubric—or, more properly still, the
stage-directions of the office) appointed for the Feast
of Asses; which was a sort of interlude performed in
some churches at Christmas. I do not know whether
it would be possible now to learn what was said or
sung by the various characters, as the account of Du
Cange contains only the rubric, and the initiatory words
of each part; but the dramatis personæ appear to have
been numerous and miscellaneous; and I can only
account for the total absence of the Virgin Mary by
supposing that it arose from superior respect. There
were Jews and Gentiles as the representatives of their
several bodies, Moses and Aaron, and the Prophets,
Virgilius Maro, Nebuchadnezzar, the Sibyll, &c. Among
them, however, was Balaam on his ass; and this (not,

one would think, the most important or striking part
of the show) seems to have suited the popular taste,
and given the name to the whole performance and
festival. I should have supposed, that Nebuchadnezzar's
delivering over the three children to his armed men,
and their burning them in a furnace made on purpose
in the middle of the church, would have been a more
imposing part of the spectacle; but I pretend not to
decide in matters of taste, and certainly Balaam's ass
appears to have been the favourite. [1] The plan of the
piece seems to have been, that each of the persons
was called out in his turn to sing or say something
suitable to his character; and among others, "*Balaam
ornatus sedens super asinam* (hinc festo nomen) *habens
calcaria, retineat lora, et calcaribus percutiat asinam,
et quidam juvenis, tenens gladium, obstet asiuæ. Quidam
sub asina dicat,* Cur me calcaribus miseram sic læditis?
Hoc dicto Angelus ei dicat, Desine Regis Balac præceptum perficere. *Vocatores Balaun,* Balaun, esto vaticinans.
Tunc Balaun respondeat, Exibit ex Jacob rutilans," &c.

I am afraid that some persons give me credit for
defending a good deal of nonsense; and, therefore, let
me say at once, that I am not going to defend this.
I acknowledge that it was nonsense—nonsense that
came very near, if not to actual, profaneness, at least
to something like the desecration of holy things. The

---

[1] Indeed, he seems to be always a favourite with the public, and
to give the tone and the title wherever he appears. The ass is the only
link which unites these two stories, and in each he seems to be put
forth as the principal character. So it was, when, in the twelfth century,
an order of monks was formed, whose humility (or at least their Rule)
did not permit them to ride on horseback. The public (I hope to
the satisfaction of the humble men) entirely overlooked them, eclipsed
as they were by the animals on which they rode, and called it *Ordo
Asinorum.*

age, I admit, was dark; the performers were probably ignorant; in short, the reader may say what he pleases of the Feast of Asses, and of all the animals, biped or other, concerned in it, if he will only bear in mind one other fact,—a fact almost incredible, perhaps, to those who do not know how Robertson muddled the chronology of his proofs and illustrations, yet very true,—namely, that, notwithstanding all he had said about the period from the *seventh* to the *eleventh* century, and the immediate connexion about heathen converts retaining their barbarous rites—notwithstanding all this, the Ordinal of Rouen, which is Du Cange's sole authority on the subject, is a MS. of the *fifteenth* century. How long the Feast of Asses had been celebrated at that time I really do not know; and I shall be obliged to anybody who will tell me [2]—nor do I know how long it was suffered to continue—but that it flourished when this MS. was written seems clear; and to bring it forward as a special and characteristic sin of the dark ages, is too bad.

Fourthly, as to the fact.—Though the Feast of Asses had nothing to do with the flight of the Virgin, yet

---

[2] The following passage from Warton's History of Poetry has been cited against me:—"Grosthead, bishop of Lincoln in the eleventh century, orders his dean and chapter to abolish the FESTUM ASINORUM, *cum sit vanitate plenum, et voluptatibus spurcum*, which used to be annually celebrated in Lincoln Cathedral, on the Feast of the Circumcision. Grossetesti Epistol. xxxii. apud Browne's Fascicul. p. 331. edit. Lond. 1690. tom. ii. Append. And p. 412." *Vol. II. p.* 367. Beside the general issue that Warton's authority in such matters is not worth a rush, it may be pleaded in this particular case, first, that Bishop Grosteste's letter does not belong to the *eleventh*, but the *thirteenth* century; and, secondly, that it says not a word of the Feast of Asses, but only of the Feast of Fools, which was a totally different matter. I believe that this blunder is corrected in the octavo edition of Warton's History, published in 1840.

that latter event was celebrated, it appears, in some churches in the diocese of Beauvais, on the 14th of January, with some of the absurdities mentioned by Robertson. This, at least, is stated by the editors of Du Cange; who give no account of their authority, or any idea of its date, except that for the "hymn no less childish than impious" which they quote, they say that they have the authority of a MS. five hundred years old; which of course throws the matter back into the *thirteenth* century. [3] They add, that the same silly ceremony was performed in the diocese of Autun; but for this they give no authority at all. Such appears to have been the extent of the custom; as to its duration I am unable to judge. It may have existed through all the dark ages, but I do not remember to have met with any trace of either custom; and the fact, that neither Du Cange nor his editors appear to have known of their earlier existence, is ground for a presumption that they did not, in fact, exist before the times which have been mentioned.

One more observation as to the fact—"The ass was taught to kneel at proper places." I must say I doubt it. It may not be impossible, but I suspect it is very difficult, to make that class of animals do such a thing. Indeed, I think the reader who turns to Robertson's authority will agree with me in supposing, that he was led to make this statement merely by his misunderstanding the marginal direction annexed to one verse of the hymn, "*hic genuflectebatur.*"

But having thus observed on the *facts,* let us now

---

[3] Should this meet the eye of any gentleman whose reading in early French has enabled him to judge, from the *language*, as to the date of the song in question, I should feel much obliged by his referring to it, and communicating his opinion.

notice the *animus* and the *modus;*—the *facts* are, as we have seen, absurdly misstated; but what are we to say of the design, and the manner, of introducing those facts? It is really necessary to say very little on this point, though it is principally for this that the matter is worth noticing at all. Who can help seeing the absurdity of introducing this asinine business by a sober reflection on the practical evils of assuming infallibility, with its attributes of perpetuity and immutability; and then telling us, that what is apparently given as an example (for why, else, is it given at all?) never was general, and was, after a while, abandoned. But what is the obvious *animus?* Why did not Robertson, instead of throwing the whole odium of this nonsense on the church, tell his readers that this ass was patronized by the people—that he was the pet of the laity—and that, with natural and characteristic obstinacy, and, cheered by the love and sympathy of his lay friends, he kept his ground against the ecclesiastical powers which would have turned him out of the church? Why did he not add the statement of those from whom he borrowed the story—"Hæc abolere censuris ecclesiasticis non semel tentarunt episcopi, sed frustra, altissimis quippe defixa erat radicibus donec supremi Senatus accessit auctoritas, qua tandem hoc festum suppressum est?"

Having said thus much of Asses, let us proceed to speak of Fools. Robertson says, just in the way of passing allusion, that the Feast of Asses "was not, like *the Festival of Fools*, and some other pageants *of those ages*, a mere farcical entertainment, exhibited in a church, and mingled, *as was then the custom*, with an imitation of some religious rites." In saying that these festivals differed, Robertson is right. The Feast of the Ass, and the more ridiculous custom of the girl at Beauvais, which he describes, were, I believe, instituted by Christians in a comparatively late age of the church. From what has been said, at least, it appears that the Feast of Asses flourished in the fifteenth, and the other follies in the thirteenth century, in some part of France. But the Feast of Fools was a more ancient and more widely celebrated festival; which may, perhaps, be more or less traced in all ages of the church, and in all parts of Christendom. Even now, I suppose, there is hardly a parish church in our protestant country which does not annually exhibit some trace or relic of it. Notwithstanding the decrees of Councils, and the homilies of Fathers, the Christmas evergreen,—the *viriditas arborum*,—which they denounced, still keeps its ground.

The Feast of Fools (the *Festum Fatuorum*, or *Stultorum*) was, in fact, the old heathen festival of the January Calends. Some ingenious persons have employed themselves in showing that every ceremony and observance of the Romish church (that is, every ceremony and observance which they do not see in their own day, and their own parish church or meeting) is a genuine pagan rite, adopted from the heathen. Others with as much facility and truth, prove that every particular is Jewish. I have neither the taste nor the learning required for such an undertaking, and if I had it would be sadly out of place here. The same persons would, I hope, be consistent enough to admit that the people of the dark ages, whatever ceremonies or observances they might introduce, did not borrow either from pagans or Jews—for who knew the classics—who read the bible—in *those* days? So it, evidently, is not my present business; but I wish that someone would give us a true and full account of the insinuation, modification, or extirpation, of gentilisms in the Christian church, at the same time tracing their causes, history, and effects. As to our present business, however, I will pass over all the earlier councils and fathers; [4] but as I should wish to give a specimen of the resistance made by the church to this pagan folly, I am glad to be able to give at the same time a farther extract (it happens to be the immediate continuation of what I gave at p. 140) from the well-known, or at least much talked-of, sermon of St. Eloy. I have already stated that, about the year 640, he became the bishop of a people, many of whom were newly and scarcely converted from heathenism. If I carry on the quotation a few lines farther than the matter for which it is especially quoted, and the immediate subject of this paper may seem to require, those who have read Nos. VI. and VII., and who at all understand my motive,

---

[4] The reader who wishes to follow out this subject will find abundant indication of sources by referring to Du Cange in v. *Kalendæ:* or by looking at Bingham's Antiquities, b. xvi. ch. iv. sect. 17, and b. xx. ch. i. sect. 4. In less than two hours, however, he may become pretty well acquainted with this part of the subject by reading the Homily of Asterius, which is, of all that I know, the thing best worth reading, and which he may find in the Bibliotheca Patrum, tom. xiii. p. 590, of the Paris ed. of 1633, or a Latin translation of it in Raynaud's edition of Leo Magnus. Next to this in value (and it may be found in the same edition of Leo, and, I believe, in the largest Bib. Pat., but I am sorry to say I have not the means of ascertaining), is the Homily on the Circumcision, by Maximus Taurinensis, at p. 198 of his Homilies; and if the reader has Mabillon's Museum Italicum, let him look at tom. i. par. ii. p. 17. The same edition of Leo also contains the sermons of Petrus Chrysologus, the 155th of which is worth reading. These, with the 62nd canon of the council in Trullo (Lab. Conc. vi. 1169), will, I think, put the reader in possession of most that is known on the subject. It may seem a good allowance for two hours; but, in fact, I might have said one, for all the things referred to are very short.

N

and the drift of these papers, will perceive my reason for doing so.

"Before all things, however, I declare and testify unto you, that you should observe none of the impious customs of the pagans; neither sorcerers, [5] nor diviners, nor soothsayers, nor enchanters ; nor must you presume for any cause, or any sickness, to consult or inquire of them ; for he who commits this sin immediately loses the sacrament of baptism. In like manner, pay no attention to auguries and sneezings; and, when you are on a journey, do not mind the singing of certain little birds. But, whether you are setting out on a journey, or beginning any other work, cross yourself in the name of Christ, and say the Creed and the Lord's Prayer with faith and devotion, and then the enemy can do you no harm. Let no Christian observe the day on which he leaves, or returns, home ; for God made all the days. Let none regulate the beginning of any piece of work by the day, or by the moon. Let none on the Calends of January join in the wicked and ridiculous things, the dressing like old women, or like stags, [6] or other fooleries, nor

---

[5] The following note was appended by Mr. Rose to this passage : —"If anyone will take the trouble to refer to the writers of the eleventh century, especially Peter of Blois, he will find a constant condemnation of superstitious usages and customs; and if he will go back much farther, to Theodore's *Pœnitentiale*, in the seventh century, he will find the same doctrine.—ED."

[6] *Vetulas aut cervolos.*—The council of Auxerre (an. 378) had decreed—"Non licet Kalendis Januarii vetula aut cervolo facere." Lab. Con. v. 917. Some would read this as *vitulas*, and suppose it to mean assuming the appearance, or sacrificing, a calf. But certainly the wearing of female attire by men was one great feature of the festival. Isidore (about the end of the sixth century) says —"Tunc enim miseri homines, et, quod pejus est, etiam fideles, sumentes species monstruosas, in ferarum habitu transformantur ; alii fœmineo gestu demutati virilem vultum effœminant." *De Eccl. Offic. lib. ii. c.* 40. (*Bib. Pat.* x. 200.) Alcuin, nearly two centuries after, has almost the same words ; but it is worth while to remark that he changes *transformantur* and *effœminant*, into *transformabant* and *effœminabant*; in fact, he says, —"Domino largiente, hæc a fidelibus pro nihilo habentur, licet quantulæcunque similitudines, quod absit, adhuc lateant in feris hominibus." *De Div. Off.* (*Ibid.* p. 229.) The reader will observe that I put some words of the extract in the text in italics without any note, by which I wish to

make feasts lasting all night, nor keep up the custom of gifts [7] and intemperate drinking. Let no Christian believe in *puras*, nor set amidst their singing, for these are the works of the Devil. Let no one on the festival of St. John, or on any of the festivals of the saints, join in *solstitia*, or dances, or leaping, or *caraulas*, [8] or diabolical songs. Let none trust in, or presume to invoke, the names of dæmons; neither Neptune, nor Orcus, nor Diana, nor Minerva, nor Geniscus, nor any other such follies. Let no one keep Thursday as a holy-day, either in May, or at any other time (unless it be some saint's day), or the day of moths and mice, or any day of any kind, but the Lord's Day. Let no Christian place lights at the temples, or the stones, or at fountains, or at trees, or *ad cellos*, or at places where three ways meet, or presume to make vows. Let none presume to hang amulets on the neck of man or beast; even though they be made by the clergy, and called holy things, and contain the words of Scripture; for they are fraught, not with the remedy of Christ, but with the poison of the Devil. Let no one presume to make lustrations, nor to enchant herbs, nor to make flocks pass through a hollow tree, or an aperture in the earth; for by so doing he seems to consecrate them to the Devil. Let no woman presume to hang amber beads on her neck; or in her weaving, or dyeing, or any other kind of work, to invoke Minerva, or the other ill-omened persons; but let her desire the grace of Christ to be present in every work and confide with her whole heart in the power of His name. If at any time the moon is darkened, let no one presume to make a clamour; for, at certain times, it is darkened by the command of God. Neither let anyone fear to set about any work at the new moon; for God has made the moon on purpose to mark the times, and to temper the darkness of the nights, not to hinder anybody's work, nor that it should make any man mad, as foolish persons think, who suppose that those who are possessed by devils suffer from the moon. Let none call

---

express that I do not know what they mean. This is not the place to discuss the conjectures of others, or to offer my own.

[7] *Strenas.*—What Asterius says on this point is worth reading. When he says that children were taught to love money by being permitted to go round from house to house collecting it, in return for nominal presents, one is led to think of *Christmas-boxes*; which, indeed, as well as new year's gifts, seem to be genuine remains of the custom.

[8] I will not here repeat the arguments of those who make this word mean *charms* or *dances*, but I cannot help thinking of and mentioning Christmas *carols*.

the sun or moon 'Lord;' nor swear by them, for they are creatures of God; and, by the command of God, they are subservient to the necessities of men. Let no man have his fate or his fortune told, or his nativity, or what is commonly called his horoscope, so as to say that he shall be such as his horoscope shall indicate; for God will have all men to be saved, and come to the knowledge of the truth, and wisely dispenses all things even as He hath appointed before the foun- dation of the world. Moreover, as often as any sickness occurs, do not seek enchanters, nor diviners, nor sorcerers, nor soothsayers, or make devilish amulets at fountains, or trees, or cross-roads; but let him who is sick trust only in the mercy of God, and receive the sacra- ment of the body and blood of Christ with faith and devotion; and faithfully seek consecrated oil from the church, wherewith he may anoint his body in the name of Christ, and, according to the apostle, 'the prayer of faith shall save the sick, and the Lord shall raise him up;' and he shall receive health not only of body but of mind, and there shall be fulfilled in him that which our Lord promised in the gospel, saying, 'for all things whatsoever ye shall ask in prayer, believing, ye shall receive.'

"Before all things, wherever you may be, whether in the house, or on a journey, or at a feast, let no filthy or lewd discourse proceed out of your mouths; for, as our Lord declares in the gospel, for every idle word which men shall speak on earth, they shall give account in the day of judgment. Forbid also the performance of all diabolical games, and dances, and songs of the heathen. Let no Christian perform them, because by them he becomes a heathen; for indeed it is not right that from a Christian mouth, which receives the sacraments of Christ, and which ought always to praise God, diabolical songs should proceed. And therefore, brethren, eschew with your whole heart all inventions of the Devil, and fly from all the impieties which I have mentioned, with horror. You must show reverence (venerationem ex- hibeatis) to no creature beside God and His saints. Destroy the foun- tains which they call sacred; forbid them to make the images of feet which they place at the parting of roads, and if you find them, burn them with fire. Believe that you cannot be saved by any other means than by calling on Christ, and by His cross. For what a thing it is that if those trees, where these miserable men pay their vows, fall down, they will not use them to make their fires. And see how great the folly of the men is, if they pay honour to an insensible and dead tree, and despise the commands of Almighty God. Let not any man, then, believe that the heaven, or the stars, or the earth, or, in short, any creature whatsoever, is to be adored (adorandam) except God; because He, by

Himself alone, created and arranged them. The heaven, indeed, is high, the earth great, the sea immense, the stars are beautiful; but He who made all these things must needs be greater and more beautiful. For if these things which are seen are so incomprehensible—that is, the various produce of the earth, the beauty of the flowers, the diversity of fruits, the different kinds of animals—some on the earth, some in the waters, some in the air—the skill of the bees, the blowing of the winds, the showers of the clouds, the noise of thunder, the change of seasons, and the alternation of day and night—all which things the human mind hath never yet been able by any means to comprehend. If therefore these things, which we see, without being able to comprehend them, are such, how ought we to estimate those heavenly things which we have not yet seen? And what is the Creator of them all, at whose nod all were created, and by whose will all are governed? Him then, brethren, above all things, fear; Him in all things adore; Him beyond all things love; cling to His mercy, and never lose your confidence in His loving kindness."

Notwithstanding the statement of Alcuin, which was, I dare say, true, as far as his knowledge went—and his means of knowledge render his authority respectable—we are not to suppose that this heathenism was entirely rooted out. If it was so modified as to be lost sight of, and to have become comparatively harmless, in old Christian societies, the accession of barbarous nations, or heathenish communities, from time to time, rendered it necessary to watch against, and denounce it. Whether on this account, or merely to make his Capitulare more complete, Atto (Bishop of Vercelli, as late as A.D. 960) inserted a prohibition against the heathenish celebration of the Calends;[9] though it is not improbable that this superstition might maintain its ground, in its more barefaced form, up to a later period in Italy than elsewhere. It is curious to observe that Boniface, the apostle of Germany, not long before the time when Alcuin wrote, found his new converts

---

[9] Can. 79, ap. Dach. Spicil. i. 410.

much scandalized by reports which travellers brought from Rome, of what went on in the pope's own city, and "hard by the church of St. Peter." In his letter of congratulation to Pope Zachary, he told his Holiness (or rather, "his Paternity"—it is the pope who calls Boniface "your Holiness") that when the laity and secular persons among the Germans, Bavarians, and Franks, saw these things performed at Rome, it was vain to denounce them as sins, or to attempt to persuade people that they had not ecclesiastical sanction. The pope replied that he considered it an abomination, and had (like his predecessor, Gregory) done all that he could to put a stop to it. [1]

But I am not writing the history of this folly. The question forces itself upon one—What had *this* heathen foolery to do with the church, more than any other invention of the world, the flesh, or the devil? It was "juxta ecclesiam sancti Petri"—"hard by" St. Peter's; but did it get in? Council after council attests that all regular ecclesiastical authority perpetually opposed it;

---

[1] The pope's reply is dated 1st of April, 743; but I do not know that the precise date of Boniface's letter can be fixed. Having inquired respecting dispensations, respecting marriage, which some maintained to have been granted by the pope, he adds—"quia carnales homines idiotæ, Alamanni, vel Bajuarii, vel Franci, si juxta Romanam urbem aliquid fieri viderint ex his peccatis quæ nos prohibemus, licitum et concessum a sacerdotibus esse putant; et dum nobis improperium deputant, sibi scandalum vitæ accipiunt. Sicut affirmant se vidisse annis singulis, in Romana urbe, et juxta ecclesiam Sancti Petri, in die vel nocte quando Kalendæ Januarii intrant, paganorum consuetudine choros ducere per plateas," &c. The pope, after expressing his abomination of such proceedings, says — "quia per instigationem diaboli iterum pullulabant, a die qua nos jussit divina clementia (quanquam immeriti existamus) apostoli vicem gerere, illico omnia hæc amputavimus. Pari etenim modo volumus tuam sanctitatem populis sibi subditis prædicare atque ad viam æternæ perducere vitæ."—*Lab. Conc.* vi. 1497 – 1500.

and, though I know less than I could wish about the particulars, and the time of its intrusion into sacred places, and its admixture with sacred things, yet I believe that it did not become "a farcical entertainment, exhibited in a church," during the period with which we are concerned. The only account which I have met with of any participation by the church in this "libertas Decembrica," as it was also called, is that which is given by a writer, who is said to have belonged to the church of Amiens, and to have been living in A.D. 1182.[2] He tells us that there were some churches in which it was customary for the bishops and archbishops to join in the Christmas games which went on in the monasteries in their dioceses, and even so far to relax as to play at ball. If I grant that this was "desipere," may I not plead that it was "in loco," and that it was not quite so bad as what went on at Rouen and Beauvais in more enlightened times?

For when did this festival become the regular Feast of Fools, with the Bishop of Fools, and the Abbot of Fools, and foolery sacred and profane in perfection? Let us hear Du Cange, to whom Robertson remits

---

[2] His words are—"Sunt nonnullæ ecclesiæ, in quibus usitatum est, ut vel etiam Episcopi et Archiepiscopi in cœnobiis cum suis ludant subditis, ita ut etiam sese ad lusum pilæ demittant;" and he afterwards says—"quanquam vero magnæ ecclesiæ ut est Remensis, hanc ludendi consuetudinem observent, videtur tamen laudabilius esse, non ludere."— *Ap. Du Cange in v. Kalendæ.* The only writer before the year 1200, mentioned in the continuation of the article by the editors, is Petrus Capuanus, who wrote in A.D. 1198. He is the earliest writer, as far as I have seen, who speaks of this, or any festival, under the title of the Festum Fatuorum. He is here said to have testified its existence in the church of Paris, and elsewhere; but with what rites it was celebrated does not appear. He wrote, as cardinal-legate, to Odo, Bishop of Paris, and to some of the canons, requiring them to put down the custom; and it appears that they issued an ordinance for that purpose.

us—"Licet, inquam, ab ecclesia non semel proscriptæ fuerint, indictis ad hanc diem jejuniis et litaniis de quibus suo loco, quibus eæ quodammodo expiarentur, et ut ludicræ et impiæ festivitatis loco vera ac solida succederet; non potuere tamen tam alte radicatæ prorsus evelli, *adeo ut extremis etiam temporibus plus solito vires acceperint,* et non a secularibus dumtaxat; sed et ab ipsis episcopis et sacerdotibus legantur usurpatæ: [imo, cum ab iis omnino abstinuissent laici, eas obstinate retinuisse clericos, atque ab iis solis usurpatas fuisse, testantur theologi Parisienses in Epist. encyclica ann. 1444. 'Quid quæso fecissent' (Episcopi) 'si solum clerum sicut hodie his observantiis vacantem vidissent?']" The part between brackets is so printed by the editors, to show that is their own addition to the statement of Du Cange, who proceeds to say that, in modern times, beside its old title, it came to be called the Feast of Subdeacons; not because that order of the clergy alone took part in it, but from the ambiguity of the word "*Soudiacres* id est ad literam *Saturi Diaconi,* quasi *Diacres Saouls.*" He also refers to the fourth council of Constantinople, to show that something like the mock consecration of the Bishop of Fools was performed in the east, in the ninth century, by some of the laity in derision of the clergy; and that it was forbidden by the church. This council declares it to be a thing before unheard of; and whether it was thence imported into the west, and, if so, at what time, it might be curious to inquire; but the editors of Du Cange skip at once from the ninth to the fourteenth century. What they quote from the Ceremonial of Viviers, written in A.D. 1365, from the council of Rouen, in A.D. 1445, or the Inventory of York, in A.D. 1350; or even the more scanty references to the council of Paris, in A.D. 1212, or that of Cognac, in A.D. 1260, and the

Constitutions of our Archbishop Peckham in A.D. 1279, it is not to our present purpose to notice; but I wish that some of those gentlemen who understand all about the march of intellect would explain, how it happened that these profane follies began—if not to exist, at least to flourish and abound—at, and after, and along with, the revival of letters. If not, I may, perhaps, attempt something of the kind; but, in the meantime, I hope (having, perhaps, said enough about popular misrepresentations for the present) to go on to some of the points which I proposed to investigate with reference to the earlier—for really, after such a discussion, I do not like to call them the darker—ages of the church.

No. X.

"Habet unumquodque propositum principes suos. Romani duces imitentur Camillos, Fabritios, Regulos, Scipiones. Philosophi proponant sibi Pythagoram, Socratem, Platonem, Aristotelem, Poetæ, Homerum, Virgilium, Menandrum, Terentium. Historici, Thucydidem, Sallustium, Herodotum, Livium. Oratores, Lysiam, Gracchos, Demosthenem, et ut ad nostra veniamus, episcopi et presbyteri habeant in exemplum Apostolos et Apostolicos viros: quorum honorem possidentes, habere nitantur et meritum. Nos autem habeamus propositi nostri principes, Paulos, et Antonios, Julianos, Hilarionem, Macarios."—HIERONYMUS.

"THE monks were abominably illiterate"—Well, good friend, and if you are not so yourself, be thankful in proportion as you are sure that you are the better for your learning. But suppose it were otherwise—suppose *you* were "abominably illiterate"—would you like me and all other writers in great books and small, in magazines and newspapers, to rail at you and run you down, as a creature not fit to live? If you were too modest to speak in your own behalf, it is likely that some of your friends might suggest such redeeming qualities as would show that you were not only tolerable, but useful, in the world. "Very true, very true," says the march-of-intellect man, "I dare say he may be a very good Christian, a good subject, a good husband or father or landlord, a person of great integrity and benevolence, and all very well in his way, but he is abominably illiterate, and I will throw it in his teeth whenever I come within a mile of him." Now surely the compassion of a mere by-stander would lead him to say, "Well, suppose he is abominably illiterate, do let him alone; he makes no pretence to learning."

But did not the monks pretend to it? Certainly not. "C'est une illusion de certaines gens, qui ont écrit dans

le siècle précédent que les monastères n'avoient esté
d'abord établis que pour servir d'écoles et d'académies
publiques, où l'on faisoit profession d'enseigner les
sciences humaines." Very true, Dom Mabillon, and it
is very right that you should contradict in plain terms
a vulgar error, which, for want of proper discrimination
on the part of the public, has been confirmed rather
than corrected, by the labours of yourself and Montfaucon, and other of your brethren in the Benedictine
Order. The "Editio Benedictina et Optima," which
figures in every bookseller's catalogue, has a tendency
to mislead even those who do not take the trouble to
inquire who the Benedictines of St. Maur were, or why
their editions of books cost three times as much as
others. This by the way, however; for it is here only
necessary to say, that the abuse heaped on monks for
being unlearned is altogether unjust and absurd.

The monastic life, whatever it might have of good
or bad, was, I apprehend, that point of rest in which
the minds of men settled after they had been driven,
partly by fierce persecution, and partly by the natural
tendency of man towards extremes, into a mode of
life purely solitary. At that stage of the world, man
might have known from experience, as well as from
the Word of God, without making a fresh trial, that
it was not good for him to be alone; and that it was
as truly, if not as great, a sin to live without man,
as without God, in the world—that is, to renounce the
second great commandment, under pretence of keeping
the first. The eremitical life was contrary to nature,
reason, and religion, and seems only to have been
permitted in order to the introduction of a system which
was, to say the least, more rational—namely, that of
societies, not individuals, forsaking the world, and living
in seclusion. The solitary ascetic, by his self-constructed,

self-imposed, rule (self in all things, self the boundary
of his horizon), was required to renounce the duties,
the charities, the sympathies, of life, and to cut himself
off from all the means of grace which God has given
to man in his fellows; but, in the monastery, the idea
was to carry out into some remote place of safety
one mind dispersed and diversified in various bodies,
guiding many hands and uniting many hearts, and
directing, sanctifying, and governing the various gifts
of the many members of one body, whose head was
Christ. Such was the idea; and when once suggested
it spread rapidly. Small companies nestled down in
solitude—to study the classics?—to stimulate the march
of intellect? No such thing—"tota rusticitas, et extra
psalmos silentium est. Quocunque te verteris, arator
stivam tenens, alleluia decantat. Sudans messor psalmis
se avocat, et curva attondens vitem falce vinitor, aliquid
Davidicum canit. Hæc sunt in hac provincia carmina:
hæ, ut vulgo dicitur, amatoriæ cantiones. Hic pastorum
sibilus: hæc arma culturæ." Solitude, labour, silence,
and prayer—these were the elements of monastic life;
and the question was not how the monk might most
effectively gather and diffuse learning, but—when,
indeed, any question came to be raised—whether he
might lawfully cultivate learning at all.

"Tout le monde sait"—says Dom Vincent Thuillier;
but it is certainly quite a mistake of his,—or if it was
true when he wrote it, it has long since ceased to be
so,—for there are plenty of people, who are very far
from being abominably illiterate, who nevertheless
know nothing about the "Contestation sur les Etudes Monastiques," of which he undertook to be the
historian. If he had said that most people have
heard of De Rancé, of his noble birth, his pro-
fligate life, his sudden and mysterious conversion, his

persevering austerities—of the solitary and silent
horrors of La Trappe, and of a great deal of picturesque
truth so like romance that one can hardly imagine the
hero sitting at a wooden table, with a real pen and ink,
writing a book—if Father Thuillier had said this, we
might have assented; but to tell us outright that
everybody knows that De Rancé's "Traité de la Sain-
teté et des Devoirs de la Vie Monastique" began the fray
between him and Dom Mabillon, is too much, seeing that
there are, as I have said, a great many very well-informed
persons, who do not know that these two famous men
ever had any controversy about monastic studies, or even,
perhaps, that there were any such studies to dispute about.

The work of De Rancé, I am told (for I have never
seen it) was professedly written for his own monks,
and represented to them that the pursuit of literature
was inconsistent with their profession, and that their
reading ought to be confined to the Scriptures and a
few books of devotion. This seemed like—some thought
it was meant to be—an attack on the Benedictine
monks of St. Maur—for that they were learned everybody knew—and they were urged to reply. They,
however, remained very quiet; and it was long before
they could be persuaded to take the field. The Benedictine historian whom I have mentioned, and to whom
I am indebted, suggests as a reason for this, that the
Benedictines really were (and everybody knew they
were) following the footsteps of their learned predecessors in the cultivation of letters, and that they thought
it quite sufficient to tell those who talked to them on
the subject, that the abbot of La Trappe had his own
reasons for what he did[1]—that he had no authority

---

[1] "Et pour toute réponse à ceux qui les excitoient à se défendre,
ils alléguèrent que le Père Abbé *avoit ses vues particulières,* qu'il n'avoit

except in his own convent—that there he really was
master—and no one had a right to blame him if, in
order to conduct his own flock to heaven, he prescribed
paths somewhat singular under the conviction that they
were the safest.

Father Thuillier is not, perhaps, quite an unpreju-
diced historian; and I hope I am not uncharitable in
thinking that he might have added, that although these
good fathers of St. Maur were in fact following the
steps of their predecessors in the order of St. Benedict,
yet, considering that they had had predecessors in that
order for nearly twelve hundred years, and that during
the lapse of that period many things had altered both
in and out of the cloister, they felt it rather awkward
to be sharply recalled to the naked letter of their Rule.
They were in no haste to meet an opponent of great
influence from family, connexion, character, and the
singular circumstances of his life—a man, acute, eloquent, fervid, and fully persuaded that he was maintaining the cause of pure and primitive and spiritual
religion, against the incursions of vain, worldly, and
mischievous pursuits. One might forgive them if they
were not eager to fight such a battle, with such an
adversary, before an enlightened public, who, whichever
side might gain the victory, would be sure to make
themselves merry with the battle of the monks.

Be this as it may, however, a considerable time
elapsed—I do not know in what year De Rancé

---

droit de décision que sur sa Maison, qu'il y étoit le maître, et qu'on
ne pouvoit trouver à redire, que pour conduire son troupeau au Ciel,
il se fît des routes singulières, puisqu'il les croioit les plus sûres."
Mabill. Op. Post. Tom. I. p. 366. The words which I have marked
by *italics* seem capable of an invidious construction; but the notorious
circumstances of the case were such that it can hardly have been
intended.

published his book, and therefore cannot tell whether
it was with a view to be specific, or to show his own
classical reading, that Father Thuillier tells us that
more than nine years had passed before the Benedictine
reply came out; but in fact Dom Mabillon's "Traité
des Etudes Monastiques" was published in the year
1691. It was, of course, learned, wise, and modest. It
proved that there had been a succession of learned
monks from almost the very beginning of monasticism,
that they had learned and taught as much as they
could, and that, on the general principles of religion,
reason, and common sense, they were quite right in so
doing; but, as to the RULE, he did not get on quite
so well; because it must be obvious to everyone who
inquires, that none of the monastic legislators ever
contemplated the formation of academies of learning
and science. This Mabillon of course knew, and I
doubt whether he could have carried on his argument
(for I do not believe that he would have done what
he considered dishonest), had it not been for a full
persuasion of his mind which, though it may not bear
to be stated as an argument, peeps out occasionally
in a very amusing manner, and gives a colour to the
whole line of defence.—"Not study? why, how could
they help it?"—or, thrown into a more logical form,
"You acknowledge that the monks lived in their
monasteries; but it is impossible for people to live
without study; therefore the monks studied." Some
caviller might say that the Rule did not tell them to
study; and the good father would perhaps have smiled
and answered that it did not tell them to breathe.

The work was, however, popular; for who would
not wish to be ranged with the admirers and advocates
of learning and science? and a second edition was
printed the next year after the first. It was quickly

translated into Italian by Father Ceppi, an Augustinian monk,[2] but was very near being prohibited, not on account of anything connected with the dispute, but for some things which appeared too liberal; among others, a commendation of Archbishop Ussher's Annals. Father Ceppi, however, managed to soften the Master of the Sacred Palace, and so got a conditional *imprimatur* in 1701. A German translation of it was published by Father Udalric Staudigl in 1702; and a Latin one by Father Joseph Porta in 1704.

It is not, however, my present business to trace this controversy through the reply of De Rancé, and the rejoinder of Mabillon. I mention it here to show that, even so recently as little more than a century ago, it was a question sharply contested between men of the highest monastic eminence, whether a monk might lawfully be a learned man. I do this with a view to remove what I believe to be a very common misapprehension as to the origin and nature of monastic institutions. I know, as well as Mabillon did—that is, as to full conviction that it was so, not as

---

[2] I learn from Father Ossinger's Bibliothecâ Augustiniana, that this Father Ceppi was, "singularis venerator nostri S. Nicolai de Tolentino," and that "ad promovendam devotionem erga hunc universæ Ecclesiæ Patronum in lingua Italica typis mandavit, 'Maraviglie trecenta ed una operate da Dio per li meriti del Santo Protettore di Santa Chiesa Nicolo di Tolentino. In Roma, 1710.'" And also another work, with the same design, "Il sangue miracoloso del Santo Protettore di Santa Chiesa Nicolo di Tolentino, dedicata all' Eminentissimo, e Reverendissimo Prencipe il Signor Cardinale Nicolo Coscia. Romæ, 1725, in 8." I acknowledge that this has nothing to do with the period under our consideration; for Ceppi wrote in the *eighteenth*, and this St. Nicholas (his patron, or patronized) lived in the *fourteenth*, century; but may I not be pardoned if, having to say so much of the dull, legendary, and lying works of the Dark Ages, I enliven the subject by an occasional reference to the wiser literature of more enlightened times? *See Note* A.

to the facts which his almost unbounded learning might
have furnished in proof or illustration—that the monks
were the most learned men ; and that it pleased God
to make monastic institutions the means of preserving
learning in the world, and I hope to show this ; but
before I do so, I wish to come to a clear understanding with those who, instead of thanking the monks
for what they did, find sufficient employment in abusing
them for not doing what they never undertook to do,
and were, in fact, no more bound to do than other
people. With this view I am also desirous to say something of the Rule of St. Benedict. "I would not have
answered him," said De Rancé to Father Lamy, when
the Duchess of Guise, who took a vast interest in the
matter, had gone to La Trappe, and got these two fathers
face to face, to fight the matter out before her [3]—"I
would not have answered him, if he had not carried
the matter up to the time of Pachomius." It *was* too
bad ; and I am not going to imitate it by speaking
here of any earlier Rule than St. Benedict's. To be
sure, even that was born before the dark ages, and has
survived them ; but its almost universal adoption in the
west, and its incalculable influence, as being the Rule
by which almost all the monasteries of Europe were
governed, and by which therefore every individual
monk in them had solemnly bound himself, render it
a matter of much interest and importance to those who

[3] Father Lamy went, because Mabillon could not be persuaded to
go ; "Il se rendit donc à la Trappe auprès de son A. R. Elle avoit
sans doute prévenu sur son chapitre le P. Abbé, car on ne peut pas
plus d'égards, plus d'honnêtez, plus de soins et d'assiduitez qu'il reçut
et de deux de ses Religieux. Après les premiers complimens son A. R.
les fit asseoir dans une ruelle, l'un, dit-elle agréablement, a titre de
goute sciatique, et l'autre a titre de pierre, et puis Elle les obligea
d'entrer en matière sur le grand différent des Etudes."—p. 376.

O

would understand the spirit of monastic institutions, and their real circumstances during the Dark Ages. For our present purpose, it may be sufficient to extract the prologue, and the fourth chapter; the former of which is as follows:—

"Hear, O my son, the precepts of a master; and incline the ear of thine heart; and cheerfully receive, and effectually fulfil, the admonition of an affectionate father; that, by the labour of obedience, thou mayest return to him, from whom thou hast departed by the sloth of disobedience. To thee therefore my discourse is now directed—whosoever, renouncing the desires of self, and about to serve as a soldier of the Lord Christ, the true King, dost assume the most powerful and noble arms of obedience.

"In the first place, you must, with most urgent prayer, entreat that whatsoever good thing you take in hand, may through Him be brought to completion; that He who hath condescended now to reckon us in the number of his sons, may not be obliged to grieve over our ill conduct. For He is ever to be served by us, with those good things which are his own; so served by us as that not only He may not, as an angry father, disinherit his sons,—but that He may not, as a Master who is to be feared, be so incensed by our sins, as to deliver over to eternal punishment, as most wicked servants, those who would not follow Him to glory.

"Let us, however, at length arise; for the Scripture arouses us, saying, 'That now it is high time to awake out of sleep;' and, our eyes being opened to the divine light, let us hear with astonished ears the voice which every day admonishes us, 'To-day, if ye will hear his voice, harden not your hearts;' and again, 'He that hath ears to hear, let him hear what the Spirit saith to the churches;' and what saith He? 'Come, ye children, hearken unto me: I will teach you the fear of the Lord'—'Run while ye have the light of life, lest the darkness of death overtake you.'

"And the Lord, seeking for his workman among the multitude of the people, whom He thus addresses, saith again, 'What man is he that desireth life, and will see good days?' And if when you hear this you answer 'I,' God saith unto you, 'If thou wilt have life, keep thy tongue from evil, and thy lips that they speak no guile. Depart from evil, and do good; seek peace and pursue it.' And when you shall have done this, 'my eyes are upon you, and my ears are towards your prayers; and before ye call upon me I will say unto you "Here am

I."' Most dear brethren, what is sweeter than this voice of the Lord inviting us? Behold, in his mercy, the Lord points out to us the way of life.

"Our loins therefore being girded, and our feet shod with faith and the observance of good works, let us, under the guidance of the gospel, go forth on his ways, that we may be counted worthy to see Him who hath called us, in his kingdom. In the tabernacle of whose kingdom, if we desire to dwell, we can by no means attain our desire, except by running in the way of good works. But let us inquire of the Lord with the Prophet, and say unto Him, 'Lord, who shall dwell in thy tabernacle, and who shall rest in thy holy mountain?' After this inquiry, Brethren, let us hear the Lord replying, and showing us the way of his tabernacle, and saying, 'He that walketh uprightly, and worketh righteousness, and speaketh the truth in his heart; he that backbiteth not with his tongue, nor doeth evil to his neighbour, nor taketh up a reproach against his neighbour.' Who turning away the eyes of his heart from the wicked Devil who tempts him, and from his temptation, hath brought him to nought, and hath taken the young thoughts which he hath bred and dashed them to pieces on Christ. [4] Who, fearing the Lord, are not puffed up by their good works; but who, considering that those good things which are in them could not be wrought by themselves, but by the Lord, magnify the Lord who worketh in them, saying with the Prophet, 'Not unto us, O Lord, not unto us, but unto thy name give glory.' Like as the Apostle Paul reckoned nothing of his preaching, saying, 'By the grace of God I am what I am;' and again he says, 'He that glorieth let him glory in the Lord.'

"Hence also it is, that our Lord saith in the gospel, 'Whosoever heareth these sayings of mine, and doeth them, I will liken him unto a wise man, which built his house upon a rock: and the floods came, and the winds blew, and beat upon that house; and it fell not: for it was founded upon a rock.' While the Lord does all this, He expects every day that we should respond to his holy admonitions, by our actions. Therefore it is, that the days of this life are extended as a respite for the emendation of what is evil; as the Apostle says, 'Knowest thou not that the long suffering of God leadeth thee to repentance?' For the merciful God hath said, 'I desire not the death of a sinner, but that he should be converted and live."

"When therefore, my brethren, we inquire of the Lord, 'who shall

---

[4] The allusion is to Psalm cxxxvii. 9. "Filia Babylonis . . . beatus qui tenebit et allidet parvulos tuos ad petram."

abide in thy tabernacle?' we thus hear the rule of habitation; and if we fulfil the duty of an inhabitant, we shall be heirs of the kingdom of heaven. Therefore our hearts and bodies are to be prepared to go forth to the warfare of holy obedience to the commandments; and, because it is impossible to our nature, let us ask the Lord of his grace that He would assist us with his help. And if, flying from the pains of hell, we desire to obtain eternal life, while yet there is opportunity and we are in this body, and space is afforded to fulfil all these things by this life of light, we must now run and labour for that which shall profit us for ever.

"We must, therefore, institute a school of service to the Lord; in which institution we trust that we shall appoint nothing harsh or burdensome. If, however, anything a little severe should, on reasonable grounds of equity, be enjoined for the correction of vices, and the preservation of charity, do not in sudden alarm fly from the way of safety, which can only be begun by a narrow entrance. In the progress, however, of our conversation and faith, the heart being enlarged with the ineffable sweetness of love, we run the way of God's commandments, so that never departing from his governance, remaining under his teaching in the monastery until death, we through patience are partakers of Christ's sufferings, that we may be counted worthy to be partakers of his kingdom."

The first chapter of the Rule is on the various kinds of monks—the second, on the qualifications and duties of an abbot—the third, on the duty of the abbot to take counsel with the brethren—and the fourth is headed, "Quæ sint instrumenta bonorum operum." This title has given some trouble to commentators; and the reader may translate it as he pleases. It is not my business to criticize it, especially as the chapter itself is intelligible enough. It contains seventy-two brief injunctions, from whence we may form some general opinion as to what those who bound themselves by this Rule did, and did not, undertake. Most of the other seventy-two chapters of the Rule consist of regulations respecting the organization and management of their society, which would, of course, occupy the most room; but it seems to me that this single fourth chapter should at least qualify the statements of those who profess to have found nothing but a body of heartless forms.[5]

" 1. In the first place, to love the Lord God with the whole heart, whole soul, whole strength. 2. Then his neighbour as himself. 3. Then not to kill. 4. Then not to commit adultery. 5. Not to steal. 6. Not to covet. 7. Not to bear false witness. 8. To honour all men. 9. And what anyone would not have done to him, let him not do to another. 10. To deny himself, that he may follow Christ. 11. To chasten the body. 12. To renounce luxuries. 13. To love fasting. 14. To relieve the poor. 15. To clothe the naked. 16. To visit the sick. 17. To bury the dead. 18. To help in tribulation. 19. To console the afflicted. 20. To disengage himself from worldly affairs. 21. To set the love of Christ before all other things. 22. Not to give way to anger. 23. Not to bear any grudge. 24. Not to harbour deceit in the heart. 25. Not to make false peace. 26. Not to forsake charity. 27. Not to swear, lest haply he perjure himself. 28. To utter truth from his heart and his mouth. 29. Not to return evil for evil. 30. Not to do injuries; and to bear them patiently. 31. To love his enemies. 32. Not to curse again those who curse him; but rather to bless them. 33. To endure persecutions for righteousness sake. 34. Not to be proud. 35. Not given to wine. 36. Not gluttonous. 37. Not addicted to sleep. 38. Not sluggish. 39. Not given to murmur. 40. Not a slanderer. 41. To commit his hope to God. 42. When he sees anything good in himself, to attribute it to God, and not to himself. 43. But let him always know, that which is evil in his own doing, and impute it to himself. 44. To fear the day of judgment. 45. To dread Hell. 46. To desire eternal life, with all spiritual longing. 47. To have the expectation of death every day before his eyes. 48. To watch over his actions at all times. 49. To know certainly that, in all places, the eye of God is upon him. 50. Those evil thoughts which come into his heart immediately to dash to pieces on Christ. 51. And to make them known to his spiritual senior. 52. To keep his lips from evil and wicked discourse. 53. Not to be fond of

---

[5] About this time the monastic rules of Benedict were established, which afterwards were received through the western churches. They are full of forms, and breathe little of the spirit of godliness. The very best thing that I can find recorded of the superstitious founder, is the zeal with which he opposed idolatry.—*Milner's History of the Church of Christ*, Cent. VI., ch. iv.

much talking. 54. Not to speak vain words, or such as provoke laughter. 55. Not to love much or violent laughter. 56. To give willing attention to the sacred readings. 57. To pray frequently. 58. Every day to confess his past sins to God, in prayer, with tears and groaning; from thenceforward to reform as to those sins. 59. Not to fulfil the desires of the flesh; to hate self-will. 60. In all things to obey the commands of the abbot, even though he himself (which God forbid) should do otherwise; remembering our Lord's command, 'What they say, do; but what they do, do ye not.' 61. Not to desire to be called a saint before he is one, but first to be one that he may be truly called one. 62. Every day to fulfil the commands of God in action. 63. To love chastity. 64. To hate nobody. 65. To have no jealousy; to indulge no envy. 66. Not to love contention. 67. To avoid self-conceit. 68. To reverence seniors. 69. To love juniors. 70. To pray for enemies, in the love óf Christ. 71. After a disagreement, to be reconciled before the going down of the sun. 72. And never to despair of the mercy of God."

I apprehend that these injunctions are better than some readers would have expected to find; and should it appear that, on the whole, they are defective either as to doctrine, or instruction, let it be remembered that St. Benedict did not intend that his Rule should supersede the Holy Scriptures. He did not mean to give his disciples the traditions of men *instead* of the word of God. He told them plainly that the most perfect Rule of life was contained in the Old and New Testament;[6] and that he expected them to be assiduous in reading the Scriptures, and the works of some of the Fathers, is clear. This species of study, and this only, he enjoined upon them; and as to their practice in this respect I hope to speak hereafter. In the meantime, I just observe that thus to read (or to be

---

[6] "Quæ enim pagina, aut quis sermo divinæ auctoritatis veteris ac novi Testamenti, non est rectissima norma vitæ humanæ," &c. *Cap.* lxxiii; which is entitled "De eo quod non omnis observatio justitiæ in hac sit Regula constituta."

read to, if he could not read) was all that was required
of a monk.

It may, however, be said, that supposing the monks
to have kept to their original state, and to have lived
in all things according to their Rules, they might not,
perhaps, have been so much to blame for the want of
learning, but that, by the times with which we are
concerned, most of them were priests, and that the
clergy—well, I fully admit that as clergy they were
bound to be more learned than other men; but at
present, as Jerome says, "quod loquor, non de episcopis,
non de presbyteris, non de clericis loquor; sed de
monacho."[7] I desire, first, to place the question on its
right footing, and trust that I shall not be found
reluctant to acknowledge that the clergy ought to be
the most learned class in the community. In fact, they
always were so, and this I hope to show.

---

[7] Ad Paulin.

No. XI.

"Alia, ut ante perstrinxi, monachorum est causa: alia clericorum. Clerici pascunt oves; ego pascor." — HIERONYMUS.

IT will be readily admitted that those who profess to teach others should be more learned than the rest of the community. This was, however, the very point of difference between the monks and the clergy—"monachus non docentis, sed plangentis habet officium," said Jerome, and a monk, as such, had no business, and did not, in fact, pretend, to teach anything or anybody. This, though strictly applicable only to the original state of things, may be, in some degree, applied to the subsequent condition of monastic institutions, when most of the monks were priests; because the real and practical difference is between those who live in the world with, and for the sake of, the cure of souls, and those who, either for devotion or for any other reason, live out of the world—in the cell or the cloister. [1]

---

[1] That which St. Jerome so pithily expressed, is more diffusely stated by St. Ambrose—"Namque hæc duo in adtentiore christianorum devotione præstantiora esse quis ambigat, clericorum officia, et monachorum instituta? Ista ad commoditatem et moralitatem disciplina, illa ad abstinentiam adsuefacta atque patientiam: hæc velut in quodam theatro, illa in secreto: spectatur ista, illa absconditur .... Hæc ergo vita in stadio, illa in spelunca; hæc adversus confusionem sæculi, illa adversus carnis appetentiam: hæc subjiciens, illa refugiens corporis voluptates: hæc gratior, illa tutior: hæc seipsam regens, illa semet ipsam coercens: utraque tamen se abnegans, ut fiat Christi; quia perfectis dictum est: 'Qui vult post me venire, abneget seipsum sibi, et tollat crucem suam, et sequatur me.' ... Hæc ergo dimicat, illa se removet: hæc illecebras vincit, illa refugit: huic mundus triumphatur, illi exsulat: huic mundus crucifigitur, vel ipsa mundo, illi ignoratur: huic plura tentamenta, et ideo major victoria; illi infrequentior lapsus, facilior custodia."—*Ep.* lxiii. tom. ii. p. 1039.

Notwithstanding—or, perhaps, I ought rather to say,· by reason of—this, the monks took the lead in learning. It is not worth while here to enter into all the reasons of this, while there is one that is so obvious—namely, that they led quiet, retired, and regular lives; and that if they could not be originally, or at all times, said to have more leisure than the secular clergy, their employments and habits were of a nature less unfriendly to study. Instead, therefore, of now entering into this matter, let us come at once to a question which must be met if we are to understand each other on the subject,—for I cannot help fearing that, while speaking of the dark ages, I and some, at least, of my readers may be thinking of very different things, under the same name—What is learning? or, to put the question in a more limited and less troublesome form—What did the people of the dark ages think on this subject? It might, I think, be shown that there were a good many persons in those ages not so destitute of all that is now called learning as some have asserted, and many, without much inquiry, believe. I might ask, how does it happen that the classics, and the older works on art or science, have been preserved in existence? and I might, with still greater force (but obviously with intolerable prolixity), appeal to the works of writers of those ages to show that they knew the meaning of that which, no one can deny, they preserved and multiplied. But this is not to our present purpose; and the proper answer is, that people in those days were brought up with views respecting profane learning which it is necessary for us to understand before we form our judgment of the men; and, as I have never seen these views clearly stated, I will take leave to say a few words about them.

"Quid ergo Athenis et Hierosolymis? quid Academiæ

et Ecclesiæ? quid hæreticis et Christianis? Nostra
institutio de porticu Salomonis est: qui et ipse tradiderat,
Dominum in simplicitate cordis esse quærendum.
Viderint qui Stoicum, et Platonicum, et Dialecticum
Christianismum protulerunt. Nobis curiositate opus non
est post Christum Jesum, nec inquisitione post evangelium. Cum credimus, nihil desideramus ultra credere.
Hoc enim prius credimus, non esse, quod ultra credere
debemus." These are not the words of a monk of the
tenth century, if not of a priest of the second. How
far it might have been better or worse if the Christian
church had maintained, and acted on, the feeling which
Tertullian expresses, this is not the place to discuss.
In point of fact, the rigour of the law here laid down
was soon softened,—or perhaps I should say that an
excuse was soon provided for those who were enamoured
of profane learning. They were not to go down to
Egypt for help. Undoubtedly, that was quite clear;
but it was equally clear that they might spoil the
Egyptians, and bring that silver and gold which,
wherever they may be found, are the Lord's, into the
camp of His people. They were not to contract alliances
with the heathen. Certainly not; but if, in the course
of war, they should see among the spoil a beautiful
captive, it was lawful to bring her home; and, when
her head had been shaved, and her nails pared, to take
her to wife. These fancies were, as far as I know,
excogitated by Origen,—the man, perhaps, of all others
most bound, and best able, to devise some excuse for
a practice which the severe and exclusive purity of
primitive Christianity had condemned. [2]

---

[2] In his letter to Gregory (tom. i. p. 30), he suggests that this might
be really intended by the command given to the Israelites to borrow
from the Egyptians. As to the captive, after quoting the law (Deut.

Whether it was entirely valid or not, however, this was, for more than a thousand years, the standing excuse for those who were conscious (not to say vain) of their heathenish acquirements. Take, for instance—

---

xxi. 10), he says—"And to say the truth, I also have frequently gone out to battle against my enemies, and there I have seen, among the spoil, a woman beautiful to behold. For whatever we find that is well and rationally said in the works of our enemies, if we read anything that is said wisely and according to knowledge, we ought to cleanse it, and from that knowledge which they possess to remove and cut off all that is dead and useless,—for such are all the hair of the head, and the nails of the woman taken out of the spoils of the enemy,—and then at length to make her our wife, when she no longer has any of those things which for their infidelity are called dead. Nothing dead on her head or in her hands : so that neither in senses, nor in action, she should have anything that is unclean or dead about her." *In Levit. Hom.* VII. tom. ii. p. 227. If Origen's plaything were not the Word of God, one might often be amused with his childish fooleries ; but when we consider what mischief has been done to truth by the way of allegorizing (or, as it is now called, spiritualizing) the Bible, it cannot be looked on without disgust. Of course, the next step is to despise and get rid of the letter of Scripture, as Jerome does most unceremoniously (not to say blasphemously) in this very case. After telling us that the husks, in the parable of the prodigal son, may mean poetry, rhetoric, and the wisdom of this world, he adds—"Hujus sapientiæ typus et in Deuteronomio sub mulieris captivæ figura describitur : de qua divina vox præcipit : ut si Israelites eam habere voluerit uxorem, calvitium ei faciat, ungues præsecet, et pilas auferat : et cum munda fuerit effecta tunc transeat in victoris amplexus. Hæc si secundum literam intelligimus *ridicula* sunt ? Itaque et nos hoc facere solemus quando philosophos legimus," &c.—*Ad Damas.* tom. iii. p. 44, M. My object here, however, is only to show whence certain opinions and feelings of the dark ages were derived. The reader who thinks what I have said insufficient may see the account which Jerome gives, in his Epistle to Eustochium, of his being brought before the judgment-seat, and punished as a Ciceronian. The story is too long to be extracted here, and too well known, perhaps, to require it. At all events, it was well known in the dark ages. He introduces it by saying—"Quæ enim communicatio luci ad tenebras ? qui consensus Christo cum Balial ? Quid facit cum

and as a specimen of the feeling at a period with which we are at present more concerned than with that of Tertullian or Origen—a letter and answer which passed between a prior and an abbot in the year 1150:—

"To his Lord, the Venerable Abbot of ——, R. wishes health and happiness. Although you desire to have the books of Tully, I know that you are a Christian and not a Ciceronian. But you go over to the camp of the enemy, not as a dèserter, but as a spy. I should, therefore, have sent you the books of Tully which we have De Re Agraria, Philippics and Epistles, but that it is not our custom that any books should be lent to any person without good pledges. Send us, therefore, the Noctes Atticæ of Aulus Gellius, and Origen on the Canticles. The books which we have just brought from France, if you wish for any of them, I will send you."

The Abbot replied:—

"Brother ——, by the grace of God what he is in the Catholic Church, to his friend R., the venerable Prior of H——, blessing and life eternal. You have rightly reminded me, brother, that though I may have the books of Cicero, yet I should remember that I am a Christian; and as you have written (and as your Seneca says of himself) I go over sometimes to the enemy's camp, not as a deserter or traitor, but as a spy, and one who is desirous of spoil, if haply I may take prisoner some Midianitish woman, whom, after her head has been shaved, and her nails have been pared, I may lawfully take to wife. And though I deserve only to be a stranger—or, indeed, an exile—in a far country, nevertheless I desire rather to be filled with that bread which came down from heaven, than to fill my belly with the husks which the swine do eat. The dishes prepared by Cicero do not form the principal, or the first, course at my table; but if, at any time, when filled with

---

Psalterio Horatius? cum Evangeliis, Maro? Cum Apostolis, Cicero?" &c.—tom. i. p. 51, C. To this we may add, the first book of Augustine's Confessions, c. 12, and thenceforth. Stronger things than these fathers wrote are not, I believe, to be found in the writings of the dark ages. Some of what Jerome says it would hardly do to produce in the present day—for instance, "At nunc etiam sacerdotes Dei, omissis evangeliis et prophetis, videmus comœdias legere, amatoria Bucolicorum versuum verba canere, tenere Virgilium; et id quod in pueris necessitatis est, crimen in se facere voluptatis," &c.

better food, anything of his pleases me, I take it as one does the trifles which are set on the table after dinner. For it is even a kind of pleasure to me not to be idle. Nor, indeed (to say nothing of any other reasons), can I bear that that noble genius, those splendid imaginations, such great beauties both of thought and language, should be lost in oblivion and neglect; but I want to make into one volume all his works which can be found; for I have no sympathy with those who, neglecting all liberal studies, are careful only for transitory things; and who collect that they may disperse, and disperse that they may collect. They are like men playing at ball—they catch eagerly, and throw away quickly; so that they have no moderation either in catching or in throwing away. Although their doctrine is praised by secular persons of bad character, yet if you love me, you will avoid it as poison, and the death of the soul. I have sent you as pledges for your books, Origen on the Canticles, and instead of Aulus Gellius (which I could not have at this time) a book which is called, in Greek, Stratege-maton, which is military."

It must be observed, however, that this excuse would scarcely serve—indeed, strictly speaking, it could not be admitted at all—for reading heathen works of fiction. The Midianitish captive might have beauty, and might be loved, if she assumed the form of philosophy or history, art or science. Truth, wherever found, is truth and beauty; but when the captive appeared in the meretricious form of poetry, and that, too, poetry about false gods—or, more plainly, nonsense about nonenti-ties—or even coarsely, as they would have expressed it, lies about devils—when this was the case they thought that the less Christians had to do with it the better. Beside this, they thought that Virgil and Horace (to say nothing of some others) spoke of things whereof it is a shame to speak—things which children should not be taught, and which it were better that Christian men should not know. This was their feeling and con-viction; and on this they acted. It was not, as modern conceit loves to talk, that they were ignorant that such books existed, or that they were men so destitute of brains and passions as not to admire the language in which the heathen poets described, and the images in which they personified, ambition, rage, lust, intemperance, and a variety of other things which were quite contrary to the Rules of St. Benedict and St. Chrodegang.

I grant that they had not that extravagant and factitious admiration for the poets of antiquity which they probably would have had if they had been brought up to read them before they could understand them, and to admire them as a necessary matter of taste before they could form any intellectual or moral estimate of them. They thought, too, that there were worse things in the world than false quantities, and preferred running the risque of them to some other risques which they apprehended; [3] but yet there are instances enough

---

[3] When our Archbishop Lanfranc was a monk at Bec, but at a time when the most renowned teachers of Latin were coming to him for instruction—clerici accurrunt, Ducum filii, nominatissimi scholarum latinitatis magistri—he was one day officiating as reader at table, when the prior corrected, or thought that he corrected, him for a false quantity. "It was," says his biographer, "as if he had said docēre with the middle syllable long, as it is; and he [the prior] would have corrected it by shortening the middle syllable to docĕre, which it is not, for that prior was not learned. But the wise man, knowing that obedience was due to Christ rather than to Donatus, gave up the right pronunciation, and said as he was improperly told to say. For he knew that a false quantity was not a capital crime, but that to disobey one who commanded him in God's stead (jubenti ex parte Dei) was no trifling sin."—*Mab. A. S.* IX. 635. By way of a set-off to some things which I have quoted, and a specimen of the exceptions of which I speak, I may add what the biographer of Herluin (who was abbot of Bec at this time) says of this confluence of learned men. He tells us that the monastery increased in a variety of ways, as to fame, revenue, &c.—"Viris litteratis undecumque confluentibus cum ornamentis et spoliis quibus spoliaverant Ægyptum, que cultui tabernaculi postmodum forent accommoda. Poetarum quippe figmenta, philosophorum scientia et artium liberalium disciplina, Scripturis sacris intelligendis valde sunt necessaria."—*Ibid.* 364.

of the classics (even the poets) being taught in schools, and read by individuals; and it cannot be doubted that they might have been, and would have been, read by more but for the prevalence of that feeling which I have described, and which, notwithstanding these exceptions, was very general. Modern, and, as it is supposed, more enlightened, views of education have decided that this was all wrong; but let us not set down what was at most an error of judgment as mere stupidity and a proof of total barbarism. If the modern ecclesiastic should ever meet with a crop-eared monk of the tenth century, he may, if he pleases, laugh at him for not having read Virgil; but if he should himself be led to confess that, though a priest of Christ's catholic church, and nourished in the languages of Greece and Rome till they were almost as familiar to him as his own, he had never read a single page of Chrysostom or Basil, of Augustine or Jerome, of Ambrose or Hilary—if he should confess this I am of opinion that the poor monk would cross himself, and make off without looking behind him.

So different are the feelings of men, and I doubt whether it is possible for any man in the present day to form a complete idea of the state of feeling on this subject which existed for many centuries; but it is very desirable that it should be understood, and perhaps it may be illustrated by a few extracts from writers of different periods.

Pope Gregory wrote a letter to Desiderius, a Bishop of Gaul, which begins thus:—"Having received much pleasing information respecting your studies, such joy arose in my heart that I could not on any account think of refusing what you, my brother, requested. But after this I was informed (what I cannot repeat without shame) that you, my brother, teach certain persons grammar. [4] At this I was so grieved, and conceived so strong a disgust, that I exchanged the feelings which I have described for groans and sadness; for it cannot be that the praises of Jupiter and the praises of Christ should proceed from the same mouth. Consider, yourself, how sad and wicked a thing it is (quam grave nefandumque sit) for a bishop to sing what would be unfit for a religious layman; and although, my most dear son, Candidus, the priest, who came afterwards, being strictly examined as to this matter, denied it, and endeavoured to excuse you, yet my mind is not satisfied. For as it is horrible that such a thing should be told of a priest (execrabile est hoc de sacerdote enarrari), so should the investigation of its truth or falsehood be strict in proportion. If, therefore, the information which I have received shall hereafter be shown to be false, and it shall appear that you are not studying trifles and secular literature, I shall give thanks to God, who has not suffered your mind to be polluted with the blasphemous praises of the wicked, and we shall then confer, safely and

---

[4] I say "teach Grammar," though it is a very absurd translation of *Grammaticam exponere.* The reader who does not require such an explanation will, I hope, excuse my saying, for the sake of others, that the "ars grammatica" comprehended something much beyond what the words would now suggest. Indeed, they might, perhaps, be more properly translated "classical," or, what is the same thing, "profane literature." The *Grammaticus* was, as his name imported, a man of letters — those letters, however, to borrow the words of Augustine, "non quas *primi magistri*, sed quas docent qui *grammatici* vocantur."—*Confess.* L. I. c. xii. How much those who lived in the dark ages knew of such literature, people may dispute; and therefore, as I know of no other alternative, I prefer using the word "grammar," though incorrect, to the appearance of exaggerating their knowledge, until I can show, as I hope to do, that they were not so entirely ignorant of the classics as some have supposed.

without hesitation, on the subject of your requests." [5]

Our countryman, Alcwin, was probably born about the year 735, devoted to the church as soon as he was weaned, and brought up in it. His biographer, who was his contemporary, or within a few years of him, tells us that, when a child, he frequented the daily services of the church, but was apt to neglect those which were performed in the night. When he was about eleven years old, it happened that a lay-brother who inhabited a cell [6] belonging to the monastery was one day, by some accident, deprived of his usual companions, and petitioned the schoolmaster of the monastery that one of the boys might come up and sleep there that night, being, perhaps, afraid to pass the hours of darkness alone. Alcwin was sent, and they retired to rest, and when, about cock-crowing, they were waked by the signal for service, the rustic monk only turned in bed, and went to sleep again. Not so Alcwin, who soon perceived, with horror and astonishment, that the room was full of dæmons. They surrounded the bed of the sleeping rustic, and cried—"You sleep well, brother!" He woke immediately, and they repeated their salutation. "Why," they added

---

[5] Lib. IX. Ep. xlviii.

[6] These cells were little establishments which rose up like offsets round monasteries, and properly consisted of a few (perhaps from two to half a dozen) monks placed there by the superiors of the monastery, and living under its rule, either that they might be on the spot for the protection and cultivation of property belonging to the monastery — or because they desired to lead a more solitary life than they could do in the monastery — or because applications for admissions were so numerous, that in order to admit those who applied it was necessary that some of the older monks should swarm out—or because those who had given certain property had made it a condition that monks should be settled on the spot. The reader will imagine that, if not so originally (as in most cases it was) the cell generally became a farm; and often the oratory grew into a church, a monastery, a town, &c.

"do you alone lie snoring here while all your brethren
are watching in the church?" Quid multa? says the
historian; and, indeed, everybody may guess what
ensued. They gave him an awful drubbing, which, we
are told, was not only very beneficial to him, but was
matter of warning and rejoicing (cautelam et canticum)
to others. In the meantime poor Alcwin, as he afterwards
related, lay trembling under the persuasion that his
turn would come next, and said in his inmost heart—"O,
Lord Jesus, if Thou wilt deliver me from their bloody
hands, and afterwards I am negligent of the vigils of
Thy church and of the service of lauds, and continue
to love Virgil more than the melody of the Psalms,
then may I undergo such correction; only I earnestly
pray that Thou wouldest now deliver me." Alcwin
escaped; but in order to impress it on his memory,
his biographer says, he was subjected to some farther
alarm. The dæmons, having finished the castigation of
his companion, looked about them and found the boy,
completely covered up in his bedclothes, panting and
almost senseless. "Who is the other that sleeps in the
house?" said the chief of the dæmons. "The boy,
Alcwin, is hidden in that bed," replied the others.
Finding that he was discovered, his suppressed grief
and horror burst forth in tears and screaming. His
persecutors being restrained from executing all that
their cruelty would have desired, began to consult
together. An unfortunate hiatus in the MS. prevents
us from knowing all that they said; but it appears
that they came to a resolution not to beat him, but
to turn up the clothes at the bottom of the bed and
cut his corns, by way of making him remember his
promise.[7] Already were the clothes thrown back, when

---

[7] As the passage now stands it is:—"Non istum verberibus, quia

Alcwin jumped up, crossed himself, and sung the twelfth Psalm with all his might. The dæmons vanished, and he and his companion set off to the church for safety. [8]

Some readers will perhaps doubt whether *all* the monks were in the church during this scene in the cell; but, without arguing on the dæmonology of the story, I quote it to show the nature of the sin which lay on the child's conscience when he thought that he was in the hands of devils. He was, as his biographer had before said, even at that early age, " Virgilii amplius quam Psalmorum amator;" but he received a lesson which he never forgot. Speaking of him in after life, and when he had become celebrated as a teacher, his biographer says:—"This man of God had, when he was young, read the books of the ancient philosophers and the lies of Virgil, which he did not wish now to hear, or desire that his disciples should read. 'The sacred poets,' said he, 'are sufficient for you, and there is no reason why you should be polluted with the impure eloquence of Virgil's language.' Which precept, old Sigulfus endeavoured secretly to disobey, and for so doing he was afterwards publicly brought to shame. For, calling his sons, Adalbert and Aldric, whom he was then bringing up, he ordered them to read Virgil with him in the most secret manner, forbidding them to let anyone know of it, lest it should come to the knowledge of Father Alcwin. Alcwin, however, calling him to him in his usual manner, said: 'Where do you come from, *Virgiliane?* and why have you begun and designed, contrary to my will and

---

rudis adhuc est, acris . . . . pedum tantum, in quibus duritia inest-calli, tonsione cultelli castigemus, et emendationem sponsionis nunc suæ confirmabimus."

[8] Mab. Acta SS. Ord. Bened. tom. v. p. 140.

advice, and even without my knowledge, to read
Virgil?' Sigulfus, throwing himself at his feet, and
having confessed that he had acted most foolishly,
humbly did penance; which satisfaction the indulgent
father, after rebuking him, kindly received, admonishing
him not to do so any more. The worthy man of God,
Aldric, who is still alive, and an abbot, declares that
neither he nor Adalbert had divulged the matter to
anyone; but had, all the time, as they were directed,
kept it secret from everybody." [9]

Passing over about a century, we are told by the
biographer of Odo, Abbot of Clugni (who lived until
942), that he was so seduced by the love of knowledge,
that he was led to employ himself with the vanities
of the poets, and resolved to read the works of Virgil
regularly through. On the following night, however,
he saw in a dream a large vase, of marvellous external
beauty, but filled with innumerable serpents, who,
springing forth, twined about him, but without doing
him any injury. The holy man, waking, and prudently
considering the vision, took the serpents to mean the
figments of the poets, and the vase to represent Virgil's
book, which was painted outwardly with worldly eloquence, but internally defiled with the vanity of impure
meaning. From thenceforward, renouncing Virgil and
his pomps, and keeping the poets out of his chamber,
he sought his nourishment from the sacred writings. [1]

After another century—that is, about the middle of
the eleventh—we find Peter Damian blaming those
monks "who go after the common herd of grammarians (grammaticorum vulgus), who, leaving spiritual
studies, covet to learn the vanities of earthly science;

---

[9] Mab. *ibid.* p. 149.
[1] Mab. *ubi sup.* tom. vii. p. 187.

that is, making light of the Rule of St. Benedict, they love to give themselves up to the Rules of Donatus;" [2] and, very near the same time, our Archbishop Lanfranc wrote to Domnoaldus—"You have sent me some questions respecting secular literature for solution; but it is unbecoming the episcopal function to be occupied in such studies. Formerly, I spent the days of my youth in such things; but on taking the pastoral office I determined to renounce them." [3] His contemporary, Geronius, abbot at Centule, was (his biographer tells us) in his youth accustomed to read the heathen poets; and had nearly fallen into the error of practising what he read. [4]

Honorius (about 1120), or whoever was the author of the Gemma Animæ, says—"It grieves me when I consider in my mind the number of persons who, having lost their senses, are not ashamed to give their utmost labour to the investigation of the abominable figments of the poets, and the captious arguments of the philosophers (which are wont inextricably to bind the mind that is drawn away from God in the bonds of vices) and to be ignorant of the Christian profession, whereby the soul may come to reign everlastingly with God. As it is the height of

---

[2] Ap. Mab. *ibid.* Sæc. III. P. I. Præf. No. 42, p. xvii.

[3] Ibid.

[4] "Sed, ut fieri solet, cum adolescens Grammaticæ operam daret, et patulo sensu ipsorum jam carminum vim perpenderet, animadvertitque inter ea quædam, quorum omnis intentio hæc est, ut aut expletas luxurias referant, aut quomodo quis explere voluerit, vel explere potuerit recenseant: et dum talium assidua meditatione polluitur juvenis mens casta, tum juvenili fervore, tum turpium verborum auditione, maxime vero diaboli instinctu ad hoc cœpit impelli, ut ea faceret quæ tantorum Poetarum æstimabat narratione celebrari."— *Chron. Centulen. ap. Dach. Spicil.* ii. 338.

madness to be anxious to learn the laws of an usurper, and to be ignorant of the edicts of the lawful
sovereign. Moreover, how is the soul profited by the
strife of Hector, or the argumentation of Plato, or the
poems of Virgil, or the elegies of Ovid, who now,
with their like, are gnashing their teeth in the prison
of the infernal Babylon, under the cruel tyranny of
Pluto? But the wisdom of God puts the brightest
honour on him who, investigating the deeds and
writings of the apostles, has his mind continually
employed on those whom no one doubts to be now
reigning in the palace of the heavenly Jerusalem, with
the King of Glory." [5]

Let me add an extract from the works of a contemporary, whose name is too well-known, and whose
words are worth copying, because he was quite a
march-of-intellect man. Peter Abelard, after quoting
the statements of Jerome, and saying that, from the
injunction laid on him, some persons gathered that it
was unlawful to read any secular books, adds, "I
conceive, however, that reading in any of the arts is
not forbidden to a religious man; unless it may be
that by it his greater usefulness may be hindered;
and we must do in this as we know must be done in
some other good things—namely, the less must sometimes be intermitted, or altogether given up, for the
sake of the greater. For when there is no falsehood
in the doctrine, no impropriety in the language, some
utility in the knowledge, who is to be blamed for
learning or teaching these things? unless because, as
I have already said, some greater good be neglected
or omitted; for no man can say that knowledge is,
strictly speaking, evil. But how greatly this may be

---

[5] Prol. Bib. Pat. tom. X. p. 1179.

done to our condemnation and confusion every reflecting person may see; since we are not only told that
'the mouth that belieth slayeth the soul' (Wisd. i. 11),
but also that an account will be required of every
idle word. If a Christian chooses to read for critical
knowledge of phrases and forms of speech, may he
not do this sufficiently without studying the figments
of the poets and foolish tales? What kind of phraseology, what ornament of language is there, which the
phrase of scripture does not supply? Full as it is of
enigmatical allegories, and abounding as it does with
mystical language, what elegances of speech are there,
which may not be learned from the mother tongue
Hebrew? especially when it appears that the common
people of Palestine were so accustomed to parables,
that it behoved the Lord Jesus to address them in
that way when he preached the Gospel to them. What
dainty can be wanting at the spiritual table of the
Lord,—that is, the Sacred Scripture—wherein, according
to Gregory, both the elephant may swim and the
lamb may walk?" Then, after proceeding to show that
as much, and as good, language as can be wanted,
may be had from Jerome, Augustine, Cyprian, and
other Christian writers, he says—"Why then do not
the bishops and doctors of the Christian religion expel
from the city of God, those poets whom Plato forbade
to enter into his city of the world?" [6]

I might go on with extracts of this kind until we
should come again to De Rancé; but I am afraid that
the reader may think that I have already cited more
testimonies than enough on this point. Should there,
however, be anything like tautology in them, I beg
him to remember that my object in bringing them

---

[6] Theol. Christ. Lib. II. *Mart.* tom. V. p. 1238.

forward is to describe and illustrate a feeling which existed very generally in the Christian Church before, and through, and after, the Dark Ages. That there were, even in those days, reading men, I hope to show; and that they did not give the first place to classical or scientific learning, I allow, though I cannot admit that it was from pure ignorance of the sources of information ; and the question naturally arises—What did they read ? This inquiry I hope to pursue, and to begin by showing that there were some persons— perhaps a good many—who read the Bible.

No. XII.

"Omissis igitur et repudiatis nugis theatricis et poeticis, divinarum Scripturarum consideratione, et tractatione pascamus animum atque potemus vanæ curiositatis fame ac siti fessum et æstuantem, et inanibus phantasmatibus, tanquam pictis epulis, frustra refici satiarique cupientem."—AUGUSTINUS.

THERE is no subject in the history of mankind which appears to me more interesting, and more worthy of investigation, than the actual state of the Christian church during the dark ages. It is, as I have already said, with a view to this that I have entered on this series of papers ; and having now, I trust, in some degree, cleared the way, by exposing some popular misstatements, I hope to come more directly to the point. To begin, then, with an inquiry respecting the Christian knowledge, or the means of such knowledge, which existed in those days ; and to begin this at the beginning—Did they know anything about THE BIBLE ?

I believe that the idea which many persons have of ecclesiastical history may be briefly stated thus : that the Christian church was a small, scattered, and persecuted flock, until the time of Constantine ; that then, at once, and as if by magic, the Roman world became Christian ; that this Universal Christianity, not being of a very pure, solid, or durable nature, melted down into a filthy mass called Popery, which held its place during the dark ages, until the revival of Pagan literature, and the consequent march of intellect, sharpened men's wits and brought about the Reformation ; when it was discovered that the pope was Antichrist, and that the saints had been in the hands of the little horn predicted by the prophet Daniel for hundreds of years without knowing so awful a fact, or suspecting anything of the kind. How much of this is true, and how much false, this is not the place to inquire; but I feel bound to refer to this opinion, because the necessity of describing the church during the kingdom of the Apocalyptic Beast in such a way as scarcely to admit of her visible existence, even when it has not led popular writers on the prophecies to falsify history, has at least prepared their readers to acquiesce without surprise or inquiry in very partial and delusive statements.

There is another point which I would just notice, because it has given colour to the statements of all the writers, who, from whatever motive, have maintained the entire ignorance of the dark ages,—I mean the complaints made by contemporary writers of the neglect of the word of God, as well as of the other sins of those ages. I have before alluded to something like this of a more general nature, and will here only give a single specimen; and that not so much to prove or illustrate what is plain and notorious, as because it is somewhat curious and characteristic in itself, and relates to one of the most early versions of the Scripture into the vernacular tongue.

William of Bamberg, as he is commonly called, who was a monk of Fulda, and afterwards abbot of St. Peter's by Mersburg (about the year 1070), wrote a translation, or rather a double paraphrase, of the Book of Canticles, in Latin verse and Teutonic prose, to which he prefixed the following preface:—

"When I look at the studies of our ancestors, whereby they became famous in respect of the Sacred Scriptures, I am forced to lament the depravity of this age, when almost every literary pursuit has ceased, and there is nothing going on but avarice, envy, and strife. For if there are any who, under scholastic discipline, are instructed in grammatical and dialectical studies, they think that this is enough for them, and entirely neglect the Holy Scripture; whereas it is on account of that only that it is lawful for Christians to read heathen books, in order that they may perceive the great difference between light and darkness, truth and error. Others, however, though they are mighty in sacred learning, yet, hiding in the earth the talent committed to them, laugh at those who make mistakes in reading and chanting, though they take no pains to help their infirmity, either by instructing them or correcting their books. I found, in France, that one man, named Lantfrid [1] (who had previously been much distinguished in dialectics, but who had then betaken himself to ecclesiastical studies), had by his own acuteness sharpened the minds of many in the Epistles of St. Paul and the Psalms; and as many of our countrymen flock to hear him, I hope that, after his example, they also will produce the fruit of their industry in our provinces, to the benefit of many. And as it often happens that through an impulse given by generous steeds the half-bred horse is set a running. (although I am not ignorant of the dulness of my poor genius, yet hoping to have a merciful God for my helper), I also have determined, according to my small means, to offer to the studious reader some little help towards improvement. I have determined, therefore, if God permit, to explain the Song of Songs, whose very name testifies its eminence, both in verse and in the Teutonic language, in such a way, that the text being placed in the middle, these two versions may accompany it down the sides, and thereby whatsoever is sought may be more easily found. I have added nothing of my own, but have compressed all I could find in the various expositions of the fathers; and, both in the verses and in the Teutonic translation, I have taken more pains about the sense than the words. Sometimes I repeat the same verses; for those things which the Holy Spirit has repeated in the same words, it does not appear improper for me to repeat in the same verses. I have thought it good to distribute the parts to the Bridegroom and the Bride, both in the translation and in the verses, as well as the text, not only that they may have the greater appearance of authority, but that the reader may be gratified by the persons speaking alternately. I do not know whether I am the dupe of a pleasing delusion; but if not, surely he who rained on Solomon hath also condescended to shed some few drops on me. Sometimes on reading what I have written I am as much delighted as if it was the work of an approved author. I offer this little work, as long as I live, to the correction of those who are more learned;

---

[1] That is, our Archbishop Lanfranc.

if I have done wrong in anything, I shall not be ashamed to receive their admonitions ; and if there is anything which they like, I shall not be slow to furnish more." [2]

To come, however, to the question—did people in the dark ages know anything of the Bible? Certainly it was not as commonly known and as generally in the hands of men as it is now, and has been almost ever since the invention of printing—the reader must not suspect me of wishing to maintain any such absurd opinion; but I do think that there is sufficient evidence—(I.) that during that period the scriptures were more accessible to those who could use them—(II.) were in fact more used—and (III.) by a greater number of persons—than some modern writers would lead us to suppose.

The worst of it is, that the proof must not only be defective—for on what subject connected with that period can it be otherwise?—but that, if by any means fully produced, it must be so voluminous as to be quite inadmissible in a work like the present. It is not by generalizing on particular cases, as has been the fault of some writers whose statements I have noticed, but by accumulating a great number of facts—facts, too, of very different descriptions, and forming totally distinct parts of the proof—that anything like a correct idea can be formed. It is absurd for Robertson to say that monasteries of considerable note had only one

---

[2] *M. & D.* I. 501. To this poor monk's own account of his performance, it is only justice to add the testimony of a learned Protestant : — "Paraphrasin Willerami mire commendat Junius, autorem vocat præstantis ingenii virum, et rerum theologicarum consultissimum, qui in hac provincia administranda, et vero sensu connubialis carminis eruendo tanta dexteritate est et fide versatus, ut paucos habuerit ex antiquis illis, quos se vidisse et legisse notat, pares ; priorem fere neminem." — *Cave, Hist. Lit.* tom. ii. p. 148.

missal, because the Abbot Bonus found only one in
the ruined chapel at Pisa. It is as absurd in Warton
to tell us that "at the beginning of the tenth century
books were so scarce in Spain that one and the same
copy of the Bible, St. Jerome's Epistles, and some
volumes of ecclesiastical offices and martyrologies, *often*
served for different monasteries," [3] because old Gennadius, Bishop of Astorga, thought fit, after dividing many
other books among four monasteries or oratories, which
he had founded in his diocese, to give them his Bible
and some other books as common property. [4] I think

---

[3] Diss. ii.

[4] Warton refers to Fleury, L. LIV. c. liv. but adds, "See other
instances in Hist. Lit. Fr. par Rel Benedict. vii. 3." To this book I
have not access at present; but I shall be much surprised to find that
it contains other instances sufficient to support this assertion.

Since I wrote this note I have received a letter from a friend whom
I requested to look out the reference, in which he says, "It is curious
that you should be again sent back to your old friend, the Homilies
of Haimo; the whole passage is not long, and I shall, therefore,
transcribe it. Hist. Lit. tom. vii. p. 3, n. 3.

"'III. A ce defaut presque generale d'inclination pour les lettres,
qui avoit sa source dans le genie de la nation, se réunirent plusieurs
autres causes, qui concoururent à entretenir l'ignorance. Le X siècle
n'avoit pas été suffisant pour reparer *les pertes de livres* qu'avoit souffert
la France, dans les courses précédentes, les pillages, les incendies, des
Sarasins, des Normans, des Hongrois, des Bulgares. *Quoiqu'on eût
travaillé à renouveller ces livres, comme nous l'avons montré,* ils étoient
encore fort rares, ce qui rendoit les études très-difficiles. D'ailleurs n'y
aïant presque que des moines qui s'occupoient à les copier, ils com-
mencerent par ceux qu'ils croïoient plus nécessaires : *la Bible* et les
livres liturgiques, les écrits des Peres, les recueils des Canons. Ainsi il
se passa du temps, avant qu'ils pussent transcrire les Historiens, les
Poëtes, les Orateurs. Et le defaut de ces ouvrages contribua beaucoup
aux mauvaises Etudes et à la barbarie qui y regnoit. On avoit cependant
de cette sorte d'auteurs : mais ils n'étoient pas communes.—(*Mab*. an. 1.
61, n. 6). Un trait que l'histoire a conservé touchant le prix excessif
des livres et ce temps-là nous doit faire juger de leur rareté. Encore

it would be quite as fair and as foolish for me to say,
"In the ninth century the bishops used to write Bibles
for their churches with their own hands," because I
find that Wicbert, who became bishop of Wildesheim
in the year 880, did so. Still such notices are not to
be passed over; and I will here offer a few, to which,
I have no doubt, many more might be added if I had
access to more books. Though I put them first, I beg
the reader not to suppose that I consider them as the
most important part of the proof, but only offer them
as notices not entirely uninteresting in themselves, and
as forming a part, though a small one, of the proof
required.

1. In the first place, then, whoever reads the writers—perhaps I should say principally the historians—
of those ages will find them not unfrequently speaking
of the Bible. I do not mean referring to it as an
authority, or quoting its contents, or, if I may so express
myself, speaking of it in the abstract (for this is quite
another part of the subject), but incidentally mentioning the existence of Bibles at various times, and in

---

s'agit-il d'un auteur ecclesiastique, le recueil des Homelies d'Haimon
d'Halberstat. Grécie Comtesse d'Anjou,' &c., &c.

"The rest of the paragraph I think I sent you before; or, at least,
you know its contents. [The reader may find it in No. V. p. 87.] And
it appears that there is nothing whatever about one book serving many
monasteries; nay, the inference from the whole passage is the very
reverse of the statement for which it is quoted by Warton; and it
relates, not to Spain, but to France. I therefore looked in the index
of the volume, in hope that the reference might possibly be misprinted;
but I find nothing at all like the statement in Warton's text."

I do not wish to lengthen this note by any remarks on this passage,
which I adduce as being the authority on which Warton relied ; but
I have marked one or two words by *italics*, which show what an
important bearing it has on the subject in general, and particularly on
that part with which we are at present engaged.

places where they were accessible to many readers. I need not repeat that the proof must be defective, not only because we may reasonably suppose that those copies of the Bible which happen to be thus incidentally mentioned, in the comparatively few documents which have come down to us, were but a very small part of those which were in existence, but because the instances which I can give are only such as I happen to have met with in circumstances not very favourable to research on such subjects.

When Aldhelm, who became bishop of Schireburn in the year 705, went to Canterbury to be consecrated by his old friend and companion Berthwold (pariter literis studuerant, pariterque viam religionis triverant), the archbishop kept him there many days, taking counsel with him about the affairs of his diocese. Hearing of the arrival of ships at Dover, during this time, he went there to inspect their unloading, and to see if they had brought anything in his way (si quid forte commodum ecclesiastico usui attulissent nautæ qui e Gallico sinu in Angliam provecti librorum copiam apportassent). Among many other books he saw one containing the whole of the Old and New Testament, which—to omit the incidents for the sake of which the fact is recorded, but which are not to our purpose—he at length bought; and William of Malmesbury, who wrote his life in the twelfth century, tells us that it was still preserved at that place.[5]

In the year 780, King Offa gave to the church at Worcester, among other things, a great Bible—magnam Bibliam.[6]

It was probably soon after—for he became bishop of Orleans about or before the year 794—that Theodulfus

---

[5] Ang. Sac. ii. 21.   [6] Ibid. i. 470.

made his great Bible, which is still in existence; at least it was so in the days of Father Sirmond, in whose works the reader may find the verses which the bishop prefixed to it, and the preface, which was written in gold.[7]

In the list of books given to his monastery by Ansegisus, who became abbot of Fontanelle in the year 823, we find "Bibliothecam optimam continens vetus et novum Testamentum, cum præfationibus ac initiis librorum aureis literis decoratis;"[8] and among those which he gave to the monastery of St. Flavian, "Pandecten a B. Hieronymo ex hebræo vel græco eloquio translatum."[9]

In a return of their property which the monks of St. Riquier at Centule made, by order of Lewis the Debonnaire, in the year 831, we find, among a considerable quantity of books, "Bibliotheca integra ubi continentur libri lxxii. in uno volumine;" and also, "Bibliotheca dispersa in voluminibus 14."[1]

---

[7] Sirm. Op. tom. ii. p. 763.

[8] Chron. Fontan. ap. Dach. Sp. ii. 280.

[9] Ibid. 281. I do not know that this name was ever general, or that it was used by any writer before Alcwin. In the verses which he wrote in the copy which he corrected by order of Charlemagne (and which the reader may find in Baronius, an. 778, No. xxiii.), he says:—

"Nomine PANDECTEN proprio vocitare memento

Hoc corpus sacrum, lector, in ore tuo;

Quod nunc a multis constat BIBLIOTHECA dicta

Nomine non proprio, ut lingua Pelasga docet.'

As to the name *Bibliotheca*, I have already had occasion to mention that it was the common name for a Bible. It seems to have arisen (I know not how properly) from the words of Jerome, who, offering to lend books, says to Florentius, "et quoniam largiente Domino, multis sacræ bibliothecæ codicibus abundamus," &c.—*Ep.* VI. *ad Flor.* tom. i. p. 19. I.

[1] Chron. Centul. ap. Dach. Sp. ii. 311.

In the year 843 the Normans came up the Loire, and laid waste Nantes, and the surrounding country. After killing the bishop in his cathedral, with many of the clergy, monks, and laity who had sought refuge there, they loaded their vessels with spoil and captives, and proceeded along the Loire to an island, where they began to divide their prey. In doing this, they quarrelled and fought, and many of them were killed. "The captives, however," says the historian, "seeing the storm, all fled into the more inaccessible parts of the island; but among them there was one who ventured on a very bold stroke (magnæ invasionis audax). He took on his back the great Bible, which is preserved to this day [probably in or before the twelfth century] in the great church of Nantes, and ran off to hide himself, with the rest, in the mines." The Normans having fought till they were tired, those who survived were seized with a panic; in consequence of which they gathered up the spoil, and set sail, without troubling themselves about the captives, who at length got safe back to Nantes, having lost much in silver, and gold, and books, and saving only their Bible, "solummodo Bibliothecam afferentes."[2]

It is somewhat curious that, among the little scraps of history which have come down to us, we find a notice of another Bible in the same year, and very near the same place. In a charter cited by Du Cange, from the tabulary of the monastery of St. Maur, on the Loire, we find—"Donum autem confirmat Bibliotheca Veteris et Novi Testamenti;"[3] the Bible having been used, I presume, in the conveyance of some property in the way which I have described in No. V.

---

[2] Frag. Hist. Armor. ap. Mart. iii. 830.
[3] Du Cange in v. *Bibliotheca*.

p. 105. Indeed, it seems as if they were in the habit of
so using their Bible at that monastery; for in another
charter, bearing date 847, and conveying property to
it, we find—"Donum autem hujus rei est hæc Bibliotheca
Veteris ac Novi Testamenti." [4]

In the short interval between the dates of these two
charters—that is, in the year 845—Hamburg was burned, and the Bible which Lewis the Debonnaire had
given to Anscharius was, with many other books,
destroyed by fire—"Bibliotheca, quam serenissimus jam
memoratus Imperator eidem patri nostro contulerat,
optime conscripta, cum plurimis aliis libris igni dis-
periit." [5]

Everhard, Count of Friuli, by his will, dated A.D.
867, divided his books among his children, leaving to
his eldest son "Bibliothecam nostram." [6] This Count,
before the time just specified, had founded a monastery
at Cisoing (a little to the south between Lille and
Tournay), and it appears that a monk named Wulga-
rius, who states that he had laboured in the monastery
ever since its foundation, presented to it several books,
among which we find "Bibliothecam 1." [7]

Wicbert, who became bishop of Hildesheim in the
year 880, I have already mentioned as writing a Bible
with his own hand. The chronicler who records the
fact, and who probably wrote in the twelfth century,
says, "Bibliothecam quæ adhuc in monasterio servatur,
propria manu elaboravit." [8]

Gennadius, who bequeathed his Bible, as part of a
sort of circulating library, to his four monasteries or

---

[4] Given by Baluze Capit. Reg. Franc. tom. ii. p. 1456.

[5] Vita S. Anscharii int. add. ad Lambecii Orig. Hamburg. c. xiv. p. 59.

[6] Dach. Sp. ii. 877.   [7] Ibid. p. 879.

[8] Chron. Ep. Hildesh. ap. Leib. Sc. Brun. I. 743.

oratories, I have also already mentioned. He describes it as "Bibliothecam totam." [9]

Olbert, who was abbot of Gembloux until the year 1048, wrote out a volume containing the whole of the Old and New Testament;[1] and the unfortunate Bonus, who was abbot at Pisa at exactly the same time, gave

---

[9] Mab. A. S. vii. p. 36.

[1] This is the person who, under the name of Albert, comes in for a sneer from Warton on the page just referred to of his second Dissertation; "Albert, Abbot of Gemblours, who, with incredible labour and immense expense, had collected an hundred volumes on theological, and fifty on profane subjects, imagined he had formed a splendid library." The "incredible labour and immense expense," and the Abbot's own imagination of the splendour of his library, are, I believe, as purely poetical as anything that Warton ever wrote. Fleury, to whom he refers, says only, "Etant Abbé, il amassa à Gembloux plus de cent volumes d'auteurs ecclesiastiques, et cinquante d'auteurs profanes, ce qui passoit pour une grande bibliotheque."—*Liv.* LVIII. *c.* lii. *tom.* XII. p. 424. The fact, however, is, that he was a monk of Lobbes, who was sent to reform and restore the monastery of Gembloux, which was in a state of great poverty and disorder—exterius ingrueret *gravis rei familiaris tenuitas*, interius autem horreret grendis irreligiositas— and he did, according to the account of his biographer, in a marvellously short time, restore discipline, build a church, and provide many things needful for the monastery, and among others the 150 volumes of books. As to the "incredible labour," we are expressly told that he set his monks to write, to keep them from being idle; and as to the "immense expense," his biographer's remark is, that it is wonderful how one man, with such slender means, could do so much as he did. "Non passus enim ut per otium mens aut manus eorum torpesceret, utiliter profectui eorum providet, dum *eos per scribendi laborem exercet,* et frequenti scripturarum meditatione animos eorum ad meliora promovet. Appellens ergo animum ad construendum pro posse suo bibliothe-cam, quasi quidam Philadelphus, plenariam vetus et novum Testamentum continentem in uno volumine transcripsit historiam; et divinæ quidem scripturæ *plusquam* centum congessit volumina, sæcularis vero disciplinæ libros quinquaginta. Mirandum sane hominem unum *in tanta tenuitate rerum,* tanta potuisse comparare, nisi occurreret animo, timentibus Deum nihil deesse."—Mab. A. S. tom. viii. p. 531. The reader will here

(as we have already seen) ten pounds for what he describes as a "liber Bibliothece." [2]

Among the books which Thierry, who became the first abbot of the restored monastery of St. Evroul, or Ebrulf, at Ouche, in the diocese of Lisieux, in the year 1050, caused to be written for that monastery, we find, "omnes libros veteris et novi Testamenti." [3]

Stephen, who became abbot of Beze, in the year 1088, gave the monastery a "Bibliotheca, tam veteris quam novi Testamenti." [4]

Wicbert's Bible, twice mentioned already, did not prevent Bruno, who succeeded him in the see of Hildesheim in the year 1153, from presenting to the library a glossed Bible— "contulit ad ipsum armarium totum Testamentum novum et vetus, utrumque glos-

---

observe that use of the phrase "divina scriptura," which I have before noticed, and of which it would be easy to give instances; one of the most curious is perhaps that in the Burton Annals (Gale, iii. 264). King John is represented as saying to the Pope's Nuncio, "unde videre potestis per *sacras scripturas* quod beatus et gloriosus rex sanctus Edwardus contulit in tempore suo Sancto Wulstano episcopatum Wigorniæ," &c.

[2] When I mentioned the Abbot's Bible before (No. IV. p. 72), I gave a specimen of his latinity; and this morsel may give me an opportunity of suggesting to the reader that we are not, in all cases, to take it for granted that there was nobody better able to understand, or to describe a book, than the person who happens to have incidentally noticed its existence, or to have made an inventory of various things, and of books among the rest. For instance, the list of books belonging to the church of St. James and St. Christopher, at Stedeburg, which Leibnitz gives us (I. 870), begins with "Liber Genesis Biblia," and contains "Liber in Principio et evangeliorum secundum Marcum." I do not mention this Bible in the text, because I do not know the date of this list. The more modern it is, the more it is to the purpose of this note.

[3] Mab. A. S. ix. 136.
[4] Chron. Bes. ap. Dach. Sp. ii. 435.

satum " [5]—and this was followed by another glossed
Bible, very carefully elaborated, and presented by Berno,
who succeeded to the see in the year 1190— "contulit
etiam ecclesiæ veteris ac novi Testamenti libros glos-
satos et magno scholasticæ diligentiæ studio elabora-
tos." [6]

To these instances I doubt not that a little trouble
would add many more ; but I am afraid that the reader
has already found them tedious, and I will here only
add some notice of a correspondence between Geoffry,
sub-prior of St. Barbara, in Normandy, and John, the
abbot, and Peter, one of the monks, of Baugercy, in
the diocese of Tours, some time between the dates just
specified, and probably about the year 1170. The sub-
prior begins one of his letters thus :—

" To his Venerable Abbot John, Geoffry, the servant of your holiness,
wishes that which is the true health. I received the letters of your
affection, which seemed to my heart to be sweetened with the honey
of love. I read them eagerly ; I now read them again gladly ; and,
often read over, they still please. Of this only I complain, that you
send so few and such short letters to one who loves you, and whom
you love, so much. You seldom converse with me, and I should like
the conversation to be longer. I should like to hear something from
you that might instruct us as to our life and conversation, relieve the
weariness of our pilgrimage, and inflame us with the love of our
heavenly country. I must also tell you that the excellent Bible (Bibliothecam optimam), of which I wrote to you long ago, you may still
find at Caen, if you wish it."

The Abbot in his reply (which I presume was not
a speedy one, for he begins it with reproaching the
sub-prior that he had been so long silent) takes no
notice of the Bible, unless it be by saying at the close
of his letter, "Peter Mangot salutes you ; to whom I

---

[5] Chron. Hildesh. ap. Leib. Sc. Br. i. 747.
[6] Ibid. 749.

wish that you would write, and comfort him in the Lord, and among other things admonish him about buying a Bible." It seems to have been the custom of these two friends to add one, two, or three couplets to their letters, in the way of marginal notes, referring to the subjects on which they were writing. The second of the two couplets on this occasion is as follows :—

> "Ardenti studio sacra perlege dogmata, si vis
> Dulcis aquæ saliente sitim restringere rivo."

This letter produced one from Geoffry to Peter Mangot, who seems to have been a monk of Baugercy, who had undertaken and obtained permission to build a monastery.

"To his beloved and friend Peter Mangot, brother Geoffry wishes health and perseverance in the work begun.

"God has fulfilled your desire, — you have what you so ardently sought. You have got what you asked from me, from the King through me, and from the chapter of Citeaux through the King's letters, and the help of others. These things, indeed, seemed very difficult at first, and, from the circumstances of the case, we were almost in despair; but God himself looked upon us with an eye of mercy, and with a strong hand made all things plain before our face. Go on, then, with increasing devotion in a work that was first conceived with a devout intention, and devoutly begun; and carefully provide all that is necessary for it. Build up a temple to the Lord of living and elect stones, who may receive you into eternal habitations. I give thanks to the grace of God which worketh in you; I give thanks also to you, who are working together with that grace; for the grace of God, which without you, wrought in you a good will, now worketh by you."

He afterwards adds:—

"A monastery (claustrum) without a library (sine armario) is like a castle (castrum) without an armory (sine armamentario). Our library is our armory. Thence it is that we bring forth the sentences of the divine law, like sharp arrows, to attack the enemy. Thence we take the armour of righteousness, the helmet of salvation, the shield of faith, and the sword of the Spirit which is the word of God. See to it, therefore, that in your armory of defence that which is the great defence of all the other defences is not wanting. That defence is the Holy Bible, wherein is contained the right rule of life and manners. There each sex and every age finds what is profitable. There spiritual infancy finds that whereby it may grow, youth that which may strengthen it, age that which may support it, — a blessed hand which ministers to all, whereby all may be saved. If therefore you have taken care to provide the arms for this warfare, you will have nothing to do but to say to him, ' Take thine arms and thy shield, and arise to my help.' Farewell! and take care that the Bible, which no monastery should be without, is bought."

To this letter three couplets are added, of which the third is as follows:—

> " Quamvis multorum multi placeant tibi libri
> Hanc habeas, sapias, sufficit ipsa tibi." [7]

It does not appear (and as our inquiry relates in a great degree to the possibility of obtaining such things in those days, it is worth while to notice the circumstance) that this recommendation to procure a Bible had anything to do with the *Bibliotheca optima* at Caen; for, in a subsequent letter, the Abbot John requests his friend Geoffry to secure it for him. [8]

---

[7] The other four lines have nothing to do with our immediate subject, but I hope the reader will forgive my quoting them, as belonging to a writer of the dark ages. From his correspondence, in which the reader who is not fastidious as to style (or, rather, as to latinity), may find much that is interesting, I hope at some future time to give farther extracts. After

> " Petrus vocaris firmus esto,"

we find these four lines, or, rather, two couplets, which seem to have reference to different parts of his letter, and to have been originally unconnected with each other, as also with the third couplet quoted above:—

> " In Christo petra fidei fundamine jacto
> Spe paries surgit, culmina complet amor.
> Vivit agendo fides; ubi non est actus amoris,
> Gignit abortivam spem moribunda fides."

[8] Mart. i. 502, 509, 514.

All the instances which I have given refer to the whole Bible, or, as it is expressed in some of them, the *Bibliotheca integra*, or *Bibliotheca tota;* but I must beg the reader's attention to one circumstance, which is important, if we would understand matters aright. Undoubtedly Bibles were scarce in those days; but we are not hastily to conclude that wherever there existed no single book called a Bible, the contents of the Bible were unknown. The canon of Scripture was settled, indeed, as it is now; but the several parts of which the Bible consists were considered more in the light of separate and independent books than they are by us. To copy *all* these books was a great undertaking; and even when there was no affectation of caligraphy or costly ornament, and when we reduce the exaggerated statements about the price of materials to something reasonable, it was not only a laborious but a very expensive matter. Of course, writing and printing are very different things. I do not pretend to speak with accuracy (for it would require more trouble than the thing is worth), but I am inclined to suppose that at this day a copy of our English Bible, paid for at the rate at which law-stationers pay their writers for common fair-copy on paper, would cost between sixty and seventy pounds for the writing only; and farther, that the scribe must be both expert and industrious to perform the task in much less than ten months. It must be remembered, however, that the monasteries contained (most of them some, and many a considerable number of) men who were not to be paid by their work or their time, but who were officially devoted to the business. Of this, however, I hope to say more hereafter, and to show that there was a considerable power of multiplication at work. In the meantime, I mention these circumstances merely as reasons why

we should not expect to meet with frequent mention
of *whole* Bibles in the dark ages. Indeed, a scribe
must have had some confidence in his own powers
and perseverance who should have undertaken to make
a transcript of the whole Bible; and that (except under
particular circumstances) without any adequate motive,
supposing him to have practised his art as a means
of subsistence. For those who were likely to need and
to reward his labours either already possessed some
part of the Scriptures, and therefore did not require a
transcript of the whole, or, if it was their first attempt
to possess any portion, there were but few whose
means or patience would render it likely that they
should think of acquiring the whole at once. It is
obvious, too, that when copies of *parts* had been multiplied, that very circumstance would lead to the
transcription of other *parts*, which would comparatively
seldom be formed into one volume. We may well
imagine that a scribe would prefer undertaking to
write a Pentateuch, or adding the two next books a
Heptateuch, or with one more an Octateuch, or a
Psalter, or a Textus containing one or more of the
Gospels, or a Book of Proverbs, or a set of the
Canonical Epistles, or some one or other of the portions
into which the Bible was at that time very commonly
divided. Of these I hope to speak hereafter, and only
mention their existence now as one reason why we
are not to take it for granted, that all persons who
did not possess what we call "a Bible" must have
been entirely destitute and ignorant of the Holy
Scriptures.

No. XIII.

"Sunk in the lowest state of earthly depression, making their pilgrimage in sackcloth and ashes, pressed by every art and engine of human hostility, by the blind hatred of the half-barbarian kings of feudal Europe, by the fanatical furies of their ignorant people, and, above all, by the great spiritual domination, containing in itself a mass of solid and despotic strength unequalled in the annals of power, vivified and envenomed by a reckless antipathy unknown in the annals of the passions,—what had they [the Scriptures] to do but perish?"

HITHERTO I have spoken only of whole Bibles; and I have observed, that it would be unreasonable to expect that we should find notice of any very considerable number during the Dark Ages; not only because all books were scarce—not only because such notices, and the finding of them, are merely accidental—but because the Bible was comparatively seldom formed into one volume, and more commonly existed in its different parts. To mention all the notices which occur of these parts, and all the proofs which exist, that they must have been numerous, would be both tedious and useless; but it will tend to illustrate, not only the immediate question before us, but our general subject, if I say a few words of copies of the Gospels; at least, of some which may be worthy of notice, from their costly decorations, or from the persons by whom they were possessed, or to, or by, whom they were presented.

I have already said something on the subject of costly books; and I only refer to it here in order to correct a mistake. I stated the case of an "Elector of

Bavaria, who *gave* a town for a single manuscript";[1] whereas I should have said, that he *offered* a town for it; but that the monks, wisely considering that he could, and suspecting that he would, retake the town whenever he pleased, declined the exchange. The MS. remained in their library in the beginning of the eighteenth century; and is, for anything that I know, still there.[2]

I have before referred to St. Jerome's testimony as to the splendour of some books even in his day; and I may just mention the present of the Emperor Justin to Pope Hormisda, made between the years 518 and 523, and including a splendid copy of the Gospels— "sub hujus episcopatu multa vasa aurea venerunt de Græcia, et evangelia cum tabulis aureis, cum gemmis preciosis pensantibus lib. 15," &c.[3]

As to the period, however, with which we are particularly engaged, Leo III., who was pope when it

---

[1] No. V. p. 92.

[2] I made the statement on the authority (as I thought) of Baring, who mention the circumstance in his Clavis Diplomatica, 2nd edit. p. 5; and the word " obtulit " conveyed to my mind, from its constant use in charters, diplomas, and all the documents to which his work has reference, no other idea than that of giving—that is, offering what was not rejected. Whether he meant this, I do not know. He might be mistaken on that point, as well as with regard to its contents; for it was not a New Testament, but a book of the Gospels, as we learn from a letter dated 3rd Oct., 1717, and published by Martene in his second Voyage Litteraire. The writer says, " Le Livre aux Evangiles que je vis dans l'Abbaye de Saint Emeram, est encore une rare et très riche antiquité, c'est un don de l'Empereur Henry IV. On m'a dit que Maximilien, grand-père du Duc de Baviere d'à présent, ne sçavoit assez l'admirer, et qu'il en avoit offert sa ville de Straubingen avec ses dépendances ; mais les bons moines, persuadez que ce Duc les leur reprendroit ensuite, quand il voudroit, trouverent convenable de refuser un si bel offre."—p. 177.

[3] Conc. iv. 1416.

began (having been raised to the pontificate in the year 795), gave to one church "Evangelium ex auro mundissimo cum gemmis ornatum pensans libras...;"[4] and to another (as I have already stated) a copy which seems to have been still more splendid.[5]

When the abbot Angilbert restored the Abbey of St. Riquier, in A.D. 814, he gave to it (beside two hundred other books) a copy of the Gospel, written in letters of gold, with silver plates, marvellously adorned with gold and precious stones.[6]

Ansegisus, who became Abbot of Fontenelle in A.D. 823, ordered the four Gospels to be written with gold, on purple vellum, in the Roman letter; and lived to see the Gospels of St. Matthew, St. Luke, and St. John completed.[7]

At the translation of the remains of St. Sebastian and St. Gregory to the monastery of St. Medard, at Soissons, in A.D. 826, Lewis the Debonnaire gave several rich presents; and, among others, a copy of the Gospels, written in letters of gold, and bound in plates of the same metal, of the utmost purity.[8]

Hincmar, who became archbishop of Rheims in the year 845, caused a Gospel to be written for his church in letters of gold and silver, and bound in gold, adorned with gems;[9] and another, specially for the crypt to which the remains of St. Remigius were translated, he bound in the same way (parietibus aureis gemmarumque nitore distinctis munivit).[1]

---

[4] Ib. vii. 1083.   [5] See No. V. p. 97.

[6] Mab. Act. Sanct. O. B. tom. v. p. 110.

[7] Mab. ibid. tom. vi. p. 597.

[8] Ibid. viii. 388.

[9] Flodoardi Hist. Remen. l. iii. c. v. ap. Sirmondi Op. tom. iv. p. 113.

[1] Ib. c. ix. p. 119.

Leo IV., who became pope two years later, gave four catholic books (quatuor catholicos libros) to the church of the Virgin Mary, thirty miles from Rome (unum Evangeliorum, alium Regnorum, Psalmorum, atque Sermonum),[2] of which I do not find that they were peculiarly ornamented; but he gave to another church a copy bound in silver plates—"codex Evangeliorum cum tabulis argenteis." [3]

Of the splendid donations of his successor, Benedict III., who became pope in A.D. 855, I have already spoken; [4] and I may here add that during his time the Emperor Michael sent as a present to St. Peter's (by the hand of the monk Lazarus, "pictoriæ artis nimie eruditi") a Gospel, of most pure gold, with divers precious stones. [5]

Everhard, Count of Friuli, whose will of the year 861 has been already mentioned, beside his Bible, bequeathed to his children a considerable number of other books, and among them a Gospel bound in gold—another in ivory—another in silver—another, which is not particularly described. [6]

A charter of William, Abbot of Dijon, relating to the monastery of Frutari, in Piedmont (and probably of the year 1014), mentions, among the presents made to the monks of Dijon, to reconcile them to the withdrawment of the recent foundation from dependence on them, "textum unum auro, gemmis et lapidibus mire ornatum." [7]

Just in the same year we find the Emperor Henry II., who has been already mentioned in connection with Meinwerc, Bishop of Paderborn, making a similar

---

[2] Conc. tom. viii. p. 22.　　[3] Ib. p. 27.
[4] No. V. p. 97.　　[5] Conc. viii. 231.　　[6] II. Dach. Sp. 877.
[7] Mab. A. S. viii. 308, et Ann. Benn. an. 1003, xxxiv.

donation to the church of Mersburg;[8] and a few years afterwards (in 1022), on occasion of his recovery from illness, at the Monastery of Monte Casino, he present- ed to it a copy of the Gospels, covered on one side with the most pure gold, and most precious gems, written in uncial characters, and illuminated with gold.[9] Returning the same year into Germany, he had an interview with Robert, King of France, on the banks of the Meuse, the common boundary of their domin- ions; but of all the rich presents offered by that king —presents of gold, and silver, and jewels, beside a hundred horses, completely and sumptuously equipped, and each bearing a knight's armour—the emperor accepted only a copy of the Gospels, bound in gold and precious stones, and a reliquary of corresponding workmanship, containing (or supposed to contain) a tooth of St. Vincent, for himself, and a pair of gold ear-rings for the empress.[1]

The biographer, and almost contemporary, of Anse- gisus (who was abbot of St. Riquier, near Abbeville, and died in 1045), informs us that he contributed greatly to the enlargement of the library, and specifies—

"Librum Evangelii, Sancti vitamque Richari
Ipsius studio mero argento decoravit.
Est et Episto-liber-larum, atque Evangeliorum,
Ipsius argento quem industria nempe paravit."[2]

Desiderius, who became abbot of Monte Casino in the year 1058 (and who was afterwards Pope Victor III.), provided his monastery with many costly books;[3]

---

[8] Ditmar. ap. i. Leib. 399.   [9] Mab. A. S. viii. 400.
[1] Glab. Rod. ap. Baron. an. 1023, iii.
[2] Mab. A. S. viii. 446.
[3] Librum quoque *Epistolarum* ad missam describi faciens, tabulis aurea una, altera vero argentea, decoravit. Codicem etiam Regulæ B. Bene-

and the Empress Agnes, who came, as Leo Marsicanus says, like another Queen of Sheba, from the remote parts of Germany, to behold another Solomon, and another temple, made many rich gifts (dona magnifica) to the church, and, among the rest, a copy of the Gospels, with one side (or, if I may so speak, one board) of cast silver, with chased or embossed work, very beautifully gilt. [4]

Paul, who became abbot of St. Alban's in the year 1077, gave to that church "duos Textus auro et argento et gemmis ornatos." [5]

In the same year a charter of Hugh, Duke of Burgundy, giving the church of Avalon to the monastery of Clugny (and containing a "descriptio ornamenti ipsius ecclesiæ"), mentions three copies of the Gospels, which, I presume, formed a part of the 115 books belonging to it; "Textus unus aureus, et unus argenteus, aliusque dimidius." [6]

In a charter of A.D. 1101, concerning the church at Beze, we find a Textum Evangelii, "coopertum de argento," used in the manner already repeatedly referred to, in the conveyance of property. [7]

The author of the history of the monastery of St.

---

dicti pulcro nimis opere deintus comtum, a foris argento vestivit; similiter fecit et de Sacramentoriis altariis uno et altero, et duobus nihilominus *Evangeliis* et *Epistolario* un." *Leo Mar. ap. Mab.* A. S. ix. 594. After this we read, "Non solum autem in ædificiis, verum etiam in libris describendis operam Desiderius dare permaximam studuit;" and in a very respectable catalogue of these books we find, "Evangelium majorem auro et lapidibus pretiosis ornatam, in quo has *reliquias* posuit : de ligno Domini et de vestimentis Sancti Joannis Evangelistæ."— *Ibid.*, p. 608.

[4] Chron. Cas. Lib. iii. c. xxx. p. 609, and Mab. A. S. ix. 602.

[5] M. Paris, Vit. S. Alb. Abb. tom. i. p. 51.

[6] Dach. Spic. iii. 412.

[7] Chron. Bes. ap. Dach. Spic. ii. 436.

Hubert-en-Ardennes (who wrote in 1106) tells us that in his time there was remaining in the monastery a very fine copy of the Gospels, adorned with gold and gems.[8]

Ralph, Bishop of Rochester, in 1114, gave a "textum pulchre deauratum" to his church;[9] but I do not feel certain that in this case the word "textus" means, as it generally does when it stands alone (as it obviously does in the cases hitherto mentioned), a copy of one or more of the Gospels.

There can, however, be no doubt as to the gift of Walter, a successor in that see, who became bishop in 1148, and gave "textum Evangeliorum aureum."[1]

Perhaps the instances which I have given are more than enough to induce a suspicion that copies of the Gospels, and even such as were of a splendid and costly description, were not unfrequently to be met with even in the Dark Ages; and yet they are not the notices which most strongly and obviously lead to such an opinion. Some may even consider the fact that a book was given to a church, or a monastery, as implying that it was not already possessed; and I will therefore add one or two instances, which show that churches not uncommonly (I believe I might say all churches that were at all

---

[8] "Superest optimus sanctorum Evangeliorum textus auro gemmisque paratus; superest psalterium auro scriptum per denos psalmos capitalibus litteris distinctum." IV. *M. & D.* 919. Martene adds, in a note on the word "psalterium,"—"Hactenus servatur in Andaginensi monasterio pretiosissimum psalterium auro elegantissime exaratum, non a Ludovico Pio, ut credit auctor, sed a Lothario ipsius filio donatum, ut probant versus qui initio codicis reperiuntur." The verses, and a full account of this psalter, with a copy of the portrait of Lothaire contained in it, he has given in his second Voyage Litteraire, p. 137.

[9] Ang. Sac. i. 342.

[1] Ibid. 345.

respectably endowed and appointed) had more than one such book.

We are not, I apprehend, to suppose that the monastery of Glastonbury had no copy of the Gospels when Brethwold (who had been a monk there, and became bishop of Salisbury perhaps in A.D. 1006) sent them two. [2]

Olbert, already mentioned (p. 227), as abbot of Gembloux until A.D. 1048, gave to his monastery (beside the Bible which is there mentioned) one gold and three silver copies of the Gospels, and one silver copy of the Epistles. [3]

Among the furniture of his chapel, bequeathed by King Robert (whose present to the emperor Henry has been noticed at p. 238) to the church of St. Anian, at Orleans, were " deux livres d'Evangiles, garnis d'or, deux d'argent, deux autres petits." [4]

John, Bishop of Bath in 1160, implied a bequest of more than one copy to the Abbey church when he left to the blessed apostle St. Peter, and to his servants the monks (inter alia), all that he had collected "in ornamentis ecclesiasticis," or, as he proceeded to specify, "in crucibus, in *textibus*, in calicibus," &c. [5] I quote this instance because the reader will observe that these costly books were considered as a part of the treasure of the church, rather than merely as books ; and, indeed, the bishop bequeathed them as a distinct legacy from his whole library (plenarium armarium meum), which he also gave to the church.

For this reason, and not for this only, I will also

---

[2] Guil. Malm. ap. Gale, tom. iii. 325.
[3] Mab. A. S. viii. 530.
[4] Fleury, t. xii. p. 491.
[5] Dugd. Mon. i. 186.

R

mention another case, although—perhaps I should say
because—it is nearly a century more modern than the
period with which we are engaged. At a visitation of
the treasury of St. Paul's, in the year 1295, by Ralph
de Baudoke, or Baldock, the Dean (afterwards bishop
of London), it appears that there were found twelve
copies of the Gospels, all adorned with silver, some
with gilding, pearls and gems; and another, which
presents an unusual feature—"Textus ligneus desuper
ornatus platis argenteis deauratis cum subtili triphorio
in superiori limbo continens xi capsas *cum reliquiis*
ibidem descriptis." [6] I call the decoration of the Gospels
with relics an unusual feature, because, though I have
not intentionally suppressed it, it has appeared in only
one of the cases already mentioned; and, common as
the custom might afterwards be, I do not believe that
it was so (if indeed it could be said to exist as a
custom at all) before the thirteenth century. I know
of only one other exception, which belongs to the
twelfth century, and will be noticed presently.

There is another circumstance which throws some
light on this point. It may be supposed that great
care was taken of these books; and in fact they were
frequently kept in cases as valuable, in respect of
ornament, as themselves. Often, indeed, I apprehend,
the case was the most valuable of the two, and is
mentioned among the treasure of the church when the
book which it contained is not noticed because there

---

[6] Dugd. Monast. iii. 309, 324. Beside the parts of the Scriptures
mentioned above, there were six Epistolaria, four Evangelistaria, two
Bibles (one "de bona litera antiqua," and the other "in duobus voluminibus nova peroptimæ literæ"), a glossed copy of the Epistles of St.
Paul, the same of the Gospels of St. Luke and St. John, two copies
of St. Matthew and St. Mark, with the commentary of Thomas Aquinas,
and the twelve prophets, glossed.

was nothing uncommon about it, and no particular
circumstance as to its writer or donor which was
thought worthy of record. From some of the notices,
however, of these cases or coverings, [7] we get farther
ground for supposing that there were not unfrequently
a good many copies of the Gospels in a church or
monastery. For instance, in the St. Riquier return,
already more than once referred to, beside the Bibles
which I have noticed, and beside three other copies
of the Gospels and five lectionaries containing the
Epistles and Gospels, we find, "Evangelium auro
Scriptum unum, cum capsa argentea gemmis et lapidibus
fabricata. *Aliæ capsæ* evangeliorum duæ ex auro et
argento paratæ." [8] A passage, too, in Ado's Chronicle,
given by Du Cange, seems to imply that the place to
which it refers had several copies, " *Viginti capsas*
evangeliorum ex auro purissimo, gemmario opere

---

[7] *Capsæ,* or *coopertoria*—for it is not necessary to speak of the
camisiæ (chemises) *librorum,* which I suppose to have been only wash-
able covers to keep the books clean,—or *thecæ,* or, as I have only
once found the word used, *bibliothecæ.* At the dedication of Ripon
church, Archbishop Wilfred (who lived till 711)

"—— quatuor auro
Scribi Evangelii præcepit in ordine libros,
Ac *thecam* e rutilo his condignam condidit auro."
(Godwin de Præs, 654.)

Or, as the prose historian who wrote soon afterwards informs us, it
was a sort of miracle such as had not been heard of before their times,
being written with the purest gold on purple vellum, and contained
in a superb case,—"necnon et *bibliothecam* librorum eorum omnem de
auro purissimo, et gemmis pretiosissimis fabrefactam, compaginare inclu-
sores gemmarum præcepit."—Edd. Steph. ap. Gale, Scr. XV., p. 60.
Another name was *cavea,* as the reader may see in Du Cange, who
quotes from Eckhardus, junior (who wrote about the year 1040), " fit
de auro Petri *cavea* Evangelii," &c.

[8] Chron. Cent. ap. Dach. Spic. ii. 310.

cælatas;" [9] and William of Malmesbury, in the account which he gives of the chapel which King Ina made at Glastonbury, tells us that twenty pounds and sixty marks of gold were used in making the "Coopertoria Librorum Evangelii." [1] Two objections which may be made to the evidence arising from these *capsæ*, though they do not seem to me to be of any weight, it may be fair to mention;—first, we are not certain that the owners always had quite as many books as they had cases for holding them; and, secondly, as these *capsæ* were very costly and ornamental, those who wrote the history of their monasteries might be tempted to pretend that they had more than they really possessed. If, however, these same monkish chroniclers, in describing their premises, had told us that the abbot's stable contained twelve or twenty stalls, we should be apt to infer, that though some stalls might be empty, or the number of the whole exaggerated, it was nevertheless no very uncommon thing for an abbot to be pretty well furnished with horses; and some such inference, confirmed as it is by direct evidence, I think we may fairlay draw with regard to books.

Hitherto I have only spoken of those costly and precious volumes which, as I have already remarked, were considered as belonging to the treasury, rather than to the library, of the church. They were, I apprehend, for the most part, brought out only on festivals, the church being provided with others for daily use. Thus Berward, who became bishop of Hildesheim in the year 993, and who was (as we learn from his fond old schoolmaster and biographer, Tangmar) a man skilful in the arts—if I may use such a word in speaking of such a period,—"fecit et ad solemnem

---

[9] In v. *Capsæ.*   [1] Ap. Gale, Scr. XV. 311.

processionem in præcipuis festis, Evangelia auro et
gemmis clarissima;"[2] and Martin, the monk of Moutier-
neuf, at Poitiers, tells us, that on the anniversary of
their founder (Count Geoffry or William, who died in
1086), they used to perform mass in much the same
way as on festivals; and he adds, "nec aureus textus
deest."[3] Indeed, I need not say that such a style of
binding could not have been adopted for books in
general, or books in common use. To have bestowed
such pains and expense on books for private use, or
for any use but that of the church, would have been
inconsistent, perhaps, with the ideas of some strict
ascetics, and at any rate it could never have become
general.[4] Others, perhaps, beside Godehard (the successor of Berward just mentioned, in the see of Hildesheim), had a fancy to adorn their books (though I
apprehend that here we must understand service-books)
with small stones of white, or black, or red, or varie-
gated hues, cut and polished after the manner of gems.

---

[2] Leib. Scr. Brun. i. 445.   Mab. A. S. viii. 184.

[3] Hist. Mon. Novi. ap. Mart. iii. 1218.

[4] Thus the Abbot Esaias, in his Præcepta, "ad fratres qui cum ipso
vivebant," and in that part which is particularly addressed "ad fratres
juniores," says, "Si librum *tibi* ipse compegeris, in eo ne elabores
exornando. Est enim vitium puerile." By the way, in that same section
he goes on to give directions as to the mode of receiving strangers,
among which he says, "et posteaquam sederit, quomodo se habeat,
quære, et nihil amplius, sed libellum ei aliquem legendum præbe;"
and afterwards "Si peregre proficiscens diverteris apud aliquem, et ille
domo egrediatur, et te solum relinquat, oculos tuos ne sustuleris, ut
quæ ibi sunt, vasa, et supellectilem aspicias. Fenestram, aut arcam, aut
librum aperias, cave."—*Bib. Pat.* tom. iii. c. 887. *Ed.* 1575. I do not
pretend to decide when these precepts were written, which have perhaps
nothing to do with the period, or the part of the world, to which my
remarks are particularly directed; but it must have been, I think, at
some time and place where books were not extremely rare things, and
where one might expect to find them lying about a room.

He used to set the children, and those paupers who were not fit for other work, to collect such pebbles; and a crippled servant of the monastery, who was glad to do what little he could, was particularly useful in that matter; [5] but generally, I apprehend, the binding of books was in parchment or plain leather.

"About the year 790," says Warton, "Charlemagne granted an unlimited right of hunting to the abbot and monks of Sithiu for making their gloves and girdles of the skins of the deer they killed, and covers for their books. We may imagine that these religious were more fond of hunting than reading. It is certain that they were obliged to hunt before they could read, and at least it is probable that under these circumstances they did not manufacture many volumes." [6] This passage I have read over many times, and I really cannot make any sense of it. *Why* should Charlemagne's grant induce such suppositions? *Why* are we to imagine that these monks loved hunting better than reading? *Why* must they hunt before they could read? *Why* is it probable that they did not "manufacture" (a strange term for binding a book, and one which

---

[5] "Quicquid tamen a pueris fieri vidit, quod vel sedendo vel proreptando agere potuit; in hoc se voluntaria utilitate studiosus exercuit, nec prorsus aliquod tempus, nisi cum somnum vel cibum caperet, transire sibi patiebatur, quin semper in aliquo utilis esse videretur. Consuetudo namque dilecto nostro pontifici fuit ut puerulos, vel etiam pauperes validiores sæpius per plateas, vel per defossas petrarum foveas ageret, qui sibi lapillos minutos quosdam nivei coloris, vel nigri, vel rubri interdum, vel varii, deferrent: quos ipse elimatos, et politos variaque collisione vel confricatione in similitudine pretiosorum lapidum redactos, aut in altaribus, aut libris, aut in capsis honeste collocavit. In quo nimirum opere, prædictus ille pauper se privatim exercuit, et cæterorum industriam utiliter prævenit, et pro curiositate tali episcopo penitus complacuit." *Vita Godehardi ap. Leib. Scr. Brun.* i. 500.

[6] Dissert. ii. prefixed to his Hist. of Poetry.

looks as if Warton supposed that they were to write
on buck-skin) "many volumes under *these circumstances*," the chief circumstances being (according to his
account) an "unlimited" right to hunt for leather, granted
by the sovereign of such extensive dominions? I cannot
help suspecting that there may be a meaning in the
passage which I am not acute enough to perceive,
for to me the grant appears rather to intimate that
the monks who obtained such a privilege must have
done (or, to say the least, must have been supposed
to do) a good deal in the way of book-binding.

But here, as in too many of the facetious anecdotes
of the dark ages, when we turn out the reference we
find that the story is false, not only as to the spirit,
but the letter. The charter stands, indeed, as Warton
tells us, "Mab. de Re Dipl. 611," but as soon as we
look at it, the "unlimited right" becomes sadly circumscribed; and as to the jolly abbot and his sporting
monks, "paf—all should be gone," like "de great
Peolphan" and his spectre train. The limitation of the
grant to the woods belonging to the monastery is
express, and is even reduced by the exception of such
royal forests as were set apart for the emperor's diver-
sion; and the fun of the religious hunt is entirely
spoiled by the fact that the permission is not for the
monks, but for the *servants*, of the monastery, to hunt
for the useful purposes specified in the charter.[7] That

---

[7] "Concessimus Autlando abbati et monachis ex monasterio Sithiu . . . .
ut ex nostra indulgentia *in eorum proprias silvas* licentiam haberent
eorum homines venationem exercere, unde *fratres* consolationem habere
possint, tam ad volumina librorum tegenda, quamque et manicias et ad
zonas faciendas, *salvas forestes nostras*, quas ad opus nostrum constitutas
habemus." The emperor then goes on to charge all his subjects, to
whom the charter is addressed (omnium fidelium nostrorum magnitudini),
that they should not presume to oppose the exercise of this privilege

charter, as far as I see, contains nothing which should lead us to suppose that the monks of Sithiu ever hunted at all, or that "these religious" were inferior to the modern priest who has held them up to scorn, either in the knowledge or the practice of that which their character and station required.

There is however another point relating to these costly books which must not be omitted. Their extraordinary value would of course lead to their being taken great care of—but then it would also render them peculiarly liable to destruction. It is probable that such books were among the "insignia ornamenta" of the church of St. Benignus at Dijon, when they were stolen on one of the anniversaries of the patron saint's day in the eleventh century; [8] and the soldiers who plundered Nigel, Bishop of Ely, in the time of King Stephen, thought it worth while to carry off a

---

by the abbot, his successors, and their men (abbate, aut successoribus suis, seu hominibus eorum—but nothing of the monks), "nisi liceat *eorum hominibus* ut supra diximus ex nostra indulgentia in eorum *proprias silvas* venationem exercere." Indeed, who that knew anything of Charlemagne or his laws could expect to find him patronizing a company of mere sporting monks? Let me give two short instances from his Capitularies, one earlier, and the other more recent, than the charter in question :—"Omnibus servis Dei venationes et silvaticas vagationes cum canibus, et ut accipitres et falcones non habeant, interdicimus." This is only a repetition of previous enactments by his predecessors, made probably quite at the beginning of his reign. In 802 we find "Ut episcopi, abbates, presbyteri, diaconi, nullusque ex omni clero canes ad venandum, aut acceptores, falcones, seu sparvarios habere præsumant; sed pleniter se unusquisque in ordine suo canonice vel regulariter custodiant. Qui autem præsumpserit, sciat unusquisque honorem suum perdere. Cæteri vero tale exinde damnum patiantur ut reliqui metum habeant talia sibi usurpare."—*Capit. edit. Baluz.* tom. i. 191, 369.

[8] "Latronum fraude in ipsius sancti festivitate, occisis custodibus furto fuerunt asportata."—*Mab.* A. S. viii. 301.

copy of the Gospels adorned with relics.[9] But beside downright and forcible robbery, or even fraudulent abstraction, there were many reasons why these books were liable to be destroyed. Though it does not enter into the design of this paper to refer to the present state, or even the present existence, of such manuscripts (and, indeed, I purposely avoid speaking of some, merely because they are known to be now in existence, and therefore belong to another part of the subject), yet as I have mentioned the Bible presented by Lewis the Debonnaire in the year 826, I may here add that Mabillon tells us that it was still in existence, with *silver* plates, which had been supplied by the Abbot Ingrannus in the year 1168, to replace the original *golden* ones which had somehow disappeared.

Of course, various things—charity and need, as well as cupidity,—were likely to produce what was then termed *excrustation*, and to risk, if not almost to ensure, the destruction of the manuscript itself. Charity,—as when all the valuables (omne ornamentum in auro et argento) belonging to the church of St. Benignus of Dijon were sacrificed to provide relief for the poor in the famine of A.D. 1001;[1] or when, five years afterwards, Odilo, Abbot of Clugni, having exhausted all other sources, was obliged to apply the sacred vessels to the same object.[2] Need,—as when, in order to meet the heavy tax laid by William Rufus to raise money for the purchase of Normandy, Godfrey, Abbot of Malmesbury (*pessimorum usus consilio, quos nominare possem, si peccantium societas crimen alleviare posset*

---

[9] Ang. Sac. i. 622.

[1] Mab. A. S. tom. viii. p. 300.

[2] "Exhaustis in egentium usus horreis et ærariis, sacra etiam vasa confregerit." — Mab. Ann. an. 1006, tom. iv. 170.

magistri, says William the historian), stripped no less than *twelve* copies of the Gospels; [3] or when William de Longchamp, who became bishop of Ely in the year 1190, contributed one hundred and sixty marks towards the redemption of King Richard, and, to raise the money, pawned *thirteen* copies of the Gospels, including one of great value which had belonged to King Edgar. [4]

That books thus pawned did not always find their way back may be imagined; and indeed we are told that three books, adorned with gold and silver and precious stones, were lost to the Abbey of Laurisheim about the year 1130, owing to their advocate, Bertolf, having been allowed by the abbot, Diemo, to raise money upon them. Whether these copies of the Gospels ever ran a risk of having the inside as well as the outside falsified, and a false reading or gem substituted for a true one, I do not know; but it is certain that a "textus aureus" belonging to the church of Ely was once pledged to the Jews of Cambridge. This, however, belongs rather to the dangers arising from cupidity, if we may trust Richard of Ely, who mentions the circumstance in his long list of the depredations committed by Nigel, already mentioned. [5] This source of

---

[3] Die uno xii. textus Evangeliorum, viii. cruces, viii. scrinia argento et auro nudata et excrustata sunt."—*Vita Aldh. ap. Ang. Sac.* ii. 44.

[4] Ang. Sac. i. 633.

[5] " Item pro parvo *textu aureo* et pro ansa argentea dedit v. marcas cuidam de Thetford; et præterea uno anno abstulit de Sacristaria xxiv. marcas et vi. solidos. Antea vero prædictam *crucem* et *textum* similiter pro nummis transposuerat Judæis apud Cantebrigge, quæ gloriosus rex sæpe dictus Edgardus ob signum libertatis suæ et munificentiæ ibi donavit : et ne tanto muniminis titulo frustrarentur, Monachi dederunt cc. marcas per manus Willelmi prioris."—*Hist. Elien.* ap. Ang. Sac. i. 625. As to the importance of the Jews of Cambridge a few years before this time, see Fuller's History of the University, p. 4, § 11, 12;

danger is indeed obvious enough; and I will here give
only one other instance, which I am unwilling to omit
because it refers to a considerable number of copies.
The historian who relates the destruction of Hide Abbey,
near Winchester, tells us that Henry, who was bishop
of that see from A.D. 1129 to 1174, got the monastery
into his hands. After it had been burned in the year
1141, the monks got out of the ashes sixty pounds of
silver, and fifteen pounds of gold, and various other
things, which they brought to the bishop, who subsequently committed the care of the monastery to
Hugo Schorchevylene, a monk of Clugni, whom he
made abbot. This monk having, by the bishop's direction, dispersed thirty out of the forty monks, laid hands
on the treasures of the church, and stripped *ten* copies
of the Gospels. [6]

It may probably be said, that too many of those
who gave and received these costly volumes thought
more of the outside than the inside, and even forgot
that the rich cover enclosed the more precious Word
of God;—it may have been so, though I hope not

---

but in his quotation from Peter of Blois he omits his testimony that a
principal object of Gislebert's preaching was the refutation of Judaism;
and that, in fact, several Jews were converted by it. „Verbum Dei ad
populum prædicans . . . contra Judaicum errorem maxime disputabat
. . . cumque nonnulli increduli et adhuc Judaica perfidia cæcati ad ejus
verba in sinum matris ecclesiæ, relicto penitus suo pristino errore,
compuncti accurrerunt," &c.— *Pet. Bles. ap. Rer. Ang. Scr.* tom. i. p. 114.

[6] "Manum in sanctuarium Domini extendens, cruces quinque, scrinia
decem, *textus totidem* auro argento gemmisque pretiosis ornatos, . . .
excrustavit."— *Dug. Mon.* i. 210. One cannot suppose that this sort of
spoliation was known to the bishop, whose taste for costly ornament
was so fully proved. In particular, Giraldus Cambrensis tells us that
"Cathedralem ecclesiam suam palliis purpereis et olosericis cortinis et
aulæis preciosissimis, *textis*, philateriis, crucibus aureis . . . usque ad
regum invidiam exornavit."— *Ang. Sac.* tom. ii. p. 421.

always,—but I beg the reader to take care that he
does not fall into much the same error. I hope he
will not forget that, whether in sackcloth and ashes,
or in gold and silver, each of the books which I
have here spoken of was the Gospel of Christ. Should
he think that, although tiresome for their sameness,
these instances are not in fact very numerous, I
would repeat that they are only such as have occurred
to me, in circumstances not the most favourable
for research; and I must add, that while I have
met with these notices of the Scriptures, and with
many others which I hope to bring forward in this
argument, I have *not* found anything about the arts
and engines of hostility, the blind hatred of half-
barbarian kings, the fanatical fury of their subjects,
or the reckless antipathy of the popes. I do not
recollect any instance in which it is recorded that
the Scriptures, or any part of them, were treated with
indignity, or with less then profound respect. I know
of no case in which they were intentionally defaced
or destroyed (except, as I have just stated, for their
rich covers), though I have met with, and hope to
produce several instances, in some of which they were
the only, and in others almost the only, books which
were preserved through the revolutions of the monasteries to which they belonged, and all the ravages of
fire, pillage, carelessness, or whatever else had swept
away all the others. I know (and in saying this I do
not mean anything but to profess my ignorance, for
did I suppress such knowledge I might well be charged
with gross dishonesty) of nothing which should lead
me to suppose that any human craft or power was
exercised to prevent the reading, the multiplication,
the diffusion of the Word of God. When, therefore,
after having written almost all the foregoing pages, a

periodical work fell into my hands containing the passage which stands at the head of this paper, I could not resist the temptation to borrow it as a motto. In so using it I mean no offence to the gentleman from whose tercentenary sermon it purports to be an extract, but only to call the attention of the public to the different views which are held, and the different statements which are made, on a very interesting subject, in the hope that truth may be thereby elicited.

Whether, however, the Scriptures were exposed to this treatment in the dark ages, or not, I hope to show as the next step in the argument that there are still in existence many copies which belonged to that period; and in the meantime to draw the reader's attention to some circumstances which, to my own mind, render it a matter of astonishment that we possess so many.

No. XIV.

"Still I am not satisfied; and the stubborn fact of *scarcity* inclines me to suspect that the pens of the monks were less constantly employed than many would induce us to believe."—BERINGTON.

WITHOUT entering into any question here as to what may, or may not, be properly called *scarcity*, in regard to ancient manuscripts, let us assume that its existence is a stubborn and undeniable fact; yet that fact may, perhaps, admit of some explanation. Suppose there are but few manuscripts in existence, it is no proof that but few were written; and, indeed, I must say, that from what I have been able to learn respecting the real number, of which this surviving *scarcity* consists, and the circumstances under which they have been preserved, I can only wonder that we have so many— or, I am almost tempted to say, that we have any— manuscripts seven or eight hundred years old. It is, however, quite clear, that if we would form any opinion of the state of literature, or means of knowledge, in the Dark Ages, we must, in some degree, enter into this question, and cannot pass it over with a slight allusion to the ravages of time. It is necessary to our design; and I am inclined to hope, that a short and superficial sketch, such as the nature of these essays admits, may not be altogether uninteresting. As a great part of my illustrations will be drawn from the reports of some literary travellers, I will first give some notice of them, in order that I may hereafter refer to them with more brevity, and that such of my readers as are not acquainted with the books may understand my references.

Between the 16th of April and the 10th of June,

1682, Dom Mabillon, accompanied by his brother Benedictine, Michael Germanus, made a journey through Melun, Sens, Auxerre, Dijon, Verdun, Chalons sur Saone, and Autun, to Lyons, and returned by way of Moulins. In the course of this excursion they visited Citeaux, Clugni, and many other monasteries, and overhauled their manuscripts; the object of their journey being to examine, or to search for, some documents relating to the royal family. How far this was openly avowed, and whether it was known even to the younger of the two travellers, I cannot tell; but Mabillon's acknowledged supremacy, in all such matters, naturally pointed him out to the minister Colbert as the fittest person to be sent on such an errand. That he executed it with skill and fidelity, and, at the same time, took an opportunity of doing a little business in his own way, of antiquarian research, nobody will doubt. Two years after, he drew up an account of his tour; and it was subsequently printed under the title of "*Iter Burgundicum.*" [1]

The next year, they went, by the same order, through part of Germany, taking the route of Basil, Zurich, Augsburg, Munich, &c. They set out on the 30th of June, and appear to have returned in October. Mabillon prefixed an account of this journey to his "Vetera Analecta," under the title of "*Iter Germanicum.*" [2]

In the year 1685, at the suggestion of Le Tellier, Archbishop of Rheims—the brother of the minister who had succeeded Colbert, and the owner of 50,000 volumes—Mabillon was sent, at the royal cost, to investigate the libraries of Italy, and to procure books for the king's library. He set out, with the same companion as before, on the 1st of April, and returned

---

[1] It will be referred to as, It. Burg.   [2] It. Germ.

in the June of the following year. The royal library was enriched by the addition of 3,000 volumes; and Mabillon published an account of the journey, in the first volume of his "Museum Italicum," under the title of "*Iter Italicum.*"[3]

Again this father set out in the year 1696, accompanied by another Benedictine—the well-known Ruinart; and, between the 20th of August and the 10th of November, they travelled through most of Alsace and Lorraine, conducting themselves, in respect of all libraries which they could meet with, in the way which might be expected from them. Ruinart drew up an account of the journey, which he entitled, "*Iter Litterarium in Alsatiam et Lotharingiam.*"[4]

When Father Montfaucon had completed the Benedictine edition of "Athanasius," he became convinced that the Greek fathers could not be properly edited without first ransacking the libraries of Italy for manuscripts; and therefore (permissu superiorum) he and Father Paul Brioys sett off for that purpose on the 18th of May, 1698, and did not return until the 11th of June, 1701. In the course of the next year he published his "*Diarium Italicum;*"[5] which was, I believe, the year after, translated into English.

The Benedictines of St. Maur—that learned body, to which all the travellers hitherto mentioned belonged —having determined to undertake a new edition of the "Gallia Christiana." resolved to send one of their number to collect what materials he could, for correction and addition, from the various libraries, churches, and monasteries of France. "La resolution," says Dom Edmund Martene, "en fut prise à Marmoutier au chapitre general de 1708, et comme j'étois sur les lieux,

---

[3] J^t. Ital.   [4] It. Alsat.   [5] Diar. It.

et qu'on sçavoit que Dieu m'avoit donné quelque petit talent pour lire les anciennes écritures, je fus un des premiers sur lesquels on jetta les yeux." Nothing could be more natural, as it respects the Chapter; and, perhaps, as to Martene, though he might sincerely feel all that he says of the vastness of the undertaking, nothing more agreeable. He set out accordingly on the 11th of June, and travelled until the 23rd of December, when he got back into winter quarters at Marmoutier, just in time to avoid being exposed to a more inclement season than any which the oldest persons living could remember. Being informed that he must set out again as soon as Easter was past, he begged to have a companion. This request being granted, he chose Dom Ursin Durand, and they set out together on the 4th of April. In short—for I am not writing the history of their travels—that year, and the four which succeeded (except when they were in winter quarters), were spent in making various circuits, in the course of which they visited a great part of France; the whole time, from Martene's first setting out to their joint return on the 16th of Nov., 1713, being five years and a half; or, so far as travelling was practicable, we may perhaps more correctly say, six years. Martene tells us, that they visited about a hundred cathedrals, and at least eight hundred abbeys; in which they failed not to examine whatever manuscripts they could find. In so doing, they not only fulfilled their commission, as it regarded the "Gallia Christiana," but met with a vast quantity of unpublished matter, of various sorts, which they gave to the world in the year 1717, in five folio volumes, under the title of " *Thesaurus Novus Anecdotorum ;*" and it is the work which (having explained myself in No. II. p. 37 *n.*) I have since frequently quoted, under the brief reference " *Mart.*"

S

In the same year that this large work was brought
out, Martene published an account of these six journeys,
in one volume quarto, entitled, "*Voyage Litteraire de
deux Religieux Benedictins de la Congregation de
Saint Maur;*" and it is to this which I now refer.[6]

Having published these collections of his journeys,
there was nothing, Dom Martene tells us, which he
less expected than to set out again on his travels:
yet so it was. A new edition of the ancient historians
of France was projected; and our two travellers were
requested to go and look for materials, to render it
as full and correct as possible. They accordingly set
out on the 30th of May, 1718, from the neighbourhood
of Paris; passed through Soissons, Rheims, Amiens,
Brussels, Liege, Aix-la-Chapelle, Dusseldorf, and penetrated as far into Germany as Paderborn—returned
by Cologne, Treves, Luxembourg—and got back in
January, 1719. By that time, the scheme of publishing
the early historians had been abandoned; but the travellers had accumulated a great quantity of curious
matter. Their former labours, and the published fruits
of them, had brought them invitations to ransack Germany and Spain; and though they could not accept
them, yet literary contributions poured in from those
quarters: much, also, that Mabillon had previously
collected, but not published, was thrown into the
common stock; and when the work came forth in
1724, the editors felt justified in calling the nine folio
volumes, "*Veterum Scriptorum et Monumentorum
historicorum, dogmaticorum, moralium, amplissima collectio.*" It is the work which I have quoted by the
reference "*M. & D.;*" but at present, our business is
with the single quarto volume in which Martene gave

---

[6] I. Voy. Lit.

an account of this journey. He published it under the
same title as the former; but, for the sake of distinction, I shall refer to it as his *second* literary tour. [7]

From these sources, it would be easy to show that
there are—or, at least, that there were, a little more
than a hundred years ago, which is quite sufficient
for the purposes of our inquiry—a good many ancient
manuscripts in existence; but for that fact there are
better proofs; and it is not my present object to prove
it. I quote these literary tourists, not to show that
manuscripts are numerous; but as incidentally furnishing
illustrations of the reasons why they are so few, and
why we may reasonably wonder that they are not
fewer still. It is grievous, for instance, to read such
notices as those which both Mabillon and Martene
have given of the state of things at Clugni. They
found the old catalogue (Mabillon says four, Martene
five or six, hundred years old), written on boards three
feet and a half long, and a foot and a half wide, and
covered with parchment—grandes tablettes, qu'on ferme
comme un livre—but of the books which it contained
(ex copiosissimo illo numero), they could find scarcely
one hundred. "On dit," says Martene, that the Huguenots carried them to Geneva; but be this at it may,
they were gone somehow. [8] Such was the case, also,
at Nonantula, where, of all its former riches (ex multis
quos celeberrima olim illa Abbatia habebat veteres
codices), Mabillon found but two manuscripts. [9] At
Rebais, Martene says, "Il y avoit sans doute autrefois
beaucoup de manuscrits dans l'abbaye, mais après des
révolutions si étranges, à peine y en reste-t-il quel-

---

[7] Il. Voy. Lit.

[8] It. Burg. 22; I. Voy. Lit. 227.

[9] It. Ital. 202.

ques-uns;" [1] and, at the Abbey of Beaupré, "Il y avoit
autrefois beaucoup de manuscrits; mais nous n'y en
vîmes que deux ou trois." [2]

But the fact that the manuscripts were gone in places
which had possessed considerable collections, will be
sufficiently proved incidentally; and my wish is rather
to call up to the reader's mind those causes which
may account for it, by a brief and superficial enume-
ration of them.

I.—I hardly know how to arrange these causes;
but, as it is of little consequence, I will first advert
to one of the most powerful, but one which, through
the distinguishing mercy of God, can hardly be appre-
ciated among us. No man living has known anything
like war in our country; and even in modern Europe
generally, the mode of warfare, the circumstances of
places taken by siege or by storm, as to their liability
to be burned or utterly destroyed, and the fact that
most books are now produced by hundreds or thousands
at a time, make so great a difference, that we can
scarcely institute a comparison. When, however, the
word WAR is mentioned, it will readily occur to the
reader, that among the desolations of fire and sword,
manuscripts did not escape destruction; but I wish to
raise a more particular idea of the dangers to which
they were exposed, and the destruction which they
actually suffered from certain wars during and since
the period with which we are engaged.

Think, in the first place, of the ravages of the Danes
and Normans in the ninth century; accounts of their
cruel desolations meet us at every turn in monastic
history. It may easily be conceived, that at all times,—
at least, all early times,—monasteries and churches

---

[1] I. Voy. Lit. P. ii. 73.   [2] Ib. 166.

were likely to form a nucleus, both from their being
the places most likely to contain spoil, and from their
being (next to those which were regularly fortified)
the places of greatest strength. Hence they became
peculiarly obnoxious to destruction, and particularly
to destruction by fire. As to the desolation of monasteries by these barbarians, however, the shortest way
to give some idea of them would be to copy the
article "Normanni," in the index of the third volume
of Mabillon's Annals, in which he gives a list of the
monasteries of his own order which were pillaged or
destroyed. Even that, however, would be too long to
insert here; but it begins, "Normanni, monasteria ab
eis incensa, eversa, direpta, —; Amausense, —; Aru-
lense, —; Arvernense S. Illidii, —; Autissiodorense
sancti Germani, —; Bardeneiense, —," &c.; and so the
index goes on through the alphabet, naming between
seventy and eighty Benedictine monasteries. It is impossible to doubt, and, indeed, in some cases it may
be proved, that there was a great loss of books. When,
for instance, the Abbey of Peterborough, in Northamp-
tonshire, was burned by the Danes in the year 870,
there was a large collection of books destroyed—sanctorum librorum *ingens bibliotheca*.[3] The language of
Ingulph may provoke a smile; and I assure the reader
that I do not want to make mountains of mole-hills,
or to catch at a word in any writer of the dark ages.
But I cannot consent to sneer away the statement to
nothing; and the rather because, though it may not
be easy to say what the abbot's idea of an "ingens
bibliotheca" was, yet, as will presently appear, he uses
no such expression in speaking of the library of seven
hundred volumes belonging to his own monastery

---

[3] Ingul. ap. Gale. V. Scr. p. 23.

which was burned in his own time—that is, in A. D. 1091.

Again, "when the black swarm of Hungarians first hung over Europe, about nine hundred years after the Christian æra, they were mistaken by fear and superstition for the Gog and Magog of the Scriptures,—the signs and forerunners of the end of the world." [4] There

---

[4] As it is a principal part of my design to draw attention to the misrepresentations of popular writers, I cannot help offering a remark or two on the note which Gibbon adds to his words which I here quote (Dec. and Fall, vol. v. p. 548):—"A bishop of Wurtzburg submitted this opinion to a reverend abbot; but *he* more gravely decided, that Gog and Magog were the spiritual persecutors of the church; since Gog signifies the roof, the pride of the Heresiarchs, and Magog what comes from the roof, the propagation of their sects. Yet these men once commanded the respect of mankind. Fleury, Hist. Eccles. tom. xi. p. 594, &c." I do not know why Gibbon says "a bishop of *Wurtzburg*," when his authority Fleury and D'Achery (Fleury's only authority) say *Verdun;* nor do I know how he learned that "*these* men" ever commanded the respect of mankind, for it seems as if there was some doubt who the bishop was—and as to the "reverend abbot," I believe no one pretends to guess who he was, or of what country. Could it be shown, therefore, that these two persons, whoever they might be, held a foolish opinion on a very obscure point, and maintained it by mere nonsense, yet that would not go far towards showing that the respect of mankind in the tenth century was misplaced, in so far as it was given to bishops and abbots. The document exists, however, merely as "Epistola cujusdam Abbatis Monasterii S. Germani ad V. Episcopum Virdunensem de Hungris." Neither the bishop nor the abbot seem to have given any credit to the notion of the Hungarians being Gog and Magog. In writing to the abbot, the bishop appears (for I believe his letter is not extant, and is only known by the answer) to have mentioned that the idea was current in his diocese, and to have desired him to look at the prophecy of Ezekiel, and let him know what he supposed to be its meaning. That the bishop did not express or imply any belief in the opinion, may be presumed from the terms in which the abbot (after saying that it was current in his part of the world also) sets it down as mere nonsense—frivolam esse et nihil verum habere—contrasted with the language of deep respect and affection in which he addresses the bishop. But farther—the sarcasm can scarcely

would be no use in detailing such particulars as are handed down to us; it is always the same horrid tale of barbarous outrage and destruction. I will here only refer to one case, partly out of respect to our friend the Abbot Bonus, who was brought up there, though it was before his time, in the days of Abbot Leopard, who presided there from the year 899 to 912; and principally because, as I have just said, Mabillon found only two manuscripts at Nonantula.[5] In the first or third year of Abbot Leopard, after a great battle on the river Brenta, in which many thousands of Christians were slain, the pagans advanced to Nonantula, killed the monks, burned the monastery with many books (codices multos concremavere), and ravaged the whole place.

---

be said to touch either of the parties; for the abbot gives the notion about Gog and Magog being the roof, and the heretics, &c., as the exposition of Jerome, without the expression of any opinion as to its correctness; unless indeed we may find something like apology in the language of the single sentence of comment which he bestows on it—"quæ quia a B. Hieronymo exposita sunt, et brevitas epistolæ plura de his dicere non permittit." He then goes on to inquire who the Hungarians really were, whence they came, and how it happened that they had not been mentioned in history, considering the extent of the Roman conquests and researches—had they been known under some other name? "sicut solent mutari urbium vel locorum seu fluminum nomina. Nam Tiberis quondam Albula dicebatur. Unde Virgilius ' amisit priscum Albula nomen;' et Italia prius Saturnia dicebatur; sicut idem poeta, 'et nomen posuit Saturnia tellus,'" &c. The letter, on the whole, is such as that I cannot but hope that the writer did command the respect of his age. Whether the wretched infidel who thought fit to sneer at him will command the respect of those who take the trouble to look out his authorities, they who see such a specimen as this may fairly question. Fleury refers to Dac. Spic. xii. 349; in the folio edition it is at tom. iii. 368.

[5] Of course I do not mean that they had none in the meantime. I hope under another head to show that they had many, of whose ate fire and sword were guiltless.

I pass over the irruption of the Saracens into Italy;
but, though it is lamentable to carry on the history
of desolation as the work of Christians, yet truth requires me to notice what may be called religious, or,
more properly and emphatically, irreligious, wars.
Happily the books which I have mentioned as furnishing illustrations relate chiefly to France, and we
will not at present look elsewhere. The Dean and
Chapter of *St. Theudere, near Vienne*, says Martene,
"nous comblerent d'honnêteté, et nous communiquerent,
de la meilleure grace du monde, ce qui leur reste
d'anciens monumens de la fureur des heretiques. Car
ces impies brûlerent en 1562, toutes les chartes."[6]
"Nous fûmes de là à *Tarbe,* où nous ne trouvâmes
pas grand travail, l'église cathédrale et tous les titres
ayant été brûlé par les Calvinistes, qui, dans toute le
Bearn et dans la Bigorre, ont laissé de funestes marques
de leur fureur."[7]—" Pour l'abbaye de *St. Jean* [at *Thoüars*],
elle est beaucoup plus ancienne, mais les ravages qu'y
ont fait les Calvinistes le siecle passé, en ont dissipé
la plûpart des monumens."[8] *Grimberg* I must reserve
for another purpose, and here only mention that it
had been destroyed and its library burned by the
Huguenots; and as I do not wish to repeat the same
cases, even for the illustration of different points, I
here only mention the neighbouring monastery of
Dilighen, of which Martene says—"Cette abbaye a
éprouvé le même sort que celle de *Grimberg.* C'est à
dire, qu'elle a été ruïnée par les heretiques. Aujourd'hui
on la rétablit, et on lui a rédonné son premier lustre;"
except, of course, in one respect, for he adds, "L'église
est fort jolie..... la bibliotheque assez bonne, mais
il n'y a que très-peu de manuscrits qui ne sont pas

---

[6] I. Voy. Lit. 252.   [7] I. Voy. Lit. P. ii. p. 13.   [8] Ib. p. 5.

de consequence." [9] At another monastery (near *Ferte sous Jouarre,* not far from Meaux), Ruinart says, "Sperabamus nos ibi in archiviis aliquid forte reperturos..... at monasterii chartas a Calvinianis penitus combustas fuisse nobis responsum..... supersunt in bibliotheca aliquot codices manuscripti;" and, after specifying a good many works, he adds, "quæ non sunt magni momenti." [1] Much the same injury had been suffered at the monastery of *Fleury,* where Mabillon found but a few relics of the vast collection which had been destroyed in the religious wars of the preceding century. [2] The effects of war were, indeed, too frequently visible; but not to tire the reader with repetition,—yet without repetition how can I impress on him the extent of the mischief?—some other notices of the destruction produced by what may be termed general or common warfare shall be thrown into a note, and I will proceed to speak of another cause of destruction. [3]

---

[9] II. Voy. Lit. 112.   [1] It. Alsat. 415.

[2] "Penes quos quidam adhuc reliqui sunt ex innumera illa veterum librorum copia, quæ superiori sæculo, furente hæresi, direpta est." It. Burg. 30.

[3] Take the following instances—Of the abbey of *Brunwillers,* Martene says, "Comme le monastère a beaucoup souffert par les guerres, et qu'il a été sujet comme les autres aux revolutions, on ne doit pas être surpris s'il n'y a plus qu'un manuscrit des lettres de Ciceron." (II. Voy. Lit. 269.) "Le Roi Louis XIV, ayant soûmis Luxembourg à la force invincible de ses armes, l'abbaye de *Munster* éprouva une seconde fois le sort de la guerre, et fut entièrement rasée ..... après tant de revolutions on ne pouvoit pas s'attendre à faire des découvertes dans la bibliotheque. En effet, nous n'y avons trouvé que cinq ou six manuscrits." (II. Voy. Lit. 302.) St. *Arnoul* at *Metz,* "Cette abbaye ..... fut entièrement rasée avec celles de Saint *Clement,* de Saint *Symphorien,* de Saint *Pierre,* et de Sainte *Marie,* au siege de Mets formé par l'empereur Charles-quint." (I. Voy. Lit. P. ii. 112.) At *Othmersheim,* "Cette abbaye, étant exposée au theatre de la guerre, a perdu ses anciens monumens, et nous n'y trouvâmes rien qui dût

II. I need not insist on the liability of manuscripts to be destroyed by accidental FIRE, especially at a time when so many were kept in wooden buildings. Our travellers, however, continually furnish us with such notices as these, most of which are quite modern. At *Rheims*, "L'église cathédrale et l'archevêché ayant été brûlez dans le douzième siècle, toutes les archives furent pour lors consumées par le feu." [4] — At *Gembloux*, "Nous passâmes la matinée à voir ce qui restoit de manuscrits de l'incendie generale du monastère." [5] —At the monastery of the Jacobins at *Liege*, "Il y avoit autrefois une assez bonne bibliotheque ; mais il y a quelques années que tous les manuscrits périrent dans un incendie, qui consuma entièrement le monastère." [6]—At *Lucelle*, "L'incendie qui consuma tout le monastère en 1699 nous priva du plaisir d'y voir une très-riche bibliotheque en manuscrits, que les flammes ont reduit en cendre, avec le religieux qui y étoit entré pour tâcher de les sauver." [7]—"Ce que nous venons de rapporter nous fait voir que les *six incendies* qui sont arrivées à *S. Wast*, n'ont pas tout consumé, et nous font aisément juger des trésors immenses que nous y trouverions, si nous avions tout ce que les flammes nous ont ravi." [8]—The abbey of *Loroy*, "Qui ayant été entièrement brulée il y a environ quarante ans, n'a conservé aucun de ses anciens monumens." [9]

---

nous arreter." (I. Voy. Lit. P. ii. 143.) *La Chartreuse*, by Liege, "Il y avoit autrefois beaucoup de manuscrits ; mais le monastère ayant esté entièrement réduit en cendres dans les dernières guerres, ils ont tous esté consumez dans les flammes. Il n'y a que les sermons de Jacques de Vitry, en quatre ou cinq volumes, qui ayant échappé à l'incendie." (II. Voy. Lit. 183)

[4] I. Voy. Lit. P. ii. 79.   [5] II. Voy. Lit. 117.
[6] II. Voy. Lit. 182.   [7] I. Voy. Lit. P. ii. 141
[8] II. Voy. Lit. 65.   [9] I. Voy. Lit. 36.

I do not wish to be tedious on this point, but I
am irresistibly tempted, first of all, just to allude to
the conflagration of the monastery of *Teano*, near
Monte Casino, which was burned, as Leo Marsicanus
says, "cum omnibus operibus suis," in the year 892,
because, among those "opera" it is said that the original
copy of the Rule of St. Benedict perished,[1] and then
to give one or two anecdotes respecting what may
be called accidental burning of monasteries, as contradistinguished from those conflagrations which took
place in the wars. I give them not as proofs that
such things happened, for that is naturally to be supposed, and is sufficiently attested by history, but as
stories illustrative both of one particular point and of
our general subject.

Thieto, who was abbot of *St. Gall's*, in the year
937, was a strict disciplinarian; and this was very
sensibly felt, not only by the monks, but by the schoolboys. St. Mark's day being a holiday, some of the
latter had got into mischief (quædam errata commise-
rant) which the monitors (censores scholarum quos
circatores vocabant) reported to the masters. Sentence
having been passed on the guilty, one of them was
sent to the upper part of the building to fetch rods.
By way of anticipatory revenge for his flogging, or
as a desperate resource to avoid one, the boy took a
brand from a fire and placed it under the dry wood
which was next to the roof. This quickly took fire,
and the flames, driven by the wind, soon seized the
tower of the church. The monastery was almost entirely
burned, and many books were lost (multi libri amissi),
though they were in time to save the church bells
and furniture. The writer who relates the story, adds,

---

[1] Mab. Ann. tom. iii. p. 263.

"that from this mischief, the monks of St. Gall took a great dislike to the scholars, and some thought that the school ought to be entirely given up, but he suggests that the loss which the monastery sustained by this occurrence was more than counterbalanced by the credit which it had gained through the scholars whom it had sent forth." [2]

If it had not happened in the same year, I should not have mentioned the burning of the famous monastery of *Fulda*, because I do not know how it happened, and cannot prove that the library was burned; and where there are cases enough of positive evidence, it is not in general worth while to notice that which is merely presumptive, however strong it may be; and of this monastery and its library I hope to find a fitter occasion to speak.

"Towards the evening of that day," says the historian of the monastery of *Lawresheim* or Lorsch (a few miles east of Worms), speaking of the 21st of March in the year 1090, "after that, following the example of the carnal Israel, the people hat sat down to eat and to drink, and risen up to play, it happened that, among other games, a disc, set on fire at the edge in the usual way, was whirled in the air by a soldier. [3] Being driven round with great force, and presenting the appearance of a circle of fire, it forms a spectacle which pleases, not only the eye by its

---

[2] Mab. iii. Ann. 407.

[3] "Inter cætera ludorum exercitia discus in extrema marginis ora (ut solet) accensus, militari manu per aera vibrabatur; qui acriori impulsu circumactus, orbicularem flammæ speciem reddens, tam ostentui virium quam oculis mirantium, spectaculi gratiam exhibet." I do not quite understand this, but I suppose it must have been some kind of circular wheel or circular frame, whirled by a strong arm, and presenting some such appearance as a Catherine wheel.

appearance, but as an exhibition of strength. This
being whirled by someone who did not keep sufficiently fast hold, it flew, by his unintentional cast, on
the top of the church. Sticking fast there, between the
wooden tiles and the old beams, it set fire to the place.
What need of many words ? In the first place, the
flame seized on the tower, which was made with admirable woodwork, [4] and in which were the bells, and
their ropes being burned they could not be used to
give the alarm. It then seized all the upper part
of the building, the towers, and the porches. At length
the dropping of the melted lead, with which all the
roof was covered, rendered it utterly impossible to go
in or get anything out. Then was the face of things
miserable—so many excellent buildings, of the church
as well as of the whole monastery—so many fine
ornaments devoured by the sudden ravages of the
flames, a few only saved with great exertion and risk,
either snatched with the hand or broken away with
the axe or hatchet from the very midst of the fire." [5]

I hope to give the reader another story somewhat
similar, and more graphic; but, though I am not apprehensive of his thinking it tedious, it would extend
this paper to an unreasonable length; and therefore,
in the meantime, and before I speak of some other
causes, I will take the opportunity of briefly adverting
to a point which cannot be fairly passed over.

---

[4] "Castellum mirabili dolatura fabrefactum." I do not undertake to
decide the precise meaning of *dolatura* in this place, and therefore
translate by general terms only; but I suppose that we may in fact
understand it to refer to those small, neat, wooden tiles (if I may use
the expression, as I have done above, in translating *tegulas*, because
the historian tells us that all the roof was covered with lead) which,
in some parts of Europe, may still be seen forming the roofs or fronts
of houses.

[5] Chron. Laur. ap. Freher. p. 81. Edit. 1600.

It is somewhat anticipating to say so, but in fact there are still so many manuscripts of some sorts in existence, that it has been very warmly contended by some learned men that a great part at least must be forgeries, because it is impossible that so many should have survived the perils to which such things have been exposed. On such an occasion as this, I must only just glance at what have been called the *Bella diplomatica*, and my sole reason for referring to them at present is, to show that those causes of destruction which I have already specified have been considered by learned men as sufficient to account for (indeed, I may say, to require) a greater *scarcity* of manuscripts than actually exists. "They say," says Ludewig, "that since all the kingdoms of Europe have carried on so many wars, and Germany in particular has been subject to such intestine commotion, no doubt all ancient documents have thereby perished, which led to the forging of new and supposititious ones. But, as nobody doubts respecting the destruction of manuscripts through these causes, so there were also reasons why they might escape. For soldiers, intent on gold and silver, and other things which they could turn to account, were, as they are now, careless about writings, especially considering the ignorance and contempt of letters which then prevailed among them. To this we may add, that even amidst the outrages of war, the soldiers were restrained by superstition from laying hands on the literary treasures of the bishoprics." He goes on afterwards to speak of fire, and represents his opponents as saying that there is scarcely to be found a city, a monastery, or a habitation of any confraternity of any kind which has not been more than once the subject of a conflagration, in which all its documents have perished. "This also," he replies, "is most true; for my own part, I declare that I have never been in any archives in Germany, though I have visited them without number, where the keepers have not attributed their deficiencies to fires which had destroyed those very documents which were most important." [He adds in a note, "The keeper at Mayence told the same story in 1705. When I inquired for their documents of earlier date than the period of Frederic I., he answered, 'that they had all perished when the castle and the court, which were of wood, were burned.'"] "But," he goes on to say, "even in the most tremendous fires, the first care is commonly to preserve the public archives from destruction; nor do I hesitate to commend the prudence of the celebrated Maskowsky, Chancellor of Darmstadt, who, when the castle and principal palace were on fire, proposed and paid a reward to those who, at the risque of their lives, went into the lowest story, which was well arched, and brought the written documents out of the archives, which were thus saved like brands plucked from the burning. The same thing we may reasonably suppose to have been done in older times by prudent keepers." [6]

I did not like to pass over this point without some notice; but the reader will at once perceive that there is an important difference between the case of which I am speaking and that to which Ludewig refers. Indeed, so far as our subject is concerned, I really have the suffrage of both parties in this diplomatic war in my favour. Those who contend that wars and fires must have destroyed the diplomas, charters, deeds, and other comparatively small and portable manuscripts of the dark ages, will readily grant that books were not likely to escape; and those who reply, as Ludewig

---

[6] Reliq. Manuscript. Pref. p. 84, 85.

justly does, that such documents would be kept with peculiar care, and saved first, and at all hazards, in case of danger, would not think of extending their argument to such manuscripts as we are concerned with.

No. XV.

"Domus sanctificationis nostræ et gloriæ nostræ, ubi laudaverunt te patres nostri, facta est in exustionem ignis, et omnia desyderabilia nostra versa sunt in ruinas."—Is. lxiv. 11.

SOMEWHAT more than eleven hundred years ago, a young man of noble family quitted the military service, and entered a monastery. By the time that he had been a monk two years he had become acquainted with the lives of the early ascetics, and, like many other monks, at various times, and especially in the earlier centuries of monasticism, he resolved to imitate them. Having discovered a wretched and solitary place, suited to his design, among the fens of Lincolnshire, Guthlac, commending himself to the special patronage of St. Bartholomew, for whom he had peculiar respect, took up his abode there on the festival of that saint, in the year 699. Some years afterwards, Ethelbald, then an exile and a wanderer, came to the hermit, with whom he was wont to consult, and whom he called his father confessor, for advice in his distress,—ut ubi consilium defecit humanum, divinum acquireret,—and received from his lips a prediction that he should come to the throne of Mercia without battle or bloodshed. Ethelbald declared that, in that case, he would found a monastery on the spot to the praise of God, and in remembrance of his father Guthlac; and when the prediction was fulfilled, in A.D. 716, he lost no time in performing his promise. Instead of the wooden oratory of the ascetic, he built a stone church, and founded

T

a monastery, which he endowed with the whole island of Croyland, on which it stood, by a charter, which begins thus:—

"Ethelbald by divine dispensation King of the Mercians, to all that hold the catholic faith, everlasting salvation. I give thanks, with great exultation, to the King of all kings, and Creator of all things, who has hitherto with long-suffering sustained me while involved in all crimes, has drawn me with mercy, and raised me up in some degree to the confession of his name. Wherefore it is good for me to cleave unto God, and to put my trust in Him. But what shall I render unto the Lord, for all things which He has given unto me, so that I may be pleasing before Him in the light of the living; since without Him we have nothing, we are nothing, and we can do nothing; For the Author of our salvation, and Giver of all things, accepts with great desire our things which are least, that He may have a cause of returning those which are greatest, and joys that are infinite. Those who follow his teaching by works of mercy, He comforts, saying, 'What ye have done unto one of the least of mine, ye have done unto me.' Hence it is, that when I had been instructed by the advise, and urged by the prayers, of my beloved confessor Guthlac, the devout anchorite, I cheerfully acquiesced," &c.

Kenulph, a monk of Evesham, was appointed the first abbot. Pega, the sister of Guthlac, who had long resided as a solitary some miles from her brother, having brought to the monastery his psalter, the scourge of St. Bartholomew, and some other relics, went back to her own cell, where she remained two years and three months; after which she went to Rome, where she spent the rest of her life. Bettelmus, Tatwin, and two other ascetics, who lived in cells by the hermitage of Guthlac, for the sake of his neighbourhood and instruction, were permitted by the abbot to remain *in statu quo*.

As I am not writing history, and am bound by no unities, let us skip over rather more than a century, and we shall find this monastery, founded by the piety of a Saxon king, become the sanctuary of more than

one of the royal race of Mercia. Etheldritha, daughter
of Offa, the betrothed of Ethelbert, king of the East
Angles (who was treacherously murdered by her father),
had retired to a cell in the southern part of the church
of Croyland. Thus she was enabled, more than thirty
years after her sad betrothal, to offer a sanctuary to a
successor of her father, Wichtlaf, king of Mercia, when
he fled from Egbert, king of Wessex, in the year 827.
The Abbot Siward, who was the only other person
privy to his retreat, negotiated for his safety and restoration as a tributary to Egbert; and the grateful,
though humbled monarch, never forgot the benefit.
Six years afterwards he gave a charter, which begins
thus:—

"Wichtlaf, by divine dispensation King of the Mercians, to all the
worshippers of Christ inhabiting all Mercia, everlasting salvation. Far
from feeling it any disgrace, I esteem it to be honourable and glorious,
to publish and set forth the wonderful works of God. Wherefore, I
will openly confess unto the Lord, who dwelleth on high, but hath
respect unto the lowly in heaven and on earth, because for a time He
was angry with me; but his anger is turned away, and He hath comforted me. In his anger, humbling the sinner unto the ground, bringing
him down even unto the dust; and again, in his mercy, raising the
needy from the dust, and lifting up the poor from the dunghill, that
I may sit with princes, and possess the throne of glory. In the day of
good things, then, let me not be unmindful of the evil things. ' I will
make mention of Rahab and Babylon, to them that know me,' not
Rahab the harlot, but the most holy virgin, my kinswoman, Etheldritha,
a recluse at Croyland for the love of her spouse, the Lamb without
spot; who, in the time of my trouble, most carefully hid me in her
cell, by the space of four months, from the face of the enemy and the
persecutor. I will make mention also of Babylon; not of the tower of
confusion, but of the most holy church of Croyland, which is a tower
reaching to heaven,—with watchings and prayers, psalms and lessons,
disciplines and penances, tears and sobs, alms, and innumerable other
acts of devotion and works of piety, offering most powerful violence to
the kingdom of heaven on behalf of a sinful world. [1] Therefore, since the

---

[1] The reader will, I trust, understand that I give this introduction,

venerable father, the Lord Siward, abbot of Croyland, hath protected me in his tabernacle in the evil day, hiding and saving me from the face of him that troubled me, beside the privileges of my predecessors, kings of Mercia, who have amply enriched the aforesaid monastery with various gifts and immunities, I also offer to the great altar of the said monastery, out of my poverty, a golden chalice, a golden cross, and a table out of my own chapel covered with plates of gold, professing that I will constantly defend the said church to the best of my power."

Then, after other matter—

"I also offer to the sacrist of the said monastery, for the service of the most holy altar, the scarlet robe with which I was invested at my coronation, to make a hood or chasuble; and for the ornament of the most holy church, my golden curtain on which is wrought the taking of Troy, to be hung on the walls on my anniversary, if they shall see fit. I also offer to the refectory of the said monastery, for the use of the president every day in the refectory, my gilded cup which is chased over all the outside, with savage vine-dressers fighting with serpents, which I am wont to call my *crucibolus*, because the sign of the cross is impressed transversely on the inside of it, with four projecting corners having a like impression; and also the horn of my table, that the elders of the monastery may drink out of it on the festivals of the saints, and may sometimes, amidst their benedictions, remember the soul of the donor, Wichtlaf."

Many other gifts are contained in this charter; and Wichtlaf, we are told, remained constant in his affection to the monastery as long as he lived, visiting it at least once a year, and always making some rich and valuable present.

As to the destruction of this monastery by the Danes in A.D. 870, I must not here run into all the

---

and some other things of the same sort, not for the taste with which Scripture language is used, but as showing the fact that it was so used, and leading to the inference that it was familiar, or, at least, not unknown. Neither do I offer any voucher for the genuineness of charters, in any case where it may be disputed. It is obvious that a forgery, if made during the period of which I write, would be of more value in my inquiry than a genuine document of earlier date could be.

details of that horrible event ; but one or two facts
I wish to mention. News of the enemy's approach was
brought by some fugitives, who arrived at the monastery while the monks were performing matins. The
abbot Theodore, who had succeeded Siward, resolving
to remain at his post with those whose advanced or
tender age rendered flight or resistance equally impossible, and might perhaps excite compassion, ordered
the younger and stronger part of the monks to escape,
if possible, into the surrounding marsh, taking with
them the reliques, principal jewels, and documents of
the monastery. The golden table given by Wichtlaf,
the chalices, and all that was metal, were sunk in
the well; but the table was so large that, place it
which way they would, it could not be prevented from
showing above water; and at length they drew it out
again ; the fires were seen nearer and nearer, and the
monks who were to fly with the other still more
valuable things, which were already in the boat, pushed
off, leaving the abbot to conceal the table as well as
he could. He, with the help of two of his old companions, did it so effectually that I believe it has never
been found to this day. Certainly it had not been two
hundred years afterwards, at which time there seems
to have been a tradition that it was buried somewhere
outside the church on the north side. After this, they
dressed themselves, and assembled in the choir to
perform divine service, which they had scarcely finished,
when the Danes broke in. The abbot was slain upon
the altar. The old men and children attempted in vain
to fly. They were caught, and tortured to make them
tell where treasure might be found, and then murdered.
All perished but little Turgar, a beautiful child, of
ten years old, who kept close to Lethwyn the sub-
prior, when he fled into the refectory, and seeing him

slain there, besought his persecutors that he might die
with him. The younger Count Sidrok was touched—
he pulled off the cowl of the little monk, threw a
Danish tunic over him, and bade him keep by his
side. Under his protection, the child, who alone survived to tell the tragic story, went in and out among
the Danes all the while they were at Croyland, went
with them to Peterborough, and while accompanying
them on their way towards Huntingdon—taking advantage of the moment when Sidrok's followers, who brought
up the rear, were suddenly called to rescue two carriages
laden with spoil, which had sunk in fording a river—
he escaped into a wood, and, walking all night, got
to Croyland early in the morning. There he found his
brethren who had fled, and who, having spent the
interval in a wood not far distant, had returned the
day before, and were engaged in attempting to
extinguish the fire which was still raging in many
parts of the monastery.

How they endeavoured to repair this desolation,
and how the exactions of Ceolwlph which followed
brought the monastery to such poverty that the abbot
was obliged to disband the greater part of the monks,
I need not here relate. All the chalices but three, all
the silver vessels except Wichtlaf's crucibolus, all their
jewels were coined or sold to satisfy his rapacity;
and the few monks who stayed by the abbot were in
the deepest poverty. When Athelstan succeeded his
grandfather, Alfred the Great, in A.D. 924, this little
company of twenty-eight had dwindled down to seven;
and when that monarch was succeeded by his brother
Edmund, in A.D. 941, the number had decreased to five.
Two of these, Brunus and Aio, after losing about the
same time King Athelstan and the Abbot Goodric,
gave up all hope of the restoration, and even the

continued existence of the monastery, and migrated, the former to Winchester, and the latter to Malmesbury. Clarenbald, Swartting, and Turgar (the child of A.D. 870, and apparently the youngest of the three) alone remained.

In A.D. 946, Edmund was succeeded by his brother Edred. If I had been writing the history of the Anglo-Saxons, I should have had much to say, in the reigns of these sons of Edward, of the old soldier Turketul, who had been chancellor to them all three, and to their father before them, and who was, moreover, their first cousin, being like them a grandson of Alfred the Great. In the second year of his reign, Edmund was threatened with invasion from the north, and Turketul was sent to York. Passing through Croyland on his way, with a great train—for he was not only the king's cousin, but himself lord of sixty manors— the chancellor was intercepted by the three old monks, who begged that, as night was approaching, he would be their guest. It is true that they had no suitable means for entertaining such a person, with such a retinue; and had it not been that in those days travellers of rank knew that they must, and therefore did, in a great measure, provide for themselves, they could never have enterprised such a matter. As it was, how they got through it is past my comprehension. But they did; they took him to prayers in the little oratory which had been got up in one corner of the ruined church, showed him their reliques, told him their story, and implored him to intercede with the king for the rebuilding of their church. He was quite taken with the old men—senum curialitatem intimis visceribus amplexatus; he promised to be their advocate with the king, and their benefactor from his private means; and, when he went forward in the morning, he ordered his servants to leave provisions sufficient for them until his return, with an hundred shillings for their expenses.

The old monks had made a strong impression, and during his whole journey the chancellor could talk of nothing, even to strangers whom he met on the way, or at inns, but the old monks of Croyland. After settling his business at York, he revisited them in his way back to London; and having passed the night there, and left them twenty pounds, he went on to tell the king, first about the northern business, and then about them. In short (I assure the reader that I am not making a long story, but, I fear, spoiling one for brevity's sake), having obtained the king's orders to do what he saw fit in the matter of restoring the monastery, he astonished his royal master by declaring his intention to turn monk. "The king hearing this, wondered beyond measure, and endeavoured by all means to dissuade him from his purpose, especially as he was now growing old, and having been bred up in ease, had not been accustomed to the rigour of monastic life. Beside this, as in the most important affairs of state everything depended on his help and counsel, he not unjustly feared that the kingdom would be endangered." The chancellor answered, "My lord the king, God who knows all things is my witness that I have fought for my lords your brothers, and for yourself, with all my might; now, for your soul's sake, let your clemency permit that I may at least in my old age fight for my Lord God. As to my counsel and every assistance that my poor means can give, it shall be promptly given to all your affairs as long as there is life in my body; but your highness must certainly understand that from this time forth I will not handle the weapons of war."

The king was grieved, but unwilling to force or to over-persuade his faithful servant—yet he did afterwards make one desperate effort to retain him; calling him one day into his private chamber, he fell at his feet, and implored him not to desert him in his distress. Turketul, however, though overcome by the unexpected proceeding of his sovereign, fell down also and besought him to spare him, nor could he be moved from his purpose. They rose, the king consented, and fixed a day for accompanying him to Croyland, in order to its execution.

In the meantime, the chancellor sent a crier round London to say, that if he was indebted to anyone he would be ready at a certain time and place to pay him, or if he had wronged any man, to restore him threefold. He then gave his sixty manors to the king, reserving only one in ten for the monastery. He also ran down with all possible expedition to pay a hasty visit to his old friends, who were over-joyed to see him—"summa celeritate de Londiniis Croylandium advolans præfatos tres senes in dicta insula latitantes devotissime visitavit, et supra quam dici potest, aut excogitari, revelato suo sancto pro-posito, in immensum lætificavit." He put them in a carriage, and rode them about into every corner of the island, exploring by the help of their memories, and the charter of foundation, the boundary of the posses-sions of the monastery, which he marked out by stone crosses. The lands had, of course, got into other hands; but it seems as if in most cases he had little trouble in redeeming them. People were not unwilling to sell him (perhaps even at a moderate price) what they knew did not belong to them; and, in fact, he appears to have failed in only two cases. Duke Osbricht had got hold of the lands of Kyrketon, Kymerby, and

Croxton; the original charters had perished; the lands were not specified in any royal confirmation; and his offer to repurchase at a fair price having been twice refused, Turketul was obliged to give them up. The other case was more difficult and delicate—Beovred, king of Mercia, had given the manor of Depyng to his chief baker, Langfer. It had descended to his two daughters, and they now belonged to a class of ladies with whom it is not always easy to deal. They would yield to neither claim nor entreaty, and the chancellor seems to have been too polite to attempt their eject-ment by any other means. He patiently hoped that they would change their minds (so I am resolved to understand his expectation of better times), but he waited all his life in vain [2].

The king went to Croyland on the eve of the Assumption in the year 948. Turketul accompanied or had preceded him. Messengers were sent for the two absent monks, who joyfully returned, and were heartily welcomed, for they were "viri literatissimi, et moribus multum honesti ac religiosi." [3] The chancellor

---

[2] "Quæ diu in cœlibatu permanentes, neque cum Turketulo voluerunt componere, nec juri suo prece vel pretio renuntiare. Expectabat itaque diutius venerabilis pater Turketulus tempora meliora; sed quamdiu vixit, vixerunt et illæ in eadem pertinacia."

[3] It is worth while, at it regards the possibilities of locomotion in those days, to observe that the king arrived at Croyland on Monday, the 14th of August. Messengers were (mox), I know not exactly how soon, dispatched to Malmesbury and Winchester, and the two monks got to Croyland on Wednesday, the 23rd of the same month. We may, in the present day, consider that as ample time for such a journey; but we must remember that the messengers had not merely to go and return a distance of at least 120 or 150 miles, but that each had to bring with him a very aged companion. We know that Turgar was at this time eighty-eight years of age, and that these travellers were his seniors, for they were among the "fortiores et adolescentiores" who

laid aside his lay habit, and received the pastoral staff from the king, and the benediction from the bishop of the diocese, and thus became Abbot of Croyland. The king took on himself the expense of building, and set about it in earnest. Leaving Egelric (a kinsman of Turketul) to act as clerk of the works, he took the new abbot, with two of his monks, Turgar and Aio, to London, where, in a public council before the archbishops, bishops, and nobles of the land, he confirmed to the monastery all its possessions. Many learned men followed Turketul, of whom ten became monks. The others had no notion of doing so (rigorem religiones abhorrentes), but only came because they did not know how to do without him (quia præsentia ejus nullo modo carere poterant). These, being numerous, he placed in a cell dedicated to St. Pega, on the east side of the monastery. He gave them the allowance of monks, built them a chapel, and appointed for them the same religious services, by day and night, as the monks performed. Many became priests, and afterwards monks, and in the meantime he employed them in school-keeping, and made a point of going at least once every day to inspect the progress of each individual child; taking with him a servant who carried figs or raisins, or nuts, or walnuts, or more frequently apples and pears, which he distributed as rewards.

But I am not writing the life of Turketul. He was succeeded in A.D. 975 by his relation Egelric, already mentioned. From being one of the *clerici* Pegelandenses, he had become a monk, and during the latter years

---

fled from the Danes, when he was left behind as a child. Yet we may reasonably hope that neither of the old gentlemen was overfatigued, as we hear nothing of it, and find one of them setting out for London on the Monday after.

of Turketul he had had the chief management of affairs,
for which he was peculiarly qualified. One point which
gained him credit was the management with which he
provided a large stock of timber, of which a great part
of the monastery was afterwards built. Of it, during
the lifetime of Turketul, the nave of the church was
built, and the tower was framed with very long beams;
and after he became abbot he erected many very fine
buildings—namely, the infirmary, of very good size,
the beams and boards of which were put together with
admirable art of carpentry. A chapel, of like workmanship, with baths and other requisites; and because they
would not have borne a stone roof, they were covered
with lead. Then he made the hall of the guests, and
two large and very handsome chambers of the same workmanship. He made also a new brewhouse, and bakehouse
all of very beautiful woodwork (omnia de lignorum pulcher-
rimo tabulato), a great granary in the same style, and
a large stable, the upper chambers for the servants of
the abbey, and the under part for the horses; those of
the abbot at one end, and those of the guests at the
other. These three buildings, the stable, granary, and
bakehouse, formed the west side of the court of the
monastery; on the south was the hall of the guests,
and its chambers; on the east the *sutrinum,* or place of
sewing, or clothes-making, the hall of the converts, with
the abbot's chamber, chapel, hall, and kitchen; and the
north side contained the great entrance, and the apartment for receiving the poor. All, except the hall,
chamber, and chapel of the abbot, and the apartment
for the poor (which had been built of stone by Turketul),
were built of wood, and roofed with stone. With Egelric's agricultural performances we are not at present
engaged, and I write under a most wretched fear of
being tedious; but I must say that they were such that

the monastery was enriched beyond measure by the produce of its lands; population gathered round, and there was soon a town in the marshy desert. It is more to our purpose to observe that Abbot Egelric "caused to be made two great bells, which he named *Bartholomew* and *Bettelmus,* two of middle size, which he called *Turketul* and *Tatwyn,* and two lesser, *Pega* and *Bega.* His predecessor had before caused to be made a very large bell, which he named *Guthlac,* which was in tune with these bells, and with them made admirable harmony; nor was there such another peal of bells in England." [4]

His successor, though he bore the same name, was a man of different disposition—vir magis libris et literis sacris deditus, quam in temporalium provisione doctus. It was well that he followed, rather than preceded, his namesake; for books and sacred literature are most advantageously studied under cover, and with places and means for physical refection; and so it is that God employs the various talents and dispositions of men; even so obviously that one would think the hand could never dream of saying to the foot, "I have no need of thee." I beg pardon for this reflection, when I

---

[4] The reader is probably aware of the custom of naming bells, and I believe that the previous history sufficiently explains who all these persons were, except *Bega,* whom one would naturally suppose to be St. Bees, but I do not feel quite certain that it was so well known a personage, and the point is not worth discussing. The great bell at Gloucester Cathedral has puzzled some antiquaries by its legend, ME FECIT FIERI MUNCUTUS NOMINE PETRI. Without disputing whether *muncutius* is an allowable poetical licence for *montacutius*—or whether, if we strain it to *monchatus,* we have got a word, and if we have, whether that word has any meaning—I beg to say that (however different they may look in Roman type) the tall, narrow, black-letter word which someone has carelessly copied *muncutus,* is in fact *conventus.* The convent caused the bell to be made "nomine Petri."

am really studying brevity, but it has been repeatedly forced on my mind in reading the brief records of whole strings of abbots, priors, &c. Egelric the Second gave to the common library of the monastery (communi bibliothecæ claustralium monachorum—I do not know whether that phrase was used to exclude the scholastic "clerici Pegelandenses," already mentioned) forty great original volumes of learned writers, and more than a hundred smaller volumes of miscellaneous treatises and histories; and besides these he made for the choir six graduals, four antiphonaries, and eight missals for the different altars.

I see that I must fairly skip over about a century, and say at once that Ingulph, to whom I am indebted for most of the foregoing particulars, was Abbot of Croyland in A.D. 1091. What I have hitherto said, though it seems to me to illustrate many parts of our subject, is given with immediate view to his account of what happened in his own time. Speaking of his beloved patron, Archbishop Lanfranc, who died in A.D. 1089, he says—

"Two years after his death, happened that which was my heaviest misfortune, which had been foreshown by so many prodigies — the total destruction of so great a monastery, so often clearly foretold in very many visions, and other apparitions—that most fierce conflagration which cruelly devoured so many and such dwelling places of the servants of God. For our plumber, being employed in the tower of the church about the repairs of the roof, and not extinguishing his fire in the evening, but fatally and most foolishly covering it with ashes, that he might the more readily set to work in the morning, went down to supper; and when, after supper, all our servants had gone to bed, and were every one of them fast asleep, a strong wind rising from the north speedily brought on our great calamity. For, entering the tower through the lattice-work, which was open on every side, it first blew away the ashes, and then drove the live coals against the nearest woodwork, where, quickly finding dry materials which were ready to catch, and thus gaining strength, the fire began to seize the more substantial parts.

The peasants, who saw for a long while a great light in the belfry, supposed that the clerks of the church, or the plumber were finishing some work; but at length, perceiving the flames burst forth, they came knocking at the gates of the monastery with great clamour. It was just about the dead of the night, and we were all resting in our beds, taking our first and deepest sleep. At length, being awakened by the loud clamour of the people, and hastening to the nearest window, I saw as clearly as if it had been noon-day all the servants of the monastery running towards the church, crying and hallooing. Having put on my slippers, and waked my companions, I hastened down into the cloister, where everything was as brilliant as if it had been lighted up with a thousand tapers. I ran to the door of the church; and, attempting to enter, I was very nearly caught by the melted bell-metal and boiling lead, which were pouring down. I stepped back, however, in time; and, looking in, and seeing that the flames had everywhere got the upper hand, I took my course towards the dormitory. The lead from the church dropping on the cloister, and soon making its way through, I was severely burnt in the shoulder, and might have been burnt to death, if I had not quickly leaped into the open area of the cloister; where, seeing that the flames that issued from the tower of the church on every side had seized the nave also, and were pointed towards the dormitory of the monks, in which direction burning materials were continually carried, I cried out to those who were still in deep sleep; and, by raising my voice to the utmost, I was scarcely able, after a long while, to rouse them. They, recognizing my voice, and leaping out of bed in great alarm when they heard that the cloister was on fire, rushed through all the windows of the dormitory in their slippers, and half-naked, and fell miserably. Many, alas! were wounded, many bruised and fractured, by the hard fall.

" The flames, however, continuing to increase, and continually throwing flakes of fire from the church towards the refectory—first the chapter house, then the dormitory, then the refectory itself, and, at the same moment, the cloisters belonging to the infirmary, and the whole of the infirmary, with all the adjoining buildings, were swallowed up at one stroke. As all our brethren collected about me in the court, when I saw most of them half-naked, I tried to regain my own chamber that I might distribute the clothes I had there to those who were most in need. But every avenue to the hall was so exceedingly hot, and such a shower of melted lead was falling on every side, that even the boldest of the young men were obliged to keep their distance. Moreover, not yet knowing that our infirmary had been seized by the flames on the other side, I was going round by the north cemetery

towards the east end of the church, when I perceived that our infirmary
was on fire, and that the unconquerable flames were raging with the
utmost violence among the green trees—ash, oak, and willow—which
were growing around. Returning, therefore, to the west side, I found
my chamber like a furnace, vomiting forth incessant flames from all
the windows; and, going forwards, I beheld, with tearful eyes, that
all the contiguous buildings towards the south (that is to say, the halls
of the converts and of the guests), and all the other buildings that
were covered with lead, were on fire. But the tower of the church
falling on the south transept, I was so terrified by the crash, that I
fell on the ground, half dead in a fainting fit. I was picked up by my
brethren, and carried into the porter's lodge; but I scarcely recovered
the use of my faculties and my customary strength before morning.

"Day breaking at length, and I having recovered from my fit, the
brethren weeping and languid, and some of them miserably wounded,
and burnt in many parts of their bodies, performed divine service
ogether with mournful voice, and lamentable wailing, in the hall of
Grimketul, our corrodiary. Having performed all the hours of divine
service, as well for the day as for the night, we went out to take a
view of the state of things throughout the whole monastery, the flames
being still unsubdued in many of the offices. It was then that I first
perceived that our granary and stable were burned; the flames being
not yet quenched, though their posts had been burned even below the
level of the ground. About the third hour of the day, the fire being
n great measure got under, we went into the church, and, extinguishing with water the fire which was already subsiding, we perceived in
the incinerated choir that all the service books, both antiphonaries
and graduals, had perished. On entering the vestry, however, we found
all our sacred vestments, the relics of the saints, and some other valuables which were there reposited, untouched by the fire, because the
building was covered with a double stone arch. Going up to our archives we found that, although they were entirely covered by a stone
arch, [5] nevertheless, the fire rushing in through the wooden windows,

---

[5] Here is an instance of that which I have already noticed—the
greater provision which was made for the security of the archives. I
have said that when Mabillon was at Nonantula, he found only two
MSS. of all its former riches; but he found " in archivo diplomata
perantiqua Ludovici Lotharii et aliorum." (*It. Ital.* 202.) Of course
they had a value far beyond that which an antiquary could discover in
them, which would account for peculiar care being taken for their preservation, and for their being actually preserved when books were lost. To this

all our deeds were stuck together, and burnt up by the extreme heat, as if they had been in a glowing furnace or oven; although the cases in which they were kept appeared to be safe and sound. Our most beautiful chirographs, written in the Roman character, and adorned with golden crosses, and most beautiful paintings, and precious materials, which were reposited in that place, were all destroyed. The privileges also of the kings of Mercia, the most ancient and best, in like manner beautifully executed, with golden illuminations, but written in the Saxon character, were all burned. All our documents of this kind, greater and less, were about four hundred in number; and, in one moment of a most dismal night, they were destroyed and lost to us by lamentable misfortune. A few years before, I had taken from our archives a good many chirographs, written in the Saxon character, because we had duplicates, and in some cases triplicates of them; and had given them to our Cantor, Master Fulmar, to be kept in the cloister, to help the juniors to learn the Saxon character, because that letter had for a long while been despised and neglected by reason of the Normans, and was now known only to a few of the more aged; that so the younger ones, being instructed to read this character, might be more competent to use the documents of their monastery against their adversaries in their old age. These chirographs, being kept in a certain old chest, which was enclosed by the wall of the church, were the only ones that were saved, and escaped the fire. These are now our chief and principal documents, which were formerly secondary, and put aside, having been long lightly esteemed and looked down upon, because of their barbarous writing; according to the saying of Job— 'The

---

their superior portability would often conduce. We have just seen that the documents of Croyland were carried into safety when it is probable that books were destroyed. Ruinart tells us that when he and Mabillon were at Morbach, something similar had occurred.— "Magnam esse ibi diplomatum copiam acceperamus, sed quod ob bellorum tumultus alio asportata essent, ea videre non licuit" (*It. Alsat.* 468); but he goes on to say—"Hanc jacturam codicum mss. Bibliothecæ abundantia resarcivit, quorum non pauci sub prima regum nostrorum stirpe litteris majusculis aut franco gallicis descripti sunt." He specifies a psalter that was 800, and a copy of St. Paul's Epistles 900 years old, and a New Testament of equal antiquity, "et alii codices optimæ notæ in quibus sacræ scripturæ libri," etc.; but these were to take the chance of war. *Ap. Mab. Op. Post.* Tom. iii.

U

things that my soul refused to touch are as my sorrowful meat.'[6]

"All our library also perished, which contained more than three hundred original volumes, beside smaller volumes, which were more than four hundred. Then, too, we lost that most beautiful and very costly table, wonderfully made with every kind of metal to distinguish the stars and the signs—Saturn was of copper—Jupiter of gold—Mars of iron—the Sun of brass—Mercury of amber—Venus of tin—the Moon of silver. The colure circles, and all the signs of the zodiac, according to their kinds, by the skilful workmanship having their proper images and colours, in various forms and figures, engaged, beyond measure, not only the understanding, but the eyes, of the spectators by the multiplicity of precious stones and metals. There was not such another nadir known or talked of in England. The King of France had formerly presented it to Turketul; and he, at his death, had given it to the common library, as well for ornament as to teach the juniors. Now it was consumed, and melted down to nothing, in the devouring fire.

"Our chapter-house was totally consumed; our dormitory, and all the beds of the monks which were in it, and the building which adjoined, perished in one conflagration. In like manner our infirmary, with the chapel, the baths, and all the adjoining offices, were burned. Our refectory and all that it contained (except a few stone cups, and the horn and *crucibolus* of Wichtlaf, king of Mercia, which were kept in stone chests), with the adjoining kitchens, and all the hall and chamber of the converts, with all that was in them, were burnt together. Our cellar, and the very casks full of beer, were destroyed. The halls also of the abbot, and his chamber, and the whole court of the monastery, which had been most beautifully surrounded with very elegant buildings through the diligence of my predecessors,—(unhappy I, that my stay there was prolonged to behold such a sight!)—perished in a miserable conflagration, the flames raging on every side with the fury of Greek fire. A few huts of our poor pensioners, and the outhouses of our cattle, and the buildings containing the other animals, being at a greater distance, and covered with stone, were all that were preserved. For, beside the north transept of the church, from whence the wind rushing forth most powerfully drove the flames towards the south, all the buildings of the monastery, especially those that were roofed with lead, whether built of wood or stone, our chirographs and valuables, books and utensils, bells and their turrets, clothes and provisions, in

---

[6] Ch. vi. ver. 7. Quæ prius nolebat tangere anima mea, nunc præ angustia cibi mei sunt.

one moment of time, while I, most unhappy, presided, were lost and consumed.

"Many signs and many portents prognosticated these fires, and nocturnal visions very often predicted them ; but all these things I understood only after the event. Not only the words of our holy Father Turketul, when he was at the point of death, earnestly admonishing us to take care of our fire, but also those of our blessed father Wulfran at Fontanelle, in a night vision, commanding me carefully to preserve the fire of the house of the three saints, — that is to say, Guthlac, Neot, and Waldev, — contained most certain admonitions. But I understand and confess all these things, unhappily, too late ; and I, who for my sins do worthily deserve to pour forth such lamentations and useless tears, am only indulging in vain complaints.

"But that we may go on, let us return to our sad history. Our great misfortune being quickly made known through the whole vicinity, many of our neighbours, having bowels of mercy for our misery, most kindly looked with an eye of pity on our destitution. For our lord and most holy father Remigius, bishop of Lincoln, graciously granted to those who should do to us, or procure for us, any good, forty days of indulgence; and beside this, he gave us forty marks of silver in money. By his advice and suggestion, also, the venerable canons of the church of Lincoln, and the citizens of that city, who were our neighbours, sent us a hundred marks. Also Richard de Rulos, Lord of Brunne and Depyng, as our faithful brother and loving friend in the time of tribulation, then gave us ten quarters of wheat, ten quarters of barley, ten quarters of peas, ten quarters of beans, and ten pounds of silver. This was the contribution of Richard de Rulos towards the restoration of our monastery. Also Haco of Multon gave us twelve quarters of corn, and twenty fine flitches of bacon. This was the contribution of the aforesaid Haco. Also Elsinus of Pyncebec gave us a hundred shillings in silver, and ten flitches. Also Ardnotus of Spalding gave us six quarters of corn, and two carcases of beef, and twelve flitches of bacon. And beside these, many other persons made us various gifts, whereby our distress was much relieved, whose names may our Lord Jesus Christ write in the book of life, and may He repay them with heavenly glory. But among so many benefactors, Juliana, a poor woman of Weston, of pious memory, must not be forgotten, for she gave us of her property, even all her living,—namely, a great quantity of twisted thread, to sew the garments of the brethren."

I pass over the arrangements which the abbot proceeded to make for raising money on the lands of the monastery, and the documents which he has inserted respecting these transactions; but I must add the short paragraph which follows them:—

"Being therefore mercifully helped by the contributions of so many of Christ's faithful people, as well our neighbours as persons at a distance, we laboured, in the first place, night and day, to rebuild the house of the Lord, lest their gifts should seem to have been cast away on a barren soil. We put in a new nave to the roof of the church, in place of the old one which had been burnt; we added also some other appendages, such as they were. Moreover, for the old tower of the church, a humble belfry, in which we placed two little bells which Fergus, the brass-worker of St. Botolph's, had lately given us, until better times, when we propose, by the help of the Lord, to renew everything in a better manner, and to raise to the Lord of majesty a worthy temple on surer foundations."

I trust that these details are not without interest in themselves, and they certainly conduce to one very principal object of these papers, which is, not merely to call the reader's attention to the facts of the dark ages, but to the writers who have recorded them. I have perhaps said more than enough of the ravages of fire and sword, and I hope to proceed immediately to the consideration of another cause to which we may ascribe the scarcity of manuscripts.

No. XVI.

"Ne toga cordylis et pænula desit olivis,
Aut inopem metuat sordida blatta famem."—MART.

THERE is an appearance, at least, of self-complacency
in an author's saying, "the reader remembers," which
may provoke a smile, that is more or less deserved,
in proportion to the importance of the matter referred
to, and its distance as to time and place. If it is a
startling fact, or a necessary argument, on the preceding
page, it is well enough; but if it is some slight matter
of passing remark, five or ten volumes off, and which
the reader cannot be supposed to have seen for a
twelvemonth, it argues that the writer has a more
accurate knowledge of his own works than of human
nature. My readers would smile if I were to assume
their recollection of what I said about a year and a
half ago, on a matter which they may think of very little
importance, but of which (it being myself) I may be
allowed to form a different estimate. I did, however,
in the very first number of these papers, avow myself
to be of rather a discursive turn; and fairly stated
that I should be sure to digress, if such a thing were
rendered possible by marking out a plan. I have no
fear that anyone will dispute that I so far spoke the
truth. But I also said, that although I had no plan,
I had a purpose, which I fully stated; and that I
have actually been following this by something like
a train of argument, may not perhaps be equally
obvious. Yet it is really true; and as I freely forgive
the reader who may not perceive it, so I trust that
if I am honoured with any reader so attentive as to

have kept it in view, he will pardon me if I here very briefly advert to the progress which I consider myself as having made in it, and the course which I hope to pursue.

As to the knowledge of the Bible in the dark ages, I stated in No. XII. an opinion that it was, in fact, much greater and more general than some modern writers would lead us to suppose. In order to support this, I began with what I did not consider as the most powerful argument, but yet as having some weight for proof, and some interest in itself,—namely, the incidental notices of existing copies of the Scriptures, which are scattered up and down in the histories of that period. In the two following papers I gave many instances; but though, with regard to the notices of *parts* of the Scriptures, they were so numerous that I restricted myself to those which challenged particular attention by their intrinsic value, or some other peculiar circumstance, yet I was afraid that even with this limitation the reader would feel the induction of cases tedious. Beside this, I thought it possible that when I had even unduly trespassed on his patience, he might say,— "Well, but now I have counted up all the Bibles, and Testaments, and Gospels, and Psalters which you have mentioned, and I know that in my little parish there are, at this moment, twice as many; and if they were as plentiful then as they are now, surely we should have more proofs of it in existence." I might reply by inquiring, how many of those Bibles in your parish are an hundred, or an hundred and fifty, or two hundred years old?—or, more strictly, by asking, how many of the Bibles which were in the parish two hundred, or one hundred, or fifty years ago, are there now to prove that they ever existed?

But the proper answer is, to call attention to the

various causes of destruction which have perpetually been at work. I wish, if possible, to make the reader partake of the surprise which I unfeignedly feel, that so many manuscripts have survived such fierce and unrelenting persecution. After this I hope to proceed to more direct evidence that the Scriptures were known and read in the dark ages than even that which is afforded by the incidental mention of them. In the meantime, in this digression (not from our subject, but from that particular argument) on the scarcity of manuscripts, I have mentioned, in the first place, the ravages of war and fire; and I hope that I shall not be thought to have wasted time in giving one or two cases somewhat in detail. There are two reasons for it—first, that a very principal object which I have in view is, to bring to the reader's notice, not merely the facts, but the writers, of the dark ages; secondly, that it is impossible, without some such consideration of details, to understand and appreciate the few words in which some of our literary travellers occasionally speak. Without some little reflection, and, perhaps, without having our minds particularly called to some such cases, we should hardly form an idea of what they mean to convey by the few words in which they allude to a whole string of desolations. It was said of a celebrated violinist that every stroke of his bow was a mouthful; something like it might be said of single sentences from the pen of Father Martene. For instance —

"Quoyque le bibliotheque ait été pilliée *en plusieurs occasions*, il y reste encore un grand nombre de manuscrits, presque tous anciens et fort beau." [1]

At the collegiate church of Romans in Dauphiny —"Elle a eu le malheur d'être ruinée *six* fois : —

---

[1] I. Voy. Lit. P. II. p. 214.

1. Par les Maures; 2. Par l'Archévêque Sebon; 3 et 4. Par le feu; 5. Par Guigne Dauphin dans le douzième siècle; et 6. Par les Calvinistes." [2]

The monastery of La Charité sur Loire, Martene tells us, "was originally built half a league from the place where it now stands, near the ancient town of Seir, which no longer exists. Having been destroyed by the Vandals, it was re-established by King Pepin, who placed Benedictine monks there. They did not continue long, because the place was soon after destroyed by the barbarians. Geoffrey of Nevers, Bishop of Auxerre, having rebuilt the church in honour of the Holy Virgin, gave it to Hugh, Abbot of Clugni, who made it a famous monastery, and the first in consequence among those affiliated to his own, and gave the government of it to Girard, his prior, who is considered a saint at Clugni. It is said that, under that illustrious prior there were two hundred monks at La Charité, who were afterwards reduced to a hundred priests and twenty novices; and successively to ninety, eighty, and at length to sixty. This number remained until the time of Robert de Lenoncour, the first prior who held it *in commendam*, who reduced them to thirty; and these, after the conflagration of the monastery, which speedily followed, were, if I remember right, still further reduced to seventeen." Can we wonder that, when Martene goes on to tell us that, through modern restoration, "Le monastère de la Charité se ressent encore aujourd'hui de son ancienne splendeur," [3] he should, nevertheless, say nothing of the library, and mention only one manuscript?

---

[2] Ibid. p. 263.   [3] I. Voy. Lit. p. 37.

At Sens, too, "L'abbaye de Saint Pierre le Vif ayant été détruite *neuf ou dix fois*, tant par les barbares et les ennemis de l'état que par diverses incendies, on est surpris qu'elle subsiste encore aujourd'hui." [4] This is very true; but one is *not* surprised to hear nothing whatever of manuscripts there.

Other instances will, however, come under notice incidentally; and having said, perhaps more than enough of fire and sword, let me mention another cause, perhaps as mighty, and more constant, which has led to the destruction of manuscripts.

III. A most effective cause may be found in the NEGLIGENCE of those who have had the care of them. As this infidelity to the trust reposed in him by the Author of every good gift is a sin of which man has been guilty in all times and places, we may very well suppose that a good many manuscripts perished in this way during the dark ages, as they certainly have done since. Yet I think I shall not be considered unfair if I suggest the probability that this cause was less operative *then* than it was when books became less scarce and valuable. I do not want to take advantage of those exaggerations as to cost and rarity which I have been endeavouring to expose; nor even of the equally fallacious statements which have been made respecting the care taken, and the precautions used, about single volumes, as if they were the only books on earth. Warton, in that "Second Dissertation," to which I have had occasion more than once to refer, tells us of a bishop who, "in the year 1299, borrows of his cathedral convent of St. Swithen, at Winchester, *Bibliam bene glossatam*, —that is, the Bible with marginal annotations,—in

---

[4] Ibid. p. 61.

two large folio volumes, but gives a bond for due
return of the loan, drawn up with great solemnity." [5]
All this is, I dare say, very true ; and, in the present
day, it may sound rather strange; but does he not
tell us that the Bible was a bequest from the bishop's
predecessor to the convent? Ought they to have
treated it just as if it had been a novel in a circulating
library?—and could the prelate who borrowed it be
offended by the care which they took of it? But when
Warton goes on to say,—"When a single book was
bequeathed to a friend or relation, it was seldom
without many restrictions and stipulations,"—it is
obviously more than he can prove, and more than
most people will believe. It is a singular circumstance
that we find another Bible just at the same time
bequeathed by the Bishop of Cambray to the Carthusians of Macour, near Valenciennes; the bishop had
died in the year 1296, on his way to the Holy Land,
and the monks, who received the twelve volumes by
the hands of the Count of Hainault, entered into an
engagement with him not to lend it without good
security; and, in case of their quitting that part of
the country, to return it to him. [6]

Such cases it is worth while to notice, for the
legitimate purpose of showing that books existed,
were valued, and taken care of; and I mention them
the more readily because they relate to Bibles. I hope
to have occasion to refer to them hereafter, when we

---

[5] Page cix. 8vo. edit. See more of Warton in *Note* B.

[6] "Promittimus bona fide, nos Bibliam in duodecim voluminibus,
quam de legato præfati pontificis per manus potentissimi principis
domini Johannis de Avesnis, Comitis Hannoniæ, ac suæ consortis
dominæ Philippæ Comitissæ nobilissimæ habemus, hujusmodi non ven-
dere, dare, vel impignorare, seu accommodare, nisi bonum correspon-
dens haberemus, quæcumque necessitas nos impellat," &c. — *Mart.* i. 1314.

shall, perhaps, be led to think that special care was
taken of such books. In the meantime, I am only
contending that, generally speaking, books were taken
care of; and if these instances are more recent than
the period with which we are engaged, let us get
back into it by noticing the case of a Gratian, presented to the monastery of Clairvaux, by Alanus,
Bishop of Auxerre (the disciple of St. Bernard), on
condition that it should on no account whatsoever
(nulla necessitate) be removed from the monastery.[7]
Martene, who relates the circumstance, and who would
not lose the opportunity of saying a word or two on
the Benedictine side of the question respecting monastic
studies, observes that the monks of Clairvaux, even
in those days, were evidently no enemies to the study
of canon law. But to this I must add a suspicion,
that books of canon law were peculiarly apt to get
out of their places, and not to find their way back.
A curious hint of this is furnished by a statute of
Mainerius, Abbot of St. Victor's at Marseilles, in the
year 1198. After premising the excellence and benefit
of peace and unity, especially among those who are
knit together by the love of Christ, and the care which
should be taken to prevent or to stop division, he
proceeds,—"Whereas all the brethren of our monastery
have complained that certain of our predecessors took
and carried away at their pleasure, from the library
of this church, which hath been furnished by the
provident and diligent care of the ancient fathers and
abbots, and adorned with books of divers arts, the
books of law, which, like the other books, belong to
the library (having, perhaps, been bequeathed by the
devotion of individuals, or having come, in some way

---

[7] I. Voy. Lit. p. 103.

or other, to the monastery), I, Mainerius, by the grace
of God, abbot of the said monastery of Marseilles,
having consulted with our elders, have determined to
pacificate and end those complaints by perpetual peace
and concord:" and he then goes on to order, that
whatever books shall be bequeathed, or given, or in
any way accrue to the monastery, shall be considered
as an inalienable and irremovable part of the library;
except only the breviaries, which properly belong to
the abbot, and the missals for the service of the church.[8]

These cases, however, as well as those cited by
Warton, and many others which might be collected,
are rather specimens of individual character than
anything else. As to general rules, I have in a former
number given a letter from the prior of a monastery
to an intimate friend, who wanted to borrow a book,
and whose request led him to state the inflexible
rule of the monastery not to lend books, without
receiving some equivalent volumes as a pledge; and
there can be little doubt that such regulations were
very general. "Our books," says Ingulph, who has
been sufficiently introduced to the reader in the preceding number, "as well the smaller unbound volumes,
as the larger ones which are bound, we altogether
forbid, and under an anathema prohibit, to be lent to
any far-distant schools, without the leave of the abbot,
and his distinct understanding as to the time when
they shall be returned. As to lending lesser books,
however, such as Psalters, copies of Donatus, Cato,
and the like poetical works, and the singing lesson-
books, to children and the relations of the monks, we
strictly forbid the cantor, or anyone who shall act as
librarian, under pain of disobedience, to allow them to

---

[8] M. & D. i. 1020.

be lent for a longer space of time than one day, without
leave of the prior. Should anyone hereafter presume
so to do, let him remain in disgrace and incapable of
office in the monastery for two years." [9] It was also
perhaps natural that those who had been at the trouble
of writing a volume should over-rate the value of their
own labours, and use such means as they could to
prevent their work from being lost, defaced, or even
removed from the scenes in which it had been for
many years in the process of elaboration, the only
companion of the silent and solitary artist—solitary,
though, like Rodulf, who was a monk of St. Wast, or
Vedastus, about a thousand years ago, he might fancy
that his well-pleased patron-saint was looking on, and
balancing the account of sins and letters. A copy of
Augustine on the Psalms, which he wrote, is still extant,
and contains a portrait of himself, and some lines, part
of which I cite, not for their poetical beauty, nor their
orthodoxy, but because they express feelings which
were, probably, not peculiar to himself; and which, so
far as they extended, would form a guarantee for some
zeal in the multiplication and preservation of books.

"Cum librum scribo, Vedastus ab æthere summo,
Respicit e cœlis quot aretur pagina sulcis,
Quot folium punctis hinc hinc laceretur acutis,
Tuncque favens operi nostro, nostroque labori,
Grammata quot sulci, quot sunt quot denique puncti
Inquit, in hoc libro, tot crimina jam tibi dono.
Hancque potestatem dat Christus habere perennem.
Nec labor iste tibi, frater, jam proderit uni,
Sed queiscumque velis detur pars magna laboris.
Hæc merces operis, quam dat scriptoribus ipsis
Sanctus Vedastus, pater optimus, atque benignus,
Hac mercede librum perscripsi sedulus istum,

---

[9] Ing. ap. Gale. p. 104.

Quem si quis tollat, tellus huic ima dehiscat,
Vivus et infernum petat amplis ignibus atrum.   Fiat, fiat." [1]

One would almost imagine that this monk, instead
of belonging to the Flemish monastery of St. Wast,
had been a disciple of Theodoric, Abbot of St. Evroul
in Normandy, two hundred years later,—that is, in the
middle of the eleventh century. Of this abbot we are
told—

"Ipse manu propria scribendo volumina plura
Ecclesiæ natis, dedit exemplum bonitatis;"—

and therein he, no doubt, did well; but when to example
he added exhortation, he seems to have gone too far.
I am not praising, or even palliating his conduct, and
I only notice it because it is evident that "the love
he bore to learning was in fault;" and it is a principal
part of our business to trace that spirit, even though
it be manifested in error. He used, we are told, to
lecture his monks against idleness, and "also he was
wont to tell them this story:—

"There was a monk in a certain monastery who was guilty of many
transgressions against its rules; but he was a writer, and being devoted
to writing, he of his own accord wrote out an enormous volume o
the divine law. After his death, his soul was brought before the tribunal of the just Judge for judgment; and when the evil spirits sharply
accused him, and brought forward his innumerable crimes, the holy
angels, on the other hand, showed the book which that monk had
written in the house of God, and counted up the letters of that enormous volume as a set-off against the like number of sins. At length the
letters had a majority of only one, against which, however, the dæmons
in vain attempted to object any sin. The clemency of the Judge, therefore, spared the monk, and commanded his soul to return to his body,
and mercifully granted him space for the reformation of his life. Frequently think of this, most dear brethren; cleanse your hearts from

---

[1] II. Voy. Lit. 64.

vain and noxious desires; constantly offer the sacrifice of the works
of your hands to the Lord God. Shun idleness, with all your power,
as a deadly poison; for, as our holy father Benedict says,—'Idleness
is the enemy of the soul.' And frequently consider, also, what is said
by a certain approved doctor, in the Lives of the Fathers,—that only
one devil tempts a monk who is employed in any good occupation,
while a thousand devils attack him who is idle, and drive him, when
stung with innumerable darts of temptation, to grow weary of his
monastery, to desire the injurious pomps of the world, and to make
trial of noxious pleasures. And since you cannot support the poor with
large alms (for you have no earthly riches) and cannot build large
churches, as kings and other great secular persons do, you, who are
shut up within the rules of the cloister, and are deprived of all power,
should, at least, as Solomon exhorts, 'Keep your hearts with all diligence', and continually use every endeavour to please God. Pray, read,
chant, write, and employ yourselves in other things of the same kind,
and with them wisely arm yourselves against the temptations of evil
spirits." [2]

---

[2] Ordericus Vitalis, quoted by Mab. A. S. ix. 137. I cannot mention
this old abbot without adding, from the same authority, on the page
preceding that just quoted, a few more words respecting his writing
himself, and being the cause of writing in others.—"Ipse scriptor erat
egregius, et inclita sibi insitæ artis monimenta reliquit Uticanis juvenibus.
Collectaneum enim et Gradale, ac Antiphonarium propria manu in ipso
cœnobio conscripsit. A sociis etiam suis, qui secum de Gemetico venerant,
pretiosos divinæ legis codices dulcibus monitis exegit. Nam Rodulfus
nepos ejus Eptaticum [Heptateuchum] conscripsit, et Missale ubi Missa
in conventu quotidie canitur. Hugo autem socius ejus expositionem
(Gregorii Magni) super Ezechielem et Decalogum, primamque partem
Moralium ; Rogerius vero presbyter Paralipomenon, librosque Salomonis,
tertiamque partem Moralium. Præfatus itaque Pater per supradictos, et
per alios, quos ad hoc opus flectere poterat, antiquarios, octo annis
quibus Uticensibus præfuit, omnes libros veteris et novi Testamenti,
omnesque libros facundissimi Papæ Gregorii Uticensium bibliothecæ
procuravit. Ex ejus etiam schola excellentes librarii; id est Berengarius,
qui postea ad episcopatum Venusiæ provectus est, Goscelinus et Rodulfus, Bernardus, Turchetillus, et Richardus, aliique plures processerunt,
qui tractatibus Hieronymi et Augustini, Ambrosii et Isidori, Eusebii
et Orosii, aliorumque doctorum, bibliothecam sancti Ebrulfi repleverunt,
et exemplis suis ad simile studium secuturam juventutem salubriter
exhortati sunt."

Those who wrote under the influence of such feelings as an address like this was calculated to produce, might very naturally add to their manuscript something like an anathema against any person who should destroy or deface their labours. Thus the writer of a manuscript in the library of St. Gal—

> "Auferat hunc librum nullus hinc omne per ævum
> Cum Gallo partem quisquis habere cupit."

The same terrible imprecations were occasionally annexed by the donors or the possessors of books. As in a Sacramentary which Martene found at St. Benoit-sur-Loire, and which he supposed to belong to the ninth century. The donor (whose name appears to have been erased) having sent the volume as a present from beyond seas, fiercely anathematizes all persons who should on any pretence remove it from the monastery without the intention of returning it, devoting them to the like destruction with Judas, Annas, and Caiaphas. [4] One may suppose that books containing such awful imprecations were the less likely to be stolen, and the more likely to be returned if they did get astray. Indeed, it was enough to frighten the possessor of a book, however honestly he might have come by it. There is a curious instance of this in a manuscript of some of the works of Augustine and Ambrose in the Bodleian library :—"This book belongs to St. Mary of Robert's Bridge; whosoever shall steal it, or sell it, or in any way alienate it from this house, or mutilate it, let him be anathema-maranatha. Amen." And underneath there follows, in another hand—"I,

---

[3] Canis. Ant. Lect. tom. ii. P. iii. p. 230.

[4] I. Voy. Lit. p. 67. "Ut si quis eum de monasterio aliquo ingenio non redditurus abstraxerit, cum Juda proditore, Anna, et Caiapha, portionem æternæ damnationis accipiat. Amen, amen. Fiat, fiat."

John, Bishop of Exeter, know not where the aforesaid house is, nor did I steal this book, but acquired it in a lawful way." [5]

As to our present point, however, it will, I apprehend, be readily conceded, that more care was taken of manuscripts during the period with which we are engaged than afterwards,—that is to say, more care was taken during what is generally considered as the darkest period than during that which followed ; and though the time when manuscripts came to be undervalued and destroyed by wholesale was that which followed on the invention of printing, yet that time had been prepared for by a long period of gradually increasing laxity of discipline and morals in monastic institutions. There had, I apprehend, long been less multiplication, less care, less use, of books ; and many a fine collection had mouldered away. There is a passage, which it may be worth while to transcribe from one of John of Trittenheim's (or Trithemius) exhortations, delivered to his monks when he was abbot of Spanheim, in the year 1486 :—

"Do you not know," he says, "that our holy lawgiver Benedict says, in the rule,—'If anyone shall do the business of the convent in a slovenly or negligent manner, let him be punished; and if he does not amend, let him be subjected to regular discipline?' And in

---

[5] "Liber S. Mariæ de Ponte Roberti, qui eum abstulerit, aut vendiderit, vel quolibet modo ab hac domo alienaverit, vel quamlibet ejus partem abscideret, sit anathema maranatha. Amen. *Aliena manu.* Ego, Joannes, Exōn Epūs, nescio ubi est domus predicta, nec hunc librum abstuli, sed modo legitimo adquisivi." Wanley (Cat. Lib. Sept. p. 152) adds, "Hic fuit Joannes Grandisonus, Exoniensis Episcopus, qui floruit circa A.D. 1327." Robert's Bridge was a Cistercian monastery, founded by Robertus de Sancto Martino in 1176, a few miles north of Battle, in Sussex (1 Dug. 916), and consisting at its surrender an. 29 Hen. VIII. of an abbot and eight monks. Burnet, Rec. to Book iii. No. i. vol. i. p. 135.

his chapter on the cellarer of the monastery, he says,—'Let him look on the vessels of the monastery, and all its property, as if they were the consecrated vessels of the altar.' In short, I cannot, and, undoubtedly, I should not, refrain from saying in how slovenly and negligent a way most of you do everything; as if they either were not observed by God, or as if their sloth did no injury to the affairs of the monastery. Know, my brethren, what I give you notice of beforehand, that for all these things, as well as for your other sins, you must give an account to the Lord God. For this reason I have diminished your labours out of the monastery, lest by working badly you should only add to your sins; and have enjoined on you the manual labour of writing and binding books. These, and similar occupations, you may carry on with tranquillity of mind and body, within the inclosure of the monastery. I wish that you may diligently perform even these works of your hands for the love of God, lest you eat the bread of idleness. There is, in my opinion, no manual labour more becoming a monk than the writing of ecclesiastical books, and preparing what is needful for others who write them; for this holy labour will generally admit of being interrupted by prayer, and of watching for the food of the soul no less than of the body. Need, also, urges us to labour diligently in writing books, if we desire to have at hand the means of usefully employing ourselves in spiritual studies. For you see, that all the library of this monastery, which formerly was fine and large, has been so dissipated, sold, and made away with, by the disorderly monks before us, that when I came I found but fourteen volumes. It is true that the industry of the printing art, lately, in our own day, discovered at Mentz, produces many volumes every day; but it is impossible for us, depressed as we are by poverty, to buy them all."—f. xvi.

I fear that this was no solitary instance, and that of many places it might be said, as Martene says of the cathedral at Auxerre, that, besides other causes, "La negligence des anciens moines ont dissipé un si grand nombre de manuscrits qu'il n'en reste aujourd'hui que fort peu," [6]—though I apprehend that those whom he here called *ancient*, should, in our inquiry, be termed *modern*, monks. But passing over all the revival period, and all the shocking stories of the state

---

[6] Voy. Lit. 56.

in which the manuscripts were found,[7] what did Martene
himself find in the *eighteenth* century? Several hints
in his literary travels show us, that many of the manuscripts which he found were in the hands of persons
by no means sensible of their value. At the archives
of the cathedral of Narbonne he and his companions
found "un fort beau manuscrit.... dont on ne faisoit
pas grand cas: mais l'estime que nous en fismes,
reveilla le soin des chanoines pour le conserver."[8] At
Albi, "beaucoup d'anciens manuscrits que nous trouvâmes la plûpart en très mauvais état. L'estime que
nous en fimes fit ouvrir les yeux aux chanoines, qui
les méprisoient; et ils nous promirent d'en avoir plus
de soin à l'avenir. La plûpart sont de 900, 800, ou 700
ans."[9] At the Abbey of St. Martial at Limoges, "on
y conserve encore près de deux cens manuscrits, la
plûpart des saints pères, sur-tout de S. Ambroise, S.
Jerôme, S. Augustine, S, Gregoire, monumens du
travail des saints *moines* Benedictins qui ont autrefois
sanctifié cette abbaye, et edifié le païs, mais aujourd'hui
fort negligée par les *chanoines*."[1] I beg the reader to
understand that I am responsible for the *italics*, which
Martene did not think of putting; but I do it as the
shortest way of conveying a hint which I do not feel
it fair to suppress. All these stories are of *canons*, and
the author is a *monk;* and from that fact I would

---

[7] Only, as we have noticed Montfaucon's journey into Italy, in the
year 1698, I must just give his description of the state in which he
found the celebrated (said to be autograph) manuscript of St. Mark's
gospel; which, without admitting all its claims, he declares to have as
great appearance of antiquity as he recollected to have seen in any
manuscript:—"Folia agglutinata simul sunt et putrida, ut non facile
possint diduci sine fractione; nam locus perquam humidus, et brevi
periturus funditus est codex si istic maneat."—*Diar. It.* p. 55.

[8] I. Voy. Lit. P. ii. p. 62.   [9] Ibid. p. 67.   [1] Ibid. p. 69.

draw two inferences,—first, that there might be some
little prejudice, if not malice (shall I say colouring?
—hardly, I hope, in stories told at the time, to say
nothing about character), in the relation of these facts,
and that therefore we must not overstrain the statements;
secondly, that, although we do not find them recorded,
there may, perhaps, have been a similar set of stories
respecting monks, if we really knew all, and so our
present argument would be strengthened. Be this as
it may, however, I make the former of these remarks
not so much with reference to the cases already mentioned, as to a case which I must give in Martene's
own words. I do not know that we can suspect it of
being much coloured, but, making every deduction,
it is quite awful. The holy chapel at Bourges was
originally founded by John, duke of that city, in the
year 1405, for thirteen canons, thirteen chaplains,
thirteen vicars, and six clerks of the choir, and enjoyed
a quasi-episcopal jurisdiction. "Next to the cathedral,"
says Martene, "the holy chapel holds the first rank in
the city of Bourges;" and, after telling us that "Le
trésor est très riche," and recounting matters of gold
and silver, pearls and precious stones, vases of agate
and rock crystal, he goes on to say—

"There was once a rich library at the holy chapel; and in order
that the books might not be dispersed, the holy pontiffs had excommunicated all who should remove them. On this account the cardinal
Amboise, legate of he holy see, when he wanted St. Hilary's commentaries on the Psalms, employed all his authority to obtain them, and
was moreover obliged to give the canons absolution from those censures
which they would have incurred by lending them. This we learn from
the following letter of the cardinal, which I copy from the original."

In this letter, which Martene gives at length, the
cardinal, after referring to his wish to borrow the book,
and the difficulty which lay in the way, says—

"We therefore absolve you from all censures and pains to which you may be exposed by the removal of this book; and by the authority with which we are invested and empowered, we declare you to be absolved; the said bull, or anything else to the contrary, notwithstanding. Given at Bourges, the 3rd of March, 1507."

What Martene professes to have found, however, at the holy chapel, after the march of intellect had gone on just two hundred and one years from that time, I must really give in his own words:—

"Ces bulles n'ont point empêché ces manuscrits d'être dispersez dans la suite. Il en reste pourtant encore environ cinquante ou soixante, que j'eus la curiosité de voir. Monsieur le procureur du chapitre me fit ouvrir le lieu où ils etoient conservez. Je les trouvai dans un état pitoyable, parce que le receveur du chapitre, à qui on avoit confié la clef de ce lieu, en avoit fait un poullalier; et que comme ils étoient ouverts sur des pupitres, les poules les avoient couverts d'ordures. Lorsque je commençois à les manier, Monsieur l'abbé Desosiers, à qui il appartient d'en avoir soin, me vint trouver; il ne fut pas moins chagrin que moy de les trouver en cet état, et fit à l'heure même netoyer la lieu et les livres, et me promet de faire relier ceux qui en auroient besoin. L'un des plus curieux manuscrits de la sainte chapelle, est celui qu'on appelle les heures du Duc Jean. C'est un pseautier latin avec une version angloise de six ou sept cens ans. Ceux qui me la montrerent, croyoient que c'étoit d'allemand ou de l'hébreu. Mais si-tot que je l'eus vû, je connus le caractère Anglo-Saxon."—*Voy. Lit.* p. 28.

Oh, the ignorance, the carelessness, the barbarian stupidity of the monks in the dark ages!—how hateful does it look beside this reverent and enlightened watchfulness of the eighteenth century!

No. XVII.

"We have set Dunce in Boccardo, and have utterly banished him Oxford for ever, ... and the second time we came to New College, after we had declared their injunctions, we found all the great quadrant-court full of the leaves of Dunce, the winds blowing them into every corner, and there we found one Mr. Greenfeld, of Buckinghamshire, gathering part of the said book-leaves (as he said) therewith to make him scuels, or blaunsheers, to keep the deer within the wood, thereby to have the better cry with his hounds."—COMMIS. LAYTON TO SEC. CROMWEL, Sept., 1535.

"Colleges, originally of popish institution, like all contrivances of that masterpiece of human policy, bear upon the great scheme of mastering down the human mind to an acquiescence in THE CRAFT." — CHRISTIAN EXAMINER, July, 1836.

IF the reader has fairly considered the probable effects of war and fire, aided by the more slow and silent, but incessant operation of Time, assisted by damp and all the auxiliaries which he has employed when the negligence of man has left manuscripts at his mercy—if he has reflected that more than six hundred years have elapsed since the close of that period of which we are speaking, during all which time the work of destruction has been going on—if he has at all realized these facts, surely I might confidently appeal to him whether it is very far short of a miracle, that *any* manuscripts of that or of an earlier period should have survived to the present time? Whether it is not absurd to talk of scarcity (at least to reason from it to former conditions) while hundreds, nay thousands, of such manuscripts repose in our libraries? Yet I should be doing great injustice to the subject if I did not mention another cause, which has probably been

as operative as either of those already adverted to ;
if, indeed, I ought not rather to say, more efficient
than all of them put together. I speak, perhaps, with
prejudice; for I certainly feel strongly on this point.
Of the desolations of WAR and FIRE, I have heard
tell; and, should the reader "bid me discourse," I
could, I think, persuade him that I have been mercifully
brief on the subject; but I have *seen* nothing of them
—not even the Cottonian Library; and to the reader,
probably, as well as myself, these matters are mere
hearsay—"demissa per aurem." But other proofs of
destruction, from other sources, are constantly at hand,
and I could set them before his eyes. Of all the
thousands of manuscripts burned by war or by accident,
by Danes or Hungarians, or housemaids, [1] the ashes
are dispersed and no trace remains. Those that were
not found by Ambrose of Camaldoli, a mouldering
part of general desolation [2]—those that were not res-

---

[1] " Bp. Earle's Latin translation of Hooker's books of Ecclesiastical
Polity," says Dr. Smith, in a letter to Hearne, " which was his entertainment during part of his exile at Cologne, is utterly destroyed by
prodigious heedlessness and carelessness; for it being written in loose
papers, only pinned together, and put into a trunk unlocked after his
death, and being looked upon as refuse and waste paper, the servants
lighted their fire with them, or else put them under their bread and
their pies, as often as they had occasion."—*Letters of Eminent Persons
from the Bodleian.* Vol I. p. 140.

[2] Mabillon says of his call at the monastery of Crypta-ferrata, " Festi
occasio in causa fuit, ut reliquias librorum videre non potuerimus.
Verum Ambrosius Camaldulensis qui ejusdem rei causa olim eo se
contulerat, nihil reperit præter ruinas *ingentes parietum et morum,
librosque ferme putres atque conscissos.*"—*It. Ital.* 87. I presume that
the words in italics belong to Ambrose, though Mabillon does not give
any reference. He certainly says much the same in one of his letters,
"ea tamen quæ vidimus ita dissipata et concisa et putrida erant, ut
miserabilem omnino faciem præferrent . . . . . monasterium omne cir-
cuivimus, immo non jam monasterium, sed ruinas lacrymabiles lacry-

cued by Poggio when he drew Quintilian to light
from a dark and filthy dungeon[3]—those that were
not saved by Father Mennitius when he gathered in
a "festiva copia" from his Calabrian dependencies,
where they were unheeded and perishing[4]—those, in
short, that have not been redeemed by individual
exertion to give us some notion of what has been
lost, have left no memorial that they ever existed.
Those which overanxiety hid too carefully, may be

---

mati sumus: sola ferme ecclesra integra, quæ et ipsa fimo plena videbatur. Servat tamen plurima vestigia antiquæ dignitatis. Verum ista
coram melius explicabimus."—*M. & D.* III. 544.

[3] "Ibi inter confertissimam librorum copiam, quos longum esset
recensere, Quintilianum reperimus, adhuc salvum et incolumem, plenum
tamen situ, et pulvere refertum. Erant enim in bibliotheca libri illi,
non ut eorum dignitas postulabat, sed in teterrimo quodam et obscuro
carcere, fundo scilicet unius turris, quo ne vita quidem damnati detru-
derentur."— *Ap. It. Ital.* 211.

[4] "Is enim, quia in variis sibi subjectis Calabriæ monasteriis codices
istos, obsoleto pene Græcæ linguæ usu, jacere intactos neglectosque
acceperat, imminenti *jam* [that is, in the latter part of the *seventeenth*
century], exitio subduxit inque Urbem advehi in usum eruditorum cu-
ravit."—*Diar. Ital.* 211. Montfaucon, in the next paragraph, mentions
a curious circumstance respecting the destruction of manuscripts. The
Archbishop of Rossano told him that his see had formerly possessed
a vast number of Greek documents (ingentem diplomatum Græcorum
numerum), as had been stated by Ughelli in his Italia Sacra; but that
one of his predecessors had fairly buried them, to be rid of the trouble
occasioned by persons coming to inspect them; "pertæsum adventantium
frequentiæ, rogantiumque ut diplomata proferrentur, suffodi omnia et
in perniciem ire curasse." Can one conceive how Father Montfaucon
looked on hearing this? Perhaps (so far as the two men could look
alike) very much as Mabillon did, when, in hunting over the library
at Monte Casino for the life of St. Placidus, he found the most ancient
of the three lives—itself a MS. of the tenth century—not as book, but
as the binding of books—"Primæ vitæ folia ante annos septingentos
descripta ad compingendos alios codices detracta invenimus."—*It. Ital.*
125.—*See Note* C.

hidden still; [5] and those that brutal stupidity buried, have perished. What the rats have eaten we know not; what the deep sea has swallowed we cannot tell, and seldom think of. All those are gone without memorial, except such scattered notices as may be gleaned from the survivors. But there are thousands equally destroyed—thousands of murdered wretches not so completely annihilated; their ghosts do walk the earth—they glide, unseen, into our libraries, our studies, our very hands—they are all about and around us—we even take them up, and lay them down, without knowing of their existence; unless time and damp

---

[5] The correspondent of the Baron de Crassier, whom I have already had occasion to quote, and to whom I shall have to refer again presently, says—"Pendant mon séjour à Wirtzbourg j'ai vû M. Siegler, secrétaire du conseil ecclesiastique.... Il a encore une collection des chartres les plus anciennes de l'abbaye de Fulde, avec les sceaux des anciens empereurs et rois très-bien dessinez : mais ce qui va vous surprendre, est qu'ayant depuis peu, de la permission de Monsieur le Baron de Hutten, grand doyen de la cathédrale, foüillé sous les toits de cette église, il y a trouvé un trésor consistant en manuscrits, qui étoient entièrement oubliés, et que l'on croit y avoir resté cachez depuis la guerre de Suede, si pas plus long-tems. Ces manuscrits, dont je n'ai scû voir que quelques-uns, sont des plus anciens et la plûpart écrits : *cum literis semiuncialibus* sans interponctions. Entre autres un *codex Justiniani* que je crois être du tems de cet empereur."—II. *Voy. Lit.* 176. Is it improbable that many such cases may have occurred ? Ingulph, for instance, tells us that when his old enemy, Yvo Tailbois (hostis semper noster implacabilis), tried first to take advantage of what he supposed to be a total loss of documents by the fire at Croyland, and then by a desperate effort to possess himself of those which he found to be in existence, he thought it best to place them in secure concealment—"Ego autem audita tanta hostis nostri malitia, tam contra incendia quam contra talia machinamenta hostilia, assumtas chartas nostras posui sub tam secura custodia, quod vita mea comite nec ignis consumet nec adversarius surripiet, Domino nostro Jesu Christo, ac beato Patrono nostro Sanctissimo Guthlaco propitiantibus et protegentibus servos suos, prout firmiter ego credo."—*Ap. Gale.* I. 107.

(as if to punish, and to mock, us for robbing them of their prey) have loosed their bonds, and sent them to confront us. But to speak soberly:—

IV. To the causes already mentioned, we must add IGNORANCE, CUPIDITY, DISHONESTY—they may all go together, for in some cases it may be difficult to say how much should be ascribed to one cause, how much to another. Nor is it very material. When we read, for instance, "Il y avoit autrefois un assez bon nombre de manuscrits au Val St. Lambert, mais la plûpart ont esté *vendus ou perdus*," [6] it is of no great consequence to settle how far either of these causes preponderated, or how far ignorance (if it had anything to do with the business) was that passive ignorance of whose effects I have already spoken, or that more homely and honest ignorance whose desolations we are now to trace. On reading such a notice, one would, indeed, like to know, why the manuscripts were sold, and for what purpose. In the present day we should take it for granted that they were only transplanted into some richer collection; but there is too much reason to fear that they were sold merely as parchment. In fact, the number of manuscripts for which bookbinders have to answer is beyond all calculation, and this, too, even in times long since the dark ages. Mabillon found many manuscripts (though happily they were not of peculair value) in the hands of a bookseller at Besançon, who had destined them to the use of the binder; and another in the hands of a physician, who had rescued it from the same fate. [7] A still more

---

[6] II. Voy. Lit. 195.

[7] It. Germ. 2. He adds this reflection—"Hæc fortuna fuisset veterum librorum omnium, nisi Deus aliam mentem in quorumdam studiosorum mentes hoc ævo inspirasset." It is impossible to say how many *authors*

recent and wholesale example is afforded by the author of a letter to the Baron de Crassier, which I have already had occasion to refer to. Writing from Nuremberg in the year 1717, and giving an account of M. Uffenbach, and his collection of books and other valuables, he says. "Parmi les manuscrits il y en a qui lui viennent du pillage de l'abbaye de S. Gal, qu'il a acheté au poids seulement, ayant fait exprès un voyage à Ausbourg, où il avoit appris, mais trop tard, qu'on y avoit amené des chariots pleins, qui furent d'abord vendus chez des bateurs d'or et des relieurs de livres, et périront ainsi misérablement." [8] Of the gold-beaters I know nothing, but all trades have probably had a share of the plunder,[9] and theirs has, I doubt not, been very considerable ; but as to the bookbinders, I repeat that they have to answer for an innumerable quantity of manuscript. Those who are at all in the habit of

---

as well as *copies* may have been lost to posterity through their ravages. Agobard had a very narrow escape. Baluze says, in the preface to his edition, "Magnam porro gratiam debemus omnes Massono, ob servatum Agobardum. Nam cum is, ut ipse scribit in epistola ad ecclesiam Lugdunensem, Lugduni in vico Mercium libros quæreret, et apud compactorem librorum versaretur ejus rei causa, compactorque ille Agobardi codicem in membranis perscriptum veteribus notis dilaniare paratus esset, cultrumque ad eam carnificinam manu teneret, vitam illi redemit Massonus ; numerato videlicet pretio libri."

[8] II. Voy. Lit. 175.

[9] "Whole libraries were destroyed, or made waste paper of, or consumed for the vilest uses. The splendid and magnificent Abbey of Malmesbury, which possessed some of the finest manuscripts in the kingdom, was ransacked, and its treasures either sold or burnt to serve the commonest purposes of life. An antiquary who travelled through that town, many years after the dissolution, relates, that he saw broken windows patched up with remnants of the most valuable MSS. on vellum, and that the bakers had not even then consumed the stores they had accumulated, in heating their ovens."—*Lett. of Em. Per. from the Bod.* I. 278.

looking at such things know how commonly early-
printed books, whose binding has undergone the ana-
lytical operation of damp, or mere old age, disclose
the under end-pieces of beautiful and ancient manuscript. They know how freely parchment was used for
backs and bands, and fly-leaves, and even for covers.
The thing is so common that those who are accustomed
to see old books have ceased to notice it; and to give
to others any idea of its frequency, or of the immense
consumption of manuscripts occasioned by it, is utterly
impossible; especially, considering that the books so
bound were principally those published during the first
century of printing, and that the volumes themselves
are now become comparatively scarce. How the bookbinders of that age came by them is another, and a
sad question; but that their part of the tragedy was
performed in honest ignorance may be believed.

And what must we say of DISHONESTY—of another
kind of dishonesty from that which has been noticed,
and which was only that of monks who sold what
they had no right to sell, to purchasers who knew
that they had no right to buy? It was bad enough,
quite bad enough; but there is another species of dishonesty belonging to the question, to which it is still
more disgusting to refer, though it must not be overlooked. Think of Sir John Cotton writing to Dr. Smith,
"I have written to John Vigures that Betty Hart should
let you into the library when you please. As for anything of a *bond*, I desire none. I know you, and confide in your worth and honesty." [1] And again, "As
for my library, it is wholly at your use and service.
The same liberty which my father gave to the learned
Mr. Selden, I give to you. But Mr. Selden was too

---

[1] Letters by Em. Per. from the Bod. Vol. i. p. 18.

free in lending out books, which, after his death, were never restored."[2] A sad thing it is that such prudence should be necessary, and that such suspicion should have grounds among men of letters; but it has ever been so. "Il est surprenant," says Martene, "que dans une bibliothèque aussi complete que celle d'Anchin on trouve si peu de manuscrits des conciles, et si peu des historiens. Il y a apparence que les manuscrits de ces matières ont été enlevez par *des curieux,* qui s'en seront rendus maîtres par la facilité de quelques abbez." [3]

The Jesuits had rather a bad name in this matter; and the same writer relates an anecdote which (though in this case the Jesuit was a "fort honnête homme") may not be out of place here. He was employed at the Cistercian Abbey of Cambron to teach the young monks philosophy, because the strictness of the abbot's discipline did not permit such exemption from monastic service as would have allowed any of the elder monks to undertake that duty. "We dined with this Jesuit," says Martene, "who appeared to us to be a good sort of man. He was in the library when we were introduced; and, taking up a manuscript, he read these words—'Liber B. Mariæ de Camberone, siquis eum abstulerit anathema sit.' On this, the monk who accompanied us said, with a smile, 'If all who have carried off our manuscripts are excommunicate, there must be a good many Jesuits in that predicament.' 'Vous nous les avez donnez,' replied the Jesuit; and this," says Martene, "might very well be true; for I am persuaded that many thefts of manuscripts are charged on these reverend fathers of which they are quite innocent; and I have found, in certain monasteries, manuscripts which have been returned, and also the letters announcing

---

[2] Ibid. 23.   [3] II. Voy. Lit. 82.

their return, though they still kept the *recepisse* of those
who had borrowed them. Those who found these *rece-
pisses* did not fail to say, without further examination,
that the fathers had kept their manuscripts."[4]

Whether the Jesuits were more or less guilty of
stealing books, it is certainly a very bad thing, even
when done from conscientious motives, as it seems to
have been by Jacob the Jew, whose memoirs Mabillon
met with in the Medicean library at Florence; and
who therein confessed that before his conversion he
had stolen the books of Christians, carrying off those
which related to either the Old or the New Testament,
but committing the works of the fathers to the flames—
thus, in his kind and degree (and perhaps as only
one out of many of his nation so employed), helping
forward the work of destruction.[5] But bad as stealing
is, there is really something which seems to me to
be still worse; or which we ought perhaps to call
the worst form of stealing, only we do not generally
consider it as such, because the mischief eclipses the
sin. I mean the mutilation of manuscripts. At Long
Pont, says Martene, "nous nous arretâmes un jour
pour voir les manuscrits, qui sont en grand nombre
et fort beaux, mais dont *plusieurs ont été tronquez*
par des gens trop hardis, à qui on a permis de les
voir trop facilement sans connoître leur caractère."[6]
I do not say that this mutilation, too, may not be very
conscientious when united with ignorance and blind
zeal, as in the case of the Oxford Commissioners,
who have furnished my motto;[7] but what is one to

---

[4] II. Voy. Lit. p. 107.   [5] It. Ital. 168.
[6] I. Voy. Lit. P. ii. p. 152.
[7] Or by their successors a few years after, who, with as great hatred
of poor Dun Scotus, "and all his blind glosses," carried their reform

say when learned men do such things from mere cupidity or idleness? Only the other day I took up a popular county history, where I met with a note in these words, relating to a work mentioned in the

---

to still greater lengths. "What mad work this Dr. Coxe did in Oxon, while he sat chancellor, by being the chief man that worked a reformation there, I have elsewhere told you," says Anthony Wood (Ath. Ed. Bliss. I. 466), referring to p. 269 of his history, where he gives an account of the visitation of the commissioners which took place in 1549. In his account of the following year, he writes to the following effect:—"To return at length to the royal delegates, some of whom even yet remained in Oxford, doing such things as did not at all become those who professed to be learned and Christian men. For the principal ornaments, and at the same time supports, of the University, that is, the libraries filled with innumerable works both native and foreign, they permitted or directed to be despoiled. Hence, a great multitude of MSS. having no mark of superstition about them (unless it were to be found in the red letters on their titles) were adjudged to the flames, or the vilest purposes. Works of scholastic theology were sold off among those exercising the lowest description of arts; and those which contained circles or diagrams, it was thought good to mutilate or to burn, as containing certain proofs of the magical nature of their contents. As to the public library, I shall speak of it elsewhere; though those which belonged to single colleges scarcely suffered less. For I find that an immense quantity, almost a waggon-load, of MSS. was carried off from Merton College," &c. I wish that I could venture to quote the whole passage — but it is perhaps more to the purpose to give part of what the learned editor of the Athenæ has added to Wood's account in the volume above cited.—"Of the various beautiful MSS. in Duke Humphrey's library, one specimen only has escaped the ravages of these monsters: this is a superb folio of Valerius Maximus, written in the Duke's age, and, probably, purposely for him. The mischief committed at this time can scarcely be conceived. 1 have seen several fine old chronicles and volumes of miscellaneous literature mutilated because the illuminations were supposed by the reforming visitors to represent popes and saints, when they were really intended for the portraits of kings and warriors; nay, some were absolutely mathematical figures! The malice of these barbarians was only equalled by their ignorance."—p. 468.

text:—"It is a quarto MS., in the Ashmolean Museum, fit for press. Dr. —— borrowed it while compiling his —— —— and cut out five leaves, which have since been recovered." Well might Cave say, "I hear many persons, indeed, frequently saying that it is hard to obtain admission into libraries—that the golden fleece (which some critics most firmly believe to have been old parchments) was literally guarded by dragons, and that we are doing just the same thing in these days. The wickedness of men has led to all this caution, and the necessity which requires it forms its excuse. Who does not burn with unbounded indignation when he sees that the best books, while their names still stand in the catalogues, are gone from the shelves? Who but must groan when he sees others mutilated, obliterated, erased, and spoiled by every kind of barbarism?"[8] Sad stories might be told on this subject, but where would be the use of telling them? It may be hoped that to most they would seem incredible.

Some readers may not, perhaps, be aware that, at no very remote period, it was customary to take the precaution of chaining the books to the shelves. A notice on this subject, which I found in a Chapter library, I thought worth transcribing. It was written in a copy of Lock on the Epistles (S. 100); I suppose because that was then one of the newest and most popular books, and therefore most likely to bring the notice under the observation of those whom it might concern.

"ADVERTISEMENT.

"Since, to the great reproach of the nation, and a much greater one of our holy religion, the thievish disposition of some that enter into libraries to learn no good there, hath made it necessary to secure

---

[8] Script. XV. præf. *a.* 2.

the innocent books, and even the sacred volumes themselves, with chains—which are better deserved by those ill persons, who have too much learning to be hanged, and too little to be honest—care should be taken hereafter, that as additions shall be made to this library, of which there is a hopeful expectation, the chains should neither be longer, nor more clumsy, than the use of them requires, and that the loops, whereby they are fastened to the books, may be rivetted on such a part of the cover, and so smoothly, as not to gall or raze the books, while they are removed from or to their respective places. Till a better way be devised, a pattern is given in the three volumes of the Centur. Magdeburg, lately given and set up. And forasmuch as the latter, and much more convenient manner of placing books in libraryes, is to turn their backs outwards, with the titles and other decent ornaments in giltwork, which ought not to be hidden— as in this library, by a contrary position, the beauty of the fairest volumes is—therefore, to prevent this for the future, and to remedy that which is past, if it shall be thought worth the pains, this new method of fixing the chain to the back of the book is recommended, till one more suitable shall be contrived." [9]

As to this difficulty of acces, everybody must see the reasonableness of it in the very lamentable fact, that it has been so unsuccessful. But there is another point of view in which it is worth our notice; and it is very principally on this account that I have said so much about it. In the first of these papers I said, "Who can take upon himself to say what is extant?" And I wrote these words under the feeling, that copies (perhaps authors) which are not known to exist may still be in being. It may seem strange that I have said so little of the Vatican, the King of France's Library, the British Museum, and other vast repositories

---

[9] This advertisement appears to have been written as recently as the year 1711, when the practice had generally gone out of fashion. Martene says of one of the libraries which he visited in 1718, "La bibliothèque est assez bonne; tous les livres y sont enchaînez selon l'ancien usage, car l'abbaye de S. Jean des Vignes a toûjours été fort attachée à ses premieres pratiques."—II. Voy. Lit. 24.

W

of manuscripts; but the truth is, that I know very little
about them beyond what is known to most persons
who are likely to take even the slightest interest in
the matter; and what is the use of telling the reader
that these and other libraries contain almost innumerable manuscripts? He knows it; · and I am rather
trying to call his attention to the fact, that so recently
as when these Benedictines made their tours, there
were so great a number dispersed up and down the
country, and still, if I may so speak, *in situ*. One
might naturally suppose that, so far as these travellers
went (how small a part of Europe) they saw all that
could be seen; and it is therefore necessary to state,
that even with their recommendations, and all the
facilities which could not be refused to men of their
character, travelling with their objects, they often
found it difficult, and sometimes impossible, to gain
access to what they were looking for. Ignorance,
suspicion, jealousy, often prevented the archives of
cathedrals and monasteries from being freely open to
them. Yet we must not ascribe every refusal to so
bad a motive. The reader will recollect, that many
manuscripts, which might be curious to the antiquary,
only as fixing a date, or illustrating a custom, or
presenting some singularity of language, or penmanship,
might be extremely valuable to the owners as a title-
deed. Suppose that, in rummaging the archives, these
prying Benedictines had filched away the diploma of
Charles the Bald, by which the abbey had held broad
lands for centuries; or suppose, what is more likely,
that in the exercise of their diplomatic skill they
should suspect it of being, if not a forgery, a second
edition, made to supply the place of what had really
existed; or suppose, what is still more probable, that
in their search they should not be able to find it at

all, and be obliged to say so in their new Gallia
Christiana?

I am not insinuating dishonesty; but everybody who
knows anything of the state of real property, even in
our own country, is aware that there is many a good
estate, held by its lawful owner, whose title no one
has a right to dispute, and which is nevertheless held
by him against his will, because he cannot so prove
his title as to be able to sell it. Indeed, it was the
shrewd remark of an able and experienced lawyer,
that the best security which any man could have for
an estate of which he was in possession, would be the
certainty that there were no title-deeds in existence.[1]
Owing to this, and the other causes to which I have
alluded, our travellers sometimes found it no easy
matter to make their way into the archives; and even
when not met by rudeness, or incivility, they could
perceive that the abbot, or canons, would gladly have
dispensed with their visit.[2]

---

[1] The reader will easily imagine something like jealousy between
orders, and even individual communities. Something like it, only on a
greater scale, might have been specified among the desolations of war,
especially when of a civil or revolutionary nature. For instance, in his
preface to the catalogue of the Cottonian MSS. Mr. Planta says—"We
are informed by Stukeley, that—Bromsall, Esquire, of Blunham, in
Bedfordshire, high sheriff for the county of Bedford in the year 1650,
was greatly instrumental in preserving this inestimable treasure during
the convulsions of the civil wars, in which all documents of a consti-
tutional and legal nature were *industriously sought after*, in order to
be destroyed."

[2] At *Verdun* the archbishop plainly refused to open his archives;
and the dean and chapter, though they opened theirs at first, shut them
the next day, and would not even grant admission to the "méchant
reste d'une bonne bibliothéque qu'ils ont venduë."—I. Voy. Lit. P. ii.
p. 93. At *Strasburg*, the personal interference of the Prince of Auvergne
(one of the twenty-four noble canons—tous princes ou comtes), was

Still, though they did not see all that might have
been seen—though their object was not precisely

---

insufficient (Ib. 145); and at *Lyons*, the strong recommendation of the
archbishop was scarcely sufficient (I. Voy. Lit. 238) to get them admitted. At *Rosseauville*, "nous n'y eûmes aucune satisfaction."—I. Voy.
Lit. p. ii. 177. At. *St. Trone*, they expected better treatment—"Nous
ne pûmes cependant rien voir, pour des raisons dont il est inutile de
rapporter les motifs et le détail."—II. Voy. Lit. 197. At *St. Bertin*,
"La bibliotheque est remplie d'un tres-grand nombre de manuscrits
fort anciens;" but they were scarcely permitted to enter, and not allowed
to examine.—I. Voy. Lit. p. ii. 184. At the Cistercian abbey of
Candelle, the abbot refused, in opposition to his monks; and Martene
was obliged to report in the Gallia Christiana that he had been there
to inspect the archives, "sed non licuit per senem abbatem, hominem
utique suspiciosum."—Ib. 68, G. C., I. c. 56. At *St. Martin de Cani-
goux*, it was just the reverse. The prior received them "assez charita-
blement, il nous ouvrit même les archives qui sont entieres; mais à
peine eûmes-nous vû quelques-uns des titres, qu'un de ses moines [before
described as 'six ou sept moines sauvages'] vint nous les arracher des
mains."—Ib. p. 60. Perhaps at such a place there was less to regret,
as Martene thought at *Brindler*, where he was plainly told that he
could not see the library. He consoled himself by remarking, that everything "parut fort petit et fort mince dans cette maison;" except, indeed,
the kitchen fire, made of whole trees, and the ten staghounds that lay
before it.—II. Voy. Lit. 248. At *Gigni* they were received politely by
the abbot, who promised that they should see everything the next day;
by which time he had changed his mind.—I. Voy. Lit. 173, 174. At
Lerins the abbot told them that the librarian had gone out for a
holiday, and would not be back for a month—"et que ainsi il n'y
avoit rien à faire pour nous à Lerins. La charité m'oblige de passer
sous silence le reste de nôtre entretien."—I. Voy. Lit. 273. Sometimes
it was managed with more politeness, as at *Lobbes*, where the abbot
was occupied in receiving the Princess of Nassau, and turned our
travellers over to the prior, who took them to his garden, and showed
them "beaucoup de puerilitez;" but they could not get a sight of the
library.—Ib. p. ii. 210. And sometimes, what might be civility, looked
very much like suspicion; as when the chapter of *Chalons*, after having,
with much difficulty, granted their request, appointed four canons,
"plutôt pour nous obseder que pour nous accompagner, qui ne nous
permirent pas de rien écrire."—Ib. 90. Nor does Martene fail to

the same as ours, and they did not think of mentioning the manuscripts of the Scriptures which they met
with, unless some accidental circumstance rendered
them remarkable, yet it would be easy to specify a
hundred copies of the whole, or parts of the Bible,
which they happen thus to mention, and which had
existed during the dark ages. I spare the reader the
details on this subject; but there is one point which
seems to me too curious and interesting to be passed
over. I have stated that, at many places, they found
no manuscripts; and perhaps I have said enough to
account for it. At other places there were one, or two,
or a few only remaining; and it is worthy of notice,
how frequently such relics consisted of Bibles, or parts
of the Scriptures. It may have been that there were
originally more of them, or it may have been that
they were better taken care of; but either way the
fact is so much to our purpose, that I must be allowed
to specify some of the cases.

At *Luxeuil,* "Il reste dans la bibliothèque quelques
manuscrits, dont les principaux sont l'ancien lectionaire
de la liturgie Gallicane, écrit en lettres merovingiennes,
un commentaire sur les pseaumes d'environ sept ou
huit cens ans, dont les premiers feuillets sont déchirez
. . . . . outre cela on voit dans la sacristie un tres
beau texte des évangiles," which had been presented
by Gerard, who was abbot in the early part of the
eleventh century.[3]

At the priory of *St. Lupicin,* near Claude in Franche

---

acknowledge the politeness of the two abbesses of "l'abbaye du
Paraclet, si fameuse par la retraite d'Abaillard et d'Eloïse"; and especially that of the younger — "qui nous fit l'honneur de ne nous pas
quitter," while searching the archives. — Ib. p. i. 85. *See Note* D.

[3] I. Voy. Lit. 168. Mab. Ann. IV. 237.

Comté, the only manuscript mentioned is a copy of the Gospels, "un fort beau livre, écrit en lettres unciales d'argent sur un velin de pourpre ou violet, dont l'écriture n'avoit gueres plus de neuf cens ans." [4]

At *St. Claude,* the only manuscripts which they mention are, "une fort belle Bible, qui a bien huit cens ans d'écriture, et un manuscrit de S. Eucher." [5]

At *La Grasse,* in Languedoc, the only manuscript mentioned is "un texte des évangiles qu'on prétend avoir été donné par l'empereur Charlemagne." [6]

At *Joüarre* the only MSS. mentioned are, "deux textes des évangiles, couverts de lames d'or," one seven, the other eight, hundred years old. [7]

At *Hautvilliers,* "Il n'y reste qu'un texte des évangiles, écrit en lettres d'or et d'une beauté charmante, qui est du temps de l'archévêque Ebon;" [8] that is, A.D. 816—845.

At the cathedral at *Rheims,* "On y voit encore plusieurs manuscrits tres-anciens, entr'autres un texte des évangiles, écrit sur du velin pourpré, et une Bible de l'archévêque Hincmar," [9] the successor of Ebbo.

At *Verdun,* though the canons had only the "méchant reste d'une bonne bibliothéque," yet they had "deux beaux textes des évangiles; l'un écrit en lettres majuscules il y a plus de 900 ans, ... et l'autre d'environ 700 ans." [1]

At *Metz,* though most of the MSS. belonging to the cathedral had been transferred to the library of M. Colbert, "Il en reste neanmoins encore quelques uns qui ne sont pas indifferens. Nous y vîmes entr'-autres une trés-belle Bible de sept ou huit cens ans; les grands et les petits prophetes écrits en lettres Saxones." [2]

---

[4] I. Voy. Lit. 175.   [5] I. Voy. Lit. 177.   [6] Ib. P. ii. 55.
[7] Ib. 74.   [8] Ib. 78.   [9] Ib. 79.   [1] Ib. 93.   [2] Ib. 110.

At *Pont à Mousson,* in the monastery of St. Mary, only four MSS. are mentioned, of which two were, "belles Bibles manuscrites d'environ 500 ans." [3]

At *St. Michel* only two mentioned, one "un tres beau pseautier, écrit en Grec." [4]

At *St. Riquier,* notwithstanding the "belle bibliothéque qui étoit autrefois," there were only two MSS. "qui méritent quelque attention." One "un texte des évangiles, écrit en lettres d'or sur du velin pourpré, donné à S. Angilbert par l'empereur Charlemagne," [5]

At *St. Vincent's,* at Metz, after repeated fires, "entre le peu de manuscrits qui restent dans la bibliothéque, nous y vîmes un tres-beau texte des évangiles." [6]

At *St. Medard,* at Soissons, "de tous les anciens monumens il ne reste à S. Medard qu'un ancien texte des évangiles, qu'on ne peut trop estimer . . . . . . c'est un present que l'empereur Louis le Debonnaire fit au monastere." [7]

At *St. Jean de Vigores,* "On y voit encore quelques manuscrits, que l'injure des tems n'a pas dissipé. Les principaux sont une Bible avec des concordances," and two others. [8]

At *St. Vaast's,* at Doüay, "Nous n'y vîmes pour tout manuscrits qu'un pseautier." [9]

"Les différentes revolutions arrivées à *Stavelo* sont cause qu'aujourd'hui on n'y trouve pas un si grand nombre de manuscrits, mais le peu qu'il y en a est bon. On y voit entr'autres une très belle Bible en deux grands volumes." [1]

---

[3] Ib. 128.   [4] Ib. 129.

[5] I. Voy. Lit. ii. 175.   [6] Ibid. 112.   [7] II. Voy. Lit. 17.

[8] Ib. 24.   [9] Ib. 76.

[1] Ib. 149.—Its date is given in the following inscription contained in it, which may also give an idea of the pains bestowed on such a work:—"Codices hi ambo quia continuatim et tamen morosius scripti

At *Malmidi,* "De tous les anciens monumens on a
à peine sauvé de l'incendie cinq ou six manuscrits
dont les principaux sont une Bible en deux volumes,
et un Joseph." [2]

At *La Val Dieu,* "Nous n'y avons trouvé pour tout
manuscrit qu'une Bible assez belle." [3]

At *Grimberg,* "La bibliotheque ayant été brûlée
par les heretiques, tous les manuscrits ont été con-
sumés par le feu. Il n'y reste aujourd'hui que deux
Bibles manuscrites, et d'anciens statuts synodaux de
l'eglise de Cambray." [4]

At *St. Pantaleon,* at Cologne, "Il y avoit autrefois
plusieurs manuscrits, mais les religieux, qui n'en con-
noissoient pas le prix, les ont vendu pour fort peu de
chose: il n'y reste qu'une très-belle Bible, l'histoire
ecclesiastique de Pierre le Mangeur et Jean Belet." [5]

"Comme tous les anciens monumens de l'Abbaye
d'Eisterbac ont été dissipez dans les guerres, nous n'y
trouvâmes de manuscrits qu'une Bible, avec les dialo-
gues et les homelies de Cesarius." [6]

"Les grandes revolutions arrivées à *Epternac* n'ont
pas tellement ruiné les anciens monumens qu'il n'y
reste encore plusieurs manuscrits;" and among them
(though only three others are mentioned) two extraordinary copies of the gospels. [7]

---

sunt per annos ferme IIII. in omni sua procuratione, hoc est scriptura,
illuminatione, ligatura uno eodemque anno perfecti sunt ambo. Licet
hic posterior qui est anterior, et ipse est annus ab incarnatione Domini
M. XCVII. indictione v. Henrico IIII. imperante, Christianorum exercitu
super paganos violenter agente. Obberto Leodicensi præsule, Rodulfo
Stabulensi abbate, Christo Domino ut semper infinita sæculorum sæcula
regnante. Amen."

[2] II. Voy. Lit. 171.   [3] Ib. 199.   [4] Ib. 112.

[5] Ib. 264.   [6] Ib. 270.

[7] Ibid. 297. It would be unpardonable not to notice that one of
these MSS. is a copy of the Gospels "écrit en lettres Saxones

I am quite aware that such details are tedious, but I do not know how I could have made out this part of the argument at all without them. Indeed, the apprehension of being charged with mere catalogue-making, has, I fear, led me to state it very imperfectly. I am, however, very anxious to get to other portions of the argument, which may, I hope, be more generally interesting, but which I could not venture upon without premising some attempt to show that a good many copies of the Scriptures did exist in the dark ages; and that, at all events, it is the most absurd thing in the world to infer their non-existence then, from their being scarce now. I hope to show not only that they existed, but that they were often in the hands of those who read and valued them.

---

corrigé à ce qu'on pretend sur l'original même de Saint Jerome; not, however, from any chance that this was actually the case, but from the real probability that it belonged to our countryman Willibrod, and was brought thither by him when he came there as a missionary in the seventh century.

No. XVIII.

"Esse niger monachus si forte velim Cluniaci,
  Ova fabasque nigras cum sale sæpe dabunt.
Surgere me facient media de nocte, volentem
  Amplius in calido membra fovere thoro.
Quodque magis nollem vellent me psallere sursum,
  Et geminare meos in diapente tonos."—BRUNELLUS.

IT may perhaps appear from the evidence which has
been adduced, that there is good ground for an opinion
that copies of the Scriptures were not so exceedingly
scarce in the Dark Ages as some persons would lead
us to suppose. I have shown that a good many existed;
and I have stated (and, indeed, given some incidental
proofs), that this existence is attested by a considerable
number which have survived those ages, and are now
in our libraries. It certainly was my intention to have
spoken much more fully on the latter of these points,
and to have afforded to the reader something like a
return of the number of copies of the bible, or of parts
of it, which are even now known to exist, and which
are believed, on good grounds, to have been written
in, or before, the Dark Ages. But I pass it over; and
I might claim the reader's gratitude for so doing, on
the ground that I have already occupied more space
than I intended, or he may have approved, in what
may be considered by many as dry details. I might
tell him, also (and very truly), that though the inquiry
would not be without interest, yet it is not very material
for my object, which is, as I have stated, to investigate
the actual state and means of scriptural knowledge
during the Dark Ages. I might add (and with equal
truth), that, having said more than enough respecting

that part of the proof which I introduced by stating, that it was in my view far from being the most im portant, I am anxious to get to some other parts, which may, it is hoped, prove more interesting to readers in general, and to some, perhaps, more convincing. All this I might say—but I had rather acknowledge the simple fact, which is, that I am unable, at present, to give anything like a satisfactory statement on the subject. I hoped that before this time I should have received information which I have not yet been able to obtain, and by which I might have rendered what I have had it in my power to glean less imperfect.

Let us, then, go to another part of the argument. I do not know whether to call it the next, for the parts are so connected, and so intimately dependent on each other, that is not only impossible to separate them completely, but extremely difficult to decide which should be taken first. Hitherto our inquiries have commonly led us to the monastery in which the books forming our subject were written and reposited ; and it may be natural to inquire next (as it is, indeed, a most important point to learn) how far we have reason to believe that the inmates of the cloister had any knowledge of the contents of those volumes of which they were confessedly the transcribers and the guardians. It will greatly promote our understanding of this, and of our subject in general, if we first take a hasty glance at one or two of the monastic institutions of the period ; especially at one, which may be called the child of those times, born and brought up in what is commonly considered as the darkest of the Dark Ages— the century which has been distinguished as the "Sæculum Obscurum."

As to the pedigree of Count Berno, it is even more obscure than the age in which he lived ; and whether

he was, or was not, of Burgundian descent, it does
not concern us to inquire. It is clear that he and
his cousin, Laifin, founded the monastery of Gigni, in
the northern part of the diocese of Lyons, between
Lion-le-Saunier and St. Amour, some time, and probably not long, before the year 896. This appears
from a letter of Pope Formosus, dated in that year,
which also informs us they had endowed it with their
property, and that Berno had become the first abbot.[1]
That it was not completed for a considerable time
we may presume from the language of a charter
granted by Rodulph, King of Burgundy, eighteen
years afterwards.[2] In consequence of Berno's appli-

---

[1] Baluz. Misc. ii. 159.

[2] The language of the charter is, "Reverentissimus Abbas adiit nostram magnitudinem petens nos ut quendam locum Gigniacum, quem
ipse Abbas et sui confratres tenent vel construunt regulariter, rebus
proprietatis nostræ ditaremus."—*Bal. ibid.* 161. I know that it is not
safe, in Latin of this period, to lay much stress on moods and tenses;
but the probability is, that the building was a long business; and even
if I misconstrue *construunt*, yet it gives me an opportunity of reminding
my readers, that in those ages to which we owe most of our churches,
and certainly the best, the building was a gradual process. To this day
it is very commonly so in the Romish church; while our way, generally speaking, is to do all at once. Yet, at a time when so much
church building is obviously wanted, and so much actually projected,
might it not be worth while to give a moment's consideration to the
old way? Generally speaking, we make the church *at once* all that it
is meant to be; and with a view to this immediate perfection all our
estimates are framed. For a given sum, say 10,000*l.*, we can have
one large church of the plan A or two small churches of the
plan B; or if we like to have something between the two, we may
have the plan C for 7,500*l.* Well, but suppose we want as large a
church as A, and have only half or three quarters of the 10,000*l.*;
how much of *that* plan can we get executed for 5,000*l.* or 7,500*l.*?
—or, if we want such a church as C, how much of *that* can we get
executed for the *full cost* of B? Can we get a place which, though
to the eye of taste and science it may be obviously unfinished, may

cation, the king granted to him and his monastery
the cell of Beaume, which he and his monks had
restored and rebuilt; and he continued to govern
Gigni and the dependent cell with strict discipline.
This, at least, we may believe, from various circumstances, and especially from one which occurred about
the year 909, when two strangers applied for admit-
tance into the fraternity of Beaume. Before they could
make the formal request, some of the monks got
about them, and drew such a picture of the abbot's
severity that one of the strangers would have turned
back. Adegrin, however, was better informed respecting the place; and, moreover, had the sagacity to
suspect that those who gave such a horrible account
of discipline might be the persons who were most
obnoxious to it; and, encouraged by him, his companion Odo entered. [3]

---

yet be so far complete as to be a respectable place for the performance
of divine worship for a few years, during which the original design
may be carried into full execution ? It is, humanly speaking, impossible
that one generation should build half the churches which are now
wanted in this country ; but we are building a good many, and we
may hope that each one will be a tree whose seed is in itself, or
which will at least have such a principle of vitality as will enable it
to grow up to maturity.

[3] I have already mentioned that our Benedictine travellers visited
Gigni, and I cannot help transcribing a few words of what they say
respecting both these places : — "Nous arrivâmes à Beaume comme on
sortoit de vêpres ; .... cette Abbaye est fort ancienne, et recomman-
dable par la retraite de Saint Odon et de Saint Adegrin, qui y ont fait
profession de la vie religieuse. La situation est des plus affreuses qu'on
puisse voir; on n'y arrive que par une gorge serrée de deux rochers
escarpez d'une hauteur prodigieuse. Le lieu même où il est bâtie est
fort étroit, et de tous côtez on ne voit rien que des rochers steriles et
élevez à perte de vûë .... *Aujourd'hui* ce lieu si saint, qui a servi de
retraite à tant de serviteurs de Dieu, et d'asile à tant de pécheurs con-
vertis, est devenu *en proye à la noblesse du païs*, qui regarde l'abbaye

In the next year, the abbot Berno laid the foundations of what afterwards became one of the most celebrated and influential monasteries, during, and beyond, the period of the Dark Ages. Under the auspices, and at the expense, of William, Count of Auvergne, commonly called William the Pious, he formed a monastery at Clugni, near Macon, in Burgundy. As to the monasteries which he afterwards founded or superintended, it is not to our purpose to inquire; for it is only as the founder of Clugni that I here introduce him. To that monastery he transferred his residence; and Odo, who accompanied him, became his successor in the year 927. The fame of this second abbot of Clugni so far eclipsed that of his predecessor

de Beaume comme *une décharge de leur famille ;* et pour y être religieux, il faut faire preuve de seize lignes de noblesse." After Beaume, they visited Gigni — "Qui étoit autrefois une abbaye illustre, fondée par S. Bernon, et ensuite réduite en Prieuré soumis à Cluni. Ce monastère, aussi-bien que celui de Beaume, sert de décharge aux familles nobles . . . . nous prîmes le chemin de S. Claude, et monsieur le Chambrier nous donna un garçon pour nous conduire à une demie lieuë de là. Ce bon enfant se mit à nous entretenir de la vie des moines de Gigny, comme ils passoient tout leur temps à se divertir : je n'entre pas dans le détail de ce qu'il nous dit, parce qu'il ne leur est pas fort honorable. Voilà la gloire que Dieu retire de ces maisons de noblesse, et l'édification qui en revient au prochain. Et on appelle un grand bien pour les familles de la Province, ce qui est capable de leur attirer la malediction de Dieu."—I. *Voy. Lit.* 171, &c. Only imagine that St. Berno could have resumed his place, and that some friendly voice had whispered to these modern religious, as the monks of Beaume did to Odo, when he applied for admission, "Nosti consuetudinem Bernonis Abbatis? At ille: Nusquam, inquit. Et illi: Heu, heu, si sciretis quam dure scit ille monachum tractare. Correptionem vero suam sequuntur verbera, et rursum quos verberat compedibus ligat, domat carcere, jejuniis affigit: et hæc omnia perpessus, nec sic suam potest miser impetrare gratiam." *Mab. A. S.* vii. 158. Making all due allowance for exaggeration, there must have been something about Abbot Berno which the merry monks of the eighteenth century would not have liked at all.

that many have erroneously considered him as the
founder; but however probable it may be that he was
the man of the most learning, the most expanded
mind, and most extensive views, and perhaps of
better informed, if not more zealous piety, yet it
were unjust to deny that what he did was built on
the foundation of his predecessor, and that he was
probably enabled to do it, not only by the property
which had been acquired, or the buildings which had
been raised, but by the rigid discipline which had
been instituted and maintained.

Odo, before he came to Beaume, had been schoolmaster and precentor of the cathedral church of St. Martin,
at Tours. While in his cradle, his father had devoted
him to that saint; and he had been brought up by
Fulk the Good, Count of Anjou, who was himself one
of the canons of that church. [4] As he grew up, his father
seems to have repented of his oblation to St. Martin,

---

[4] "In monasterio beati Martini apud Turonos collegio fratrum adscrip-
tus, Canonicus ibidem esse, et dici, gaudebat. In festis etiam ejusdem
Sancti in choro inter psallentes clericos cum veste clericali, et sub
disciplina eorum astabat." The count's pithy letter to Lewis the Fourth
of France, who had ridiculed him for this, is well known — "Regi
Francorum Comes Andegavorum: Noveritis, Domine, quod Rex illiteratus est asinus coronatus." It is to the credit of Lewis, who, if he
was an illiterate king, certainly was not merely an ass with a crown
on, that he observed on reading it, "It is true that wisdom, and eloquence,
and letters, are especially becoming in kings and counts; for the more
exalted any man is in point of station, the more eminent should he
be in respect of morals and learning." The historian adds, that those
who laughed at the pious and book-learned count, were constrained to
respect the soldier:—"Factum est ut omnes qui Deo dignum ac litte-
ratum Consulem ac strenuum militem illudendo caput agitabant, postmodum eum in reverentiam haberent, qui licet litteris regulisque grammaticæ artis, Aristotelicis Ciceronianisque ratiocinationibus perspicacius
peritissime eruditus esset, inter majores et meliores ac strenuos milites
optimus habebatur."— *Gesta Cons. Andegav. ap. Dach. Spicil.* iii. 245.

and to have wished to bring up his son to a military life; and for that purpose, he placed him in the service of the Count of Auvergne, who has been already mentioned. But military exercises and field sports seem soon to have become wearisome to young Odo. An inveterate headache, which, from his seventeenth to his nineteenth year defied all the medical skill which his parents could procure for him, seems to have at length awakened the father's conscience, and to have reminded him that his suffering son had been devoted to St. Martin; and superstition suggested that the sickness was judicial, and indicated the anger of the saint. The vow was performed, and, perhaps, without much reluctance by the father; who, though a layman, and tempted for awhile to devote his handsome and accomplished son to that which was then considered the most noble profession, was himself a learned and a reading man. "My father," said Odo, in reply to the inquiries of the monk to whom we are indebted for his life, "was named Abbo, but he seemed to be a different sort of person, and to have acted differently, from men of the present day; for he had by heart the histories of the ancients, and the Novellæ of Justinian. At his table there was always the reading of the gospel. If at any time a dispute arose, there was such a general opinion of the soundness of his judgment, that people came to him from all parts to obtain his decision; and on this account, he was much respected by everybody, and particularly by the most puissant Count William." Odo seems to have inherited the taste for reading. I have, in a former paper, mentioned how he was deterred from the study of heathen literature, [5] but it was only to pursue sacred

---

[5] No. XI. p. 212.

knowledge—relictis carminibus poetarum, alti edoctus spiritu consilii, ad Evangeliorum, Prophetarumque expositores se totum convertit—and when he entered at the priory of Beaume he brought with him his private stock of books, amounting to a hundred volumes. He succeeded Berno as Abbot of Clugni in the year 927. My object is not to write the history of the monastery, or the lives of its abbots; my reason for mentioning the place at all will soon be obvious; but I wish first, as briefly as possible, to give the reader some idea of the persons whose names I am obliged to mention, and to state some few circumstances respecting them which have reference to my object. With this view I give the following anecdotes of Odo:—

"At that time," says his biographer, "when we were crossing the Cottian Alps, with Gerald, Bishop of Riez... in that same journey there was a feeble old man, who was passing over that part of the Alps at the same time with us. He was carrying a bag full of bread, and garlic, and onions, and leeks, the smell of which herbs I could by no means endure. But the pious father no sooner saw the old man than he made him get on his horse, and undertook to carry the most vile-smelling bag himself; and I, unable to bear such a stink, dropt away from the side of my companion. Having got over the steepest part of the Alps and beginning to descend, I saw him from a distance yield to the importunity of the old man, and remount his horse; but even then he did not give back the bag to its owner, but hung it at his saddle bow. I then set forward, passing those who were before me; and when I got near to him I went hastily, and with a sense of shame, and presently after I had come up with him, he called to me, 'Come here, for there are still some psalms remaining which we have to chaunt;' and when

I told him that I could not bear the stink of that bag,
he immediately rebuked me, saying, 'Alack-a-day, what
you call stinking the poor man can eat, while you
cannot bear to smell it; the poor man can carry it,
and you say you cannot bear to look at it.' But this
he said with reference to himself, who was one of the
true poor of Christ; and with these, and the like sayings,
he reproved me, and so cured my sense of smelling,
that I was no longer sensible of any ill savour." [6]

I mention this circumstance principally for the sake
of noticing the custom of repeating the psalms on a
journey, which was by no means a peculiarity of Odo.
It might, indeed, in this case, be the office for the
canonical hours; but, independent of this, I believe
the custom of repeating the psalms under such
circumstances to have been very frequent. The biographer of Odo tells us, that being obliged to travel
about a great deal on diplomatic business (pro pace
regum et principum), as well as for the reformation
of monasteries, thieves lay in wait for him; and once
a banditti of forty were on the point af attacking
him; but when one of them who was their leader,
named Aimon, saw him, and the monks who were
with him, persist in chanting the psalms without interruption, and go on their way thus chanting, he was
immediately struck with compunction, and said to his
companions, "I do not remember ever to have seen
such men as these, and I do not think that such have
been seen anywhere else;" nor could the entreaties
of his comrades persuade him to attack them. [7]

---

[6] Mab. A. S. Tom. vii. p. 165.

[7] There may, perhaps, appear, to enlightened readers of the present
day, something very ridiculous in the perpetual psalmsinging of the
monks; and, in fact, it has been a very common topic of pleasantry.
Were it not that the malignity is as disgusting as the absurdity is

Odo was succeeded by Aymard, who was an old man at the time of his election; and who, becoming blind six years afterwards, resigned the office of abbot, in the year 942, in favour of Maiolus, or, in more modern language, St. Mayeul. Aymard, however, lived many years after this, and appears to have considered himself as still abbot, and on one occasion to have vindicated his authority in a manner which may be worth noticing, as it gives a lively picture of the discipline and subordination kept up in the monastery.

"From the monks of the venerable monastery of Clugni," says Peter Damian, who visited the place in the year 1062, "I happened to learn two remarkable instances of holy humility, one of which may be extremely edifying to prelates, and the other to subjects. Aymard, who was abbot of that monastery, made Maiolus his substitute; and sought repose in his old age. While he was living as a private person in the infirmary, he sent one evening for some cheese, which the cellarer, being as usual very busy, not only did not give, but bestowed some uncivil speeches on the messenger, complaining that there was such a multitude of abbots, and that he did not know how to manage with so many masters. The old man having heard of this, was not a little offended; and, being entirely blind, the vexation took the greater hold on

---

amusing, one must needs laugh at the motive which Tyndale, the reformer, assigns for the practice:—"Your singing is but roaring, to stretch out your maws (as do your other gestures and rising at midnight) to make the meat sink to the bottom of the stomach, that he may have perfect digestion, and be ready to devour afresh against the next refection."—*Expos. on Matt.* vii. 15. It does not enter into our present purpose to discuss their motive—the *fact* that there was one very large portion of the scriptures which they were expected to know by heart, and which they were continually repeating, is obvious and important.

his mind; for blind persons, from the very circumstance of their want of sight, ruminate more deeply
in their hearts on what they hear, and it acts as
a greater stimulus to resentment, because the impression is not weakened by the sight of external objects.
In the morning, however, he ordered his servant to
lead him into the chapter, and being come there, he
addressed the abbot to this effect— 'Brother Maiolus,
I did not set you above myself that you might persecute me, or rule over me as a buyer does over his
slave, but I chose you that you might feel for me as a
son for a father;'—and, after a good deal to the same
purport, being nearly overcome, he added, ' Are you, I
beg leave to ask, my monk ?' and the other replying,
,I am, and I profess that I was never more so than I am
at this moment,'—'If you are my monk,' said Aymard,
,instantly quit your seat and go to the place which you
used to occupy.' Maiolus, on hearing this, immediately
rose, and, as he was ordered, took a lower place;
and Aymard, as if he had come home again after an
absence, took the vacant seat. He stated his charge
against the cellarer who had offended him, and while
he was prostrate, sharply rebuked him, and then enjoined him such penance as he thought proper. Then,
having performed allthe duty for which he had resumed
that brief authority, he immediately dethroned himself,
and ordered Maiolus to resume his seat. He did so
without the slightest hesitation." [8]

---

[8] Opusc. 33, c. 7, cited Mab. A. S. Tom. V. p. 233. The Liber
Ordinis S. Victoris Parisiensis, cited by Du Cange in v. *Infirmaria*,
says, " In infirmaria tria sunt genera infirmorum. Sunt enim quidam qui
lecto prorsus decubant. Sunt alii qui de infirmitate convalescunt, et jam
surgere et ambulare possunt : sed tamen pro reparatione virum adhuc
in Infirmaria sunt. Sunt alii qui hujusmodi infirmitatem non habent, et

Maiolus, soon after his entrance into the monastery, had been appointed librarian, and held some other

---

tamen in Infirmaria assidue comedunt et jacent ut senes, et cœci, et debiles et hujusmodi."

Turketul, who has been already mentioned (No. XV. p. 283) was Abbot of Croyland at the same time that Maiolus presided at Clugni. Ingulph gives us an interesting account of the classes into which he divided his monks. First, the juniors, who remained in that class during the first twenty-four years after their profession. Secondly, those who had passed through that period, and were for the next sixteen years excused from certain services and severities of monastic discipline, but bore the labour and responsibility of the general management of the monastery — "cum istis magnitudo negotiorum, et providentia consiliorum, ac totius loci solicitudo specialiter incumbit." Thirdly, those who had passed through both these periods, and had therefore been monks forty years. These were called the seniors, and were for the next ten years entitled to greater indulgences. Indeed, after the two first years of the ten, they were excused from all official duties of a secular nature, except in cases of emergency. "He who has attained the fiftieth year of profession," continues Ingulph, "shall be called a *Sempecta*, and he shall have a good chamber assigned to him by the prior, in the infirmary; and he shall have an attendant or servant specially appointed to wait on him, who shall receive from the abbot an allowance of provision, the same in mode and measure as is allowed for the servant of a knight in the abbot's hall. To the Sempecta the prior shall every dag assign a companion, as well for the instruction of the junior, as for the solace of the senior; and their meals shall be supplied to them from the infirmary kitchen according to the allowance for the sick. As to the Sempecta himself, he may sit or walk, or go in or go out, according to his own will and pleasure. He may go in and out of the choir, the cloister, the refectory, the dormitory, and the other offices of the monastery, with or without a frock, how and when he pleases. Nothing unpleasant respecting the concerns of the monastery shall be talked of before him. Nobody shall vex him about anything, but in the most perfect peace and quietness of mind, he shall wait for his end."

There is something in this arrangement, this care "to rock the cradle of declining age," so beautiful that I do not like to suppress it, especially as it throws light, which some readers may want, on the fact of the old abbot's residence in the infirmary; but the worst of these long notes is, that they do themselves want notes; at least I do not like to

important offices; but, as I am not writing his memoirs,
I say nothing of the various transactions in which he
was engaged, of the monasteries which he reformed,

---

give this passage without two. First, if any reader does not understand
what is meant by the word *Sempecta*, I wish him to know that I am
in the same predicament, having never seen any etymology which was
at all satisfactory. Secondly, I hesitated a good while before I could
bring myself to translate *froccus* by *frock*, though I believe that to be
the right word, and that the garment was so called by the monks of
France in the vulgar tongue, merely because (notwithstanding some recent
changes in clerical costume) I do not like to suggest the idea of a
person so aged, and circumstanced, in a frock coat. As to the garment
itself, not having the artist, whom Ingulph calls the "Serviens Cissor
de Sartrina," of Croyland, at my elbow, I am not sure that I could
describe it with technical accuracy; but it may perhaps be enough to
say that it was the upper garment, differing only from that commonly
used by the monks from its having no cowl. Another evil of these
long notes is, that one gets into a gossiping way, and one story leads
to another. I cannot fancy this Sempecta rambling about the monastery
at his pleasure without being reminded of an old soldier of my acquaintance, who, after gaining great reputation, but losing his two sons,
in the crusades, took refuge in a cloister — or, as a monk of the house
says:—

> "Ipse post militiæ cursum temporalis,
>   Illustratus gratia doni spiritualis,
>   Esse Christi cupiens miles specialis,
>   In hac domo monachus factus est claustralis.
> Ultra modum placidus, dulcis et benignus,
>   Ob ætatis senium candidus ut cygnus,
>   Blandus et affabilis, ac amari dignus,
>   In se Sancti Spiritus possidebat pignus.
> Nam sanctam ecclesiam sæpe frequentabat,
>   Missarum mysteria lætus auscultabat,
>   Et quas scire poterat laudes personabat,
>   Ac cælestem gloriam mente ruminabat.
> Ejus conversatio dulcis et jocosa,
>   Valde commendabilis et religiosa,
>   Ita cunctis fratribus fuit gratiosa,
>   Quod nec gravis extitit nec fastidiosa."

of the preferment (including the papacy) which he
refused—but I will notice one or two things respecting
his literary character. I have said that Odo (one of
his predecessors) had been deterred from the study of
profane learning by a dream; and Maiolus seems,
without any such intimation, to have renounced it, so
far, at least, as poetry was concerned. It may be a
sufficient proof that he was a reading man, if I say
that it was his custom to read on horseback. [9] There

We may easily suppose that the old crusader, who had gone to the
Holy Land "Equis et divitiis satis sublimatus, et præclara militum
turba stipatus," and who had himself been employed as an ambassador
to the Soldan, had tales of travel and danger which would make him
a very acceptable companion in a monastery; and we may imagine
him roaming about it like the old Sempecta—

> "Hic per claustrum quotiens transiens meavit,
> Hinc et hinc ad monachos caput inclinavit,
> Et sic nutu capitis eos salutavit,
> Quos affectu intimo plurimum amavit."

I am ashamed of the length of this note—but I must add what really
relates to our subject. I do not know whether this old gentleman was
generally quartered in the infirmary, or whether it was only so when
he was ill; but we are told that, in that case—

> "Ipse nihilominus missas frequentabat
> Unde Infirmarius ipsum increpabat,
> Et ut requiesceret eum exorabat.
> Dicens, 'Franco, remane, vinum tibi dabo
> Et te bonis epulis pascam et cibabo.'" &c.—*Mart.* iii. 1333.

I cite this that the reader may see, by the argument of the Infirmarius,
that the young brother who was appointed in turn to spend the day
with the Sempecta, was not sent on an unpleasant duty. All was, of
course, subject to rule, but there was more licence as to good cheer
in the infirmary than in any other part of the monastery; and, in fact,
sham *ægrotats* were among the little tricks against which the superiors
in monasteries had to be on their guard.

[9] "Adeo lectioni semper erat deditus, ut in itinere positus libellum
sæpius gestaret in manibus. Itaque in equitando reficiebatur animus

is certainly a story of his falling asleep over the works
of Dionysius the Areopagite—a thing which might be
forgiven, if for no other reason, to men who never

---

legendo."—*Mab. A. S.* VII. 771. The same thing (and, omitting *semper*,
in the same words) is told of Halinardus, who became Abp. of Lyons
in A.D. 1046. Ibid. IX. 35. I do not wish to anticipate what I hope
to say of *reading-men* in the Dark Ages; but of course it is impossible
to prevent their making their appearance incidentally from time to
time. I cannot, however, mention their equitation without annexing
some kind of protest ; and, to say the least, an expression of doubt
whether they ought to ride on horseback at all without some good
reason. This same Abbot Maiolus nearly lost his life by going to sleep
on his horse, who happily stopped just in time to save him from being
struck by the projecting branch of a tree. Ibid. VII. 384. And Thierry,
afterwards Abbot of St. Hubert's, in the forest of Ardennes (born 1007),
got into circumstances of still greater peril. While he was a monk at
Stavelo he was attending his Abbot Poppo to Liege, and somehow
("forte intentus cantico psalmorum," says his biographer), he suffered
his horse to wander from the company, and follow a by-path, just
as they were coming to the Ambleve. Though the river was swelled
with the winter's rain, and the foaming torrent was rolling forward
stones and uprooted trees, the abbot and the rest of his train passed
over the ford in safety; and having arrived at the other side they saw
the poor monk, still muffled in his hood, and wholly unconscious of
his situation, riding on a lofty wooden bridge, constructed for foot
passengers only, and supposed to be altogether impassable for any
others (pons ligneus, in medios quidem agros ab utraque fluminis ripa
distentus, in medio autem propter hibernas aquas longe elatus ; sed ita
angustus, ut neque equis, neque bobus, neque asinis possit esse aliquo
modo pervius). Thierry, we are told, never once looked about him ;
and to this, humanly speaking, he seems to have owed his preservation.
He knew nothing of the danger in which he had been placed, until
he had descended among his anxious companions, in whose thankful-
ness and astonishment he heartily joined when they had explained to
him the cause of it—mirantibus et prædicantibus sociis divinæ virtutis
gratiam in suo facto ipse stupuit.—Ibid. IX. 566. A more prudent man
was Gerard Bishop of Csannad in Hungary (cir. A.D. 1048), who
always rode in a carriage, reading his own works—non jumento uteba-
tur sed vehiculo, in quo sedens, libros quos Sancti Spiritus gratia
composuerat, relegebat.—Ibid. VIII. 551.

had a night's rest; especially if, as one of his biographers tells us, he had been preaching; "distributa in monachos substantia verbi Dei, et sermoni ad eos habito."

One other circumstance of his life I must also mention. Returning from Rome, he and his companions were set upon in one of the passes of the Alps, and taken prisoners by the Saracens. Of course they were plundered; and the abbot's biographer tells us that he lost all the books which he had with him except one—cæteros sacros codices cum omnibus quæ hic habebat. That one was a book on the Assumption of the Virgin, which he seems to have had in his bosom at the time (vestis sub tegmine) and which escaped the search of the enemy. [1] The hope of ransom gained him permission to send a monk to Clugni with the following pithy epistle, manu propria conscriptam,—

"To the lords and brethren of Clugni, the wretched Maiolus, a captive and in chains.

"The floods of ungodly men have compassed me about; the snares of death prevented me. [2] Send, if you please, the price of ransom for me, and those who were made prisoners with me."

This letter produced grief and consternation among the brethren; and the next day a large sum (infiniti ponderis pecunia), which was raised by almost stripping the monastery of whatever could be turned into money, was sent off, and the abbot regained his liberty. Moreover, as his biographer tells us, the outrage was revenged by the Christians, who slew the Saracens,

---

[1] Mab. A. S. VII. 779. The learned Benedictine does not lose the opportunity of stating that there had been a controversy in the ninth century between Hincmar, Abp. of Rheims, and "nostros Corbeienses," in which the latter had maintained that this book was not a genuine work of St. Jerome.

[2] *Torrentes Belial*, as in the Vulgate and Heb. II. Sam. xxii. 5, 6.

and took great spoil, which they divided among themselves. They considered, however, that the Abbot Maiolus had a right to a share; because, though absent, there could be no doubt that the victory was in some degree owing to his merits; and therefore (either from a knowledge of his taste, or more probably under the guidance of their own) they assigned to him all the books of which he had been plundered—"propterea sacros codices, quos barbari rapuerant beato viro, sua pro parte miserunt."

I wish Brother Syrus, to whom we are indebted for this account, had told us what the books were, especially as it appears from another source that the single book which he mentions as having been saved was not the best which the abbot had in his travelling library. Glaber Rodulphus incidentally mentions that while he was in the hands of the Saracens, one of them, who was smoothing a piece of wood, grieved him by putting his foot on the Bible, which, "according to custom, he was in the habit of carrying with him." [3] That he was, indeed, with whatever mixture of superstition, in the habit of deferring to the Word of God, may be charitably hoped from another fact incidentally stated by his biographer—or, if this be thought too much, it will at least show that he had the Word of God at hand, and thought it worth while to appear to consult it. I have already said that he refused the papacy—the Emperor Otho II. and the Empress so strongly urged him to accept it, that he knew not what to do; for, says his biographer, "he would not leave the little flock which it had pleased Christ to

---

[3] "Alius quoque Saracenorum eorumdem cultro deplanans ligni castulam, posuit incunctanter pedem super viri Dei codicem, bibliothecam scilicet, quam ex more secum consueverat."—*Mab.* A. S. VII. 756.

commit to him; and desired to live in poverty with Him who descended from the height of heaven, and became poor. But, being pressed by both these great persons, he endeavoured to obtain some delay. Then he betook himself to the refuge of prayer, hoping, through that means, to obtain the divine guidance as to what he should do, and what answer he should make to such powerful importunity. As he rose from prayer, a copy of the epistles happened to catch his eye; and having opened it, a passage presented itself at the top of the page, which he looked upon as a word of instruction from heaven. What he thus found he began reading to those about him. 'Beware, lest any man spoil you through philosophy and vain deceit, after the tradition of men, after the rudiments of the world, and not after Christ.' He confessed to his companions that he ought, with all his soul, to practise that which this text of Scripture taught him;" and in fact he did so—he remained Abbot of Clugni as long as he lived.

In the year 990, when Maiolus had governed the monastery two-and-forty years, Odilo was associated with him (as Maiolus had been with Aymard), and in the year 994 he succeeded him. The only points of his history which I will here mention bear a considerable resemblance to those just mentioned with respect to Maiolus. The monastery of Nantua had been placed under his care; and once, in going over Mount Jura, in his way to Geneva, he was obliged to cross a river which ran down the side of that mountain. The mule which carried his bed and his books (qui lectulum hominis Dei ferebat simul cum libris) being without a guide, missed the proper ford, and began to get into deep water. All the company ran together, shouting, and the animal, by a strong effort, raised itself, and reached the bank with outstretched neck. A servant put forth his hand to catch at the bridle, but the mule, misconstruing the action, turned about, swam across the stream, with only its head above water, and, on reaching the opposite bank, was with some difficulty rescued. Brother Jotsald (the contemporary biographer of Odilo) mentions these circumstances on account of the miracle which followed. On opening the package which the mule carried, the cloths, such as napkins, towels, &c., alone were wet, and the bed (I suppose I should say mattress) and books were dry. Master Peter, who had charge of the abbot's things, and who had been in a dreadful fidget while the mule was in the water, pushed forward, and was the first to tell the abbot what he could not be brought to believe, until, on their arrival at the quarters for the night, he ordered the books to be brought to him. Whether he then supposed that there had been any miracle I do not know; but all that he is recorded to have said is, "Oh, my dear brethren, you see the wonderful mercy of God to us. Indeed, he has preserved to us unhurt those things which would have been irrecoverably spoiled by being wet, and has suffered those things to become wet which could sustain no injury from it." Whatever view the abbot, or his biographer might take of the matter, the modern reader will perhaps be most disposed to find a miracle in the fact that the books were there at all.

On another occasion, while passing over the same mountains, a horse, who bore a variety of packages, lost his footing, and slipped down the side, until he reached the deep valley, full of sharp rocks. It was with much difficulty that they could get to him; but when they did, they found him unhurt, and part of his burthen with him; but the abbot's sacramentary, written

in letters of gold, and some glass vessels with embossed
work were missing—quæ res non parum viri Dei mæs-
tificavit animum.[4] It could not, however, be helped,
nor could the rain and snow which followed; but when
the abbot arrived in the evening, at a cell belonging
to the Abbey of St. Claude, he besought the brethren
to institute a search, which they cheerfully undertook
to do. Here accounts differ; but (whether on the next
day, or two months after, when the snow had thawed
and the lost goods were forgotten) all agree that the
book and the glasses were found uninjured. If he resembled his predecessor in thus carrying about books,
he resembled him also in refusing—seriously and
absolutely—very high preferment when urged upon him
by almost irresistible authority. The pope would have
made him Archbishop of Lyons, sent him the pall and
ring, and peremptorily ordered him to assume the office.
He positively refused; and, notwithstanding the most
urgent entreaties and menaces of the pope,[5] he continued
Abbot of Clugni.

---

[4] This was part of his travelling *capella*, as they called the collection of all things necessary for the performance of divine offices which
prelates and ecclesiastics of rank took with them on their journeys.
For instance, Ekkehard, junior (who wrote about 1040), mentions, in
speaking of an Archbishop of Treves, "capellam qua itinerans uteba-
tur cum reliquiis, et libris, et omnibus utensilibus sacris." — Ap. *Gold.
Scr. Rer. Al.* I. p. 15. Many other instances are referred to by
Du Cange in v. *Capella*, No. 3.

[5] See the pope's letter, Dach. Sp. III. 381, and Lab. Conc. IX. 858.

No. XIX.

"Sicut tibi notum est, sacra lectio et oratio in nostro ordine sibi invicem succedunt. De lectione itur ad orationem, ab oratione reditur ad lectionem; et sicut vester ordo [Cisterciensis] est activus, quia elegit sibi justum laborem cum Martha; ita noster ordo est contemplativus, quia elegit sibi sanctum otium cum Maria, quæ quia elegit sibi, Christo teste, partem meliorem, non dubito nostrum ordinem vestro ordine esse digniorem."—DIAL. INT. CLUNIAC. ET CISTERCIEN. MON

ONE might easily say a great deal about Hugh, Abbot of Clugni, for he held the office sixty years; that is, from A.D. 1049 to 1109, and was engaged in many of the most important transactions of his time; but of the ten thousand monks who are said to have been under his superintendence, my present business is with one, for whose sake I have given this slight reference to the history of Clugni and its abbots. Let us come to him at once.

Ulric was born of a noble family at Ratisbon. His father, Bernold, was high in the favour of the Emperor Henry III., and he was himself brought up in the court. His disposition to letters was manifested very early; and his constant attendance on divine service, and the interest which he took in it (though, in his case, it seems to have been self-devotion), has led his biographer to compare him to the child Samuel.[1] He

---

[1] "Divinæ legis præcepta, docente eum intrinsecus Spiritu-sancto, intentissime legebat, legendo intelligebat, intelligendo conservabat, conservando summa mentis alacritate, quantum in ipso fuerat, operibus implere satagebat. In templo Domini crebro aderat, ac laudes supernæ majestati pro modulo suo devote celebrans, in conspectu Domini Sabaoth, velut alter Samuel, simplici mente ministrabat." — *Mab.* A. S. IX. 777, 778.

became a favourite with the Empress Agnes, whom I have had occasion to mention once before. [2] That she was the consort of Henry III.,—that after his death, in the year 1056, she acted as regent,—that she had the management of her son, Henry IV., then only five years old, until, six years afterwards, he was taken from her by stratagem,—and that she subsequently devoted herself to a religious life, are facts which may be found in most histories of the period; but as she has thus come in our way, I wish to speak of her somewhat more particularly, for there are one or two documents relating to her history which seem to me very interesting. The first is a short letter (or rather a part of one, but, I believe, all that has been published) to the abbot and monks of Frutari, which strongly, though briefly and unaffectedly, describes the unhappy state of mind under which she pursued that migratory course of devotion, which, though complimented as resembling the journey of the Queen of Sheba, was, in fact, leading her about from shrine to shrine, from one broken cistern to another, ignorant of the rock which followed her:—

"Agnes, empress and sinner, to the good father Albert, and the brethren assembled in the name of the Lord, at Frutari, offers the service of an handmaid, whose eyes are unto the hands of her mistress.

"My conscience terrifies me worse than any spectre, or any apparition. Therefore I fly through the places of the saints, seeking where I may hide myself from the face of this terror; and I am not a little desirous to come to you, whose intercession I have found to be a certain relief. But our ways are in the hand of God, and not left to our own will. In the meantime, I do in spirit kneel at your feet, [3] &c."

Peter Damian, whom she met with at Rome, and to whom she made a general confession, bears witness to the deep anguish with which she detailed what

---

[2] No. XIII. p. 239.   [3] Mab. Anal. I 164.

seemed to him to amount only to vain thoughts and childish levities, for which he knew not how to assign any penance. What she gained from him I know not; but I am inclined to hope and believe that her troubled spirit was afterwards under the instruction of one who was, in some degree, qualified to lead her feet into the way of peace. I form this opinion of John, who was Abbot of Fescamp, in Normandy, for fifty years, from a few scraps which have been published from his neglected, and almost unknown, manuscripts. [4] One is entitled "Thanksgivings for the Benefits of the Divine Mercy." But it seems rather to have been a prayer, composed when he entered on the office of abbot. The marks of omission I give as I find them, without knowing whether they indicate that the MS. was imperfect or illegible, or that the transcriber intentionally omitted the intervening words:—

"Christ God, my hope........ I pray, entreat, and beseech thee, that thou wouldst perfect in me that work of thy mercy which thou hast begun. For I, the lowest of thy servants, not forgetting those benefits of thy compassion which thou hast granted to me, a sinner, do give thee thanks, that through thy mere mercy thou hast freed me, unworthy as I am, from the bonds of original sin, by the water of sacred baptism, and by the renewing of the Holy Ghost...... Thou shepherd and ruler of all, Christ God, who, for no worthiness of mine, but only by the condescension of thy mercy, hast called my littleness to this pastoral office, for thine own sake, and for the sake of thy holy name, fit me

---

[4] He was a native of Ravenna, and had been a monk of St. Benignus, at Dijon; and his biographer, a contemporary monk of that society, after celebrating his erudition, his knowledge of medicine, and other good qualities, tells us that, on account of his being a very little man, he was called Johannelinus, or Johnny—"ab exilitate JOANNELINUS diminutivo nomine est dictus; sed humilitatis, sapientiæ, discretionis et ceterarum virtutum tanta in eo refulsit gratia, ut, sicut sanctus refert Gregorius in libro Dialogorum de Constantio Presbytero, ita in hoc mirum esset intuentibus, in tam parvo corpore gratia Dei tanta dona exuberare."— *Ap. Mab. ibid.* 167.

for this service, that I may govern thy house wisely, and may be
enabled to feed thy flock according to thy will in all things. Grant,
for the honour of thy name, that, with much fruit of this brotherly
society, I may attain to thy glory . . . . . . I know, and am assured, that
thou canst produce good and great increase of thy flock by me, little
and weak as I am; for I am but a child, and a little man of no
strength, having none of the qualities which should be required, or
which are worthy of such an office. Despairing, then, of my own
littleness, I breathe only in thy mercy. But though thou art great in
the things which are great, yet thou dost still more gloriously work
out great things by those which are least. Surely thy praise will be
the sweeter, and, after the manner of men, more full, if by me, little
as I am, thou shalt condescend to work out great things for thy
flock . . . . Give to me a full sufficiency of heavenly and of earthly
things, that I may have wherewithal to feed and to maintain thy flock,
both in soul and body, and without hesitation to receive those who
shall come in thy name; and, at the same time, to regulate the places
committed to my charge, and to provide in a fit and becoming manner,
for the peace and welfare of the brethren . . . . Two things I beg of
thee; one of them, do not, for thy mercy's sake, refuse me. I beseech
thee, by all thy compassions, give me thy heavenly consolation in my
many troubles; for that most heavy burden which is placed upon my
weak shoulders I cannot bear, and I am afraid to put down I
give thee thanks, O Lord, who hast separated me from the company
of this vain world, and hast brought me into thy holy service," &c.

From this little abbot the empress sought instruction; and he wrote a book for her use. It exists only,
I believe, in manuscript; but the preface, which has
been published, is as follows:—

"Long since, imperial lady, you were pleased to signify your desire
that I should collect from the sacred writings some short and plain
discourses, from which you might learn, according to your order, and
without wearisome labour, a rule of good life; for every rank, age,
and sex, has its own peculiar instruction for conduct in the sacred
books; so that each one, walking rightly in the vocation in which he
is called, may arrive at the kingdom in which there are many mansions.
At length, after the decease of your late consort, of revered memory,
the most illustrious and wise Emperor Henry, you cordially embraced
the praiseworthy design of active widowhood; and though rank, wealth,
and youth, might have prompted you to a second marriage, yet you

Y

did not incline your heart to the words of men speaking falsehood for truth; but you rose up and stood firmly on your feet, with your loins girded, so that, in contempt of carnal and worldly allurements, you might serve the Lord Christ in chastity, and set to other matrons an example worthy of imitation; namely, that being provoked by your continuance to better things, they may maintain their fidelity to their deceased husbands, and through the heavenly sacrifice, and by constant works of mercy, seek from the Lord the remission of their sins. How decent and becoming is it for a Christian woman, who cannot claim the higher reward of virginity, to study to live thenceforth chastely and soberly, so that, by God's help, she may be called, and may really be, the wife of one husband. If I mistake not, the propriety of maintaining this glorious excellence of single wedlock is taught us by the single rib taken from the side of man for the formation of woman. [5]

"As soon as I knew the pious desires of your heart, I set to work, and quickly culled some passages from the works of the Fathers, that wherever you are you may have with you some veracious documents, which may more fully point out the way in which a faithful widow ought to walk in righteousness and piety. Moreover, I added another discourse, on the life and conversation of virgins, for the instruction of the nuns who are collected in your monastery. And having found you to be much given to works of mercy, I did not hesitate to write this; namely, that, without all doubt, the proper objects of eleemosynary gifts are not ecclesiastics, who are already possessed of large property, but widows, orphans, sick persons, foreigners, and specially those who are truly the poor of Christ. In doing all this, through all my labours, my value for you has prevented my feeling it any trouble.

"Be dumb, ye dogs of Scylla; I shall go on, turning a deaf ear to the noisy rage of your abuse. I understand that, in your little cabals (in conventiculis vestris) something like this drops from your canine jaws—'While you profess to be a monk, and silence is the peculiar characteristic of monastic life, what have you to do with women? Whence have you such authority, that you should sit in the seat of the learned, and teach even women with your written scraps?' Be silent, wretched men. You say this because you are blind leaders of

---

[5] Ad legem semel nubendi dirigam. Ipsa origo humani generis patrocinatur, constans quid Deus ab initio constituerit, in formam posteritatis recensendum. Nam quum hominem figurasset, eique parem necessariam prospexisset, unam de costis ejus mutuatus, unam illi fœminam finxit, &c.—*Tertull. Exhort. ad Castit.* Cap. V.

the blind. 'Return, ye transgressors, to the heart,' [6] and diligently
consider the filthy condition in which you are lying. I wish that your
wicked mind may repent, and may study, in some degree, to imitate
the pious works of good women. Is not this woman worthy to be had
in all reverence, who has preferred the love of Christ to riches and
honours? Therefore it was, that while she was the mistress of kingdoms,
she humbled herself and became the servant of the poor. I say nothing
of her having traversed almost all Italy, most devoutly visiting the relics
of the saints, and offering to them precious gifts, and giving great alms
in the cities and towns, and in all places which she visited to pay her
devotions; and because the narrow limits of a letter will not permit
me to dwell longer on her praise, I will also pass over the fact, that
on her return into France she has, in like manner, comforted the poor
and the churches of God with a liberal hand; as it is written, 'She
hath dispersed, she hath given to the poor, her righteousness remaineth
for ever.'

"But setting aside these persons, who blow on the earth, and raise
a dust to blind their own eyes, lest they should see themselves, I
return to you, venerable handmaid of Christ, that my discourse, which
I began for your instruction, as if I had been present conversing with
you, may, by the help of God, be carried forward to the completion
of that design. Therefore, though I should have thought that those
little compilations, made according to my poor ability, might have
sufficed for your safety; yet since I understand, through some friends,
that you wish and require that I should also copy for you what I
have published on Divine Contemplation, and the Love of Christ, and
concerning that heavenly Jerusalem which is the mother of all the
faithful, I confess that my heart does greatly rejoice, and magnifies,
in you, God the giver of all good things. For were it not that, under
the leading of Christ, you had risen to higher things, going from
strength to strength, you never could have had the power to ask such a
thing. Who will not admire to see a soul so fervent, which, still drinking
the streams of sweet waters, ceases not to thirst? Very foolish and
very obstinate is he who despises the prayers of such a woman, and
does not accede to her most proper requests. As to myself, revered
mother, here I am quite ready, according to the degree of knowledge
which God has given me, cheerfully and joyfully to fulfil your wishes
in all things. I would He may be a spark of fire within me, which
may add somewhat to my mind, warmed by its influence.

---

[6] Is xlvi. 8. *Douay*. Redite prævaricatores ad cor. *Vulg*.

"Receive, therefore, O excellent soul, noble example of holy widow-hood, accept, with a watchful mind, this little work, which you desired, and which, by the grace of Christ, I have compiled, which you will find to consist chiefly of sweet words of heavenly contem-plation. These are to be reverently read, and meditated on with due fear, lest coming to them in a cold and undevout frame of mind, you be judged guilty of rashness. From this you will understand, that this book is chiefly intended for the use of those who do not suffer their minds to be darkened with carnal desires and worldly lusts; and when these things are read with tears and great devotion, then the meek reader tastes, with the palate of his heart, the inward sweetness which is hid in them. If it be thus, or rather, since it is thus, let not the proud and fastidious mind presume to meddle with the secret and sublime words of the divine oracles, lest it fall into error; for with blind eyes it cannot behold the light. Hence it comes that many rush, through heresy, into the abyss of eternal damnation, drawing down others along with them to death; because the mysteries of holy scrip-ture, which are rooted in heaven, are not fully intelligible even to any of the perfect in this world. Only they who, being wise with the wisdom of God, bring forth the fruit of profound humility, understand so much as the Holy Spirit condescends to reveal to them. Therefore read these things often, and especially when you feel your mind to be under the influence of heavenly desire; for right it is that you, whose practice in active life is so good, should take the wings of contemplation, and, soaring upwards, should drink of the fountain of celestial sweetness, saying with the prophet, 'With thee is the fountain of life, and in thy light we shall see light: my soul hath thirsted for God, the living fountain. Lord, I have loved the beauty of thy house, and the place of the habitation of thy glory:' and, what we find in the song of love, where the soul which loves God only addresses Christ her beloved, saying, 'Thy name is as ointment poured forth; therefore do the virgins love thee. Draw me, we will run after thee. (i. 3.) My beloved is mine, and I am his: he feedeth among the lilies. Until the day break, and the shadows flee away.' (ii. 16).

"With regard to this matter, however, it must be known, that that chief and unchangeable being, who is God, can by no means be seen by mortal eyes in this land of the dying, nor has been ever seen by any mortal, since the time when our first parent was driven out from the beauty of paradise into this state of trouble. Hence it is that the contemplative life begins here; but it is perfected only there, where God is seen face to face. For the meek and simple mind, when it is raised into contemplation, and, overcoming the hindrances of the flesh, penetrates into the things of heaven, is not permitted to remain long thus above itself, but is drawn back to inferior things by the burthen of the flesh. Yet, though it is quickly recalled to itself, struck back by the infinite splendour of the heavenly light, still it gains great strength even from this one thing — that it is enabled to obtain some foretaste of the divine sweetness; for being presently fired with great love, and being raised by it, it perceives the impossibility of seeing what it ardently loves, yet could not so ardently love if it did not catch some glimpse of it. There are some persons, less instructed, who conceive of God as like an image, because, being unhappily scattered abroad amidst the things of the world, they are incapable of the intellectual contemplation of that wonderful and unbounded light. To such, what is the eye of contemplation but a snare of perdition? Persons of this description are to be warned that they content themselves with the exercises of active life, without presuming to ascend the mount of contemplation; for as it is written, 'The carnal mind receiveth not the things of the Spirit of God;' and, 'to be carnally minded, is death.' For the human mind, unless it repels the desire of external things, does not penetrate those which are internal; because the more clearly it discerns invisible things, the more perfectly it despises the things which are seen. Therefore, although God is in his nature invisible and incomprehensible, yet by the purified and holy mind, which seeks only the things that are above, he is, even here, seen without sight, heard without sound, received without motion, touched though immaterial, present though not circumscribed by place.

"Having premised these necessary things, I beseech you, dear lady, that if you find any persons who wish to have this book, you would admonish them to copy it carefully, and to read it over several times after they have written it, so that they may not suffer anything to be added, omitted, or altered. We say this because of the carelessness of book-writers, who not only corrupt the truth, but add lie to lie. May God be with you, and may his hand strengthen you, that, becoming like the living creature with wings and eyes, you may every day make progress in both modes of life—now with Martha actively serving Christ in his members, now with Mary sitting in contemplation at the feet of the Lord, and intently listening to the words of his mouth—so that, by well doing and pure contemplation, you may arrive at that beatific vision in which the Son speaketh openly of the Father. And to this, for his mercy and his goodness sake, may he vouchsafe to lead his servants and his handmaids—He who descended to these things that are below, that we might rise to those which are above, who stooped that he might raise us, who became weak that he might make us strong, who took our life that he might give us his—for He, the only begotten, is co-eternal with the Father, who liveth and reigneth with him in the unity of the Holy Spirit, God throughout all ages. Amen.

"I, John, the lowest of the servants of Christ, and the brethren who are with me, salute you in Christ; O blessed lady, pious mother of the poor, and noble ornament of widowhood, farewell.

"May the Omnipotent Trinity ever keep you in its will." [7]

Digression? this is anything in the world but a digression. I am telling a plain story in the most straightforward way imaginable. To be sure, the story, as far as I have yet got, might have been comprised in three words, "Udalricus monachus Cluniacensis;" or, I might have said, "At *Clugni* there was a *monk* named *Ulric*"—for this is, I admit, all the progress which we have yet made in the story, without having even explained how he came there; but then my readers would have slipped over it at once; and, as it respects too many, I might quite as well have been more brief still, and (giving letters instead of words to represent what were, in fact, unknown quantities) I might have said, "at x there was a y named z." This would have conveyed to many persons, whose knowledge on other subjects is accurate and extensive, nearly as much information as to the where, the what, and the who. Yet it is most particularly this which I wish to be understood; and, therefore, as to the first, I have very slightly traced Clugni up to the time in question; I have endeavoured, by the way, to give some idea of what it was to be a monk there, and now we are arrived at the who—who was Ulric? and how can I answer the question without saying something of his royal patroness? and what would be the use of only saying that Ulric was the favourite of the Empress Agnes, when not one man in a hundred has

---

[7] Mab. ubi sup. p. 133.

taken the pains to satisfy himself of her existence, and
fewer still have formed any opinion whether she was
likely to patronize a young courtier for his virtues or
for his vices? And how could I speak of her without
saying something about the little abbot, even supposing
that I had no wish to bring him in, or to give the
reader an incidental peep at the mysticism (I use the
word with reverence, of the dark ages?—a subject
which seems to me most interesting and instructive,
of which I have hitherto said nothing, and of which
I believe little, if anything, ever has been said in our
language. But, without any such collateral view, it
was quite necessary to mention the little Abbot John;
and, indeed, I had it in my mind to have said something about his correspondence with William the Con-
queror; only then I thought some persons would really
charge me with digression—especially those for whose
sake I thought of doing it, and who might not be
aware that I only went out of my way in order to
hook the matter over one of the very few pegs which
the minds of people in general present, on which to
hang the occurrences of the dark ages.

So I say nothing of it; but go straight on with
Ulric, who was (though not yet) a monk of Clugni.
I wish I knew more of his uncle, who was Bishop of
Frisingen; but all that I find is, that (led, I presume,
by the disposition of the youth which has been described) he invited him to come to him, ordained him,
and at length made him Prior of the Canons. While
he held this station, he was accompanying the Emperor on a journey into Lombardy, with a view to
proceed into Italy, when he learned that the body of
which he was a member was in great distress, through
a famine which extented over several districts. He obtained reluctant permission from the Emperor, and

returned in haste, mortgaged his hereditary possessions, and relieved the distress of others beside his own brethren. After this, he determined on a pilgrimage to Jerusalem. "The anxieties and labours which he underwent by the way," says his biographer, "namely, in the badness of the roads, by perils from men and by sea, I pass over briefly, lest the prolixity of my narrative should tire the reader. But this I ought by no means to omit, that every day, before he mounted his horse, he repeated the Psalms." On his return he found that his uncle was dead, and that the see of Fri-singen, as well as his own priorate, was filled by a suc-cessor. He had, as has been already stated, mortgaged his private property, and he was therefore somewhat at a loss for a maintenance. The prior of the canons of Ratisbon, however, who was his relation, kindly took him in until he could redeem his estates. Having at length effected this, his first idea was to found a monastery; but the circumstances of the times, and the irreligion of the bishops (says his monkish biographer), prevented his fulfilling that design, and he therefore determined to devote himself, and all that he had, to the Lord, and to embrace the monastic life. He began, therefore, to distribute his goods to the poor, among whom he very justly numbered the nuns of a convent near Ratisbon, whose finances were so low that they were obliged to be content with an allowance of half a pound of bread (part white and part black) per day. He gave them land enough to provide them with a pound of white bread per day, and also to enable them to maintain seven poor persons. Having thus disposed of all his property, except so much as was necessary for the effecting his purpose, he resolved to enter into a monastery. He was unwilling to go alone, and persuaded Gerald, a scholar of Ratisbon, to accompany him; and having formed this resolution, they first made a pilgrimage to Rome, and then, having heard a high character of Clugni (cujus religionem longe lateque prædicari audierant), they determined to go thither. There they were received by the Abbot Hugo, who, as I have already said, had obtained that office in the year 1049.

We may dismiss Gerald at once by saying that he afterwards became Bishop of Ostia. As to Ulric, I need not repeat all that his biographer tells us of his mild, humble, and affectionate disposition; he loved, and was beloved by, all, but especially showed his constant care and kindness to the novices. Considering them as persons peculiarly in want of instruction and consolation, he sent for them and taught them with assiduous benevolence. Indeed, he seems to have had not only a talent, but a taste, for this sort of teaching, which led him into a practice somewhat out of the common way, and which gave offence to some of his brethren. He used to write "sweet and salubrious" letters of advice, and to send them privately to abbots and monks, confirming the moral and religious, and recalling those who had erred from the way of truth. Some of the monks made a formal complaint, but the "abbas discretissimus" seems to have thought that there was no great harm in the matter; and, in fact, the next thing of which we read shows that his confidence in Ulric was undiminished—perhaps increased—by what transpired during the inquiry. Ulric was sent to take the superintendence of a nunnery which the abbot had founded at Marcigni. While there, owing to his long vigils and his continual writing (per scribendi laborem continuum), he suffered from pain in his head. To relieve this, he washed his head with wormwood, and on one occasion he managed so to get a fragment

into his eye that he could not get it out. Having
suffered from it for six months, he returned to Clugni,
and begged leave to resign his charge.

Shortly after this, Lutold, the rich and powerful
lord of the castle of Rumelingen, and his wife, having
no children, signified their intention of devoting their
property to the service of God, and offered it on the
altar of St. Peter and St. Paul, at Clugni. On his
request that some of the brethren might be sent with
him to found a monastery, Ulric and another were
deputed for that purpose. They chose a site; but,
winter coming on, they were obliged to defer the
building until the spring; and in the meantime, declining
the society of the laymen among whom they were cast,
they retired to a cave about two miles off, where
they proposed to live in solitude. In this they were
disappointed; for Ulric having preached to some few
strangers who came to look at them from curiosity,
the numbers increased, and he was soon surrounded
by multitudes of the rude natives, Christians only in
name, to whom he had an opportunity of making
known the gospel.

After the winter, they set to work, and were cordially assisted by all the neighbourhood, except two
priests, who were afraid that they should lose their
fees by the erection of this monastery, and who
therefore did all they could to set the people against
the monks and their design. One of these priests told
his congregation in the course of a sermon, that a
certain poisonous herb was springing up in that part
of the country, which, if it came to bear fruit, would
fill the whole land with its poison. The simple people
were horror-struck, and inquired if there were no
marks by which they might distinguish, and no means
by which they might eradicate, such a perilous plant;

and the preacher enlightened them by saying, "Those monks coming into these parts from the monastery of Clugni, full of deceit, avarice, and envy, expose you to great danger; for if they get a footing among you, and cause the hurtful seeds of their preaching to grow up in your hearts, whatever good work may have been wrought in you by my care will soon be destroyed, and you will bring forth no fruit of virtue. Having, therefore, prayed to God that his divine goodness would vouchsafe to remove them from you, earnestly pray also that their deceitful doctrine and feigned sanctity may not deceive your senses, and (which God forbid) draw you aside from the way of salvation." Some of his hearers implicitly followed his directions, and forthwith began to pray, but the more prudent hesitated. Soon after, the priest was benighted, and fairly lost his way, and saw no alternative but to ask for shelter from the monks, who were perfectly aware of his feelings and practices against them. Between hope and fear, he resolved to try the experiment. Ulric went out to meet him, received him cheerfully, and, according to monastic rule, first led him to prayers, then embraced him, and gave him the kiss of peace, talked kindly with him, and showed him all hospitality. The next day, after having been kindly dismissed, the priest's conscience smote him, and on the succeeding Sunday he frankly told his congregation that he had been to blame in abusing the monks, and instead of telling them as before, to pray against Ulric and his companion, he besought them to pray that God would pardon the sin which he had committed in defaming them. Sincere friendship ensued, and the priest and his parishioners set to work with all their heart to help the monks build the monastery.

I mention these circumstances because they throw

light on our general subject; but it would be tedious
to particularize all that Ulric did in this way. He
was evidently considered a peculiarly fit person to
be employed in founding cells and monasteries, and
bringing them into order, being, as his biographer
says, "in omni norma cœnobialis vitæ ad unguem
edoctus." Yet, with all his engagement in active
business, Ulric was a reading, thinking, praying man;
and his biographer recounts the circle of his principal
employments as prayer, reading, teaching, copying,
and composing. It is enough here to say, that he
founded the monastery of La Celle, and presided over
it from its foundation until his death. He had long
lost the sight of one eye, and two years before his
death he became totally blind. During that period he
devoted himself, with less avocation, to prayer, psalmody,
and listening to sacred reading; and he died, at an
advanced age, in the year 1093.

Ulric was a monk of Clugni—that is all which I
wish the reader to take with him, and we will at once
change the scene for the Black Forest, in the diocese
of Spier. At the same time that Hugo was Abbot of
Clugni, and was extending its fame and dependencies
by the ministry of Ulric, the monastery of Hirschau
was governed by the Abbot William. He was a Bavarian
by birth, and born of honest parents, who offered him
in his childhood at the monastery of St. Emmeram, in
Ratisbon, where he was educated, and made great
proficiency both in sacred and profane learning—tam
in divinis scripturis, quam in sæculari philosophia doc-
tissimus evasit. "No one," adds Trithemius, the historian
of his monastery, "ever saw him idle, no one engaged
in frivolous pursuits; he was always devoted to prayer
and reading, or some manual occupation which his
obedience required. He became very learned in all sorts

of knowledge, and in a short time made such progress
in what are called the liberal arts, that he got beyond
his teachers. In philosophy he became a most acute
disputant; in music he was unusually learned, and
composed many and various chants in honour of the
saints. How skilful he was in astronomy, mathematics,
and arithmetic, his works testify : on these subjects he
bestowed much pains." [8] I need not add to this all that
we are told of his virtues as an abbot, or of his fame,
honour, and extended influence.

Still less need I recount the miracles which he is
said to have performed, or even notice any but one,
which Trithemius himself, though he records the others,
declares to be the greatest. Indeed, I see no reason to
believe that the abbot ever pretended to any such
power as some of his admirers seem to have supposed
that he must have possessed; but Trithemius, after
mentioning some wonderful things ascribed to him,
while for the sake of brevity he omitted others, adds—
"But of all his miracles I consider this to have been
the greatest—that, in the midst of a perverse nation, he
shone forth as a most excellent man ; and in so dangerous
a time of discord between the church and the state, he
maintained an unspotted course in the paths of righteousness." He goes on to say that the Abbot William
restored the order of St. Benedict, which had almost
fallen into ruin in Germany; and that he was, either by
himself or his agents, the means of founding eight
monasteries, and restoring more than an hundred ; so
that, next to the reformation wrought by the foundation
and influence of Clugni, his work of reform was the
most important which was to be found in the annals
of his order. The monks of his own monastery (whom,

---

[8] Chron. Hirsaug. Tom. I. p. 221, sub an. 1070.

notwithstanding that he was continually sending them
out to the monasteries which he founded or restored,
he contrived to keep up to the number of an hundred
and fifty) "were perpetually employed, either in the
performance of divine service, or in prayer, meditation,
and sacred reading. Those who appeared less fit to be
employed in sacred things were appointed to perform
such manual labours as were necessary, so that none
of their time might pass in idleness. The holy father,
knowing, moreover, what he had learned by laudable
experience, that sacred reading is the necessary food
of the mind, made twelve of his monks very excellent
writers, to whom he committed the office of transcribing the holy scriptures and the treatises of the
fathers. Beside these, there were an indefinite number
of other scribes, who wrought with equal diligence
in the transcription of other books. Over them was a
monk well versed in all kinds of knowledge, whose
business it was to appoint some good work as a task
for each, and to correct the mistakes of those who
wrote negligently. In the course of time" [for William
was abbot two and twenty years] "the monks wrote
a great many volumes; but a very small part remained
at Hirschau; for the holy father, who was always more
anxious to win and to profit souls than about all things
else in the world, whenever he sent forth any of the
monks to other monasteries to reform them, cheerfully,
and of his own free will, gave them books, and
whatever else they thought necessary; and forasmuch
as the monasteries which he reformed were many, a
very small part of the great multitude of books which
he caused to be transcribed remained at Hirschau. Oh,
every way praiseworthy man, who preferred souls
redeemed by the blood of Christ to the advantage of
transitory gain, and consulted the benefit of others

instead of seeking the perishable riches of the world!
Truly this is a virtue to be found in few—that abbots
should strip their own monasteries, either of ornaments
or books, to supply the wants of others." [9]

The Abbot William himself may now tell that part
of his history, for the sake of which I have introduced him:—

"After that I, brother William, had been called, by the providence
of God and the election of the brethren of Hirschau, to the government of that place, I appointed for them, in the first instance, those
customs of monastic life which I had learned from my childhood in
the monastery of St. Emmeram; but as, through the gradual negligence
of monastic rigour which succeeded, there seemed to be in many things
a degeneracy from that high tone of life and conversation which it
imparts, I resolved that, wherever, either by seeing or hearing, or by
reading sacred books, I should meet with things tending to improve
the conversation of the brethren, I would collect them together, as
living stones for the erection of a spiritual building. And while I
commended this my resolution with earnest and constant prayer to Him
'who fulfils the desire of his faithful in good things,'[1] through the
wonderful and merciful providence of God, that venerable man, worthy
to be had in remembrance by all good men, Bernard, Abbot of Marseilles, having executed his office as apostolical legate, came to us, and,
owing to the difficulty of prosecuting his journey as he desired, stayed
with us nearly a year. After he had particularly examined the mode
of life pursued by our monks, and the state of our monastery, he one
day, in the course of conversation on other matters relating to a spiritual life, thus addressed me:—'I see, my dearest brother, that this
place is remarkably adapted to monastic life, and the monks appear to
be animated with a most ardent desire to lead a life of holiness
and righteousness; but I should like to know by whom you have
been chiefly guided as to your regulations, and from what monastery
in particular you have derived those customs which are traditional?'
I replied:—'It is our desire, as far as we can, to imitate all the religious men of our order; but if, in any point where we have erred,
you will condescend to bring us back into the right way, you may
rest assured that we shall be most prompt to follow wherever your

[9] Trith. ubi sup. 227.
[1] Qui replet in bonis desiderium fidelium suorum. — *Vulg.* Ps. cii. 5.

good counsel may lead us.'—'Your manner of life,' said he, 'as far
as my poor judgment goes, seems to be such as must be acceptable to
God, and admirable in the eyes of all wise men; but even if it were
more glorious, and (if I may so speak) were shining forth with apostolic
signs and powers, yet, to those who are simply looking for the perfection of monastic life, it would be rendered more graceful and acceptable if it were assimilated to regularly constituted monasteries in dress,
tonsure, and other customs. And, if you ask my opinion, among all
the monasteries of Cisalpine Gaul I should most particularly recommend
you to select Clugni, where, both by the authority of the most perfect
monks, and the lapse of a great length of time, the monastic life
has grown up to such a degree of strength and splendour, that
if there are still any traces of holiness to be seen in other monasteries, there can be no doubt that these little streams have flowed
from thence as from a living and inexhaustible spring.' In these and
similar admonitions he was, as we say, spurring the free horse; and
having finished the diplomatic business for which he had come, he
returned home. By the way, he visited Clugni, and most particularly
commended us to the abbot, so as to predispose him to show us all
kindness, in case we should apply to him. About the same time, Ulric,
a senior monk of Clugni, who was, through the providence of God,
sent into Germany on some business relating to his monastery, stayed
some time with us; and as we had formerly been on the most intimate terms, and he had had long experience in the discipline of Clugni,
I asked him to write out their customs for our benefit. He consented,
promised, and, according to his promise, he wrote two books concerning those customs for us. Afterwards, considering that many things
were wanting in those books for a full knowledge of the customs, I
first sent two of our monks, then two more, and afterwards a third
couple, to Clugni, who so thoroughly investigated all the most obscure
things of that order, that their teachers, in whose hearing they recited
what they had written on the customs, affirmed that there had never
been any scholars in that spiritual school who had more fully or more
truly understood the nature of their institution." [2]

---

[2] Mab. Anal. p. 154.

No. XX.

"The abbots took the scriptures from their monks, lest some should ever bark against the abbot's living, and set up such long service and singing, to weary them withal, that they should have no leisure to read in the scripture but with their lips, and made them good cheer to fill their bellies, and to stop their mouths."—TYNDALE'S PRACTICE OF PRELATES.

WHEN Ulric (who, the reader may recollect, was a monk of Clugni) had written his book, he sent it to the Abbot William, at whose request, and for whose benefit, he had composed it. With it he sent a letter, some part of which is so much to our purpose that I must make an extract:—

"To the most reverend lord, and most pious father, William, Abbot of Hirschau, and to the holy company of monks under his government, brother Ulric, a monk, such as he is, wishes health in the Lord, and his most speedy blessing here and hereafter.

"The daily remembrance of yourself, and of your monastery, dearest father, has really become so habitual to me that now, through the mere force of habit, as well as of affection, it would be impossible for any day to pass over without it. Sometimes, too, I have the very agreeable and grateful recollection of your promise that you would be on your guard against the disposition of some secular persons who, caring very little for aught but the things of this world, when they have got a house, as I may say, full of sons and daughters—or if any of their children should be halt, or maimed, or deaf, or blind, or deformed, or leprous, or with anything about him that may render him less acceptable to the world, they are wonderfully anxious to devote him to the service of God, and make a monk of him; though it is obviously not for God's sake, but only that they may rid themselves of the burden of educating and maintaining such children, or be able to do more for their others. To say nothing, therefore, of those who do not want bodily health and sound limbs, what evils have we known to arise from those who can only be called half-men, or, at least, only half-alive? Were it expedient, it would be easy to name one who was induced to adopt the habit of sanctity by no other holiness than

Z

the reproach of scurvy; and another who, had it not been that his foot [something wanting in the manuscript], both of whom, as you can testify, set no very good example. How much less, then, can we expect from those who are in good health, wherever they are collected together in such number, and with such influence, that the regulation of the monastery is in their hands? Truly, everybody may know what sort of life and conversation, and what degree of regular discipline, is maintained, if he does but know that monks of this description are at the head of affairs. In fact, it is a thing obvious and notorious, that if any strict discipline, in this our spiritual warfare, is to be maintained among the pollutions of our time, it can be only where those who have renounced the world, and embraced the monastic life, not in the age of caprice and levity, or by command of their parents, but of their own free will, at mature age, and in single obedience to the command of Christ, are predominant in number and authority.

"Your prudence duly weighing this—although you were yourself brought up in a monastery (for it does sometimes happen that the lily will spring up among thorns), and being careful for nothing so much as to take all measures of caution, and such as might conduce to the solid establishment of religion, you have made a law in your monastery which compels the secular persons whom I have mentioned to seek some other nest wherein to deposit their abortive and disinherited young ones. By God's providence, they will no longer be able to carry on their practice of laying (as the prophet speaks) cockatrice eggs, and that which 'shall be hatched into a basilisk,'[1] and giving them in charge to pious men, devoted to the service of God, perverting their office into that of serving-maids and nurses. Others may form what opinion they please on the subject; but, for my own part, I am certain that you have struck at the root of that evil by which all those monasteries have been ruined which have fallen either in France or Germany.   *   *   *   *   *   *   *   *   *   *

You will observe, that, in what I have written, I have represented us as talking together; for, if you recollect, we did converse a great deal on the subject. And if I should seem to have added anything, yet even this your mouth and your tongue hath spoken, for not only my tongue, but my whole self, is yours; not to say that Christ had bound us to each other in the unity of the Spirit, in one body, that is the church—under one Head, that is Himself. Yet, since personally I am inconsiderable and obscure, barbarous in name, and rude in style, it has appeared to me that it would be unbecoming to mention such a name

---

[1] Is. lix. 5.

as mine, or to follow the usual course of prefixing a preface. Nevertheless, as this compilation, such as it is, consists of three parts, I have begun each of them with some sentences which may pass for a sort of procemium, chiefly on your account, and that of our other brethren, whose good example, having seen it, I could not willingly pass over in silence."

Ulric's book is still in existence; [2] and though we may easily imagine that, when the Abbot William came to act upon the written descriptions of rites and ceremonies and customs (minute and even prolix as those descriptions may appear to us), doubts would frequently arise, yet the work is one of the most valuable and useful relics which time has spared, for giving us an insight into the real nature of monastic life, in the tenth and eleventh centuries. Its actual composition appears to have taken place between the years 1077 and 1093, but it must be recollected that it was not so much intended as an account of new inventions, as of long-established customs. In fact, it consisted of the reminiscences of an old man, and had reference to regulations most of which were probably as old as the monastery of Clugni itself. The brief procemium prefixed to the first book is as follows:—

"Our senior lord abbot once sent me into Germany, on what business it is not worth while to state; what is to the present purpose is, that on that occasion I took the opportunity of visiting that venerable man the Lord Abbot William, whose monastery is situated in the Black Forest, in the diocese of Spier. This father having been known, and very much attached, to me from a child, received me joyfully; and when I would have gone further, like another Cleophas, he made me stay some days longer with him. During this period, I had a great deal of discourse with him (indeed, so far as he could manage, it was continual), respecting the customs of our monastery; a subject which he introduced by saying, 'Your monastery, my dearest brother, through God's mercy, has acquired a great character for religion in our parts;

---

[2] Dach. Spicil. I. 641.

and we are inclined to think that, among all those of which we have any knowledge, there is none which can compare with it in rule and discipline. You will do us a great favour if you will make us acquainted with the customs and regulations of your predecessors. For even if we do not ourselves practise them, it may tend to our edification, in humility, to know that your life and conversation is such as our infirmity is unable or unwilling to attain to.' I replied, 'I am going to eat your bread, and it were unreasonable that I should hesitate to fulfil your wishes. At the same time, one who has only lived in our monastery as almost a barbarian unto them in respect of language, and not brought up there from childhood, cannot be expected to have such a perfect knowledge on all points as if he had been a native of the country, and educated in those customs from infancy. You must not, therefore, be surprised if I do not know much, who, during almost the first thirty years of my life, cared but little for aught but the things of this world. What I do know, however, I shall willingly tell : what, then, will you put as your first question?'"

The first chapter, which is entitled *Quomodo Testamentum legatur utrumque,* then begins in the following manner :—

"*Question.*—I hear that your lessons in the winter and on common nights are very long; will you be pleased to state at once the manner in which the Old and New Testament is read, both in summer and winter ?

"*Answer.*—To begin with the most ancient of all the books, that is, the Octateuch—this book, according to general custom, and as it is in other churches, is appointed to be read in Septuagesima. On the Sunday itself there are but short lessons ; except, that, for the first, the whole of that prologue, *Desiderii mei,* [3] is read. During the following nights, the lessons are so much increased, that in one week the whole book of Genesis is read through in the church only. On Sexagesima, Exodus is begun, and together with the other books which are read, it also is read, both in the church and in the refectory; so that where the lesson finished one day shall be the beginning of the lesson for the next; and the whole Octateuch is read through, if not before, by the beginning of Lent. Lessons are, however, taken from it for the Sundays in Lent; but on the other nights during that period, St. Augustine's exposition of the Psalms, and especially of the Songs

---

[3] That is, St. Jerome's.

of Degrees, is read; and as the nights then grow shorter and shorter, so do the lessons. Care must, however, be taken that they are not so abbreviated as not to allow sufficient time for the brother who goes the round, both within and without the choir, with his dark lantern [4] to see if anyone has gone to sleep during the lesson. In the passion of our Lord, the prophet Jeremiah is read; and, as before, the prologue forms the first lesson. It is, however, read in the church only, and so as that before Holy Thursday it is finished as far as Lamentations. In Easter Week, the Acts of the Apostles are read; and for one week only; during which, from the shortness of the nights, it is impossible that much should be read. After this, for two weeks, the Revelation, and the canonical epistles, until Ascension Day. Then the Acts of the Apostles are again appointed, and are again read (as if they had not been read before), from the beginning, until Pentecost. These same books, however, are not the less read regularly and throughout in the refectory; where, also, are read, in their appointed seasons, the books of Kings, of Solomon, of Job, of Tobit, Judith, Esther, Ezra, and the Maccabees, which are all read only in the refectory, and not at all in the church; except the short extracts which may be made from any of them for the Sundays. From the calends of November, the lessons for common nights are doubled. The prophet Ezekiel is appointed to be read in the church only; and is customarily finished before the feast of St. Martin; and although we celebrate the octaves of that

---

[4] Perhaps it is not quite correct to call it a "dark" lantern; but I suppose it to have been a light so enclosed as to shine only in one direction, or through a single aperture, so that it might be thrown on any particular object. Ulric's words in this place are, "qui circam facit cum absconsa;" but in the 8th chapter of his second book, entitled, "Quomodo laternam ligneam portare debet ad Nocturnos," he gives a further account of the matter. Describing what ought to be the conduct of a monk, under various circumstances, he says, "If, however, during the lessons, he who carries round the wooden lantern should come to him, and, supposing him to be asleep, should throw the light on his face, let him, if awake, bow reverently. But, if he was asleep, and the lantern shall have been placed before him, as soon as he is waked he must take it up, and first examine the right side of the choir; and then, returning through the middle, do the same in the outer choir, and lastly, the left side. Should he find anyone asleep, he must throw the light in his eyes three times; if on the third time he does not wake, he must place the lantern before him, that when he is awaked he may take it up, and carry it in like manner."

feast with singing, and with other solemnities, yet the prophetical lessons are not changed, nor, indeed, are they on other octaves, unless they would make twelve lessons. Then the prophet Daniel and the twelve minor prophets, which would not hold out if we did not add, after the last of them, from the homilies of the blessed Pope Gregory on Ezekiel. In Advent, Isaiah the prophet is appointed; and when I inquired about this, and wished to learn in how many nights it ought, in strictness, to be read through, I could not learn from anybody, and I can only say what I recollect to have heard and seen. When I was there, it was sometimes read through in six common nights. After this, follow the Epistles of Pope Leo on the Incarnation of our Lord; and other discourses of the holy fathers, and chiefly of St. Augustine. The epistles are appointed for that Sunday which first occurs after Innocents' Day, provided that day is neither the Circumcision nor the Anniversary of the Lord Odilo. And here, again, I must say as I did of the prophet; for different persons think differently; and I must again state what I saw. Such an epistle as that to the Romans was read through in two common nights; and when one of the monks who portioned out the lessons had made them shorter, he was prohibited by our seniors in chapter. If, however, it should happen that the epistles were finished before Septuagesima, they read John Chrysostom's Exposition of the Epistle to the Hebrews. Now, you see, I have in some fashion gone round the circle of the year; and let us, if you please, go on to something else."

The Abbot William then proceeds to elicit a very minute, and (to say the truth) prolix, account of the psalmody at Clugni, which it would be useless to extract, because that matter may be settled in a very few words, so far as is necessary for our purpose. A monk was expected to know the Psalter by heart. Martene, in his commentary on the rule of St. Benedict, quotes and acquiesces in the observation that the words "legantur" and "dicantur" had been used advisedly, and with a design to intimate that the lessons were to be read from a book, but the psalms were to be said or sung by memory. He also quotes, from several of the ancient Rules, proofs that means of instruction were used, which render it probable that this was practicable, and was required. From Pachomius, "He

who will renounce the world . . . . must remain a
few days outside the gate, and shall be taught the
Lord's Prayer, and as many psalms as he can learn;"
and again, "There shall be nobody whatever (omnino
nullus) in the monastery who will not learn to read,
and get by heart some part of the scriptures; at the
least (quod minimum est) the New Testament and
Psalter." St. Basil, "If anyone who is in good health
shall neglect to offer prayers, and to commit the psalms
to memory, making sinful excuses, let him be separated
from the society of the others, or let him fast for a
week." St. Ferreol, "No one who claims the name of
a monk can be allowed to be ignorant of letters.
Moreover, he must know all the psalms by heart."
He gives several instances which it is not worth while
to quote, but one incidental proof which he produces
is curious; because, though I really believe that it is
to his purpose, yet it might appear, at first sight, to
wear a contrary aspect. Referring to the catalogue of
the library of the monastery of St. Riquier, which I
have more than once had occasion to notice, he observes that in this monastery, where there were at
least three hundred monks and one hundred boys,
there were but seven psalters. As to the number of
psalms which were daily repeated by the monks of
Clugni, it may be sufficient, instead of the more particular account of Ulric, to give the statement of the
biographer of Abbot Odo, whom I have had repeated
occasion to quote. He tells us that, in his time, they
had, in compassion to infirmity of weak brethren
(propter pusillanimorum animos) abbreviated the daily
course by taking away fourteen psalms from the original
number of a hundred and thirty-eight.[5]

---

[5] Mab. A. S. vii. 159. I have said something before, and it would

There is another point referred to in the extract
from Ulric, of which it may be right to take some

---

be easy to say a good deal, about repeating the Psalms. Ulric himself,
as I have stated, spent the extremity of his old age in psalmody, as
well as in prayer and hearing sacred reading; and I am tempted to
add another case of an old monk, not because I believe the thing to
have been at all singular, but through some circumstances connected
with the man. When Hugh, Bishop of Lincoln, was travelling in France,
in or soon after the year 1195, an old monk at Clairvaux, so well
known as St. Bernard's monastery, sent to say that, if he could make
it convenient to give him a call, he should be glad to see him, for
he had long desired it. I rather think that they were old friends : but
I cannot take upon me to say. However, the biographer of the Bishop
of Lincoln records that he did go to see this old monk, "who, being
of a great age, had resigned his pastoral charge, only retaining (by
the pope's order) the insignia of his former rank [the author of the
article in the Gallia Christiana, iv. 128, to whom I am indebted for
the extract, here inserts, in a parenthesis, that he had learned elsewhere
that this monk had also a reserved pension of thirteen pounds], devoted
himself, in that monastery, to holy contemplation." He adds, that on
the bishop's inquiring what part of the scripture was the subject of his
meditation, he replied, that meditation on the Psalms had come to
engross all his thoughts—"Psalmorum meditatio sola jam penitus totum
sibi me vindicavit." I do not know why he retired to Clairvaux, unless
it was from respect to the memory of St. Bernard, for whom he seems
to have had a peculiar veneration. He was the spokesman when, between
forty and fifty years after the canonization of Bernard, the monks of
Clairvaux wished to have a collect and prayers drawn up by the pope
for the commemoration of the good abbot. Innocent III. granted the
request, and sent the prayers to our old monk, with a letter, in which
he said, "Petisti namque rogatus a fratribus ut ad honorem Bernardi
primi Clarevallensis Abbatis, quem apostolica sedes sanctorum adscrip-
serat catalogo venerandum, nos ipsi collectam et alias orationes ore
proprio dictaremus tum propter auctoritatem dictantis, tum propter stylum
dictaminis, cum majori devotione dicendas. Et ecce sicut potuimus,"
&c.—*Lib*. v. *Ep*. 60. It is not, however, by anything which he did
after he got to Clairvaux that this old monk is known to the world.
Those who have read the very interesting papers on the history of
Thomas à Becket in the British Magazine, may remember John Bishop
of Poitiers, the friend of the Archbishop, of John of Salisbury, and

notice. He speaks of some books of scripture which
were read in the refectory, as contradistinguished from
others which were read only in divine service. This
custom of reading at meals was not exclusively
monastic, and is too important a feature, in a view
of the literature of the Dark Ages, to be passed over
without some notice. Eginhart tells us that Charlemagne, while at supper, heard either some diverting
story or a reader. Histories and the deeds of ancient
kings were read to him. He delighted, also, in the
books of St. Augustine, and especially in those which
he entitled "*De Civitate Dei.*" I have before referred
to the custom, in the case of a layman of less distinction; [6] and if it existed among the laity, we shall not
wonder to find it among the clergy. As to bishops,
it was directed (I do not mean to say, as a new thing)
by the second Council of Rheims, in the year 813.
The seventeenth canon directs, "That bishops and
abbots shall not allow low buffooneries to be acted
in their presence, but shall have the poor and needy
at their table, and that sacred reading shall be heard
there"[7]—lectio divina ibi personet. The same thing
was enjoined, also, by the Council of Pavia, held
about the year 850, and I think that the reader who

Stephen of Tournay. But neither is it for anything that he did as
Bishop of Poitiers that he is particularly known, nor is it under that
name that he has been, and continues to be, held up to the horror
and execration of Christians, for his malicious fierceness against the
true doctrine of Christ, and as one of the members of antichrist, "who
could neither abide that the scriptures should be declared by any other,
nor would they take the pains to declare them themselves;" in short,
he was the very man who excommunicated Peter Waldo—that is, if
(as is commonly said) Peter Waldo was excommunicated by Jean aux
Bellemains, Archbishop of Lyons.

[6] See p. 336.   [7] Conc. vii. 1256.

wishes to form an idea of that period will not be displeased to see the three first canons of that council:—

"I. The holy synod has decreed that the domestic and private life of a bishop ought to be above all scandal and suspicion, so that we may (according to the apostle) provide things honest, not only before God, but before all men. It is meet, therefore, that in the chamber of the bishop, and for all more private service, priests and clerks of sound judgment should be in attendance; who, while their bishop is engaged in watching, praying, and searching the scriptures, may constantly wait on him, and be witnesses, imitators, and (to the glory of God) setters forth, of his holy conversation.

"II. We decree that bishops shall perform mass, not only on Sundays, and on the principal festivals, but that, when possible, they shall attend the daily sacrifice. Nor shall they think it beneath them to offer private prayers, first for themselves, then for their brethren of the priesthood, for kings, for all the rulers of the church of God, for those who have particularly commended themselves to their prayers, and especially for the poor; and to offer the sacrifice of the altar (hostias offerre) to God with that pious compunction, and deep feeling of holy devotion, which belongs to more private ministration, that the priest himself may become a living offering, and a sacrifice to God of a broken spirit.

"III. It is our pleasure that a bishop should be content with moderate entertainments, and should not urge his guests to eat and drink; but should rather at all times show himself a pattern of sobriety. At his table let there be no indecent subjects of discourse; and let no ridiculous exhibitions, no nonsense of silly stories, no foolish talking of the unwise, no buffoon tricks, be admitted. Let the stranger, the poor, the infirm, be there, who, blessing Christ, may receive a blessing from the sacerdotal table. Let there be sacred reading; let *viva voce* exhortation follow, that the guests may rejoice in having been refreshed not only with temporal food, but with the nourishment of spiritual discourse, that God may be glorified in all things through Jesus Christ our Lord." [8]

With regard to monks, however,—at least the monks of the order of St. Benedict, of whom we are speaking, [9]—it was a part of their rule which they were

---

[8] Conc. viii. 61.

[9] For brevity's sake, I say nothing here of canons, or nuns, or of

not at liberty to dispense with. The thirty-seventh chapter, "De Hebdomadario Lectore," describes the manner in which the reader for the week should perform his office, expressly requires that there should be reading at all their meals, and directs that the reader's voice, and his only, should be heard on such occasions, unless the abbot, or other president authority, should choose to offer any brief remark for general edification. It also orders that the brethren shall not read in turn, but such only as may edify the hearers.

Hitherto I have spoken only of what may be termed public and, with some modifications according to time and place, general means, afforded to the inmates of monasteries for obtaining some knowledge of the Word of God. I have said nothing of the means or encouragements for private study, but have simply referred to such as were used in the community for the benefit of all. Will it be seriously contended that these men were peculiarly ignorant of the scriptures?— that special means were taken to prevent them from knowing the revealed will of God? "Yes," replies the zealous anti-papist, "but that was all a trick of the pope—the abbots actually set them to this continual reading of the Bible with their lips, to prevent their having leisure to read it in any other way."

Well, that was certainly a very deep trick of the pope; but I expect to show, by a distinct species of evidence, that it did not succeed with all the poor simple monks on whom he tried it.

---

the various other rules beside that of St. Benedict. If the reader wishes to see how general the custom was, and how frequently the injunction was reiterated, let him look at the "Codex Regularum," or those parts to which Martene refers in his comment on this chapter of the rule of St. Benedict.

No. XXI.

"It may be proper just to mention Peter, abbot of Clugny, surnamed the Venerable. That so ignorant and so trifling a writer should have been honoured with a title so magnificent, is one of the strongest marks of the low state of religious knowledge in general at that time."—MILNER.

IT may be proper;—but really, when I sent the preceding paper to the press, I had no idea of saying anything about the abbot Peter. On the contrary, having been led to say so much more than I at first intended about Clugni, I resolved to get away from that subject, for the present, at least, fearing that my readers would be tired of the very name.

I hope, indeed, that they are aware of my expectation that they may find matter of argument in extracts and anecdotes not less easily, and perhaps more pleasantly, than in systematic arrangements of rules and customs; yet, for all that, I resolved to be somewhat more methodical in offering a few remarks on what may be called the private reading of the monks, as distinguished from the public reading in the church and refectory. I did not think this necessary in order to rebut the suggestion contained in the motto of the preceding paper, that the monks were kept reading the Bible over and over in public, that they might have no opportunity for reading it in private, or for meditating on its contents; but I thought it was a very important part of our subject, and that we had fairly arrived at it. In the former part of this supposition, I am sure that I was right; in the latter, it appears that I was wrong,—for, no sooner had I drawn out a regular skeleton—I. What books did the monks read? II. How did they get them, that is, under what restrictions were they allowed to have the books of the monastery for private use? III. What time had they for private reading? IV. In what places did they read?—No sooner, I say, had I made out this skeleton from Martene's book, "De Antiquis Monachorum Ritibus," and set to work very methodically to treat first of the first, than I was turned back by my references to Clugni, and found myself involved in a correspondence of Peter the Venerable. It gave a somewhat different direction to my thoughts, and led me to reflect whether (considering the object of these papers) I ought to say so much about Clugni, without one word of that abbot who is perhaps the only one known, even by name, to many readers of ecclesiastical history, and who is known to many of them only by the sneer of a writer who does not pretend to have seen a line of his works. I say, "considering the design of these papers," for that is, very principally, to meet the general deductions and broad statements which ignorance, infidelity, prejudice, and party, have all, in their turns, and to their mutual edification, drawn from mistaken words, misunderstood or purposely distorted facts, and even mere falsehoods, for which tiresome investigation can hardly find a shadow of foundation.

The reader may perhaps remember—though, under a full persuasion that he does not, I will repeat it— that the Abbot Hugh, whose history I deserted at p. 350 to follow that of his monk Ulric, presided over the monastery of Clugni for sixty years. In A.D. 1109, he was succeeded by Pontius de Melgueil, whom it is necessary to mention, not only as a connecting link, but for other reasons which will appear. He was the son of the Count of Melgueil, and is said to have been a godson of Pope Paschal II., and to have been educated at Clugni by his command.[1] The same writer who tells us this, goes on to inform us that Pontius "was, from his childhood, docile, affable, and steadfast in virtues; of middle stature, and pale-faced." Perhaps his noble birth, his relation to the pope, and these popular qualities, may account for his having been elected, at a very early age, to succeed an abbot, during the latter part of whose very long reign it seems probable that some degree of laxity had crept into the monastery. The fact, however, of his youth at the time of his election, is certain, and it is just to him to state it; though Peter the Venerable, to whom we are indebted for most of what we know about Pontius, allows that for some years, he conducted himself with considerable moderation and propriety—"satis modeste ac sobrie."

But somehow (and I really do not know how), he became involved in disputes with his monks, and, in process of time ("multis ac diversis casibus vel causis," Peter says, and it was not necessary, when he wrote, to explain), he contrived, on some ground or other, to quarrel with them all. The dissension, which had been growing for ten years, and which had been kept as quiet and as private as it could be, at length broke out into a public rupture. Pontius hastened to Rome, and begged the pope to allow him to resign his charge. Calixtus would not hear of such a thing; but Pontius was resolute and prevailed. He then set out for Jerusalem, with a professed intention (if we may credit a succeeding pope, under a vow) to spend the

---

[1] Odericus Vitalis says—"Consulis Merguliensis filius Regum et Imperatorum consanguinitate proximus, Paschalis (II.) filiolus, cujus imperio inter Cluniacenses educatus est."—*Hist.* L. xii. *ap. Gal. Chr.* IV. 1134.

remainder of his days there. [2] Calixtus informed the monks of Clugni of their abbot's resignation, and directed them to choose another; on which they selected Hugh, prior of Marcigni, a nunnery in the diocese of Autun, already mentioned in the history of Ulric. [3] He held the office only a few months; and on his death, a large assembly, consisting of several bishops and abbots, and a great multitude of monks (multus monachorum populus) chose Petrus Mauricius de Monte-Buxerio, or Pierre Maurice de Montboissier, or, as he has since been generally and justly called, PETER THE VENERABLE, to succeed him.

He was of a noble family in Auvergne, and was one of several brothers who filled important stations in the church. Heraclius was archbishop of Lyons; Pontius, abbot of Vezelai; Jordanus, abbot of La Chaise-Dieu; Armannus, prior of Clugni, and afterwards abbot of Manlieu. Peter himself was offered by his parents, in his childhood, at the priory of Soucilanges, or Sauxillanges (belonging to Clugni, and about thirty miles S.E. of Clermont in Auvergne), and, during the abbacy of Pontius at Clugni, he was first prior of Vezelai, and then of Domaine, a considerable cell, dependent on that monastery, but in the diocese of Grenoble. [4] It was in this character,

---

[2] Honorius says—"Se perpetuo Jerosolymis victurum voto adstrinxerat." —*Gal. Chr.* I. 1136.

[3] See p. 361.

[4] "Qualis fuerit infantia, quantaque assiduitas legendi seu discendi, postea rei probavit eventus. Nam ad tantam scientiæ plenitudinem, Dei gratia, in brevi evectus est, quod in ipsa juventutis adolescentia in Viziliacensi monasterio seniorum doctor et custos ordinis constitutus est. Quod cum strenue et religiose tenuisset, et novellam plantationem secundum formam religionis sacri eloquii imbre ad plenum irrigasset, promotus est in Priorem de Domina, in quo non est oblitus scientiam

and when he was about thirty years of age, that he attended the election at Clugni, on the 22nd August, 1122; when, as I have already stated, he was chosen abbot, and received the benediction from the archbishop of Besançon on the same day.

It may well be supposed, that a house divided against itself for ten years had not prospered; and Peter found it in a sad state at his accession. In a document written long after, he says—

"When I was raised to the office, twenty-six years ago, I found a large monastery, religious and famous, but very poor ; with great expenses, and, comparatively speaking, scarcely any revenue whatever. There were three hundred monks, or more, and the monastery was not able, from its own resources, to provide for more than one hundred. A crowd of guests, and always an infinite number of poor." [5]

By his judicious measures, however, he soon put things in a train for amendment. Old quarrels subsided, and Peace sat quietly waiting for Plenty, when, all at once, with unexpected violence, she was driven from the place. Pontius, it would seem, got tired of living at Jerusalem. He returned to Italy, and set up a little monastery near Ravenna; but this did not succeed, or was perhaps only intended as a temporary residence ; and he soon quitted it, and returned to France.

"Having at length," says the Abbot Peter, " gained information that I was from home (for I was absent in *Aquitania Secunda*, on the business of Clugni), [6] pretending that he would not come to Clugni,

---

et disciplinam, sed magis et magis in Deum proficiens, in annis juvenilibus assidue meditabatur, quod postea in senectute devotus impleret. Lectioni et orationi vacabat, et ita sapientiæ splendore fulgebat, ut amabilis omnibus videretur. Suavis eloquio, decorus aspectu, sermone admirabilis, facundia insuperabilis, benignitate singularis, misericordiæ visceribus affluens, universis compatiebatur."— *Vita, auctore Rudolfo Mon. ejus Discip. ap. M. & D.* vi. 1189.

[5] Baluz. Miscel. tom. V. p. 443.

[6] This is not a very precise statement, as that district includes the

he, nevertheless, by degrees, came nearer and nearer. Having been joined by some deserters from thence, and being supported by the arms of the rabble whom he had collected, he came suddenly to the gates of Clugni. These being forced, and the venerable old Prior Bernard, and the monks, put to flight in all directions, he entered the monastery with that mixed multitude of armed men, even women rushing in along with the rest. Immediately on his entrance, he took possession of everything, and those whom he found there he compelled, by threats and torments, to swear fidelity to him. Such as refused, he turned out, or subjected to severe imprisonment. He instantly laid hands on the sacred things. He seized golden crosses, golden tablets, [7] golden candlesticks, golden censers, and all the other vessels, many in number and of great weight. He also took the most holy chalices, and did not spare the gold and silver reliquaries and shrines, containing the bones of many saints and martyrs. These and the like he melted down into a vast sum of money, with which he invited the knights of the neighbourhood, and all the robbers who were greedy of gain, to the war. Protected by them, he invaded the towns and villages round the monastery; and, endeavouring, in a barbarous manner, to subdue the religious places [that is, the dependent cells and priories], he laid waste all that he could with fire and sword. He abstained from no species of warfare; plunder and slaughter, by soldiers hired with consecrated gold, raged everywhere.

"In this manner, all the summer, from the commencement of Lent to the beginning of October, was passed, withhout any respite, of even a few days, from these calamities. During this time, Bernard the prior, already mentioned, and the noble, religious, and great men, were out of Clugni, wherever they could find places more secure; and there they defended themselves, as well as they could, against the attacks of such enemies. Thus, by the inscrutable, but just judgment of God, Satan, being loosed for a time, raged in that holy and most famous house of Clugni; but, according to the book of the blessed Job, 'He that made him, made his sword to approach unto him;' [8] and soon put a happy termination to such great evils.

"The venerable Pope Calixtus, already mentioned, had departed this

---

dioceses of Bordeaux, Agen, Angouleme, Saintonge, Poitiers, and Perigeux.

[7] That is, what we should call the "boards" of books. See what is said of "excrustation," in No. XIII. p. 248, 249.

[8] Job xl. 19.

A A

life, and had been succeeded by Honorius, who was not his inferior. Hearing of such disorder in so great a monastery, and having sent the Lord Cardinal Peter, as his legate *a latere*, with whom was joined Hubald, archbishop of Lyons, he condemned Pontius and all the Pontians (as they were then called) with a terrible anathema; but having shortly after appointed a day for both parties to appear before him, for the hearing and decision of that important cause, he cited them by his apostolical letters.

"All our side obeyed immediately; and, among innumerable priors of monasteries, that one on whose account I insert these particulars, the venerable Prior Matthew, was present. Pontius, although against his will, was there also with his party, and was cited to the trial on the day appointed. As, however, he could not be a party in any suit, nor be canonically subjected to any judgment, while excommunicate, he was ordered first to make satisfaction, and, by so doing, to free himself from the bond with which he had been legally bound. Messengers were sent by the pope, who, in the name of him who sent them, ordered him to make satisfaction for such enormities. This he refused to do; and affirmed that he could not be bound by the anathema of any man living. He would acknowledge that power to belong to St. Peter in heaven, and to him only. The Lord Pope, being still more incensed by such an answer, and all the city being in an uproar, there was an universal outcry that he was not only an excommunicate person, but a schismatic. And because, as has been said, he could not be admitted to trial until the excommunication was taken off, the Lord Pope, by his messengers, desired an answer from those who had come with him, whether they were willing to make the satisfaction which he had refused? They immediately replied that they were prepared to submit to his authority. They all, therefore, entered the palace barefoot; and, publicly confessing themselves guilty, were immediately absolved; and, being absolved, they were admitted to trial, and left nothing unsaid that could be said for themselves, or for him on whose behalf they appeared. On the other side, the venerable Matthew acted as spokesman for the party, and went through the whole business with great wisdom.

"The pope having heard both sides, instantly rose; and, being accompanied by the whole court of Rome, retired to consider the matter in private. He stayed a long while; but, returning with them all, after some hours, he resumed his seat, and commanded the bishop of Porto to pronounce the sentence which had been agreed on. He, as he was directed, pronounced the sentence; and to give his very words:—' The holy Roman and apostolic church,' said he, ' deposes for ever from all ecclesiastical honour and function, Pontius the usurper, the sacri-

legious person, the schismatic, the excommunicate ; and has restored to
the present abbot (from whom they have been unjustly taken away)
Clugni, its monks, and all things pertaining to the said monastery.' This
sentence having been given, the divided parties were united, and the
body of Clugni being healed, as it were in one moment, this great
and protracted storm of evils was appeased." [9]

Pontius remained at Rome, where he did not long
survive the papal condemnation ; and Peter, returning

---

[9] Bib. Clun. 552. I have said that this is Peter's account ; and perhaps we must make some allowance for feeling ; other accounts, too
general to give any satisfaction, lead us to hope that there were some
redeeming qualities about Pontius. At all events, it is quite to our
purpose to give a short extract from the Chronicle of Clugni, which
may tend to show that, if he was not himself as much under the influence of the Word of God as he should have been, he yet took
some pains to preserve the letter of scripture :—"Albert was a monk
of St. Hugh, worthy of an honoured memory by those who are fond
of copying books, or making them for themselves. For his glory in
that volume [*hiatus* [*in MS.*] is to be found at the entrance of the
library of Clugni, which he wrote with the help of Peter, the librarian,
also called the rector of the choir, or chanter. For it is that volume
of the Bible, great, wonderful, and precious for the writing, and the
correctness, and also for the binding, adorned with beryl stones, whose
eulogy or commendation is written in the same volume, in manner
following :—'This book was written by a certain monk of Clugni,
previously of Treves, named Albert, by the order and at the expense
of the Lord Pontius, the venerable abbot. Peter being also at that time
librarian, and providing, according to his office, all things necessary,
with joy and diligence. But the father of the aforesaid monk, named
Andrew, came with him to Clugni, and both (that is, the father and
son), through the Holy Spirit's assistance and illumination, received the
monastic habit from the holy father Hugh. But the father died long
since, at Clugni. Moreover, the aforesaid monk, associating with himself
a certain religious brother named Opizo, read through this book twice,
with great diligence, that he might improve it on the authority of other
books, and twice he corrected it. Therefore the brother Albert, a sinner,
prostrating himself at the feet of the seniors of Clugni, humbly entreats
that they would obtain from God, for himself and his father, the pardon
of their sins. Amen.' "— *Chron. Clun. ap. Biblioth. Clun.* p. 1645.

to Clugni, pursued his quiet plans of reform in peace,. until circumstances arose which, in a view of the dark ages, with reference to ecclesiastical history, would claim our attention, even if they had not been the immediate occasion of Peter's being exhibited as an ignorant person, the respect entertained for whom is of itself evidence of the irreligion of the age ; but, to understand it, we must look back a little.

While Peter was a child, a monk, named Robert,. who was prior of the Benedictine monastery of Moutier-la-Celle, close to Troyes, [1] became abbot of St. Michael's at Tonnere, in the diocese of Langres. That this monastery required some reform, there is reason to believe ;. and that Robert's ideas of discipline and monastic austerity were unusually strict, is certain. He could not manage the monks, who led him a sad life ; and he was tempted to listen to the invitation of some recluses in the desert of Colan, to whom his austerities seem to

---

[1] Or perhaps it would be more correct to say, in the suburb of Troyes. The reader will find most of the places mentioned in this paper in the little map (or skeleton of a map, or, more properly still, index to a map) which is annexed. It is copied, as to scale and the site of places, from the map of France published by the Society for Promoting Useful Knowledge; but instead of roads, rivers, and departments, I have marked the boundaries of dioceses. These are reduced (without any pretence of minute accuracy) from the Gallia Christiana ; and from that work, and M. Bonne's map of France, in the Abbé Grenet's Atlas Portatif, some places are inserted. Whether *Coulanges* is the ancient *Colan*, and *Ricey le Haut*, the ancient *Haut*, I do not pretend to determine ; but it seems to me so probable, that I have put them in. Perhaps I need not say that the suffragan sees are united to their metropolitans by a dotted line. [My principal reason for giving this little sketch was to furnish a specimen of a sort of map which would, I believe, be very useful to readers of ecclesiastical history. I cannot help thinking that anybody who would even reduce and republish the maps already given in various *Sacras* would be doing such readers a very great service.]

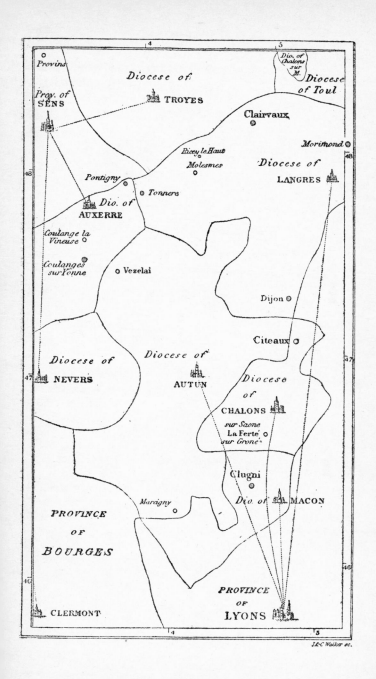

Provins

Prov. of
SENS

Diocese of
TROYES

Ricey le Haut
Molesmes

Clairvaux

Morimond

Dio. of
Chalons
sur M.

Diocese
of Toul

Diocese of
LANGRES

Pontigny

Tonnere

Dio. of
AUXERRE

Coulange la
Vineuse

Coulanges
sur Yonne

Vezelai

Dijon

Citeaux

Diocese of
NEVERS

Diocese of
AUTUN

Diocese
of
CHALONS
sur Saone
La Ferté
sur Grone

Clugni

Dio. of MACON

Marcigny

PROVINCE
OF
BOURGES

CLERMONT

PROVINCE
OF
LYONS

J.& C. Walker sc.

have recommended him, and who wished him to come
and take the government of them. The prior of St. Michael's, however, and some of the elder monks, were
unwilling to lose him ; and, to please them, he agreed
to stay there, and to confine himself to epistolary correspondence with the hermits. But it would not do :
after a while, the conduct of the greater part of the
monks (that is, I believe, their insubordination and
refusal to submit to certain strict regulations, for I do
not see any charge of immoral conduct, and in writing
on such a subject it is necessary to say so) drove him
away. Why he did not then go to the hermits, I do
not know ; but, in fact, he returned to the monastery
where he had been brought up, and of which,
as I have said, he had been prior. From thence he
was soon sent to take charge of the monastery of St.
Aigulph, at Provins, which was dependent on Moutier-la
Celle.

The solitaries of Colan, however, did not choose that
he should escape them so. I do not find that they said
anything to him, but they applied to the pope, and got
an order directed to the abbot of Moutier-la-Celle,
directing him to give up Robert to them, on the ground
that they had elected him as their superior; and in
this he appears to have very cheerfully acquiesced. He
accompanied his new subjects to their desert; but, finding
it to be a very unhealthy place, he transplanted them
to the forest of Molesme. There they built cells with
the branches of trees, and an oratory, dedicated to the
Holy Trinity, and for some time went on very well.
But it seems that some of their rich neighbours, who
admired their zeal and self-denial, destroyed, or at least
diminished, both those virtues, by the presents which
they heaped upon them ; and the monks of Molesme,
when they became comparatively rich, were as hard

to govern as those of Tonnere. At all events, Robert could not keep them up to what he considered the proper standard in ascetic life, and he fairly ran away from them to some recluses in a solitude called Haut. These seem to have been simple, industrious men, who lived by the labour of their hands, in great harmony, and they considered Robert such an acquisition, that they chose him for their abbot.

But the monks of Molesme were not willing to part with him now any more than they had been before; and having succeeded so well on the former occasion, they again applied to the pope (and this time to the bishop of Langres also) to order him back. Their request was granted, and he returned; but there is too much reason to fear that their anxiety to regain him arose chiefly from secular motives, and indeed it may be well imagined that both their character and revenue suffered from its being known that they had driven him away. Things, therefore, soon became as bad as before. The greater part of the monks were ungovernable; but there were some who felt conscientiously distressed by the consideration that they were not living in conformity with the rule of their order, which they daily heard read in their chapter, and which they had bound themselves to obey. They conferred among themselves on the best means of remedying the evil, and relieving their consciences; but the matter soon transpired, and the other monks took the alarm, and opposed them with all their might. Under these circumstances, they thought it would be best to retire, and seek for some place where they might serve God according to their consciences, without such disturbances. They asked the abbot's permission; and he not only granted it, but expressed his willingness to accompany them. In order to do this with perfect regularity, he took six of them

with him to Lyons, that he might explain the matter
to the archbishop (who was also legate of the Holy
See), and obtain his sanction. The abbot stated his wish
to institute an exact practice of the rule of St. Benedict,
such as he had found himself unable to produce at
Molesme, which he desired permission to quit; and he
obtained from the archbishop letters patent, approving
his design, and counselling him to persevere in his holy
resolution. [2] Returning to Molesme, he selected those
monks who were most zealous for exact discipline, and
with them, to the number of twenty, he set out to form
a new settlement. He fixed (I know not why) on a
desert spot in the diocese of Chalons-sur-Saone, about
five leagues south of Dijon; and there, on Palm-Sunday,
in the year 1098, being St. Benedict's Day, and the
2nd of March, he and his companions settled down in
that place, and so laid the foundation of that Monastery and of that Order, from whence were to issue
unnumbered popes, cardinals, and prelates, to say nothing of more than three thousand affiliated monasteries.

But when Robert had thus founded what he named
the New Monastery, afterwards called the monastery
of Citeaux, he could not stay there; and whether he
should be called the first Cistercian abbot is a point
which has been disputed, and in which writers vary.
However, it is certain that, before he had been long
there, he was reclaimed by his old subjects at Molesme,
who made a fresh application to the pope, and were
again successful. They seem to have felt that there
was no living with him, nor without him; and they

---

[2] The Archbishop says—"Vos..... in nostra præsentia adstitisse,
ac Regulæ Beatissimi Benedicti, quam illic hucusque tepide ac negligenter
in eodem monasterio tenueratis, *arctius* deinceps atque *perfectius*
inhærere velle professos fuisse," &c.—*Exord.* c. ii. *ap. Nomast. Cister*

set off to Rome, where Urban II. was then holding
a council. By great clamour and vehement importunity,
as the pope says, they prevailed on him to restore
their abbot; and he wrote a letter to the archbishop
of Lyons desiring him to manage the business.[3] Robert
accordingly returned to Molesme, where he presided
during the rest of his life; and Alberic became abbot of
Citeaux. He framed some regulations for the government of the monastery, which are still extant, and
which partake of the austere character which he (as
well as Robert) had endeavoured to give to monasticism
at Molesme. After he had governed for nine years
and a half, he was, in the year 1109, succeeded by
our countryman, Stephen Harding, who was also one
of the original settlers.[4]

In fact, they had not gained a single recruit, and
so many of their number had died, during the first
fifteen years from the foundation, that there was some
apprehension that the community would become extinct,
when, all at once, it received an accession of more
than its original number. In 1113, St. Bernard, who
was then but twenty-two years of age, brought with
him thirty companions, and seems to have had the
power of making men fall in love with that rigorous
and austere mode of life, which, though hitherto per-

---

[3] The pope begins his letter by saying, "Molismensium fratrum
magnum in Concilio clamorem accessimus, abbatis sui reditum vehemen-
tius postulantium. Dicebant enim religionem in suo choro eversam,
seque pro abbatis illius absentia odio apud principes et ceteros vicinos
haberi."—*Ep.* xx. *Conc.* x. 444.

[4] I do not like to mention him without saying that the great Bible,
in six volumes, which he caused to be written, and which, by the help
of learned Jews, he collated with Hebrew MSS., was at Citeaux, little
more than a hundred years ago, and is, I presume, still in existence.—
See I. *Voy. Lit.* 221; *Gal. Chr.* iv. 984.

severed in by its originators, had been so repulsive to all others. Citeaux revived,—it flourished,—it sent forth its branches, and before it was fifty years old it numbered more than five hundred affiliated abbeys. It is not necessary to give a detailed account of all and each of them; but it would be uncourteous not to name the "quatre premieres filles." Stephen Harding, who appears to have had ideas of centralization which would not have disgraced a more enlightened age, and who seems almost as if he had anticipated the extensive increase of the order, published what he denominated a "Charta Caritatis." It is a brief set of regulations, chiefly designed to promote uniformity in the understanding and practice of the rule of St. Benedict in the Cistercian monasteries, and to guide the mutual connexion, dependence, and intercourse between them.[5] To the "quatuor primi abbates" of the order is given the honour of being the visitors of the chief monastery of Citeaux, and of governing it during vacancies. These four filiations were, first, Ferté sur Groné, in 1113; secondly, Pontigny, in the year following; thirdly, Clairvaux, in 1115; and, fourthly, in the same year, Morimond.

There is no need to enter into details about it—no necessity to trace Cistercian history from St. Michael's at Tonnere to La Trappe,[6] in order to show that the spirit of the order was austere and ascetic. No doubt it was originally, in its conception and first spirit, a plan of reform; and if it was not meant particularly

---

[5] See Paris, Nomast. Cist. 65.

[6] Of course I mean La Trappe in the days of De Rancé, for the monastery was one of the earliest affiliations of Citeaux. That reformer had, I believe, no idea of going beyond what he considered (and, I believe, rightly) as required by the Cistercian order. Perhaps he mistook

and pointedly to reflect on Clugni and its connexions,
yet it can hardly be wondered at that jealousies arose.
I hope that I do them no injustice by the suggestion,
—but really I have often wondered why these monks
of Molesme should travel a distance of, I suppose, at
least seventy or eighty miles, to set themselves down
in a swampy thicket,[7] so bad that, after a short time,
they were obliged to remove a quarter of a league,
unless it was that all that distance brought them
almost as much nearer to Clugni. Surely, whatever
nicety of taste they might have in such matters, they
might have been accommodated with a suitable wilderness nearer home. If that was really all they wanted,
surely they must have seen "quod petis est hic"
inscribed in characters not to be overlooked or mistaken,
on some part or other of almost every league which
they travelled. I do not dispute, either, that Alberic

---

in that point in which he differed from Robert. He desired to reform
the Cistercian order, and might have had better success, if, instead of
setting about it under that name, he had founded a new order, as
Robert did. Fuller is not a writer whom I would quote as an authority
about "the several orders of monks and nuns," but a remark made by
him in his attempt "confusedly to shovel up these vermin," contains
much truth and much history:—"As mercers, when their old stuffes
begin to tire in sale, refresh them with new names to make them more
vendible; so when the Benedictines waxed stale in the world, the
same order was set forth in a new edition, corrected and amended,
under the names, first, of Cluniacks—these were Benedictines sifted
through a finer search, with some additionals invented and imposed
upon them by Odo, abbot of Clugni, in Burgundy, who lived, Anno
Domini 913. . . . Secondly, Cistercians, so called from one Robert,
living in Cistercium, in Burgundy aforesaid; he the second time refined
the drossie Benedictines," &c.—*Ch. Hist.* B. vi. p. 266.

[7] "Qui locus in Episcopatu Cabilonensi situs, et præ nemoris spi-
narumque tunc temporis opacitate accessui hominum insolitus, a solis
feris inhabitabatur."—*Exord.* c. iii. *ap. Nomast. Cister.*

might dream that the Virgin Mary directed that his
monks should wear white garments; but it leads me
to suspect that he might have been thinking on the
matter when he was awake; though even then, perhaps,
it was not because the monks of Clugni wore black
ones. Nor do I take upon me to say that he was
thinking of the fine chandelier, composed of brass,
gold, and silver, which hung from the roof of the
church at Clugni, when he gave special directions that
the Cistercians should have none but iron candlesticks
in their churches; nor, indeed, that he meant to be
personal in the minute directions which he gave
respecting various little matters, wherein grounds
of accusation against the monks of Clugni were afterwards found; but it seems impossible not to believe
that there was, from the first, something like a design
on the part of the Cistercians to reform (not to say
rival, or humble) the monks of Clugni.

Be this as it may, jealousies did arise: the Cistercians murmured that the Cluniacs were lax, and the
Cluniacs hinted that the Cistercians were upstart
pharisees; and in the course of a few years these
feelings had become strong, undisguised, and even
noisy. Look for a moment at the real state of things:—
during that period, Bernard, at the age of four and
twenty, in the ardour of youthful zeal, and in the
practice of austerities which he lived to regret and
condemn, had set out in the government of one of
the first offsets of a severe Order, even younger than
himself; while Pontius, probably not much his senior,
was at the head of a monastery nearly two hundred
years old, where, perhaps, the protracted abbacy of
his predecessor, or the mere lapse of time, had produced
some relaxation, and where, during his dissensions
with his monks, every kind and every consequence

of misrule might naturally be expected. By the time
that Bernard had been ten years at Clairvaux (that
is, in the year 1125, just when Peter was settling
down quietly at Clugni, after the irruption of Pontius),
William, Abbot of St. Thierry's, near Rheims, one of
Bernard's dearest and most intimate friends, and himself a Cluniac, urged him to publish some statement
on the subject; letting people know authentically what
he had, and what he had not, said about it, and what
charges the Cistercians really did mean to bring against
their Cluniac brethren. Bernard accordingly put forth
what is called his Apology, but what is, in fact, a
vehement attack on the monks of Clugni.

That this work contains much important truth and
much fervent eloquence, and that it was dictated by
a. true zeal for the glory of God and the welfare of
his church, Bernard's enemies will scarcely venture to
deny; but that it was vehement beyond the occasion,
that his zeal for God was not merely intemperate, but
misguided (as such intemperate zeal too frequently is)
into something too much like judging another man's
servant, even his friends must admit. The tone is like
that which we expect from a man who would think
it wrong to write in anger, but who tells us (and
very sincerely) "I am not at all angry, but I certainly
do feel very much hurt." In fact, this is so apparent,
and this tone in an aggressor, who might rather have
been expected to write with feelings of quiet self-
complacency, is so singular, that I cannot help noticing a circumstance which, if it does not entirely excuse,
may perhaps account for, some appearance of personal
feeling in the matter. A young cousin of St. Bernard,
named Robert, for whom he seems to have had a
most tender and paternal affection, had accompanied
or followed him to Citeaux, during the time that

Pontius governed the abbey of Clugni. This latter
monastery claimed him, on the ground that his parents
had promised (not, St. Bernard contends, offered) him
there in his infancy; and the prior of Clugni came to
Citeaux, and persuaded the youth to quit the place,
and come to the monastery for which he had been
originally destined. Their claim to him was affirmed
by the pope; but it was done on an ex-parte statement,
if we may place entire reliance on St. Bernard's account
of the matter, in a letter which he wrote to his cousin,
with the hope of moving him to a voluntary return.
This letter is a singular composition of wrath and
tenderness; of rebuke to the youth, whom he treats
as a prodigal gone to indulge in riotous living, and
of self-reproach for the harsh enforcement of austerities
such as he might have known that a lad, brought up
in the softness of secular life, could not bear. And
as to the prior of Clugni (magnus quidam prior, ab
ipso principe priorum: foris quidem apparens in vestimentis ovium, intrinsecus autem lupus rapax) and
his monastery, they are treated with all the bitterness
of bereaved affection. But it was in vain; as long as
Pontius remained abbot of Clugni, Robert was not to
be regained. When, however, Peter succeeded him,
he gratified his friend Bernard by restoring his young
kinsman, who expiated, we may hope, a comparatively
short absence by sixty-seven years of submission to
the Cistercian order.

That Bernard had forgotten all about this when he
wrote his Apology—that he did not naturally feel
bound to follow up and support the charges which he
had made in that letter—and that he did not bring
to the work some of the feelings which had been so
strongly excited, is more than can be believed; and,
as I have already said, the Apology is, in fact, a vehe-

ment invective. It would exceed the bounds of this
paper even to mention the charges which he makes;
but, as people in the present day form the most gross
ideas on the least hint of irregularity in a monastery,
I must just say, that he charges them with nothing
which in the common and gross sense of the term we
should call immorality, nothing more nearly approaching
to it than such a degree of luxury in eating and drinking, and dress, and in the ornament of their buildings,
as he considered inconsistent with strict monastic life.
It is as Benedictine monks, it is for their Benedictine
irregularities, and for departures from the Rule which
they professed (that is, however, we must recollect, for
perjury), that Bernard attacks them. In fact, Milner, or
more properly the writer from whom he borrowed, is
in some sort a voucher for this; for, from Peter's
reply, he characterizes the matters in dispute as "frivolous punctilios and insignificant ceremonies." His
testimony as to the merits of the case may be admitted, though he happened to mistake between the
plaintiff and defendant; for it is obvious that Bernard
if either, was the trifler, and that Peter was only replying to his charges; that Bernard was the person
insisting on punctilios, and that Peter was in some
cases repelling charges of perjury, and in others assert-
ing his Christian liberty, and claiming a right to modify
such small matters according to his discretion. This is,
I say, obvious; and if it should not immediately appear
so to any reader, I hope to make it plain; for the
contention and correspondence of two such persons,
and so situated, as Bernard and Peter, is quite worthy
of further discussion.

In the meantime, it may be right to explain how
the historian from whom I have borrowed my motto
came to entertain the opinion which is there expressed.

He was too much in the habit of forming his opinion of authors from the brief accounts and extracts which he found in the English translation of Dupin's Bibliotheque des Auteurs Ecclesiastiques,[8] to which work he very honestly refers us on the present occasion. *The works of Peter he does not profess to have seen.* As printed in the Bibliotheca Cluniacensis they extend from col. 621 to col. 1376,—that is to say, they occupy about 377 folio pages, which are not, I believe, defrauded of their full measure by a single note. Dupin's account of the life and writings of Peter, in this English translation, does not fill quite seven folio pages, not so large, but,' owing to a smaller type, containing rather more than an equal number of the others. Of these seven pages, a large, though I do not know that we should say a disproportionate, share is given to an abstract of the letter which Peter wrote in Reply to Bernard's Apology. Dupin naturally thought this letter one of the most curious among nearly two hundred of Peter's

---

[8] I do not know how far this translation is faithful, not being much acquainted either with it or with the original work ; and I shall be very much obliged to anyone who can communicate the history of this version. I have seen two or three persons named as translators, but, I suspect, incorrectly. The tenth volume, with which we are at present concerned, is, as far as I see, anonymous ; and so is the ninth ; but the eighth is dedicated to the Bishop of London, by William Jones, in terms which distinctly imply that he was the translator. Some of his notes look as if he might be the person whom Watt mentions as the author of a "Poem on the Rise, Progress, and present State of the New Reformation. Lond. 1691, fol." Whoever he was, I cannot help suspecting, from the little which I have seen, that he was not very familiar with ecclesiastical matters and language. In this present article he tells us that Peter wrote "Several pieces of prose," which he certainly did ; and perhaps without being aware of it. But the translator (for the mistake can hardly be Dupin's) does not seem to have known that *a prose* was something in verse—especially as he goes on to say that Peter wrote "a discourse *in prose* on the Virgin Mary."

B B

which are extant; and the abstract which he gave of it, including the translator's addition, occupies exactly two pages out of the seven. Yet, long as it is, this is a very brief abstract of Peter's long letter, and, compared with it, little more than a table of contents, stating the points in dispute. Immediately after it, comes what would be called a note, if it were not inserted in the text in manner and form following;—

[*And now upon this whole Debate or Controversie between the Monks of Cisteaux and those of Cluny, we cannot forbear making this one Remark, that, according to our old course* English *Proverb, here has been a great Cry, but little Wool; a great noise and clamour about the Externals, but scarce one Word said, Pro, or Con, about the Internals, of Religion; which sufficiently shows, that when Men are once wedded to any party in Religion, their greatest Heats happen about the Circumstantials of Religion to which that Party adheres, and that they have little or no Concern for the Fundamentals of the truly Catholic and Christian Church.*]

Mr. William Jones, in all probability, knew nothing whatever about the matter but what he found in Dupin, and did not consider that Peter was replying to the particulars of a charge of perjury, urged with great heat by a man whose character and station made it necessary that every such charge should be fairly met and discussed. He only thought, perhaps, that the bookseller who employed him wanted to have Dupin's work "turned out" of French into English, as he tells us that Peter the Venerable "procured the Alcoran to be turned out of Arabick into Latin;" and having learned and taught his readers in the foregoing chapter that St. Bernard "touches the heart with his movements," he perhaps expected to produce the same effect in the present case; or, more probably, only took the opportunity of showing his zealous protestantism.

The passage, however, inviting attention by the

indicating hand and the brackets, and by being printed
almost entirely in italics, probably caught Milner's eye
as he turned over Dupin, just as its reprint here may
arrest the attention of someone carelessly turning over
the leaves of this book; and it is, most likely, to this
effusion of Mr. William Jones that Peter owes the
notice which he received from the historian. It is
evidently on this suggestion, and almost in the language, of this absurd and ignorant translator, that
Milner says, "He takes large pains to vindicate the
manners and customs of his monastery against objections; and in doing this he is so verbose and circum-
stantial, that he may seem to have placed the essence
of Christianity in frivolous punctilios and insignificant
ceremonies." [9] It is not wonderful that, in the practice
of these *sortes Dupinianæ*, Milner sometimes formed
wrong opinions respecting the character and writings
of authors of whose history and works he knew
nothing. But, surely, if the matter is to be decided
by a casual dip, it should at least be made in the
author's own works; and who will venture to say
that Peter would have been pilloried as an ignorant
and triffling writer, if Milner had happened to open
on col. 865, and to have read in one of his epistles,
"Libri, et MAXIME AUGUSTINIANI, ut nosti, apud nos
AURO PRECIOSIORES sunt?"

---

[9] Cent. XII. Chap. viii. See Dupin, vol. X. p. 82 of the English
Translation. Lond. 1698, fol.

No. XXII.

"It is most deeply to be lamented that your lordship should not have thought proper to acquaint yourself with some of the most general and notorious provisions of our collegiate statutes, before you hazarded against those bodies a charge which, under whatever name it is disguised, cannot be less than PERJURY . . . . . . Is your lordship aware that, for the most part, these trivial matters are expressly placed by the statutes themselves at the discretion of the governing body; that if they are absurd and impracticable (palpably absurd, and wholly impracticable—for very little licence indeed is to be granted in our notions of absurdity), there is a dispensation in the very nature of the oath; sometimes in the law of the land; always in the law of interpretation prescribed by the founders themselves?"—SEWELL.

I HOPE I shall not be understood to insinuate, that Bernard had no more information respecting matters which he wished to mend, than what is considered in the present day quite sufficient for a zealous reformer. But really, after I had selected and translated what I am about to lay before the reader, I took up the letter from which I have made free to borrow a motto, and there seemed to be such a resemblance between the circumstances which called it forth, and those which led to Peter's defence,— such a similarity in the charge, the manner of making it, and the mode of meeting it,—that the abbot might have written, and almost did write, the very words which I have quoted. Indeed, I am afraid that I shall hardly be believed when I say, that I took the motto because it seemed so applicable to the extracts which I had already made, and did not select or modify them to suit the motto.

Before, however, I call the reader's attention to

the dispute between Bernard and Peter (or rather between their respective "Orders"— for I must use that word though in some degree by anticipation), it may be necessary to remind him, that the two men hold very different places in history from those which they actually occupied among their contemporaries. They were of nearly the same age. Bernard was born in A.D. 1091; and Peter, perhaps three years, or more probably only one year, after. They were both of noble family, and had received the best education which the times afforded. So far they were alike; and so they were as to some points of personal character, which it is not to our present purpose to discuss. But as to official station they differed widely.

CLUGNI, the "Caput Ordinis," had long been the most important monastery in the world. I have already said that the abbot Hugh was supposed to have under his government ten thousand monks; and of these Peter found three hundred at Clugni on his accession in A.D. 1122; and a general chapter, which he held ten years after, was attended by two hundred affiliated priors. I have not such accurate information as would enable me to say whether those from Mount Tabor, or the valley of Jehosaphat, or Constantinople, were there; for I am not sure whether they were then affiliated; but the Order had spread far and wide, and its abbots had long been men of the highest station and most eminent influence in all matters, both ecclesiastical and secular.

The dependencies of CITEAUX, of course, bore no comparison. Clairvaux was, indeed, its most important filiation, and had, even when Bernard wrote his Apology, in 1125, put forth some shoots, but nobody then knew that it was to be (either by adoption or foundation) the parent of eight hundred monasteries.

It had only three, [1] new, of course, and, I apprehend,
poor, and at no great distance from the parent
monastery, which had scarcely risen into wealth or
importance of any kind, except what it derived from
the personal character, the uncommon abilities, and
the singularly influential qualities, of Bernard himself.
No man, I think, can read his history and writings
without feeling that he was one of those few men who
seem as if they could carry all the rest with them
wherever they please, if they could only once get them
within the sphere of their personal influence. I have
said that Peter could not have been attacked by
anyone whom he would have been more imperatively
called on to answer fully; and perhaps I may add, on
the other side, that there was no one whom, under
all the circumstances, it required more boldness to
attack than the abbot of Clugni. Not that we are to
regard it as a personal attack. Bernard, as I have
already stated, had written a most severe and impas-
sioned letter concerning the abduction of his cousin
Robert, while Pontius was abbot of Clugni; and when
(six years after) he wrote his Apology, it does not
appear that he knew much of Peter, and it seems
pretty clear that they had never met. Indeed, Bernard
was particularly anxious to disclaim anything like
personal feeling, or hostility to the Order; and though
his Apology is certainly sharp enough, yet it is evident
that one object was to disclaim feelings and opinions
which, being avowed by others of his Order, had been,
or might very naturally be, attributed to him. In what
may be considered as the introduction, he says—

---

[1] They were — Trois Fontaines, in the diocese of Chalons, founded
in 1118; Fontenay, in the diocese of Autun, founded in the same
year; and Foigny, in the diocese of Laon, founded in 1121; but, in
fact, the church was only dedicated in November, 1124.

"Who ever heard me openly attacking, or privately whispering against, that Order? What man belonging to it did I ever see without pleasure, receive without honour, speak to without reverence, admonish without humility? I said, and I still say, that their mode of life is indeed holy, honest, adorned with charity, distinguished by prudence, instituted by the fathers, foreordained by the Holy Spirit, and greatly conducive to the good of souls. Do I either despise or condemn that of which I speak in such terms? I remember to have been, on some occasions, received as a guest in monasteries of that Order. May the Lord reward his servants for the even superabundant kindness which they showed me in my illness, and the respect, beyond my deserts, with which they honoured me. I commended myself to their prayers, I was present at their collations; frequently I discoursed with many of them on the scriptures, and on the salvation of souls, both publicly in their chapters, and privately in their chambers.

"Whom did I ever, either publicly or privately, dissuade from entering that Order, or solicit to enter ours? Have I not rather repressed many who wished to come, and even driven away those who did come and knock for entrance? Did I not send back brother Nicholas to St. Nicholas's, and two monks to your monastery, as you can bear witness? Moreover, were there not two abbots of that Order (whose names I will not mention, but you know them very well, and you know that they are my intimate friends [2]) who wished to migrate to another Order (which you also know), and who, while they were actually deliberating upon it, were prevented by my advice, and persuaded not to quit their posts? Why then should I be thought, or said, to condemn an Order in the service of which I persuade my friends to remain, to which I restore its monks when they come to me, and whose prayers for myself I anxiously solicit and devoutly receive?

"Or is it because I am myself of a different Order that I am suspected? Why, on the same grounds, all of you who differ from us may be said to reflect on us. Then those who live in celibacy, and those who are married, may be said to condemn each other, because each forms a part of the church, subject to its own laws. The monks too, and the regular clergy, may be said to reflect on each other, because they are distinguished from each other by peculiar observances. Indeed, we may suspect that Noah, Daniel, and Job, could not bear

---

[2] One of them being the abbot William himself. The monastery of St. Nicholas here mentioned was that of St. Nicholas aux Bois, in the diocese of Laon. Simon, its abbot, was the brother of William.

to live together in that one kingdom, because we know that they have not reached it by precisely the same path of righteousness. We must suppose, also, that either Martha or Mary displeased our Saviour, whom both were trying to please by modes of service so different. On this principle, too, one cannot conceive of anything like peace or concord in the whole church, which is distinguished by so many and such different Orders, like the queen of whom we read in the Psalm, 'clothed round about with varieties.' [3] For what secure tranquillity, what safe state, can be found in it, if each man, choosing some one Order, either despises all the others or suspects that they despise him? especially when it is impossible for one man to belong to all the Orders, or for one Order to comprehend all the men.

"I am not so dull as not to know Joseph's coat—not his who saved Egypt—but his who saved the world; and that, not from bodily hunger, but from the death of both soul and body. Everyone knows that it is a coat of many colours, that is, diversified with beautiful variety. But it shows, too, the stain of blood—not indeed of a kid, the type of sin, but of the lamb, the figure of innocence; that is, his own, and not another's. He is truly that most meek Lamb who was dumb, not indeed before the shearer, but the slaughterer; who did no sin, but took away the sins of the world. They sent, too, those who should say to Jacob, 'We have found this; see whether it is thy son's coat or not.' And see thou, O Lord, whether this is the coat of thy beloved Son. Acknowledge, O Father Almighty, that coat of many colours which thou madest for Christ thy Son, giving some apostles, some prophets, some evangelists, others pastors and teachers, and those other things which thou hast beautifully appointed for his singular ornament, for the perfecting of the saints, coming to a perfect man, to the measure of the stature of the fulness of Christ. Vouchsafe, also, O God, to acknowledge the purple of that most precious blood with which it is stained, and, in that purple, the illustrious sign, the most glorious token of obedience. 'Wherefore,' saith he, 'art thou red in thine apparel?' and he answers, 'I have trodden the wine-press alone, and of the people there was none with me.'

"Therefore, since he hath become obedient unto the Father, even unto the wine-press of the cross which he trod alone (for it was his

---

[3] The Vulgate reads, "Circumamicta varietatibus." Ps. xliv. 15. Eng. Version (xlv. 14) "In raiment of needlework." I give the Douay version here and in some other places as the only way of rendering the reference intelligible.

own right arm that helped him), according as it is written in another
place, 'I am alone until I pass;'[4] now, therefore, exalt Him, O God,
and give unto Him a name that is above every name, that at the name
of Jesus every knee should bow, of things in heaven and things in
earth, and things under the earth;—let him ascend up on high, lead captivity
captive, and give gifts to men. What gifts? Let him leave to his spouse the
church that coat of many colours, but 'without seam, woven from the top
throughout!' Of many colours, from the various distinctions of the many
Orders which compose it; but without seam, by reason of the indivisible
unity of indissoluble charity. 'Who,' saith he, 'shall separate me from the
love of Christ?' Hear how it is of many colours:—'There are,' he
says, 'diversities of gifts, but the same Spirit; and there are diversities
of operations, but the same Lord;' and then, having enumerated various
gifts, as it were the colours of the garment, to show that it is a coat
of many colours, he adds, in order to show that it is without seam,
and woven from the top throughout, 'But all these worketh that one
and the self-same Spirit, dividing to every man severally as he will.'
For 'the love of God is shed abroad in our hearts by the Holy Spirit
which is given to us.' Let it not then be divided; but let the church
obtain it whole and entire, by her hereditary right; for of this it is
written,—'the queen stood on thy right hand in clothing of gold,
surrounded with variety.'[5] Therefore it is that different persons receive
different gifts—one thus, and another thus—whether monks of Clugni
or of Citeaux, or canons, or even faithful laymen, in short, every Order,
every tongue, each sex, every age and condition, in every place, through
all time, from the first man to the last. For it is on this account too
that it is described as a long garment,[6] because it reacheth unto the
end (as the prophet saith, 'there is no one that can hide himself from
its heat'), suited to him for whom it was made, of whom another
scripture testifieth that he 'reacheth therefore from end to end mightily,
and ordereth all things sweetly.'[7]

"Let us all therefore unite under one garment, and out of all let
one be made. Of all, I say, one—for though made up of many, and
those differing, my dove, my perfect one, is *but* one;[8] that is, not I

---

[4] "Singulariter sum ego donec transeam." Ps. cxl. 10. In our version,
"Whilst that I withal escape." Ps. cxli. 10.

[5] "In vestitu deaurato circumdata varietate," v. 10.

[6] "Nudaverunt eum tunica talari et polymita."—Gen. xxxvii. 23.

[7] Wisd. viii. 1.

[8] Cant. vi. 8, Douay.

alone, nor you without me, nor he without either of us; but we are
all, and at the same time, ONE, if we are but careful to maintain the
unity of the Spirit in the bond of peace. It is not, I say, exclusively
our Order, or exclusively yours, which constitutes that ONE, but yours
and ours together—unless (which God forbid) envying one another, and
provoking one another, we bite one another, and are consumed one of
another, and so make it impossible for the apostle to present us as a
chaste virgin to Christ, that one husband to whom he espouses us.
Yet that *one* saith in the canticle, 'He set in order charity in me;' [9]
that, although one in charity, it might be diverse in ordination. What
then? I am a Cistercian—do I therefore condemn those of Clugni?
God forbid; but I love, I praise, I magnify them. 'Why, then,' you
will say, 'do you not take upon you that Order, if you so praise it?'
Hear—because the apostle says, 'Let every man abide in the same
calling wherein he was called.' [1] And if you ask why I did not originally choose it, if I knew it to be such as I have stated, I answer,
because the apostle again says, 'All things are lawful for me, but all
things are not expedient.' Not, that is, that the Order is not holy
and just, but that I was carnal, sold under sin : and I felt that my
soul was so diseased as to require more powerful medicine. Now,
for different disorders, different medicines are proper; and for
more powerful disorders stronger medicines. Suppose two men to have
quartan and tertian ague; he who has the quartan recommends for
the tertian, water, pears, and all sorts of cold things, while he abstains
from them himself, and takes wine and other warm things as more
suitable for him. Who, I ask, can properly blame him? If the other
should say to him, 'Why do not you drink the water which you so
praise?'—would he not rightly answer, 'I prescribe it faithfully in your
case, and abstain from it beneficially in my own.' But suppose it be
asked, 'Why, as I praise all the Orders, I do not keep them all?'—for
I do praise and love all the Orders, wherever they live piously and
righteously in the church. I do hold one in practice, the others in
charity—and charity will be a means (I speak confidently) that I shall not
lose the fruit of those whose customs I do not adopt. I will say something
further—do you take care of yourself; for it may happen that you may
have laboured in vain, but that my love to your good works should be
vain is impossible. Oh! how great confidence may we have in charity :

---

[9] "Ordinavit in me caritatem." Cant. ii. 4. We translate "His banner
over me was love."
[1] 1 Cor. vi. 10.

one man works without charity, while another with charity does nothing but look on; the one loses his labour, the other's charity never faileth."

Bernard proceeds to rebuke, with great asperity, those members of his own Order who brought railing accusations against the monks of Clugni; and then goes on to point out what he considered wrong or defective in the customs of that monastery. This he does, it must be admitted, not so much in the style of brotherly expostulation, as of passionate invective. I should like to give the whole of this Apology, and, indeed (if I may so speak), all the pleadings of the case, of which this Apology formed the declaration; but though they appear to me to be most curious and valuable documents, throwing great light on the period, and especially on our subject, yet I do not know that others might think them equally interesting; and, moreover, as Peter himself quietly observes, in one of his letters:—"Additur difficultati studium brevitatis, qua MODERNI nescio qua innata segnicie delectantur." Were I, however, to transcribe the whole of Bernard's work, I do not think that it would give the reader so clear an idea of the matters in dispute as may be conveyed by extracting the brief statement of them with which Peter introduces his reply. This, though it is in the form of a letter to Bernard, professes not so much to be an answer to his Apology, as to the charges commonly brought by the Cistercians.

"Some of your monks, however, object to ours in this manner:— You, say they, do not keep the Rule which you have professed to follow, as may be seen by your works. On the contrary, your feet have turned aside into unknown paths, and devious tracks of all sorts. For, having made laws for yourselves, according to your own liking, you call them most sacred. You renounce the precepts of the fathers for your traditions; and, what seems monstrous, you act in one and the same matter both as masters and disciples. Moreover, to increase your sin and the Divine displeasure, you bind yourselves by a vow before

God and his saints, and, transgressing it, you show yourselves, without all doubt, guilty of breaking a vow. You promise to fight in the heavenly camp under the rule of St. Benedict, and to maintain a perpetual obedience to his regulations. This is your promise—let us see whether your manner of life corresponds to it.

"And that we may take up these points in regular order, how do you keep the Rule as to the admission of novices, when it directs that they shall not be received until after a year, during which their spirits shall be tried whether they are of God, [2] and you receive them without hesitation, and (if we may so speak) the very moment that they apply? Whence it happens that, having been carelessly received, they live still more carelessly after their reception; and because when they came they did not understand what they were coming to, when they are associated with the rest they know not what to do; and, not having been previously trained in the stadium, when they come to the real conflict they fly instead of fighting, or if they fight with a bravery which should ensure conquest, their inexpertness renders them an easy prey to the enemy.

"By what authority, also, do you defend the use of leather garments, and of skins of various sorts, when that Rule contains nothing about any such things?

"It commands, also, that those who are sent abroad shall receive breeches from the wardrobe, and shall replace them there on their return, not allowing anyone but those who are so circumstanced to wear them. [3]

"As to your bed furniture, judge for yourselves whether you follow the master, while you certainly put both under and over you more things, and different things than those prescribed by the Rule. [4]

"In that Rule, so often mentioned already, you read that all the monks should be satisfied with two dressed dishes; or that, if there be means for providing a third, it shall be of fruit, or pulse; [5] whether you adhere to this, is known to yourselves.

"It commands that monks who are transgressors and apostates from their profession,—that is, those who withdraw their necks from the yoke of the Rule, run away from monasteries, and return to secular life—shall, if they express their repentance and desire to return, be received to the third time; [6] and that if after that they repeat the

---

[2] "Noviter veniens quis ad conversionem, non ei facilis tribuatur ingressus: sed sicut ait apostolus 'probate spiritus,'" &c. *Cap.* lviii.

[3] Cap. iv.   [4] Ibid.   [5] Cap. xxxix.   [6] Cap. xxix.

offence, they shall not be again received. You, however, set at nought this regulation, as you do the others, and receive them as often as they choose to come, contrary to the command of the Rule.

"What shall we say of the regular fasts which you have so set aside, and so changed according to your own will and pleasure, that you scarcely retain some small remains of them — and those, perhaps, more from shame towards man than from the fear of God? For whereas the monks are commanded to fast on Wednesdays and Fridays, from Whitsuntide to the 13th of September, they should fast till the ninth hour, unless they have work to do in the fields, or the heat of the weather should be very oppressive. And whereas it is also enjoined, that from the 13th of September to Ash-Wednesday, they should always take their meal at the ninth hour, [7] you, on the contrary, throughout the summer, make all the days of the week alike, and keep the prescribed fast by eating twice every day, and the remainder of the time, by keeping or neglecting the fast at your pleasure. Instead of submitting yourselves to the Rule, you make the Rule submit to you.

"Manual labour, which the holy fathers, the hermits, always used — whereby even the apostles provided the means of sustenance for themselves and others — concerning which, while visiting the sin of the first man with this punishment, God said, 'in the sweat of thy brow thou shalt eat thy bread,'—of which, also, David, 'Thou shalt eat the labours of thy hands; blessed art thou, and it shall be well with thee;' you have so renounced, that not even all these authorities have power to make you labour, nor can the obedience which you promised to render to God, according to the Rule, prevail to draw from your bosom, and set to work, hands that have become delicate through idleness.

"You know that it is there also commanded, that on the arrival or departure of guests, Christ, who is received in them, is to be worshipped by the monks, with bowing of the head, or the prostration of the whole body on the ground. Neither are you ignorant that it is there commanded—'The abbot shall pour water on the hands of the guests; the abbot and the whole congregation shall wash the feet of all the guests;' [8] but you, despisers of your vow, do not care to keep it even in that small matter.

"The abbot is directed to keep an inventory of the implements and various things belonging to the monastery; [9] but either through negligence he does not care, or through pride he does not condescend, to do it.

"Moreover, whereas it is commanded that those who are not able

---

[7] Cap. xli.   [8] Cap. liii.   [9] Cap. xxxii.

to attend the church to join in divine worship, shall bow their knees with godly fear in the place where they may happen to be ; [1] you (according to your custom, following your own rule and despising the common one) neglect this, though there is nothing very burdensome in it ; and, making some devices of your own, you put contempt on this little commandment, just as you do on those which are greater.

"Also, it commands that the abbot shall always take his meals with the guests and strangers, [2] that so he may always have Christ as his guest, who declares that he will say, 'I was a stranger, and ye took me in.' This so great benefit, and one so easily obtained, you despise, as if you thought it of no value.

"It is commanded that wheresoever the brethren meet each other, the younger shall ask a blessing of the elder; [3] and this, also, is not done among you.

"It is commanded that a wise old man shall be put at the gate of the monastery, [4] which is not done.

"It is directed that the porter shall answer, 'Deo gratias,' or give his blessing to everyone who shall knock or call; and this is not observed.

"This, however—this, I say, opposed to all reason and authority, how do you defend—that those who have already made profession of steadfastness, and conversion, and obedience, in one place, should again, in another place, repeat the vow of steadfastness, conversion, and obedience ; and you compel them to make void their former faith; so that you thus environ those who give way to you with such inevitable peril, that, turn which way they will, they cannot escape sin. For if they will keep the first vow, they are guilty as to the second; if they keep the second, they are entangled by the first. Nor do they alone suffer, but the same chain will bind yourselves, perhaps even more severely; for deceivers ought to suffer a greater punishment than those who are deceived.

"But, besides, give, if you can, any excuse for this—that, contrary to your Rule, so often mentioned (*yours*, certainly,—*yours*, either to save or condemn you), you receive, indifferently, monks of another, and of a known monastery, without permission of their own abbots, or letters of recommendation ; and thus you do to others what you would not have done to yourselves. [5] In this, also, you show a want of regard to brotherly love, nor do you love your neighbours as yourselves, according to the divine precept, which says, 'This is my commandment, that ye love one another.'

---

[1] Cap. i.   [2] Cap. lvi.   [3] Cap. lxiii.   [4] Cap. lxvi.   [5] Cap. lxi.

" Beside all this, there is one thing which you pertinaciously maintain, which everyone must plainly see to be unjust, and contrary to
the decrees of the church, and such as might lead all persons justly
to condemn you. Contrary to the custom of the whole world, you
refuse to have any bishop of your own. How absurd this is, even the
ignorant must see. For whence are you to get chrism? whence holy
orders? whence the consecration of churches, and the benediction of
burial places? whence, in short, all things which, in order to canonical
performance, require the presence or direction of a bishop? Certainly
in these points you break the Rule, not only of monks, but of all
Christians.

"On what ground do you hold parish churches, first fruits, and
tithes, when, according to the canons, all these things pertain not to
monks, but to clerks? That is, they are granted to those whose office
it is to baptize, and to preach, and to perform whatever else belongs
to the cure of souls, in order that they may not be necessarily involved
in secular business; but that, as they labour in the church, they may
live by the church, as the Lord saith, ' The labourer is worthy of
his hire.' But why do you usurp these things, while it is not your
place to do any of the duties which we have mentioned? and while
you do not perform that labour, why do you take the wages thereof?

" But what will you say concerning those secular possessions which
you hold after the manner of secular persons, from whom, in this
particular, you seem not to differ at all. For towns, villages, and
peasants, servants and handmaids, and, what is worse, the proceeds of
tolls and taxes, and almost all revenues of that kind, you receive indifferently, hold them unlawfully, and, when they are attacked, you do
not scruple to use all means to defend them. Hence it is that, contrary to the laws of monastic order, ecclesiastics carry on secular
causes, monks turn advocates, accuse and are accused, become witnesses (contrary to the apostle's injunction), are present at trials, and,
under pretext of maintaining their rights, they do, in heart, return into
Egypt. After having left Sodom, they turn to behold its conflagration.
Having put their hand to the plough, they look back, and therefore
cannot be fit for the kingdom of heaven. In all these things we have
very clearly shown that you are transgressors of your profession, and
of your vow; for if it is certain that your Rule has commanded these
things, and that you have made a vow to keep it—if it shall appear that
you have not hitherto done this—it is clear, as we have said, that you
are guilty of breaking your vow. But *we* observe *all* these things as
they are commanded; and keep, without exception, whatsoever is in
the Rule which we promised to God that we would keep.

"To these things our monks reply—Oh, oh! a new race of pharisees has risen up in the world, who separating themselves from others, and setting up themselves before all, say what the prophet foretold that they would say, 'Touch me not, for I am clean.' But to answer first to that which you have put last—say, you true observers of the Rule, how is it that you boast of keeping it? when, as your very words show, you do not even keep that short paragraph in which it is said that a monk is not only to declare with his lips, but to feel in his inmost heart, that he is the least, and meanest of men? [6] Is this to believe and to declare yourselves inferior, when you disparage the deeds of others and extol your own, despise others and magnify yourselves, while the scripture directs—'when ye shall have done all those things which are commanded you, say, We are unprofitable servants?' 'In thy sight,' says the prophet, 'shall no man living be justified;' and Isaiah, 'All our righteousnesses are as filthy rags.'"

Having thus briefly stated the charges, the abbot proceeds to answer them in detail, and at considerable length; but one or two extracts will enable the reader to judge of the style and spirit of his reply, and how far it was just (even supposing that he had not written anything but that single letter to Bernard) to characterize him as an ignorant and trifling writer, who "may seem to have placed the essence of Christianity in frivolous punctilios and insignificant ceremonies."

"It is objected to us that, on every arrival or departure of guests, both the abbot and the whole congregation do not prostrate themselves on the ground, or bow all their heads in the sight of all the guests, that the abbot does not pour water on the hands of the guests, and that he, as well as the whole congregation does not wash all their feet. It is affirmed by the objectors, that the salvation of monks depends on their keeping these things to the letter; but, oh! men, like children running after butterflies, fighting, yet beating not us but the air, making frivolous objections, not following the path of discretion, the mother of virtues, and therefore turning aside from the right way; tell us, we beseech you, is the congregation of Clugni or any other congregation to be adjudged to have broken its vow, and therefore to

---

[6] In cap. vii.

be deprived of eternal salvation, unless, with its abbot, it bows or prostrates itself before all guests who come and go? Shall it be consigned to perdition if it does not wash the hands and feet of all the guests? If it be so, either the whole body of monks must be at all times in the house appropriated to guests, or the guests must be lodged in the cloister and in the apartments of the monks; for it is quite impossible that the injunction should be literally fulfilled unless they actually live together. For the continual coming and going of visitors will require the constant attendance of those who are to wait upon them.

"Hence it will happen that those whom you wish to be monks can no longer be so, but, always living with secular persons, will lose both the name and the true life of monks; and while they are labouring unwisely to keep this part of the law, they must give up all the rest of it, without even attaining what they aim at. Thus, plainly thus, it will happen—this will be the consequence—monks must live with clerks, soldiers, peasants, clients, players, and men of various conditions, and even (for they are not shut out from hospitality) with women; and these peculiar persons, these who are dead to the world, these to whom even the free use of the common air is not allowed, are to be again mixed up in promiscuous intercourse with mankind, from whom they have separated. Undoubtedly the number of visitors is almost always so great that if we must bow and prostrate ourselves before them all, and if we must wash the hands and feet of all, it will be necessary, as I have said, that all the monks should be with them from the rising of the sun to its setting, and spend the whole day in genuflections and in washing hands and feet, and very often they would not be able to go through the business in the day. Let them, then, give up all divine service; let them give up all the other parts of the Rule; let them give up even their meals; let them not trouble themselves about prime, or tierce, or sext, or nones, or vespers, or complin, or the celebration of mass; let them give up all these things for the washing of hands and feet, and either let the church be silent, or let some other persons be found to do the duty of the monks. Does not this appear very ridiculous? Would not even the most stupid protest against such a proceeding? Would not even the brute beasts cry out against it? We do, however, what we can; and on every day in the year we do wash the hands and the feet of three strangers, and offer them bread and wine, the abbot taking his turn, and none except those who are disabled by sickness being excepted.

"Thus we fulfil what we can of the Rule, and do not, for the sake of this, break the other parts of it; for it behoves us, as our Lord saith, to do these things and not to leave the others undone. And

C C

though, as I have shown, reason itself, even without our adding anything, exclaims against your objection, and completely makes an end of it, yet it behoves us to recur to what we before stated, and from thence to show that we fully keep the Rule. St. Benedict says, 'Let the abbot so temper and dispose all things as that souls may be saved.' He said 'all things,' and excepted nothing. If, therefore, the abbot is allowed, for the good of souls, to temper and dispose all things, it is lawful for him so to temper these things that have been mentioned as that the guests shall want nothing that is necessary, but shall be received and provided for with respect, brotherly love, and diligence; while, at the same time, the Church of God shall not be defrauded of its proper services, and no part, even the least, of regular observance shall be intermitted."

I think this will appear to most readers to be a sensible and sufficient reply to the charge. His defence on another point certainly seems less satisfactory if we look at the strict letter of the Rule; but it is perhaps on that account the more to our purpose. It shows the abbot contending not for punctilios, but for such a discretionary dispensing power as might indeed have been long used in his monastery, but has perhaps scarcely ever obtained in any other, where the Rule of St. Benedict was professed. The passage is, moreover, very characteristic of the man.

"You say that the Rule directs that we should place a wise old man at the gate of the monastery, and that we omit to do so. But we reply—supposing us to have a porter who is a wise man, though he does not happen to be an old one, are we to be condemned as breakers of the Rule, and on that account deserving of hell? Suppose we should not be able to find old age and wisdom in the same person? Is he on this account—because he is not both old in years and wise in conduct—incapable of acting as porter? What says the scripture?—'Wisdom is the grey hair unto men, and an unspotted life is old age.' [7] Beside this—unless he answers, 'Deo gratias,' to all who knock or call, or bawls out a benediction, even though he should perform all the offices of kindness to those who come, yet, according

---

[7] Wisd. iv. 9.

to you, it profiteth nothing; and not even the whole Rule, kept most strictly in all other points, can suffice to save us, unless the aforesaid porter cries out with a loud voice, 'Deo gratias.' Let reason consider this, let truth consider, let the lovers of truth consider, and without our saying a word, let them tell us what they think. But why are *we* to place a porter at *our* gate, when *we* have no gate? For our gates are not shut by day; but, always standing open, they admit all comers, without respect of persons. No one is obliged to knock or call, because he finds, not only the outer gates, but the entrance to the hospitium open; and, seating himself there, he sees that every necessary preparation has been made for his reception. Lest, however, the monks should be kept out of their own houses, we cause a wise and honest servant to remain, and to lie at hand; who, at noon, or at those times when all the gates of the monastery are by custom closed, may answer to those who knock or call, not so much by the clamour of his voice, as by the performance of his duty. Then, certainly, thus doing, we are not breakers, but, according to our power, keepers of our Rule."

These extracts will not, I trust, be found uninteresting by the reader. I give them not only as a matter of justice to Peter, but as directly bearing on our subject.

No. XXIII.

"Pontio Clarevallensi successit Petrus, cujus meminit Trithemius, libro de scriptoribus Ecclesiasticis, floruitque hoc duodecimo seculo. Is unus eorum est qui Romanam tyrannidem animadvertit et accusavit."—CAT. TEST. VERIT.

IN the preceding paper I have exhibited Bernard and Peter, not, indeed, as enemies—for, to the credit of both parties, there does not seem to have existed any-thing that could be called enmity between them, even in the height of their dispute—yet in something like a hostile position towards each other. It is but justice to show them as friends; and happily we have the means of doing this from some of the letters which passed between them.

It may perhaps be remembered, that I was led to speak of Peter by getting unexpectedly involved in his correspondence; and, in truth, it was with an intention of producing some extracts from his letters that I brought him forward. I meant to have prefaced those extracts by some remarks on the value of the epistolary correspondence of the dark ages; but in this point I have been very agreeably anticipated by an able and extended discussion and illustration of the subject. I take it for granted, that all who may trouble themselves to read what I write will be acquainted with the article to which I refer,[1] and I will therefore here only offer one remark on the subject. I am so fully convinced of the value and importance of the immense number of middle-age

---

[1] In the recent number of the Quarterly Review. [That is, "recent," in July, 1837.] *See Note* E.

letters which are still in existence, and of their not
having been yet made to yield anything like all the
very interesting materials which they contain for
history, that it has appeared to me most desirable to
obtain something like a chronological arrangement of
them. The full value of such a thing cannot be esti-
mated until it is done; but even a slight acquaintance
with comparatively few of them is sufficient to persuade
me that, when brought together by the chronology
which we have, one of the first effects would be a
correction of that chronology in almost innumerable
instances.

Beside this, letters passing at a certain time between
A and B, with more or less reference to the events
of the period, being thus placed beside those which
passed at the same time between C and D, and half-
a-dozen other couples of correspondents in different
places, who had never heard of A and B, or of each
other,—these letters having no common tie as to their
writers, their locality, or their professed subjects, and
now suffered to lie in a wide dispersion, would, if
collected and arranged *in order of time,* be found to
dove-tail in an infinite variety of circumstances, and
thus throw light on facts and motives, fix dates, iden-
tify persons, explain contradictions,—in a word, illustrate history in every way, and that, perhaps, to a
greater degree than we can at present imagine, or
could by any other means perform.

"I wolde wyshe," says Bale, "som learned Inglish-
man (as there are now most excellent fresh wyttes)
to set forth the Inglish Chronycles in their right shape,
as certein other landes hath done afore them, al affections set a-part. I cannot think a more necessary thing
to be laboured to the honour of God, bewty of the
realme, erudicion of the people, and commoditie of

other landes, next the sacred scriptures of the Byble, than that worke wold be." [2]

Of the truth of this I am very fully convinced; and I cannot but wish to see something effected on a larger scale. I have long, and often, and earnestly thought, how good a thing it would be, if the chronicles which we possess, and many of which have been edited, either separately or in various larger or smaller collections, with much learning, industry, and critical skill,—which, nevertheless, lie so wide that one can scarcely hope to see them all, or even any considerable proportion of them, anywhere but in a public library, —which, even when found, require him who would collect, and compare, and weigh their testimony on any point, to cover something less than an acre with outspread folios, and wander to and fro among them, carrying about collations in his head, till his patience and his shoes are very considerably worn in the business,—which, on this very account, have never yet, I believe, been fairly placed side by side, so as to show the full extent of reiteration, concordance, and discrepancy, and to reflect on each other that light which obscure, and even unintelligible passages, often do throw on each other; if, I say, we had these, which are, in fact, not only the sources of history, but all, and more than all, the *real* history which we have, brought into something like what theological writers call a " Harmony," with the letters chronologically arranged, as I have already suggested, by way of a running commentary, I really believe that we might very easily know more of history than anybody has ever known yet.

It would, to be sure, be rather a large work, but

---

[2] Brief Chron. of Sir J. Oldcastle, Har. Misc. ii. 237.

a very noble one; and then, if people liked to write
what is commonly called History, they would know
where to find materials on their own terms (that is,
without trouble), or, if they still preferred, as too many
have done, making it out of their own heads, others
would know where to find an antidote to their misrepresentations. I do not think that Bale has stated the
matter too strongly, and I really doubt whether any
competent man could be better employed (I do not
mean merely for the cause of literature, or general
truth, but specially for the cause of Christ's Church
on earth), than in thus arranging and editing the
records, and in particular the letters, of the dark ages;
and, as to these latter, I heartily wish that the writer
who has shown such a sense of their value, and such
a capability for the work, would undertake it.

It is very pleasant to run on imagining the supply
of *desiderata;* but perhaps some sedate reader may
have already asked, "What would be the expense
of such an undertaking?" I am sure I do not know;
but I am inclined to think that those who have not
turned their attention to the subject would be surprised
to see in how small a compass all that may be called
original histories, or sources of history, would lie. Still
I acknowledge that it would be rather a large work;
and if it be asked, "Who will buy it?" I feel some
hesitation about an answer. I have no such certainty
to fall back upon as George Stevens's projector had,
when he proposed to pay off the National Debt by
bottling the River Thames, and selling it as Spa-
water: "But you say, 'Who'll buy it?'—Who'll buy
it? why, the Waterman's Company *must* buy it, or
what will they do with their boats?" There is no
chartered company on the stream of history. Any
speculator may launch his barge or his wherry; he

may take in whatever company he can get for Richmond, but there is nothing beyond their own sagacity to prevent their being floated down the stream, and floundered out on the Isle of Dogs, and there left to make the best of their bargain; and truly (if I may trust the popular opinion) when they have got upon their legs, and settled to their own satisfaction whether the Tower is Somerset House or Greenwich Hospital, they may feel thankful that matters have been no worse,—that they were not run down by some dashing steam-boat or crossheaded lighter, and that they are where they are, to comfort themselves with the reflection that, for all the *really useful* purposes of air, and exercise, and pastime, it does just as well as if they had gone where they thought they were going. This, however, by the way;—it being only a little reflection suggested by the sudden (and to myself very unexpected) mention of the Waterman's Company; it is my hope and belief that a work which would be obviously for the whole world, and which must maintain an undiminished value as long as the world lasts, would meet with support. I do not say that any particular individual or body *must* buy it; but I cannot help very thankfully expressing my conviction that something like a *must* is growing up among the more educated classes, who (one sees proof of it every day) are prying into the original sources of history, both secular and ecclesiastical, and who, if such a scheme were proposed by capable men, would feel that they *must* support it. [3]

---

[3] I believe that at the time when this suggestion was made, the English Historical Society was just being formed, though I was not aware of that fact. Since then the Camden, the Irish Archæological, and the Ælfric have been added.   might perhaps fairly add the Anglo-

But as to Bernard and Peter; there are two passages in this letter of Peter which I must add to those already given.

"After this, you adduce some very strange and unheard-of charges, — insomuch that we hesitate to answer, through mere astonishment. You blame us, and say that we are just like secular persons, because we have castles, towns, peasants, servants, and handmaids, and (worse still) revenues arising from tolls; and we accept property of almost every such kind without distinction, hold it unlawfully, and defend it by all sorts of means against those who attack it. You add, that on this account, laying aside our monastic character, we assume that of lawyers, accuse and are accused, produce witnesses from our own body, are concerned (contrary to the apostle's injunction) in judicial proceedings, and cannot therefore be fit for the kingdom of heaven.

"It would be proper for you who make these charges to substantiate them by some written authority, to which we must yield, and not let them rest on your bare assertion, by which we are not greatly moved. For thus the law requires, that he who accuses anyone should prove his charge, since the burthen of proof always lies on the accuser. Nevertheless, we will here act contrary to this judicial method; and, sparing you, whom we know to be unable to prove your case, we will prove our own in the following manner:—

"We know, indeed, that 'the earth is the Lord's, and the fulness thereof; the world, and they that dwell therein;' but, beside this, we read elsewhere in the same Psalms, 'The heaven, even the heavens, are the Lord's; but the earth hath he given to the children of men.' It is plain, then, that both the heaven and the earth are the Lord's; but that he has given the earth unto men for a time, that, if they use it well, they may, after the earth, attain unto heaven, [4] and that what

---

Catholic and the Parker Societies; both formed exclusively for the reprinting old books, and both (the latter one more directly and in a greater degree) tending to illustrate the history of the Church by giving us the works of contemporary writers. Are not these new Societies sufficient (without saying anything of what has been done by the government or by private individuals) to warrant my suggestion that a spirit of investigation was arising?

[4] "Post terram *mererentur* et cœlum, et quæ sua erant ex potestate, hominum fierent ex ipsius benignitate." I believe that I give the true sense of the author, that is, the true sense of *mereor*—as commonly

was his by sovereign power, may become man's through his benignity. By which most merciful benignity and most benign mercy, though he 'hath poised with three fingers the bulk of the earth, and weighed the mountains in scales, and the hills in a balance,' [5] he nevertheless accepts that same earth, and those earthly gifts, from those same men to whom he had given them, and (if I may so speak) allows the kingdom of heaven to be bought at his own expense. Nor does he thence seek profit for himself, but the salvation of man, and esteems that his own gain. Hence it is, that, while he orders that meat should be given to the hungry, and drink to the thirsty, he previously creates bread in the corn, wine in the grape, and loads the trees with fruit, and the animals with offspring. The very water, for a cup of which given to the needy he has declared that a reward is laid up, he makes to rise from springs, and flow through all the rivers. And, in a word, all the things with regard to which he rewards the goodwill of those who give them, he does himself, first of all, give to those givers. Hence the Church of God, grounding its right as well on the Old Testament as on the New, receives all things that are offered, not to her, but to God, as his representative; and thence charitably maintains those of her members who are in want, and have no property of their own in the world; as clerks, and monks, or paupers, or whomsoever she knows to suffer the need of such things. Monks, therefore (for at present we speak of them only), receive all the offerings of the faithful, whether in moveable or immoveable property; and repay the donors by a perpetual course of prayer, fasting, and good works. But as it is respecting the acceptance of immoveable property that we are now called in question, I will at present answer to that point.

"In the first place, then, we plead our Rule. For, in treating of the reception of novices, it says—'If he has any property (res si qaus habet), let him either first give it to the poor, or, by a solemn act of

---

used by writers of the dark ages —which is (as I think I could show by a good many examples, which some criticisms that I have seen have led me to notice, but which it would be out of place here to transcribe), to *arrive at,* or *obtain,* or *come to the possession of,* some honour or benefit, without reference to personal desert, or what a protestant would understand to be referred to in the popish doctrine of *merit.* Indeed, whoever understands Peter as affirming that none but those who have *merited* heaven shall obtain it, must understand that none do obtain the earth until they have previously merited it. And this is, in fact, true, according to his use of the word, and his meaning.

[5] Douay vers. Isa. xl. 12, "Appendit tribus digitis molem terræ."—*Vulg.*

donation, confer it on the monastery.'[6] By saying, 'if he has any
property,' it excepts nothing; but if it excepts nothing, it does not
except any landed property, or town, or peasants, or servants, or handmaids, or anything of that kind. But clearly nothing is excepted, and
therefore it is obvious that these things which we have mentioned are
not excepted. And what I have before quoted from St. Gregory agrees
with the command of our Rule; wherein he forbids that any bishop
or secular person should presume, in any way, or on any occasion,
either by fraud or force, to take from the revenues, or property, or
muniments of monasteries, or of cells, or towns belonging to them.
For, by forbidding that anyone should take away any of these things,
or presume to employ fraud or force against them, he most evidently
shows that monks might lawfully possess revenues, property, cells, and
towns; as he would, by no means, have forbidden that they should
be disturbed in the possession of those things, if he had known that
they held them unlawfully. And, since the revenues arising from land
are of different kinds, and property is of various descriptions, and since
there cannot be towns without inhabitants (that is, men and women,
of different conditions), and the words of Gregory contain no exception
with regard to them, it is plainly shown that monks may rightly possess
all sorts of revenues, without any exception,—any kind of property,
any towns; and, by a parity of reasoning, any inhabitants of the different conditions, that is, free or servile.

"But you will, perhaps, object, that without the help of all these
things, monks ought to provide what is needful for them, by agriculture,
and the labour of their own hands. I think, however, that no one can
fail to see how indecent and impossible this would be; and, in the
first place, I shall show that it is impossible. How are a languid set
of men, confined to a vegetable diet, that imparts scarcely any physical
strength, and, in fact, hardly keeps them alive, and who are, on that
account, in a state of great debility, to endure agricultural labours,
which are found most oppressive by hinds and peasants, and to do the
hard work of ploughmen, exposed sometimes to scorching heat, sometimes to rain, snow, and intense cold? And how are they who, by
religious fasting, commonly diminish even their poor weakly food, to
bear such hard and continual labour? And if, as to bodily strength
they could bear all this, why should they do it, when, without the help
of others, they can obtain sufficient food and clothing?

"Having shown that it is impossible, I will show that it would be
indecent. Does it not appear indecent—yes, most indecent—that monks,

---

[6] Cap. lviii.

who are directed always to keep in the cloister, devoting themselves
most intensely to silence, prayer, reading, and meditation, and the other
precepts of the rule and services of the church, should throw up all
these things for vulgar and rustic labour? that those who, like the fine
linen of the tabernacle, should adorn its interior by their value and
their fine texture (that is, by the subtle contemplation of heavenly
things), should like hair-cloth on the outside, have to bear the wind
and rain, and all the storms, — that is, too great occupation in worldly
affairs drawing them away from internal things?

"And since this, as I have said, is proved to be both indecent and
impossible, you must of necessity allow monks some other means of
maintaining their order above absolute want; and indeed, if you refuse
your permission, we shall nevertheless, relying on the authority of the
saint, continue our practice. You have just heard that St. Gregory
allowed these things to monks; now observe that he *gave* them; for
thus we read in his life: — 'When Gregory came to have the full power
of disposing of his property, he built six monasteries in Sicily, and
stocked them with a sufficient number of monks, to whom he gave as
much landed property as might provide a daily maintenance to those
who were there serving God.' And of St. Maur we read: — 'The next
day St. Maur went to see and take possession of the royal estate which
the king had given to the monastery.' And again—'At the same time,
Lothaire, coming to Angers, sent word to the man of God that he
wished to come to the monastery. And when the man of God returned
an answer that he might come, he set out with a few attendants. And
when he had come there, he gave to that place an estate belonging
to the royal property, called Blazon; and there, also, by royal authority, he gave the town called Longus-campus.' We find, too, that almost all the things which you think that monks ought not to have,
were possessed by St. Columban and many other holy monks, whose
merits God attested by many and great miracles, and whom the church
solemnly commemorates.

"And now, to add another argument to what we have premised
—who will not think it more right, more expedient, more useful, that
every one of those various things which have been specified should be
in the hands of those whom the Order which they have assumed, and
the monastic vow which they have made, bind to a lawful use and
possession of them, than of those who, through negligence, and being
under the influence of less strict obligation, not merely despise the
trouble of good management, but also from an undue love of the things
themselves, and by ill management of them, bring on their own
destruction? For as we see commonly, and in almost every case, as long

as they are held by secular persons, they are dealt with in a secular manner; but when the property in them is transferred to the religious (if they are such, not in name only, but in fact), then by the religious they will be religiously dealt with. And, for instance, let me specify some things:—Suppose a castle is given to monks, it immediately ceases to be a castle, and becomes an oratory; nor does anyone after that fight against corporeal enemies, in a corporeal army, but is employed in repelling spiritual enemies, by spiritual weapons. And thus it comes to pass, that what was before fighting for the devil, now begins to fight for Christ; and what was before a den of thieves, is made a house of prayer.

"The same argument may be used as to peasants, servants, and handmaids; and by it we may most excellently prove that monks have a legitimate right to possess them. For everybody sees how secular masters rule over their peasants, servants, and handmaids; for they are not satisfied with their accustomed and due service, but always unmercifully claim their persons with their property, and their property with their persons. Hence it is, that, beside the accustomed payments, they three or four times in the year, or as often as they please, spoil them of their goods; they oppress them with innumerable claims of service; they lay upon them grievous and insupportable burthens. Hence they force many to leave their native soil and fly to foreign parts, and (what is worse) their very persons, which Christ has redeemed with so rich a price—even his own blood—they are not afraid to sell for one so mean, that is, for money. Now, monks, though they may have such possessions, do not possess them in the same way, but very differently; for they employ only the lawful and due services of the peasants to procure the conveniences of life. They harass them with no exactions, they impose no intolerable burthens, and if they see them in want, they maintain them at their own expense. They have servants and handmaids, not as servants and handmaids, but as brothers and sisters; and, receiving from them reasonable service according to their ability, take care in return that they shall suffer no want or injury; so that they are (to use the words of the apostle) as having nothing, yet possessing all things. By the authorities and arguments which I have adduced, therefore, it is, I think, clear, even to the blind, that monks may not only lawfully possess such things, but even more lawfully than laymen.

" And why are we to be prohibited from receiving the proceeds of tolls, when it is acknowledged that the princes of this world hold them lawfully? Or, is it thought unlawful for them to possess what the apostle directs their subjects to pay to them—'tribute, to whom

tribute, custom to whom custom?' Truly we consider that to be lawful
which is done all over the world without reproof from the Church of
God, which passes by no unrighteousness : nobody is excommunicated,
nobody is even called in question for it. And since, without the contradiction of anyone they receive them as they do their other rights,
why may they not, in like manner, give them to churches and monasteries of God? Why may not monks rightly receive these from them
as well as other things? If you object that St. Matthew, being called
by the Lord from the receipt of custom, did not afterwards return to
it, as an unrighteous calling, while Peter and the other apostles, who
were fishermen, after being in like manner called, were found afterwards
fishing, whereby they proved the lawfulness of that occupation, we
reply that this does not in any way help your argument, or weaken
ours, for we are not defending violent exactions, such as Matthew
relinquished, but just, customary, prayments, which the church receives.''

There are several reasons, which will, I hope, be
apparent, for my quoting this passage; but one of
them is so important that I cannot help distinctly
calling attention to it. It gives us a glimpse of one
of those features of the dark ages which are the least
known, and by many most reluctantly acknowledged.
It goes to show that, at the darkest periods, the
Christian Church was the source and spring of civilization, the dispenser of what little comfort and security
there was in the things of this world, and the quiet
scriptural asserter of the rights of man. Whether,
strictly speaking, the monks of the order of St. Benedict
had a right to dispense with manual labour, I very
much doubt, notwithstanding the abbot Peter's defence
of them, which I quote principally to show that he
was not quite the person that he has been represented
to be; but it was, and we ought gratefully to acknowledge that it is, a most happy thing for the world that
they did not confine themselves to the possession of
such small estates as they could cultivate with their
own hands.

Without at present entering into a subject which

is extremely interesting, and for the illustration of
which materials are very abundant, I may just observe
that the extraordinary benefit which they conferred on
society by colonizing waste places—places chosen
because they were waste and solitary, and such as
could be reclaimed only by the incessant labour of
those who were willing to work hard and live hard—
lands often given because they were not worth keeping
—lands which, for a long while, left their cultivators
half starved, and dependent on the charity of those
who admired what we must too often call a fanatical
zeal—even the extraordinary benefit, I say, which they
conferred on mankind by thus clearing and cultivating,
was small in comparison with the advantages derived
from them by society, after they had become large
proprietors, landlords with more benevolence, and
farmers with more intelligence and capital, than any
others.

One thing, however, is worthy of notice, as showing
that one eccentricity (I do not like to call it a fault,
or even a folly, though it seems likely to be punished
as a sin) of the church is not peculiar to modern times,
but at least as old as the beginning of the twelfth
century,—namely, that these ecclesiastical landlords did
not make so much of their property as they might
have done, or as would have been made of it by the
unprincipled and tyrannical laymen by whom they
were surrounded, and too frequently robbed. I think
we may infer, from Peter's way of alluding to their
mode of dealing with their tenants, and those serfs
over whom the law gave them so great a power, that
though, in one sense, very careful of their property,
they were not careful, or had not the wisdom, to make
the most of it. I do not remember to have seen it
assigned as a reason for taking away their property,

but then (as philosophical historians say) we must consider the spirit of the age. The conservative power which offered the only opposition to brute force in those days was an odd compound of elements. Beside some codes of laws, more or less comprehensive, and extending, with more or less influence, over larger or smaller districts, they had the Bible, and what was, or came to be, the Canon law, and the testimony of history, a great deal of superstition, perhaps some religion, and certainly some (if but little) common sense and conscience, all and each of which would have been separately outraged by such a pretext; and they were so blended together, that barefaced and comparatively honest spoliation found it necessary to cut the knot with brute force. It was not merely that fire and sword did the work more speedily and effectually, but men really had not learned how to meet the spirit of the age, as (could it be revived) it would now be met. People had not then learned that "the lands of the church, destined for the support of public servants, exhibited none of the characters of property. They were inalienable, because it would have been not less absurd for the priesthood to have exercised such authority over these lands, than it would be for seamen to claim the property of a fleet which they manned, or soldiers that of a fortress they garrisoned."[7] This is a recent discovery; and indeed the illustration would not have held good in the dark ages, when soldiers and sailors received pay.

---

[7] I extract this from a paper in the Congregational Magazine for June [1837] p. 363, entitled, "Are the Lands occupied by the Church of England the Property of its Members?" As this has, I believe, ever since its commencement, been considered as the organ of the most educated part of the orthodox dissenters, the discussion of such a subject in its pages is worth notice on many accounts.

I must, however, add another extract from this letter of Peter's, concerning his Rule, not merely to show that he did not place all his religion in the punctilios and pharisaical observance of it, but as throwing light on the state and spirit of monastic institutions in his time, as well as the opinions of men concerning them.

"You have said, 'St. Benedict framed his Rule either with or without charity. But that he framed it without charity none of you will dare to affirm, and therefore you do not deny that he framed it with charity. Now, since the Rule was framed by charity, it was not meant to be altered; and if not to be altered, then to be kept. Therefore you either act injuriously towards the saint by changing it, or you keep it by entire obedience.' And to this we reply — It is clear that the rule was framed by charity, but it is not clear that on that account it is unalterable; nay, from its having been framed by charity, it follows that it may be altered. And to make this evident, let us inquire into what is the office of charity. And what is the office of charity? The one and single office of charity is to seek the salvation of men by all means. Our Lord himself, the apostles, all the saints, cry aloud that this is its office. All holy scripture, as I have already repeatedly said, testifies that whatsoever it commands is just; and (what is a still greater argument) the Lord has declared that on it hang all the law and the prophets. This the apostle calls the fulfilling of the law, and the end of the commandment. Of this St. Augustine says, 'If this one thing be wanting, all things are vain; if this only be present, all are complete.' Of this, too, he says elsewhere, 'But the whole fruit is charity, without which, whatever else a man may *have*, he *is* nothing.' And in another place, 'Have charity, and do what ye will.' And therefore, to promote the salvation of men, it doth what it will; and if it be lawful for it to do as it will, it was lawful for it to make a law, and lawful also to change it. Nor can it be said that any injury is done to the saint, for it is not altered by another; but by that which, being shed abroad in his heart by the Holy Spirit given to him, used him as an instrument for the composition of that Rule. And since it envieth not, is not puffed up, doth not behave itself unseemly, seeketh not her own, those who are filled therewith know nothing of such things; and, being without envy, inflation, and ambition, they know not how to take offence. No injury, then, is done to the saint, for it made his Rule according to the circumstances of that time, and when it saw it would be useful so to do, altered what it had itself made, retaining

D D

whatever it seemed proper to retain. And as it would be absurd to
say that an injury was done to a notary, if he who dictated any document to him should choose afterwards, for some reason known perhaps
to himself only, either by his own or another's hand, to alter what
he had written, so it would be to say that St. Benedict is injuriously
treated, if Charity either by him, if she had so pleased, or by any
other whom she shall see fit to employ, should, on sufficient grounds,
alter all or any of the things which she originally wrote by him."

Surely such language is sufficient to clear the abbot
of Clugni from the charge brought against him; is it not
(to say the least) going as far as any honest friend of
expediency would venture to go? But though, from
finding that other matter, which I did not like to pass
over, has taken up more room than I expected, I have
hitherto said nothing of the more agreeable part of
his correspondence with Bernard and others, yet I
hope to show, not merely for his sake, but for the
illustration of his age, that he truly deserved his title
of "Venerable," by the promotion of religion and
learning.

I suppose that when I wrote this paper, I did not
recollect (for I had been obliged to do so much with
the book for other purposes, that I think I must have
seen it) that Peter the Venerable, who appears in
Milner's Church History as "so ignorant and so trifling
a writer," that he seems "to have placed the essence
of Christianity in frivolous punctilios and insignificant
ceremonies," had previously figured, and was, of course,
still figuring in the Catalogus Testium Veritatis of
Flacius Illyricus, as one of the witnesses against the
Romish Antichrist. The passage which I have now given
as a motto to this paper is from the enlarged folio
edition of that work published in 1608. In the original
octavo edition of 1556, the passage stands, "Petrus

Cluniacensis, abbas, floruit ante 400, et paulo amplius annos. In ejus epistolis quædam ab instituto nostro haudquaquam aliena invenio, quæ adscribam," &c. As one object of these papers is to show how Church History has been written, it may not be useless to say a few words on this matter.

Of the dispute between Bernard and Peter, which has occupied so many of these pages, Illyricus professes to have known but little. "There was, indeed," he says " in the time of this man, a very great contention be- tween the Cluniacs and the Cistercians, during the life of a certain abbot of theirs, Bernard, concerning some, I know not what, tithes, of which the Cistercians wished to deprive the Cluniacs. I do not know much about the controversy, and it is of very little consequence for our purpose to understand it thoroughly." This candid admission of ignorance is not retained by M. Simon Goulart, the editor of the folio edition, but I believe that he gives all the extracts from Peter's works which were in the first edition, as well as a good many more.

I will beg the reader's attention to one extract, which, with its comment, appears in both editions; and for the sake of that I will set before him the whole of Peter's letter, for it is not very long. I will mark by brackets that part which is extracted by Illyricus.

"*To the supreme Pontiff, and our special Father, the Lord Pope Eugenius, Brother Peter the lowly Abbot of the brethren of Clugni, sends devout obedience with sincere affection.*

"I am troublesome, no doubt, in writing to you so often; but I am afraid that continual apologies for it would only make me still more troublesome. What shall I do then? If I am silent, I shall injure myself and many others; and if I speak I shall be, as I have said, tiresome. But of these alternatives I will choose the latter. I had rather (saving the reverence due to your paternal character) appear loquacious or officious in your eyes than remain silent respecting many things which ought not to be concealed from you. What I am about to speak of is not, indeed, my own business; yet how is it quite alien from me, if it is in anywise yours? But it is your business to hear the causes of the whole Church of God that is on its pilgrimage in this vale of tears, when heard to discuss them, and when discussed to decide with apostolical judgment. And although your high office is appointed [8] over 'the nations, and over kingdoms to root up, and to pull down, and to waste and to destroy, and to build and to plant,' yet as you are not God, nor Jeremiah the Prophet to whom this was addressed, you may be led into error. You may be deceived by those who seek their own and not the things which are Jesus Christ's. That this may not happen it is the duty of every faithful son to communicate to his father what he knows, and you perhaps do not know; and to take all such measures as are in his power to prevent those of whom it is written 'the poison of asps is under their lips' from infecting your purity with their poison. For it is no small gift of God to be delivered from such; especially when the well-known Psalm says, 'O Lord, deliver my soul from wicked lips and a deceitful tongue.' [9] But how is this—perhaps I am again running on too much, still guilty of the very fault for which I have just apologised. I restrain my pen therefore; and when I wish, and think I ought, to say a great deal, I will briefly state the point at which this introduction aims. For there is one point in particular, though it is not the only one. This I will now state, and reserve the others for their proper time.

"How much I have loved, and do love, the regulations of the Carthusian Order and system, how I reverence, how I embrace them, many know; but I more, God most of all. For if my own soul does not deceive me, if my conscience bears witness to me of the truth, if in fact the divine word is true, which says, 'No man knoweth the things of a man save the spirit of a man that is in him,' I confess that for now nearly thirty years, that is, even from before the time when I became Abbot, I have loved the Order, revered the sincerity, embraced the truth of the Carthusians, more than almost all other mortals. [I thought, and I do not believe I was wrong, that their's was the best of all the Latin systems; and that they were not of

---

[8] This is, I believe, the true rendering of "Et licet persona vestra constituta sit."

[9] Ps. cxx. 2.

those who strain at the gnat and swallow the camel; that is, who make void the commandment of God for the traditions of men; and, tithing mint, and anise, and cummin, and (according to one evangelist) every herb, neglect the weightier matters of the law, judgment, mercy, and faith. For they do not consider the kingdom of God as consisting principally in meats and drinks, in garments, in labours, and the like, though these, wisely managed, may do that kingdom of God good service; but in that godliness of which the apostle says, 'Bodily exercise is profitable to little, but godliness is profitable to all things, having promise of the life that now is, and of that which is to come.']¹—Those truly holy men feast at the table of wisdom, they are entertained at the banquet of the true Solomon, not in superstitions, not in hypocrisy, not in vanities, not in the leaven of malice and wickedness, but in the unleavened bread of sincerity and truth. They are great, therefore, to be loved, to be embraced. And what shall I say? Against my will I state what I feel; forced by conviction, I say what I would not. I seem as if I were touching the ark of God, and as Uzzah of old, when the oxen were unruly, upholding it with a presumptuous hand. But I am not presumptuous; I am not, as concerning this matter, worthy of death as he was; for I am secured by His words who has said, 'If thine eye be single thy whole body shall be full of light.' I will speak therefore without more delay. May the father grant a favourable ear to the words of his son; and not suspect them of concealing anything crafty or deceitful; for as I remember, in a letter I lately addressed to your highness (*sublimitati vestræ*), I said I would as soon die as tell you a falsehood.² In the

---

¹ The passage enclosed in these brackets is that quoted by Illyricus; and the remark which he appends is curious, coming as it does from one of the most fiercely zealous, not to say ferocious, of the protestant party in the sixteenth century. "Whence it may be understood that even then there were some monks who made the whole of religion consist in a superstitious observation of days, meats, garments, and gestures; but that this father and others of a sounder description, were very far from holding that opinion"—*ex quibus licet cognoscere jam tum quosdam monachos in superstitiosa dierum, ciborum, vestium ac gestuum observatione pietatis summam constituisse: sed hunc patrem, aliosque saniores longissime ab ea opinione fuisse.*

² This refers to a letter in defence of the Archbishop of Vienne, in which he had said, "Novit Pater, ut credo, filii cor; novit si recordatur, quæ ei Antisiodori, vel apud Barum secreto suggessi; quod pene

matter of the Grenoble election which is still agitated, it seems to me
that a sudden whirlwind has destroyed the serene day of the Carthusian
Order ; and a little cloud, that has risen up I know not whence, has
obscured the hithertho crystalline splendour. It is divided against itself,
and the holy congregation, which up to this time has been more
remarkably than others, one in Christ, is by this business engaged in
intestine feud. Hence Chartreuse, Excubiæ, Durbonum, hence Portæ,
Majorevum, Sylva, Alverium, [3] and if there be any other places belonging to that sacred order, stand as diverse walls ; and one party, as
well as the other, profess according to the Prophet to go up 'for the
house of Israel to stand in battle for the day of the Lord.' One party
says, that the person elected ought not to be a bishop ; and puts forth
certain reasons which it is not my place to repeat. On the contrary
others say—' What is that to you ? It is a rule of the Carthusian Order
to give information of anything wrong which it may happen to know,
to those whom it concerns ; but not to be litigious. Their part is to
state what they think in simplicity, but not to get into palaces to
gossip. It does not belong to our wild solitude that we should be
attending courts of justice ; it is not the business of those who are
dead to the world to be plaintiffs and defendants in public business.
Our simplicity has nothing to do with worldly craft ; nor is it becoming
that we who, while we were in the world, chose the desert, should
now return from the desert to the world. But if it is not becoming
to return even when drawn thither, is it becoming to thrust ourselves
into courts of justice of our own free will, everybody opposing, everybody protesting against it ?' This is the cause, not indeed of open
quarrel, but of secret grudge among the holy men ; which would be
better known to our Father if I could speak, as well as write to your
majesty (*majestati vestræ*). For there are some things which I do not
like to commit to writing ; but them, as I did not think fit to write
them, I have placed in the mouth of our beloved brother and your
son Arnald, that they may be imparted to you."

Is it not really strange, that at a distance of seven
hundred years one should be occupied in refuting two

---

idem esset, quantum in libro conscientiæ meæ legere poteram, vobis
mentiri quod mori."—*Lib.* VI. Ep. x. *Bib. Clun.* col. 903.

[3] I suppose the Pope knew what all these places were ; but as I
do not (except Chartreuse itself, and that I suppose Portæ to mean
Portes Chartreuses some leagues to the N.N.W. of that place) I do not
attempt a translation.

such opposite statements, against a man well known in his day, and whose works are still extant and accessible to all moderately-educated persons? Was the person who was thus writing to the Pope a heartless formalist, or a witness against the Romish Antichrist? Or was he neither? and what was he?

No. XXIV.

"Scriptores recta linea
Veraces scribant literas,
Distinctiones proprias
Usque in finem compleant."

PETRUS DAMIANI.

CONSIDERING that he appears to have felt no reluctance to speak on the subject, I wish that the Secretary Nicholas had given us a fuller account of himself; and, indeed, that I had the means of referring to all that he actually did write. He was, I imagine, a very extraordinary person; and, at all events, he had very peculiar opportunities of gaining, not only all the learning which was to be had in the twelfth century, but a vast deal of information which would be most curious and interesting. In a letter to Henry, Count of Champagne, written about the year 1170, he says, "From my youth I have pleased great men, and the chief princes of this world. But to you in particular, by right of dominion, I owe all that I am, and, by duty of friendship, all that I can.[1] And a wise man has said,

'Principibus placuisse viris non ultima laus est.'"[2]

---

[1] So Mabillon understands him to mean by "Tibi singulariter, ex dominio naturæ debeo quicquid sum, et ex officio amicitiæ quicquid possum."

[2] Baluz. Misc. ii. 236. It may seem odd to find Nicholas quoting Horace under such a respectful title, especially if we consider that, according to the customs of Clugny, under which he was brought up, he could never have asked for his works without a most significant, though somewhat comic, expression of contempt for the author. To preserve silence, the monks communicated by signs, by which they were taught to express almost everything which they could wish to say. Of

Indeed, this seems to have been the case with Nicholas, in an extraordinary degree; for though strong feeling and ardent expression are very striking features in the letters of the Dark Ages, yet I know of no man whose correspondents seem to have loved him with more ardent affection. One of those friends was Peter, Abbot of Moutier-la-Celle, by Troyes (a monastery which I have already had occasion to mention at p. 368), who has from that circumstance retained the name of "Cellensis," though he afterwards succeeded our countryman John of Salisbury as Bishop of Chartres. A specimen may be taken from one of his letters:—

"Whenever you write, your letters are composed with an admirable relish to meet my eager appetite. So that (to say the truth to a true friend) it seems as if it might almost be said of them as a peculiar characteristic, 'They that eat me, shall yet hunger; and they that drink me, shall yet thirst.' (Eccles. xxiv. 29.) I, however, unskilful as I am as to style in answering, know how to return your affection. I know whom I ought to love, and why, and how much, and how long. Whom, if not the servant of God; if not him who loveth righteousness and hateth iniquity; if not, in short, him who abideth in God, and God in him? Why, if not because he is a fellow servant, and a brother, and one for whom Christ suffered? How much, if not as much as the Son of God hath loved me, as much as myself, as much as the hand loves the eye? How long, if not until death, if not through all ages, through all eternity, and beyond it? This is the common feeling of those who

---

course, there was a sign for "a book." "Pro generali signo libri, extende manum et move sicut folium libri moveri solet." This general sign being made, another was added to distinguish the sort of book wanted; and there were distinct signs for the Missal, the Gospels, the Epistolary, the Psalter, the Rule, and so on; but to distinguish a book written by a heathen, the monk was to scratch his ear like a dog. "Pro signo libri sæcularis, quem aliquis paganus fecit, præmisso generali signo libri, adde ut aurem tangas digito sicut canis cum pede pruriens solet, quia nec immerito infideles tali animanti comparantur." — *Mart. de Antiq. Mon. Rit.* 885.

seek not their own, but the things of Jesus Christ; and who being filled with charity and love, lie down or feed at noon in the chambers, or in the gardens of spices." [3]

This was Peter's phrase for living in a monastery; but it is more to our purpose to state how Nicholas lived in his; and particularly to transcribe his sketch of what he calls his *Scriptoriolum*, or little writing-cell, a retired apartment, shut in and concealed on every side by the various parts of the monastery:—

"Its door opens into the apartment of the novices, where commonly a great number of persons, distinguished by rank as well as by literature, put on the new man in newness of life . . . , . . On the right, the cloister of the monks runs off, in which the more advanced part of the community walk . . . . . . There, under the strictest discipline, they individually open the books of divine eloquence, not that they may winnow forth the treasures of knowledge, but that they may elicit love, compunction, and devotion. From the left projects the infirmary, and the place of exercise (deambulatorium) for the sick, where their bodies, wearied and weakened by the severities of the rule, are refreshed with better food; until, being cured, or at least in better health, they may rejoin the congregation, who labour and pray, who do violence to the kingdom of heaven, and take it by force. And do not suppose that my little tenement is to be despised; for it is a place to be desired, and pleasant to look upon, and comfortable for retirement. It is filled with most choice and divine books, at the delightful view of which I feel contempt for the vanity of this world, considering that, 'vanity of vanities, all is vanity,' and that nothing is more vain than vanity itself. This place is assigned to me for reading, and writing, and composing, and meditating, and praying, and adoring the Lord of majesty."

It was not as a common scribe or writing monk that Nicholas occupied this apartment, but because he was my lord abbot's secretary, and conducted his extensive and important correspondence, of which I hope to say more presently; but in the meantime I am irresistibly led to say something about the *scriptoria* of monasteries in the Dark Ages.

---

[3] Ep. Lib. iv. ep. iii. ap. Sirmondi Op. iii. 734.

I am inclined to suppose, that at a period somewhat later than that to which I generally refer, the
writing performed in monasteries was carried on in
small apartments or cells, which could not (perhaps
at all, or at any rate without inconvenience) contain
more than one person; and that, owing to such a use
being so generally made of them,—that is, owing to
the great quantity of writing, the number of hands
engaged in it, and the places occupied by it,—owing,
in short, to its being the chief and almost only in-
doors business of a monk out of church,—cells, or
small rooms, or even larger apartments, which had
no other particular name or use, were commonly called
scriptoria, even when not actually used, or particularly
intended, for the purpose of writing. Thus we are told
that Arnold, Abbot of Villers, in Brabant, from A.D.
1240 to 1250, when he resigned his office, occupied a
scriptorium, where he lived as a private person in his
own apartment.

In fact, it seems to have been a custom, principally
and perhaps exclusively in the Cistercian order, to
grant such cells as a privilege to certain monks for
their private study or amusement.[4] Jacobus, a successor
of Arnold, who became abbot in the year 1276, made
scriptoria round the calefactory, and his immediate
successor added two, adjoining the house of the sacrist.[5]
The former was the better place, undoubtedly; as the
scribes probably obtained some benefit from the apartment which was heated on purpose that the monks

---

[4] "Monachi quibus ad studendum vel recreandum scriptoria conce-
duntur, in ipsis scriptoriis non maneant illis hoiis quibus monachi in
claustro residere tenentur, &c."—Stat. selecta Cap. Gen. Ord. Cisterc.
A.D. 1278, ap. Mart. iv. 1462.

[5] Mart. iii. 1298.

might go there to warm themselves. Many a scribe has,
I dare say, felt what Lewis, a monk of Wessobrunn
in Bavaria, records as his own experience during his
sedentary and protracted labours. In an inscription
appended to a copy of Jerome's commentary on Daniel,
among other grounds on which he claims the sympathy
and the prayers of the reader, he says—

> "Dum scripsit friguit, et quod cum lumine solis
> Scribere non potuit, perfecit lumine noctis." [6]

I do not take upon me to say that these cells were
warmed by hot air from the stove in the calefactory,
though that is not so completely a modern invention
as some people may think. The monks in the Dark
Ages were not quite incapable of conceiving and
executing such an idea; and it is not going out of
our way to mention a proof, which has a moral beauty,
far more valuable than its evidence respecting their
knowledge and ingenuity. When Bernard, owing to
the illness produced by his early austerities, was compelled by the Bishop of Châlons to retire to a cell,
he could not be persuaded so far to relax the severity
of his asceticism as to allow any fire, or even fire-
place, in it. His friends, with pious fraud (if there ever
was such a thing), contrived to heat his apartment
without his knowing it, by introducing hot air through
the stone floor under his bed. [7]

But the *scriptorium* of earlier times was obviously
an apartment capable of containing many persons;
and in which many persons did, in fact, work together,
in a very business-like manner, at the transcription of
books. The first of these points is implied in a very

---

[6] Pez, Thes. Anec. Noviss. Diss. Isag. in tom. i. p. 20.
[7] Voy. Lit. p. 99.

curious document, which is one of the very few extant specimens of French Wisigothic MS. in uncial characters, and belongs to the eighth century. It is a short form of consecration, or benediction, barbarously entitled, "Orationem in Scripturio," and is to the following effect— "Vouchsafe, O Lord, to bless this scriptorium of thy servants, and all that dwell therein; that whatsoever sacred writings shall be here read or written by them, they may receive with understanding, and bring the same to good effect, through our Lord," &c. [8]

That the scriptorium was larger than a mere cell, is also obvious from an anecdote of the ninth century, which is very well worth transcribing on many accounts, though I confess that it has been brought to my mind on this occasion by what has just been said of the *scriptorium* and *calefactory* in juxtaposition. Ekkehard, junior, the historian of the monastery of St. Gall, who wrote in the earlier half of the eleventh century, after a chapter concerning Solomon, who had been abbot in the latter part of the ninth century,—another chapter respecting Magister Iso, a monk of the same monastery, and a "doctor nominatissimus," who had that Solomon, together with Notker, Tutilo, Ratpert, and some others, for his pupils,—and further telling us how the latter three of the pupils just named somewhat grudged at the more indulgent treatment which Solomon received from their master ("delicatius quasi canonicum educaverat,"—a monkish hit), —and further still how this old grudge had led to some unpleasant collisions after Solomon had risen to be Bishop of

---

[8] Nouv. Tr. de Diplom. iii. 190. See also Du Cange in v. *Scriptorium*, and the supplement in v. *Scripturium*; why the authors of this supplement should say that it is given in the two other places "ipsismet verbis" I do not know. I here follow Du Cange's text, "opere perficiant," instead of the other, "ore percipiant."

Constance, while his three school-fellows remained still mere monks of St. Gall's, proceeds :—

"These having been thoroughly instructed in divine things by Iso, became (as I have said) scholars of Marcellus; who, being equally versed in sacred and secular learning, taught them the seven liberal arts, but especially music, which being more natural than the rest, and though more difficult in the learning yet more pleasant in the use, they made such progress therein as may be seen by their respective works, of which I have already said something. But these three, though of one heart, were yet, as sometimes happens, very different persons.

"Notker was weak in body, not in mind ; and in speech, not in spirit, a stammerer. In spiritual things firm, in adversity patient, mild to all, a severe disciplinarian, timorous in any sudden alarm, except of demons, whom he used to combat manfully. In ornamenting, reading, and composing, assiduous; and, briefly to comprehend all his sacred endowments, he was a vessel of the Holy Spirit not less eminently than anyone of his time.

"But Tutilo was very different. He was a good and useful man ; as to his arms and all his limbs, such as Fabius teaches us to choose for a wrestler. He was eloquent, with a fine voice, skilful in carving, and a painter. A musician, like his companions; but in all kinds of stringed and wind instruments (for in a place appointed by the abbot he taught the children of the nobility to play on stringed instruments), he excelled everybody. In building and in his other arts he was eminent. He was, by nature, powerful, and ready at singing in either language ; cheerful, whether in jest or in earnest ; so that Charles [the Gross] once cursed him for making a monk of such a person. But, with all this, what is of more consequence, he was powerful in the choir, and in secret given to tears, very skilful in making verses and melodies. Chaste as a disciple of Marcellus, who shut his eyes against women.

"Ratpert was, however, something between the two whom I have mentioned. He had been the schoolmaster from his youth, a straight-forward, kind teacher, very strict in discipline, more rarely than any of his brethren putting his foot out of the cloister, and making one pair of shoes last a twelvemonth. He said that going out was destruction ; and frequently admonished Tutilo, who was given to travelling, to mind what he was about. Fully occupied in the schools, he commonly neglected the services and mass ; ' for,' said he, ' we hear good masses while we are teaching how they should be performed.' And although he used to say that impunity was the greatest disgrace of a monastery, yet he never came to the chapter unless he was sent for; because, as he observed, that most painful office of reproving and punishing was laid upon him.

" Such being three of the senators of our republic, they were, as happens to all learned and useful men, exposed to the detraction and backbiting of the idle and frivolous; and chiefly the holy Notker (as I may truly call him), because he took less pains to contradict it. Tutilo and Ratpert, indeed, who dealt more harshly with such persons, and did not take injuries so patiently, were less frequently attacked; but Notker, who was the meekest of men, learned by his own experience to know what such injuries were; of which I wish to introduce one, that you may learn by a single instance how far Satan presumes in such things.

" There was a monk named Sindolf, who was the *Refectorarius*; but at length, with feigned obsequiousness (his only merit) telling lies of the brethren, Solomon made him clerk of the works (decanus operariorum). While he was refectorary, however, he made himself as annoying as he dared, particularly to Notker. Solomon, however, being much occupied, and unable to attend to everything, when it sometimes happened that the food of the brethren was deficient or bad, many exclaimed against the injustice; and it appeared that, among others, the three whom I have mentioned had said something.

" Sindolf, who was always making mischief, knowing the cause and origin of the old grudge on the part of these companions, got the ear of Solomon, as if he was going to inform him of something in which his honour was concerned; and he, though he knew that nothing is more mischievous to bishops than listening to the whispers of their inferiors, inquired what news he had to communicate. On this Sindolf falsely told him that those three were always talking against him, and that the day before they had said such things as must be intolerable to God. He believed these tales, and bore malice against those who thought no ill, and at length he showed it. They, however, not being able to learn from him what was the ground of offence, guessed that they had been brought into it by some trick of Sindolf. The matter being at length discussed among the brethren, when they, with the concurrent testimony of all the rest, proved that they had said nothing against the bishop, everyone called for justice against the false informer; but as the bishop would not give him up, they silently acquiesced.

---

⁹ That is, it was his duty to superintend the refectory, and see that all things belonging to it were properly provided and taken care of.

"It was the invariable custom of these three, by permission of the prior, to meet in the night in the interval before lauds [1] in the *scriptorium*, and to discourse together on such scriptural subjects as were most suited to such an hour. Sindolf, knowing the time and the fact of these conversations, went out one night and came privily to the glass window against which Tutilo was sitting, and, applying his ear to it, listened to catch something which he might carry in a perverted form to the bishop. Tutilo, who had become aware of it, and who was a sturdy man, with full confidence in the strength of his arms, spoke to his companions in Latin, that Sindolf, who did not understand that language, might not know what he said. 'There he is,' said he, 'and he has put his ear to the window; but do you, Notker, who are timorous, go out into the church; and you, my Ratpert, catch up the whip of the brethren which hangs in the calefactory, [2] and run out; for when I know that you have got near to him, I will open the window as suddenly as possible, catch him by the hair, drag in his head, and hold it tight; but do you, my friend, be strong and of a good courage, and lay the whip on him with all your might, and take vengeance for God on him.'

"Ratpert, who was always most alert in matters of discipline, went softly, and catching up the whip ran quickly out, and came down with all his might like a hailstorm on the back of Sindolf, whose head was dragged in at the window. He, however, struggling with his arms and legs, contrived to get and to keep hold of the whip; on which Ratpert, catching up a stick which he saw at hand, laid on him most lustily. When he found it vain to beg for mercy, 'I must,' said he, 'cry out'; and he roared vociferously. Part of the monks, astounded at hearing such a voice, at such an unwonted time, came running with lights, and asking what was the matter. Tutilo kept crying out that he had caught the devil, and begging them to bring a light, that he might more clearly see whose shape he had assumed; and turning the head of his reluctant prisoner to and fro, that the spectators might the better judge, he asked with affected ignorance whether it could be Sindolf? All declaring that it certainly was, and begging that he would let him go, he released him, saying, 'Wretch that I am, that I should have laid hands on the intimate and confidant of the bishop!' Ratpert,

---

[1] As to the mode of spending that interval required by the rule of St. Benedict, see Martene in cap. viii. p. 249.

[2] Here called *Pyrale*. He afterwards says that it was adjoining to the scriptorium, "proximum pyrali scriptorium," cap. xi. p. 52.

however, having stepped aside on the coming up of the monks, privately withdrew, and the sufferer could not find out who had beaten him." [3]

I do not undertake to defend all Tutilo's proceedings in this affair; especially his going on to persuade the monks that the flagellator, who had performed so strenuously, and then suddenly vanished, must have been an angel. Notker, it will be observed, had nothing to do with the business, and Ratpert was merely executive in the way of his calling; but, without canvassing the matter too strictly, I am content to feel as a Swedish clergyman did, when a friend of mine, who happened to have been present at the service in his church, remonstrated against what appeared to him to be a prayer that ships might be wrecked on their coast. The good priest assured him, that it was no such thing, and that they were not such wretches as to harbour any wish of the kind; but only prayed, that *if* ships *were* to be wrecked, *they* might have the benefit of it. In like manner, though I doubt the lawfulness of wishing that any Christian man should either give or take such a beating as Sindolf received, yet *if* somebody *was* to have it, I am glad that it fell to his share; and that not so much for his dirty tricks which have been just mentioned, as for a villany which I unaccountably omitted to notice in a former paper, where it would have been more in place. I had him (that is, a memorandum of him), literally pinned down to my desk much longer than Tutilo held him at the window, but somehow he escaped. What do you think he did? Why, when Notker, with great labour and pains (multis sudoribus), had made a fair copy of the Canonical Epistles in Greek—having borrowed them

---

[3] Ekkehardus Jun. de Casib. Mon. S. Galli. ap. Gold. Scr. Rer. Alem. i. 24 et Ekkardus Minimus in vita Notkeri, ibid. 226.

for that purpose from Luitward, Bishop of Vercelli—
"behold, Sindolf, now (as I have said) a great man,
and of much consequence in the place [for it was in
consideration of the beating that the bishop preferred him
to be the *decanus operariorum*], lighting by chance on
that delicately written book, carried it off, and having
cut out all the leaves, tore and spoiled them, as is to
be seen at this day, and then folded them up, and put
them where he found them." [4] What do you think of
that ? Would a second edition of Ratpert's performance have been half enough for such a villany ?

The scriptorium where these three friends used to
meet was obviously something very different from
what we now call a cell, or what is now sometimes
described or shown as a writing-place of the old times.
And I doubt not that the twelve expert scribes, to
whom, as I have already said, [5] the Abbot of Hirschau
committed the work of transcribing the Holy Scriptures and the writings of the fathers, as well as the
indefinite number of inferior scribes, worked in company. Indeed, if we were always to understand that
the scribe was sitting alone, it would be difficult to
comprehend the direction of the general chapter of the
Cistercian Order held in A.D. 1134, directing that the
same silence should be maintained in the scriptorium
as in the cloister. [6]

The same thing appears from the Abbot Heriman's
account of the restoration of St. Martin's at Tournay.
He was himself the third abbot, and he tells us that
his predecessor, Odo, who has been already mentioned

---

[4] Ekk. Jun. ubi sup. p. 29.

[5] No. XIX. p. 366.

[6] "In omnibus *scriptoriis* ubicunque ex consuetudine Monachi Scribunt,
silentium teneatur sicut in Claustro."—Cap. lxxxvii. ap. Nomast.
Cisterc. 272.

(p. 78) as the first, and who entered on that office
about the year 1093, showed himself no good manager
in temporal things, and was glad to confide the management of them to Ralph the Prior, who showed peculiar
talent and zeal in such matters:

"In which the abbot greatly rejoiced, and used to thank God, who
had given him a man that had relieved him from the anxiety and
bustle of worldly affairs. For, committing to him the whole charge of
the external affairs of our monastery, he gave himself up so entirely
to the duties of a monk, and to silence, that frequently he did not
go out of the monastery for a month together, but, being devoted to
reading, he took the utmost pains to promote the writing of books.
He used, in fact, to exult in the number of writers which the Lord
had given him; for if you had gone into the cloister, you might in
general have seen a dozen young monks sitting on chairs in perfect
silence, writing at tables carefully and artificially constructed. All
Jerome's Commentaries on the Prophets, all the works of St. Gregory,
and everything that he could find of St. Augustine, Ambrose, Isidore,
Bede, and the Lord Anselm, then Abbot of Bec, and afterwards Archbishop of Canterbury, he caused to be diligently transcribed. So that
you would scarcely have found such a library at any monastery in that
part of the country, and everybody was begging for our copies to
correct their own. Our monastery was at that time in great reputation,
and in a high state of discipline; for in the whole province of Rheims
there were at that period only three monasteries which followed the
customs of Clugny—namely, Anchin, Afflighem, and our own. The
monastery of Clugni at that time excelled all others belonging to the
kingdom of the Francs in monastic order; for the rigour of the Cistercians had not then sprung up, and the Lord Norbert had not as yet
been heard of." [7]

---

[7] Herimanni Narratio Rest. Abb. S. Martini Torn. § 79 ap. Dach.
Spicileg. ii. 913. One of the original companions of Odo was Godfrey,
who was, says Heriman, "a very skilful scribe, and left many manuscripts in our church—namely, the Morals of St. Gregory on Job in
six volumes, an excellent history, which, beginning at the Proverbs,
contains the prophets, the Acts of the Apostles, and the Epistles, a
missal from which each mass is every day performed in the convent, a
copy of the gospels, Augustine on the City of God, and his Enchiridion,
and many other books which may be easily distinguished as his by

I do not wish unnecessarily to multiply instances or illustrations which must possess a sameness of character that may render them tedious; but there is one idea which I am very desirous to impress on the reader, as applying generally to the whole subject.

We are, on the one hand, familiar with the press; used to see its rapid multiplication, and filled with the idea of its almost unlimited powers—we are, on the other, but little accustomed to read any large mass of manuscript, or to write continuously anything which could be called a book—we can, moreover, set the press in motion so easily, and so cheaply, that even a third-rate shopkeeper who is advertising simply because he has nothing to do, would not think of writing a hundred circular letters—the question, how much an expert scribe could write in a given time is so seldom presented to our thoughts, that we feel scarcely able to give any opinion—we almost lose sight of the fact, that all the books which are *printed* have been *written* (and, if worth printing, more than once written) by their authors—we hardly realize the idea which our words express when we say that an author "wrote" such and such works, which were afterwards published in so many volumes folio—and further, though it would

---

the handwriting," § 76, p. 912. One of the first who joined Odo was Alulfus, who was, during forty-seven years afterwards, the *armarius* or librarian of the convent. "He frequently read over all the works of St. Gregory; and, in imitation of Paterius, extracting all the passages of the Old and New Testament which he had expounded, he made three volumes, to which he added a fourth, consisting of miscellaneous and very useful sentences, and entitled the whole work *Gregorialis.*" § 38. It may interest the reader to know, that several MSS. of this period, and this monastery, and in all probability the identical works written in Odo's scriptorium, and in particular the fourth volume (apparently the autograph) of Alulfus's Gregorialis, are now the property of my learned friend Dr. Todd, of Trinity College, Dublin.

not call for the reading, the thinking, the correcting, the rewriting, or any of the intellectual labour which not only produced the most fatigue, but took up the most time, yet would not you feel rather unwilling to undertake such a job as merely writing out a copy of Archbishop Ussher's works, or Lord Bacon's?

Thus, I suspect, we are apt to be led into error when we think we are comparing the respective powers of hand-writing and the press. Not perhaps into theoretical error, for, without forming anything like a theory, we may say at once that the things are not to be compared at all; seeing that the power of multiplication by the press exceeds that of the slower process of hand-writing out of all proportion. But we are liable to practical error, because we are apt not to consider the different degree in which those powers are put out. The press does a great deal, and it might do a great deal more. It could easily as far outdo its present self, as it now outdoes manuscription; but it has never been, and most likely never will be, called on to do this; and the probability (almost certainty) is, that in proportion as it approximates to anything like it, the works which it produces will have less and less connexion with learning. I believe that the history of printing will bear me out in this; and we come, I think, fairly to the idea that, although the *power of multiplication* at work in the Dark Ages was infinitely below that which now exists, and even the whole *actual produce* of the two periods not to be compared, yet, as it regards those books which were considered as the standard works in sacred and secular literature, the difference was not so *extreme* as may have been supposed. Perhaps I may illustrate my meaning by asking what proportion the copies of Gregory's "Morals," or Augustine's "City of God," *printed* between the years

1700 and 1800, bear to those *written* between the years 1100 and 1200.

But, as I have said, we have perhaps a very imperfect idea of what may be done by the labour of an individual. We must think of writing as a business; as one generally taken up by choice, and very commonly pursued with a degree of zeal and indefatigable perseverance, which in the present day seems almost incredible. We find notices on the subject, which appear to me very interesting; and the point is so important to our getting a clear idea of the matter which is now in hand, that I will mention two.

Othlonus, a monk of St. Emmeram's, at Ratisbon, was born about the year 1013; and in his book, "De ipsius tentationibus, varia fortuna, et scriptis," he has given us an account of his literary labours, and of the circumstances which led to his writing the various works of his which we possess. Of his original compositions, however, it is not to our present purpose to speak; but, after enumerating a good many, and saying, "As the Lord commanded the Dæmoniac in the gospel to go to his own house, and show how great things God had done for him, I also would relate how great benefits God has vouchsafed to me," he goes on—

"For the same reason I think it proper to add an account of the great knowledge and capacity for writing which was given me by the Lord in my childhood. When as yet a little child, I was sent to school, and quickly learned my letters; and I began, long before the usual time of learning, and without any order from the master, to learn the art of writing. But in a furtive and unusual manner, and without any teacher, I attempted to learn that art. From this circumstance I got a habit of holding my pen in a wrong manner; nor were any of my teachers afterwards able to correct me in that point; for I had become too much accustomed to it to be capable of altering. Many who saw this unanimously decided that I should never write well; but, by the grace of God, it turned out otherwise, as is known to many persons. For, even in my childhood, and at the time when, together with the other boys, the tablet was put into my hands, that I might learn to write, it appeared that I had some notion of writing, to the no small surprise of those who saw it. Then, after a short time, I began to write so well, and was so fond of it, that in the place where I learned, that is, in the monastery of Tegernsee [in Bavaria, almost in a line between Munich and Innspruck], I wrote many books. And being sent into Franconia while I was yet a boy, I worked so hard at writing while I was there, that before I returned I had nearly lost my sight. This I resolved to mention, in the hope that I may excite some others to a similar love of labour; and that, by recounting to others the grace of God which has granted to me such benefits, I may lead them to magnify that grace of God with me. And the better to do this, I think it proper to relate how I laboured in writing afterwards, when I had returned from Franconia, for I was there when the Emperor Henry died, and Conrad came to the throne [in the year 1024].

"Then, after I came to be a monk in the monastery of St. Emmeram, I was soon induced, by the request of some of them, again to occupy myself so much in writing that I seldom got any interval of rest, except on festivals, and at such times as work could not be performed. In the meantime, there came more work upon me; for, as they saw that I was generally reading, or writing, or composing, they made me the schoolmaster. By all which things I was, through God's grace, so fully occupied, that I frequently could not allow my body the necessary rest. And when I had a mind to compose anything, I very commonly could not find time for it, except on holydays, or by night, being tied down to the business of teaching the boys, and the transcribing which I had been persuaded to undertake. Therefore, beside the books which I composed myself, which I wrote to give away for the edification of those who asked for them, and of others to whom I gave them unasked, I wrote nineteen missals—ten for the abbots and monks in our own monastery, four for the brethren at Fulda, five for those in other places; three books of the Gospels, and two with the Epistles and Gospels, which are called Lectionaries; besides which I wrote four service books for matins. Afterwards, old age and infirmity of various kinds hindered me; especially the tedious interruption which lasted for a very long time through various anxieties, and the grief which was caused by the destruction of our monastery; but to Him who is the Author of all good, and who alone governs all things, and who has vouchsafed to give many things to me unworthy, be praise eternal, be honour everlasting.

"I think it right also to relate, as far as I am able to recollect, how many books I have given to different monasteries and friends; and first I would mention the monks at Fulda, because, as I worked a great deal in their monastery, writing many books which I sent to our monastery, so in ours I wrote out some books which they had not; and, if I remember right, I sent them seven. To the monks of Hirschfeld, two books; and when I returned from those parts and came to Amarbach, I gave one to the abbot of that place. Afterwards, being under obligation to brother William, I gave him four books, among which there was a very valuable missal. To the abbot of Lorsch, one book; to certain friends dwelling in Bohemia, four books; to a friend at Passau, one book; to the monastery of Tegernsee, two books; to the monastery of Pryel, near us, one volume, in which were three books. And also I gave one book, and various epistles, to my sister's son, who was living there. To the monastery of Obermunster I gave three books; and to that of Nidermunster, one book. Moreover, to many others I gave or sent, at different times, sermons, proverbs, and edifying writings." [8]

One would like to know what books they were which Othlonus thus multiplied; but this is perhaps now impossible. With regard to another case, however, which I have particular pleasure in producing, we are in no doubt. An anonymous monk of Wessobrunn, a place already mentioned and also in Bavaria, has preserved an account of a nun whose labours quite eclipse those of Othlonus. The historian, who seems to have begun his work in the year 1513, says—

"Diemudis was formerly a most devout nun of this our monastery of Wessobrunn. For our monastery was formerly double, or divided into two parts,—that is to say, of monks and nuns. The place of the monks was where it now is; but that of the nuns where the parish church now stands. This virgin was most skilful in the art of writing. For though she is not known to have composed any work, yet she wrote with her own hand many volumes in a must beautiful and legible character, both for divine service and for the public library of the monastery, which are enumerated in a list written by herself in a

---

[8] Mab. Anal. iv. 448 (fol. ed. 119), Conf. B. Pez in Diss. Isagog. in Tom. iii. Thes. Anecd. Noviss. p. x.

certain plenarius. [9] For in that list the following books pertaining to divine service are enumerated :—

A Missal, with the Gradual and Sequences.

Another Missal, with Gradual and Sequences, which was given to the Bishop of Treves.

Another Missal, with the Epistles, Gospels, Gradual and Sequences.

Another Missal, with the Epistles and Gospels for the whole year; and the Gradual and Sequences, and the entire Service for Baptism.

A Missal, with Epistles and Gospels.

A Book of Offices.

Another Book of Offices, with the Baptismal Service, which was given to the Bishop of Augsburgh.

A Book with the Gospels and Lessons.

A Book with the Gospels.

A Book with the Epistles.

These books she wrote, as I have said, for the use and ornament of divine service. With the following she adorned our library, of which only those that are marked thus § still remain there. [1] For the others have perished and are lost, either through the burning of the monastery (which is said to have happened twice), or by the negligence and sloth of subsequent monks; as the list already mentioned specifies the following books belonging to the library :—

A Bible, in two volumes, which was given for the estate in Pisinberch.

A Bible, in three volumes.

The Morals of St. Gregory [that is, his Commentary on Job], in six volumes, the first and third of which are lost.

St. Gregory ad Regaredum. [2]

St. Gregory on Ezechiel, and some other things, in one volume.

Sermons and Homilies of Ancient Doctors, three volumes.

Origen on the Old Testament.

---

[9] The writer probably means (as this term frequently does) a missal containing, besides its proper contents, the Epistles and Gospels; but the word is used so variously, that it is impossible to feel certain.

[1] I translate as it stands; but I do not see that any books in the list are so marked, or in any way distinguished from the others.

[2] I do not know what this means; but I am not so familiar with Gregory's works as Alulfus was. I do not recollect that any of them are addressed to anyone so named.

Origen on the Canticles.

Augustine on the Psalms, iii. volumes.

————— on the Gospel, and the first Epistle of St. John, ii. volumes; the first missing.

————— Epistles, to the number of lxxv.

————— Treatises, 'De verbis Domini,' 'De Sermone Domini in Monte,' 'De opere Monachorum,' and 'De Agone Christiano,' 'De Adorando,' 'De Professione Viduitatis,' 'De Bono Conjugali,' 'De Virginitate.'

St. Jerome's Epistles, to the number of clxiv.

The Tripartite History of Cassiodorus [that is, the compendium of ecclesiastical history which he made, in the sixth century, from Epiphanius's Latin Version of Socrates, Sozomen, and Theodoret.]

Eusebius's Ecclesiastical History.

St. Augustine, Fifty Sermons; the Life of St. Silvester; Jerome against Vigilantius, and 'De Consolatione Mortuorum'; The Life of St. Blaise; The Life of St. John the Almoner [Patriarch of Alexandria early in the seventh century. I presume, from the way in which they are put together, that these formed only one volume, as also the following:—]

Paschasius on the Body and Blood of Christ; The Conflict of Lanfranc with Berengarius; The Martyrdom of St. Dionysius; The Life of St. Adrian, pope, &c.

St. Jerome 'De Hebraicis Quæstionibus,' and many other works by him and by other writers.

St. Augustine's Confessions.

Canons.

The Gloss, alphabetically arranged [I suppose this is meant by 'Glossa per A. B. C. composita.']

These are the volumes written with her own hand by the aforesaid handmaid of God, Diemudis, to the praise of God and of the holy apostles, Peter and Paul, the patrons of this monastery. But at what period she lived I could never discover, since, in all the books (we charitably hope from humility), she omitted to mention her name and the time when she finished." [3]

That, however, which her anonymous biographer could not discover, Pez learned from a MS. account of the Abbots of Wessobrunn, which he found in

---

[3] Pez Diss. Isagog. in Tom. i. Thesaur. Anecd. Novis. p. xx.

the neighbouring monastery of Tegernsee. The author of it states that Diemudis lived in the time of Gregory VII. (who became pope in A.D. 1073), and therefore, though probably somewhat younger, she was contemporary with the monk of Ratisbon, whose labours I have just mentioned. The same writer says, that Diemudis carried on a correspondence by very sweet letters (epistolæ suaves valde) with Herluca, who was for thirty-six years a nun at Eppach, a mile (I suppose a German one) from Wessobrunn; and that the letters were then extant in the monastery of Bernried. Pez, however, who went there to look for them, could obtain no information. Without giving any improper sanction to the popish doctrine of transferred merit, may we not allow this indefatigable "exaratrix" (as her bio-grapher calls her) to make up, in some degree, for the deficiency of her pious founder, who has been a standing jest among writers on the Dark Ages, because he could not write his name? [4]

But readers will ask questions; or, at least, writers cannot help imagining it, especially when they feel that they are at all discursive. Somebody may say, "What has this to do with the Secretary Nicholas?" To which I answer—If the reader can imagine him out of, and without reference to, a *scriptorium*, well and good—it is more than I can do; and believing such powers of abstraction to be very rare, I have thought it right, in introducing him, to say a few words on that subject. Again, it may be asked, "What had Nicholas to do with Bernard's letters to Peter the Venerable?" To do with them? why everything: he wrote them; he carried them; he was the depository of the "verbum secretum" which accompanied them,

---

[4] Of Tassilo, Duke of Bavaria, see No. II. p. 34.

and which correspondents frequently sent by the trusty
messenger before post-offices came into fashion; he
was the connecting link between the abbots, the bosom
friend of both; in short, he was a person worth knowing, and I hope to make him better known.

No. XXV.

"Amantium iræ amoris integratio est."—LAT. GRAM.

"Is it thus that you think fit to joke?" says Bernhard
to his friend Peter of Clugny, who, notwithstanding
his title of "Venerable," and his being scarcely known
in the present day except as a monk of the Dark Ages
(that is, in the minds of many, a mere vegetation of
over-fed stupidity), was certainly a very facetious
person—

"Is it thus that you think fit to joke? It is all very proper and
very friendly, provided only that it is not meant to take me in. Do
not wonder at my saying this ; for the very circumstance of your sudden
and unexpected condescension makes me suspect it. It is not long ago
that I wrote to salute your greatness with all due reverence, and you
did not answer me a word. Not long before, also, I had written to
you from Rome, and then too I did not get a single syllable. Do you
wonder that on your recent return from Spain I did not intrude my
nonsense upon you? At any rate, if it is a fault merely not to have
written, whatever may have been the cause, surely some blame attaches
to unwillingness, not to say contemptuous neglect, in answering. Observe
what I might say on the score of justice (as you put me on that) were
it not that I desire rather to meet returning kindness, than to retard
it either by useless excuses or recrimination. But I have said this, that
I may not keep shut up in my mind anything which I have not fairly
spoken out; for that is inconsistent with true friendship. As to the rest,
since charity believeth all things, let every remnant of suspicion be
removed. I rejoice that you have again warmed to the remembrance
of former friendship, and even to the recalling of your friend, injured
as he is. I come gladly as soon as I am called, happy that I am
called, and have quite forgotten all my wrongs. Here am I, that used
to be, and am, the servant of your holiness. [1] I am thankful that I am

---

[1] The difficulty of translating letters of this period is much increased
by the titles; which, though common at that time, can now scarcely be
put into English without some appearance of burlesque, not to say

excellently well situated, being, as you are pleased to write, an actual
inmate of yourself (intimus vobis factus), for if, as you charge me, I
should become cold, I shall undoubtedly soon grow warm again, thus
cherished by your bowels of charity.

"And now as to what you were pleased to write—I received it with
outstretched hands, I read it eagerly, I love to reperuse it, and, after
often reading over, it still delights me. I confess, I love the humour
of it. For it is delightful in its mirth, and serious in its gravity. I
know not how it is that, in the midst of your jocularity, you do
somehow manage your discourse so judiciously, that the humour has
not the appearance of levity, and yet the dignity which you preserve
does not diminish the freedom of your humour. In fact that dignity is
kept up in such a way that one might fairly apply to you what was
said by the holy man : 'If I laughed on them they believed it not.'"
[Job xxix. 24.]

One would like to see Peter's letter to which the
foregoing was an answer (or part of an answer, for
I am afraid of tiring the patience of my readers by

---

derision. This is the case with "your holiness," which some protestants
know only as a title of the Pope, and suppose to belong exclusively
to him. The thing, however, was common, and sufficient specimens
might be furnished from the correspondence of Bernard and Peter alone
to show that it was so. Geoffry of Chalons writes to Peter, "rescribat
humilitati meæ *Sanctitas* vestra." (*Bibl. Clun.* 781.) How is one to
translate such terms as "humilitas mea," "prudentia," or "beatitudo,
vestra," &c.? I must really request the reader's instruction, or his
indulgence, in what follows in this paper, and on all similar occasions.
The title of *Sanctitas* is also given to Peter by Sugerius, Abbot of St.
Denys. (Ib. 961.) But perhaps what may appear the most singular
instance is Peter's thus addressing the unfortunate Heloise—"Gavisus
sum et hoc non parum, legens *Sanctitatis* vestræ literas." (Ib. 920.) As
to the Pope's exclusive right, we may say the same of his being "Vicar
of Christ." Jacobus de Vitriaco (who wrote early in the thirteenth
century) says, "Ipsa terra Jerosolymitana patriarcham habet, qui et fidei
peritus, et Christianorum pater, et *Vicarius Jesu Christi.*" Hist. Orient.
ap. Mart. iii. 277. Solomon, too, Bishop of Constance, at an earlier
period (whom I hope the reader will always remember as the patron
of the abominable Sindolf), addressed Bishop Dado, "Discrete Antistes,
venerande *Vicarie Christi.*" Bib. Pat. Supp. ii. 825.

giving whole letters, except when they are very important or very brief), but I believe that it is not
known to be extant. The simple fact seems to be,
that Peter had felt, and expressed, though in a playful
manner, some sense of neglect, owing to his not having
heard from Bernard since his return from Spain; and
some *amantium iræ* had certainly ensued. My object,
however, is not so much here to enter into the personal history of these abbots, as to give the reader
(as far as I know how to do it by translation, which
those who have tried it will know to be very difficult,
and at the best very inadequate) some idea of their
correspondence, many years after the dispute about
their respective Orders, in which we have seen them
engaged in the characters of plaintiff and defendant.
Peter begins his reply by saying—

"Your shrewd holiness will perhaps wonder that I have been so
long in answering such a sweet and pleasant letter of a friend, to which
I ought cheerfully and quickly to have replied; and will, I am afraid,
impute it to sloth or contempt. Far be both—both are far—from me;
for I scarcely ever received anything in the nature of a letter with
more pleasure, or read it with more interest. The delay has been partly
caused by the messenger; who, coming to Clugny, and not finding me
there (though I was not very far off, being only at Marcigni), neither
brought on nor forwarded your letter, but left it at Clugny. And that
I may not even appear to be finding fault with a good man, I must
say that I believe him to have been called away by business, or
deterred from attempting to reach me by the extreme severity of the
winter. I was myself detained there both by snow and business for a
month, and scarcely got home by the beginning of Lent. At length I
got your letter from the Sub-Prior, to whom it had been intrusted.
Immediately my mind was drawn out, and glowing as it was before
with affection to you, when so much more enflamed by the breath of
your bosom through that letter, it could no longer harbour any feeling
of coldness or lukewarmness. Drawn out, I say, and so drawn out
that I did what I never remember to have done, except in reverence
to the Holy Scriptures—as soon as I had read your letter, I kissed
it. And that I might, according to my custom, excite as many as I

could towards you (for all at that time I could not) what I had read
to myself, I read over again to those around me; and endeavoured
as much as possible to excite in them a greater kindness for you.
Then immediately I laid it up with the gold and silver which, according to the custom delivered to me by my fathers, I carry about with
me for the purpose of charity. [2] And not incongruously; for your
regard, your affection, is precious to me beyond all gold and silver.

"I determined to write what was in my mind the very next day,
but I was kept silent by my daily—nay, my continual taskmaster, [3]
who made me do other things. My most severe tyrant, whom I could
not resist, commanded silence, and multifarious care about an infinite
number of matters kept me silent not one, but many days. Sometimes
fifteen days, sometimes a whole month, sometimes several months,
during all which I was trying to write, passed over; but the tyrant
already mentioned did not permit. At length I broke this tiresome
chain; and, though with difficulty, I have overcome the burdensome
yoke and sceptre of the exactor by writing clandestinely and at intervals. And lest I should seem to say too much in excuse of [my slow-
ness in replying, you have forced it upon me by saying, 'It is not
long ago that I wrote to salute your greatness [4] with all due reverence,
and you did not answer me a single word. Not long before, also, I
had written to you from Rome, and then, too, I did not get a syllable.
Do you wonder that on your return from Spain I did not intrude my
nonsense upon you? At any rate, if it is a fault merely not to have
written, whatever may have been the cause, surely some blame attaches
to unwillingness, not to say contemptuous neglect in answering.' This
is what you say. Now what do I say? Plainly this—I say that I could
by no means have denied the fault which you impute, if I had dis-
dained to reply to such a friend when he had written first. For I
confess that I ought to have written to one who had first written to

---

[2] That is, he put it in his *eleemosynaria*, or *almonaria*, or, in plain
terms, his purse, which, in those days, and with regard to such matters, answered the purpose of what we call a pocket. See a story of
Simon de Montfort during the Albigensian crusade, "qui ad hanc
vocem protulit literas de sua almoneria, dicens," &c.; and afterwards,
"reposuit literas in bursa diligenter." *Gul. de Pod. Laur.* § xxi.

[3] There seems to be here, and in what follows about his taskmaster,
some allusion to the contents of the letter which had produced that
to which Peter was now replying.

[4] The text of Bernard's letter, as it stands in this copy of Peter's,
is *coronam* instead of *magnitudinem*.

me ; but, as far as I can remember, while you were staying at Rome I wrote first, and you replied. To be sure, I might have rejoined ; but your full answer, so completely satisfactory as to what I had written, made me silent. Now if this be the case, the fault with which I am charged seems to turn from me, and look towards you. For you have been trying to convict the blameless, and to load the shoulders of an innocent brother with a burden which does not belong to him— not to say, which does belong to yourself. As to my having done the same thing on another occasion, I do not know how to answer, for I cannot recollect the circumstances. If I could, there should certainly be either a fair excuse, or a humble apology.

"But you add, 'Observe what I might say on the score of justice'; and I say, for the reasons just stated, it appears that justice is on my side, for I am not convicted of any fault. Now if I were not merciful, I might call myself (as you call yourself) an injured friend, and justly require that the injury should be punished. But, according to my custom, I spare you, and forgive you even unasked. I, as you have said, remember no injuries. For this also pertains to what follows, [5] for as I am anxiously endeavouring, not in jest, but in earnest, to exclude the well-known jealousy from many hearts (and wish to excite you also to exclude it), I would first exercise indulgence to all, and what I labour to make others do, I would first do myself.

"But perhaps you will say again, 'Is it thus that you think fit to joke?' Yes, I do think it fit, with *you*. Certainly, with *you*, though not with others. For with them, if I were to pass the bounds of seriousness, I should be afraid of incurring the charge of levity ; but with you I am under no apprehension about levity, but follow after charity lest that should slip away. Therefore it is always delightful to me to talk to you, and to keep up by pleasant discourse the honied sweetness of charity between us. For I take all possible pains not to be of the number of those brethren who hated Joseph in their heart, and could not speak peaceably to him."

If a soft answer turneth away wrath, we may hope that this reply from Peter produced the effect. There was, indeed, such a fervour in the whole character and style of Bernard that those who knew him personally

---

[5] That is, I presume, to the sequel of the letter, which relates to the differences existing between the Orders, and was written to promote peace between them.

must have been aware that, in matters of feeling at least, he was liable to be drawn into saying rather more than would bear the cool examination of after-thought, or the strict anatomy of malice. Yet perhaps another of his letters to Peter may lead us to doubt whether he is really responsible for every expression which may be found among his epistles. He says—

"I wish I could send you my mind just as I send you this letter. You would, I am sure, read most clearly what the finger of God has written on my heart, has impressed on my marrow, of love to you. What then? Do I begin again to commend myself to you? Far be it from me. Long since has my mind been agglutinated to yours, and equal affection makes equal souls in unequal persons. Else what could my lowliness have done with your eminence, if condescension had not bowed your dignity? Ever since, both have been mingled, both my lowliness and your eminence, so that I cannot be humble without you, nor you exalted without me. I say this because my Nicholas (yes, and yours too) being vastly moved in spirit himself, has moved me; affirm-ing that he saw a letter from me addressed to you, which contained some unkind expressions. Believe one who loves you, that there neither rose in my heart, nor issued from my lips, anything which could offend the ears of your blessedness. The fault is owing to the multitude of business; so that my scribes do not well remember what I tell them. They sharpen their style too much; and it is out of my power to look over what I have ordered to be written. Spare me this time; for however it may go with others, I will see yours, and will trust no eyes or ears but my own. Other matters this common son of ours will more clearly and fully tell you by word of mouth. You will hear as myself, him who loves you not in word nor in tongue, but in deed and in truth. Salute for me that holy multitude of yours, and entreat them to pray for their servant."

Peter, as I have elsewhere stated, was liable to be rather prolix whenever he took his pen in hand. He seems to have eyed with a calm, quiet, somewhat ad-miring look, that impatient love of brevity and con-densation, and knocking off matters in a *verbum sat* manner, which had made such progress in his modern days. I have no doubt that he was a man of business,

and got through a great deal, in a very clear-headed
way; and he could write very short letters. But when
his feelings were moved, they were apt to overflow,
and cover a great deal of parchment. They *were* touched
by this letter of Bernard, which produced a reply five
times as long as itself; so that brevity, or rather moderation, admits of only an extract in this place. After
discoursing on the titles of "Most Reverend," of
"Father," and of "Friend," by all of which Bernard
had addressed him in the superscription of his letter,
Peter adds—

"But what shall I say of what follows? 'I wish,' you say, 'that I
could send you my mind, just as I send you this letter': and immediately after, 'you would, I am sure, read most clearly what the finger
of God has written on my heart, has impressed on my marrow, of
love to you.' Truly these words (if I may say it without irreverence
to the greater sacramental mystery to which the passage applies) are
like ointment on the head, which descended from the head of Aaron
to the skirt of his garment—truly this is the dew of Hermon, which
descended on Mount Zion—truly, also, thus do the mountains drop
sweetness, and the hills flow with milk and honey. Do not wonder
that I scrutinize, and lay hold on your words. For I know that they
proceed not from a common mouth; but from his who knows not
to speak but from a pure heart, and good conscience, and love unfeigned. I know this, I say, and the world knows, as well as I, that
you are not of the number of those who, according to the Psalm,
have spoken vain things, every one to his neighbour; that you are
not one of those who have spoken with deceitful lips and a double
heart. Therefore, whenever your holiness is pleased to write to me,
I receive, and read, and embrace, your letters, not carelessly or negligently, but studiously and with affection. For who would not read
with interest, who would not embrace with deep affection, what I
have already quoted, and what follows—'Long since has my mind
been agglutinated to yours, and equal affection makes equal souls in
unequal persons. Else what could my lowliness have done with your
eminence, if condescension had not bowed your dignity? Ever since
both have been mingled, both my lowliness and your eminence, so
that I cannot be humble without you, nor you exalted without me?'
Are words like these to be negligently read? Ought they not to fix

the eye of him who reads them, to ravish the heart, to unite the
soul? You, my dearest friend, who have written these things, may
think of them as you please; but for my part, I cannot take them
otherwise than simply according to the letter—than as the declarations
of such, so true, so holy a man. Nor, as you have yourself said, do
I begin again to commend myself to you. While we were young men
we began to love one another in Christ; and now that we are old
ones, or not far from it, shall we call in question a love so sacred,
and of so long standing? God forbid; believe one who loves you
(to borrow your words) that no such thing ever arose in my mind,
or issued from my lips, as any kind of doubt about anything which
you had ever seriously said. What you wrote, therefore, in this letter,
I received, I keep, I preserve. It would be easier to rob me of a
thousand talents of gold, than that these things should be torn from
my heart by anything that could happen—but enough of this.

"As to the rest, what your prudence conceives might have offended
me was this:—As to the affair of a certain English abbot (which you
know very well), your letter contained these words: 'As if, say they,
judgment were subverted, and justice had perished from the world,
and there were none who would deliver the needy from the hand of
him that is stronger than he, the poor and the destitute from them
that spoil him.' But, if you will believe me, you may rest assured that
I was only moved by them, as the prophet (though I am not a prophet)
says that he was. 'But I, as a deaf man, heard not; and as a dumb
man, not opening his mouth; and I became as a man that heareth
not, and that hath no reproofs in his mouth.' [Psalm xxxvii.] Indeed,
I was not offended by them. But, even if I had been, you have made
full amends, by saying, 'the fault is owing to the multitude of business; so that my scribes do not well remember what I tell them.
They sharpen their style too much, and it is out of my power to
look over what I have ordered to be written. Spare me this time, for
however it may go with others, I will see yours, and will trust no
eyes or ears but my own.' I do spare you, then. Even in matters of
serious offence (I say it with humility), I do not find it difficult to
forgive one who seeks forgiveness, or grant a pardon to one who asks
it. And if in serious things it is no hardship to forgive, how much
less, how nothing, is it in trifles?

"As to the will of Baro, the Sub-Deacon of Rome, which he is
said to have made at the time of his death, in favour of your monastery of Clairvaux and of Citeaux, respecting property which he had
deposited with us, some persons, who say that he enjoined them so
to do, have written to me. I wish you, however, to know, that accord-

ing to the testimony of some whom I believe to be credible witnesses, you are more indebted in this case to the Abbot of Clugny's good will than to the testament of Baro. I knew, indeed, for I am not so unacquainted with divine and human laws as to be ignorant, that a will or a legacy for pious uses, or a trust *causa mortis*, is to be judged according to posteriority; but I read elsewhere that nothing is so agreeable to natural law as that the will of a proprietor, desiring to transfer his property to another, should take effect. I say this, therefore, because (as the aforesaid witnesses confess) whatever he had deposited at Clugny, he had given the whole of to Clugny, unless he should himself resume it in his lifetime. I have not, however, chosen to insist on this right; but what, from their testimony, I believe to be my own, I have given up to you and yours. As to the Grenoble election [of a bishop to succeed Hugh, translated to the Archbishopric of Vienna] which our Carthusians are opposing, I have carefully deposited my opinion in the mouth of my most dear, and your faithful, Nicholas, in order that he may inform you. Hear him, and what he repeats to you as having been said by me, believe without the least hesitation. If I have forgotten anything which I ought to have said, when I recollect it, I will mention it to my most dearly-beloved in Christ. In fine, I most earnestly ask and entreat you (what I have already asked by some persons of your Order) that in this so great assembly of holy men as has met together at Citeaux, you will remember me as one belonging to yourself, and will strongly commend me and the whole body of the Cluniac congregation to their prayers."

With this letter to Bernard, or, I am inclined to think, more probably before this was answered, with another letter on the old and difficult subject of the differences between their respective Orders, Peter sent one to the Secretary, in which he says:—

"As I love you with unfeigned affection, I cannot long together forget you. I loved you when you where of our colour [a black monk of Clugny], and now having, as regards myself, changed only your colour [by becoming a white monk at Clairvaux], and not your heart, I love you not the less. I had rather that you belonged to me than to anybody else; but since wherever you are you are God's, so I still consider you mine. Make a due return and love him who truly loves you; for as not the whole world with all its powers could alter those feelings in me, so let nothing draw you away from the like affection. You know that it was not to gain any temporal advantage,

you know that no other cause moved me to love you, but only what
was amiable in yourself. But you ask, what was that? Because I knew,
or believed you to be learned, able, and, what is more, religious,
though only in time, and not from eternity. [6] But enough of this; to
come to the point—I am writing a letter to my lord of Clairvaux
which I want you to present to him. Read it to him carefully and
studiously, and exhort him as much as you can, that what I have
written with a view to charity may be brought to good effect. Urge
him, for he must be urged on account of the shortness of the interval,
that in the next feast of All Saints he may do what I wish, and if he
finds persons objecting he may bring them over to my (and, I think
I may call it, his) view. The King's brother [Henry, brother of Lewis
the young, then a monk of Clairvaux] whom I sincerely love, Galcher
the Cellarer, our Garner, Fromund the warden of the guests, and the
other brethren whom you know better than I do, salute affectionately
on my behalf."

To this, Bernard, by the hand of the Secretary Nicholas, replied—

"I saw your letter only for a moment, but with no little interest;
I was occupied with so much business, as you, most loving father,
know, or may know. However, I tore myself away, and escaped from
the solicitations of everybody, and shut myself up with that Nicholas
whom your soul loveth. I read over again and again the sweetness
that flowed from your letter. It was redolent of your affection, and it
moved mine. I grieved that I was not able to answer according to my
feelings; because the evil of the day, which was great, called me away.
For a vast multitude, out of almost every nation under heaven, had
assembled. It was my place to answer every one; because, for my
sins, I was born into the world that I might be confounded with
many and multifarious anxieties. In the meantime, I write this scrap
to him who is my own soul, but when I can get time I will dictate
a letter more accurately, and which shall more clearly express the
feelings of one who loves you. As to the will of Baro, which you

---

[6] "Quia te literatum, quia strenuum, quia quod plus est, religiosum:
licet ex tempore non ab æterno esse aut cognovi, aut æstimavi." I give
this as it stands and as it is pointed in the *Bib. Clun.* p. 901, but I
confess that I do not understand it, and can only conjecture that it
may refer to some dispute which might exist between them, as to what
is now called Calvinistic doctrine.

sent to us, in truth we give you credit for it, for we receive it not as a debt, but as a gift. I am glad to know the truth concerning the Grenoble business. I would have you to know, too, that my heart was much moved by the words of our common son, which he brought to me from you. I am not disturbed by it, but prepared to do what you wish wherever I can. You, as a most special lord and father, and most dear friend, and your monks both alive and dead, are remembered at Citeaux. The Bishop of Beauvais elect [that is, the King's brother Henry, just mentioned], as one of your own, which indeed he is, salutes you. I your Nicholas salute you for ever and beyond it, and the household that cleaves to your body and spirit."

PETER TO BERNARD.

"If it were allowed, if the providence of God did not prevent it if a man's way were in his own power, I had rather, most dearly beloved, cleave to your blessed self with an indissoluble union, than be a prince or a king anywhere else. And why? Ought I not to prefer, before all earthly kingdoms, your society, which is delightful not only to men, but to the angels themselves? I should not be wrong were I to call you their fellow citizen, though through God's mercy hope has not passed into reality. If indeed it were given me to be with you here till your last breath, perhaps it would be granted to me to be with you for ever. Whither should I run but after you, drawn by the odour of your ointments? [Cant. i. 3.] But as this is not granted constantly, I would it were frequently; and since even that is not the case, I wish I could at least have frequent messengers from you. And since that very seldom happens, I desire that your holiness will, as soon as possible, visit one who loves you until the Christmas week, by your Nicholas, in whom it appears to me that your spirit in a great measure reposes, while mine does so altogether. I shall see you, holy brother, in him, and hear you, by him; and some things which I wish to communicate privately to your wisdom, I shall send by him. To your holy soul, and to the holy ones serving Almighty God under your government, I commend myself, and ours, with all possible energy and devotion."

PETER TO NICHOLAS.

"If you are mine, as I call you—if I do not deceive myself—although you are a man under authority, yet I command, and absolutely will, that you come here. I have for a long time deferred issuing this command, though I had most fully resolved in my own mind to do it, not from dissimulation, but because I waited for a fit opportunity. For I am always, as you know, moving about, not knowing how long I may have to stay in any particular place, or when, or whither, I may get away from it. But now, as an accident which I have met with will compel me to remain at Clugny, at least until Christmas, you must come, and make no excuse; for, perhaps, if you delay, you may not find me there, for I know not how long. When you come, I will explain to you why I am so urgent. I have written to your Lord Abbot another letter, more in the nature of a command than a request, to send you to me. The History of Alexander the Great, our Augustine against Julian (if the correction of your own by it is completed), and any other good things which you may have, bring with you."

BERNARD TO PETER.

" What are you about, my good man? you laud a sinner and beatify a miserable creature. You must add a prayer, that I may not be led into temptation. For I shall be led into it, if, feeling complacency in such compliments, I begin not to know myself. How happy now might I be, if words could make me happy. Happy nevertheless I shall call myself, but in your regard, not in my own praises. Happy that I am loved by, and that I love, you. Though, indeed, this morsel, sweet as it is to me, must be a little modified. Do you wonder why? It is because I do not see what claim I have to such affection, especially from such a man. You know, however, that to desire to be more beloved than one deserves is unjust. I would that I might be enabled to imitate as well as to admire that mark of humility. I would that I might enjoy your holy and desired presence, I do not say always, or even often, but at least once a year. I think I should never return empty. I should not, I say, look in vain at a pattern of discipline, a mirror of holiness. And (that which, I confess, I have as yet but too little learned of Christ) I should not quite in vain have before my eyes your example of meekness and lowliness of heart. But if I go on to do to you what I have complained of your doing to me, though I may speak the truth, yet I shall act contrary to the word of truth, which commands us not to do to others what we would not that they should do to us. Therefore let me now reply to the little request with which you concluded your letter. He whom you order to be sent to you is not at present with me, but with the bishop of Auxerre, and so ill, that he could not, without great inconvenience, come either to me or to you."

I have no doubt that the reason assigned by Bernard for not sending the Secretary was true and sufficient; but we may perhaps find ground to doubt whether it was the only reason. It is, however, corroborated by a letter of Nicholas, which begins thus :—

"' Show me, O thou whom my soul loveth'—when shall I come and appear before thy face, when shall I see thee, ' when wilt thou comfort me?' Comfort me, I say, for 'comfort is hidden from mine eyes' until I see your desired and desirable presence; and my soul is sorrowful even unto thee. To be sure, wherever I go, the most delight-ful remembrance of you follows me; but in proportion as that recollection is sweet, so is absence the more grievous. Far be it from me to receive comfort from that specious, but false sentiment, which tells us that those are more really present who are so to the mind, than those who are before our eyes, and that there is more in the union of hearts than of persons. As if, indeed, the look and speech had not something of living pleasure, which the absent cannot give. But I think this was said rather from system than from feeling, by that splendour of Roman eloquence with whom eloquence was born and brought to light—that is, Tully, of whom it is said, that what he had framed in thought he enforced in action, followed up with art, transferring with the utmost ease his heart to his tongue. What am I about? I have wandered from my business, and am guilty not only of a digression but a transgression. Who will make up to me for not having seen together those two great lights, [7] and that too in the firmament of heaven, namely, in that place which the Lord hath chosen from among all the places of the earth to set his name there? I am angry with my occupations through which it occurred, not that I was unwilling, but unable, and that I did not even know of it. It was caused by the business of your brother, my Lord Abbot of Vezelai, in which, by your command, I had to fight with beasts that man might not prevail," &c.

It is quite clear that Nicholas was as anxious to go to Clugny as Peter was to get him there. His letter is too long to admit of my here inserting the whole, and it may be sufficient to say that he begged Peter to write again to his Abbot, to the Prior, and to Galcher the Cellarer (for he was involved in the business

---

[7] Alluding, I apprehend, to a recent visit of Bernard to Clugny.

of each—horum enim omnium negotiis intricatus et
implicatus sum), and promised to bring Alexander the
Great, Augustine, and any other good thing which he
could lay his hands on. "I know," he says, "that my
Lord Abbot told you not to send for me without necessity, and he said the same thing to me; but there
is necessity, the greatest necessity, to see you, however
busy I may be. What need of many words? Order me
to come." Peter wrote as he was desired to all the
parties; and his letter to Bernard is characteristic and
worth transcribing:—

"If it be lawful to complain of a friend, and of such a friend, I
do complain; and I say what was once said to a certain person,
'Father, if thy friend had bid thee do some great thing, surely thou
shouldst have done it;' how much more then when, first by writing,
and then by word of mouth, he bade, entreated, with familiar boldness
ordered—'Send your Nicholas to Clugny?' I do not deny that the
thing itself is great; but it is no great journey. What if you had only
once written to me, 'send me' this, or that person, or ever so many?
What should I—I say, what should I do, but what I am wont to do?
I am in the habit not only of granting your requests, but of obeying
your orders. But you want to know my reason. Is it not reason enough,
to see a person whom one loves? He is yours indeed, but he is very
dear to me, and are you not pleased with my liking what belongs to
you? Does it not please you that one whom I believe you love more
than many who belong to you, should be still more dear to me? And
what greater proof of true friendship is there than to love what my
friend loves? I love him for his own sake, and for yours too. For
your sake, because he is attached to you; for his own sake, because
ever since the time of the Lord Bishop of Troyes, he deserved it on
many grounds. Hitherto I have made him no recompence for all these
things, except that I have always sincerely loved him in the Lord.
While others make a practice of repaying one service or benefit by
another, would it not seem beyond all measure ungrateful in me to
deny to one who loves me such kindness as costs nothing? Is it
strange, if, in order to prove to him that this kindness does not wholly
evaporate in written representations of words, I desire at least once a
year to see him, to talk with him, to delight myself in the Lord with
him concerning those writings both sacred and philosophical, of which

he is full to the brim? If it is not idle to converse of God, of divine things, of those which are most profitable to the soul, then Nicholas's visit is not an idle one. If the cultivation of personal regard for you in our own hearts, if the commendation of your order to all men, if at length to unite your whole body to our congregation with the cement of charity, is idle, then Nicholas's visit is an idle one. His heart is always inditing some good matter of you and yours; he seeks the good of his people; he prays for the peace of Jerusalem. These are the ridiculous, vain, frivolous occasions of Nicholas with us. Why, then, my dearest friend, cannot he be granted to me for a month, when I, from mere affection, gave up to you Peter and Robert your kinsmen, and Garner, and others, not for a month, but for ever? How many abbots, how many monks, have I granted to other, not to say strange, monasteries (aliis, ne dicam alienis, ecclesiis), under the influence of your letters and counsels? Nor do I repent of having yielded to my friend, to whom I am prepared to yield a great deal more. But it is right that he should make a return; it is right that, to one who is always giving up to him, he should yield something. This thing is more profitable to your congregation than to us ; for there is no person, unless it be yourself, venerable man, there is, I say, no person through whose advocacy they could more persuasively plead their cause, and no hook with which they could more effectively fish in the sea or in the river of Clugny.

"But I remember that when your holiness was at Clugny lately, you said, 'What do you want with Nicholas?' I answered, 'It is of no consequence, no great matter.' But I confess to you, dearest friend—if I sinned, forgive me—they were rather the words of wounded feeling than of truth. Truly I was then deceitful. I know not how it happened, for it is not often the case with me, that I used deceitful language. I had one thing in my heart, and another on my tongue. This is what my mind tacitly suggested, 'Why should you repeat your wishes so often? Perhaps, as you have been denied your request twice before, you may now be denied a third time. You have asked, and have not been listened to ; why should you go on entreating?' I felt inclined to answer, as the man born blind did to the Pharisees, 'I have told you already, and you have heard ; why would you hear it again?' I was inclined to answer thus, but I did not like to do it. Now, you see, I confess. Let my confession avail me — let it avail me that I have not covered the truth with a veil of falsehood — let it avail me that, as it is said all is naked among friends, so I have stripped before my friend what was disguised in my bosom. Let it, I say, avail me — but for what? That you should take anything for my sake out of your barns? or anything out of your cellars? that you should diminish your treasures of gold and silver, if you had them? What then? That you should send Nicholas; and not only now, but whenever I shall send for him. For I will take care, as far as possible, not to ask anything that can be reasonably denied, or which may in any way annoy you, not to say myself. Let it be, then, let it be, as I wish, that Nicholas may spend next Easter with us, and, according to his custom, pour out your heart to me, and mine on his return to you."

No. XXVI.

"I can only say, in the praise of Peter, that his manners were gentle, his temper very mild and humane, and that he had what in common language is concisely called A GOOD HEART." — MILNER.

WE must not, however, lose sight of books in this correspondence, for so did not even the Secretary Nicholas, who was so much occupied by it: in addition to all his business, as the abbot's amanuensis, he had what Mabillon calls a "librorum commercium" with various persons. Thus, in his thirty-fourth letter, addressed to Amedeus, Bishop of Lausanne, he says, "I send you the book of Master Anselm, well pointed, if I mistake not, and corrected." By another letter, it appears that he used to lend books on condition that a copy should be returned with the volume lent. When Peter of Celle had borrowed two volumes of St. Bernard's works, he wrote to him, "Make haste and quickly copy these, and send them to me; and, according to my bargain, cause a copy to be made for me. And both those which I have sent to you, and the copies, as I have said, send to me, and take care that I do not lose a single tittle." Writing to the Dean of Troyes, he says, "Send me the Epistles of the Bishop of Le Mans, for I want to copy them;" and, indeed, he seems to have had a constant eye to the acquisition and multiplication of books. When Philip, prior of the cathedral church of Cologne, and the emperor's chancellor, was going to Jerusalem, he put in for his "noble library," which he had so wonderfully and incomparably collected, assuring him that his poor brethren would pray for his prosperous voyage. [1]

But, to say the truth of the Secretary Nicholas— and I suppose it ought to be said of him, as well as of other people, and it may as well be said in plain terms, though I am sorry to be obliged to use them —he was a great rogue. Enjoying, as he did, the most affectionate confidence of these two good abbots, and professing the greatest attachment to them, and the highest reverence for those things which they held most sacred, he was a hypocrite, a cheat, and a thief. I am afraid that I do not exaggerate the fact, and that he might be called with peculiar propriety "graphicum furem." But then how far the inconsiderate and confiding kindness of his patrons conduced to spoil a clever, conceited, ambitious young man, is more than I can pretend to say. Certain it is, however, that when Peter was writing of Nicholas, in the affectionate terms which I have quoted in the preceding number, or, at the utmost, very soon after, Bernard had begun to suspect him of duplicity and fraud. In a letter to the Pope, principally about the Archbishop of Rheims,

---

[1] As to his "commercium librorum" (see before, pp. 79, 80, 81), it would be easy to multiply illustrations and examples. One offers itself immediately in a letter of the abbot Peter to Guigo, prior of Chartreuse, in which he tells him that, according to his direction, he had sent him the lives of those saints, Nazianzen and Chrysostom, and Ambrose against Symmachus. That he had not sent Hilary's work on the Psalms, because he found the same fault in their copy as was in the prior's, but that if, knowing that, he still wished for it, he would send it. That they had not got Prosper against Cassian, but he had sent into Aquitaine for it, and would, if needful, send again. He begs him to send the greater volume of St. Augustine, containing the letters which passed between him and St. Jerome, because a great part of their copy, while lying at one of their cells, had been eaten by a bear (casu comedit ursus).—*Lib.* I. *Ep.* xxiv. *Bib. Clun.* 653.—See Note F.

Bernard says, "We have been in peril by false brethren, and many forged letters, under counterfeits of our seals, have gone forth into the hands of many. And (what I am more afraid of) it is said that the deception has extended to you. Thus compelled, I have laid aside that seal, and use the new one which you see, containing both a figure of me and my name. The other seal, therefore, you will not receive as coming from me, except in the matter of the Bishop of Clermont, to whom I gave a letter sealed with the other seal, because I had not then got this one." [2]

In another letter to the pope, of the same year, Bernard speaks more plainly—"That Nicholas has gone forth from us, because he was not of us; and he has gone out, too, leaving very dirty footmarks behind him. And I had seen through the man a long time, but I waited in the expectation that either God would convert him, or that he, like Judas, would betray himself: and that has happened. Beside books, money, and a good deal of gold, there were found upon him when he went away: three seals—his own, the prior's, and one of mine, and that not the old, but the new one which I had been lately forced, by his tricks and rogueries, to alter. This is what, I remember, I wrote to you about, without mentioning any name, only saying that we were in peril by false brethren. Who can say to how many persons he has written just what he pleased, in my name but without my knowledge? I would that your court may be thoroughly purified from the defilement of his falsehoods. I would that the innocence of those about me may be able to clear itself with those whom he has deceived and prejudiced by his most impudent lies. It has been partly proved,

---

[2] Ep. 284. Tom. i. p. 275.

and he has partly confessed, that he more than once wrote to you in this fraudulent manner. As to his vile tricks, with which the country is filled, so that we are a byeword to everybody, I feel it unnecessary to pollute my own lips or your ears. If he comes to you (for he boasts of doing so, and is confident on the strenght of his having friends in the court), remember Arnold of Brescia, for a greater than Arnold is here. No man is more worthy of perpetual imprisonment— nothing could be more just to him than the imposition of perpetual silence." [3]

Whether Nicholas ever made any such appeal as he threatened does not appear; but if he did, it certainly was not followed by the consequences which Bernard suggests, for he was living many years after as a monk in his old monastery of Montier Ramey, as appears by a letter which we have from him to William, Archbishop of Rheims, who dit not attain that dignity till the year 1176. [4]

But let us (as Bernard did) abruptly dismiss Nicholas, and look at the Abbot of Clugni's own notary, Peter of Poictiers, who was afterwards grand prior of Clugny, and who seems to have shared, and better deserved, the affectionate kindness of Peter the Venerable. I was originally led to mention this abbot by a reference

---

[3] Ep. 298. The Cistercians were more cautious at a later period. Among the Statuta Selecta of the General Chapter of that Order, in A.D. 1223, we find the following:—"Abbas de Ponte, Obran, qui literas quas non inspexit sigillavit, tribus diebus sit in levi culpa, uno eorum in pane et aqua: et monachus qui ei litteras obtulit, eadem pœna puniatur, et in Capitulo vapulet."—No. xxiii. ap. Mart. IV. 1337.

[4] The reader will, I believe, find most of the particulars relating to Nicholas, for which I have not otherwise accounted, in Mabillon's discourse, "De Nicolao sancti Bernardi Notario," prefixed to the third tome of his edition of St. Bernard's works, Vol. i. 712.

to one of his letters bearing on the question of monastic studies, and showing his opinion as to *what* monks ought to read. In what sort of books his own "commerce" lay, may in some degree appear from what I have just given in a note; and his doctrine on the subject will appear from the following letter; though, not having Martene's book at hand, I am not sure whether it is that to which he refers:—

"To his beloved son Master Peter, Brother Peter the humble Abbot of Clugni wishes the seeing eye and the hearing ear:

"Pitying you, my most beloved son, labouring as you are in acquiring the knowledge of secular literature, and burthened with the heavy load of profane studies, and foreseeing no reward for your labour, no relief for your burthen, I grieve to think that you are spending your time in vain. For, if the single and definite object of the true philosopher is to learn wherein real blessedness consists, and having learned that, to attain to it, so that instead of being miserable he may be blessed,—and if that is not worthy to be called blessedness in which any good thing is wanting, but that the *summum bonum* is a blessed eternity,—who will dare to say that he is a philosopher who, by all his labours, is not advancing to eternal blessedness, but to eternal misery? The wise men of antiquity laboured in a search after this blessedness, and set to work vigorously to bring to light what was hidden in profound depths, as it were from the very bowels of the earth. Hence the invention of arts, hence the multiplied perplexities of argumentation, hence the innumerable dissensions of sects disputing with each other; some of which placed happiness in sensual pleasures, others in the capabilities of the soul, others thought it was to be sought in something above man, others with some other opinion opposed them all.

"Seeing that these erred, and that they were seeking among things below for those which are hidden above, and that mortals in this world were straying in the confusion of falsehood, Truth, looking from heaven, and compassionating their misery, arose from the earth; and having taken the likeness of sinful flesh, in order to render Himself visible to such creatures, He cried to those labouring under these and the like evils, 'Come unto me, all ye that labour and are heavy laden, and I will give you rest; take my yoke upon you.' And, because he saw that they were tied and bound by deep ignorance of truth, assuming the character of a teacher, he added, 'Learn of me, for I am meek and lowly, and ye shall find rest to your souls.' And, in his

sermon on the mount, he plainly taught not only where true blessedness
is to be found, but also the means by which it is to be obtained; and
at once put down the curious trifling of those who are searching after
happiness, saying, 'Blessed are the poor in spirit, for theirs is the
kingdom of heaven.'

"See now, without the study of Plato, without the disputations of
the Academy, without the subtleties of Aristotle, without the teaching
of philosophers, the place and the way of happiness are discovered.
Let human presumption, then, be silent, now that the Divine Master
has been heard. Let Falsehood hold its peace, for Truth teaches. Let
man quit the teacher's chair, for the God-man sits down to teach — 'Blessed,'
saith he, ' are the poor in spirit, for theirs is the kingdom of heaven.'
Why is it then, my most dearly beloved, that you run from school to
school? Why are you labouring to teach and to be taught? Why is
it that you are seeking, through thousands of words and multiplied
labours, what you may, if you please, obtain in plain language, and
by little labour? Why, vainly studious, are you reciting with the come-
dians, lamenting with the tragedians, trifling with the metricians, deceiving
with the poets, and deceived with the philosophers? Why is it that
you are now taking so much trouble about what is not philosophy,
but should rather (if I may do it without offence) be called foolishness. I say, foolishness; for this is the declaration of the true philosopher — 'Hath not God made foolish the wisdom of the world?' Run,
then, my son, to that blessedness of the kingdom of heaven which is
proposed to you by the heavenly Master, as the one single fruit of all
philosophy, and which you cannot obtain except by true poverty of
spirit. For, as I have already said, the true Master, presiding in the
school of the whole world, and overthrowing the seats of the false
teachers, has declared him that is poor in spirit to be blessed, because
for him is laid up the highest blessedness, that is, the kingdom of heaven.

"Enter the way of poverty, wich leads to the blessedness of the
kingdom of heaven. Enter, I say, the way of poverty, not so much
of the body as of the soul; not so much of possessions as of humility; not so much of the flesh as of the mind. You will then be
the true philosopher of Christ, when he shall have made the wisdom
of the world foolishness in you. For, according to the same apostle,
if you will be wise, become a fool, that you may be wise. And
do not glory in your knowledge of the vain talk of logic, or the
curious trifling of physics, or in knowing anything else but Jesus
Christ and him crucified. If, through his gift, you attain to this, there
will be joy over you among the angels of God, who rejoice over
every sinner who repents, and there will be much joy among

the saints, for when one member rejoices, all the members rejoice with it. And to me it will be a joy beyond everything; for I will receive you as an only son,—I will nourish you with the milk of piety,—I will cherish you in the bosom of love,—I will bring you up among the little ones of Christ; among the multitude of recruits I will arm you with heavenly weapons, and, as far as I can, will animate you to the spiritual warfare, and will fight by your side against the enemy. We shall have help from above, that as fellow-soldiers in the heavenly camp we may conquer the enemy, and, conquering, may be crowned; and, truly philosophizing, may arrive at the true object of philosophy — eternal blessedness.

How these promises were performed by the kind and warm-hearted abbot, and how affectionately he was attached to this son, we may learn from a letter which he wrote to him when he had permitted him to go and reside elsewhere (I presume at some cell belonging to Clugni), and missed him so much that he repented of the leave which he had given. It is long, but some part is so characteristic of the writer, and otherwise so illustrative of our subject, that I must give an extract. After saying a good deal about the elevated situation of his retirement, and reminding him of the purposes for which Moses ascended the mount, and our Lord went up into the mountain, the abbot adds—

"Since then, most dear son, in going up into a mountain, and in solitary retirement, you do, according to the grace given you, imitate the Lord and his servant, see that you do as far as you can imitate them in other things; that, as I have met your good desires by providing for you the peace of solitude, so you may procure some alleviation of my labours by your prayers. For to that affection with which, as you know, I embrace you in the love of Christ with my whole soul, you owe, not only your prayers, but (as St. Paul said to Philemon) your own self also. What, indeed, do you not owe to me, you whom I have loved almost beyond any other? What do you not owe to me, who never thought more even of myself than of you? And it is no wonder that you have gained this place in my regard, when it was hardly possible for me to make any adequate return for your life and conversation. For, to say nothing of your other virtues, where or at what price shall I ever be able to procure anybody so assimilated and conformed to my own ways ? If I wanted to investigate any of the deep things of holy scripture, I always found you most ready and prepared. If I wanted to look out anything in profane literature (for the sake of that which is sacred), I found you prompt and shrewd. If our talk happened to be (as our most familiar talk most frequently was) on the contempt of the world and the love of heavenly things, your words seemed so separate from earthly things, and so full of immortality, that you appeared to be saying to me, 'That my mouth speak not the works of men.' [5] And me, coming from worldly occupations, and, as it were, frozen up with the cold of the north wind, they thawed as. with the warmth of the southern breeze, in such a way, and so melted me by the heat of their breath into divine love, that even to them the words of the Psalmist might be applied — 'Send forth thy word, and thou shalt melt them; his breath hath blown, and the waters shall flow'; [6] —and I may sing with the spouse in the Canticles, 'My soul melted as my beloved spake.' [7] All things were wearisome to me, I felt everything a burden, I was groaning like one bowed down under a heavy load of punishment. I was like those of whom we read in Job, 'Behold, the giants groan under the waters.' [8] I had no rest, no relief from anybody, until my very necessity suggested to me to go to you. But as soon as I could get a little leisure with you, and have, if only a little, conversation, I rose up again with renewed powers, and more alacrity, to my labours, like one strengthened with much meat, and you had performed that divine injunction, 'If thou shalt see thy neighbour's ass fallen in the way, thou shalt not pass by, but thou shalt help with him.' [9] By your care, undoubtedly, like the cable of an anchor (as Gregory says) I was prevented from being driven out to sea by contrary winds, and, though much tossed, kept into the shore.

" Have you forgotten these frequent and earnest conversations ? Have

---

[5] Ps. xvi. 4.—*Douay.*

[6] Ps. cxlvii. "He shall send forth his word, and shall melt them : his Spirit shall blow, and waters shall flow." — *Douay.*

[7] Cant. v. 6. "My soul melted as he spake."—*Douay.*

[8] Job. xxvi. 5.

[9] Exod. xxiii. 5. "If thou see the ass of him that hateth thee lie underneath his burden, thou shalt not pass by, but shalt lift him up with the same."—*Douay.*

you forgotten my tears and lamentations over my personal dangers ?
Have you lost all recollection of the frequent repulses with which you
met my desire to fly from all earthly things and devote myself entirely
to God? Oh, how often, when the door was shut, and every mortal
excluded, and He alone who is always in the midst of those who
think or speak of Him was witness, have we held awful discourse on
the blindness of the human heart and its hardness ; on the snares of
various sins ; on the different kinds of crafts of demons ; of the depths
of God's judgments, and 'how terrible in counsels over the children
of men,'[1] that on whom he will he hath mercy, and whom he will
he hardeneth, and that man knows not whether he is counted worthy
of love or hatred ; of our uncertain and fearful calling ; of the scheme
of man's salvation wrought out by the incarnation and passion of the
Son of God ; of the tremendous day of the final judgment, of the
incomprehensible severity of the divine trial whereby he punishes the
wicked everlastingly, and the unspeakable mercy wherewith he gives
eternal rewards to the good.

"Conversation on these and similar subjects, when the noise of the
world was shut out, formed a sort of hermitage for me in the midst
of men, and was like the tabernacle of the Lord, to which (like Moses
from the stones of the Jews) I fled for refuge from the tumult of the
world. Tired with the litigation of men and the arguments of law-suits,
here I rested. Worried about the petty cares of domestic management,
and worn out with various dissensions, here I was refreshed. Annoyed
by the irruption of those who spoiled us, by the slaughter of our
people, by the devastation of various places, here I put off my sadness.
The spots contracted from the filth of the world, I here washed away,
and purged out the old leaven which is opposed to the unleavened
bread of sincerity and truth. And, what need of many words ? Truly,
according to Isaiah, this tabernacle was to me 'a shadow in the daytime
from the heat, and for a place of refuge, and for a covert from storm
and from rain.'

"Nor was this only here at home, but wherever I went. You were
my companion. This, as we travelled together through various parts,
neither the scorching sun, nor the freezing north wind, nor the tempest,
nor the cloudy day, nor the muddy earth, nor the steep mountains, nor
the deep valleys, could deprive us of. Everywhere, when the waves of
the great sea were a little still, this secret place remained to us. I had
you so unanimous in all things, I was so sure that what I found in

---

[1] Ps. lxv. 5.—*Douay.*

my own mind was in yours also, that in you, almost alone and without exception, I found that friendship which is truly defined as identity of will; so that nothing could possibly please me which was displeasing to you, nor displease me if agreeable to you,—according to what we read, that a certain person once said, there were not two souls to two bodies, but one soul seemed to inhabit both. But if such affection could exist among those who knew not God, as that, without confounding the substance and only uniting the will they could express such an idea as this, what wonder is it if the love of God, which is shed abroad in men's hearts by the Holy Spirit, hath united us in Him who maketh of both one, and who said to his Father, of his disciples, 'that they may be one, as we are?'

"But it is time to begin complaining, that I may bring forth that wherewith I have so long travailed. For you, you, I say, have offended against this love; you have severed this divine union; you have rescinded this heavenly contract, when, as a friend, your friend—as an intimate, your intimate—and (to come to the language of authority) as a subject, your superior—as a disciple, your master—as a monk, your abbot—not to say as a servant, your lord—has been deserted by you. But if I were to call you a servant, should I go too far? for the Rule prescribes that a monk shall submit to his superior with *all* obedience. If with *all*, then with servile; but with *all*, therefore with servile; so that you are my servant. I complain then of my servant's flying from his master, seeking out a lurking place, refusing to follow him, being unwilling to serve him."

But there are two more folio pages of this letter, and, instead of pursuing it, it seems more to our purpose to extract part of another to a monk named Gilbert, of whom I am sorry that I know little more than that he seems to have adopted a very secluded (if not absolutely solitary) life in some remote cell, and to have written to the Abbot of Clugni for advice and instruction. If I pass over what Peter replied in the way of general advice, or with respect to the peculiar temptations of his circumstances, and what he says of the employment of his time in prayer and meditation, it is not because I think it uninteresting, or less scriptural or sensible than what he might have

written if he had been reserved to our enlightened age.
But, in fact, the letter fills nearly five folio pages, and
one must select; and the reader will remember that
my present subject relates more directly and immediately to the knowledge, than to the piety, of the Dark
Ages. Having spoken of prayer and meditation, he
adds, referring to the latter—

"But since she [for he has compared her to a handmaid, whose
mistress is Prayer] is wholly spiritual, she requires the support of
something else, and something inferior, and let her have the help of
sacred reading. Refreshed with this, and having shut her book, she
reflects upon what she has read, and after long reflection, ministers as
a handmaid to prayer. For as the fire, when the fat is cast into it,
from receiving that rich food, breaks forth in greater flames, so the
fervour of prayer, enriched by the fatness of meditation and reading,
rises to the greatest heat of divine love. These are the dainties of the
king's sons. This is the table prepared by the mother, Wisdom, to
which, crying in the streets, she invites the little, not the great ones,
saying, 'If any be a little one, let him come to me;' and again,
'Come, eat ye my bread, and drink the wine which I have mingled.' [2]
This bread no man eats who is not fasting from all the food of man.
This wine, unless he abstains from all other drink, he cannot drink.
For, according to St. Gregory, he who feeds on sensual pleasures shall
be counted unworthy of those feasts of eternal dainties.

"But I know, my most dearly beloved, that these things are difficult
of attainment; and that it is not easy for everybody to pass his
life in these pursuits only. Let these three things, therefore [that
is, prayer, meditation, and reading] be followed by manual labour;
that when the mind is fatigued with spiritual things, and, being cast
down by the weight of the flesh, falls from the highest to the lowest
things, let it be turned, not to the vain conversation of men, but to a
blessed exercise of the body. Trees cannot be planted, fields cannot be
watered, and no agricultural work can be carried on, consistently with
perpetual seclusion; but, what is more useful, instead of the plough,
you may take in hand the pen, and instead of marking the fields with
furrows, you may score page after page with sacred letters, and the
Word of God may be sown in the parchment, which, when the harvest

---

[2] Prov. ix. 4, 5.—*Douay.*

is ripe, that is, when the books are completed, may fill hungry readers with abundant fruits, and so heavenly bread may dispel the deadly famine of the soul. Thus plainly, thus you may become a silent preacher of the divine word; and while you hold your tongue, your hand will sound aloud with uplifted voice in the ears of many people. You will be shut up in your hiding-place, while in your books you traverse sea and land. Like the watchman from the high-place, you will cry aloud by the mouth of the reader in the public assemblies of the church, and whisper the same things to the silent servants of God in the recess of the cloister and the corner of the house. Profession will have made you a hermit,—devotion, an evangelist; so that what you could not do yourself, you may do by your labours. Be encouraged to this work by considering the great reward that will accrue to you on account of all whom you may help by this praiseworthy course. For all who, by reading your books, have conquered pride, subdued luxury, despised avarice, restrained wrath, have abstained from or repented of any sins, will help to fill the barns of your eternal harvest, as handfuls gleaned by the sweat of your brow. And while, for the most part, the works of men end with their lives, and cease when they do, you will not die even when you are dead; and even ceasing to live, you will not cease to do good, while by your works you are recalling the dead to life. And the gain of your good works in the sight of God will be extended even after your death, as long as (if I may so speak) the life of your books endures.

"If, however, from its injuring your sight, or from headache, or from its wearisome sameness, you cannot, or will not, be content with this one manual employment, make a variety by other handyworks. Make combs for combing and cleaning the heads of the brethren; with skilful hand and well-instructed foot, turn needle-cases, hollow out vessels for wine, such as they call *justitiæ*, or others like them, or try to put them together. And if there are any marshy places near, weave mats (an ancient monastic employment) on wich you may always or frequently sleep, may bedew with daily or frequent tears, and wear out with frequent genuflexion before God; or, as St. Jerome says, weave little baskets with flags, or make them of wicker. Filling up all the time of your blessed life with these and similar works of holy purpose, you will leave no room for your adversaries to intrude into your heart, or into your cell; but that, when God hath filled all with his virtues, there shall be no room for the devil, none for sloth, none for the other vices."

I cannot help hoping and believing that a reader

(if I am so happy as to have such an one) who has candidly considered the extracts which I have given from the letters of Peter the Venerable will have formed a less despicable opinion of him than he would have done had he merely known him by the brief and ignorant sneer of Milner. Whatever might be right or wrong in Peter's religion, he certainly was not a heartless formalist, absorbed in frivolous punctilios.

But I hope, too, that the reader has not been misled to think (and that I am not helping the delusion by what I have just said) that I am taking, and giving him, all this trouble merely with a view to defend an individual from such silly censure. If that were my object, I should not wonder if I might be able to show a probability that Peter was a man, if not of more critical knowledge, yet not deficient in secular learning, and certainly of more extensive reading, and real knowledge of the history of the church to which he belonged, than the historian who has held him up, not merely to scorn, but as a sort of proof and specimen of the barbarism of his age. If I were his panegyrist I should claim some respect for the literary enterprise (even from those who would not give it to the Christian zeal) of the man who gave to the west a translation of the Alcoran.[3] I should express my

---

[3] In a letter to St. Bernard, from which I have already quoted, he says — "Misi et novam translationem nostram contra pessimam nequam Mahumet hæresim disputantem, quæ dum nuper in Hispaniis morarer meo studio de lingua Arabica versa est in Latinam. Feci autem eam transferri a perito utriusque linguæ viro, Magistro Petro Toletano. Sed quia lingua Latina non adeo ei familiaris vel nota erat ut Arabica, dedi ei coadjutorem doctum virum dilectum filium, et fratrem Petrum notarium nostrum, reverentiæ vestræ, ut æstimo, bene cognitum. Qui verba Latina impolite vel confuse plerumque ab eo prolata poliens et ordinans : epistolam, immo libellum, multis, ut credo propter ignotarum rerum notitiam perutilem futurum perfecit. Fuit autem in transferendo hæc

belief that his Treatise against the Jews is not much
less wise and scriptural than what many persons have
written since, and would even write in the present
day on the same subject; but on that point, or any
other relating to rabbinical polemics, I should not like
to speak positively, without consulting my very excellent and learned friend, Dr. M'Caul; and of his poetry
(as of some other good men's) I should say nothing,
because I find that compliments to their sense, and
piety, and good intention, are not generally acceptable
to poets.

But I am not the biographer or the eulogist of the
Abbot Peter; and I say so much about him just for
two reasons,—first, to show the reader, and to beg
him very seriously to consider, how history, and history
even of the most sacred character, is too often written.
If there is any subject which should make the historian's hand tremble, even while he guides the pen
of truth, it is the Church of Christ, which he has purchased with his blood, which is, by his dispensation,
militant here on earth, dispersed through this naughty
world, and every page of whose history is rendered
obscure by the craft and assaults of the devil, the
weakness and the wickedness of the flesh, the friendship and the enmity of the world, the sins of bad
men, the infirmities, the follies, the fancies, of good
ones, and by the divine ordinance that it shall ever
be a body consisting of many members, often, perhaps

---

mea intentio, ut morem illum Patrum sequerer, quo nullam unquam
suorum temporum vel levissimam, ut sic dicam, hæresim silendo
præterirent : quin ei totis fidei viribus resisterent, et scriptis ac disputa-
tionibus esse detestandam ac damnabilem demonstrarent," &c.—Lib. IV.
Ep. xvii. Bib. Clun. 843. I wonder how many people at this time,
between Hyde Park Corner and Whitechapel Church, know more of
the Alcoran than Peter and his secretary did.

always, incapable not merely of executing, but of appreciating, the office of each other. Whatever else may have contributed to perpetuate and increase this obscurity, it has, I fear, done little in comparison with presumptuous ignorance.

But, in the second place, I think the reader will perceive that the abbot Peter was not a solitary being who had some knowledge of the Scriptures, while everybody else was ignorant. I do believe that it was uncommon in extent, and that his secretary Peter meant, if not quite all that his words might be made to say, yet something very strong, when he talked of the abbot's having the scriptures always ready—"utrumque Testamentum memoriter retinendo;" [4] but that it was not so uncommon in kind as some persons have supposed the reader has probably been led to suspect; perhaps he has anticipated, and wondered that I have not noticed, an argument which is one of the most obvious and the most powerful, and to which I hope to proceed.

---

[4] Bib. Clun. 619.

No. XXVII.

"Deinde etiam certis horis, certæ lectioni vacandum est. Fortuita enim et varia lectio, et quasi casu reperta, non ædificat, sed reddit animum instabilem; et leviter admissa levius recedit a memoria. Sed certis ingeniis immorandum est, et assuefaciendus est animus. Quo enim spiritu scripturæ factæ sunt, eo spiritu legi desiderant: ipso etiam intelligendæ sunt. Nunquam ingredieris in sensum Pauli, donec usu bonæ intentionis in lectione ejus, et studio assiduæ meditationis, spiritum ejus imbiberis. Numquam intelliges David, donec ipsa experientia ipsos psalmorum affectus indueris. Sicque de reliquis. Et in omni scriptura tantum distat studium a lectione, quantum amicitia ab hospitio, socialis affectio a fortuita salutatione."—GUILIELMUS REMEN.

IF the scriptures were as little known in the Dark Ages as some writers would have us believe, it would be hard to account for one very common feature in the biography of ecclesiastics of that period, written by those who were quite, or almost, their contemporaries, and who therefore, according to the popular notion, participated, and gloried, in the same ignorance and hatred of the word of God. Treating the history of those times as it has been too often treated, we may, indeed, whenever we meet with anything opposed to our previous opinion, set it down at once as an exaggeration, or falsehood, or some absurd fruit of inconceivable ignorance and stupidity. But in a great many cases this will not help; and at the same time will not prevent the statement from being of great value; for I need scarcely say that we may often learn nearly as much from falsehood as from truth, though the information may be very different in kind from that which it was the writer's intention to convey.

It is, for instance, obvious, that if a contemporary biographer describes the subject of his memoir as pulling down an old wooden church and building a stone one, so much to the satisfaction of the patron saint that he came himself in the night, and set up three great bells in addition to the three little ones of the old church—if, I say, we are told this, all or any part of it may be untrue, and the untruth may arise from the intention or mistake of the writer; but at least we attain a high probability that there were wooden churches and stone churches in his days, and that both might have bells. Indeed we are apt to suppose, that what a legend writer (I use the word in its popular sense, for a writer of something little better than romance) tells us of his saint is somewhat adapted to the taste and knowledge of those for whom he wrote, and that, even while we disbelieve his facts, we may gather from him some idea of the opinions and feelings of society in his time. Perhaps we are even liable to carry this too far; but when we do, the fault more commonly lies in building on single instances, or generalizing from a few particular cases, than in the original principle and ground of judgment. That ground is solid, and by these remarks I do not mean to throw suspicion on the statements of which I am about to avail myself, but only to remind the reader that for our present purpose it really matters but little, if at all, whether the biographers of the Dark Ages whom I have occasion to quote were scrupulously correct or not. As to the fact, I dare say that a great deal of their biography was affected by passion and prejudice, some intended to deceive, and some written in error, —some, in short, as bad in every variety of way as anything in our days,—but I really believe that a great part of it is more simple, and therefore more credible;

except on those points respecting which the writer was, from the superstition of the time, more likely to be deceived himself.

Be this as it may, it is certain that a very common subject of eulogium on the ecclesiastics of those times is that they were much devoted to the study of the scriptures, and possessed a great knowledge of them. Several instances of this have occurred already incidentally; and I will here add a few others.

The biographer of St. Luidger, bishop of Munster, who died in the year 809, tells us that he was well instructed in the sacred writings; and did not neglect to lecture his disciples daily; and whatever he found to be enjoined in the holy books, he studied to practise and teach. [5] I have already, I believe more than once, cautioned the reader that even such terms as *scripturæ sacræ* in writers of the Dark Ages do not always mean the Bible; but it may be well to repeat it here, and when the expression is ambiguous he will judge for himself, whether it is used with that laxity by which it sometimes includes the writings of the fathers, and ecclesiastical historians. It may probably do so here; but I should not mention St. Luidger where doubtful instances are not worth quoting, if I really doubted the fact in his case, and also (to say the truth) if it were not for a little anecdote which his biographer records, and which it is to our general purpose to mention. We may perhaps assume that this pupil of Alcuin (who after spending three years and a half

---

[5] " Erat sanctus Lutgerus in Scripturis sacris non mediocriter eruditus, sicut in libro ab eo composito . . . . probatur . . . . Discipulis etiam suis mane diebus singulis tradere per se lectiones non neglexit, et quicquid in sacris codicibus faciendum invenit, illud instantissime studuit observare et docere."— *Leib.* Sc. Br. I. 93. See also *Mab.* Act. SS. V. 27.

with him at York, returned "habens copiam librorum")
was not unacquainted with the scriptures, especially
as his master's eminence in such learning is recorded; [6]
but his biographer tells us that—

"As soon as he could walk and talk he began to collect the rind
and bark of trees, such as we use for lights, and everything of that
sort which he could find. And while the other children were playing
he used to make himself little books of what he had gathered. And
when he could get any fluid, he imitated those who write, and used
to carry them to his nurse to take care of, as if they were useful
books. And when anybody said to him, 'What have you been doing
to-day?' he would say that he had been all day making books, or
writing, or reading. And when he was further asked 'Who taught
you?' he would answer 'God taught me.' He was in fact meditating
in his tender age what he afterwards devotedly performed." [7]

One could imagine him accepting little Hannah
Mora's invitation, and accompanying her in her anticipatory journeys. [8] But the reason why this puerile
circumstance is worth mentioning is, that it indicates
a state of things in which the child was familiar with
books, and reading and writing. If he had not seen

---

[6] " Qui erat in omni latitudine scripturarum supra cæteros moderno-
rum temporum exercitatus," says the monk of St. Gall. Canis. Lect.
Ant. tom. ii. P. iii. p. 57. I give this, which is a testimony to his
general learning, merely for the phraseology which illustrates what I
have just said. Of Alcuin's biblical learning and labours I have spoken
in a former number [see p. 209, 224]; but they are notorious, and
the reader will perceive that my object is rather to show, by scattered
and incidental notices, the probability that there were many biblical
students among the comparatively obscure.

[7] Leibn. Scr. Brun. i. 87.

[8] "Among the characteristic sports of Hannah's childhood, which
their mother was fond of recording, we are told, that she was wont
to make a carriage of a chair and then to call her sisters to ride
with her to London to see bishops and booksellers; an intercourse
which we shall hereafter show to have been realized."—Roberts's Memoirs
of Hannah More, vol. I. p. 14.

it practised, he would have no more thought of writing than Philip Quarl's monkey did before his master came to the island.

Of St. Dunstan, who became archbishop of Canterbury in the year 961, his biographer tells us that he used to spend such leisure as he could retrieve from public affairs in religious exercises, and among other things in reading the divine writings (divinas scripturas) and correcting the copies of them. [9]

Of Maiolus, abbot of Clugni, who died in the year 994, I have already spoken—ut speculi fieri solet inspectione, ita se interius divina considerabat lectione, &c. [1]

Of Lambert, abbot of the monastery of Lobbes, about the year 1094, his biographer tells us that "of his love of the word of God and his knowledge of the scriptures; to the study and comparison of which, whenever opportunity was afforded, he gave himself wholly . . . there is much which might be worthy of mention." [2]

Anselm, bishop of Lucca, who died in the year 1086, according to his contemporary biographer, "Knew almost all the holy scriptures by heart; and, as soon as he was asked, would tell what each and all the holy expositors thought on any particular point." [3]

I think that I have referred to what William of Malmesbury, who lived within fifty years of the time, says of Wulstan bishop of Worcester's custom of repeating the whole psalter on his journeys, to keep his attendant clerks from such vain talk as is the

---

[9] Mab. Act. SS. vii. 663.
[1] See p. 344.
[2] Dach. Spic. ii. 753.
[3] Mab. Act. SS. ix. 480.

common snare of travellers; but I will here add his testimony, that "lying, standing, walking, sitting, he had always a psalm on his lips, always Christ in his heart." [4]

Hariulf, abbot of Aldemburg, and Lisiard, bishop of Soissons, contemporaries and biographers of Arnold, bishop of Soissons, who died in the year 1087, tell us, that he did not speak a single word to any creature during three years and a half which he spent in constant reading of the word of God and meditation upon it. [5]

The contemporary biographer of Thierry, abbot of St. Hubert in the Ardennes, says, that he was so assiduous in reading the holy scriptures that he knew them by heart, and could quickly resolve even the most difficult, and obscure, questions respecting them. [6]

Of Wolphelm, abbot of Brunwillers near Cologne, who lived until the year 1091, his disciple says, that he so profited in the reading of the scriptures that what he once read he never forgot. This may perhaps be meant to refer to more general theological

---

[4] William of Malmesbury says — "Ascenso animali, continuo psalterium incipere nec pausam nisi ad finem facere ... si via protelaretur ad sufficientiam horarum repetebatur psalterium. Adequitabant clerici et monachi, vel seriem versuum excepturi, vel amminiculaturi memoriæ, si quando videretur titubare, hoc ideo ut dediscerent inanes fabulas, quæ potissimum se viantibus ingerunt"—and he afterwards adds, "jaceret, staret, ambularet, sederet, semper in ore psalmus, semper in corde Christus."—*Mab. A. SS.* ix. 834, who refers to *Ang. Sac.* ii. 240.

[5] "Tribus igitur annis et mensibus sex, nullum mortalibus locutus est verbum, continuo strictus silentio, et delectatus in cælesti contemplatione atque assidua verbi Dei meditatione, quam solus legens ex divinorum copia librorum ubertim hauriebat."—*Mab. A, SS.* ix. 514.

[6] "In lectione sanctarum scripturarum ita erat assiduus, ut eas memoriter teneret, et earum quæstiones quamvis difficillimas et obscuras, cito evolveret."—*Mab. A. SS.* ix. 565.

H H

reading; but he adds, "It is also worth while to mention that this man of the Lord caused the whole of the Old and New Testament to be read through every year. The four gospels, however, as they could not be read at the same time, and in the same order, as the other books, he appointed to be read at four periods of the year, by four deacons, in the four sides of the cloisters." [7]

I suppose it would not be difficult to give enough examples to tire the reader, if I have not done it already; but I will here add only that of Aufridus, a man of high rank and military education, because his anonymous biographer tells us, that while a layman his table-talk was always seasoned with references to the holy scriptures. I mention this because he was a layman, while the others of whom I have spoken were ecclesiastics. Of course instances among the laity are less frequently met with, for two very obvious reasons. In the first place, the ecclesiastics were the reading men, and the writing men, and it is therefore likely not only that there should be more matter of this sort to record of them than of the laity, but that, as the reading men and writing men thus formed one class, they should know and care more about each other's

---

[7] "Operæ pretium est, illud etiam non reticere quod singulis annis vir Domini, Novi ac Veteris Testamenti paginas ex integro faciebat legendo revolvi: quatuor vero evangeliorum libros quoniam non eo loco, vel ordine, quo reliquos, competebat expleri, statuit quatuor temporibus recurrentibus anni in quatuor plagis claustri singulos a singulis diaconibus recitari." He also gives these verses of Wolphelm :—

Late diffusus sit ecclesiasticus usus.
Se testamentis exercet Omnipotentis.
Ut legat hæc ambo, sed et omni compleat anno
Sicut in hebdomada psalmorum clauditur ordo.

Mab. A. SS. ix. 686.

personal and individual characters, and therefore more
facts (not only in quantity, but in proportion) should
be recorded. Secondly, these laymen who had particular
knowledge of the scriptures, and of ecclesiastical books,
were very likely to become ecclesiastics, and to be
principally known in that character. I have mentioned
St. Eloy the goldsmith; and perhaps some others; and
so this Aufridus, after having been a soldier of rank,
became, in the year 994 or 995, bishop of Utrecht. [8]
Others too there were, many of whom, though equally
learned and diligent, did not rise to such high station;
and I will run the risque of specifying one, partly because he was a man not much known out of his own
circle, and who as far as I know never wrote anything;
partly, because he lived in the very darkest period, for
though there may be some difficulty in fixing the minu-
tiæ of his chronology, it appears that he was an old
man in the year 973; and partly also because his
affectionate disciple and biographer has mentioned several
particulars which illustrate not only his personal history, but the times to which he belonged.

The monastery of St. Gorgonius at Gorze, originally
founded by Chrodegang bishop of Metz, was a few
miles to the south-west of that city. Its abbot, John,
whom I desire to introduce to the notice of the reader,
was born, most probably in the early part of the tenth
century, at Vendiere, of parents who were, to say the
least, in very respectable circumstances. His father, at
a somewhat advanced age, married a young woman
of good family, by whom he had this son and two
other children. John was sent to school at Metz, and

---

[8] "Quicquid vero in jugi et quotidiana confabulatione loquebatur,
hoc divinarum scripturarum exemplis blande leniterque condiebat."—
Mab. A. SS. viii. 78.

also spent some time at the monastery of St. Michael
on the Moselle, where Hildebold a grammarian, one
of the disciples of Remigius the most learned master
of that age, kept school. From his learning, however,
as he afterwards frequently said, whether it was through
carelessness, or, as it seemed more probable, from a
sort of pride, he gained very little, though his father
paid very liberally for his instruction. Soon afterwards,
while he was quite a youth, his father died, and his
mother, who was much younger, marrying again, the
care of his brothers and all the family devolved upon
him. How he excelled in the knowledge of business,
and in domestic economy, how prudent he was and
what ability he showed, his biographer thought it need-
less to state particularly, and contented himself with
referring his readers to many persons who were then
living for testimony.

It is still less our business than it was his biographer's
to trace the future abbot of Gorze through all these
circumstances, and it may be enough to state that,
having by these pursuits lost what little learning he
had gained at school, he went to read with Berner, a
deacon at Toul, who was much celebrated for both
piety and learning. With him he studied the elements
of grammar and read the first part of Donatus;[9] but
he was quickly satisfied, or dissatisfied with these

---

[9] A very fashionable work in those days, but since so neglected
that the name has puzzled the modern editor of an ancient chonicle,
who takes some trouble in conjecturing who the *Donati* given by
somebody to a monastery could be. He had heard of *Oblati* who
offered themselves, or were offered by their parents while children, but
as to *Donati* they were a class of whom he had not heard, any more
than he had of the book in which grammar was at that time commonly
studied. It has found its way several times into the foregoing pages.
See p. 206. n., 213, 300, and probably elsewhere.

studies, and devoted himself entirely to sacred literature, in which he soon made extraordinary progress.
For brevity's sake I pass over all the intermediate steps
between this, and his being called to the nunnery of
St. Peter, at Metz, to take his turn there as officiating
priest. His biographer says—

"In the company of nuns, belonging to that place (which still
through the mercy of God continues to prosper), there was one named
Geisa, distinguished from the rest by her manners and conversation.
She was still quite a girl, and her aunt (she was named Fredeburg),
who was herself one of the nuns, was bringing her up under her own
particular care. This Geisa, therefore, who was daily making progress
in the strictness of holy conversation, amongst the other ornaments
of her sacred purpose, also wore hair cloth under all her garments.
John, who scarcely knew, if indeed he knew at all, of the existence
of any such practice, while he was one day, I know not where, talking
familiarly with her as he used to do with the others, got an indistinct
view through her linen, which was very thin, of the hair cloth which
was next the skin on the damsel's neck. Having put his hand upon
it to find out what it was, and discovering by its asperity, he was
struck with amazement and trembled all over. On his enquiring what
this kind of dress could mean, she was shy and blushed ; and after
remaining silent for sometime she replied, 'Do you not know that we
ought not to live for this world, or to serve it ? Those things to which
I see most people devoted appear to me to be altogether vain and the ruin of
souls ; a contrary disposition of mind makes me solicitous only concerning
my own personal danger.' When, in the language of holy zeal, she
had replied to him more than this, John was moved and sighed deeply ;
'Woe is me,' said he, 'miserable and most sluggish, who have so long
dragged on a life, not merely fruitless but even wicked. I, a man, ought
to take the lead of the weaker sex in virtue; but, to my great disgrace
and shame, I not only do not follow them who are already on the
way, but, slothful and altogether cleaving to the earth, I make no
progress whatever and do not in any degree imitate them.'

"Being therefore greatly stimulated by them, and more inflamed
than he had ever been before by any example of virtue, he deliberated
with a fixed mind on a plan for a more perfect life. He therefore
immediately began with these handmaidens of God, a course of divine
reading with all his might. Having first read through the whole of
the Old and New Testament, he committed to memory (accurately,

so that no one could have done it better) all the lessons which are appointed for certain times in the divine service in the church, which are contained in the book called ' Comes;' the prayers and whatever is appointed for particular occasions in the Sacramentary; the rules for the computation of times, which he had for the most part previously read over with the aforesaid Berner the deacon. The canonical laws, that is to say, the decrees of councils, the judgments for penitents, the mode of all ecclesiastical proceedings, and beside all these, the secular laws he treasured up in his mind (if I may so speak) word for word. Of homilies, sermons, and divers treatises on the epistles and gospels, as well as of whatever is memorable in the lives of the saints, he acquired such a knowledge, that whenever he subsequently had occasion to refer to them he would repeat them in the vernacular tongue straightforward from the beginning to the end as if the book had been before him, and he was actually reading from it. About the same time he laboured hard at the ecclesiastical music, without being ashamed or despairing; although some were inclined to laugh at him for enterprising what seemed unsuitable to his age. Nevertheless the perseverance of good desire, though with much labour, was completely successful. Thus were the leisure intervals of his sacred duties with the aforesaid handmaidens of God employed." [1]

We shall not surely be told that such stories as these are either fictions or very singular cases—or even that they are to any important extent coloured and exaggerated. * It would be easy to multiply them, and not easy to escape the inference that a familiar knowledge of the word of God was possessed and valued by many in those ages, which have been represented not merely as without light, but as so fiercely in love with darkness that they were positively hostile to the scriptures, and not only virtually destroyed them and made them void by their wicked doctrines and practices, but actually hated and destroyed the very letter of the Bible. There is, however, as I said before (for the reader may perceive that I have been led into what is not a digression, but certainly a parenthetical

---

[1] *Mab. A. SS.* vii. 370.   * See Note G.

paper which I did not think of when I wrote the preceding), an obvious and powerful argument—perhaps it would have been more correct to have said a plain and convincing fact—which I have not hitherto noticed, and which I hope to state and to illustrate.

Circumstances which would have rendered it difficult, if not impossible, for me to carry on this series of papers, as I had intended, are sufficiently known to my friends, and are not of a nature to interest the public. I meant, indeed, to have taken up some other points among the great variety which are intimately connected with the subject, and for which I had collected materials. These I may, perhaps, some day use; but beside that they would have required a good deal of time and trouble for their arrangement, they would have increased this volume to a very inconvenient size. I do not, however, like that this reprint should be issued without a few words to explain an allusion which I have once or twice made in the foregoing pages to an argument in proof of the scriptural knowledge existing in the Dark Ages, which had not been stated; which, in fact, I have not stated at all; but which is, I believe, altogether unanswerable.

I could not but suppose while I was writing these papers that some readers would anticipate me, and wonder why I did not at once appeal to what was so obvious to everyone possessing even a superficial knowledge of the subject. I might perhaps have done so if my only object had been to give in as few words as possible, a decisive proof that the Bible was better known in the Dark Ages than some writers would have us believe. But it was my wish, not only to state the proofs which exist, but to state them in such a manner as that they might be most intelligible and useful. I am not without hope that the contents of the preceding pages, beside having communicated to some readers information on several collateral subjects, and many incidental proofs and illustrations respecting that which is the main one, will have rendered some, who would otherwise have been unprepared, capable of appreciating that which is, when properly understood, the strongest proof of all. The proof lies in a simple fact, and the fact is before our eyes; but to those who have never looked at the writers of the period, and have imbibed all their ideas of the Dark Ages from modern declamation, there is too much reason to apprehend that without considerable preparation it must seem unintelligible or incredible.

I am not such an enthusiast as to suppose that a series of papers in a magazine, desultory and superficial as I sincerely acknowledge these to be, can do much to stop the perpetual repetition of falsehood long established, widely circulated, and maintained with all the tenacity of party prejudice. If I were, the occurrences of almost every day would, I hope, teach me wisdom. While these sheets have been going through the press they have brought me a specimen quite worthy of Robertson, and so much to our present purpose that I cannot help noticing it. Even since the foregoing paragraph was written, a proof sheet has come from the printing-office, wrapped in a waste quarter of a sheet of a book which I do not know that I have seen, but the name of which I have often heard, and which I have reason to believe has been somewhat popular of late. The head-line of the page before me is

| The University. | | Discovery. |
| Luther's piety. | D'AUBIGNÉ'S REFORMATION. | The Bible. |

Among the contents of the page thus headed, and

in the column under "Discovery. The Bible," we find the following passage relating to Luther:—

"The young student passed at the university library every moment he could snatch from his academic duties. Books were still rare, and it was a high privilege in his eyes to be enabled to profit by the treasures collected in that vast collection. One day (he had then been studying two years at Erfurth, and was twenty years of age) he opened one after another several books in the library, in order to become acquainted with their authors. A volume he opens in its turn arrests his attention. He has seen nothing like it to this moment. He reads the title—it is a Bible! a rare book, unknown in those days. [2] § His interest is excited to a high degree ; he is overcome with wonder at finding more in the volume than those fragments of the Gospels and Epistles, which the Church had selected to be read in the temples every Sunday throughout the year. Till then, he had supposed these constituted the entire Word of God; and now behold, how many pages, how many chapters, how many books, of which he had not before had a notion."

Is it not odd that Luther had not by some chance or other heard of the Psalms ?—but there is no use in criticising such nonsense. [3] Such it must appear

---

[2] On this word is a reference to a note in German at the foot of the page, which the English reader (and for such I presume the translation is made) will, of course, suppose to be a voucher for the fact that the Bible was unknown in those days ; but which is, in fact, neither more nor less than the following :—

§ Auf ein Zeyt, wie er die Bücher fein nach einander besieht . . kommt er über die lateinische Biblia . . (Mathes. 3.)

[3] After I had written this I was curious to see how Milner (in this case, the Dean) had stated the matter ; and I was surprised to find the following passage, with the capitals. as I here give it :—

"In the second year after Luther had entered into the monastery, he accidentally met with a Latin Bible in the library. It proved to him a treasure. Then he first discovered that there were MORE scripture-passages extant than those which were read to the people : for the scriptures were at that time very little known in the world." — *Vol.* IV. p. 324. Really one hardly knows how to meet such statements, but will the reader be so good as to remember that we are not now

to every moderately informed reader, but he will not appreciate its absurdity until he is informed that on the same page this precious historian has informed his readers that in the course of the two preceding years Luther had "applied himself to learn the philosophy of the middle ages in the writings of Occam, Scot, Bonaventure, and Thomas Aquinas,"—of course none of those poor creatures knew anything about the Bible.

The fact, however, to wich I have so repeatedly

---

talking of the Dark Ages, but of a period when the *press* had been *half a century* in operation; and will he give a moment's reflection to the following statement, which I believe to be correct, and which cannot, I think, be so far inaccurate as to affect the argument. To say nothing of *parts* of the Bible, or of books whose *place* is uncertain, we know of at least *twenty* different *editions* of the *whole* Latin Bible *printed* in *Germany only* before Luther was *born*. These had issued from Augsburg, Strasburg, Cologne, Ulm, Mentz (two), Basil (four), Nuremberg (ten), and were dispersed through Germany, I repeat, before Luther was born; and I may add that before that event there was a printing press at work in this very town of Erfurt, where, more than twenty years after, he is said to have made his 'discovery.' Some may ask what was the Pope about all this time? Truly one would think he must have been off his guard; but as to these German performances, he might have found employment nearer home if he had looked for it. Before Luther was born the Bible had been printed in Rome, and the printers had had the assurance to memorialise his Holiness, praying that he would help them off with some copies. It had been printed too at Naples, Florence, and Placenza; and Venice alone had furnished eleven editions. No doubt we should be within the truth if we were to say that beside the multitude of manuscript copies, not yet fallen into disuse, the *press* had issued fifty different editions of the whole Latin Bible; to say nothing of Psalters, New Testaments, or other parts. And yet, more than twenty years after, we find a young man who had received "a very liberal education," who "had made great proficiency in his studies at Magdeburg, Eisenach, and Erfurt," and who, nevertheless, did not know what a Bible was, simply because "the Bible was unknown in those days."—See Note H.

alluded is simply this—the writings of the dark ages are, if I may use the expression, *made of the scriptures.* I do not merely mean that the writers constantly quoted the scriptures, and appealed to them as authorities on all occasions, as other writers have done since their day—though they did this, and it is a strong proof of their familiarity with them—but I mean that they thought and spoke and wrote the thoughts and words and phrases of the Bible, and that they did this constantly and habitually as the natural mode of expressing themselves. They did it, too, not exclusively in theological or ecclesiastical matters, but in histories, biographies, familiar letters, legal instruments, and documents of every description. I do not know that I can fully express my meaning, but perhaps I may render it more clear if I repeat that I do not so much refer to direct quotations of scripture, as to the fact that their ideas seem to have fallen so naturally into the words of scripture, that they were constantly referring to them in a way of passing allusion, which is now very puzzling to those who are unacquainted with the phraseology of the Vulgate, and forms one of the greatest impediments in the way of many who wish to read their works. It is a difficulty which no dictionary or glossary will reach. What the reader wants, and the only thing that will help him, is a concordance of the Vulgate, in which to look out such words as seem to be used in a strange and unintelligible way. Without seeing them in their original context there is little chance of discovering their meaning—but then is it not clear that the passage was present to the mind of the writer, and that he expected it to be so to those of his readers? How could it be otherwise?

It will, I hope, be understood that I am not setting

forth all these writers, or all those for whom they wrote, as persons having a very full and clear understanding of the Bible, who had imbibed its spirit, steadfastly believed its doctrines, and punctually obeyed its precepts. I would as soon answer for all Cromwell's lambs.

I grant too that scriptural quotations and allusions were often made in the worst possible taste, and sometimes with the grossest absurdity. The specimen which I have given at p. 275, will I trust prevent my being suspected of any wish to deny or conceal this. What could be more unlucky than the allusion to Rahab and Babylon? What but inveterate habit could have seduced any man into such absurdity? But, among the extracts which I have given, the reader will easily find more creditable illustrations of my meaning; and if he suspects them of having been partially selected, or thinks (as he justly may) that they are not of themselves sufficient to constitute a full proof—for how can the matter, from its very nature, be proved by extracts however numerous and varied?—let him take the first half dozen writers of the period which he can lay his hands on, and resolve on making out the sense of half a dozen pages in each, and I have no doubt that he will find enough to make him suspect that further inquiry would prove the truth of what I have been stating. In the meanwhile I beg him to remember, that not having distinctly stated this fact in the foregoing papers, I have not there brought forward such extracts as I should have given in proof and illustration. One therefore, and I freely confess that it is rather a singular one, I will here give, and beside its bearing on the precise point under discussion, it may carry with it some ground for reflection on several questions of some interest—what was the feeling of the period? what could, and did, an archbishop preach before an Emperor, in the Dark Ages? and how was it received?

Bardo was born in or about the year 981 at Opershoven in Weteravia, or, as it would have been described in more modern times, in the upper circle of the Rhine. At his baptism one of his godfathers gave him a helmet, a lamb, and a psalter. His biographer (who appears to have been almost, or quite, his contemporary) tells us that the first of these three things prefigured the arms which he should successfully use in his spiritual warfare, the second his patience which was remarkable even from his earliest years, and the third the great profit which he would receive by the study of Psalmody. As soon as he was weaned his parents (et in divina sapientes, et in humana prudentes) sent him, with his psalter, to an old woman named Benedicta to learn his letters. She became fond of the child, and while he lay in her bosom she taught him all she knew herself. Thus in a short time, and as in play, he had learned to repeat all his psalter. He never forgot her affection and services; and, when he was an archbishop, he became, as his biographer expresses it, a nurse to his old nurse, and liberally provided for her.

When he had learned his Psalter, his parents sent him to school at the famous monastery of Fulda, then governed by Abbot Archanbald, where he made great progress. But though, through fear of the schoolmaster, he worked at secular learning, his mind was engrossed by the Psalter, the hymns of the church, [4]

---

[4] "In ecclesiastica tamen simplicitate toto mentis versabatur tenore in psalterio, Ambrosiano, Evangeliis, et talibus ceteris." As to the *Ambrosianum*, see Martene on the Rule of St. Benedict, ch. ix. p. 266.

the Gospels, and the like. In short, he became a monk at Fulda; and gained the high character of being an useful, peaceable, and peacemaking member of the society, loved and respected by all his brethren, as one who learned by reading and taught by practice. His biographer assigns to him, even at this early period of his life, the gift of prophecy, and adduces the following proofs. One of his favourite books was St. Gregory's on the Pastoral Office; and he was always reading it. Some of his friends, one day, asked him the reason of this. "Oh!" replied he, "when some foolish king comes here, and finds nobody who will consent to be an archbishop, he may perhaps make me one, and I must be prepared for it;"—on which they all laughed. His biographer gives Bardo credit for a foreknowledge of that which he affected to say in jest; but knowing as we do, and as Bardo did, the extreme probability that the Emperor should look to Fulda for an archbishop, we are not bound to suppose anything very wonderful. We must, however, I think, at the same time, acknowledge, that if the young monk had any suspicion of what really befel him more than twenty years afterwards, there was nothing discreditable in the way in which he was actuated by it.

So things went on. His influence increased and he became Dean; and when, in process of time, the abbot founded a small off-set, which he called the New Monastery in honour of St. Andrew, Bardo was sent to preside over it. While he held this office the Emperor • Conrad came to Fulda. The Abbot Richard, among other things, took him to see the New Monastery, and Bardo came forth to meet his majesty with prompt duty and reverence. After prayers, when they had quitted the church, the emperor inquired minutely about the place, what were the services, who were the monks, who the father,—and when he heard Bardo's name, and found that he was a person who had long been well known to him by reputation, he was seized with sudden joy, repeatedly saluted, embraced, and kissed him, and assured him that, on the first occasion that might offer, he should feel bound to promote him.

The biographer ingenuously tells us that this promise was the more easily to be accounted for, from the fact that Bardo was related to the empress; and adds that he dit not omit, so far as he was able, to make a proper offering to the imperial dignity, for he gave the emperor a *Kliotetra,*[5] of workmanship worthy of royalty, which, by leave of his abbot, he had prepared for the occasion of the imperial visit. Not long after the emperor sent for him to court, and received him with great respect. He introduced him to his friends, saying, "Have you heard of Bardo of Fulda?" "A great deal," said they. "What?" asked the emperor. They replied, "All that is good." "If you have," said the emperor, "believe it, for it is all true. If this is not a man whom we may praise with truth, we know not who is;" and proceeding to speak of the civilities which he had received from the pious father, he brought him into favour with them all.

It was not very long before Bardo was the abbot of two monasteries; and in process of time the archbishopric of Mentz became vacant. It would have been the natural course of things, or rather it would have been according to the course of alternate proceeding that the abbot of Fulda should have succeeded to it;

---

[5] Mabillon follows Father Papebroche in supposing this to mean a faldstool. He adds "Vide Glossarium Cangianum;" but that does not help much.

but he was passed over. In this he appears to have acquiesced, whether simply on the ground of a dream which he is reported to have had, may perhaps be questioned. But it was so in fact, and the clergy and laity of the diocese, few of whom perhaps knew as much about Bardo as the reader and I do, seem to have been quite at a loss to know by whom the archiepiscopal chair was to be filled.

It was the month of June, and the feast of St. Peter and St. Paul drew near. On the eve of that festival, it was whispered that the appointment would be made next day. As soon as it was light the emperor and empress entered the church. After prayers offered for divine direction in the business, they came forth; and, a multitude being assembled, they sat down to consult on the matter. Much murmur there was in the crowd; among the assembled prelates also each one was suggesting this or that person on account of some virtue or qualification, except indeed those who knew the mind of the emperor, and they waited for him to declare it. When, however, the day had made some progress and nothing had been decided, silence was made, and the emperor said, "Fathers and brethren, we announce to you that which we have heard and proved. I know a man of illustrious virtue, perfect holiness, singular talent, a vessel of chastity, a son of wisdom, one that has his body in subjection, eminent in charity, poor to this world, rich unto God, to whom our authority, if there be any weight in human judgment, inclines."

This speech of the emperor all the great men repeated to those around them; but still as no name had been mentioned they were asking one another who was meant. Having made this favourable impression on their minds, the emperor called for Bardo by his name and said, "Father!" at the same time beckoning him to draw near. How did he look then? How constant in mind, how unchanged in countenance, how firm in step. As he came near all the courtiers pointing him out to one another said, "This, this is he;" and all turned their eyes upon him, and their ears to the emperor. When he stood before the throne the emperor said, "We know the privilege of Fulda, and do not infringe the law of our predecessors; but there are those who know the reason why we do not promote the abbot, and we appoint you, one of that house, to be prelate according to the will of the pious." I do not know whether Bardo or any of his friends thought of a young monk who had once said something saucy about Gregory's Treatise on the Pastoral Office; but that was an old story, for he was about fifty years old when he was consecrated on the 29th of June in the year of our Lord 1031.

He went straightway to his see, and set to work zealously; but the emperor keeping the ensuing Feast of the Nativity at Goslar, he attended him there. On Christmas day he, as his rank required, performed mass, and delivered a sermon which seems to have been so brief and simple that it disappointed his audience. [6] Indeed, his biographer tells us, "there were some there who seized the occasion to vomit forth the gall of their malice, murmuring that such a rustic little man should have been made the prelate of so great a see, but in fact jealous because he was

---

[6] "Sermonem declamavit verbis non pluribus (quam ordinabatur) ad vesperam." In a note on the words in the parenthesis Mabillon says, "Et hæc quoque supplevit Papebrochius ob codicis legendi difficultatem." I suppose this means that he did not make more of a sermon on this great occasion, than might have been expected at vespers. But I do not pretend to understand it.

II

a monk. The emperor also was sorry that he had so
highly extolled him in public, and repented that he had
raised him to that most celebrated archbishoprick. So
in that day some were heard saying, 'He is a monk,
he might be good for something in his own little
monastery, but he is not fit to sit in that seat.' And,
whoever had a fling at him, ' Mo' [*i.e.* the first syllable
of 'Monachus'] was at the tip of his tongue, so that
it was easy to see where the chief offence lay. The
emperor ate scarcely any dinner, and took no thought
of delicacies, for he was hurt by the biting sarcasms
of the prelate's enemies."

"The next day came, and Dioderich, bishop of Metz,
performing mass, poured forth all his learning with lavish
prodigality. All extolled him saying, 'This *is* a bishop.'
The holy man [Bardo] however, who was not ignorant
that 'a fool uttereth all his mind: but a wise man keepeth it in till afterwards,'[7] and who was neither elated by
favour nor depressed by the carping of envy, took it patiently, having made up his mind what course to pursue.

" The third day arrived, and a message was sent to
the pious father to know who should perform mass.
He intimated that he meant, by the divine assistance,
to do it himself. His friends craftily endeavoured to
divert him from his purpose, recommending him to
order somebody else to do it on account of the fatigue;
but, in truth, being ashamed of the sermon which he
had delivered two days before. But he thinking within
himself 'my glory will I not give to another,' said
humbly, 'Every one shall bear his own burthen;'[8] and

---

[7] Prov. xxix. 11.

[8] My object in relating this history leads me to call the reader's
attention to this writer's use of scripture phraseology. He has just told
us what the Archbishop *knew* when the Bishop of Metz preached, and
now he tells us what he *thought* when asked to appoint somebody

when they talked of the trouble, he said, 'Which is best, for me to take trouble in doing what ought to be done, or to give way to negligence?' And so being prepared, he went, with the fear of God, to the altar."

On this occasion he delivered a sermon which I should be glad to give entire; but even in the smaller type used in this volume for extracts, I apprehend that it would occupy nearly fourteen pages. It is therefore out of the question.

And what is the sermon about? Thus stimulated, how did the archbishop endeavour to regain his ground, and please his noble, and critical, and now prejudiced audience? Was his sermon a highflown invocation of all the saints in the calendar? Not a word of any saint but those mentioned in the Bible, and not a word of invoking them. Was it a discourse on transubstantiation, purgatory, pilgrimages, penances, relics, images, indulgences? I do not think there is an allusion to one of those subjects. Was it a string of fulsome compliments to his imperial patron? It does not recognize the fact of his presence. Was it something in the "good-christian" way, about tithes and "presents to churchmen?" No hint of the kind that I see. Was it a catena from the fathers, or a cento from the classics, to show his learning? No uninspired writer is named, no book is quoted but the Bible.

What, then, was it? The reader wil not perhaps be much forwarder for being told that his text was, "Præ fulgore in . conspectu ejus nubes transierunt," Ps. xvii. 13, which the Douay version renders "At

else to say mass. If there is in the latter of these anything approaching to profaneness, the blame is with the writer, who probably used the words as those which occurred to his own mind, and not on Bardo. What he *knew*, or *thought*, he would perhaps have expressed better; and what he *said* was quite unobjectionable.

the brightness that was before him the clouds passed."
Our translation (which makes it Ps. xviii. 12) has
"At the brightness that was before him his thick clouds
passed." But the subject of the sermon was the pre-
eminent and excellent glory of Him whose advent in
the flesh they were celebrating—the Brightness of the
Sun of Righteousness which at once, as it were, gives
and eclipses all the radiance of those clouds which
shine with borrowed lustre, and which, brought into
comparison with him, are as nothing. Should the notion
that the clouds represent saints appear fanciful, it
would be easy to justify the archbishop, so far as
that can be done by patristic authority;[9] but my
object is not to defend his choice of a text, but to
show how he treated it; and that principally as it
regards the knowledge of the scriptures which he
displayed.[1]

The archbishop began his sermon by a reference

---

[9] I think St. Jerome makes the clouds in this text to be the prophets
who "passed" over from the Jews to the Gentiles at the coming of
Christ; but it is sufficient to mention Origen's eighth homily on
Jeremiah.

[1] In doing this, however, I am conscious that the preacher will be
presented to the reader under a twofold disadvantage. First, Father
Papebroche, as I have mentioned in a preceding note, seems to have
found it rather difficult to read the manuscript; and I have no doubt
that in some places the text is corrupt, and does not do justice to the
author. Secondly, as the point, and application, of a passage of scripture
would sometimes be greatly diminished, if not entirely lost, by giving
our translation, and as, with very little exception, it supplies a literal
translation of the texts as quoted in the sermon, I have given most of
the passages from the Douay version. These will seem strange and
unnatural to those who are accustomed only to our version, but perhaps
the variations which they perceive may tend to illustrate what I have
said respecting the necessity of being familiar with the language of the
Vulgate, before we can appreciate the scriptural knowledge of these
writers.

to St. John, and to the fact that it was his day; and after stating that the Evangelist would explain the language of the Psalmist, and having entered at some length into an inquiry respecting his character and authority, he proceeded thus:—

"After that this great steward of the Lord has received the treasure wherewith to make gain—not I think in three, or in five, or even in ten,—but, as I believe, a thousand *talents* [2] committed to him—generous to his fellow servants, he immediately gives forth a grand doctrine, *In the beginning was the Word, and the Word was with God, and the Word was God. The same was in the beginning with God.* [3] And after he had added somewhat respecting this divine Brightness, that he might declare its greatness by a similitude, he presently introduced a great cloud, or rather light, which in comparison with this Brightness he declared to be no light; for, saith he, *There was a man sent from God, whose name was John,* [4] and then he adds, *He was not light.* [5] It is indeed written of John, *He was a burning and a shining light;* [6] but John the Evangelist says, *He was not light.* [7] And if he, than whom *none born of woman was greater,* [8] was not light, then is none born of woman who was less than he; for if the greater is not, much less is the lesser. John has explained the meaning of the Psalmist, who said, 'At the brightness that was before him the clouds passed.' What is this Brightness? the Evangelist says that when Jesus transfigured Himself in the mountain *his face did shine as the sun.* [9] Here is the Brightness; and of the clouds Isaiah says, *Who are these that fly as clouds?* [1] The assemblies of the saints, says he, shine as clouds; yea, more than clouds, as it is written, they shall *shine as the sun in the kingdom of their father.* [2] They shine; one in chastity, another in simplicity, another in poverty of spirit, another as a peacemaker so as to deserve to *be called a Son of God,* [3] another is crowned in blood, another clothed in the white garments of virginity, another meek so that he will hurt no one, another wise so as to teach the ignorant, and to conclude generally, each one specially shines with some particular virtue.

"But whatsoever the measure of this may be, at the same time,

---

[2] Matt. xxv. 15. [3] John i. 1. [4] John i. 6.
[5] Ibid. 8. [6] Ibid. v. 35. [7] Ibid. i. 8.
[8] Matt. xi. 11. [9] Ibid. xvii. 2. [1] Is. lx. 8.
[2] Matt. xiii. 43. [3] Ibid. v. 9.

the whole is in God. For that Brightness, Light of light, God of
God, God the Son of God the Father—that Brightness, I say, of
which John saith that He *was the true light, which enlighteneth
every man that cometh into this world* [4] — the sower of all virtues,
the giver of all piety, the author of all holiness, He himself had
as a whole that which he imparted to each. What he disseminated
in parts abounded as a whole in Him. Whatever be the goodness
of any one, he cannot be compared with Him *who did no sin,
neither was guile found in his mouth.* [5] *There is no man that sinneth
not,* [6] not even an infant of one night, if its life be on the earth. *For
the heavens are not clean in his sight,* [7] how much more shall men
*who dwell in houses of clay, who have an earthly foundation, be con-
sumed as with the moth?* [8] Of whatsoever splendour and holiness the
elect may be, they cannot be compared with that divine Brightness,
for in comparison of Him they are as nothing. They are sanctified, it
is He that sanctifieth. They are luminous, He illuminates. They partake,
He imparts. Whatever they are He is also; but they are not all that
He is. Whence it is well said in the book of Job, *both the innocent and
the wicked he consumeth.* [9] That He should consume the wicked is plain
enough, but his consuming the innocent, though it may seem doubtful,
is equally true. He consumes the innocent because He converts him into
Himself, because he who is innocent is innocent in God, that none
may presume on his merits, *but he that glorieth let him glory in the
Lord.* [1] Or thus, He consumes the innocent because by comparison
with Himself He brings him to nothing; whence it is written, *Shall
man be justified in comparison of God, or shall a man be more pure
than his Maker?* [2] (factore suo purior erit *vir*) and the Psalmist says,
In thy sight no man living shall be justified [3] (non justificabitur in
conspectu tuo omnis *vivens*). 'Living,' he says,—for whether he is a
'man' (vir), or whether he is 'living' (vivens), he shall not be justified.
For he that is illustrious in virtue shall not be compared. He does
not say no man (omnis homo) shall be justified in his sight, but no
'vivens,' for by that word he draws no limit ; but he would only
have been superfluously stating what nobody doubted if he had said
that no man (homo) should be justified in his sight. But he has plainly
defined his meaning, by saying 'living' (omnis vivens). Living, he saith,
simple, innocent, chaste, meek, modest, poor in spirit, humble, or
alive in any holiness, shall not be likened. Why?—because, *Who in*

---

[4] John i. 9.   [5] 1 Pet. ii. 22.   [6] 1 Kings viii. 46.
[7] Job xv. 15.   [8] Ibid. iv. 19.   [9] Ibid. ix. 22.
[1] 2 Cor. x. 15.   [2] Job iv. 17.   [3] Ps. cxlii. 2.

the clouds can be compared to the Lord: or who among the sons of God shall be like to God? God, who is glorified in the assembly of the saints, great and terrible above all them that are about Him. [4] Who, he saith, in the clouds can be compared to the Lord? None.

"Behold the clouds, but at the Brightness that was before Him they have passed away; that is, the illumined clouds could not equal the illuminating brightness. Take away that which enlightens, and wat is enlightened becomes obscure. Take away the sun, and the clouds are in darkness. Restore the sun, and the clouds are in their beauty. Take away what is divine, and what is human is nothing. Add what is divine, and what is human is great. Nor let us be staggered at that which is written, *for both He that sanctifieth, and they who are sanctified, are all of one;* [5] for it is one thing to be so adoptively, and another to be so substantially. For many are called 'sons of God,' as it is said of the peace-makers, *Blessed are the peace-makers: for they shall be called the children of God;* [6] and many also 'gods,' as it is said, *I have said: You are gods, and all of you the sons of the most High.* [7] But this adoptively, and not substantively. There is but One who is the Son of God substantively, many adoptively; neither one adoptively nor many substantively. The adoptive indeed partake with the substantive, but the substantive imparts to te adoptive; neither does he partake nor do they impart; but they partake and He imparts.

"This is the Apostle's meaning, though he might seem to be stating something contrary, when he says, *Thou hast loved justice, and hated iniquity: therefore, God, thy God, hath anointed thee with the oil of gladness above thy fellows.* [8] He saith 'above thy fellows' (præ participibus tuis), which sounds as if he meant that God was a partaker, and took a part, which is altogether contrary to truth; for, according to the Apostle, *In Him dwelleth all the fulness of the Godhead corporally.* [9] But let us attend to the first part that we may fully understand what follows; for he saith, 'Thou hast loved justice,' and presently after 'God hath anointed thee with the oil of gladness above thy fellows,' and the prophet, *With my holy oil I have anointed him, the enemy shall have no advantage over him;* [1] for since the Son of God loved justice by his gift others loved it also, and were partakers of Him who loved. But He was anointed above all, because the enemy hath no advantage over Him.

"Or, if you will rather have it that in his assumed human nature He is a partaker (as the Apostle says, *He is not ashamed to call them*

---

[4] Ibid. lxxxviii.   [5] Heb. ii. 11.   [6] Matt. v. 9.   [7] Ps. lxxxi. 6.
[8] Heb. i. 9.   [9] Col. ii. 9.   [1] Ps. lxxxviii. 21, 23.

brethren, saying, Behold I and my children, whom God hath given me ;[2] and again, *Because the children are partakers of flesh and blood, he also himself in like manner hath been partaker of the same*),[3] we must recur to the same point, that *in him dwelleth all the fulness of the Godhead corporally ;*[4] but as to them, *to one is given by the Spirit the word of wisdom: to another the word of knowledge, to another the discerning of spirits, to another the grace of healing,*[5] to another something else; and it is divided unto each according to His will, and thus they partake, and He imparts. And therefore though it is said of the saints, *You are the lights of the world,*[6] it is but by participation, and not substantially, for they partake from Him who is *the true light which enlighteneth every man thath cometh into this world.*[7] For although it is written of John the Baptist, *He was a burning and a shining light,* this too is only adoptively, and not substantively; whence it is that the Evangelist has in some degree exposed the weakness of John, when he introduces our Lord speaking of him, and adding, *And you were willing for a time to rejoice in his light.* They 'were willing,' He says; but He is silent as to whether they did it or not, that He might after a sort suggest by his silence that they would have rejoiced, but were not able; for he was a ligt burning, but not kindling; shining, but not enlightening. And this cloud, so great and luminous, has passed away before the divine Brightness, because it could not be compared unto it. For he himself said, *I am not worthy to loose the latchet of his shoes.*[8]

"Great clouds, and magnificently radiant, there have been from the beginning of the world; but, how great soever, they have passed away before the divine Brightness. For I say nothing here of the difference between that which is from eternity, and that which is limited by time," &c.

The preacher then proceeded to speak of the ineffable glory of God, and the mystery of the Trinity in Unity, and the essential Deity of Christ; after which he continued thus:—

"Saying nothing, I repeat, of Him whom no clouds how radiant soever with light can approach, this we will endeavour to teach. He of whom it is written, *There is no beauty in him, nor comeliness: and we have seen him, and there was no sightliness, that we should be desirous*

---

[2] Heb. ii. 11, 13.   [3] Ibid. ii. 14.   [4] Col. ii. 9.
[5] 1 Cor. xii. 8, 10.   [6] Matt. v. 14.   [7] John i. 9.
[8] Mark. i. 7.

of him: despised, and the most abject of men, a man of sorrows, and acquainted with infirmity: and his look was as it were hidden and despised, whereupon we esteemed him not, how it is that He is also that Brightness, and that before Him the clouds have passed away. First among the first are angels, archangels, thrones, dominions, principalities, powers, virtues, ardent cherubim, burning seraphim — great clouds — always in light, always of light, always with light — yet not themselves light, or if light not unlimited, not incomprehensible. Of those it is written, *He that maketh his angels, spirits, and his ministers, a flame of fire.*[9] Of that Brightness it is written, *Who being the brightness of his glory, and the figure of his substance.* They are made; He is substantive. They innumerable; He is one. They great; He greater; as it is written, *Upholding all things by the word of his power.*[1] Upholding by the word of His power all things; angels as well as others."

After discoursing on the superiority of the glorified Redeemer over the angels, the preacher went on:—

"But why do we depress the angelic dignity by that ineffable majesty? let us make the comparison with Him in whom there was no beauty nor comeliness. The Apostle saith, *Again when He bringeth in the first begotten into the world He saith; And let all the angels of God adore him.* Who is that first begotten? Is it He of whom it is said that God *spared not even His own Son?*[2] Surely it is He. *Surely He hath born our infirmities, and carried our sorrows: the chastisement of our peace was upon him.*[3] Surely *He was reputed with the wicked,*[4] and yet of Him it is said, *And let all the angels of God adore Him.* Where now, I pray you, is that cloud? From the brightness that is before Him it has passed away.

"Now let us ascend, my brethren, *let us mind the things that are above, where Christ is sitting at the right hand of God,*[5] and let us say in words plain, and full of the Holy Spirit (for *no man can say, the Lord* JESUS, *but by the Holy Ghost*), that this is that Brightness, proceeding from the true sun of the Father's majesty, and enlightening every man that cometh into the world, of whom the Psalmist said, *He shall continue with the sun, and before the moon.*[6] He says He shall continue with the sun; for none other is there found that hath not past away at the brightness that is before Him, for at the brightness that is before Him the clouds pass. The sun continues with the sun;

---

[9] Heb. i. 7.   [1] Ibid.   [2] Rom. viii. 32.
[3] Is. liii. 4, 5.   [4] Ibid. 12.   [5] Col. iii. 1, 2.
[6] Ps. lxxii. 5.

and shall continue with the sun; for it is said, *He shall come down like rain upon the fleece.* [7] That He might show that He had so chosen a mother of the earth, as not to quit His Father in heaven, He first says, 'He shall continue with the sun,' and then adds, *in his days shall justice spring up.* [8] In his days, in his saints; that they may be not only clouds, but days, of which days He may be the sun, that there may be none among the sons *of God, like unto him.* [9] *This is our God, and there shall no other be accounted of in comparison of him. He found out all the way of knowledge and gave it to Jacob his servant, and to Israel his beloved. Afterwards he was seen upon earth, and conversed with men.* [1] Of whom the Father's voice said, *This is my beloved Son, in whom I am well pleased.* [2] And the Apostle to the Ephesians, *Who hath predestinated us unto the adoption of children through Jesus Christ unto himself; according to the purpose of his will; unto the praise of the glory of his grace, in which he hath graced us in his beloved Son.* [3]

"Let us say JESUS; *for there is no other name under heaven given to men, whereby we must be saved.* [4] *In the name of Jesus every knee should bow, of those that are in heaven, on earth, and under the earth, and that every tongue should confess that the Lord Jesus Christ is in the glory of God the Father.* [5] Therefore from the brightness that is before Him the clouds have passed. They have passed, — the clouds have not been found; all the sons of GOD in his presence, when brought into comparison with his Brightness, before his Deity, for in the name of Jesus every knee of those in heaven, on earth, and under the earth is bowed. This is that *bread of angels* which *man eat;* [6] who saith Himself, *I am the living bread which came down from heaven;* [7] of whom John says, *He that cometh from heaven is above all.* [8] How great is He, Lord in heaven, on earth a servant, as it is written, He *emptied himself, taking the form of a servant.* [9] In heaven the Creator, on earth created, as it is written, *Drop down dew, ye heavens, from above, and let the clouds rain the just: let the earth be opened, and bud forth a Saviour: and let justice spring up together;* [1] and immediately, *I the Lord have created him.* [2] *Who is like unto thee among the strong, O Lord? who is like to thee, glorious in holiness, terrible and praiseworthy, doing wonders.* [3] *Hast not thou struck the proud one, and wounded the*

---

[7] Ibid. 6.
[1] Baruch iii. 36.
[4] Acts iv. 12.
[7] John vi. 51.
[1] Isaiah xlv. 8.

[8] Ibid. 7.
[2] Matt. iii. 17.
[5] Phil. ii. 11.
[3] Ibid. iii. 31.
[2] Ibid.

[9] Ps. lxxxviii. 7.
[3] Ephes. i. 5.
[6] Ps. lxxvii. 25.
[9] Phil. ii. 7.
[3] Ex. xv. 11.

dragon? hast not thou dried up the sea, the water of the mighty deep, who madest the depth of the sea a way, that the delivered might pass over? [4] *They that hope in the Lord shall renew their strength, they shall take wings as eagles, they shall run and not be weary, they shall walk and not faint.* Whither shall they run? *To thy holy habitation,* [5] *which thy hands, O Lord, have established,* [6] taken up on thine outspread *wings,* [7] that they may be *carried in thy strength.* [8]

"When he had said this, the holy Bishop groaned within himself; and his eyes filling with tears, and despising his earthly habitation, he exclaimed: '*For what have I in heaven? and besides thee what do I desire upon eärth?* [9] and again, *But it is good for me to adhere to my God, to put my hope in the Lord God: that I may declare all thy praises, in the gates of the daughter of Sion.* [1] *Dearly beloved,* he resumed, *we are now the sons of God; and it hath not yet appeared what we shall be. We know, that, when he shall appear, we shall be like to him: because we shall see him as he is.* [2] We shall see Him. Whom? That divine Brightness, or that true Sun of which it is written, *Unto you that fear my name the Sun of justice shall arise,* [3] and we shall *shine as the sun in his kingdom* [4]—his, *of whom all paternity in heaven and earth is named,* [5] this Sun having risen upon all who have *increased even to perfect day* [6] from the beginning of the world. Our Fathers, who were worthy to be called *Stars, have given light; they were called and they said, Here we are: and with cheerfulness they have shined forth to him that made them.* [7] None is found who in anything excelled Him who for our sake was made man, so as among the glorious to excel Him in glory, or among the lowly in humiliation.

"Of ABEL indeed it is written that because of his innocence after he had been slain *his blood cried from the earth to heaven.* [8] A wonderful thing, that the silent blood of one thus silent should cry out; but what saith the apostle of Jesus? *You are come to Jesus the Mediator of the New Testament, and to the sprinkling of blood which speaketh better than that of Abel.* [9]

"NOE *was a just and perfect man in his generations, he walked with God;* [1] to whom God after the deluge was abated," &c.

---

[4] Isa. li. 9.　　[5] Ex. xv. 13.　　[6] Ib. xv. 17.
[7] Ib. xix. 4.　　[8] Ib. xv. 13.　　[9] Ps. lxxii. 25.
[1] Ibid. 28.　　　[2] 1 John iii. 2.　　[3] Mal. iv. 2.
[4] Matt. xiii. 43.　[5] Ephes. iii. 15.　[6] Prov. iv. 18.
[7] Baruch iii. 34.　[8] Gen. iv. 10.　　[9] Heb. xii. 22, 24.
[1] Gen. vi. 9.

The preacher then went on with the history of
Abraham, Isaac, Jacob, Joseph, Moses, Aaron, Samuel,
Solomon, Elijah, and Elisha; and having said something of each of these, in a style which may be
imagined from the foregoing extracts, he asked—
"But why should I enlarge? Those clouds are great,
but from the Brightness that was before Him they
have passed away;" and thus proceeded:—

"There is also another way of explaining this saying. You know
the sun, you know its rays, you know the clouds. The clouds which
are at a distance, opposite to the sun's rays, shine as long as they
are thus before the sun, and as they approach nearer, so much the
more brightly do they shine; but if the sun and the clouds come to
be in the very same place, so that where the sun is above there the
clouds are below, they are neither called clouds, nor are they so in
fact, but all the brightness is ascribed to the sun. What shall we call
this, my brethren, but in some sort a type of the kingdom of heaven?
What do the clouds (so called from nubilo, i.e., from obscurity) represent, but the human race, beclouded with the night of sin? What
does the splendour of the sun represent, but the light of the divine
Brightness? What the rays, but the illuminating works of Christ? The
cloud then, in their own nature obscure, shine when breathed on by
the rays of the sun, because human littleness shines when illuminated
by the works of Christ. The nearer it appproaches to the true Sun, so
much the brighter will it be; and powers which by its own nature it
had not, it receives by the illumination of Christ the true Sun; but if
it shall attain to that same point of divine operation, which is perfectly to give up the world, and with sedulous contemplation to look
only to the divine will, and, with the Apostle, to say, *But our conversation is in heaven*;[2] then it partakes in the name of Deity, so that
it ought to be called, not man, but even God. Whence our Lord, in
the gospel, when He had prayed for his disciples, said, *Not for them
only do I pray, but for them also who through their word shall believe
in me; that they all may be one, as thou, Father, in me, and I in thee:
that they also may be one in us.*[3] Not only that they may be called
one in us, which is great, but that they may be one in us, which is

---

[2] Phil. iii. 20.	[3] John xvii. 20.

greatest. That they may be, he says, one in us, that is, that these
clouds following me, the sun may, in my brightness, lose the nature
of clouds, and be sun."

These extracts may give the reader some idea of
the sermon, and whatever a severe criticism might find
to say respecting the taste or the truth of some of the
applications, I feel that I may confidently ask, whether
it does not imply a greater familiarity with the scriptures in both the preacher and the hearers, than most
people would give them credit for? When it is considered how small a part I have given, and that the
whole is characterized by the same biblical phraseology,
it really does appear to me surprising how any man
could, on such notice, put together such a string of
texts, at a period when concordances, commonplace
books, and other "pulpit assistants" had not been invented. Yet where is there ground for any suspicion
of fraud? I am almost ashamed to say such a thing
of Mabillon, who has printed the Sermon;[4] but still,
as many good protestants know nothing of him, or
only know that he was a papist, I must ask what he
could get by misrepresenting the matter, and printing
a long sermon by a canonized saint of the eleventh
century, based on the scriptures only, and containing
nothing in favour of any one of those things which
protestants justly consider as the corruptions of popery?
Still less can we imagine fraud on the part of a contemporary biographer; or, if we can, it is obviously a
greater wonder that some anonymous monk should
have forged a sermon of such a description, than that
it should have been actually made by a prelate who
had some reputation for talent, piety, and learning.
There is only one other supposition, namely, that it

---

[4] Act. SS. Ord. Ben. Sæc. VI. P. ii. p. 14.

was forged by some person or persons unknown
between the supposed time of the biographer and that
at which the manuscript containing it was discovered
by Father Papebroche; and of the three suppositions
this is perhaps the most improbable, not to say, absurd.

But what did the audience think of the sermon?
Was the unhappy preacher really casting pearls before
swine, in thus profusely quoting a book the very
existence of which was unknown to them? Surely, if
they knew nothing of the Bible, they must have wondered what he was talking about, and what he was
driving at; and have sorely repented that they had
expressed discontent with his former brief performance.
Surely if the emperor participated in "the blind hatred
of the half barbarian kings of feudal Europe," and the
audience in "the fanatical furies of their ignorant
people,"[5] by which we are told that the scriptures
were so cruelly and hatefully oppressed, such a preacher was likely to be torn in pieces. But nothing of
the sort appears to have happened. The people certainly were astonished, and it is said that they unanimously agreed, that the preacher was a highly fit man
to be archbishop.[6] "But," says his biographer, "his
detractors were covered with shame;" and when the
company sat down to table the emperor said, with a
cheerful countenance, "'I must keep the feast of the
Nativity to-day, for the company of those who were
tearing us to pieces is silent in confusion.' And then
again, as if his great joy made him talk nonsense (ex

---

[5] See page 234.

[6] In the first edition I said "Pope;" I now alter it in deference
to a learned friend; though I do not feel absolutely and entirely convinced that I am making it more correct. The words are " voce omnium
prædicabatur dignus esse, qui summus fieret Episcopus."

nimia lætitia quasi desipiens), 'Where,' said he, 'are our detractors?' and he ordered that water should be poured on the bishop's hands first of all. But the bishop, who had exhibited no sadness two days before, made no show of joy on this day. As he was then silent respecting those who blamed him, so he was now of those who praised him; which rendering him more and more an object of admiration, from that time forth he became very great." He was indeed for twenty years in that high office; whether he went on preaching the Bible, whether nobody but himself understood his sermons, and whether he was the only person who preached in that way, are matters worthy of inquiry.

NOTES.

Note A. on p. 192.

Father Ceppi and Mabillon.

WHEN I originally published these essays, and when I reprinted them, I took the "Historia Dissidii Litterarii," which Father Porta annexes to his translation of Mabillon's book, for an original work, and quoted it as such. I might have known better if I had carefully dissected the long title-page of the Appendix containing that History, which was, I suppose, unobserved from its occurring near the middle of the volume. That would have told me that the account of the controversy had been "gallice concinnata" by Dom Vincent Thuillier, and only translated into Latin by Father Porta. I have altered the passage accordingly.

I have also corrected another mistake. I said that Father Ceppi's work was "very near getting into the Expurgatory Index." I was probably led to use that phrase by the specification which I found of the particular passages which were objected to, and on the removal of which the publication was allowed; the case really being (as I have now stated it), that he had difficulty in getting permission to print it at all. My error was pointed out by a writer under the signature of R. G. in the Irish Ecclesiastical Journal for April, 1844.

Note B. on p. 297.

Warton's History of English Poetry.

I HAVE given several specimens of the inaccuracy of Warton's statements, feeling it to be the more necessary because he is one of the popular writers whose works are read by many, who, though well informed on other subjects, are wholly unacquainted with the dark ages, and not really studying, or particularly inquiring about them. They do, however, almost unconsciously, or at least unintentionally, form an opinion respecting that period from broad general statements, and little detached facts, one being very commonly given as if it were a sufficient voucher for the other, and both coming in quite incidentally as matters perfectly notorious—as things so far from wanting proof themselves, that they are only brought in to prove other things.

It is clear that in this way errors of a very gross kind are likely to become more popularly diffused, than if they were found in works formally didactic, and read only by those who would bring some spirit of inquiry, and probably some previous knowledge, to the study of them. If, for instance, a writer on Gardening tells his readers that they must not expect China roses to retain in England all the fragrance which belongs to them in their native country, where the thermometer is never below 200^0 Fahrenheit, and in another part of this work explains that the reason why China asters do not grow spontaneously in this country is, that we are not subject to heavy rains continuing without intermission for five or six years at a time, so that our daisies never grow to that enormous size—if there is not a word more about China in his book, or a thought or idea about China in his reader's mind, the probability is that that reader will carry away a very strange notion of the country; and, if the gardening book is popular, it is probable that more persons will be misled than if the same statements were made in a scientific work on the climate and produce of China, which would scarcely be opened by any who were not capable of detecting such gross absurdities. Gross they are, but not more so than Warton's. Take, for instance, one or two of his statements:—

"Alfred, while a boy, had himself experienced the inconveniences arising from a want of scholars, and even of common instructors, in his dominions: for he was twelve years of age, before he could procure in the western kingdom a master properly qualified to teach him THE ALPHABET. But, while yet unable to read, he could repeat from memory a great variety of Saxon songs." *Diss.* II. Sig. d.

The authority for this plain broad statement is given thus in a note:—

"Flor. Vigorn. sub ann. 871. Brompton, Chron. in ALFR. p. 814. And MS. Bever, ut supr."

How many of Warton's readers have turned to Florence of Worcester and John Brompton (to say nothing of the MS. at Oxford), to see whether they were fairly quoted, and do really say what Warton professes to state on their authority? Whoever does so will surely be astonished to find them expressly contradicting what they are said to affirm, and will wonder how any man could so misrepresent their statement   Florence of Worcester [1] says that through the neglect of his parents, and those who had the care of him (he does not say for any want of teachers), Alfred remained unlettered till his twelfth year. He then tells the well-known story of his mother's promising to give a book to that one of her children who should first be able to read it, and of Alfred's gaining the prize. We are not told how he learned to read that book, or the other which from that time he used to carry about in his bosom; but we are told that when he wished to proceed farther in learning (liberalem scilicet artem), he could not have his desire because there were no " grammatici " at that time in the kingdom of the West Saxons. How is it possible to account for so gross a misrepresentation? It may be said that the statement that there were not teachers of the liberal arts implies a low state of learning among the West Saxons at that period; but why is that fact to be exaggerated? Are we when we want to make a fine story about the wealth of England in these days, to say that at the accession of George the Third the people of England had not a morsel of bread to eat? Is it any excuse that when we are charged with lying, and pushed hard, we are able to say, " Well, but really now you must yourself

---

[1] Florence of Worcester says:—"Sed (proh dolor) suorum parentum et nutritorum incuria usque ad 12. ætatis annum illiteratus permansit. Saxonica tamen poemata die noctuque solers auditor, relatu aliorum sæpissime audiens, docibilis memoriter retinebat." He then relates the story of his mother's showing to him and his brothers a book, and promising to give it to that one which should first be able to read it, and tells us that Alfred obtained it, and afterwards always carried a book in his bosom, &c., and then he adds "sed (proh dolor) quod maxime desiderabat, liberalem scilicet artem, desiderio suo non suppetebat eo quod illo tempore grammatici in toto regno occidentalium Saxonum non erant."

John Brompton's account is much the same. His words are "Cum autem plus cæteris fratribus ab utroque parente dilectus, usque ad xij. ætatis annum in paterna curia illiteratus mansisset, Saxonica tamen poemata docilis puer memoriter tenuit, in arte venatoria summus, psalmos et orationes in unum libellum compegit, quem secum jugiter circumduxit, grammaticam tamen minus perfecte attigit, eo quod tunc temporis in toto occidentali regno nullus grammaticæ doctor extitit, quamobrem ad consilium beati Neoti abbatis, quem crebro visitaverat, scolas publicas variarum artium apud Oxoniam primus instituit," &c.—*Apud X. Scrip.* col. 814.

The reference "MS. Bever, ut supr." relates to a fuller reference, "MS. Bever. MSS. Coll. Trin. Oxon. Codd. xlvii, f. 82." A friend has been so kind as to look at the MS. and send me an extract, which is almost in the very words of John Brompton.

acknowledge that game was hardly to be procured for love or money."
That may be true and singular, but the marvel of a nation subsisting
without bread, and all the marvellous deductions from that marvellous
fact, are clean gone, and our confidence in the historian must surely go
with them.

But let us take another matter of fact; at least what is set forth as
one by Warton in the same simple, concise, unqualified manner. It is
just one of the things which speak volumes to the meanest capacities.
The reader sees at once in what a pretty state things must have been:—
"About the year 1120, one master Hugh, being appointed by the
convent of St. Edmondsbury in Suffolk, to write and illuminate a grand
copy of the Bible for their library, could procure *no parchment for
this purpose in England."* *Diss.* II. Sig. g.

The authority for this is contained in a note at the foot of the page,
which is as follows:—

"Monast. Angl. i. p. 200. In the great revenue roll of one year
of John Gerveys, Bishop of Winchester, I find expended 'In parchea-
mento empto ad rotulos, v*s*.' This was a considerable sum for such
a commodity in the year 1266. But as the quantity or number of the
rolls is not specified, no precise conclusion can be drawn. Comp. MS.
Membran. in Archiv. Wulves. Winton. Compare Anderson Comm. i.
153. sub ann. 1313."

It is true enough that "no precise conclusion" can be drawn from
such premises. What indeed but confusion of ideas can be drawn from
attaching to a statement so plain and unequivocal, other matter so
vague and so irrelevant? Here is in the text a plain fact stated,—
that in 1120 Master Hugh could procure no parchment in England to
write a Bible on; and what is the use, or the sense, of telling us in
a note that one hundred and forty-six years afterwards the Bishop of
Winchester paid five shillings for an unknown quantity of parchment,
which, for anything that appears, he did not get "in England" any
more than Master Hugh?

This may probably seem to the reader like quibbling, and he may
be ready to say, "Oh, of course, if Master Hugh could not get parchment in England he could not get it at all; indeed it is not likely
that the stupid monk knew that there was any place in the world
except England—'the monks of Ferrieres, in the diocese of Sens, did
not know that there was such a city as Tournay in Flanders'—and
Master Hugh, of Bury St. Edmond's, was not likely to be better informed;
and of course the romantic idea of writing a Bible was abandoned."
Now it is just in this way that falsehood is engendered. The story

as Warton tells it is not only a foolish, but a false one. The gist of
it is to show the barbarous destitution of the period; and this is very
much assisted by turning this Suffolk monk's own neighbourhood (which,
one can hardly doubt, was all that was meant by "in partibus nostris")
into all England, and cutting the story short without telling us (as
Warton's authority does) that what Master Hugh could not get in his
own neighbourhood he did get from Scotland. There was parchment
there it seems, and the English monk knew it, and knew how to get
it, and did get it, and the great Bible was written; and if we are to
wonder and be confounded at the thought that there was no parchment
in England, let us equally wonder and be amazed that there was
parchment in Scotland, and that there was this traffic between the
places – but this part of the business is not stated.

Yet that even this is not the whole story, will, I think, be apparent
to anyone who fairly considers Warton's authority. It is probably one
of those little facts (like Haimon's Homilies) which have come down
to us so briefly and imperfectly told that without some explanation we
cannot fully understand them. [2] It seems that the Sacrist thought fit to
make a present of a great Bible to be written for the use of the
monastery, and incomparably illuminated by Master Hugh, and that he
wanted vellum, and not what we now call parchment. [3] That the word
"parchamentum" might be used with more laxity to describe the
material by the writer who relates the story of Master Hugh, in order
to avoid repetition, is very possible; but he says expressly, that what
was not to be found "in partibus nostris" was not parchment but
vellum, "pelles vitulinas;" and it is reasonable to suppose that it was
something out of the common way that was wanted for the incomparable
artist on so important an occasion.

Let us, however, look at another of Warton's stories :—

"Towards the close of the seventh century, even in the Papal
library at Rome, the number of books was so inconsiderable, that pope
St. Martin requested Sanctamand, Bishop of Maestricht, if possible, to

---

[2] I do not know whether anything is to be found respecting this occurrence, except in Dugdale's Monasticon, to which Warton refers. At page
300 (not 200) of the first volume we have the following brief statement:—
"Iste Harveus, frater Taleboti Prioris omnes expensas invenit fratri suo
Priori in scribendo magnam bibliothecam, et manu magistri Hugonis incom-
parabiliter fecit depingi. Qui cum non inveniret in partibus nostris pelles
vitulinas, in Scotiæ partibus parchamentum comparavit."

[3] "Among traders the skins of sheep are called parchment, those of calves
vellum."—*Johnson.*

supply this defect from the remotest parts of Germany." *Diss.* II.
Sig. a. 3.

The authority given for this is : —

"Concil. Tom. xv. p. 285. edit. Paris, 1641."

How Warton could write this, or how anyone possessed by the
popular notion of the dark ages could read it, without being staggered,
I am at a loss to conceive. Surely their previous idea would be that
"towards the close of the seventh century" if there were books anywhere
it was at Rome, and in the Pope's Library, if he had one. They might
not, perhaps, have been surprised to learn that he had none ; but even
then to find him, instead of rejoicing in his darkness, anxious to remedy
such a state of things amidst all the trials and troubles of his sad and
turbulent pontificate—to hear him crying and craving " Books, books,
prithee Sanctamand send us books, from the remotest part of Germany"
—truly this must be a matter of great astonishment. For to be sure,
he did not send there only, or as the place of all others, but everywhere, and would have sent to the back settlements of America if
there had been any; but then such an œcumenical and fervent search
for books, carried on by the Pope of Rome, would equally cross the
popular view of the Dark Ages.

But the follower of Warton must take the fact as he finds it, logic
and all. The number of books in the Pope's Library, in the seventh
century, was *so* inconsiderable that he requested Sanctamand to supply
the defect "from the remotest" parts of Germany, "if possible"—a
sly clause put in to save his infallibility in case anything in, or beyond,
nature should have exhausted that great storehouse of literature, remotest
Germany. If the number of his books had not been *so* inconsiderable,
he might, perhaps, have contented himself with sending to the less
remote parts of Germany; for the bishop of Maestricht, who lived in
the very least remote parts of Germany, would have to send a good
way in order to execute his Holiness's commission. One hardly knows
whether to say that the story would have been rendered more or less
credible if Warton had added that the Pope knew that Sanctamand
was in the habit of attending the Frankfort and Leipsic fairs, and
could therefore get him the newest books and best editions at a liberal
discount for ready money, and send them without much trouble by
the Parcels Delivery Company.

But the oddest part of some of these stories is the way in which
they vanish, when once they are fairly looked in the face. One may
sometimes meet with an exaggeration, and perceive clearly the temptation that the writer was under to embellish, or one may detect a

mistake, and see how a man might naturally fall into it; but some of these stories seem positively to have no ground or origin, and the authorities afford no explanation of the way by which they came into existence. There certainly is extant a letter—and I believe but one— from Pope Martin to St. Amand, Bishop of Maestricht, and it is given along with the rest of that pope's letters in the Councils : and I dare-say it would have been given in the edition of Paris, 1641, if there had been such an edition, for it is given (I learn by the kindness of a friend) in that of 1644, which is no doubt the edition meant by Warton. But really when I originally referred to the letter in my own copy of Labbe and Cossart, I could only imagine that in some other edition to which I had not then access, there must be something quite different from what I found, and I said nothing about the matter. Having, however, now learned that in the edition of 1644, Vol. XV. p. 285 (agreeing with Warton's reference), the letter stands just as it does in my own copy, I can only say that I am at a loss to account for so extraordinary a misstatement. In that letter the Pope is so far from begging books from the remotest part of Germany, or anywhere else, that he makes an apology, plainly indicating that St. Amand had been begging books from him. St. Amand had sent a letter to the Pope, the principal object of which was to obtain permission to resign his see. The Pope sent him a long reply, in which he encouraged him to persevere, and took the opportunity of writing to him on one or two other points; but I do not see one word in the letter which can possibly have any connection with the matter now before us except the following :—

"Reliquias vero sanctorum, de quibus præsentium lator nos admonuit, dari præcepimus. Nam codices jam exinaniti sunt a nostra bibliotheca, et unde ei dare nullatenus habuimus; transcribere autem non potuit, quoniam festinanter de hac civitate regredi properavit."—*Lab. Conc. VI.* 385.

Now how was it possible for any man to make up such a story from these materials? One could more easily have imagined a hasty writer to have taken up the notion that the Pope actually had no books, though the difference between "having nothing" and "having nothing to give" is very plain in itself, and very well understood by suitors; and it is rendered perfectly obvious here by the statement that the messenger was only hindered from transcribing by his haste to return. There were books to copy, it seems, if there were none to give. [4]

---

[4] Since this was written I have looked into Fleury, who gives the meaning of the passage thus, with the same remark on it:—"Nous avons fait donner

It is only when we keep in mind such specimens of qualification as these that we are not surprised, and scarcely offended, to find the Oxford Professor talking of "Voltaire, a writer of much deeper research than is imagined, and the first who has displayed the literature and customs of the dark ages with any degree of penetration and comprehension."—*Diss.* I. Sig. c. *b.*

Note C. on p. 312, n.

Destruction of MSS.

It seems worth while to add two instances, one English and the other French, of the destruction of MSS. by those who were their guardians, and who seem to have been influenced by religious (if one ought not rather to say, party) feeling. It is the more necessary because it is hard to conceive of such things; and the circumstances of the latter case in particular lead one to apprehend that the matter was not the act of a stupid fanatical individual, but a practice encouraged by those who had it in their power to do, and certainly did, much mischief; and that not only openly, but by private means, less easily detected.

Henry Wharton, in the preface to his *Anglia Sacra,* after stating the impossibility of rivalling works of a similar nature which had been published respecting France and Italy, owing to the destruction of manuscripts at the suppression of monasteries, &c., says, that he had met with a case in which a bishop avowedly, with the design of getting rid of popery, had burned all the Registers and documents belonging to his see.[5] He does not name him; and, without inquiring who he was, we will charitably hope that he acted in stupid sincerity, and was the only English prelate that ever did such a thing, or anything like it.

But there is a French story, more surprising and pregnant, and forming a valuable commentary on many sad passages in Martene's

---

au porteur les reliques qu'il a demandées. Car pour les livres, nous n'avons pû lui donner, parce que nôtre bibliotheque est vuide: et il étoit si pressé de s'en retourner, qu'il n'a pû en transcrire." He adds, "Ces dernieres paroles font voir, qu'il restoit des livres dans le bibliotheque du pape, mais qu'il n'y avoit pas assez d'exemplaires du même auteur, pour en donner ou en prêter aux étrangers."—*Hist. Eccles. Liv.* XXXVIII. § lvi. Tom. VIII. p. 488.

[5] "Comperi enim Episcopum quendam ante centum et quod excurrit annos, avitæ superstitionis delendæ prætextu, omnia Ecclesiæ suæ monumenta et Registra igni tradidisse." *Vol.* I. p. x.

literary tour, which might otherwise be thought to bear marks of prejudice against the protestant party. But this fact, coming as it does from themselves, is beyond suspicion; and it is briefly as follows:— At the "Quatrième Synode National des Eglises Reformées de France, tenu à Lion le 10 Août, 1563, L'An III. du Règne de Charles IX., Roi de France. Monsieur Pierre Viret, alors Ministre de l'Eglise de Lion, élû pour Moderateur et pour Sécrétaire," among the "Faits particuliers" which were discussed and decided, No. XLVII. is thus stated:—

"Un Abbé parvenu à la connoissance de l'Evangile, aiant abatu les Idoles, *brulé ses Titres,* pourveu aux besoins de ses moines, sans qu'il ait permis depuis six ans qu'il se soit chanté Messe dans son Abbaye, ne fait aucun exercice du service de l'Eglise Romaine, mais au contraire s'est toûjours montré fidele, et a *porté les armes* pour maintenir l'Evangile. On demande s'il doit être réçu à la Cene? *Réponse.* Oüi." *Aymon, Syn. Nat.* Tom. I. p. 45.

We cannot here indulge any such charitable hope as that which I suggested in the preceding case; for the point which seizes our attention is not the act of the individual, but the approbation of the National Synod. The matter is quaintly entered in the Index, and in plainer terms than those in which it was submitted to the assembled divines:—"Abbé reçû à la Cene *pour avoir* brulé ses Titres, abatu les Images de l'Eglise de son Convent, et porté les Armes *pour maintenir les Predicateurs* Reformés. Pag. 45."

NOTE D. on p. 323, n.

Difficulty of access to MSS.

I LATELY found among my papers a fragment which appears to have been cut off from the Note at p. 323. The Note was certainly long enough without it; but as the fragment contains some further illustrations of the subject, and of rather a different kind, I here subjoin it:—

"Indeed they had sometimes a little difficulty in dealing with Abbesses, whose suspicions, considering their helpless condition, may be forgiven, though they sometimes produced amusing results. The Abbess of *S. Menoust,* (a niece of the Père de la Chaise) could do nothing without consulting her superior, the Cardinal de Bouillon, and therefore did nothing at all." [6] When Martene paid his compliments to the superior of the Carmelites at *Nevers,* and inquired their founder's name

---

[6] I. Voy. Lit. 45.

and the date of their foundation, "cette proposition démonta tellement cette bonne fille, qu'elle s'écria : 'Hé pourquoy me demandez-vous cela, mon pere ? n'est-ce pas pour mettre encore de nouveaux impôts sur nôtre maison ? nous en avons déja tant payé que nous avons été obligées pour y satisfaire d'emprunter une somme considerable, dont nous payons la rente [7];' " and it was not until after consultation with her "directeur," and his assurance that it would be an honour for her convent to be noticed in the learned work which was projected, that she produced the deed of foundation. The old Cistercian Abbess of *Ostine* took fright, and could scarcely be beaten out of her notion that these Benedictine monks were going to claim a visitatorial power, which she declared that none but those of her own order should ever exercise in her house; [8] and two out of three Abbesses at *Metz* refused positively. The other "communiqua tout ce qui étoit dans ses archives, parce qu'elle aime sa maison, et qu'elle est bien-aise qu'on sçache ce qu'elle a toûjours été." A pretty strong hit at the other two; but in fact he goes on to tell the world that they wanted to secularize into canonesses, and to conceal that they were properly and originally nuns. "Mais elles ont beau faire," says the malicious monk, "toute la posterité sçaura que sainte Waldrade, premiere Abbesse de S. Pierre, étoit religieuse; and he goes on to show that he could prove all that they wished to conceal, without being indebted to their manuscripts. [9]

Note E. on p. 420.

Dovetailing of Letters.

When I said that old letters, if brought out from various sources, would "dove-tail" greatly to the illustration of each other and of history, I might (if I had then known it) have quoted a singular instance which had recently occurred.

In the "State Papers published under the authority of his Majesty's Commission, Volume I., King Henry the Eighth, Parts I. and II. 1830," there are (Part II. p. 883) two letters from Gardiner, Bishop of Winchester; one to the king, and the other to Sir William Paget, requesting him to deliver it to his Majesty. Both letters are dated December 2. A note on the letter to the king says, "This letter is holograph, and a contemporary indorsement fixes its date to 1546." Another note says, "The tenth instrument signed by stamp in December, 1546, is a letter to the Bishop of Winchester in answer to his letters

---

[7] Ibid. 50.   [8] Ibid. P. ii. 187.   [9] Ibid. 115.

to the king, concerning an exchange of land desired by the king."
The reader will remember that Henry VIII. died on January 28,
1547, and that during some time previous, the royal name was af-
fixed to instruments by a stamp, because, as was said, the king
could not write his name. But where is this No. 10? where is the
stamped instrument containing the king's answer to Gardiner? Why it
had been printed and published hundreds of years before these State
Papers were issued. It is not wonderful that it should have been long
unobserved, not only because it is not a document of much interest,
or very intelligible, in itself, but because it existed only, so far as I
know, in the first edition of Fox's Martyrology, which is a very rare
book. Having had a good deal to do with that work, I have happened
to see it. It stands at p. 801, and purports to have been " Yeuen vnder
our signet, at our maner of Otelands, the iiii. of December the xxxviii.
yere of our reigne." It was, I believe, omitted in every subsequent
edition, until it was recently restored in the comic edition of Messrs.
Seeley, which was not begun till after the publication of the volume
of State Papers alluded to. The letter and answer therefore may now,
after a separation of nearly three hundred years, be placed side by
side; and though, as I have said, the subject matter is not very intelligible or of any great consequence, yet I venture to say that, from
other circumstances, which it would be tedious here to detail, these
three letters are amongst the most important documents which exist
with reference to the History of the Reformation.

[Since this note was added to the second edition I have printed
both the Letters, with some remarks tending to show their importance,
in my Essays on Subjects connected with the Reformation in England,
No. XVI. p. 330.]

NOTE F. on p. 478.

Commercium Librorum.

ANY reader who may wish to pursue this subject, which is surely one
of the most interesting connected with the history of the dark ages,
will find a great deal of curious matter in Pez's " Codex Diplomatico-
historico-epistolaris," which forms the sixth volume of his " Thesaurus
Anecdotorum Novissimus."

I have had occasion to speak of the monastery of Tegernsee at p.
455. According to Pez, it was under the government of the Abbot
Gozpert from A.D. 983 – 1001; and he gives a good many letters by
and to him and his monks. The reader will therefore bear in mind

that the writers of all those which I here mention lived in the *tenth century*.

A letter from the Abbot Romuald, Abbot of St. Emmeram's at Ratisbon, requesting the loan of a " Librum plenariæ collationis," in order that it might be copied. *Col.* 121.

Another to "Domnus H.," to borrow the third part of the Tripartite History for the same purpose. *Col.* 127.

Froumond (a monk of Tegernsee, but who seems to have been at, and quitted, another monastery) to Gozpert, begging parchment. *Col.* 158.

The same to the same, vehemently protesting that he had not stolen the abbot's book, "librum vestrum M." *Col.* 159.

Reginbald (probably, says Pez, a monk of St. Emmeram's), to Froumund (not, as Pez entitles it, sending him a Persius, but), returning him some book which he had borrowed, and asking for a Persius. *Col.* 160.

The same to the same, sending him the remainder of a book which he had asked for, desiring that he would make his copy and return it as soon as possible, because he had yielded to his importunity, and sent it without the knowledge of its owner — that he could not at that time meet the wish of Froumund and Master Meginhelme, because though the book thus wanted was in their library, he doubted of its correctness; but he would see, and if it appeared that it would be of service to them, would endeavour to bring it when he should come to them. *Col.* 162.

Froumund to Reginbald, to lend him a Horace to copy a morsel which their book did not contain—if he had not that at hand to send some other book that would be useful to them, and to return a book of his which he had, by the bearer. *Col.* 163.

The same to the same, rebuking him for sending back his book in such a condition—crumpled, dirty, and without the map of the world which had been at the beginning: "totum rugosum, cœnosum, parteque disruptum . . , circulus continens scripturam quatuor plagarum mundi." *Col.* 164.

The same to the same, begging him to lend a Statius, or, if offended, to return him his book. *Col.* 164.

The same to P. (probably his Abbot) relates to the transcription of Boethius, and about copies of Juvenal and Persius, Arithmeticæ Boethii, and the liber Invectivarum Tullii Ciceronis in Salustium. *Col.* 166.

Note G. on p. 501.

John of Gorze.

It may amuse the reader to know, and it is peculiarly characteristic of the mode in which the history of the Dark Ages has been treated, to observe, that John of Gorze is coupled with Meinwerc, by Brucker, as a specimen of those deplorable blockheads who "infantum more balbutiebant summamque exosculabantur ignorantiam." After speaking of the numerous proofs of darkness collected by the learned, and giving a general reference to their works, he says:—

Nos speciminis loco unnm modo alterumque adducimus exemplum Ioannem abbatem Gorziensem (cujus vitam scripsit Ioannes abbas S.; Arnulfi Metis, quam exhibent Bollandus et socii et Mabillonius), neglecto non modo quadrivio sed et trivio, 'primas tantum partes Donati ex Bernero audivisse, eaque introductoria aspersione contentum divinis se omnino transtulisse scriptis:' et Meinwercum episcopum Paderbornensem ne recte legere quidem potuisse, et in psalterio legisse : ' Benedic domine regibus et reginis mulis et mulabus tuis, pro famulis et famulabus tuis.' Unde vix credi potest, quod idem vitæ Meinwerci scriptor refert, ' studiorum multiplicia sub eo floruisse exercitia, et bonæ indolis juvenes et pueros fuisse institutos.' *Neque mirum ;* puerum *enim* quinquennem Eriberti Aquitaniæ ducis filium adhuc ἀναλϕάβητον archiepiscopum Remensem constitutum fuisse, narrat, et indignatur Baronius."[1]

But in what different lights people view the same thing. I should have thought that the acquirements which I have mentioned in the text might have constituted John of Gorze something like a learned man, but his unfortunate confession about Donatus seems to have satisfied the Historian of Philosophy that he must have been a blockhead.

NOTE H. on p. 505.

D'Aubigné's History of the Reformation.

THE following letter appeared in the Record Newspaper for December 12, 1844. It is so curious and so characteristic of the school of

---

[1] Hist. Phil. Tom. iii. p. 634. Brucker's explanation of the cause of this desperate ignorance is worth notice. A child of the Count of Vermandois (not the Duke of Aquitaine of all people) is elected Archbishop of Rheims, that being his father's way of seizing the power and property of the see. The King of France supports him. A vicious pope is brought to allow it, but has the decency to insist on delegating the spiritual function to the contiguous bishop of Soissons. No wonder John did not read Donatus, and Meinwerc could not read the Psalter—but did Brucker mean that Baronius was more indignant than the *contemporary* historian of this scandalous usurpation?

writers to which M. D'Aubigné and his newspaper friends belong, that I am desirous to preserve it, and lay it before my readers, few of whom are likely to have seen the unfortunate publication in which it appeared. [2]

LETTER TO AN ENGLISH CLERGYMAN, IN REPLY TO HIS INQUIRIES RESPECTING SOME REMARKS OF MR. MAITLAND IN HIS WORK ON "THE DARK AGES," AGAINST D'AUBIGNÉ'S "HISTORY OF THE REFORMATION.."

" Geneva, Dec. 2, 1844.

"Dear Brother,—Nothing equals the ignorance, the levity, and the bad faith, that the greater part of the Popish writers on the Continent show on the subject of the Reformation and the Reformers. They repeat incessantly the most ridiculous stories, the falsity of which has been proved a hundred times. Will your Crypto-Papists of England enter the same course ? I should not be surprised. I have already had many attacks against my *History of the Reformation*, proceeding from the Tractarian party, either in Great Britain or America. I have no intention of replying to them, but I will however say some words upon that which you communicate in your last letter.

"It appears that Mr. Maitland, in his work on the *Dark Ages*, throws doubt on my account of the manner in which Luther found the Bible in the University of Erfurth. He seems to think (his book has not yet reached Geneva) that the Holy Scriptures were too generally spread under the Papacy before the Reformation, for Luther not to have been already acquainted with them. The argument which he makes use of is remarkable. 'Luther,' says he, 'had read the writings of Occam, Scot, Bonaventura, and Thomas Aquinas. These Doctors knew the Bible ; Luther must then have heard it spoken of.' But I have said much more myself ; I have said that he had read the fragments of the Gospels and Epistles that the Church has chosen for each Sunday of the year (vol. i. p. 156). This was more than having heard the Bible spoken of.

"What I have said is, that Luther had never until then seen an entire copy of the Holy Scriptures. Now, in advancing this fact, I have cited my authority in a note (Mathesius). An exact and conscientious critic would have had recourse to this authority ; he would have examined it, and if he had found good, criticised, or he would have opposed other authorities. But not a word of all that. Mr. Maitland prefers to throw himself into suppositions which have no weight. Probably he does not know Mathesius. I am,

---

[2] In case such readers should observe certain peculiarities in the German or Latin, it is due to myself and to the printer to say that we have endeavoured to give the letter most exactly. It may be doubted whether the Record ever had any person connected with it who was capable of correcting the press in any language but his own, if even in that.

nevertheless, told that Mr. Maitland is librarian to one of your Bishops. Here is a librarian who seems to know very little of books.

"I will say, then, that John Mathesius, one of the most respectable eccle-siastics of the first half of the sixteenth century, came to Wittemburg in 1529; he was a disciple of Luther, lodged many years in the house of the Reformer, and ate every day at his table, *usus est convictu ipsius Lutheri*, says Melchior Adam, in his *Vitæ Germ. Theolog.* There is no contemporary historian of the Reformation whose testimony has more authority where the person of the Reformer is concerned. Now, here is the literal translation of the passage to which I have referred in my *History of the Reformation*. (He writes in German.) Luther was often in the library of the University; one day, as he examined the books one after another, in order to learn to know the good, he falls upon the Latin Bible which he had *never seen* before, all the time of his life. (Die er yuvon die yeit seines lebens *ine geschen*.) He remarks, then, with great astonishment, that many more texts, epistles, and gospels, are to be found there than in the ordinary postils, and in the texts they were accustomed to explain in the churches from the pulpits. As he was running through the Old Testament, he falls upon the history of Samuel and his mother Hannah; he reads it quickly with a heart full of emotion and joy; and as all that was new to him, he began to desire from the depths of his heart that our faithful God would one day give him such a book for his own. Oh! how richly have this desire and sigh been granted.

"Thus speaks Mathesius, in his *Memoirs of the Beginning of the Life and Death of Martin Luther*, first discourse, pp. 3, 4. The edition from which I have quoted is that of the sixteenth century. (Of the year 1566.)

"Melchior Adam, in his *Lives of German Theologians*, p. 103, speaks thus:—'Lutherus incidit in exemplar Latinorum Bibliarum *quæ nunquam antea viderat, etc.*' It is useless to bring more quotations. I add only that all the historians are unanimous on this fact. I do not know that it has ever been contested by anyone, even by avowed Papists.

"There had been doubtless many editions of the Bible since the invention of printing, but we find few or no traces of them among the people. The Holy Scriptures appear to have had no influence upon the instruction either of the Church or of the school. Let us leave what the Reformers may have said, and let us search for what has been written before the Reformation, not only by men of the opposition, such as John Huss and Savonarola, but by Doctors of calm spirit, and invested with the highest ecclesiastical dig-nities, such as Matthew of Cracow, Bishop of Worms, in his *Tractatus ob Squaloribus Romanæ Curiæ*, Pierre d'Ailly, Archbishop of Cambray, John Gerson, and the respectable Abbot of Spanheim, John Tritheim. Here are some features of the picture which this last has drawn for us of the state of the Romish clergy before the Reformation in his *Institutio Vitæ Sacer-dotalis*. I will leave in Latin what it would not be decent to translate— 'Ignorant men, coarse, without merit, come to the priesthood. They ask neither a holy life, nor literary culture, nor a pure conscience. Our priests entirely neglect the study of Holy Scripture, but in compensation they occupy themselves in bringing dogs and birds *pro libris sibi liberos comparant pro studio concubinas amant*. They sit with drunkards in the public-houses, and give themselves up to play and debauchery. They do not know how to speak or write in Latin, and can scarcely explain the Gospels in German. It is not astonishing that simple priests should be so ignorant and so opposed to the study of the Holy Scriptures, for in that they have the Prelates for their example. It is not the wisest that are elected, but those who can best pay for their place. These Prelates have themselves *few or no Bibles*, and show a great hatred against instruction. Here are the blind guides who, instead of guiding the people, lead them astray.'

"What a frightful picture! Here is the state from which the Reformation has rescued the Church. Is it the state in which the Tractarians and the Crypto-Papists, who so strongly regret the Reformation, would replunge it? Dear brother, the state of the English Church becomes ever more alarming to Christians on the Continent. The evil appears to us to have reached the highest degree, and we do not see that the Church does anything to remedy it. We ask if the Episcopal system is then inefficacious to govern the Church? The Church of Scotland has repressed the reveries of Irving, and nevertheless, those reveries were less dangerous than those of Pusey, Newman, and Maitland. We love the Church of England, on account of the word of God on which it rests; of its Articles, the faith of which is so pure; of all the works, and of all the men of God that it has given birth to. But one of your colleagues, a zealous Episcopalian, who boasted to us recently of the excellencies of this system, can tell you, that we have been unanimous in opposing to him the actual state of your Church. If nothing is done against the Popery of Oxford, the cause of Episcopacy is lost upon the Continent; it is lost in the Church of God. If the Bishops continue to sleep, remember that the Church is the judge of controversies, and that the Church, according to your articles, is the assembly of faithful men. Let faithful men then rise and speak.

"Dear brother, I pray for your Church that He who is with us continually, even to the end of the world, may himself fight against the servants of human traditions, and that the victory may abide with the word and the blood of the Lamb.

"Your devoted Friend,

"MERLE D'AUBIGNÉ, D.D."

I have given the whole of M. D'Aubigné's letter, not only because, as I have already said, it is so curious and so characteristic of the class of writers to whom he belongs, but that I might not be charged with garbling it. As to great part of it, it seems to me quite a sufficient answer to say, that specific statements such as that the Bible was a rare book, UNKNOWN in the early days of Luther, and that "the Holy Scriptures appear to have had NO INFLUENCE upon the instruction either of the CHURCH or the SCHOOL," which are broad falsehoods on the very face of them, are not to be supported by little scraps of declamation from early writers such as M. D'Aubigné has thought it worth while to string together. I refer the reader to what I have said on this subject at p. 52.

Another great portion is, I imagine, sufficiently answered by saying, that if it should be proved that I am a Crypto-Papist, and a Tractarian, and the properest person in the world to be triplicated with the gentlemen whom he has named, yet that does not affect the matter. Such evasion is too gross and palpable. There is no question about doctrine between us. It is merely as to matter of fact. It is not at what he has written as a theologian, but as an historian, that I have taken the liberty to laugh, and respecting which I have cautioned people not to believe him; and a man looks rather ridiculous, who tries to conceal ignorance and blunders by assuring his friends that the person who points them out is a Hottentot.

There are, however, one or two things which require more specific notice.

1. M. D'Aubigné professes to give my words. He puts a passage in marks of quotation, and moreover adds "says he." Of course one cannot tell what representation the "English clergyman" might make, and therefore I do not mean to charge M. D'Aubigné with the stupidity or guilt of this impudent misrepresentation.

2. M. D'Aubigné says of his own work, respecting which he must surely be supposed to know the truth, "WHAT I HAVE SAID IS, that Luther had never until then, seen an entire copy of the Holy Scriptures." This is really enough to frighten one. Does not M. D'Aubigné know, did not the "English clergyman" know, (the Record is not suspected of knowing anything), that M. D'Aubigné said something more than this, and something very, very, different? His statement is express, that Luther having taken down the Bible, "a rare book, *unknown* in those days," was "overcome with wonder at finding *more in the volume* than those fragments of the Gospels and Epistles which the Church had selected to be read in the temples every Sunday troughout the year." And as if this did not state the fact with sufficient force and precision, he adds, "*Till then he had supposed* these constituted the *entire* Word of God." Even this is not all. As if to cut off the possibility of any such disgraceful retreat as he is now attempting, he went on, "and now behold, how many *pages*, how many *chapters*, how many *books*, of which he had not before *had a notion!*"

And yet after all this M. D'Aubigné says, "What I have said is, that Luther had never until then, seen *an entire copy* of the Holy Scriptures." Even this would have been next to incredible, but it is altogether different from saying as M. D'Aubigné *did* say, that Luther did not know that there was any Word of God in existence except the selected Epistles and Gospels. This was outrageous; and I do not wonder that M. D'Aubigné should very much wish it to be thought that he had not said anything betraying such monstrous ignorance. I really was so staggered by it that I thought I might be doing the author injustice through some fault of his translator; and I resolved to see the original. But the passage actually stands as I give it below in the third edition of Paris, 1842. [3]

Let it only be considered that these statements of M. D'Aubigné relate to a man of whose father he has previously told us that "possessing a higher degree of mental cultivation than most men of his class, he *read a great deal.* Books were scarce in those days, but John let pass no opportunity of procuring them." It is rather surprising that no Bible or Testament or Psalter came in his way; especially as he is said to have been a religious man. His wife "was endowed with the virtues that adorn chaste and pious women. In particular, she was remarkable for modesty, her fear of God, and her spirit of prayer;" and therefore it is no wonder that "the first thought of his pious parents was to consecrate to God by baptism the infant he had just given them." During his childhood his father rose in the world, and being made councillor of Mansfeld, "availed himself of his new situation to seek the society he preferred. He set great store by men of information, and often invited the clergy and schoolmasters of the place to his table." We are not surprised to hear that "the child profited by

---

[3] "Le jeune étudiant passait à la bibliothèque de l'université tous les moments qu'il pouvait enlever à ses travaux académiques. Les livres étaient encore rares, et c'était pour lui un grand privilége de pouvoir profiter des trésors réunis dans cette vaste collection. Un jour (il y avait alors deux ans qu'il était a Erfurt, et il avait vingt ans), il ouvre l'un après l'autre plusieurs des livres de la bibliothèque, afin d'en connaître les auteurs. Un volume qu'il a ouvert à son tour frappe son attention. Il n'en a point vu de semblable jusqu'à cette heure. Il lit le titre . . . (*sic*) c'est une Bible ! livre rare, inconnu dans ce temps-là. [1] Son intérêt est vivement excité; il se sent tout rempli d'admiration de trouver autre chose dans ce volume que ces fragments d'évangiles et d'épîtres que l'Église a choisis pour les lire au peuple dans les temples, chaque dimanche de l'année. Il avait cru jusqu'alors que c'était là toute la Parole de Dieu. Et voilà tant de pages, tant de chapitres, tant de livres, dont il n'avait aucune idée !" Vol. I. p. 197.

---

[1] Auff ein Zeyt, wie er die Bücher fein nacheinander besieht . . . (*sic*) kombt er über die lateinische Biblia . . . (*sic*) (Mathes. 3).

L L

it," and that "as soon as he was of age to receive some instruction, his parents sought to instil into him the knowledge and fear of God, and to form him to the Christian virtues." While he was "still very little... his father wishing to see him acquire the rudiments of those studies he prized so highly, invoked upon him the blessing of heaven, and sent him to school." This was after "the piety of his parents, their active habits and austere virtue" had "had a happy effect on the boy," and had given "his mind a grave and attentive cast." At school "they taught him the chapters of the Catechism, the Ten Commandments, the Apostles' Creed, the Lord's Prayer, Canticles, Forms of Prayer," beside other things more easily taught without allusion to the Old or New Testament—"in short," says M. D' Aubigné, "they taught him all that was known in the Latin school of Mansfeld." So when he was fourteen he was sent to Magdeburg, and his mind being of a grave and attentive cast, "he examined, he *listened*. Andreas Proles, the provincial of the order of Augustinians, was then preaching with great warmth the necessity of a reform in religion and in the Church." But the young listener never caught a hint that there were any pages, chapters, or books in the Word of God except what were read for Epistles and Gospels on Sundays. Well, then he was sent "to Isenach where there was a celebrated school," and where he was received as an inmate in a Christian family; where "his whole being warmed beneath the mild rays of charity, and began to bound with life, joy, and contentment. His prayers were more ardent; his thirst for knowledge greater; he made rapid progress." Still he managed to steer clear of any suspicion that there was such a Book as the Bible. [4] However, in his eighteenth year Luther arrived at the University of Erfurt; after being there two years, after studying "the Philosophy of the Middle Ages in the writings of Occam, Scot, Bonaventure, and Thomas Aquinas," he made the astonishing discovery that though "unknown in those days" there was such a Book as the Bible—very odd, was it not?

---

[4] It may be observed, not as a statement of what was done, but of what at a great distance of time we are able to trace in the history of that period, that for the year 1497, which seems to have been the year in which Luther went to Isenach, Le Long gives editions of the whole Bible printed at Strasburgh, Cologne, Venice, Paris, and Nuremberg, beside three Psalters, one with no place named, and the others from Nuremberg and Augsburgh. Of course I do not mean to represent this as more than may have been done in years recently before, or soon after, but one would not have been surprised if some one copy of the Bible had found its way to the "celebrated school of Isenach."

3. There is something very comic in the manner in which M. D'Aubigné complains of my venturing to doubt that for which he actually gives an " authority."

Now, in the first place, M. D'Aubigné did not give any authority for that part of his statement which I impugned. On the words, " a rare book, unknown in those days," he put a few German words, simply stating, that as, once on a time, Luther examined the books on the shelves, he came to a Latin Bible. These words were, of course, quite irrelevant, and only conveyed the idea, that by some mistake of the printer the note had got out of its place. But what would have been said of my folly and unfairness, if I had treated that reference to Mathesius, coupled as it was with his quoted words, and given, as it seemed to be, by way of authority for *them*, as containing a statement that Luther had never seen the book of Psalms, and did not know that there was a book of Genesis in the Bible ? How was I to guess that it was meant to certify all that, and a great deal more ?

But M. D'Aubigné seems to think that whatever has been once said by ignorance, fraud, or folly, may be said again with impunity. He gave an "authority" — why so did Robertson, and Henry, and Warton, for various absurd falsehoods, as has appeared on turning to those authorities; but some things are so plainly false, that one does not need to look at the authority on which they are stated. If M. D'Aubigné had said, that by some singular infelicity the Saxon Reformer had been educated in an atheistical manner, and until he was twenty years old had been studiously prevented from coming to the knowledge of the fact that the Bible existed —that he had been kept by his father in the woods, never taught to read, or allowed to go to church, or converse with Christians, — if M. D'Aubigné had told us even this, strange as it is, upon respectable contemporary authorities, it would of course be our duty to look at them; but when the story is told of a young gentleman whose religious education had been particularly attended to, and who had of his own free will been working hard at Occam, Scot, Bonaventure, and Thomas Aquinas, it is too much. We do not need to look at the authority. We can only lament the pitiable ignorance of the writer who could repeat such nonsense, and commend him to the patronage of the Record.

I do not know that I have ever seen the work of Mathesius, and I am not better acquainted with it than, I suspect, M. D'Aubigné is with the works of Occam, Scot, Bonaventure, and Thomas Aquinas. But I do know one little thing, on the authority of Melchior Adam, a writer whom M. D'Aubigné quotes with respect, which makes me believe that Mathesius is an authority not to be implicitly trusted on such

a point.   I suspect that he was a little in M. D'Aubigné's way of
rhodomontade and talking big for effect, and perhaps if his words had
been contradicted on the spot, he might have been as prompt to eat
them as M. D'Aubigné has been.   Melchior Adam says that Mathesius's
account of *himself* was, that having been brought up among the papists
until he was twenty-five years of age, he had never heard in any of
their churches, *any mention* of the *Ten Commandments*, the *Creed*, the
Lord's Prayer, or *Baptism*. [5]   I think we may let such an "authority"
say what he pleases of Luther, or anybody else.   Perhaps, if called on
for an explanation, he would have told us, " What 1 said is, that it
was not customary for preachers in the Romish Church to repeat all
the Ten Commandments, the Creed, the Lord's Prayer, and the Form
for Baptism, in every sermon."   M. D'Aubigné may perhaps learn
that authorities will not shelter everything, and are apt to expose those
who have not sufficient information to know how to use them.

---

[5] After speaking of the education of Mathesius, and telling us that he
had learned the Catechism at School, Melchior Adam proceeds to say, that
certain doctrines continued to be taught in the schools, when they were not
heard of in the churches "in templis altum de iis silentium. Ipse Mathesius
[*marg. note* Concione 6. de vita Luth. p. 59] alicubi fatetur, se, qui inter
Pontificios ad annum usque ætatis vigesimum quintum egerit, nullam unquam
audisse mentionem, fieri Decalogi, aut Symboli Apostolici, aut precationis
Dominicae, aut Denique Baptismi." Vit. Germ. Theol. p. 404. Some may
think that I have improperly limited his words by the context ; and perhaps
I have, but the case will well afford it.

INDEX.

THE END.

Printed by H. C. A. Thieme at Nimeguen (Holland) and Billiter Square Buildings, London E. C.